MW00336022

FRANCE OVERSEAS: STUDIES IN EMPIRE AND DECOLONIZATION

The French Navy *and the* Seven Years' War

JONATHAN R. DULL

University of Nebraska Press   Lincoln & London

⊗

Library of Congress Cataloging-in-Publication Data
Dull, Jonathan R., 1942–
The French Navy and the Seven Years' War / Jonathan R. Dull.
p.   cm.—(France overseas. Studies in empire and decolonization)
Includes bibliographical references and index.
ISBN 0-8032-1731-5 (cloth: alk. paper)
ISBN 978-0-8032-6024-5 (paper: alk. paper)
1. France. Marine—History—18th century.   2. France—History, Naval—18th century.
3. Seven Years' War, 1756–1763.   4. France—History—Louis XV, 1715–1774.   I. Title.   II. Series.
DC52.D895   2005
940.2'534—dc22
2004030729

Set in Minion and Palatino by Bob Reitz.

For the Kruger family, especially my wonderful wife, Susan Kruger, our children, Max and Anna Kruger-Dull, and my wife's parents, Stan and Alice Kruger

Contents

Maps

Preface

The Seven Years' War consisted of two great conflicts, each containing seven years of hostilities. The bloodshed in the first of these conflicts, which Americans often call the French and Indian War, began in Pennsylvania in 1754 and largely concluded in 1760. The bloodshed in the second began in Bohemia in 1756 and concluded at the end of 1762. The conflicts resulted in a set of treaties in 1763, whose impact was perhaps even greater on American history than on European. Few wars prior to the twentieth century were as complex as these two or involved as many combatants—Great Britain, France, Prussia, Russia, the Austrian Empire, Spain, Sweden, dozens of American Indian nations, and numerous principalities in Germany and on the subcontinent of India. What makes their history so challenging is that they were so closely interconnected that they must be studied as a single war. It has been eighty years since the great historians Richard Waddington and Sir Julian Corbett did so. (Intervening histories of the "French and Indian War" by Lawrence Henry Gipson, Guy Frégault, Francis Jennings, Fred Anderson, and others largely have neglected Europe.) With the 250th anniversary of the war having arrived, another such attempt is overdue.

The most important link between the wars in Europe and North America (and for that matter in Asia and Africa) was the conflict between Great Britain and France. Fighting between the two occurred on all these continents and interacted with the conflicts between the other combatants, although with strange gaps, France fighting but never declaring war on Britain's ally Prussia and Britain carefully avoiding even the hint of hostilities against France's allies Austria and Russia. The French navy played a critical part in the war between France and Britain, particularly in North America. Moreover, after 1760 the dominant issue in the Franco-British conflict became the question of whether France would continue to be a major naval power or for the indefinite future would leave uncontested command of the seas to her rival. The present book is, as far as I know, the most complete treatment of the navy's role in the war (as James Pritchard's superb study of the navy during this period does not cover naval operations). To place that role in context it has been necessary to provide a complete survey of the war, chiefly from the French side, but also paying attention to Britain and the British colonies, as well as the other belligerents.

Many French Canadian historians have tended to look at the war of 1754–63 with anger, feeling France let herself become distracted by a European war and did too little to save Canada. Many French historians have looked at the war with disgust or embarrassment, blaming the French king, Louis XV, or the French army or navy for its dismal outcome. Many British and American historians have looked at the war in a celebratory mood, treating it as a victory for republican government. None of these emotions are warranted. France made great, perhaps excessive efforts to save Canada, *including* becoming involved in a European war. Louis XV's role in the war ultimately was heroic, for he more than anyone else was the savior of the French navy. By his perseverance he was able to preserve France's share in the Newfoundland fishery and give the French navy a chance for rebirth and revenge. Without the fishery to train French sailors, it is highly doubtful France could even have participated in the War for American Independence. The French army, too, played a major role in the navy's salvation; by its efforts in Germany it helped drive Britain to surrender its monopoly of the fishery and make a compromise peace. Even the French navy performed reasonably well against an enemy that far outnumbered it. The war was only marginally a victory for republican government. The similarities between France and Britain were greater than their differences, and the outcome of the war was the establishment of a government in Canada which was far less representative in reality than it appeared. Finally the war should not be a cause for celebration unless it be for the heroism and sacrifice of those who fought on each side. The war was needless, horribly bloody, and expensive. It is difficult to judge any of its participants a real winner, considering the price that each paid (in addition to the loss of many lives)—the destabilization of relations between Great Britain and British North America, the wrenching effects on the society and culture of French Canada, and the loss of Indian autonomy.

By taking a less romantic view of this war and by emphasizing its tragedy rather than its glory, I hope that this story will be both more accurate and more interesting. Its heroes are flawed but all the more human for that (and perhaps all the more heroic for what they accomplished in spite of their flaws). Not all wars have "good guys" and "bad guys"; this is one in which it is particularly hard to tell the difference, because France and Britain would have been far better off being friends.

Many people have given me their support during the writing of this book, particularly my wife, Susan, our children, Max and Anna, my adult children, Robert Dull and Veronica Lamka, my son-in-law, Todd Lamka, my sister, Caroline Hamburger, and my nephews, John and Peter Hamburger. I dedicate this book to the members of the Kruger family, my wife and our children, my wife's parents, Stan and Alice Kruger, as well as Steven Kruger, Josh Kruger, Diane Bassett, Glenn Burger, David Kruger, and Jessica Kruger.

I have had many wonderful colleagues during twenty-seven years working at the Papers of Benjamin Franklin, including the present staff, Ellen Cohn, Karen Duvall, Kate Ohno, Michael Sletcher, and Jennifer Macellaro. I would like to pay particular tribute to a friend of twenty-five years standing, current chief editor Ellen Cohn: historical editors, bosses, and friends come no better. I have also benefited from the friendship and advice of a number of fellow historians, beginning with my teachers at the University of California at Berkeley, particularly the late Raymond J. Sontag, who introduced me to diplomatic history, Gerry Cavanaugh, Richard Herr, Robert Middlekauff, and others. Thanks too for various kindnesses extended by historians Paul Bamford, Orville Murphy, Larry Kaplan, Paul Kennedy, Max Mintz, Joel Blatt, Tom Beck, Peter Ascoli, Jeremy Black, Hamish Scott, Jim Pritchard, Roger Knight, Fred Anderson, and particularly Nick Rodger, who read and criticized my manuscript, and Jan Glete, who kindly provided me with information on the Portuguese navy. Finally I would like to thank the helpful staffs of the Yale University Library, the Service Historique de la Marine, the Archives Nationales, the Archives du Ministère des Affaires Etrangères, and the Public Record Office.

NORTH AMERICA

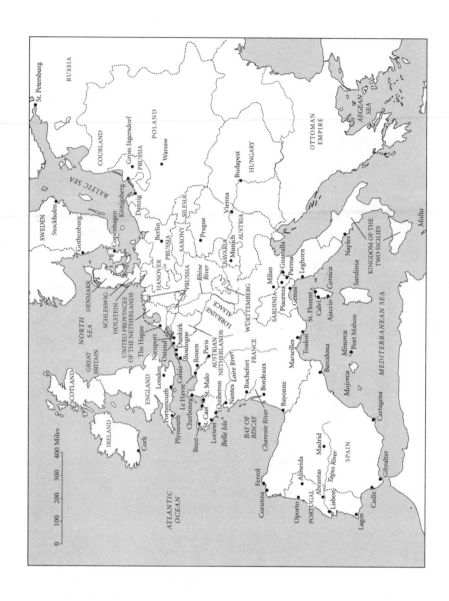

EUROPE

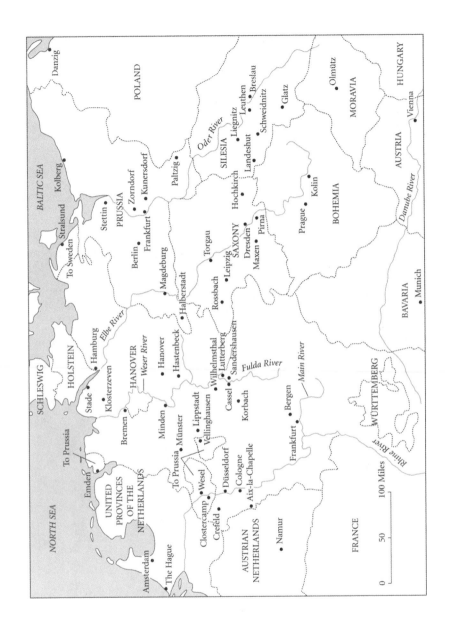

CENTRAL EUROPE

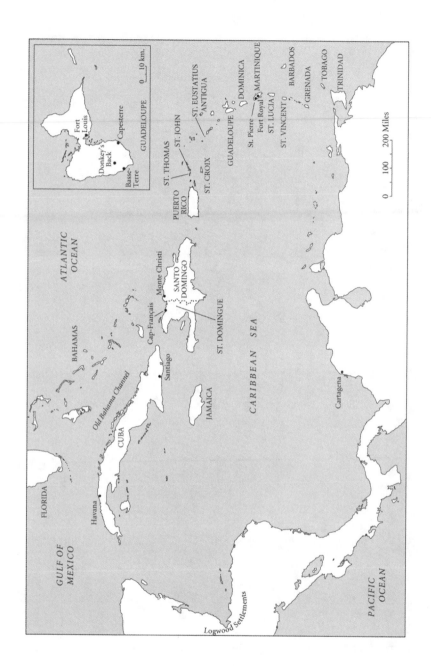

THE CARIBBEAN

Plassey

BENGAL
Chandernagore
Calcutta

Bombay

Masulipatam

BAY OF
BENGAL

ARABIAN
SEA

Madras (Fort St. George)
Wandiwash
Pondicherry
Fort St. David

C A R N A T I C

CEYLON

To Mascarene Islands
(2,100 Miles)

0   100   200   300 Miles

INDIAN OCEAN

INDIA

The French Navy and the Seven Years' War

1748-1754
An Uneasy Peace

THE WAR OF THE AUSTRIAN SUCCESSION AND THE
DECLINE OF FRANCO-BRITISH RELATIONS

As the eighteenth century reached its midpoint, the governments of France and Great Britain viewed each other with suspicion. For example, Thomas Pelham-Holles, Duke of Newcastle, one of the two British secretaries of state and, after 1754, prime minister, considered the two states as inveterate rivals, if not quite inevitable enemies. [1] Historians generally treat this animosity as one of the few constants during this century of shifting alliances. [2] Indeed, British-French relations between 1688 and 1815 have been described as a "Second Hundred Years' War." [3] On the surface this comparison to the Hundred Years' War of the fourteenth and fifteenth centuries seems plausible. Between the Glorious Revolution of 1688 and the Battle of Waterloo, Britain and France fought seven wars; hostilities occurred in some 60 of the 127 years. Significant differences, however, existed between this period of frequent conflict and its predecessor. Although what medieval historians call the Hundred Years' War was punctuated by periods of peace, it essentially was a single war with a common cause, the irreconcilable dynastic claims of the English and French ruling houses.

The so-called Second Hundred Years' War was far more complex. Some historians argue it had an underlying cause, colonial rivalry, particularly the battle for supremacy over the balance of power in America. [4] This, however, overstates the importance of American affairs. Over the course of the eighteenth century, the English public and the British Parliament took an increasing interest in the Western Hemisphere, [5] but even at the height of the War of the Austrian Succession (in which Britain participated from 1742 to 1748) elections to the House of Commons were dominated by local issues. [6] Most Frenchmen generally had scant interest in the rich sugar-producing islands of the Caribbean, let alone the

North American mainland, which produced little of any interest to them except tobacco (and, for the better off, furs).[7] The French and British monarchs of the period usually showed a far greater interest in European affairs than in American. This was especially true during the reigns in Britain of George I (1714–27) and George II (1727–60), who were obsessed with the north German electorate of Hanover, which they also ruled. Newcastle may have believed the American balance of power could decisively affect the balance of power in Europe,[8] but in 1755 his French counterpart questioned whether colonial issues were sufficient cause for war.[9]

If not the rivalry to gain colonies, what accounts for the nearly continuous suspicion and frequent hostility between Britain and France? At times Britain feared a French threat to its system of government, as in the 1740s when France supported the restoration of the Stuart dynasty or in the 1790s when Britain feared French revolutionaries. More often, however, the friction between the two powers was based on geopolitical factors, such as rivalry in the Mediterranean or in the Baltic, a region that supplied timber and masts for the navies of both Britain and France. The most serious source of reciprocal concern was the area along France's northern border, the provinces of the southern Netherlands (today's Belgium), which were ruled until 1714 by Spain and thereafter by Austria. These provinces could form a staging area for the invasion of France as they did in both the first and the last decades of the eighteenth century. Conversely this area could provide ports to assemble a flotilla to invade the vulnerable eastern coasts of England and Scotland.[10] When the French threat to the area receded after 1815, other conflicts between France and the United Kingdom were insufficient to cause war.[11] In spite of colonial rivalry that intensified in the late nineteenth century, the two states have not fought a war for almost two centuries. Indeed, outside threats to Belgium eventually turned them into allies.

This area was key to Franco-British relations in the eighteenth century, too. When the southern Netherlands fell under Austrian control, French and British anxieties about the Low Countries receded, and Franco-British relations improved. The Habsburg dynasty of Austria was a traditional enemy of the French monarchy, but it regarded the Austrian Netherlands, isolated from its other possessions in Germany, central Europe, and Italy, as a strategic encumbrance. (The Austrians did attempt briefly to exploit the potential of the ports of the southern Netherlands, but the British prevented it.) Indeed, when France and Austria went to war in 1733 (the War of the Polish Succession), France effectively neutralized the area to avoid antagonizing the Dutch.[12]

With the southern Netherlands in the hands of such a distant power (and, furthermore, one without a navy), it threatened neither Britain nor France. It posed no obstacle when in 1716 George I and the duc d'Orléans, regent for the young king, Louis XV of France (1710–1774, reigning from 1715), chose to become allies, chiefly to provide reciprocal support against dynastic rivals (the exiled Stuarts of Britain and, in France's case, Louis XV's uncle, Philip V of Spain). For the next fifteen years the Franco-British alliance benefited not only the rulers of Britain and France but also the peace of Europe at large. Austria, Russia, and even the relatively small north German state of Prussia had large armies, but their economies were not strong enough for them to fight a major war unaided. Britain and France with their more developed economies briefly became the joint arbiters of Europe.[13] For the dozen years after mid-1721 no major war occurred on the continent, the longest period of peace during the century. Eventually the Franco-British alliance broke down, because Britain withdrew support from France in its continuing rivalry with Austria.[14] Britain remained neutral during the War of the Polish Succession that France and Spain fought against Russia and Austria in 1733–35, but the Franco-British alliance became a dead letter. A war between the two remained unlikely, however, as long as British and French politics were dominated by their peace-loving chief ministers, Robert Walpole and Cardinal André-Hercule Fleury. France and Britain even remained at peace when in 1739 Britain went to war against France's real ally, Spain. France sent a large fleet of observation to the Caribbean the next year, but it returned to France without becoming involved in hostilities.[15] A Franco-British war still seemed inevitable, but a transformation of the European diplomatic scene postponed it.

In October 1740, Charles VI, archduke of Austria and head of the house of Habsburg, died without a male heir. France was pledged to recognize his elder daughter, Maria Theresa, as heir to his possessions in Germany, Bohemia, Moravia, Hungary, Italy, and elsewhere, although as a woman she was ineligible for election to succeed him as Holy Roman Emperor. (The election, for life, was by nine rulers or electors within the empire, including George II, elector of Hanover, one of the nine electorates.) Louis XV, however, was faced with a great temptation. The 1648 Treaty of Westphalia had precluded the development of a modern, unified Holy Roman Empire (including not only today's Germany but also Habsburg possessions in what now are southwestern Poland, the Czech Republic, Slovakia, Austria, Slovenia, Belgium, and part of Croatia). Since then, however, the Habsburgs, while continuing to be elected as Holy Roman Emperors, had greatly strengthened themselves by expanding their possessions to the south and east of the empire. If France dismembered the patrimony of the Habsburgs, it would permanently disable its greatest rival.

Louis XV was too inexperienced and too anxious to rival the successes of his great-grandfather and predecessor, Louis XIV, to be able to resist the temptation. When the new king of Prussia, Frederick II, seized from Maria Theresa the rich province of Silesia, in what today is southwestern Poland, the temptation became too much for him. Louis disregarded the advice of Fleury, his chief minister and mentor, [16] and sent armies that captured Prague in November 1741 and almost took Vienna. In response, Britain sent an army to the Austrian Netherlands to support Maria Theresa, virtually guaranteeing eventual war with France and driving Walpole from office.[17] Meanwhile, Philip V of Spain, wishing a principality in Italy for his youngest son, Philip, also went to war against Maria Theresa.

Louis XV made a number of miscalculations during his reign, but the attack on Austria probably was the worst. He drastically underestimated Maria Theresa's courage, ability, and popularity. She drew support from her own subjects and from Britain, the United Provinces of the Netherlands (Holland and its six sister provinces), and eventually the Kingdom of Sardinia (most of whose lands were on the Italian mainland). By the end of 1743, French armies had been driven from Austrian territory and back across the Rhine. Deserted by Frederick II of Prussia, Louis XV now faced attack from Austria, supported by contingents of British and Dutch troops. At the end of the year and the beginning of 1744, he made four major decisions that not only expanded the war's scope but undermined for decades to come any hope of restoring good relations with Britain. He elected to enter the war in northern Italy between Spain and the British-supported alliance of Sardinia and Austria, to attempt an invasion of England (before a formal declaration of war), to support the claims of the Stuarts to the British throne, and to invade the Austrian Netherlands. By attacking not only British vital interests but even Britain itself, he revived British fears from the days of Louis XIV that France wished to dominate Europe.

Again the French plans largely miscarried. The war in northern Italy was unsuccessful, a storm broke up the attempt to invade England, and Prince Charles Edward Stuart's 1745–46 campaign in Scotland and England was defeated, in part because of the French inability to send him support. [18] Only in the Austrian Netherlands was France successful. Fortunate to find a skilled commander, Maurice, comte de Saxe, an illegitimate son of the elector of Saxony, French armies repeatedly defeated the combined armies of Austria, Britain, and the United Provinces of the Netherlands, captured the Dutch-held border fortresses of the Austrian Netherlands, and even penetrated Dutch territory. In desperation the British and Dutch hired 30,000 troops from Empress Elizabeth of Russia, an Austrian ally. When the Dutch withdrew from the arrangement, the British negotiated with France a preliminary peace agreement at the neutral German city of Aix-la-Chapelle. The Dutch, Austrians, Sardinians, and Spaniards had to accept its terms.

France secured the agreement by promising to evacuate both the Austrian

Netherlands and the small portion of United Provinces of the Netherlands it had occupied. Conquests that would have dazzled even Louis XIV thereby were surrendered. So, too, was the great trading post of Madras in India, which had been captured from the British. In return France regained the fortress of Louisbourg on Isle Royale (Cape Breton Island), which New England militiamen had captured in 1745. In spite of the unequal exchange (unavoidable if peace were to be made), the Treaty of Aix-la-Chapelle largely accomplished the most important desire of France, which had not aimed at permanent conquests in the Low Countries. Its war effort instead was directed at weakening Austria's position in the balance of power and thereby indirectly improving its own. In this, France was in good part successful, even though Maria Theresa continued to rule much of central Europe and her husband, Francis, was elected Holy Roman Emperor. Prussia, which had already extricated itself from the war for a second time by a separate agreement with Austria, retained Silesia, thereby increasing its prewar population of 2.5 million by nearly half.[19] Because of the reputation of its army, Prussia achieved the great power status it sought even though Frederick ruled less than a third as many subjects as George II, king of England and elector of Hanover, a quarter as many as Maria Theresa, a fifth as many as Empress Elizabeth of Russia, or a seventh as many as Louis XV.[20] With a balance of power established between Austria and Prussia in Germany, France's role as an arbiter in Germany (which it had exercised since the Treaty of Westphalia exactly 100 years earlier) was greatly strengthened and the danger to its eastern provinces reduced. Moreover, before evacuating the Austrian Netherlands, France demolished its principal fortresses, leaving it temporarily defenseless.[21]

Austria's position in Italy also was weakened. Some of the territorial concessions in Italy that it made to gain the Sardinian alliance were kept by Sardinia. Maria Theresa also surrendered the duchy of Parma to Prince (Infante) Philip, half-brother of the new king of Spain, Ferdinand VI, and husband of Louis XV's eldest and favorite daughter, Marie-Louise-Elisabeth. Finally, the Austrian alliance with Britain was wrecked by Britain's rush to make a separate peace. Realizing Britain's limited usefulness in recovering Silesia from Prussia, Maria Theresa in 1750 appointed as her diplomatic representative in Paris Wenzel Anton von Kaunitz-Rietberg, who although reluctant to abandon connections with Britain was the chief advocate of improving relations with France.[22]

Besides weakening Austria, the French had other reasons to congratulate themselves. The Treaty of Aix-la-Chapelle weakened the restrictions imposed in 1713 upon French fortification of the great privateering port of Dunkirk, thereby restoring some of France's lost sovereignty over one of its own cities. Her allies, such as Spain and Genoa, either made minor gains or recovered their war losses.

Superficially France seemed even more powerful than she had been after the successful conclusion of the War of the Polish Succession thirteen years earlier.

Louis XV, however, paid dearly for his victory. The war was much bloodier than the limited conflict of the mid-1730s and cost France almost a billion *livres tournois*, which was equivalent to almost four years of the French royal income (or in contemporary purchasing power to perhaps $10 billion). [23] Thanks to heavy borrowing, the French government paid for the war but had to end its program of gradual debt reduction. Unknowingly, it began the slide that, accelerated by the even more expensive wars of 1755–63 and 1778–83, led it by 1787 to diplomatic paralysis and impending bankruptcy. Politically, too, the French government paid a price in lost prestige; the public, initially glad to see peace return, soon questioned the returning of the Austrian Netherlands and the costs of a war that brought France no direct gains. The general contempt for the peace terms was epitomized by the expression "stupid as the peace." The need for increased taxes to pay for the war also discredited the monarchy. [24] Even diplomatically the victory over Austria was expensive. In several important ways the War of the Austrian Succession weakened France's position in the balance of power.

First, the war increased Russia's importance. Empress Elizabeth renewed Russia's alliance with Austria in 1746; two years later, a sizable Russian army (subsidized by Britain) entered Germany en route to the Netherlands. This new prominence posed a threat to French interests in eastern Europe; over the next forty years, concern about Russia was the most common theme in French foreign policy, chiefly because of the nature of its alliance system. France based its security on several different, although interconnected, systems of formal and informal alliances. First, of course, were French alliances with one or more of the four other great powers: Austria, Britain, Prussia, and Russia. France, however, also depended on the support of lesser powers. Some of these were immediate neighbors who formed a buffer along its southern and eastern borders. Spain was the most important of these, but France also maintained close relations with Genoa, Geneva, the Swiss cantons, and a number of German principalities, such as the Palatinate and other small states near the Rhine. France took particular care, however, also to befriend the large but militarily backward powers of eastern Europe: Sweden, Poland, and the Ottoman Empire (which included not only today's Turkey but most of the Balkans). This eastern barrier helped protect France from Austria, Russia, or Prussia by forming a potential second front to draw troops away from the French border. (France attempted to create a similar eastern barrier during the years between the First and Second World Wars.) As the Russian threat to the Swedes, Poles, and Turks increased during the eighteenth century, French anxiety mounted. In 1748 the Russians sought, but did not obtain, British support for an attack on Sweden.[25] Repeatedly they intervened whenever Poland, an elective monarchy, selected a new king (who served for life). In 1733 they had driven Stanislas Leszczynski, Louis XV's father-in-law, from the Polish throne to which he had recently been elected, and substituted a candidate of their own liking. In the ensuing war they defeated a small French expeditionary force sent to Danzig while they sent 12,000 troops into Bavaria in support of Austria.[26] The most common target of Russian expansionism in the eighteenth century, however, was the Ottoman Empire. In the 1730s the Turks had regained some of the territory taken earlier by Austria; the new Austro-Russian alliance posed a particular threat to them.

Unsurprisingly, French diplomats concentrated in the years immediately after 1748 on forming alliances to contain Russia. Such alliances were contracted with Sweden, Denmark, and Prussia, and were contemplated with Poland and the Ottoman Empire.[27] This policy was in harmony with a personal project of Louis XV, a project he concealed from all but a few French diplomats. In 1745 several important Polish noblemen wrote to the prince de Conti, a distant cousin of Louis and a grandson of a French-born king of Poland who had been driven from his throne in 1697. These Polish magnates feared that their current king, Augustus III, wished to make the throne hereditary, thus costing the nobility its right to elect each king. They hoped that upon Augustus's death Conti would put himself forward as a candidate for the throne in opposition to a son of Augustus.

Informed by Conti of the request, Louis XV was highly supportive. Augustus, however, was also ruler of Saxony, a medium-sized German principality on the border of Prussia, which because of its strategic position was of considerable importance in the current Franco-Austrian war. Louis, moreover, hoped Augustus would be elected Holy Roman Emperor; even after Maria Theresa's husband was elected instead, Augustus was still influential in German politics. Not only was Louis willing to pay him a subsidy, he even agreed to the marriage of his only son, the dauphin Louis-Ferdinand, to Augustus's daughter Maria Josepha.[28] Since it would be disastrous if Augustus discovered that Louis was willing to support a rival to his son for the Polish throne, the French king could not openly assist Conti. He decided, however, to work in secret among the Polish nobility to build support for Conti and so informed his diplomatic representatives in Warsaw and in Dresden, the Saxon capital. Gradually this secret network expanded to bring in others, sometimes ambassadors and sometimes subordinate embassy officials, in order to gather information about Polish or Russian affairs. Informally known as the "Secret du Roi" (the king's secret), this organization as yet posed no threat to the established French diplomatic service, because each in its own way sought to counter Russia's increased strength and influence.[29]

The growing Russian threat was not the war's only unfortunate consequence. France's neglect of Spanish sensibilities during the peace negotiations angered Louis' cousin Ferdinand VI, just as Britain's conduct had angered Maria Theresa. Furthermore the results of the peace agreement made the Family Compact (as the Franco-Spanish alliance was called) less necessary to Spain. Although the Spaniards' gains may not have been worth their long war with Britain, Sardinia, and Austria, they did aid in resolving old issues rather than, as in France's case, creating new problems. First, the peace settlement laid the basis for ending Spain's long Italian rivalry with Austria. By the 1752 Treaty of Aranjuez the two states normalized their relations and so neutralized Italy that for the next forty years it remained at peace. Moreover, the peace settlement imposed such restrictions on the British right to sell slaves and send supplies to Spain's Caribbean colonies that in October 1750 the British government surrendered its remaining rights in exchange for a cash settlement. This eliminated the problem that had led to the British-Spanish war of 1739–48. Although Spain continued to resent the British occupation of Minorca and Gibraltar and British timber cutting in central America, tensions were so reduced that Spain could now balance between Britain and France in hopes of extracting concessions.[30] France thus could no longer count on the large Spanish navy's help in case of a war with Britain.

With the Family Compact largely a dead letter, France became virtually isolated. Except for minor powers like Sweden and Denmark, its only ally was Prussia, which had betrayed France in 1742 and 1745 by making separate peace agreements with Austria and was ready to betray France again. In 1748 Frederick unsuccessfully solicited an alliance with Britain.[31] The war destroyed the freedom of movement France needed to find a more reliable ally. Closer relations with Russia were unthinkable, and an alliance with Austria could be purchased only by helping it regain Silesia and thereby undoing the major accomplishment of the war, the establishment of a balance of power in Germany. Louis-Philogène Brûlart, marquis de Puyzieulx, the moderate and able French foreign minister from 1747 to 1751, wished for better relations with Britain and was a good friend of the Earl of Albemarle, the British ambassador at the French court.[32] Any return to even the nominal alliance of the 1730s was impossible, however. The British public's Francophobia had been fanned by the French attempt to invade England, their support for the Stuarts, and their conquest of the Austrian Netherlands. Furthermore, the capture of Louisbourg intensified its desire for colonial expansion; the British public was greatly disappointed when at Aix-la-Chapelle the government surrendered the fortress.[33]

The Duke of Newcastle overestimated French power and mistakenly saw it as basically hostile to Britain; thus he centered his foreign policy on opposing

France. Newcastle failed, however, to restore the alliances with Austria and the United Provinces of the Netherlands by which he hoped to counter France, so Britain, too, remained isolated.[34] Newcastle feared the French army as much as Louis XV's ministers feared the British navy, and he believed that France planned to encircle British North America, Hanover, and even Britain itself.[35] This sterile and dangerous stalemate made it possible for a colonial skirmish to engender a new war. Although French statesmen would sometimes hope, as had Puyzieulx, for improved relations with Britain, several more wars followed. The most long-standing result of attacking Austria was seventy years of suspicion and conflict with Britain.

THE FRENCH NAVY AND ITS LEGACY OF FAILURE

In case of war with Britain, France would be heavily dependent on its navy. It no longer was the weapon it had been when Louis XIV was at the height of his power a half century earlier. In the early 1690s France had the world's most powerful navy. Louis XIV, engaged in war against a coalition of much of Europe, chose, however, to demobilize his fleet and greatly reduce naval construction in order to concentrate his limited financial resources on the French army.[36] A similar coalition against France was formed during the first years of the eighteenth century in a new war fought over whether Louis' grandson would become king of Spain; again, Louis made the understandable decision to subordinate naval power to the increasingly desperate need to counter the dangers posed by the armies of Austria, Britain, and the Netherlands.[37] Naval construction failed to keep pace with attrition, such as the blow suffered in 1707 when the French Mediterranean fleet was scuttled during an attack on Toulon. (Toulon and the Atlantic ports of Brest and Rochefort were the navy's three major bases.) Most of the ships subsequently were raised, but some ten to fourteen ships of the line (warships of 50 or more cannon, capable of fighting in a line of battle) were subtracted permanently from the navy's rolls.[38] Louis XIV died in the autumn of 1715, soon after the return of peace. By then the French navy consisted of only forty-eight ships of the line, and many of these were ready for retirement. This was fewer than half the number France had possessed twenty years earlier.[39]

During the first few years of Louis XV's reign, much of the fleet was decommissioned and not replaced because of the French government's concern with reducing the huge debts inherited from the previous reign.[40] A modest replacement program was instituted during the 1720s, as twenty-five ships of the line were launched between 1720 and 1728.[41] During the next nine years, however, only four ships of the line were launched and one was purchased,[42] as

France concentrated its financial resources on fighting Austria, which had no navy. As tension between Spain and Britain increased and then turned to war, France began a small building program, launching nine ships of the line from 1738 through 1743.[43] On the eve of war with Britain, however, the French navy possessed only thirty-eight ships of the line (with three more in construction).[44] Of these, nine were incapable of service or had to be taken out of service after one or two campaigns. (Spain began the war with about forty ships of the line and finished with about twenty.)[45] In contrast, the British navy had seventy-seven ships of the line in service by the beginning of 1740 (just after initiating hostilities with Spain); during the 1744–48 war with France and Spain, it maintained a strength of eighty to ninety ships of the line.[46] Moreover, even though a veteran naval minister, Jean-Frédéric Phélypeaux, comte de Maurepas, directed the French navy, its performance was unimpressive.[47]

The war opened with the attempt to invade England discussed earlier. The same storm that damaged the transports assembled at Dunkirk also saved from attack their escort of fifteen ships of the line.[48] Meanwhile in the Mediterranean a fleet of fifteen French and twelve Spanish ships of the line fought thirty-four British ships of the line (including six 50-gun ships, some of which were not in the line of battle). This indecisive battle, fought off the French port of Toulon on 22 February 1744, was embarrassing to the French navy because the Spaniards carried the brunt of the fighting.[49] Subsequently the French navy undertook only one major fleet operation, an unsuccessful attempt in 1746 to recapture Louisbourg which resulted in the loss of three of the ten participating ships of the line and the death of thousands of sailors and troops from a shipboard epidemic.[50] The same year the French fought a naval battle in the Indian Ocean and captured Madras, but the participating ships were from the French East India Company.[51] The French navy provided only token support for Prince Charles Edward Stuart and for Franco-Spanish military operations in Italy. Its major function for most of the war was escorting convoys. For the first three years of the war it generally was successful, but in 1747 the British assembled a substantial fleet in the western approaches to the British Isles, gained control of the Bay of Biscay, and intercepted two major convoys. The warships escorting those convoys sacrificed themselves to give the merchant ships a chance to escape, costing the navy another nine ships of the line.[52]

By the beginning of 1748 French commerce was at the mercy of the British navy and privateers, adding to the pressure on Louis XV to make peace. Frederick II of Prussia mocked the French plight, but the disruption of the French economy, particularly in the Atlantic port cities, was quite serious. It is unlikely, however, that this seriously affected the peace settlement. There was little possibility that France would be allowed to retain its conquests in the Low Countries, and peace was made largely on the terms France demanded. The war, however, ended with the French navy humiliated and powerless and thousands of its sailors in English prisons.[53]

Structural reasons helped account for the French navy's failure. As during the reign of Louis XIV, the huge expenses of the French army left little money for the navy, whereas Britain, protected by its navy from invasion, did not have to maintain so large an army. By the summer of 1745 Maurepas was already complaining that the navy's credit was exhausted and it could barely pay its bills.[54] As already mentioned, the navy was badly outnumbered by the British, even with the help of the Spaniards. Moreover, it lacked heavy ships for fighting the British in fleet actions, having been built mostly to escort merchant convoys or capture enemy merchant ships; Maurepas and the French government largely had followed the advice of Lieutenant General of the Fleet René Du Guay-Trouin to refrain from building ships large enough to fight the huge 90- and 100-gun ships that usually formed part of the wartime British home and Mediterranean fleets. (During 1742 the navy demolished the *Foudroyant*, 110, while the *Royal-Louis*, 118, accidentally burned during construction.)[55]

For the British their naval victories in 1747 were of great importance. Until then the British public had been disillusioned with their navy's performance, particularly the failure of joint operations with the army.[56] Only the Louisbourg attack was an unqualified success, and it had been undertaken by *American* militia with the help of the British navy. The captures of the two groups of convoy escorts on 3 May and 14 October 1747 demonstrated French vulnerability, restored the navy's confidence, and gave the public two heroes in Vice Admiral George Anson and Rear Admiral Edward Hawke. Already famous for his circumnavigation of the world, Anson greatly influenced the young first lords of the admiralty John Russell, Duke of Bedford (serving from December 1744 to February 1748) and John Montagu, Earl of Sandwich (February 1748 to June 1751) when he served as a member of the Board of Admiralty. In 1751 Anson became first lord himself. The entire British navy now benefited from the innovations he had introduced as a fleet commander.[57] Its deficiencies in the war of 1739–48 were serious enough to stimulate reform, but not so serious as to undermine its self-confidence. Under Anson's leadership it became an even more formidable opponent.

Although the postwar French navy lacked a reformer like Anson, it did benefit from good administration. Maurepas was dismissed in April 1749 after quarreling with his colleagues in the Council of State or Higher Council (*conseil d'état* or *conseil d'en haut*), the king's chief advisory body on security matters.[58] His successor, Antoine-Louis Rouillé, proved a surprisingly able administrator, even though he had no prior experience in naval affairs.[59] Between the beginning of 1749 and the end of 1754, the navy launched thirty-four ships of the line (compared with twenty-six Spanish and fifteen British) and approached its authorized strength of sixty of the line.[60] However, this program was not a threat to Britain. Only the four new 80-gun ships could challenge British 90- and 100-gun ships. (These splendid French ships seem to have been intended chiefly to stiffen convoy escorts.) More importantly, even if all its ships were put into service, the French navy would be only about half the size of the British (and it had little immediate hope of Spanish assistance). Finally, Rouillé's parallel program of replenishing the naval supplies needed by the great ports of Brest, Rochefort, and Toulon, which had made considerable progress, was virtually suspended at the end of 1752 by financial constraints.[61] During the next two years work in the dockyards slowed and the navy's contract to obtain critical naval stores from the Baltic was not renewed. At the beginning of 1755 the fleet faced severe shortages of cannon and naval supplies and was at least two years away from being ready for full mobilization.[62]

By now, Rouillé's responsibility was preventing war rather than directing any naval mobilization. Puyzieulx had to resign as foreign minister in September 1751 for reasons of health. His replacement, François-Dominique de Barberie de Saint-Contest, continued his policies, but died on 24 July 1754.[63] Rouillé replaced him, turning the naval ministry over to Jean-Baptiste de Machault d'Arnouville. As finance minister (controller general of finances) Machault had made himself detested and feared by his attempts to increase royal revenue. He had requested permission to leave this thankless job,[64] but as naval minister he soon was faced with a similar problem, the constraints on expenditures caused by the monarchy's seemingly intractable financial problems.

Meanwhile at the foreign ministry Rouillé quickly earned the reputation of being honest and peaceable but lacking in ability.[65] He had his own intractable problems to face, particularly a dispute with Britain over their competing territorial claims in North America. This dispute led to a war that France wished to avoid, a war for which its navy was unprepared.

FROM COMPETITION TO CRISIS IN NORTH AMERICA

The French colonies in North America, known collectively as New France, differed widely. Most similar to Britain's heavily populated North American colonies was Canada, whose agricultural heartland, containing also the population centers of Quebec, Trois-Rivières, and Montreal, stretched along the St. Lawrence River. Canada, however, also included a vast area to the west and south, the Upper Country (*pays d'en haut*), populated almost entirely by various

Indian nations. They sold furs to the French, whose presence was centered around fortified trading posts, usually situated near rivers, such as the Wabash. Along these rivers traveled the boatmen (*voyageurs* or *coureurs de bois*), chiefly based in Montreal, who like the garrisons of the forts were intermediaries in the fur trade.

Although subordinate to the governor general of New France at Quebec, Isle Royale (now Cape Breton Island) had a completely different economic base. Although it produced some of its own food, its economy was based on fishing, and its governor, situated at Louisbourg, enjoyed a degree of autonomy. The populations of nearby Isle St. Jean (now Prince Edward Island) and of the French portion of Acadia (now New Brunswick) were mostly agricultural and were militarily dependent on Canada, but because of their location they were also economically connected with Isle Royale. Virtually autonomous from the rest of New France was the huge but sparsely populated colony of Louisiana, which produced some agricultural goods and traded for furs. Particularly active in the fur trade were the posts of the Illinois country along the upper Mississippi and Illinois River valleys, which economically and militarily were tied more closely to Montreal and Quebec than to New Orleans.[66]

All of these areas were under close political supervision from their mother country. Administered by the French naval ministry, they had a dual bureaucracy that closely resembled that of a great naval port like Brest, Rochefort, or Toulon. Senior naval officers filled the post of governor general or governor and, like port commandants, were responsible for military security and military operations. Civilian employees of the naval ministry, the *intendants* and their staffs, handled finances and a variety of administrative tasks. New France came close to achieving the unity needed for imperial defense that the British Board of Trade vainly sought from the often divided and uncooperative British North American colonies.[67]

Of the various parts of this North American empire, only one could rival in importance to France its rich sugar-producing Caribbean colonies such as Martinique, Guadeloupe, and St. Domingue (now Haiti): Isle Royale, with its great cod fisheries off Newfoundland and in the Gulf of St. Lawrence. The furs of Canada, chiefly beaver, had a limited market. Canada was an economic liability whose reason for being was strategic, that of diverting British forces from Europe and checking British North American expansion. In contrast, salt cod was both consumed in France and exported in great quantity; modern estimates are that such exports at midcentury were worth almost 2 million livres per year.[68] Even more important to the French government, however, was the contribution of Isle Royale and its fisheries to the French navy. As the navy could not afford to keep ships at sea during peacetime, it was unable to train its own sailors. Instead it conscripted them from the French merchant and fishing fleets during wartime. The Newfoundland and St. Lawrence fisheries with their harsh conditions were considered the best place to train seamen; a leading modern expert estimates that they accounted for perhaps a quarter of France's 40,000–60,000 sailors and trained 2,000 new sailors a year.[69] Without both the fisheries and its Caribbean colonies, France could not hope to construct a navy capable of fighting the British. The 1713 Treaty of Utrecht, which ended the War of the Spanish Succession, had threatened the French position in the fisheries by transferring to Britain most of the settlements near the fisheries, on Newfoundland itself and on Nova Scotia, the major portion of Acadia. Quickly the French government moved to establish settlements on Isle Royale as a substitute and, Acadia not being precisely defined, to deny the British access to the strategically important Bay of Fundy.[70]

Naval Minister Maurepas took great care to protect the fisheries. At enormous expense he built a huge (but badly situated and poorly constructed) European-style fortress to protect Louisbourg, the chief port of Isle Royale. He justified the project by claiming it would shield not only the fisheries but also the French settlements of the St. Lawrence valley.[71] Meanwhile the governors general of New France used the thirty years of peace with Britain to build other forts in order to protect Canada from the nearby British colonies. The most important of the French fortifications included Fort St. Frédéric on Lake Champlain, Fort Niagara on the Niagara River, and Fort Detroit on Lake Huron. Other posts protected Louisiana from the Spanish colonists of Florida and Texas and from the British colonists of South Carolina and Georgia. French construction disturbed British Americans, but colonial legislatures, largely responsible for their own defense, did not attempt to match it.[72] Their most extensive fortification system was directed against Spanish Florida, although the French river-and-lake communication and defense system was breached by a post at Oswego on Lake Ontario.

As long as Britain and France remained allies, even nominal ones, British colonists were unable to respond by force to the French presence in areas they considered belonged to them. They could expect no support beyond diplomatic protests from Walpole's peace-loving government; even the British navy took little notice of New France.[73] The outbreak of war in 1744, however, released both sides from their restraints. The French took the first steps by seizing a British fishing port near Isle Royale and by making use of local Indians to threaten Annapolis Royal, the capital of Nova Scotia. The British response, although approved in London, was largely the work of its local officials, particularly Governor William Shirley of Massachusetts and Commodore Peter Warren, commander of the British navy's North American station. Making use of 3,000 militia from the various New England colonies and a small covering squadron of colonial and British warships, they captured Louisbourg in June 1745.[74] This accomplishment was not followed by an attack on Quebec as Warren and Shirley wished; an expeditionary force was assembled in England in 1746, but fearing the French force en route to Louisbourg, it was diverted to an unsuccessful raid on the French port of Lorient.[75] The Treaty of Aix-la-Chapelle returned Louisbourg to France, while border disputes affecting Canada and Acadia were referred to a joint British-French commission. Such commissions had been established after the peace settlements at Ryswick (1697) and Utrecht (1713). They were the usual way of preventing contentious issues from delaying a peace settlement. The present commission, however, included extremists like Shirley and helped greatly to poison French-British relations.[76]

The duc de Choiseul, the French foreign minister during the darkest period of the Seven Years' War, later would blame France's plight on the French negotiator at Aix-la-Chapelle, the comte de Saint-Séverin. Choiseul criticized Saint-Séverin for failing to include a border settlement in North America among the preliminary peace terms, thereby laying the groundwork for a new war in 1755.[77] Time, however, was pressing during the negotiations at Aix-la-Chapelle. Having agreed to return Louisbourg, Britain was unlikely to make further concessions in North America. France was willing to surrender the immensely valuable Austrian Netherlands to avoid the risks of an indefinite war. The French government hardly would take such risks to resolve the disputed borders of an economically marginal colony across the Atlantic Ocean, which mostly served to distract British forces from Europe.[78]

Although the peace brought the return to the *status quo ante bellum* (the condition before the war) in North America, it proved impossible to return to the limited competition of the 1720s and 1730s. Both sides during the war of 1744–48 employed irregular warfare including the use of their Indian allies, which greatly added to reciprocal hatred and fear.[79] French fears for the survival of Canada had been aroused. So, too, had been British fears for their own colonies,[80] as well as the desire for territorial expansion. Although French policy did not threaten existing British American settlements, it was opposed to their expansion into areas France considered its own. To avert conflict would require foresight and strong leadership.

Initially the most dangerous dispute concerned Acadia's precise border. Here, along the peninsula joining Nova Scotia to the mainland, the French and British constructed opposing forts just a few miles apart. Although blood was shed in 1750, the French government was sufficiently impressed by British protests to urge moderation on its local commanders.[81] An informal truce greatly reduced tension, and the British concentrated their attention on constructing a great naval base at Halifax on the east coast of Nova Scotia and on bringing Protestant colonists to counterbalance the native French-speaking Acadians (who still formed the majority of the population of Nova Scotia). Neither side considered the conflict resolved, however, and the French pressured the Acadians in the English-controlled area to emigrate across the de facto border.

The chief danger now shifted to the wide area between Lake Erie and the Allegheny Mountains that was drained by the Allegheny, Monongahela, and Ohio rivers. Before the war of 1744 this region had not been a source of competition. Pennsylvania settlements lay a considerable distance to the east, and the main French passage route between Canada and Louisiana lay to the west along the Maumee, Wabash, and lower Ohio rivers. [82] The war, however, had a major impact on French relations with Indian villages throughout the Great Lakes region, relations on which the economy and military defense of Canada depended. French alliances with the various nations tottered as the French government recoiled from the heavy expenses attendant on "gift-giving," the psychological and economic foundation of relations with the Indians. The war made it both more expensive and more difficult for the French to procure and distribute "gifts" such as guns and blankets on which the Indians depended. (The "gifts" essentially were in exchange for furs.) The war thus accelerated the penetration of rival traders from Pennsylvania and Virginia, particularly into the region's nearby eastern portion, which for logistical and economic reasons was the weakest part of the area of North America claimed by France. Hitherto the French largely had ignored it because the furs of the upper Ohio, Allegheny, and Monongahela river region were considered inferior and because its forests did not produce the right kind of wood for the canoes needed to transport them. Its rivers, however, were part of the Great Lakes and Ohio-Mississippi River watersheds, all of which were claimed by France. The governors general of New France mistakenly saw the English (rather than their own parsimony) as the cause of their difficulties.

After the war the naval ministry sent a series of inexperienced governors general or acting governors general to Canada who lacked the wisdom to pursue a policy of generosity and fairness to allies in the Upper Country. Instead the successive governors general La Galissonnière, La Jonquière, Longueuil, and Duquesne resorted to a policy of force and intimidation after the failure of a farcical attempt to claim the area by burying inscribed lead plates in various locations. In 1753 Duquesne began constructing a chain of forts linking Lake Erie and the Allegheny River, using an army of Canadian militiamen reluctantly drafted into service. [83]

Duquesne was following rigidly the orders of Naval Minister Rouillé, who seems to have been convinced by La Galissonnière that British penetration of the area threatened communications between Canada and Louisiana. [84] Duquesne's expedition intimidated local nations such as the Shawnee and Delaware into joining an alliance against the British, but only in hopes of later driving the French, too, from the region.

In retrospect this expedition was a disaster, causing a cascade of events leading to a war that France did not want and for which it was not prepared. Like the decision a dozen years earlier to attack Maria Theresa, it resulted from a combination of ignorance, fear, and impatience. In the earlier case, Louis XV acted himself, but in the present case the king, perhaps distracted by his secret diplomacy in eastern Europe, left the matter to his ministers. Rouillé acted in ignorance of the repercussions the fort building would have both on the Indians and on the British and in exaggerated fear of the urgency of the British threat. Unfortunately France did not have a strong foreign minister to intervene. Saint-Contest failed to prevent Rouillé's action, even though it was contrary to France's overall policy of cultivating better relations with Britain and whoever else might be of assistance against Russia.

Meanwhile the British were about to launch their own expedition into the upper Ohio valley, in part for financial gain. Lieutenant Governor Robert Dinwiddie of Virginia and other speculators in the Ohio Company hoped not only to forestall the French but to earn large profits by attracting settlers to the area where the Allegheny and Monongahela joined to form the Ohio River. [85] Had the French been wise enough to refrain from penetrating the area by force themselves, they could have left any British incursion for the Indians to repulse. This would have had little subsequent danger of European repercussions.

In early 1754 Dinwiddie sent an advance party of 160 Virginia volunteers to protect a fort that the Ohio Company was constructing at the forks of the Ohio. Duquesne moved to counter the Virginians, leading to a confrontation that played into the intense British anger and distrust of France stemming from the recent war. Before the Virginia troops could reach the area, a party of 1,000 Indians and Canadians arrived from the new French forts 100 miles to the north. They drove off the forty Virginians constructing the Ohio Company fort and began building a larger fort of their own. The Virginia military detachment, commanded by George Washington, established a base some fifty miles to the south to await reinforcements. As had happened on the borders of Acadia, the two positions were too close to avoid a confrontation, in this case Washington's attack on a Canadian patrol and a retaliatory attack on Washington's encampment. The outmatched Virginians surrendered their camp and retreated across the mountains. [86]

News of the attack on the French patrol reached Europe just as Rouillé was taking up his new duties as foreign minister. For several reasons this gradually developing crisis proved more dangerous than the one caused by the skirmishes along the disputed Acadian border four years earlier.[87] Both Britain and France were so concerned about dominance over the Indian nations of the Ohio region that arranging a buffer zone was difficult; both parties felt that the other's presence posed an unacceptable threat to long-established areas of settlement (Canada on one side, Pennsylvania and Virginia on the other). Several years of bickering over disputed borders in North America and over the contested "neutral" Caribbean islands of St. Lucia, St. Vincent, Dominica, and Tobago had increased suspicions between the two governments,[88] and the lack of cooperation in European affairs reduced the incentive for a comprehensive settlement of differences. The British government, outraged by the introduction of Canadian troops south of Lake Erie and by the confrontation with the Virginians, responded by escalating the conflict. It sought not only to drive the French from the Ohio and Allegheny River valleys and the borders of Acadia but also to force them to destroy forts built over the preceding forty years.

The Duke of Newcastle, who in spite of his exaggerated fears of the French really wished for a peaceful resolution of the crisis, planned a gradual increase of force. First, the forts south of Lake Erie would be attacked, then Fort St. Frédéric on Lake Champlain (which Indian raiders had used in the recent war)[89] and Fort Beauséjour on the border of Nova Scotia. He assumed that at some point the French would make concessions. To win the approval of George II for sending troops, he enlisted the support of the king's favorite son, William Augustus, Duke of Cumberland, who was captain general of the British army. Cumberland and his political ally Secretary at War Henry Fox won the approval of the king and the cabinet not only for sending two regiments from Ireland as Newcastle wished but also for raising two regiments in New England. This expansion of force was dangerous enough, but Cumberland and Fox soon outmaneuvered Newcastle and jettisoned the idea of gradually applying force as a negotiating tactic. Supported by Anson and Paymaster of the Forces William Pitt, they won approval in November 1754 of a plan to resolve simultaneously *all* the border disputes in North America by sweeping away the French forts blocking the expansion of the American colonies. The overall commander, Cumberland's protégé Major General Edward Braddock, would bring the Irish regiments to Virginia under the escort of two ships of the line and two frigates. Augmented further on arrival they would attack the new French forts between the forks of the Ohio and Lake Erie. As soon as they were ready, the two New England regiments would attack Fort Niagara and Fort St. Frédéric, while three British regiments presently in Nova Scotia would deal with Fort Beauséjour, perhaps with the help of New England volunteers. Braddock would coordinate all of these operations and personally lead a column into the Ohio country.[90]

In effect Braddock's task was rolling the border of New France back to the St. Lawrence and the Great Lakes, leaving New France virtually indefensible. This, moreover, would be a terrible blow to French prestige in Europe, and given the largely lawless character of eighteenth-century diplomacy, such an appearance of weakness would threaten French security. In December 1754 the French government learned of Braddock's expedition, and in early January it received intelligence of his plans to attack the new fort at the forks of the Ohio (although not of his subsequent objectives).[91] It would have to conduct any negotiations in London, as the Earl of Albemarle, the veteran British ambassador to the French court, died suddenly on 22 December. Eight days later, France ordered back to England the duc de Mirepoix, the French ambassador to the British court, who had been home on leave.

2

1755
Countering the British Assault

In retrospect, the Franco-British negotiations of 1755 seem to have had little chance of success. The French government's miscalculations over the preceding fifteen years had created a war party in Britain strong enough to impose its will on the British government in spite of Prime Minister Newcastle's desire for peace. It had attacked Austria in spite of its promises to recognize Maria Theresa and had taken actions that it considered only expedients of war but which Britain considered mortal threats—the attempted invasion of England, the assault on the Austrian Netherlands, the support given to the Stuart uprising of 1745. Since the end of the war it had failed to use the border commission to resolve disputes in North America and had moved a large body of Canadian troops into an area that important British and British-American officials considered vital. Meanwhile for the last two years it had let the readiness of the French navy deteriorate, so that when an outraged Britain prepared to use force, one of France's chief means of resistance was not fully available. By the beginning of 1755 France was left little choice between a humiliating diplomatic surrender or a last-minute attempt at resistance. From a French perspective, the story of the last few months of peace is a dual one, that of a fruitless attempt to resolve the crisis by negotiation and that of belated preparations for war.

No member of the British government understood that French policies in North America were basically defensive and that the French government considered Russia rather than Britain the chief threat to its interests. The hostilities in 1754 between the Canadians and the Virginians seemed confirmation of Britain's long-standing fear of French aggression. Even the Duke of Newcastle saw them as the result of a calculated policy of confining the British colonies in North American to a strip of land along the Atlantic coast and of rendering them defenseless. He seems to have believed that only British firmness could force the French to back down and thus prevent war,[1] while several members of the British government were anxious to begin military operations. From what we now know of French policy, however, the present crisis was more the result of weak French leadership than of calculated aggression. This failure of leadership affected the foreign ministry, which had not insisted on the importance of better relations with Britain and thus had not acted to prevent the crisis before it began. It also affected the naval and colonial ministry, which had drifted into the crisis while simultaneously cutting back on naval preparedness. The chief responsibility for the contradictory policies, however, was that of Louis XV.

Louis was neither the menacing figure feared by Newcastle nor the ludicrous one historians often have portrayed. He was not as strong a person nor as dynamic a ruler as was, for example, Empress Maria Theresa. Moreover, he does seem to have had some of the faults commonly attributed to him. He was sexually compulsive and chronically unfaithful to his wife; he was secretive and often suspicious of those who served in his government; he was prone to morbid superstition; all too frequently he proved incapable of supporting a policy or one of his ministers in the face of public opposition. There are other sides to him, however, that have been noticed less often. He was exceptionally intelligent and often astute. Moreover, he took very seriously his duties to France and the Bourbon monarchy. What is perhaps most unusual in an eighteenth-century ruler, however, was the tenderness and humanity he was capable of showing even in public life. His experience of war in the 1740s had left him with a dislike of human bloodshed. His eventual alliances with Maria Theresa and his cousin Charles (who became king of Spain in 1759) were grounded not only on reason of state (*raison d'état*) but on his genuine personal affection for them. As we shall see later, his love for his eldest daughter and his grandchildren would play a part in his diplomacy. Although capable of cruelty when he felt injured or insulted,[2] Louis had far more in common with the peaceable Duke of Newcastle than he did with the mean-spirited George II of Britain, the arrogant and bullying William Pitt, or the cynical Frederick II of Prussia.[3] Such men were remorseless enemies. Given the questions about Louis' resolve raised by the peace he had rushed to make in 1748, there were reasons to doubt his capability for fighting another war.

Louis' dislike of confrontation of any kind and his weak self-confidence, so dangerous in a war leader, already had undermined the functioning of his government. When his mentor Fleury died in 1743, Louis refused to appoint a chief minister and chose to direct the government himself. It was a task for which he was ill-equipped. Freiherr Jean Le Chambrier, the astute and experienced Prussian minister to the French court before his death in 1751, analyzed the king and his chief ministers shortly after the end of the last war. He blamed Fleury's training for the king's aversion to work and low self-esteem. Doubting himself, he was reluctant to criticize those who served in his government. Le Chambrier also commented on the king's reserve, secretiveness, and hot temper, but praised his humanity toward those who served him. This assessment resembles that of the Cardinal de Bernis, Louis' foreign minister in 1757 and 1758, who described him as the best master in the world but ignorant of how to exercise power; he also said Louis was a man of honor who desired to do good.[4]

Lacking someone like Louis XIV with the strong self-confidence to impose his authority, the unity of the French government collapsed. The problem was compounded by the structure of the French governmental system. The Bourbon monarchy did not have a cabinet to coordinate the great administrative departments. The major heads of government departments—the secretary of state for war, the secretary of state for the navy and colonies, the secretary of state for foreign affairs, the secretary of state for the king's household (or director of the interior), the controller general of finances—did not meet regularly as such. Instead, the king regularly consulted with these men, among others, in a series of councils organized around different governmental functions. The most important of these was the Council of State, which met at least twice a week to discuss foreign policy and matters of national security. The prestige of sitting on the Council of State was shown by the title of "minister of state" given to its members, who were all appointed for life. Heads of departments, particularly ones new to their post, were not necessarily ministers of state, whereas men no longer holding other responsibilities sometimes still were. (Thus technically one should not use the terms "foreign minister," "naval minister," or "army minister"; for brevity's sake, however, we will continue to do so.) Without a strong king or first minister, the Council of State could degenerate into a forum where ministers of state either tried to impose their will on the king or tried to demonstrate their subservience to his wishes. Such rivalries had affected the conduct of the War of the Austrian Succession and were a continuing problem.[5]

In January 1755 the Council of State contained in theory nine members (including one who joined during the month), all of whom were older than the king, who was forty-four. Four of them served without portfolio. One of these, the once-powerful Pierre Guérin, cardinal de Tencin, although still a member, had retired to his see in Lyons and no longer attended meetings of the council.[6] Two others had been exiled from the court because of disagreements with the king and council: Louis-Philogène Brûlart, marquis de Puyzieulx and Alphonse-Marie-Louis, comte de Saint-Séverin d'Aragon.[7] These two friends had functioned well together in negotiating the Treaty of Aix-la-Chapelle (the former as foreign minister, the latter as plenipotentiary at the peace conference), partly because their temperaments were complementary. According to Le Chambrier, Puyzieulx was modest and gullible, while Saint-Séverin was brave and firm, but also proud, haughty, and poorly educated.[8] Still attending meetings although he was approaching retirement was Adrien-Maurice, duc de Noailles, a marshal of France, the highest of military ranks, and a former private adviser of Louis XV who had played an important part in Louis' decision to serve as his own chief minister. An expert on foreign policy, he was deeply suspicious of Britain, which he claimed was France's most dangerous enemy.[9] He still enjoyed the king's respect and exercised great influence in the council.

The other members of the council were the heads of the five great governmental departments. Foreign Minister Rouillé was considered by Newcastle a man of peace,[10] but he did not have the experience, reputation, or forcefulness to impose his views on his colleagues. Louis Phélypeaux, comte de Saint-Florentin, the secretary of state for household affairs, chiefly was concerned with domestic policies, particularly religious matters; in 1757 he was assigned responsibility for overseeing the administration of Paris. Even when serving in 1771 as interim foreign minister he refused to make decisions on foreign policy.[11] Naval Minister Machault was unpopular with the public, but had earned the king's affection and esteem. Although honest, honorable, and forceful, he lacked the affability to win friends on the council or the experience of foreign affairs to lead it.[12] The leading member of the council was Pierre-Marc de Voyer de Paulmy, comte d'Argenson, who had been army minister for the last dozen years. Le Chambrier had considered him an adroit politician, although lacking in diligence and excessively prone to delegate authority.[13] On 12 January his position on the council was strengthened when Controller General of Finances Jean Moreau de Séchelles was named minister of state. Although Séchelles was a friend of Newcastle and was respected by Machault, he was regarded as a follower of Argenson.[14]

Louis also turned for advice to two people who were not on the council, although neither had the influence in foreign affairs that many observers believed. One was his distant cousin Louis-François de Bourbon, prince de Conti, whom the king consulted frequently and whom, as already noted, he wished eventually to place on the throne of Poland. Conti's ambitions were unlimited—he even considered attempting to win the hand in marriage of Empress Elizabeth of Russia[15]—but he lacked ability, political judgment, and loyalty to the king, and soon would lose Louis' trust.

More enduring was the influence of Jeanne-Antoinette Poisson, marquise de Pompadour, who was still regarded as the king's mistress even though by now she satisfied his guilt-ridden sexual desires by providing him with women of lower social status, who would be no rivals to her influence.[16] Dodo Heinrich,

Freiherr von Knyphausen, who arrived at the French court in June 1754 as the Prussian minister plenipotentiary, accused her of dominating French foreign policy. [17] At least at this period of her life, however, she was less interested in diplomacy than in acquiring material possessions and assisting her friends (one of whom was Machault). [18] Her inclinations in foreign policy were toward peace, and in general hers was a voice of common sense and moderation. In this she resembled Amalie Sophie Marianne von Wendt, Countess of Yarmouth, George II's former mistress and continuing friend. Neither made policy, but each usually offered good advice and could provide access to the king and valuable political support.

Of more immediate influence on the coming negotiations were Rouillé's chief assistants at the foreign ministry. As naval minister Rouillé had been very dependent on advisers, including La Galissonnière. [19] This also was true of him as foreign minister. The most important of his subordinates were his three *premiers commis* for policy matters, equivalent to what would today be called undersecretaries of state. There was an important shift at this level soon after the negotiations with Britain began. Responsibility for drafting Rouillé's correspondence with the ambassador to Britain was shifted from Premier Commis François de Bussy to Premier Commis Jean-Ignace, abbé de La Ville. [20] Bussy was a protégé of Noailles and had been a premier commis since 1749. His prior career had included four years' service as minister plenipotentiary to the British court (1740–44), where he became a British spy and leaked information about French invasion plans. Bussy had virtually directed the foreign ministry during the tenure of the weak Saint-Contest and was regarded by his colleagues as a bully. The British approached him without success to resume his spying in 1755 and again in 1761, when he was sent to England to conduct peace negotiations. [21]

La Ville, who had been a premier commis since the end of 1745, had been expelled from his post during the years of Bussy's ascendancy. It was due to Madame de Pompadour's intervention that he was restored to office. He was known for his prodigious capacity for work and for his honesty, although he had a bad reputation with the British government because of his outspoken opposition to Britain's colonial ambitions. He soon became Rouillé's chief adviser. [22] Although his experience and energy were valuable, he was considered to lack originality of thought, [23] and he was not capable of substituting for a strong foreign minister. The third of the premiers commis was Jean-Pierre Tercier, who had been Saint-Séverin's secretary during the negotiations at Aix-la-Chapelle. Although he was assigned responsibility only for correspondence with the Swiss cantons, Russia, Poland, and the Ottoman Empire, he had an importance unknown to Rouillé. He recently had been inducted into the "Secret du Roi" and handled the king's private correspondence with its members; he was also in charge of the foreign ministry's ciphers.[24]

Rouillé's desire to avoid war if possible was shared by the ambassador to the British court, Gaston-Charles-Pierre de Lévis de Lomagne, duc de Mirepoix, a lieutenant general in the French army. Mirepoix, who had occupied his diplomatic post for the last six years, was dedicated and sincere; Newcastle said he had never dealt with a diplomat of his rectitude and courtesy. He did not have the reputation, however, of being a particularly skilled negotiator.[25] Before returning to London he was given new instructions to demand an explanation of the British military preparations, to convey France's desire that the governors of the British colonies in America refrain from violence and return matters to their prior condition, and to suggest that the disputes be referred to the border commission. He arrived in London on 8 January 1755.[26]

Five days earlier the king had approved plans for reinforcing Quebec and Louisbourg, and Machault had selected the ships to do so. Nine ships of the line would carry four battalions of troops to Quebec and two to Louisbourg, a total of 3,650 officers and men. (French regiments usually consisted of two battalions, each of which was slightly smaller than a British regiment. The battalions for New France were taken from the Artois, La Reine, Bourgogne, Languedoc, Guyenne, and Béarn regiments.) These ships, some of which were among the oldest in the navy, would have to remove most of their cannon to accommodate the troops; in the terminology of the time they were *en flûte*, i.e., serving as *flûtes*, or transport ships. Four fully armed ships of the line would accompany them to New France. After crossing the Atlantic together, the various ships would split into two squadrons, one for Quebec and the other for Louisbourg. The squadron for Quebec was commanded by Chef d'éscadre (Rear Admiral) Emmanuel-Auguste de Cahideuc, comte du Bois de la Motte, and the one for Louisbourg by Chef d'éscadre Antoine-Alexis Périer de Salvert. The troops for Quebec were led by Maréchal de camp (Brigadier General) Jean Erdmann, baron de Dieskau, a highly respected former aide to the great Saxe and an expert in small unit warfare. Six more ships of the line under the command of Lieutenant General of the Fleet (Lieutenant general des armées navales, roughly comparable to a British vice admiral) Jean-Baptiste MacNemara, the naval commandant at the great naval base of Brest in Brittany, would escort them clear of the French coast and then return to port.[27] It was not, however, until 20 January that Rouillé wrote to inform Mirepoix that a dozen ships of the line were being put in armament. Within weeks, the British had a highly detailed and accurate list of them.[28]

The forces being sent to New France were not a menace to the nearby British colonies. The troops being sent to Louisbourg would double the size of the present 1,200-man garrison; Canada, hitherto defended only by marines, would receive about 2,400 regulars, little more than Braddock's force. (Braddock's two regiments were expected to total about 1,500 men after finishing the recruiting in America needed to bring them to full strength.) Moreover, the size of the French garrison would be miniscule compared with the population of the British colonies in North America, perhaps 1.2 million (whereas Canada had barely 60,000 people, including 8,000 in Quebec and 5,000 in Montreal, and all of New France had fewer than 100,000).[29] The French government's decision to send troops, taken a few days before it learned of Braddock's first objective, seems to have been basically defensive. Machault ordered Governor General Duquesne to support the king's rights but to avoid confrontation.[30] Although Rouillé predicted to Prussian minister Knyphausen that the news would cause a great surprise in England,[31] Knyphausen's later speculation that the French armament was designed to intimidate the British[32] seems uninformed, given how small were the forces sent to Canada. Instead the armament seems to have been aimed at permitting the French to negotiate on roughly equal terms with Britain and, should the negotiations fail, to defend New France. It, however, had a far greater impact on British military and naval operations than on the negotiations themselves.

NEGOTIATIONS FAIL AND BOTH SIDES PREPARE FOR WAR

On 16–17 January, after a week in London, Mirepoix reported to Rouillé the results of his initial discussions with Prime Minister Newcastle and the secretary of state for the southern department, Sir Thomas Robinson (who dealt with France, Spain, and the states of western Europe).[33] Mirepoix was optimistic, believing that Newcastle feared war and that the British public, devoted to commerce, wished to avoid it. The discussions themselves, however, consisted largely of the same sterile arguments that had characterized the Franco-British boundary commission. Mirepoix proposed to Robinson that both countries send orders to their governors in North America to take no further action, that the Ohio valley be returned to the condition of 1744 (before the War of the Austrian Succession), that the dispute be referred to the boundary commission, and that Britain provide an explanation of why it was arming troops and where they were being sent. Robinson in return demanded the French demolish their new forts and evacuate the area.

The overall British negotiating position was far more ominous, however, than Mirepoix initially realized. On 16 January this position was established by a meeting of the British inner or secret cabinet, a powerful but informal body whose membership slightly varied. On this day it was attended by Newcastle, the two secretaries of state (Robinson and Robert Darcy, Earl of Holdernesse, the secretary of state for the northern department, who dealt with the states of eastern Europe), First Lord of the Admiralty Anson, and Philip Yorke, Earl of Hardwicke, Newcastle's chief adviser. They decided to demand a return to conditions in North America at the time of the Treaty of Utrecht of 1713, thereby forcing the French to demolish all the forts they had built since then.[34] Moreover, the British intended to respond to Mirepoix's claims that France had a legal right to the area between Lake Erie and the Ohio valley by their own claims that the area belonged to the nations of the Iroquois Confederacy, which the 1713 Treaty of Utrecht said "were subject to the Dominion of Great Britain." For years the British representatives on the border commission had been making such claims, which by now were very dubious; the Iroquois Confederacy's pretensions to overlordship of the area had become hollow as the nations actually living there asserted their independence.[35] Repeating these claims was an invitation to the pedantic Rouillé to conduct a debate on legal rights. This could turn the negotiations into a repetition of the sterile discussions of the border commission, and make it far more difficult to find a compromise on the basis of pragmatic considerations. Ominously, too, a few days later the inner cabinet ordered seventeen ships of the line placed in armament in response to the squadrons being prepared by Machault.[36]

A memoir incorporating the British demands was presented to Mirepoix on 22 January. The following day, his optimism shaken, Mirepoix reported that the situation was highly dangerous. He warned that the British refused to refer matters to the border commission, insisted on an explanation of French armaments, and were arming thirty ships of the line themselves.[37] A few days later Newcastle told Sir Benjamin Keene, the British ambassador in Madrid, that France and Britain were arming against each other and might be on the brink of war, although he was still optimistic that war could be avoided; he refused, however, to permit Keene leave to visit home.[38]

Rouillé's response, given the dangerous turn the negotiations had taken, offered little new. On 3 February he sent Mirepoix the full powers he had requested to make an agreement, ordered him to find out the extent of British pretensions, and told him that France was unwilling either to accept the conditions of Utrecht as a basis for discussions or to suspend the border commission. He said that although Louis XV wished to avoid war he was determined to protect his subjects in New France, who were menaced by the British threat to the supply line between Canada and Louisiana (unlike the British colonists who were separated by the Allegheny Mountains from the area in dispute). He sent a memoir for Robinson proposing a reversion to the conditions of 1744 and suggesting that orders be given to the respective governors to undertake no new operations.[39]

Mirepoix's next move was an attempt to buy time. Immediately after receiving the dispatches from Rouillé, he proposed a two-year convention regarding the Ohio area during which time both parties would evacuate the area, cancel all commercial concessions, and refrain from offensive action. It is possible, suggests the great historian Richard Waddington, he may have been acting on secret orders sent by Louis, bypassing Rouillé.[40]

The inner cabinet decided to accept Mirepoix's idea in principle, but it also called for the destruction of Fort St. Frédéric and Fort Niagara, British freedom of navigation on Lake Erie and Lake Ontario, and British occupation of the west shore of the Bay of Fundy. Mirepoix was hopeful that an agreement could be reached to defuse the crisis in the Ohio area, leaving time to discuss the other British demands, but he warned Rouillé that moments were precious and that France should take precautions.[41]

At this moment peace was still possible, as even the bellicose Duke of Cumberland admitted.[42] In his counterproposal of 19 February, Rouillé was even willing to accept demolition of the French forts provided the British demolish the forts such as Oswego that they had constructed over the last forty years.[43] Before this reply arrived, however, the British drastically altered the terms they were prepared to accept, thereby dooming the negotiations. They shifted the proposed demilitarized area to the west, leaving the area at the junction of the Allegheny and Monongahela rivers under British control. This change was not the work of Newcastle, who desired a compromise with France, but of hardliners in the British cabinet like George Montague Dunk, Earl of Halifax, head of the Board of Trade, who were able to force Newcastle into more drastic policies than he wished.[44] The revision of terms was both an insult to France and a threat to French security, since accepting them would be a dangerously humiliating retreat before the eyes of Europe; moreover, Mirepoix believed that the shift postdated the concessions France had made in her counterproposal, thereby making the insult appear all the more calculated.[45] On 17 March Rouillé ordered Mirepoix to make no new proposals.[46] For all practical purposes, the negotiations were dead, although Mirepoix remained in London, thus giving the British the opportunity to prolong the discussions while they prepared for war.[47]

These preparations already were well advanced. Exaggerated British intelligence reports had indicated France was readying thirty-two ships of the line for service at Brest and Rochefort; by mid-March Britain had commissioned thirty-five ships of the line and established bounties for volunteers in order to raise crews; this was always a problem for Britain at the start of a war, since so many sailors were abroad.[48] Meanwhile, Lieutenant Colonel Ruvigny de Cosne, the British chargé d'affaires at the French court, reported that the French public desired peace. He believed their navy was in no condition for war.[49] On 18 March the inner cabinet decided to assemble a strong squadron on the southwest coast of England; ships from it could be detached to intercept French ships and troops being sent to North America. The inner cabinet rejected, however, the idea of attacking Montreal or Quebec, as this would interfere with the military operations already planned. Six days later the inner cabinet ordered a small squadron to cruise off Louisbourg. Soon the squadron was increased, and Vice Admiral Edward Boscawen was appointed its commander. On 27 April he sailed for North America with eleven ships of the line. His instructions were to seize any French warships or transports he encountered; if they resisted he was ordered to capture or destroy them. The following day the king left for Hanover to arrange for its protection, leaving decision making in England to a group containing Robinson, Newcastle, Hardwicke, Cumberland, Fox, Anson, and Lord President of the Council John Carteret, Earl Granville.[50]

Meanwhile, on 20 February Braddock arrived in Virginia aboard a ship of the line, followed over the next several weeks by another ship of the line and transports carrying his two regiments, the 44th and the 48th Foot. In April he met at Alexandria, Virginia, with the governors or lieutenant governors of Massachusetts, New York, Maryland, Virginia, and Pennsylvania to plan the overall campaign. Commanders were assigned for the various attacks, but the colonial governors were as dissatisfied with him for refusing to shift his objective to Fort Niagara as he was with them for failing to provide him financial support. His main army was reinforced by colonial troops, however, and counted more than 2,000 men fit for duty. On 10 June it began its 110-mile march from its base camp on the upper Potomac River to the junction of the Allegheny and Monongahela.[51]

On the French side Machault ordered Governor General Duquesne to observe Braddock's movements, to make use of Indians to destroy the new fortifications that Governor William Shirley of Massachusetts was reportedly constructing along the Kennebec River, and to prepare for the arrival of troops.[52] He also ordered Capitaine de vaisseau Maximin, comte de Bompar, the governor at Martinique, to be prepared for all events; if he learned of a rupture with the British, he should send troops to occupy the neighboring island of St. Lucia (which, although inhabited by Frenchmen and their slaves, was by treaty neutral).[53] By the middle of April, frigates sailed for Quebec and Montreal to inform them that troops soon would be under way.[54] In spite of ill health, Machault had assembled 5,400 naval crewmen, six battalions of soldiers, and uniforms, blankets, and other supplies for the expeditionary force.[55]

Aboard du Bois de la Motte's flagship was a new governor general for New France, Lieutenant General of the Fleet Pierre de Rigaud de Vaudreuil de Cavagnial, marquis de Vaudreuil, whom Machault had chosen to replace the unpopular Duquesne. Vaudreuil's experience and qualifications made him an obvious choice for directing the overall operations of both Canadian militia and French army troops (with Dieskau commanding on any battlefield). Born and raised in Canada as the son of a governor general, Vaudreuil had researched sites for forts, fought alongside and negotiated with Indians, and served as provincial governor of Trois Rivières and governor of Louisiana. During his years in New Orleans (1743–53), he had been popular with native Frenchmen and conciliatory toward France's Indian allies. His knowledge of Canadian geography was unsurpassed and, unlike most French-born officers, he was appreciative of the abilities and understanding of the shortcomings of Canadian and Indian warriors. Although his grave demeanor was not endearing to French officers, his choice proved very popular with Canadians. In time he would reveal limitations of mind and character, particularly pride, but he also would demonstrate an unparalleled mastery of the strategy of North America warfare.[56]

Traveling with Vaudreuil was François Bigot, the *intendant* of New France, who was responsible for civil administration and who had been in France on leave. Machault chose to retain in his post this charming, experienced, and efficient but corrupt man. The honorable and religious Vaudreuil later tolerated Bigot's financial machinations because of the latter's energy and ability and because financial matters were not Vaudreuil's responsibility.[57]

Vaudreuil was given orders to remain on the defensive as long as the British did not attack.[58] On 2 May Rouillé gave Mirepoix permission to leave England whenever he wished.[59] On the following day the squadrons of MacNemara, du Bois de la Motte, and Périer de Salvert sailed jointly from Brest. MacNemara's six ships of the line returned to Brest on 20 May after escorting the other two squadrons for the first 600 miles of their voyage. As they continued across the Atlantic, Rouillé wrote the French ambassador in Stockholm that Louis XV had done only the necessary minimum to protect his subjects from the British, but that if the British acted against his colonies, navy, and commerce, he would have to do what was necessary to protect the dignity of his crown and French security.[60] France soon would learn whether that necessary minimum had been adequate.

Boscawen's eleven ships of the line, given a week's head start, were able to reach North America before the arrival of du Bois de la Motte and Périer de Salvert's thirteen, only four of which were fully armed.[61] Boscawen elected to lie in wait off Newfoundland to intercept the French. As they approached Louisbourg, however, they were scattered by bad weather and fog, which shielded most of their ships from discovery. Boscawen found only three ships of the line, which were traveling together: the Quebec-bound *Alcide*, 64, and *Lys*, carrying only 22 cannon, and the Louisbourg-bound *Dauphin-Royal*, carrying 24. On the morning of 10 June the *Dunkirk*, 60, opened fire on the *Alcide* after her captain, Richard Howe, had told the French ship that Britain and France were still at peace. She and the *Lys* were captured, along with ten of the fifty-two infantry companies for Quebec. The *Dauphin-Royal* escaped. Two days later she and the remainder of Périer de Salvert's squadron (the *Bizarre*, *Défenseur*, and *Espérance*) arrived safely in Louisbourg with their twenty-six infantry companies. Boscawen, having no orders to attack Louisbourg itself, could do nothing but sail futilely off Isle Royale; he was joined on 21 June by six ships of the line from England and on 11 August by two from Virginia. Most of du Bois de la Motte's squadron reached Quebec on 23 June, followed soon by the remainder.[62]

The naval action of 10 June was an ignominious way for Britain to begin the war. Moreover, by capturing only two French ships instead of two entire squadrons (as Anson had expected), Britain had no spoils to go with her shame; as Newcastle's astute friend Hardwicke said, they had done too much or too little.[63]

Meanwhile, Braddock was marching across the Allegheny Mountains to attack Fort Duquesne, the new French outpost at the forks of the Ohio. As late as 1 July the fort was defended by only 300 Indians and marines (*troupes de la marine* under the control of the navy ministry, consisting of French-born soldiers and Canadian officers). Just as Braddock's column approached, however, it was reinforced by some 800 Indians.[64] Nevertheless, even though Braddock had left behind a third of his troops, his army substantially outnumbered the 900 Indians and marines who on 9 July came to attack him before he could besiege them. By now he was about ten miles from the fort, and the forest had begun to thin. Overconfident at the lack of prior resistance, he failed to secure a key hill overlooking his line of march. Surprised at being attacked, his column became entangled and was unable to form a line of battle against an enemy enveloping it on three sides and taking advantage of the terrain. For three hours the British and Americans withstood an attack they could not counter; only headlong retreat saved them from annihilation. Barely a third of the 1,500

Britons and British-Americans engaged in the battle escaped death, wounding, or capture. Braddock himself was mortally wounded, and his army ceased to exist as an effective military force. The Indians and Canadians suffered only about fifty casualties. They captured fifteen cannon, several hundred horses and oxen, and the complete British campaign plans for the year.[65]

The plans were invaluable to Vaudreuil, who arrived at Quebec on 23 June. Although Duquesne reassured him that Canada was safe, he soon learned that a week earlier Fort Beauséjour on the Acadian border had been captured by 280 British regular troops and 2,000 New England volunteers; outnumbered by five to one, the garrison surrendered without a fight.[66] The destruction of Braddock's army now meant that the western flank of Canada was safe; although the Indians who had defeated Braddock returned to the Upper Country, other Indian attacks soon swept the frontiers of Virginia and Pennsylvania. Vaudreuil encouraged the attacks, although they were not under his control; indeed, the Delaware and Shawnee intended eventually to drive the French from the Ohio country.[67] The governor general now learned that both Fort Niagara and Fort St. Frédéric were threatened, the former by two newly raised regiments of regulars, the 50th and 51st Foot, commanded by Governor Shirley, the latter by 4,400 colonial volunteers commanded by Indian Superintendent William Johnson.[68]

Vaudreuil had only a limited number of troops to defend Canada, the newly arrived four battalions of regular infantry (numbering about 2,000 officers and men) and thirty companies of marines (numbering about 1,500), although he could supplement them with Indians and militia. (In theory he had 160 militia companies, numbering more than 13,000 men, including some at Louisbourg, but until the final crisis of 1759 he was unable to muster more than 4,000 a year for Canadian service.)[69] Hitherto he had concentrated on protecting Fort Niagara, upon which his posts in the Ohio country depended for supplies. His plan had been to send all his regular infantry, 1,800 marines and militiamen, and 500 Indians to seize Oswego on Lake Ontario, the staging point for an attack on Niagara. The first units were already in movement when Vaudreuil learned that Fort St. Frédéric on Lake Champlain also was endangered. This threat was more immediate, as the fort was little more than 100 miles from Montreal. In mid-August Vaudreuil suspended the plans to attack Oswego and sent Dieskau with 3,000 men to attack Johnson, who had assembled 3,500 Americans at a partially fortified camp on the shores of Lake George.[70]

Johnson was able to repulse the 8 September attack, partly because Dieskau disobeyed Vaudreuil's orders by dividing his forces; only half of his men saw combat. Johnson was slightly wounded, while Dieskau was severely wounded and then captured. Each side suffered several hundred casualties.[71] Although the battle was a tactical defeat for the French, it halted the British advance. Both sides went into winter quarters and began building forts, Fort William Henry on Lake George by the British and Fort Carillon on Lake Champlain (some ten miles south of Fort St. Frédéric) by the French.[72]

Meanwhile, Shirley's drive against Fort Niagara also halted. Slowed by daunting logistical difficulties and Johnson's lack of cooperation, Shirley's 1,500-man army did not reach Oswego until mid-August. Short of provisions, arms, and small boats to carry his troops across Lake Ontario, he could not undertake the 120-mile voyage to reach Fort Niagara. He, too, went into winter quarters and began new fortifications to replace the antiquated British fort at Oswego.[73]

New France had been fortunate to escape so lightly from the first British and American attack. The next offensive was certain to be larger and more ambitious. The British colonies in North America raised large numbers of volunteers to serve in Shirley and Braddock's regular regiments (about 7,500 during 1755 and 1756), in the colonial regiments serving with Johnson, and in other colonial regiments raised for frontier defense; excluding soldiers recruited by regular regiments, Massachusetts contributed 8,000 men in 1755, Connecticut about 3,000, and Virginia 650. The other colonies also raised troops. For the following year the number of volunteers surely would increase.[74] It would not be easy to coordinate such large military efforts; both the Board of Trade and a meeting of colonial leaders at Albany devised plans to do so, but the American colonies were as reluctant to risk their autonomy as the British government was to risk its authority.[75] Nevertheless, the American colonies possessed resources in men, food, and supplies far beyond those of New France.

Britain itself also planned an increased commitment. After learning of Braddock's defeat, Newcastle wanted to use only Americans to fight in America,[76] but his view had not prevailed. The British army already had been expanded considerably from the 42,000 officers and men (some 12,000 of which were paid by the Irish Parliament) in service after the last war. In November the government proposed that the British Parliament pay for an additional 17,000 troops in 1756. On 5 December Parliament was informed of the king's intention to enlarge the army; eleven days later the inner cabinet decided to raise ten new infantry regiments and some light dragoons. It hoped that 6,700 reinforcements could be sent to America.[77]

British war objectives also were increasing. In spite of Newcastle's reservations, the British government by the end of 1754 had moved beyond the aim of controlling the upper Ohio valley. It now intended to seize the entire area south of the St. Lawrence River. As Newcastle told Hardwicke on 4 August 1755, the idea of taking all of New France was in the air.[78] Expansionists like the Duke of Cumberland may not have yet created a consensus for their views,[79] but their influence was increasing. In America, Governor Shirley argued not only for capturing Fort Niagara, Fort Duquesne, and Fort St. Fréderic but also for seizing Fort Frontenac on the north shore of the St. Lawrence (where it empties into Lake Ontario) and for sending an army up the Kennebec River to attack Quebec.[80]

Questions remained about the command, financing, and objectives of the British army.[81] There were ominous warnings, however, of the dangers it posed to the inhabitants of Canada. Charles Lawrence, the acting governor of Nova Scotia, feared that his province would not be safe after the departure of the New England volunteers who had helped him capture Fort Beauséjour. In retrospect his fears were unjustified. He retained three regiments of regulars, the 40th, 45th, and 47th Foot, against which the 10,000 to 18,000 French-speaking Acadians who still lived in the Nova Scotia region offered no resistance; like the colonists of Pennsylvania, they had acquired a reputation for avoiding fighting. Lawrence waited until they had harvested their crops and then seized their lands and forcibly deported them. Many escaped, but some 6,000 or 7,000 were sent to British colonies from Massachusetts to Georgia (and sometimes thereafter to England). Treatment varied, but in some instances families were separated or people were placed in involuntary servitude.[82]

Even during the eighteenth century, wars were brutal and civilians often were victimized. People of European origin did not generally treat each other with quite such undisguised cruelty, however, and Lawrence's cold-bloodedness was exceptional by the standards of the time. Governor General Vaudreuil was particularly outraged. His own record was far from spotless; as a young man he had been introduced to the brutalities of the frontier and had participated in the campaigns against the Fox, an Indian people whom the French attempted to annihilate. In all likelihood he would have had little compunction about offering support in any case to the Indian attacks on British-American colonial settlements. But the treatment of the Acadians contributed to the enthusiasm he and many Canadians shared for the merciless war fought on the frontier.[83] (It should be noted that the treatment of Indians by American frontiersmen was equally merciless.) Lawrence, like Vaudreuil, shares considerable responsibility for instigating the war's remarkable cruelty.

In France, too, there was outrage both at the unprovoked seizure of the *Alcide* and *Lys* and the treatment of the Acadians. British ruthlessness, however, was not restricted to the Western Hemisphere; in the waters off the French coast they also did not concern themselves with diplomatic niceties before beginning war.

By sending Périer de Salvert to Louisbourg and du Bois de la Motte to Quebec, the French navy countered the danger to New France, but Britain posed other threats. Much more economically important than New France were the three great French sugar-producing colonies in the Caribbean: Martinique with a population of about 80,000, Guadeloupe with a population of about 60,000, and St. Domingue with a population of about 190,000 (their population being 90 percent slaves); in 1754 French imports from these colonies were worth about 75 million livres and exports about half that. [84] For years their defense had been neglected and they were helpless if the British attacked. Before the British turned their attention to the Caribbean, France occupied the neutral islands of St. Lucia and Dominica (which adjoined Martinique to the south and north) and recalled to France the two ships of the line on station. A British squadron containing the *Anson*, 60, *Bristol*, 50, and *Winchester*, 50, arrived in September and began seizing merchant ships, but no troops accompanied it. [85] For the time being the French islands were safe from attack.

The British navy posed a more immediate threat to merchant shipping, particularly ships returning to France from the West and East Indies with rich cargoes and sailors needed by the French navy. The only ships Machault had immediately available to protect them were the six ships of the line that had accompanied du Bois de la Motte and Périer de Salvert to sea. Perhaps with the help of his chief adviser, Sébastien-François-Ange Lenormant de Mézy, Machault devised a clever plan to divert British attention. He decided to send the French squadron to Lisbon and Cadiz, which would place it out of harm's way, awaken British fears that it would return to France to pick up troops for a surprise invasion, and impress the Portuguese (a potential British ally) and Spaniards with French naval strength. [86] It then would cruise off Cape Ortegal (on the northwest coast of Spain) before sailing back to an area near Brest to meet Périer de Salvert and du Bois de la Motte's squadrons as they returned from North America; the rendezvous was scheduled between 15 August and 5 September. All of the French warships then would proceed to Brest, taking care to avoid the British or, if meeting them, to avoid combat without compromising the honor of the flag. [87]

When the squadron sailed from Brest on 2 June, it no longer was under the command of the aged MacNemara, who reported his health inadequate for another mission at sea. He was replaced by Chef d'escadre Hilarion-Josselin, comte du Guay, a veteran officer with a reputation for courage and seamanship. [88] After a sixteen-day passage the squadron reached Lisbon. Joseph I of Portugal was flattered by the visit, which lasted until 7 July; the squadron then left for Cadiz, arriving a week later. A courier reached it there on 31 July with news of Boscawen's attack.[89]

The capture of the *Alcide* and *Lys* was reported in London on 14 July and at the French court four days later.[90] The British government had assured Mirepoix that Boscawen had no orders to act offensively.[91] According to Knyphausen, the news took Rouillé by surprise.[92] Rouillé, desperate to avoid war, had trusted the British enough to send Bussy to Hanover in order to meet with George II and Secretary of State Holdernesse. The attack destroyed his illusions; immediately he sent Mirepoix a passport to return to France and ordered Bussy to return as well.[93] Louis XV chose, however, not to declare war. For the moment, a French chargé d'affaires remained in London, and France did not embargo the British ships in its ports.[94] France did put its army on alert and began to fortify the port of Dunkirk (a violation of the Treaties of Utrecht and Aix-la-Chapelle).[95] Although du Guay was sent orders to seize British warships (although not merchant ships), these orders soon were countermanded. Indeed, when du Guay, who had not received the counterorders, returned to Brest on 4 September with a captured British frigate, it was released.[96]

There were good reasons for such caution. A delay might buy time for French shipping to arrive home and for France to prepare for war. Moreover, by France's refusing to respond to the British provocation, all the more blame would fall on Britain for beginning the war.[97] The king, too, needed time to make critical decisions on the course to pursue in Europe.

Over the next few days Louis met with the Council of State and his leading generals; the marquis d'Argenson (brother of the war minister and himself a former foreign minister) commented on Louis' appearance of sadness and his ministers' air of consternation. The decisions they made guided French diplomacy for the next seven and a half years until peace finally was made. Although Louis often was vacillating in the means he took to reach his objectives and in the people he chose to implement his policies, he was not lacking in vision and logic. The remarkable consistency in the underlying direction of France's wartime diplomacy was based on Louis' understanding of several key facts and his courage and cold-bloodedness in acting upon them. First, neither Louis nor anyone in his council seems to have questioned the assumption that a French defeat in North America would do unacceptable harm to the king's honor and to French prestige and hence to French security. Second, it seems to have been equally clear that a purely naval and colonial war was certain eventually to end in failure; although the French navy could buy time to reinforce and defend Canada, in the long run it could no more match Britain's superior resources than New France could hope to match the superior resources of the British colonies in North America. Unless France obtained naval superiority, Britain sooner or later would triumph, but in spite of Machault's hopes for strengthening the French navy, the king does not seem to have expected that France could seriously challenge Britain at sea. Third, it also went without question that France could obtain restoration of any British conquests in North America only by making conquests of her own in Europe, as had happened in 1748. Fourth, the conquests most likely to accomplish this were either the Austrian Netherlands, which would threaten Britain's security, or the electorate of Hanover, which would threaten not only George's interests but also the economic interests of Great Britain (as Hanover bordered the North Sea and lay between two major rivers, the Weser and the Elbe, that gave British trade access to much of Germany). The only real debate during the second half of 1755 was over which target France should choose.

That debate initially was framed in terms of whether France should immediately seize the Austrian Netherlands. The conquest would be easy. The Austrians pointedly had reduced the number of their troops to 12,000, and the Dutch, who still garrisoned a number of fortresses within the Austrian Netherlands, had withdrawn from all of them except Namur. Army Minister Argenson was in favor of taking the offensive, as were Rouillé (with some ambivalence), Puyzieulx, and Saint-Severin (the latter two of whom had rejoined the council). It was also favored by Marshal of France Charles-Louis-Auguste Foucquet, duc de Belle-Isle, the most respected senior officer in the French army. Opposed to such an attack were Machault, Madame de Pompadour, and the duc de Noailles. The king decided in favor of the latter; on 2 August the Austrian ambassador informed his court that France would not invade the Austrian Netherlands without giving prior warning.[98]

With someone as secretive as Louis XV we never can be certain of his thinking, but we can surmise his policies by observing his actions. The rejection of an attack on the Austrian Netherlands was not yet definitive at the beginning of August 1755, but the possibility of such an attack gradually receded. Conversely, France soon turned its attention to how to attack Hanover, which became the central element in French strategic thinking and remained so throughout the war. In coming chapters we will see how the need to conquer Hanover led Louis XV to change his European allies and how he persevered in the attempt when even his own foreign minister lost heart. Finally, we will see his steadfastness rewarded. Although the loss of New France could not be avoided, the pressure of the continuing war for Hanover broke Britain's will to pursue a monopoly of the Newfoundland fisheries, which would have destroyed the foundations of French naval power. This accomplishment came at a terrible price in not only French but also German blood and money, but it made it possible for France twenty years later to participate in the War of American Independence.

The diplomatic and military preparations for an attack on Hanover would take many months. This was all the more reason for the French government to maintain a policy of caution and restraint. The British were perplexed by France's failure to respond to their provocation. When Mirepoix and Bussy were recalled, Britain responded by withdrawing the British chargé d'affaires from the French court,[99] but the inner cabinet was divided about what to do next. Had France declared war, Britain would have been free to intercept French shipping with its rich cargoes and irreplaceable sailors; to do so now, however, would undermine the British claim that its military and naval actions merely were responses to French aggression in North America. Unless Britain could pose as a victim, it would be difficult to ask the assistance of the Austrians and Dutch; conversely, British hostilities in European waters would help France invoke its defensive alliance with Spain. Moreover, Britain was unclear of du Guay's plans; although his squadron was small, it might be awaiting reinforcements from Toulon or even Brest or Rochefort in order to provide an escort for an army invading England.

After the departure of Boscawen and his reinforcements, the British navy manned a powerful fleet of sixteen ships of the line with a veteran commander, Vice Admiral Edward Hawke. The Duke of Cumberland favored declaring war and immediately sending Hawke to attack French commerce; Newcastle, more cautious, favored waiting. Anson, surprised that France had not declared war, won approval for a compromise, by which Hawke was authorized to capture French ships of the line but not smaller warships or merchant ships. He sailed on 28 July for the Bay of Biscay, where he could intercept du Guay.[100]

The inner cabinet soon changed its mind. Eight days after Hawke sailed, he was sent authorization to capture privateers and merchant ships. Because of Newcastle's objections, it was not until 27 August, however, that this authorization was extended to other British warships and privateers. Meanwhile, Hawke did not receive his new orders until 23 August. France's restraint had bought a month's respite for French shipping and even for French warships, such as the returning *Arc-en-Ciel*, 50, which was stopped by the *Vanguard*, 70, and released; more than 80 million livres worth of cargoes arrived safely.[101]

Even with the delay, the attack on French shipping, made without a declaration of war,[102] caused terrible losses to France, perhaps as many as 300 ships and their cargoes, worth 30 million livres. Some 7,500 sailors and apprentices, more than half of them trained seamen, were brought to England as prisoners in 1755 (including 1,600 captured on warships).[103] The French navy was more fortunate. Hawke failed to find du Guay, whose six ships of the line returned safely to port in early September. With his squadron battered by weather and his crews weakened by sickness, Hawke had to return to port himself in late

September. The fleet sailed again on 14 October, now under the command of Vice Admiral John Byng. In the interim all but one of du Bois de la Motte and Périer de Salvert's thirteen ships of the line arrived at Brest or Rochefort, having eluded the British off Louisbourg. Byng managed to capture a number of merchant ships but only one ship of the line, the *Espérance*, one of the oldest warships in the French navy. Boscawen, too, returned to Europe, leaving behind four ships of the line to spend the winter in Halifax.[104] With all its ships of the line except the *Alcide, Lys,* and *Espérance* safely back in France, the French navy could prepare for further campaigns. Great Britain had failed to inflict major damage on either New France or the French navy. Soon the British government had to be concerned not only with striking a heavier blow in North America but also with defending Hanover.

THE QUESTION OF HANOVER

During his trip to Germany, George II had only limited success in arranging for the defense of Hanover. The Hanoverian army was expanded by 8,000 men to a strength of 29,000, using George's own income. On 18 June he signed an agreement with the Landgrave of Hesse-Cassel, a nearby principality, to provide a contingent of 8,000 troops if needed; in exchange Britain would give him a subsidy for four years. Arrangements were also made for 4,000 troops from the Margrave of Ansbach and the bishop of Würzburg, although ultimately the troops were not used. An attempt to hire troops from Denmark failed, however, and the Dutch refused to provide 6,000 men under the terms of the Anglo-Dutch defensive alliance, claiming that since Britain had initiated hostilities the treaty was inapplicable.[105] Hanover had not been endangered during the last war, but Mirepoix frequently had warned Newcastle that France would not let a new war be confined to America, if Britain gained an advantage there.[106] Although Hanover was not part of George's British domains, Newcastle felt a moral obligation to defend it; moreover, as already noted, the electorate was of considerable importance to Britain.[107] Parliament, however, was unlikely to approve sending British troops to Germany under the present circumstances, and even if the political situation changed, it would be impossible to find enough troops to match the French. The British army as yet had only about 60,000 soldiers, and they were needed in North America and to defend the British Isles, the West Indies, and the other parts of the British Empire. In contrast, the French army by 1756 was expanded to some 220,000 regular soldiers, including 242 infantry battalions, most of which soon contained 715 officers and men. It also had the support of 60,000 militia.[108]

There were three other great military powers in Europe: Russia with an army of some 260,000 regulars and 70,000 irregulars and militia, Austria with about 150,000 regulars and 45,000 militia, and Prussia with nearly 150,000 regulars.[109] Prussia was allied with France, leaving Austria the obvious choice to help Britain. It would be risky for France to attempt an invasion of Hanover without conquering or securing the neutrality of the Austrian Netherlands, situated near its supply lines into Germany. Newcastle negotiated for months with Maria Theresa to reconstruct the coalition which had fought the French in the Austrian Netherlands during the previous war, but by August the negotiations had failed. Newcastle was able to promise the help of Hanoverians and other German troops to defend the Austrian Netherlands, but was unwilling for political reasons to commit British troops to Europe.[110]

Newcastle also had been negotiating with Russia; these negotiations now became the chief focus of British diplomacy. On 30 September Sir Charles Hanbury Williams, the British representative in St. Petersburg, signed an agreement to subsidize a corps of 55,000 Russians for defending Hanover and to procure them a passage through Poland.[111]

Williams's treaty did not specify against whom Hanover was to be defended. This lack of specificity reflected an underlying difference of viewpoint between the British and Russians. Newcastle with his usual diplomatic myopia saw the Russians as mere auxiliaries against France, as they had been in 1748. Empress Elizabeth of Russia, who hated Frederick and coveted his possessions, saw the treaty as the beginning of an anti-Prussian alliance. In case of war with Russia, she and George were natural allies. Prussia bordered Russia's Baltic client state Courland (in what today is western Latvia) on the northeast and Hanover on the west; in addition, the detached Prussian provinces of Cleves and Guelders, in the region of the lower Rhine, were vulnerable to an attack from Hanover. In early October, Elizabeth's advisers drafted plans for an invasion of Prussia, provided that Maria Theresa, who wished to recover Silesia, also went to war against Frederick.[112] Newcastle's astute friend Hardwicke had unsuccessfully warned him of the dangers of courting Russia,[113] but Newcastle now was prepared to make use of the Russians in an even more contemptuous and dangerous way.

At the beginning of June, Newcastle had learned that Frederick II had suggested meeting with his uncle George II during the latter's visit to Germany. Although the meeting did not occur, Newcastle saw an opportunity to use Prussia to protect Hanover.[114] Over the summer he devised a plan by which Prussia would guarantee the neutrality of the Holy Roman Empire, including both the Austrian Netherlands and Hanover, during Franco-British hostilities. George's Hanoverian advisers, anxious to avoid involvement in the war, encouraged the plan, and Frederick's brother-in-law, Duke Karl of Brunswick, welcomed the opportunity to act as a mediator. (He hoped it would further his own plans to marry one of his daughters to George's grandson and heir, George, Prince of Wales, a plan ultimately foiled by the opposition of the prospective bridegroom's widowed mother.)[115] Because Frederick distrusted George II and was suspicious of the rather vague British proposal, the negotiations progressed slowly until Newcastle made use of Frederick's fear of the Russians. At the end of November Holdernesse gave a copy of the British-Russian agreement to Abraham Michell, the Prussian diplomatic representative at the British court. At the same time he offered to resolve Britain's financial disputes with Prussia and to guarantee Prussia (including Silesia) against attack.

The implicit threat of British support for a Russian attack caused Frederick to quickly accept an agreement. He insisted only that the Prussian neutrality guarantee be restricted to Germany proper, thereby excluding the Austrian Netherlands, which was part of the Holy Roman Empire but was not German-speaking. On 4 January 1756 he sent his approval of the revised agreement, and twelve days later at the palace of Westminster Michell signed on his behalf. By the Convention of Westminster Britain and Prussia agreed to oppose the entry or passage of foreign armies in Germany and to guarantee Hanover and Prussia against attack.[116]

Newcastle hoped that the agreement with Prussia would free Britain from the expense of defending Hanover and would guarantee peace in Germany. The Russian corps would no longer be needed. Although the Austrian Netherlands would receive no protection, the Austrians would at least have the benefit of seeing Germany kept free of French troops. Newcastle still hoped for a British alliance with Austria, disregarding the possibilities that Austria and Russia would attack Prussia or that Austria would abandon its traditional friendship with Britain to reconcile with its long-standing rival, France. The Convention of Westminster increased the possibilities of both, rather than lessening the danger to Prussia and Hanover. Deeper issues were involved than Newcastle's misguided treaty. Prussia was endangered because Frederick had seized Silesia fifteen years earlier, whereas Hanover was endangered because of the war in Canada. Meanwhile the Prussian-French alliance was insecure even before the Convention of Westminster because it no longer served French needs.

The first need of France, given the decision not to seize the Austrian Netherlands, was to gain control of Hanover. Only thus could France be able to prevent the loss of territory in North America and the loss of status in Europe (which would reduce its ability to protect itself and its allies). The Prussians and French were in basic disagreement, however, on how this could be accomplished. It might have been possible to pressure Frederick into cooperating in some kind of joint plan to seize Hanover provided that France agreed also to attack the

Austrian Netherlands (as Frederick continued to urge in hopes it would divert the Austrians from attempting to regain Silesia). [117] Louis XVI, undoubtedly remembering the huge expenses of the last war, rejected the idea of an Austrian war. It was not practical, however, for France to attack Hanover unaided (as Frederick, who wished to avoid any involvement in the war, also suggested), since this would arouse the opposition of the smaller principalities of Germany. It would also risk starting an unwanted war with Austria, as French armies would have to enter Germany by passing down the Rhine near the border of the Austrian Netherlands. Conversely, if Prussia itself seized Hanover (as Rouillé suggested to Frederick), [118] Britain could do little to retaliate directly, but it could subsidize an Austrian war against Prussia. Frederick dared not take the risk. Moreover, he did not trust France. Poorly advised by Baron von Knyphausen, his young and inexperienced minister at Versailles, he perceived France's restraint toward Britain as a sign of weakness. Furthermore, the 1741 treaty of alliance between France and Prussia was due to expire in June 1756.

Louis XVI had received Frederick's permission in July 1755 to send a special minister plenipotentiary to Berlin to join the regular French minister, Charles-Nicolas, chevalier de La Touche. He earlier had hoped to send one of his most distinguished generals, Marshal of France comte Ulrich Frederick Waldemar Lowendahl. But Lowendahl had died unexpectedly, [119] so Louis chose the most prestigious of his diplomats, Louis-Jules-Barbon Mancini-Mazarini, duc de Nivernais, a grandnephew of Cardinal Mazarin, a member of the French Academy, and a friend of Madame de Pompadour. It was not until the middle of November, however, that Nivernais' orders were approved and, because of illness, he was not able to leave Paris until 22 December. [120] Frederick rushed to complete his negotiations with Britain before Nivernais arrived, while denying their existence to Rouillé. [121] Why did the French government take so long to send Nivernais to Berlin? It has been argued that it was from overconfidence, [122] but given the impasse with Prussia about Hanover, it seems more likely that the delay was deliberate, Louis seeking to keep his options open as long as possible. One option encouraged by Frederick was obtaining help from Denmark, but Rouillé could obtain no promise of assistance. [123] Another was finding a new partner, Austria.

Kaunitz, the longtime advocate of a reconciliation with France who now was Austrian chancellor, saw the French decision not to attack the Austrian Netherlands as an invitation to open discussions. Maria Theresa had learned of Britain's negotiations with Prussia and decided to make an offer to France in the hope that if France were given sufficient inducement it at least would agree to remain neutral while Austria and Russia fought Prussia. At best France might agree to replace Britain as Austria's banker. The negotiations were entrusted to the able Austrian minister plenipotentiary at Versailles, George Adam, Graf von Starhemberg. Louis XV agreed to the discussions, but chose not to entrust them to Rouillé, who was strongly pro-Prussian. Instead he selected as his negotiator a protégé of Madame de Pompadour, the abbé François-Joachim de Pierre de Bernis, a member of the French Academy, former ambassador to Venice, and ambassador designate to Spain.[124] (Rouillé recently had recalled the French ambassador to Spain, who had insulted Spanish chief minister Ricardo Wall in brusquely demanding Spanish assistance against Britain.)[125] The negotiations were kept so secret that a special committee of the Council of State was established to oversee them, in which War Minister d'Argenson, the head of the pro-Prussian party, was excluded.

These negotiations often are portrayed by historians as a seduction of the naïve French by the wily and duplicitous Austrians. It would be more apt to compare them to an elaborate courtship dance between two eager but suspicious partners. In his memoirs Bernis claimed that Louis XV's motives for beginning the negotiations were personal and religious, the French king having developed a personal animosity toward Frederick and preferring an alliance with a Catholic ruler like Maria Theresa. Bernis' memoirs, however, are extremely unreliable.[126] Moreover, these motives seem insufficient to cause Louis to put at risk the only real accomplishment of the War of the Austrian Succession, the establishment of a balance of power between Austria and Prussia. The Austrians were willing to support Conti's candidacy for the Polish throne, to offer France the use of the ports of Ostend and Nieuport in the Austrian Netherlands during its war with Britain, and to exchange a portion of the Austrian Netherlands for the Italian possessions of Louis' son-in-law Duke Philip of Parma. It is doubtful, however, that Louis would even have considered the Austrian offer were it not for his need to capture Hanover. What is certain is that once France learned of Britain's agreement with Russia, French diplomacy, including the negotiations with Austria, became dominated by the need to keep the Russian corps away from Hanover. On 28 December 1755 France proposed to Austria a defensive alliance based on cooperation against the Russians (or other troops in British pay); if Russian troops in Germany attacked France or a French ally, Austria would provide free passage through the Austrian Netherlands to a French army.[127] The distinction between an offensive and defensive alliance in the eighteenth century often was artificial, since it was common for a state undertaking offensive operations to claim it was the victim of an attack. France certainly did not wish Russian troops so close to her border, but the real danger posed by Russian troops in Hanover was not to France or France's friends in Germany but rather to France's ability to attack Hanover.

The need to counter the Russians also appears in Nivernais' instructions, where joint Franco-Prussian military operations were discussed in the context of a Russian, British, or Hanoverian attack in Germany. Rouillé, hostile to the Austrian negotiations, did not answer directly Nivernais' queries about France's own intentions in Germany, but did tell him Louis would employ all the means God had given him to avenge his injuries, by attacking either London or Hanover.[128]

Several other diplomatic missions were anti-Russian and hence likely were related to France's desire to seize Hanover. Louis-Auguste-Augustin, comte d'Affry, was sent as extraordinary ambassador to the Netherlands to work with the regular ambassador, François-Armand d'Usson, marquis de Bonnac, for a commercial treaty and a convention of Dutch neutrality should France send an army into Germany.[129] Charles Gravier, chevalier de Vergennes, was sent to Constantinople to negotiate with the new sultan of the Ottoman Empire, Osman III; he was also initiated into the "Secret du Roi" and ordered to work with an agent sent by Grand-General Jan Klemens Branicki, head of the pro-French party in Poland. It was hoped Vergennes would obtain a strong declaration from the Turks that they would not tolerate a Russian violation of Polish territory or independence, but Osman was suspicious of France and ineffectual, and his government was paralyzed by rioting, inflation, and famine.[130]

It is not surprising, given the anti-Russian thrust of the "Secret du Roi," that it also played a major role in trying to win support from Augustus III of Poland against Russian troop movements. These negotiations were conducted by the energetic and resourceful Charles-François, comte de Broglie, the French minister in Warsaw and a leading member of the "Secret du Roi." The Poles were not in a position militarily to resist a Russian army moving through Poland toward Hanover; Frederick II estimated it would take the Russians no more than fifteen days to crush the Poles if they were refused passage (which was guaranteed to them by the 1744 Treaty of Warsaw).[131] Moreover, there were a number of opponents to the project: Frederick II, who considered Augustus (who was also ruler of the Electorate of Saxony, which adjoined Prussia) a rival, the prince de Conti, whose ambitions on Poland also made him a rival of Augustus, and Augustus's chief minister, Graf Heinrich von Brühl, who wished an alliance with Prussia and Britain. On 12 January 1756 Broglie had to suspend discussions.[132]

The "Secret du Roi" even had an agent, the chevalier Alexander Peter Mackenzie Douglas, spend sixteen days in St. Petersburg before being expelled. He was able to make contact with Vice Chancellor Mikhail Illarionovich Vorontsov, a rival to the pro-British Grand Chancellor Aleksei Petrovich Bestuzhev-Riumin. Vorontsov encouraged France to make an attempt to establish better relations with Russia.[133] Events would soon turn this seemingly bizarre suggestion into a proposal worth serious consideration by the French government.

All of the French attempts to block the dispatch of a Russian corps to Hanover were ineffective; even the Austrians were unwilling to help, as they needed Russian cooperation in regaining Silesia even more than they needed the French. At the end of January 1756 they rejected either resisting the Russians themselves or helping the French do so.[134] Newcastle, however, ended the threat by abandoning the Russians. In so doing he traded one danger for another. Had he persisted in his plan to send Russian troops into Germany, Britain eventually would have risked becoming implicated in a Russian attack on Prussia; Frederick in response would have had no choice but to request French help and Hanover would have come into danger from both France and Prussia. By instead abandoning the Russian initiative in order to sign the Convention of Westminster with Prussia, Britain not only alienated the Russians but rescued the Austrians from their dilemma of having to choose between France and Russia. Once France and Austria learned of the Convention of Westminster, they were free to work jointly toward an agreement which would leave them both free to pursue their offensive objectives, Austria's against Silesia and France's against Hanover. During the autumn of 1755, however, France was not yet aware of the impending shift in British foreign relations. While she pursued help against the Russians, she also made a final attempt to negotiate a halt to her war with Britain and began preparations for another naval and colonial campaign.

PREPARING THE FRENCH NAVY FOR WAR

Diplomacy seldom can be planned several moves in advance. It is a process rather than a program, a continual adjustment to an ever-changing range of options; the wise statesman keeps his options open as long as possible, particularly in a situation as fluid as France faced during the second half of 1755. Louis XV did not want war in Germany any more than he wanted war in North America, and he was reluctant to strengthen France's ancient rival, Austria. Although the underlying realities of France's strategic needs drove him to a European war, the process was not always smooth. There were hesitations and occasional steps backwards which, added to Louis' secrecy and difficulty in reaching decisions, make it impossible to trace precisely the expansion of the war from a colonial dispute to a general war in Europe. Louis' reluctance for war is demonstrated by his attempt to renew negotiations with Great Britain in late 1755. The French government made use, among others, of Etienne de Silhouette, a former member of the Canadian boundary commission, and the wealthy London merchant

Sir Joshua Van Neck to make contact with the British government. According to the always suspect later testimony of Bernis, Machault was not only involved in the attempt but, alone in the Council of State, opposed to breaking it off (which apparently happened as a result of George II's bellicose message to Parliament on 13 November). The negotiation was terminated by sending a set of peremptory demands whose rejection gave France an excuse to begin open warfare; in late December Rouillé sent them via Sir Joseph Yorke, the British representative at The Hague, to Henry Fox, the new British secretary of state for the southern department who had replaced Robinson in a governmental reshuffle.

The negotiations had been hopeless from the beginning. There was no one in the British government ready to return Fort Beauséjour or to offer adequate concessions on the dispute in the Ohio country. France also could not back down without suffering a humiliation that would do serious harm to her reputation. After the Convention of Westminster, Frederick II attempted to mediate (as did Ferdinand VI of Spain), but France refused any discussion until Britain returned the ships it had seized.[135]

As the negotiations proceeded, the French government had little choice but to prepare for another campaign of naval and colonial warfare. The first problem was finding the money to pay for it. The campaign of 1755, limited as it was, had been expensive. The king had authorized the navy and colonial department more than 31 million livres, almost twice the 17.5 million livres allotted it the preceding year, and it overspent that amount by several million livres; meanwhile, the French army's budget was about 75 million livres.[136] Fortunately, the government was able to increase its income so it could make a larger naval effort in 1756. During the last five years of peace Louis' annual net income (excluding overhead and revenue unavailable for general use) had averaged about 260 million livres. For 1756 he obtained an advance from the Farmers General (the consortium of bankers that paid for the right to collect and keep a major share of the government's taxes), as well as a gift of 16 million livres from the French clergy. The government also increased both the number of Farmers General and the amount of the lease that each of them paid, and established a lottery. Overall it was able to raise an additional 120 million livres; a recent study estimates its total revenues at 540.5 million livres.[137] The French government could not count on further such successes, however, nor would it be easy to borrow money if taxes proved insufficient. The government's ability to raise loans was only as good as its credit, and this was dependent on the state of the French economy as well as on the reputation of the government abroad. It did not bode well that French exports in 1755 declined by 10 percent compared with the preceding year and imports by 2 percent.[138]

Although the British government's annual income from 1750 to 1755 was substantially smaller than the French (on average about £7 million or, at an exchange rate of 24:1, some 168 million livres), its nonmilitary expenditures traditionally were far lower than those of France with its larger area and population. Moreover, throughout the century it proved far more successful than was France at increasing taxes and raising loans when needed. In large part this was because British merchants and other taxpayers felt they had a direct part in governing the country. Indeed, the financial capabilities of the British government were shown at the very beginning of the present hostilities when Parliament granted an extra £1 million for war expenses and the British public subscribed to a loan of almost £4 million.[139]

For the moment, however, the French navy could plan for the coming year in the expectation that its credit would hold good. By October 1755 the navy was receiving 4.5 million livres worth of bills of exchange monthly from the royal treasury.[140] The navy launched three ships of the line during 1755 (*Hector*, 74, *Sphinx*, 64, and *Vaillant*, 64) exactly matching the number the British had captured; at year's end it had 57 in port or at sea (including perhaps a dozen needing major repair), plus another nine in construction (*Océan*, 80, *Diadème*, 74, *Glorieux*, 74, *Souverain*, 74, *Zodiaque*, 74, *Belliqueux*, 64, *Célèbre*, 64, *Modeste*, 64, *Raisonnable*, 64). On 6 September the king selected names for six new ships of the line to be constructed in the near future; Nivernais was given a memoir to take to Frederick II that predicted 45 ships of the line would be ready to serve during the next campaign and that the navy eventually would contain 80 to 100 of the line.[141] Even if the predictions for 1756 were met, however, the French navy would be badly outnumbered by the British, who had 88 ships of the line in service by the end of 1755. The size of the British navy was restricted chiefly by the number of sailors it could press (conscript); on paper it had nearly 120 ships of the line available in 1755 (although this includes some needing repair). Although it launched only two during that year, another 22 were in construction or on order at year's end, including two 100-gun ships, five 90's, and seven 74's of the new *Dublin* class. To man its fleet Britain could draw on a pool of 80,000 trained sailors and fishermen, many of them involved in the trade between British ports.[142]

For Machault to place 45 ships of the line in service during 1756 he would need far more than the 7,800 petty officers and trained sailors the navy had used in 1755. According to a recently completed survey there were 52,466 sailors registered for naval service, an increase of more than 7,000 from the period of the previous war. In theory the navy could summon a portion of these men for service, as sailors were divided into "classes." This would leave sufficient sailors available to man merchant ships; during the past war the navy used about 20,000 men per year. As the present war continued, the system collapsed under the pressure of the navy's huge loss of manpower, but for the moment it operated adequately. By the beginning of the summer of 1756, when his armaments were complete, Machault found 11,000 petty officers and trained sailors for the Atlantic fleet and detached squadrons and 5,000 for the Mediterranean fleet. [143] To ease the navy's manpower needs, Machault doubled the number of the marines in French ports by doubling the size of each company. He also increased the number of men from 45 to 65 in each company of marines in Canada. [144]

A more pressing need was that of officers to command them. There was such a shortage of junior officers at Brest in 1755 that officers had to be brought from Rochefort and Toulon; in the navy as a whole there were fewer than 800 officers of all ranks, plus 200 or so *gardes de pavillon* and *gardes de la marine*, or what today would be called midshipmen. [145] The navy's flag officers (those commanding a squadron or fleet) gave no cause for complaint in 1755—du Guay, du Bois de la Motte, and Périer de Salvert had all performed superbly—but, as promotions generally were made by seniority, the navy's senior officers were extremely aged: its two vice admirals were in their eighties, and its five lieutenants general of the fleet and fourteen chefs d'escadre averaged about sixty-five years old. Eventually Machault would have to force into retirement those too old for service, but for the moment his chief concern was increasing the supply of flag officers; between September and November he appointed one vice admiral (to replace one recently deceased), two new lieutenants general of the fleet (du Bois de la Motte and La Galissonnière) and three new chefs d'escadre (Duquesne, Jean-François Bertet de La Clue-Sabran, and Joseph de Bauffremont, prince de Listenois). [146]

Perhaps the most critical of Machault's problems were the shortages in the navy's arsenals and storehouses. In July Rouillé placed an order on his behalf for wood from Sweden, and two boatloads full left for France in November; meanwhile, Machault took the cannon foundry of Ruelle under state control. He also introduced new technology in the ports, began construction of barracks, warehouses, and drydocks, assembled workers and soldiers, reorganized the coastal militia, and collected frigates to meet the incoming Newfoundland fishing fleet. [147]

Even Machault could not remedy the navy's deficiencies on such short notice; the shortage of cannons persisted for years and Machault was unable to fulfill his promises to protect commerce from the British. [148] Meanwhile, the navy had to begin preparing for its operations for the coming year. On 1 August Machault warned Toulon of the possibility of major armaments. Three weeks later he ordered that Toulon begin preparing a dozen ships of the line; the response was so enthusiastic that Machault had to warn the port officials at Toulon not to disrupt commerce by pressing the work too rapidly. As news arrived of the British attacks on French commerce, orders were also sent in September to Brest and Rochefort to prepare a dozen ships of the line for service.[149] Most of these ships, however, would not be needed until the spring. More urgent was the need to prepare the defense of St. Domingue and Martinique for the coming year. On 18 October three ships of the line and two frigates were selected from the fleet being prepared at Brest to sail to St. Domingue; a ship of the line and a frigate from Rochefort were ordered to Martinique. These ships would sail in early 1756; in the interim, dispatches and emergency supplies were sent to Canada and the West Indies by individual warships.[150] Machault informed the islands that help was coming (and that the squadrons would seize any British warships they could); in December he retroactively approved the seizure of St. Lucia and made arrangements for a Bordeaux merchant, Abraham Gradis, to send supplies to Canada on commission, the navy assuming the financial risks.[151]

By now the final hopes for peace were disappearing. On 2 January 1756 Rouillé read to an audience of ambassadors his ultimatum to Fox, which arrived in London the following day. To avoid Britain's being labeled the aggressor, the British inner cabinet again rejected the idea of declaring war,[152] but in spite of the Prussian mediation there was no longer any chance of a reconciliation; during 1756 diplomats no less than generals and admirals would be occupied with the business of war. France did not, however, concern herself solely with defending her possessions in America and looking for a way to attack Hanover as she had during 1755. Britain had vulnerable possessions of her own. By taking the offensive, France might be able to disrupt British strategy and even force Britain to reconsider continuing the war. The French navy would play a major part in that offensive and in the process would win its first battle since the days of Louis XIV.

3

1756
France Takes the Offensive

When the French government chose to take the offensive, it picked a logical but extremely dangerous target. Some 220 miles southwest of Toulon lay the island of Minorca. A British possession since 1708, it was a major privateering center that menaced not only Toulon but also the nearby great commercial port of Marseilles. (Privateering was the capture of merchant ships by privately owned but government licensed warships.) Although its garrison contained only four regiments with a total of about 3,000 men,[1] its major harbor, Port Mahon, was protected by the great fortress of St. Philip with 800 cannon. In case of attack it could withstand a siege until a squadron arrived from England. Given the superiority of the British navy, there was danger that the British would send enough ships to destroy the French Mediterranean fleet and trap a besieging French army, dependent for ammunition, food, and even water from the French mainland. France's only hope was to convince the British that it was planning to invade England as it had attempted in 1744. Hopefully the attention of the British navy would be so fixed on Brest and Rochefort (from which the escort for such an invasion would come), that its reinforcement for the Mediterranean would be too small to save Minorca.

At the end of 1755 Louis XV appointed senior army officers to command his troops along the Atlantic coast and along the Mediterranean coast. His choice as commander of the former was the duc de Belle-Isle, who began collecting a huge army of ninety-one battalions of infantry (about 65,000 officers and men) and twenty-two squadrons of cavalry (about 3,500 officers and men); no real attempt was made, though, to collect troop transports. Nevertheless, this effort caused the British to fear an invasion of England, and they diverted their attention from Minorca.[2] Rumors of an attack by 60,000 or 65,000 men did not impress Frederick II of Prussia, but by February Newcastle and Anson, knowing how few troops were available in England, were apprehensive.[3] A second factor contributed to the British government's fear. Typhus and scurvy aboard the ships of Boscawen, Hawke, and Byng had cost the lives of 2,000 men, and another 1,200 had been discharged from service; at year's end only 36,000 crewmen (including sailors, marines, and apprentices) were still available, including 6,000 who were ill. Barely a dozen warships in English ports were ready for immediate use, and the navy at large was almost 15,000 men short of the complement needed by the ships in commission. By March 1756, the navy collected forty-six ships of the line in home ports to counter an invasion, but their crews were short 10,000 men.[4]

France thus had an opportunity to invade Minorca before the British could send reinforcements. The landing force was commanded by Marshal of France Louis-François-Armand Vignerot du Plessis, duc de Richelieu, whom Louis had placed in command of the Mediterranean coast.[5] The escorting fleet was commanded by Lieutenant General of the Fleet, Roland-Michel Barrin, marquis de La Galissonnière, former acting governor general of New France. It took a huge effort to collect and man the large forces they were given to command; Richelieu's landing force of some 15,000 men (twenty-five infantry battalions and a battalion of artillery) required fifty transports and 130 supply ships. Meanwhile La Galissonnière had to find sailors for his five frigates and twelve ships of the line. Amazingly, the task was accomplished in time for them to sail on 12 April.[6] Late on the 17th they reached the western coast of the island. La Galissonnière's orders were to give priority to the protection of the troops,[7] and he devoted his entire force to covering the landing, permitting three British ships of the line (the *Princess Louisa*, 58, *Deptford*, 50, and *Portland*, 50) to escape from Port Mahon on the eastern coast. Richelieu met no resistance during his landing and his fifteen-mile march across the island because Lieutenant General William Blakeney chose to pull all his troops into Fort St. Philip. As Richelieu's army began its siege, Blakeney awaited the arrival of a squadron from Britain.

The inner cabinet took a very long time to send help to him, and the help it sent was too small. Anson was largely responsible for this failure. As early as January Cumberland called for reinforcing the island, but Anson considered the threat to Minorca only a feint. Warnings of the French preparations were sent by Blakeney, Ambassadors Joseph Yorke at The Hague and Benjamin Keene at Madrid, British consuls at Genoa and elsewhere, and British intelligence sources. It was not until 9 March, however, that the inner cabinet decided to send ten ships of the line to the Mediterranean under the command of John Byng, who was promoted to full admiral. The ships and their captains seem to have been inferior to those assigned to Vice Admiral Edward Hawke's squadron of fourteen ships of the line, which cruised off the French coast; moreover, Byng's crews were still shorthanded when he finally sailed on 6 April. Byng surely would have been given a larger squadron had Anson not been so worried about an invasion of England, since there were a number of ships of line manned and ready which did not accompany him; as it was, Anson gave Byng orders to stop at Gibraltar before proceeding to Minorca in order to make sure the Toulon squadron was still in the Mediterranean.[8]

Byng encountered bad weather and took twenty-six days to reach Gibraltar. He found there the three small ships of the line which had escaped from Minorca and added them to his squadron. The governor of Gibraltar, however, refused to put troops aboard Byng's squadron to reinforce Minorca, and the dockyard was too empty to provide materiel for repairs. Byng left for Minorca in less than a week, but his squadron still was undermanned, and the only troops he had available for Blakeney were a regiment of fusiliers who were serving aboard his ships in place of marines. When he reached Minorca on 19 May, La Galissonnière prevented him from making contact with Fort St. Philip. Not knowing how long Blakeney could hold out, Byng had little choice but to attack the French fleet.

The battle took place the next day, after the British had gained the advantage of the wind, a prerequisite to initiating an action between groups of warships under sail. On sea as well as on land it took great skill to make a cohesive attack. Byng made a complicated approach that he had failed to explain properly to his captains. His first six ships (*Defiance*, 58, *Portland*, 50, *Lancaster*, 66, *Buckingham*, 70, *Captain*, 70, and *Intrepid*, 64) came under heavy fire as they approached the French line of battle (*Orphée*, 64, *Hippopotame*, 50, *Redoutable*, 74, *Sage*, 64, *Guerrier*, 74, *Fier*, 50, *Foudroyant*, 80, *Téméraire*, 74, *Content*, 64, *Lion*, 64, *Couronne*, 74, and *Triton*, 64). When the *Intrepid*, crippled by the French fire, dropped out of line, the captain of the next ship, *Revenge*, 70, failed to close the gap. Hence the *Revenge* and the remainder of the British line (*Princess Louisa*, 58, *Trident*, 64, *Ramillies*, 90, *Culloden*, 74, *Kingston*, 60, and *Deptford*, 50) saw little action, with only the *Princess Louisa* suffering any casualties. Nevertheless it was La Galissonnière who broke off the action. His ships of the line suffered 213 casualties compared with Byng's 207, but they, unlike Byng's, were divided among all his ships. Two of Byng's ships, the *Intrepid* and *Portland*, sustained considerable damage. After consulting with his captains, Byng retreated to Gibraltar for repairs rather than risk a second battle. Even though La Galissonnière had not captured a single ship, he, like de Grasse off the Virginia Capes twenty-five years later, won a major victory. In both cases, the French navy prevented a besieged British garrison or army from receiving assistance, thereby enabling the siege to succeed, a result far more important than capturing a few ships.[9]

This result, however, was as yet far from certain. Richelieu encountered great difficulties from the terrain and from Blakeney's defense. He received another five battalions from Toulon, but it appeared likely the British could hold out until another British squadron appeared. Richelieu decided to risk an immediate assault. On the night of 27–28 June his troops stormed the outer portion of Fort St. Philip. Although the attack was only a partial success, Blakeney began negotiations to surrender. Terms were quickly reached to send the entire garrison under flag of truce to Gibraltar. The French government had planned to demolish Fort St. Philip and then evacuate the island, but with most of its walls and cannon still intact, the great fort was still defensible. Richelieu left behind eleven of his battalions as a garrison. With the remainder he and La Galissonnière quickly returned to Toulon before the British navy could reappear.[10]

It was a wise decision to avoid the risk of a second naval battle. On 6 May the British government learned that three weeks earlier the French had landed on Minorca. Two days later it ordered a new squadron of five ships of the line (*Prince George*, 80, *Hampton Court*, 70, *Ipswich*, 70, *Nassau*, 70, and *Isis*, 50) under the command of Rear Admiral Thomas Brodrick to reinforce Byng; they sailed on the 20th, the same day as Byng's battle. It also ordered three regiments to reinforce Gibraltar, and on 17 May King George II declared war on France. (King Louis XVI reciprocated on 9 June.)[11]

At the beginning of June the British government received from the Spanish envoy to the British court an extract of La Galissonnière's report of the recent naval battle. In response, the inner cabinet ordered Hawke, recently returned from his cruise, to sail immediately for Gibraltar aboard the *Antelope*, 50, to relieve Byng and save Minorca. Hawke reached Gibraltar in early July to find Byng and Brodrick still making repairs. On the 11th, just after he had sailed for Minorca, he met the flag of truce ships carrying Blakeney's garrison. When he reached Minorca eight days later, La Galissonnière and Richelieu were gone; the last stragglers from the convoy arrived safely in Toulon on 21 July.[12] Hawke cruised off Minorca and the French coast, disrupting shipping until he finally departed in October; although the Toulon fleet was reinforced by the *Hector*, 74, *Achille*, 64, *Hercule*, 64, *Vaillant*, 64, and *Oriflamme*, 50, it still was too weak to challenge Hawke. The long stay in port led to desertions, and on 30 October the original dozen ships of the line were ordered disarmed.[13]

By this time the fleet was under the command of Claude-Louis d'Espinchal, marquis de Massiac, who as port commandant had been responsible for its preparation and who now was promoted to lieutenant general of the fleet.[14] La Galissonnière became ill and went ashore at the beginning of August. On 26 October he died while traveling to the French court. Like de Grasse twenty-five years later, his real distinction was not in handling ships in battle but in his willingness to subordinate his concerns as a fleet commander to the greater strategic needs of his country, a grandeur of spirit that was rare in the eighteenth century.

In their joy at the news of Minorca, many Frenchmen briefly entertained the hope that Britain now would make peace.[15] There were those in Britain ready to do so; even Hardwicke for the moment believed the war lost. The British public, however, responded to the news not with discouragement but with rage. When Newcastle appeared in public, his carriage was pelted with mud. The prime minister shared Hardwicke's fears, but he realized the government dared not think of peace.[16] With no hope of a diplomatic solution, the government focused on dealing with the political consequences of the defeat. It already had altered one of Byng's dispatches before it appeared in the press in order to make him bear greater blame for the catastrophe. Now the government court-martialed him and seems to have made efforts to ensure a conviction. These efforts proved successful—Byng ultimately was sentenced to death, and George II refused clemency—but the government could not escape its own responsibility for sending inadequate forces to the Mediterranean. Amid the continuing political panic, it was deserted in mid-October by Henry Fox, Newcastle's spokesman in the House of Commons.[17] By then more bad news had arrived. The French had taken the offensive in North America, too, and another British fortress, although a far smaller one, had fallen.

THE CAPTURE OF OSWEGO

Except for the capture of Fort Beauséjour, Britain's 1755 campaign in North America was a series of missed opportunities: Braddock's defeat by an outnumbered enemy, Boscawen's failure to intercept the reinforcements for Canada, Johnson's inability to capture Fort St. Frédéric, Shirley's stalled offensive against Fort Niagara. The British government intended to devote a far larger force to ensure against similar failures in 1756. It hoped to rebuild by local recruiting the four regiments it had used in 1755 in Pennsylvania and New York, to send two additional regiments from Ireland (the 35th Foot and 42nd Highlanders), and to raise a huge four-battalion regiment of sharpshooters in Pennsylvania and adjacent colonies, preferably with Swiss, Dutch, and German emigrants (the Royal Americans or 60th Foot, initially named the 62nd Foot). If recruiting went well, there could be as many as 13,000 regulars available, including three regiments in Nova Scotia and seven independent companies based in New York and South Carolina. During 1755 the British colonies in North America had raised more than 12,000 men for provincial regiments; it was hoped that they too would do even better during 1756. Such a large force could hardly be entrusted to Governor Shirley, even though he already had made plans to send a force up the Kennebec River against Quebec and to personally lead attacks on Fort Niagara and Fort Frontenac. (He also had appointed Maryland governor Horatio Sharpe to attack Fort Duquesne.) On the urging of the Earl of Halifax, the inner cabinet decided to send a lieutenant general and two major generals to take command in America. The American colonies would be compensated for their expenses, but the government recalled Shirley, who had disagreed with Johnson and was suspected of war profiteering. It also ignored Shirley's elaborate plans.[18]

The choice of generals was left to the Duke of Cumberland, as it had been in 1754 when he selected Braddock. This time he chose as overall commander another of his protégés, John Campbell, Earl of Loudoun, a Scottish peer with a reputation for being a good organizer; Loudoun also was named governor of Virginia. Loudoun's interest in frontier warfare, based on his experience of the Scottish uprising of 1745, was reflected by his support for the creation of Major Robert Rogers's force of rangers to practice Indian-style warfare. In spite of his considerable administrative abilities, Loudoun was too timid and plodding to be an effective army commander. The major generals who accompanied him, Daniel Webb and James Abercromby, were even less competent.[19]

The French also needed a new commander. After Dieskau's capture, Vaudreuil wished to take personal command of the field army, but Argenson was hardly prepared to make such a concession to a naval officer (or to his rival in the Council of State, Machault). He chose Louis-Joseph, marquis de Montcalm de St.-Véran, as the new army commander and promoted him to *maréchal de camp*. Montcalm had a reputation for exceptional personal courage and extensive experience in siege warfare. Although he was an admirable person, his abilities as a general were limited; a competent, if conventional, tactician, he had little understanding of strategy. Fortunately his orders placed him firmly under the authority of the experienced Vaudreuil, and he was accompanied by a superb group of subordinate officers including Brigadier François-Gaston de Lévis, Colonel François-Charles de Bourlamaque, and Louis-Antoine de Bougainville, a young aide.[20] Less fortunately, Montcalm's appointment presented the possibility of conflict with Vaudreuil, who was disappointed not only because he himself did not receive command of army troops but also because his younger brother, François-Pierre de Rigaud de Vaudreuil, the governor of Trois-Rivières, did not receive an appointment as troop commander or as governor of Montreal, which would have put him in line to become governor general. The younger Vaudreuil, commonly known as the chevalier de Vaudreuil, had been captured on the *Alcide* and later released.[21] He now accompanied Montcalm.

The French navy was involved in outfitting squadrons at Brest and Rochefort and already had sent reinforcements to the West Indies. Thus it could not spare as many warships for transporting troops as it had in 1755. It was able to outfit *en flûte* only the ships of the line *Héros*, 74, *Illustre*, 64, and *Léopard*, 64, and the frigates *Licorne*, 32, *Sauvage*, 32, and *Sirène*, 30. Machault intended all of them to return immediately to France except for the elderly *Léopard*, which Machault wished demolished. Its crew would be transferred to the frigate *Abénakise*, 36, which was scheduled to be launched at Quebec. The six ships carried two 525-man battalions of regulars (from the regiments of La Sarre and Roussillon) and 1,000 recruits for the marines and the regulars already there. On 3 April the squadron, commanded by Capt. Louis-Joseph Beaussier de L'Isle, sailed from Brest. It became scattered because of fog as it approached the Gulf of St. Lawrence, but all its ships reached Quebec safely between 12 May and 31 May. They departed for France on 5 July, three weeks later skirmished briefly with the British ships of the line *Grafton*, 70, and *Nottingham*, 60, and reached Brest safely in September. Less fortunate was the *Arc-en-Ciel*, 50, carrying recruits for Louisbourg, which left Brest on 20 April and was captured on 12 June by the *Litchfield*, 50, and *Norwich*, 50. Later in the year the *La Rochelle*, 4, was sent to New Orleans.[22]

The first meeting between Montcalm and Vaudreuil was polite,[23] but it was only with great apprehension that Montcalm followed Vaudreuil's bold plans for the coming summer campaigning season. Boldness was needed because British and American forces in North America outnumbered by about two to one the approximately 11,000 to 12,000 men available (exclusive of the garrison of Louisbourg), to defend Canada and attack the American colonial frontier (Montcalm's 3,000 regulars, 2,000 marines, 3,000 or 4,000 militia, and about 3,000 Indians, although their numbers were severely diminished by the outbreak of smallpox in the Upper Country). Because of the enemy's difficulties, however, the situation proved less dire than might have been expected. Recruiting to fill out the regiments of British regulars took more time than anticipated, and the regiments at Nova Scotia barely were used. British-American provincial regiments from Pennsylvania to South Carolina were so involved in defending the frontier from Indian attacks[24] that Fort Duquesne was not threatened and, except for 200 provincial troops from North Carolina, the only provincial troops available on the Lake Champlain and Lake Ontario fronts were from New York and New England.[25] The severity of the Indian attacks prompted countermeasures. A chain of new fortifications was begun along the frontier from New York to South Carolina, ranging from simple blockhouses holding about twenty soldiers to major forts like Fort Augusta, Pennsylvania, and Fort Loudoun, Virginia. Once these were finished and adequately manned, Indian raiding parties usually had to bypass them as the fortifications generally were difficult to capture without artillery. Ultimately, however, it was not the forts but disease and hunger that ended the raiding.[26]

During 1756, however, several of the new forts, such as Vause's Fort in Virginia and Fort Granville in Pennsylvania, were taken by Indian or Indian-Canadian raiding parties. The most strategically important of these was Fort Bull, situated at the portage between the Mohawk River and the approaches to Oswego. On 27 March a force of 360 Indians, Canadian militia, and marines captured the eighty-man garrison and burned the fort.[27] In spite of the loss of valuable supplies, the British continued work at Oswego both on new fortifications and on a small fleet to control Lake Ontario. This was due chiefly to a highly effective force of 2,000 armed boatmen under Lieutenant Colonel John Bradstreet, which kept open the Mohawk River supply line.[28] Once the Oswego fleet was finished, the French supply lines to Fort Duquesne and Fort Niagara could be cut. Governor Shirley, still commanding British forces in America until the arrival of a replacement, now made a serious mistake, however. At a 25 May council of war held at Albany, he decided to switch two regiments, the 44th and 48th, from Oswego to the Lake Champlain region. A few weeks later General Abercromby, sent ahead from England, arrived at Albany and relieved Shirley.

The departing governor had presented Vaudreuil with a great opportunity. Some 7,000 British and American troops were concentrated at Fort William Henry and Fort Edward near Lake Champlain, but fewer than 1,500 were left at the Oswego fortifications (the 50th and 51st regiments, about 200 New Jersey provincial troops, and some artillerymen).[29] Vaudreuil now split his forces, expecting the British would delay any attack in the Lake Champlain region until they finished assembling their huge army, which grew to 12,000 men by mid-September. He kept three battalions of regulars with Lévis, Montcalm's second-in-command, to finish construction of Fort Carillon, south of Fort St. Frédéric.[30] He sent Montcalm with the other three battalions to Fort Frontenac on the northern shore of Lake Ontario in order to attack Oswego. Montcalm was right to be concerned about the dangers of the operation. Wind conditions kept the small French fleet on Lake Ontario from accompanying him, and he had to move his army by night in small boats along the shores of Lake Ontario in order to avoid detection by the Oswego fleet. On 10 August he reached Oswego undetected and met a detachment that had been sent ahead to establish a hidden camp near Oswego. With his 1,300 regulars, about 1,500 militia and marines, and 250 Indians, it took him only four days to force the British to surrender. Montcalm destroyed the British fortifications and took his prisoners to Montreal. He needed to end the campaign so that his militia could return home to harvest their crops. Moreover, by departing the area he avoided alienating the Iroquois.

Further action against the British was unnecessary. General Webb, leading the 44th regiment to rescue Oswego, retreated in panic, destroying British supply posts.[31]

The victory at Oswego also doomed the British offensive on Lake Champlain. Time was wasted while Abercromby relieved Shirley and then while Loudoun relieved Abercromby. Meanwhile a major disagreement developed concerning the relationship between British officers and the officers of the American provincial regiments. Finally it was decided that British troops would be used only in reserve and the attack would be led by an American officer, Provincial Major General John Winslow. Orders were not issued to begin the advance until 19 August. News of the fall of Oswego arrived the next day. The advance was suspended and then abandoned after the troops suffered heavy losses from disease. Loudoun went into winter quarters, engaging in a bitter dispute with American officials about housing for his British regulars.[32]

Oddly, the campaign ended in bad feelings in Canada, too. The Oswego victory started the deterioration of relations between Vaudreuil and Montcalm, who each claimed credit for the great triumph. Even more disturbingly, Montcalm praised French regulars and downplayed the contribution of Vaudreuil's beloved Canadians.[33] There were more immediate problems, however. At least a dozen ships reached Quebec between May and June, including four sent from Bordeaux by Abraham Gradis. Only two ships arrived from the West Indies, however,[34] so it was difficult to find enough food for civilians, soldiers, and France's indispensable Indian allies. Bigot had to take several measures to stretch the supplies, including adding oats to flour. Trade goods for the Indians also were in short supply; as a result, some of the Susquehanna branch of the Delawares initiated negotiations with Indian Superintendent Johnson and Deputy Governor Robert Hunter Morris of Pennsylvania.[35]

Recriminations and bad feelings were not restricted to North America. The fall of Oswego was fatal to the beleaguered government of Newcastle. He resigned in mid-November, six weeks after learning the news. Although the titular head of the new government was First Lord of the Treasury William Cavendish, Duke of Devonshire, its real leader was William Pitt, the new secretary of state for the southern department.[36] The Duke of Cumberland remained as head of the army and Holdernesse as the other secretary of state, but Anson was replaced as first lord of the admiralty by Pitt's brother-in-law, Richard Temple Grenville, Earl Temple, an arrogant civilian ignorant of naval matters. There were three admirals among the six other members of the Board of Admiralty, however.[37]

The new government was unsure of itself politically, but it had none of Newcastle's ambivalence about war objectives in North America. Loudoun had already sent plans for outflanking the outer defenses of Canada—Forts Duquesne, Niagara, St. Frédéric, and Carillon—by embarking 5,500 of his regulars at New York and striking directly up the St. Lawrence River at the heart of Canada; this also had the advantage in Loudoun's eyes of relegating provincial American troops to a supporting role. He needed reinforcements, however, along with an escorting squadron from England. Pitt responded enthusiastically, promising him 8,000 men. So large a number was impractical, however, as Parliament authorized only 19,000 of the 51,000 men on the British establishment to serve outside Britain. Cumberland reduced the size of the force. He chose for it two new 1,000-man regiments of Scottish Highlanders and five regular 750-man infantry regiments.[38] Other needs also required attention. During 1756, as will be discussed later, Britain drew troops from Hanover to reinforce its own soldiers defending England from invasion. The Hanoverians were now returning to Germany and needed to be replaced. Pitt, opposed to asking for new troops from Germany, therefore decided to ask parliamentary authorization for a militia of 50,000 or 60,000 men. He ultimately received permission for 32,000, who proved difficult to find, as the militia was unpopular.[39]

France could not hope to match the British increase of strength. Although Vaudreuil appealed for 1,800 army recruits and marines,[40] there was barely enough food to feed the soldiers already in Canada. Moreover, the supply line to Canada and the defense of Louisbourg were dependent on French naval strength. The badly outnumbered French navy, moreover, had to defend not only New France but the rest of the French empire, particularly the West Indies. In 1756 one of Machault's great accomplishments as naval minister was keeping open the supply lines not only to North America but also to the Caribbean.

MACHAULT'S ACCOMPLISHMENTS

Long before Beaussier de l'Isle sailed for Canada or La Galissonnière for Minorca, the French navy sent help to the West Indies. On 30 January 1756 a squadron of the *Prudent*, 74, *Atalante*, 34, and *Zéphir*, 30, under the command of Capitaine de vaisseau comte Charles-Alexandre Morel d'Aubigny sailed for Martinique from the roadstead of Rochefort. Just before reaching its destination on 12 March, it captured the *Warwick*, 60. Learning of the British declaration of war, d'Aubigny spent five months in the West Indies before returning to Rochefort with his prize via the Spanish port of Corunna, although a convoy he was escorting was dispersed and suffered heavy losses.[41] A larger squadron, consisting of the *Courageux*, 74, *Protée*, 64, *Aigle*, 50, *Amphion*, 50, *Fleur-de-Lys*, 30, and *Emeraude*, 28, sailed from Brest for St. Domingue on 23 February under the command of Périer de Salvert's older brother, Chef d'escadre Etienne Périer.

Because of bad weather it took him two months to reach Cap-Français, but his stay there was successful. He terrified the British squadron commander at Jamaica, took a dozen prizes, and returned to France in the late autumn with a convoy of thirty-five ships.[42] Machault was particularly concerned about the food supply of the West Indies, since most of the available land was planted in sugar. He approved opening the islands to neutral ships, but this policy met opposition from French shippers unwilling to surrender their monopoly. After learning there was as yet no problem, he backed down.[43]

The French navy also was active in the Mediterranean during 1756, except for the three months that Hawke exercised control of the area near Minorca, Toulon, and Marseilles. Once the British squadron returned to Gibraltar, the French navy resumed its activities, although on a far smaller scale than during the Minorca expedition. On 14 August France signed a treaty with Genoa to whom belonged the island of Corsica, a potential privateering center should Britain capture it (as Newcastle unsuccessfully proposed). France agreed to provide Genoa an annual subsidy and received the right to send garrisons to the major ports on its western coast, St. Florent (San Fiorenzo), Calvi, and Ajaccio.[44] The *Junon*, 40, *Gracieuse*, 24, and *Topaze*, 24, escorted 3,600 troops there; meanwhile, a squadron consisting of the *Hercule*, 64, *Pléiade*, 26, and *Nymphe*, 24, was sent to protect Minorca.[45]

The least successful area of operations for the French navy was that to which the largest number of ships was committed, the coastal waters of France itself. A squadron from Rochefort successfully reached Brest on 15 April, but even so the combined French fleet there reached a total of only a dozen ships of the line.[46] The fleet was commanded by the most respected figure in the French navy, Lieutenant General of the Fleet Hubert, comte de Conflans-Brienne, a humane and intelligent officer who had nineteen years' experience at sea and who had captured two British ships of the line during the previous war.[47] By its presence in Brest it helped to prevent the British from detaching ships overseas, but it could do no more than act as a fleet in being. It was too small to challenge the squadrons of fifteen or so British ships of the line that cruised in succession off Brest under a series of British admirals, Henry Osborn in January, Hawke in March, Boscawen in May, Francis Holburne in September, and Charles Knowles in November. In the autumn, all but four of Conflans' ships of the line were disarmed for the winter to save money. The French navy had only fifteen frigates at Brest and Rochefort for protecting the coast and escorting convoys; not surprisingly, shipping suffered heavy losses from British warships and privateers.[48] As a result insurance rates rose to as much as 30 percent, and some French ships began sailing under foreign flags. At Bordeaux the departure of ships for the colonies dropped by about a third between 1755 and 1756; the decline of shipping at Le Havre and Nantes was even more severe. Overall, the value of colonial trade dropped by 60 percent. French imports in general declined by almost a third and exports by more than a tenth.[49]

After the British declaration of war in May, the French government authorized privateering, as well as the sale of British ships detained in French ports.[50] Most French privateers were outfitted at ports like Bayonne (which sent out more than 300 during the war) and Dunkirk (where the government planned a major reconstruction of port facilities). These ports were exempt from the registration of sailors for service in the navy and close enough to the French border to attract foreigners. Within a few weeks the Dunkirk privateer captain François Thurot outfitted a squadron containing a 40-gun ship and a 36-gun ship and captured the British privateer *Hawk*. Although profitable, privateering was economically destructive and often inhumane and did little good for the French navy.[51]

The French navy could take satisfaction from the results of the 1756 campaign in spite of its failure to protect French shipping or to attain the forty-five ships of the line in service that Nivernais' memoir had predicted. It helped capture Minorca and protect Canada and the West Indies while suffering the loss of only three ships of the line, the *Arc-en-Ciel*, captured off Louisbourg, the *Léopard*, deliberately destroyed at Quebec, and the *Hercule*, which was condemned soon after its arrival at Minorca. This was more than compensated by the capture of the *Warwick* and the launching of five ships of the line, the *Océan*, 80, *Diadème*, 74, *Glorieux*, 74, *Zodiaque*, 74, and *Belliqueux*, 64. On the other hand, only two of the six ships ordered the previous year were begun (*Centaure*, 74, and *Minotaure*, 74) and only one more ordered (the *Impétueux*, 90). The British navy launched only three ships of the line during the year but placed eight more on order (as well as fifteen frigates).[52] The dockyards of Brest, Rochefort, and Toulon were operating at their limits and faced severe shortages of cannon and naval materiel. Cannon were in such short supply that Conflans had to substitute 18-pounders (i.e., cannon firing cannon balls weighing 18 pounds) for 24-pounders on some of his ships. French ambassador Havrincourt was ordered to procure 700 in Sweden, but only 400 were purchased, and it was 1759 before they were sent via the Netherlands; some were still there in May 1760. Coastal defense batteries were stripped of their cannon, leaving the coast from Poitou to Normandy virtually defenseless.[53] The delivery of masts to Rochefort virtually ceased after June, and on 5 July a fire destroyed 1.2 million livres worth of stores; even obtaining timber and masts from French suppliers was a challenge.[54]

Human shortages also were a problem. Between May 1756 and April 1757, four of the navy's most distinguished flag officers died: Charles-Félix, comte de Poilvilian de Cresnay (a vice admiral of high reputation),[55] MacNemara, La

Galissonnière, and Périer de Salvert. Machault selected seven capitains de vaisseau for promotion to chef d'escadre, but the new flag officers enjoyed markedly
less successful careers than their predecessors. In early 1757, the French navy had
twenty-seven flag officers—one admiral (a largely ceremonial office), two vice
admirals (including Conflans), six lieutenant generals of the fleet (including
Vaudreuil, Massiac, and du Bois de la Motte), and eighteen chefs d'escadre; the
British navy in 1756 had an admiral of the fleet, six admirals, eight vice admirals,
and fifteen rear admirals. The entire French naval officer corps in 1756 contained
about 1,000, excluding midshipmen.[56]

Another serious problem was the continuing loss of current or potential
crewmen; another 6,500 to 7,000 were captured by the British during 1756,
almost half of them trained sailors and petty officers, and attempts to replace
them by expanding the registration of sailors encountered local resistance.[57]
Perhaps most threatening of all, however, was the navy department's growing
financial difficulties. Although it was allocated 40 million livres, it spent 50
million or more compared to the British navy's £3.9 million (equivalent to 93.5
million livres); by August the intendant of Brest was borrowing money from
the city treasury because his reserves were reduced to 30,000 livres.[58]

Louis XV hoped to raise money by adding a second *vingtième*, one of the
government's chief direct taxes; according to Knyphausen he sought 24 million
livres, including 14 million for the navy.[59] The increase, however, needed to be
registered by the Parlement of Paris, the most important of France's judicial
bodies. Louis' attempts to bully it into doing so led to the resignation of most
of its 200 magistrates in December 1756.

The last such political crisis had occurred in 1753–54. The Parlement contained an influential minority of Jansenists, an unofficial group of Catholics
whose strict religious views and reservations about papal authority were considered heretical. Christophe de Beaumont, the archbishop of Paris, forbad the
administration of last rites to suspected Jansenists, arousing the ire of the Parlement. On that occasion Louis unsuccessfully tried to force the Parlement to
accept a compromise; instead it was able to assert its authority over the clergy.
Louis compounded the current crisis by attempting to reorganize the Parlement
and by reopening its dispute with Beaumont. Although Machault had been
regarded as sympathetic to Parlement rather than the archbishop, he became
the chief agent of the king's hard line, in large part because he needed to raise
money for the navy.[60]

For 1757 Machault planned to have fifty-six ships of the line in service, including two ready for launching—nineteen at Brest, sixteen in the Mediterranean,
and twenty-one abroad.[61] He intended to send detachments to protect Canada
and the French West Indies, but he also hoped to maintain the initiative by

carrying the war to new areas. One such area was the Indian Ocean, where the British as yet had only a squadron of four ships of the line. Before the war the French government had regarded the hostilities in India between the French East India Company and the British East India Company as an expense rather than an opportunity. Now its attitudes had changed, particularly since the French East India Company could contribute its own fleet, including lightly built but large and fast ships of the line. (The British East India Company also had a fleet, but made little use of it.) [62] One such ship of the line already was in the Indian Ocean at the French-held Mascarene Islands (Ile de France and Bourbon, now Mauritius and Réunion). Machault planned to send three squadrons to the Mascerenes, one consisting of three French navy ships of the line from Brest, the other two containing six East Indian company ships of the line from Lorient (three of them *en flûte*). They and accompanying transports would carry six battalions of troops to attack Madras and the other British trading posts of the Coromandel coast of southeast India. The entire naval force would be commanded by Chef d'escadre Anne-Antoine, comte d'Aché. [63]

Machault also planned to send two small squadrons to disrupt the British slaving trade in Africa before proceeding to the French West Indies. The *Intrépide*, 74, *Opiniâtre*, 64, and *Licorne*, 32, would operate along the coast of Guinea and the *Saint-Michel*, 64, and *Améthyste*, 32, off Angola, each attempting to destroy British establishments and capture slave ships; if possible, they then would rendezvous before crossing the Atlantic. [64] On 23 November the *Saint-Michel*'s squadron sailed from Brest, followed a day later by the *Intrépide*'s squadron. [65] The first squadron for India (three East India Company ships of the line plus frigates and transports) departed Lorient at the end of December. It carried the first troop contingent, two battalions of the regiment of Lorraine. [66]

Even with such sweeping plans, the French navy basically was buying time until Britain could be forced to the negotiating table. As the loss of Oswego and Minorca had not accomplished this, France could hardly expect decisive results from faraway India; even if the French were successful, it would take many months for news to reach Europe. By the end of 1756, however, France was preparing an offensive against Hanover in order to change the attitudes of George II and the British government. This involved major new spending on the army, which Machault opposed. Argenson and Belle-Isle were triumphant in obtaining it from the Council of State, but Machault received a promise of 66 million livres for the French navy during the coming year. [67] France would not be acting on its own in Germany. In 1756 it found a new ally, Austria.

THE FIRST STAGE OF THE DIPLOMATIC REVOLUTION

Newcastle believed that all Europe shared his fear of French aggression and that he could create a coalition similar to those which had opposed Louis XIV. After the 16 January 1756 Convention of Westminster, he even hoped that both Prussia and Austria would join Britain and the Netherlands in an anti-French alliance; if not, he was still ready to support Austria against a Prussian attack.[68] While he awaited a working alliance in Germany, he took advantage of Hanover's freedom from the fear of French invasion. In February the Dutch again refused to contribute troops in response to Britain's claim that the mobilization of Belle-Isle's army was an act of aggression.[69] The British already had sent empty troop transports to the Netherlands to embark the Dutch troops. These vessels now proceeded to the Hanoverian port of Stade, where they embarked 8,600 Hanoverians (twelve battalions of infantry and five companies of artillery) and 6,500 Hessians (eight infantry battalions). In mid-May 1756 these troops joined the Duke of Cumberland's 35,000 British soldiers, which were defending England from invasion.[70] Although Pitt mocked the Newcastle government for needing foreign troops, and public opinion generally was hostile toward them, they greatly eased the government's fears.[71]

The other consequences of the Convention of Westminster were less favorable to Britain. Maria Theresa felt betrayed by the British because the convention exempted the Austrian Netherlands; by failing to guarantee its neutrality, Britain and Prussia seemed to be inviting France to attack it.[72]

Surprisingly, Frederick II also misinterpreted the consequences of the convention. Within hours of its signing, the British-Prussian agreement was public knowledge. Louis XV did not express his feelings when the news reached France, but, as Knyphausen reported, the king and his ministers were gravely insulted by the disrespect shown to French honor and by the humiliation suffered by Nivernais. Rouillé explained to Knyphausen that, although Louis had no immediate intentions of making war in Germany, he could not be indifferent to losing the means of attacking Hanover in case the naval operations he planned (obviously the invasion of Minorca) did not have the success he anticipated. Amid the general anger, pro-Prussian ministers like Argenson were ridiculed, and they lost their influence in the Council of State.[73]

Frederick's goal in making the convention had been to escape war with Russia and Britain; he certainly did not want to risk war with France. He subsequently claimed that the convention was not directed against France and was not prejudicial to French interests because France had shown no interest in attacking Hanover. He attempted to mediate the Franco-British conflict (as discussed above). He also vigorously pursued the renewal of his alliance with

France, even hinting he was prepared to violate his obligations to Britain.[74] Surprisingly, he had support from Nivernais, who still hoped to make his mission a success. Nivernais was sent recall orders on 19 February, but he remained in Berlin until the arrival of Guy-Louis-Henri, marquis de Valory, an elderly general who had been minister to Prussia during the previous war. Valory had been sent at Frederick's request to replace Charles-Nicolas, chevalier de La Touche, as France's minister plenipotentiary. He, too, worked for a reconciliation with Prussia, but the task was hopeless. The sending of German troops to Britain was a fresh reminder to France of the limited usefulness of its Prussian alliance.[75] There were questions, however, of whether the mutual obligations of France and Prussia would end with the expiration of the fifteen-year alliance treaty of 1741, as France was also a party to a ten-year Prusso-Swedish treaty concluded in 1747; Frederick claimed that it required him only to remain neutral if France was attacked.[76] Meanwhile, keeping the alliance in force gave France time to await the results of her attack on Minorca and to negotiate with Austria.

Hitherto, France had needed an Austrian commitment to oppose the planned dispatch of Russian troops to Hanover. With the Convention of Westminster this requirement disappeared immediately, as Russian troops were prohibited from entering Germany. On 4 February 1756 the king and his council, rejecting the advice of Belle-Isle, decided against renewing the Prussian alliance; instead, France would resume negotiations with Austria. This was a victory for Machault, Madame de Pompadour (who had been mocked by Frederick and flattered by Marie Theresa), and the advocates at court of devoutly Catholic policies. It was a defeat for the remaining supporters of Protestant Prussia.[77] The negotiations were entrusted to both Bernis, who had handled the earlier discussions with Starhemberg, and Rouillé, who, like his adviser Premier commis La Ville, feared a long war in Germany and distrusted the Austrians. Henri-Joseph Bouchard d'Esparbès, marquis d'Aubeterre, the French ambassador in Vienna, was not even informed of the discussion. On 9 August he was appointed as the French minister in Spain, it now being intended that Bernis would replace him in Vienna.[78]

The negotiations did not begin smoothly. Starhemberg was reluctant to put anything on paper and, fearing the reaction of the Russians, Swedes, and Danes, discouraged the idea of a French attack on Hanover, an idea, moreover, to which Maria Theresa was increasingly hostile.[79] His task was difficult because he was under orders to pursue simultaneously an offensive alliance (in hopes of acquiring French financial assistance) and a defensive alliance (in order to protect both the Austrian Netherlands from France and Austria itself from Prussia). Bernis fell ill, and Controller General of Finances Séchelles, a strong advocate of the Austrian alliance, suffered a stroke. (Séchelles was replaced by his brother-in-law, François-Marie Peyrenc de Moras, who became adjunct controller general on 17 March and took over the department on 24 April.) Machault, although also pro-Austrian, was more cautious than were Bernis and Séchelles. Bernis later claimed that Machault blocked his admission to the Council of State to avoid embarrassing Rouillé.[80]

The impasse was overcome by Chancellor Kaunitz, who insisted that France sign a defensive alliance before continuing discussions for an offensive alliance. He even threatened a renewal of Austrian ties with Britain. Starhemberg presented his ultimatum on 16 April, and three days later Louis discussed it with his Council of State. Argenson, Machault, Rouillé, and Saint-Florentin were joined for the critical meeting by Puyzieulx, who had been on sick leave, and Noailles, by now deaf and recently retired. (Saint-Séverin had died the previous month, and Belle-Isle didn't join the council until 16 May.)[81] Opinion was unanimous that France should accede to the Austrian demands, although Argenson warned that the treaty was liable to lead to a general war, perhaps even a religious one, as Prussia, Hanover, and Britain were Protestant. Negotiations now proceeded quickly. According to Starhemberg, Madame de Pompadour helped to overcome the king's last-minute hesitations. On 1 May a defensive treaty and a convention of neutrality were signed at Rouillé's estate of Jouy near Versailles. The defensive treaty, known as the Treaty of Versailles, called for each party to contribute an auxiliary corps of 18,000 infantry and 6,000 cavalry (or a financial equivalent) if the other was attacked. The neutrality convention called for France to respect the integrity of the Austrian Netherlands and other Austrian possessions during the current war with Britain and meanwhile for Austria to maintain strict neutrality. A number of articles in the treaty were kept secret, even from Valory, including Austria's obligation to assist France if she were attacked by an ally of Britain, the prohibition of either party's making or renewing a treaty without the other's consent, an agreement to invite other parties such as Spain to join, and a promise to discuss other matters (i.e., an offensive alliance) as soon as possible.[82]

The treaty was greeted by many, including Rouillé, as if it were a guarantee of peace on the European continent.[83] It seems unlikely, however, that Louis XV shared in the optimism or that, as Bernis later claimed, Germany would have remained at peace if Prussia had not decided later in 1756 to attack Austria.[84] It does seem fairly certain, however, that Louis had little desire to help Austria regain Silesia and thereby disturb the balance of power in Germany; moreover, at least according to Bernis, he had moral qualms about going to war with Frederick while their countries still had treaty obligations toward each other.[85] Finally, with the invasion force having sailed for Minorca, France still had reason to hope Britain could be driven into making peace before the war spread to the

European continent. Thus the Treaty of Versailles was a way of buying time. Should the hopes of a quick peace with Britain be frustrated, a French attack on Hanover would become almost inevitable. To obtain Austrian consent, France would need to assist an Austrian attack on Prussia, although perhaps the attack could be delayed until the Franco-Swedish-Prussian alliance ended in 1757. For France no less than for Austria, the Treaty of Versailles was a step on a path toward war in Germany rather than toward peace.

Evidence for this is provided by how quickly France moved to begin negotiations for an offensive alliance. The day after the treaty was signed, Starhemberg sent to Vienna a list of French demands and questions. Louis wished to know how great a financial contribution Austria expected from France for recapturing Silesia and what steps should be taken to prevent British or Dutch intervention to help Prussia. France expected Austria to grant it the temporary use of the ports of Ostend and Nieuport in the Austrian Netherlands and wanted assurances that Austria was still prepared to make an exchange of territory with Louis' son-in-law Duke Philip of Parma. France also expected a promise of cooperation in the next Polish royal election, although nothing was said of the prince de Conti.[86] The negotiations promised to be lengthy and difficult. Ironically, it would be Prussia who would guarantee their success.

THE OPENING OF HOSTILITIES IN CENTRAL EUROPE

The Treaty of Versailles transformed French politics, turning representatives of the army like Argenson and Belle-Isle into advocates of the new system, while in reaction Machault cooled toward Austria.[87] Elsewhere in Europe, many were stunned that two such long-standing rivals should reach an agreement. Frederick II took the news calmly, having given up hope of restoring ties with France,[88] but Britain responded angrily. When British Minister Plenipotentiary Robert Keith confronted Maria Theresa with the accusation that Austria had thrown herself into France's arms, she replied that Austria was not in France's arms but by her side.[89]

Spain, already distressed at France's invasion of Minorca (with its predominantly Spanish population), was upset by France's reconciliation with Austria, Spain's rival in Italy. Maria Theresa wrote in vain to Ferdinand VI's wife, Queen Maria Magdalena Barbara, to appeal for an Austrian-French-Spanish alliance in defense of Catholicism. Britain, in contrast, took great pains to improve relations with Spain at this critical moment, avoiding the seizure of Spanish ships trading with France or French colonies and releasing Spanish sailors captured aboard French ships. The British campaign was successful. Spain remained neutral throughout the rest of Ferdinand's reign, thereby depriving France of the assistance of some forty-five ships of the line.[90]

Other states also took care to avoid being caught up in the Franco-British war. The Dutch refused to allow their army to protect Hanover and issued a declaration of neutrality on 25 May, but continued to trade with France and the French West Indies. Sweden agreed to a subsidy treaty with France after its Council of State foiled a plot by Queen Louisa Ulrika, a sister of Frederick II of Prussia. The Danes and Swedes signed a joint declaration of neutrality on 12 July and even outfitted a squadron of six Swedish and four Danish ships of the line to protect neutral shipping in the Baltic. The Dutch planned to outfit their own squadron but had difficulty in paying for it.[91]

Separately, the Russians sent out nine ships of the line, almost half of their Baltic fleet, to protect their shipping, but Russia's attitude during the impending crisis differed from that of the other neutral powers of Europe. Empress Elizabeth had been outraged by the Treaty of Westminster, news of which reached St. Petersburg only two days after she had ratified her own treaty with Britain. She established a war council to prepare for war against Prussia and began mobilizing her army. Although negotiations with Britain continued until September, she rejected the offer of a British subsidy. On 10 April she approved coordinating plans with Austria for a joint attack on Prussia, based on a secret clause of the 2 June 1746 Austro-Russian Treaty of St. Petersburg; she was willing to double the 30,000-man contingent required from her in case of war with Prussia if Maria Theresa did the same, but she requested an Austrian subsidy of 2 million florins (equivalent to about 5 million livres). She also approved making conciliatory gestures toward France and France's eastern European friends, Sweden, Poland, and the Ottoman Empire, whom she hoped would remain neutral when war with Prussia began. Thus, Austria did not risk alienating Russia by making an alliance with France, Russia's rival for influence in eastern Europe.

Elizabeth responded positively to the Treaty of Versailles, distancing herself further from Britain. She was prepared to establish closer ties with France, and she offered Austria 80,000 men for a joint attack on Prussia. On 10 May, however, Maria Theresa learned that only 67,000 Austrian troops could be ready for a summer campaign. Moreover, Austria was not yet sure of France's reaction to an attack on Prussia. Three weeks later Maria Theresa asked Russia to postpone the attack until 1757. Elizabeth, dependent on the Austrian subsidy, reluctantly agreed (and on 2 February 1757 signed an extension to the alliance). The delay, however, worked to her good fortune as the Russian mobilization went more slowly than expected.[92]

Meanwhile Austria had begun its discussions with France for an offensive alliance. Day-to-day negotiations with Starhemberg were entrusted to Bernis. The two met at Versailles, and when the court moved to the palace of Compiègne for the next hunting season, they made use of a nearby convent.[93] The two sides had huge differences to resolve.[94] Austria was opposed to a French attack on Hanover, fearing it would bring Britain, Hanover, and the Protestant principalities of northern Germany into the war that it planned against Prussia for the recovery of Silesia. France for its part did not wish to become involved directly in Austro-Prussian hostilities. Austria wished France not only to provide direct financial assistance but also to subsidize an army of troops from various German principalities to cooperate with the Russian and Austrian armies; France in return wanted a portion of the Austrian Netherlands for itself and all the remainder for Duke Philip of Parma. Moreover, France did not wish to see Prussia lose more than Silesia, whereas Austria (as France suspected) had made a promise to Russia that in exchange for her help in attacking Frederick II Russia would receive Courland. The eastern portion of Prussia would be given to Poland in compensation (Courland being technically still a part of Poland).

By late August partial agreement had been reached. Maria Theresa's income of 40 million florins (100 million livres) a year, while twice what it had been in 1745 and still increasing, was still substantially inferior to Louis XV's.[95] To enable her to attack Prussia, France agreed to furnish her an annual subsidy of 12 million florins and to subsidize an auxiliary corps of 25,000 to 30,000 German troops. Duke Philip of Parma would not receive the Austrian Netherlands in exchange for his Italian possessions, nor would France make peace with Britain until Austria recovered the duchy of Silesia and the adjacent principality of Glatz. The French and Austrian rulers would work together during the next Polish election and would also cooperate to resolve a potential succession dispute in the Kingdom of the Two Sicilies (consisting of the Kingdoms of Naples and Sicily). Austria and Spain had agreed in the Treaty of Aranjuez that if King Ferdinand VI died without children the Spanish throne would be inherited by his older half brother King Charles of the Two Sicilies, while his younger half brother, Duke Philip, would inherit the Kingdom of the Two Sicilies and Philip's territories in northern Italy would revert to Austria. Charles, however, had refused to sign the treaty, not wishing to disinherit his own children. Presumably his wishes would be accommodated after Philip was in Brussels.[96]

Many questions remained unresolved. France wished to receive directly half a dozen fortresses and Ostend and Nieuport, the seaports of the Austrian Netherlands, but the compensation for France was yet to be determined. It was also undecided whether France would furnish an auxiliary corps of her own troops to Austria in addition to the German troops for which she was paying, whether Austria would repay part of the subsidy if the attack on Prussia was unsuccessful, or whether Austria would close to Britain its ports of Ostend,

Leghorn (in the Mediterranean), and Trieste and Fiume (in the Adriatic). Most difficult of all, France still wished to minimize the losses of Prussia and preserve the balance of power in Germany.

As the astute Starhemberg had predicted, the impasse in the Austro-French negotiations was broken by the actions of King Frederick II. The Prussian king had known for several years that the Treaty of St. Petersburg contained secret clauses that threatened Prussia. [97] In early June he began receiving warnings from his extensive spy network about the military preparations of Austria and Russia. He realized he was going to be attacked, although he mistakenly blamed Austria as the instigator. He learned by late July, however, that the attack was postponed until 1757. This made him all the more eager to strike first against Austria. [98] He had already notified Britain of his intention to do so, warning of the danger to Hanover and asking for a British squadron in the Baltic to protect against a Russian army arriving by sea. [99] Newcastle still believed he could reach an agreement with the Russians and wished to avoid alienating Empress Elizabeth by sending a squadron to the Baltic. He argued that British ships of the line were of too deep a draft to use in shallow waters against an invading force escorted by galleys. He was able to avoid committing British ships and to convince Frederick, who wished a full-scale military alliance with Britain, to delay his attack until August. This not only gave Britain more time for its negotiations with Elizabeth, which Frederick naïvely hoped might keep Russia out of the war, but also temporarily protected defenseless Hanover. [100]

Over the summer Prussia moved closer to war with Austria, even though the Prussian army and financial reserves had not yet reached the size Frederick wished. Nevertheless he now could put 150,000 men in the field (exclusive of troops to garrison his fortresses), and he estimated that Austria could put only 100,000 men in the field against him; moreover, he had enough money for three years of war if needed. [101] He issued a series of ultimata demanding that Maria Theresa demonstrate her peaceful intentions; she scornfully refused. In his eagerness to attack first, Frederick disregarded Valory's warnings that France would honor its commitments to defend Austria, and he misperceived Russia's intentions. [102]

The first Prussian blow was delivered on 29 August not against Austria itself but against Prussia's neighbor to the south, the Electorate of Saxony. The Saxons wanted nothing more than to remain neutral, having little weight in the balance of power with their population of 2 million and army of only 23,000 effectives (3,000 of which were in Poland, which Elector Augustus ruled as king). Saxony, however, blocked direct Prussian access to the Kingdom of Bohemia (today the western portion of the Czech Republic), which was part of Maria Theresa's domains; conversely, if Saxony should join Frederick's enemies or be occupied by them, it would pose a great threat to Prussia, as its capital, Dresden, was only 100 miles from Berlin and its northern border was only 50 miles from it. Frederick instead could have chosen to invade Moravia, just east of Bohemia, which bordered Prussian Silesia and was even closer to Vienna. Maria Theresa's army had only 15,000 troops stationed there, compared with 31,000 in Bohemia. This would have exposed the Prussian heartland to an Austrian attack through Saxony, but it is most unlikely Maria Theresa would have violated Saxon neutrality.

When Augustus refused Frederick's demands for safe passage across his territory, the Prussians invaded Saxony with 62,000 troops. The Saxon army retreated to a mountain fortress near Dresden which it took the Prussians seven weeks to capture; they then incorporated the Saxon army into their own, although most of the troops soon deserted. Frederick continued into Bohemia via the valley of the Elbe River and even won a skirmish against the Austrians. It was too close to winter to continue the campaign, however, so Frederick had to retreat to Saxony.[103]

The invasion of Saxony was a diplomatic and public relations disaster. It reinforced the reputation for ruthlessness Frederick had acquired in 1740 from seizing Silesia; Rouillé told Knyphausen that the English spirit seemed to have spread to Prussia, which practiced the same violence on land that English did at sea.[104] It made Maria Theresa and Elizabeth all the more eager to crush him. It brought the armies of a number of German principalities into the coalition against Prussia (under the authority of the Holy Roman Empire) and deprived Prussia of having Saxony as a neutral buffer state. Furthermore, nothing could have been better designed to embitter Louis XV. The Prussians detained the French minister to Saxony and even forced their way into Augustus's wife's bedroom in search of evidence of Saxon collaboration with Austria. Her daughter Maria Josepha was married to Louis' son Louis-Ferdinand, the dauphin. Maria Josepha's anguish at the news of her parents and her birthplace had a great impact on the tenderhearted French king, contributing to his decisions to recall Valory from his diplomatic post in Berlin and to begin preparations for joint Austro-French operations against Prussia and Hanover. The members of his court and the French public shared his outrage.[105] Even George II was angered at his nephew Frederick for violating the territory of a fellow imperial elector.[106] Frederick thus increased his peril; moreover, by making Austria more dependent on French help, he inadvertently assisted the Franco-Austrian negotiations and placed Hanover in greater peril, too. The occupation of Saxony was financially beneficial, the Saxons being forced to bear a considerable portion of Prussia's war expenses, but Frederick henceforth would have to defend it as well as Silesia from Maria Theresa's armies.

The failure of his initial campaign made Frederick desperate for British help. He called on them not only for assistance in Germany but also for diversionary attacks against the French coast and Corsica.[107] As even Pitt, a former opponent of "diversions" in Europe realized, Britain did not have the luxury of abandoning Frederick, however reprehensible was his conduct. (Pitt seems to have conditioned his support, however, on the inner cabinet's sending reinforcements to Loudoun.) Moreover, in spite of his attack on Saxony, Frederick was still immensely popular with the English public, although the English opposed sending troops to Germany. With the return of the Hanoverian and Hessian troops that had helped defend England from invasion, there was a reasonable nucleus for an army in Germany, and Frederick was willing to lend the army troops over the winter. On 31 December Holdernesse informed Andrew Mitchell, the British minister in Berlin, that Britain would assemble an army to defend Hanover. George, however, hesitated to mobilize more Hanoverian troops or to accept Frederick's troop offer, still hoping to preserve his electorate's neutrality.[108] The need to defend Hanover and Silesia, however, was gradually drawing former enemies Britain and Prussia together, just as the desire to attack them was drawing former enemies France and Austria together. What historians now call the Diplomatic Revolution thus corresponded to diplomatic logic.

In order to help defend Bohemia and Moravia, Austria wished France to send the 24,000 troops required under the terms of their defensive alliance, besides paying as promised for a supporting German army. Maria Theresa did not wish, however, to become involved in hostilities with Britain, Hanover, or the neutral Protestant principalities of northern Germany. France had its own priorities. Rather than sending troops across Germany, the French government wished to send a large army into western Germany, first to seize on Austria's behalf Wesel, the great Prussian fortress on the Rhine (in the isolated Prussian province of Cleves), and then to capture Hanover. France wished Maria Theresa to break relations with Britain, to close her ports to British shipping, and to admit French garrisons into the Austrian Netherlands ports of Ostend and Nieuport.

While Bernis continued diplomatic negotiations with Starhemberg, Louis sent Lieutenant General Louis-Charles-César Le Tellier, comte d'Estrées, one of the most highly regarded generals in the French army, to Vienna to conduct military discussions. At the beginning of January 1757, the Austrians abandoned hope of receiving a major French auxiliary corps and agreed that France could send an army of 40,000 to capture Wesel. The French would keep it there while Austria negotiated with Hanover about that electorate's neutrality; should the negotiations fail, the French would reinforce it to 105,000 men. It would attack Hanover and then the great Prussian fortress of Magdeburg, eighty miles west of Berlin (although the Austrians continued to argue that the French should bypass Hanover and attack Magdeburg directly). France agreed to pay for 10,000 troops from Bavaria and Württemberg to support the 110,000-man army Maria Theresa was preparing for use against Frederick II. Meanwhile, on 2 January 1757, Bernis, who had tried unsuccessfully to limit the size of the French force being sent to Germany, was named to the Council of State. His discussions with Starhemberg about an offensive alliance continued while Austria negotiated with Hanover. [109] In January Maria Theresa proposed a convention by which George would remain neutral in his capacity as elector, giving Frederick II neither direct nor indirect aid and permitting Austrian and French armies "innocent passage" through his territory. [110]

France also experienced difficulties in reaching an understanding with her other former rival, Russia. Even before the Prussian invasion of Saxony, Russia was ready to join the Franco-Austrian defensive alliance, but France sought only Russian neutrality. The Prussian attack on Saxony was regarded by Elizabeth as a personal affront, since she considered Augustus's Poland to be a client state. With the likely entrance of Russia into the war, Louis soon would need to reconsider his policy of keeping the Russians out of Poland; for the moment France encouraged Russia to attack Prussia by sending an army via the Baltic rather than through Poland. Meanwhile the prince de Conti irreparably damaged his relations with Louis by his maladroit attempts to secure a military command in Germany (and perhaps by his contacts with Louis' opponents in the Parlement of Paris). The king elected to keep the "Secret du Roi" in existence, but he replaced Conti with Tercier as its director.

France's relations with Russia evolved more quickly than the French government expected. Its diplomatic representative in St. Petersburg was the inexperienced Chevalier Douglas, who returned to Russia on another secret mission at Vice Chancellor Vorontsov's suggestion. On 22 January 1757 (or by the Russian calendar 11 January 1757) Douglas, who had been named French chargé d'affaires, signed an agreement by which Russia joined the Austro-French defensive alliance; he did so at the urging of the Austrian minister at the Russian court. Unfortunately the agreement did not exempt France from assisting Russia in case of war with the Ottoman Empire, whose friendship was vital to France for both economic and strategic reasons. This matter would have to be resolved, as would the question of how to subsidize Russian participation in the coming war. There also were reasons for concern in the slowness of the Russian mobilization and in Elizabeth's ill health, as her nephew and heir, Crown Prince Peter, was sympathetic to Prussia. Nevertheless, the final piece in the Diplomatic Revolution was falling into place. [111]

France thus could hope that in 1757 Britain would be forced into a peace by which the French conquests of Minorca and Hanover could be exchanged for reasonable borders for New France. In the interim France would have to take great care that Britain's ambitious plans for conquests in North America were frustrated. The responsibility of protecting New France from further losses would fall in large part on the French navy. Unfortunately Machault, who thus far had performed so masterfully, soon would be unavailable to direct its operations.

4

1757
To the Edge of Victory

THE KING SACRIFICES MACHAULT

In spite of his successful direction of the French navy, by the beginning of 1757 Machault was the most unpopular member of the French government. As controller general before 1754 he had made himself the symbol of high taxes. He resurrected this association by his support in mid-1756 for imposing the second *vingtième*. The public suspected, moreover, that the government intended to make at least one *vingtième* permanent rather than using it just to pay war expenses. Finally Machault was blamed for the attempt to reorganize the Parlement of Paris and to limit its prior victory over the archbishop of Paris in the Jansenist dispute. The current fight with the Parlement had been occasioned by its refusal to register the new tax, but it had become intertwined with the other disputes, which involved the king's authority over judicial and religious affairs. In the process Louis and Machault had made themselves appear much more extremist in political and religious matters than they really were. Unsurprisingly, the king did not like checks on his authority. But, conservative and traditionalist by nature, he did not want to overthrow the established political order. He merely wished to alter the balance of power within it. Even less was he a religious zealot like Archbishop Beaumont. His chief desire was to end the feud between Parlement and the archbishop and restore religious peace to Paris.[1]

Machault was fiercely loyal to the king, but he too was a moderate in religious matters. In addition to his post as naval minister, he was keeper of the king's seals of office, a position which involved regulation of judicial affairs. By attacking the Parlement he hoped to increase the king's influence over parliamentary decision making, to ensure the collection of taxes needed by the navy, and to solve the religious disputes of Paris. Pursuing such an ambitious agenda made him hated by taxpayers, by the supporters of Parlement, and by Jansenists and their sympathizers. Machault put himself in such a dangerous position partly in order not to antagonize his political patroness, Madame de Pompadour. Won over by the flattery of Maria Theresa, she recently had joined the "devout" party at court, which was loyal to Austria and the pope, while being opposed to both Protestant Prussia and supposedly crypto-Protestant Jansenism. Although unenthusiastic about the Austrian alliance, Machault apparently felt he had to follow her lead.[2]

With the resignation in December 1756 of most of the judges of the Parlement of Paris, Louis and Machault provoked a political crisis, which endangered public compliance with collection of the two *vingtièmes*. It did not endanger the monarchy itself. Louis no longer enjoyed the public adulation of the early part of his reign, which had led to his being called "Louis the Beloved" (le Bien-aimé). But few people desired any fundamental changes in the basic political institutions of France. Although the public itself was as traditionalist as Louis, wanting him and the Parlements only to follow their customary roles, moments of public outrage carry the risk of individual acts of violence. No one seems to have expected one now, it having been almost 150 years since Henri IV was assassinated by a religious fanatic. The French generally regarded themselves as more civilized than the English, who in the interim had executed one king and driven another into exile. Even they were not immune from violence, however.

On 5 January 1757 Robert-François Damiens, a mentally unstable supporter of the Parlementary cause, stabbed Louis with a small knife as the king was leaving the royal chateau of Versailles. Damiens was acting alone and apparently wished not to kill the king but rather to attract his attention to the Parlement's demands. Although the wound was not serious, the king and court were panic-stricken at the possibility the knife might have been poisoned. (It was not, but the king was very fortunate to avoid a potentially fatal infection from the wound.)[3] Louis' terror probably was compounded by psychological shock. He had not fully outgrown his cosseted childhood; basically a kindly and sentimental man, he was used to being loved and admired. The attack brought out his streak of morbid and superstitious religiosity. Briefly it was generally thought that Madame de Pompadour would be exiled. Friends like Bernis and her favorite general, Charles de Rohan, prince de Soubise, rallied to her and earned her gratitude. Machault, however, made the mistake of advising her to leave the court.[4] Although she was no longer Louis' mistress (except in the eyes of the public), the king needed her love and comfort more than ever, and she quickly returned to his favor. Observers as late as 1761, however, noticed Louis' melancholy.[5] His initially timid response at the end of 1757 to setbacks in the war may have been partly a product of his weakened self-confidence. Louis' wounding brought expressions of concern from other monarchs, including George II, but not from Frederick II, whom Louis never forgave.[6]

The attack by Damiens and its aftermath were costly both for the Parlement of Paris and for those who failed to support Madame de Pompadour. For the Parlement the effects were only temporary. Initially its dispute with Louis was worsened, as the king exiled or imprisoned the leading judges of the court. The torture of Damiens before his trial and execution failed to reveal any outside complicity in his crime, however. Soon the Parlement's dispute with the king resumed a normal course. Bernis, more than ever in Madame de Pompadour's favor, eventually took over negotiations with the Parlement. He saved the second *vingtième*, but abandoned the attempts to reorganize the court and to interfere with its authority over the actions of the clergy. The exiled and imprisoned judges were restored to office, and the Parlement returned to work in September 1757. To complete its victory, Archbishop Beaumont was exiled to his estate in rural Perigord in early 1758.[7]

Those whom Madame de Pompadour considered rivals or false friends were not so fortunate. On 1 February Louis removed from office and exiled to their country estates both War Minister Argenson and Naval Minister Machault, the former with a curt message, the latter with expressions of gratitude and a pension. The king further spared the feelings of Machault by not appointing a successor to him as keeper of the royal seals. In the opinion of the astute Starhemberg, Argenson was knowledgeable, diligent, and able, but Madame de Pompadour's dislike of him finally proved politically fatal. Machault, according to Starhemberg, was liked and respected by the officers of the navy in spite of his lack of charm (not surprisingly given his generosity and deference to them). Hated by the public and lacking Madame de Pompadour's support, however, Machault shared the fate of his political rival.[8]

Machault was succeeded as naval minister by François-Marie Peyrenc de Moras, who for the next six months also retained his position as controller general of finances. Moras, moreover, immediately entered the Council of State. The new naval minister lacked his predecessor's genius, but he was honest and conscientious and, as we shall see, he attempted to pursue Machault's policies. The navy, moreover, benefited at least indirectly from being in the hands of the person directing French finances; although it did not receive all the money it had been promised, it escaped close scrutiny when it overspent its budget.[9] Argenson's successor was his nephew, Antoine-René de Voyer d'Argenson, marquis de Paulmy. Paulmy was the friend of Bernis, who regarded him highly, but he was four years younger than Moras, and his only independent position of authority had been as ambassador to Switzerland.[10] With a wider war impending, it was highly dangerous that the army, too, was being placed in inexperienced hands. Paulmy, too, entered the Council of State, which during the immediate aftermath of the attack on the king had been directed by his pious and timid son, Dauphin Louis-Ferdinand. The dauphin handled the responsibility well enough for his father to give him the right henceforth to attend its meetings, although he was too exalted a personage to be considered an official member.[11]

Without the rivalry of Machault and Argenson, meetings of the Council of State became more peaceful, but it suffered from their absence. The dominant figure in the Council henceforth was Bernis, who as yet lacked a department to administer. Belle-Isle's advice on military matters was invaluable, but the old soldier was no longer the dominant figure he had been fifteen or twenty years earlier. Rouillé and Saint-Florentin lacked the ability and Moras and Paulmy lacked the experience to provide leadership, and Puyzieulx had retired because of ill health.

It is understandable that following his wounding the king should have desired calm, both inside and outside his government, but it was dangerous to make changes that might adversely affect the French war effort. The political crisis between the Parlement and the Archbishopric had been in large part the result of poor personnel choices by the king, such as the choice in 1746 of Beaumont as archbishop. So too had been the disastrous interwar Canadian policy. The expanding war in Europe would place extraordinary demands on the new heads of the war and naval ministries. Moreover, with the king's self-confidence shaken, he would be more dependent than ever on the advice of the Council of State, which had just lost two of its most distinguished members. If the diplomats and generals were successful and Hanover were captured, the war might yet be brought to a quick conclusion, but neither the government's finances nor the quality of its leadership held much promise of success if the war lasted much longer. Until the attempt was made to conquer Hanover, the main burden in holding back the British assault on the French empire would fall on the navy and on the officials of New France. Machault virtually had completed preparations for the campaign before his removal from office; whatever success the navy and Vaudreuil enjoyed would be in large part the final legacy of his all-too-brief tenure as naval and colonial minister.

NEW FRANCE SPARED

At the end of 1756 the British government accepted Loudoun's plans for striking up the St. Lawrence at the Canadian heartland and promised to send him nearly 6,000 reinforcements. The threat to Hanover briefly put the government's decision in doubt, but it was able to save the plan by sending troops from Ireland instead of England and Scotland. The troops were the second battalion of the 1st regiment and six one-battalion regiments, the 17th, 27th, 28th, 43rd, 46th, and 55th. Two Highland regiments of an oversized battalion apiece, the 77th and 78th, came later. Also, the 22nd regiment had arrived in December 1756, and the 80th light infantry was raised in America during 1757; each had a single battalion. The 50th and 51st had been disbanded, but eleven battalions remained from previous campaigns (four from the 60th, and one apiece from the 35th, 40th, 42nd, 44th, 45th, 47th, and 48th). By the autumn of 1757 British regular units in North America were, on paper, more than 20,000 officers and men strong, although only 16,000 were fit for duty.[12]

The troops from Ireland were escorted by a squadron under the command of Vice Admiral Francis Holburne.[13] Pitt insisted on a significant change in Loudoun's plans, however; after the troops from New York and Ireland rendezvoused at Halifax, they first would capture Louisbourg, which Pitt assumed would occur by late May or early June. Only then would they proceed up the St. Lawrence to attack Quebec. (This, in fact, proved prudent, as Loudoun's troops would have been in great peril sailing up the St. Lawrence with a French squadron at Louisbourg athwart their supply line.) Subsequently, Cumberland persuaded the inner cabinet to allow Loudoun the choice of attacking Quebec directly, but the changed orders arrived too late. Meanwhile Loudoun wrote Cumberland that he was bringing seven battalions from New York (comprising 5,500 men) to join the three battalions already in Nova Scotia.

It took far longer than anticipated for the forces from the British Isles to reach North America. They did not leave Cork until 8 May and reached Halifax only on 9 July. Loudoun had arrived there ten days earlier, having embargoed American shipping (over American objections) to collect 100 ships to use as transports. He manned them by impressing 800 sailors and then sailed to Halifax under the escort of a single ship of the line, the *Sutherland*, 50. He now was prepared to attack Louisbourg with more than 11,000 regular troops, against some 3,000 defenders (1,000 regulars, 800 marines, 600 disembarked sailors, and at least 500 militia).

Loudoun's advantage was wasted because his naval escort was too weak to challenge the French. Holburne brought fourteen of the line and found two more waiting for him, but there were sixteen French ships of the line at Louisbourg and they were defended by shore batteries. Holburne cruised off the approaches to the fortress, but he did not risk an attack. His plans foiled, Loudoun had to return to New York with most of his troops.[14] As at Minorca the year before, the British navy had sent too small a force.

The French arrived at Louisbourg in three squadrons. The first, including the *Tonnant*, 80, *Défenseur*, 74, *Diadème*, 74, *Eveillé*, 64, and *Inflexible*, 64, was commanded by Chef d'escadre Joseph, prince de Bauffremont de Listenois. It sailed from Brest on 30 January, the same day a British blockading squadron left port for the approach to Brest. It reached St. Domingue on 19 March after capturing the *Greenwich*, 50. Leaving his prize there, Bauffremont sailed for Louisbourg on 4 May and arrived on the last day of the month.[15]

The second squadron, with the *Hector*, 74, *Achille*, 64, *Sage*, 64, and *Vaillant*, 64, was commanded by Capitaine de vaisseau Jean-François de Noble du Revest, who had commanded the *Sage* during the Battle of Minorca. It was sent its sailing orders on 22 January, sailed from Toulon on 18 March, passed through the Straits of Gibraltar on 5 April (outrunning a British squadron of five ships of the line), and reached Louisbourg on 15 June.[16]

The third squadron originally consisted of the *Duc-de-Bourgogne*, 80, *Glo-rieux*, 74, *Hardi*, 64, and two frigates; commanded by Chef d'escadre Aubigny it sailed from Rochefort for Martinique and then Louisbourg at the end of December 1756 but was forced to return to port.[17] Moras gradually increased its size, dropping the *Hardi* but adding the *Formidable*, 80, *Héros*, 74, *Superbe*, 74, *Dauphin-Royal*, 70, *Belliqueux*, 64, *Bizarre*, 64, and *Célèbre*, 64. He placed the squadron under the command of Lieutenant General of the Fleet du Bois de la Motte, who had performed so brilliantly in 1755. Du Bois de la Motte had orders to take command of the entire fleet in North America and, at his discretion, to undertake offensive operations. While the British blockading squadron was in port temporarily, he sailed from Brest on 3 May in company with a squadron for India. He arrived at Louisbourg on 19 June, sending on the *Bizarre* and *Célèbre* to Quebec with troop reinforcements. Vaudreuil and Montcalm received two battalions of the Berry regiment originally intended for India, eight companies from the regiments of La Reine and Languedoc to replace those captured by Boscawen, and ten companies of marines.

Unfortunately an epidemic of typhus had broken out aboard du Bois de la Motte's squadron; 400 of his crewmen already were dead and another 1,200 were sick. The epidemic spread throughout the rest of the fleet, which was also weakened by scurvy, malaria, and yellow fever brought from St. Domingue. It was unable to put to sea until a hurricane on 25 September crippled Holburne's fleet (which had been reinforced by the *Prince Frederick*, 70, *Somerset*, 70, *De-vonshire*, 66, and *Eagle*, 60, while the French received only the *Apollon*, 50). The *Tilbury*, 60, sank, and the rest were driven to Halifax. As soon as he finished his own repairs from storm damage, du Bois de la Motte sailed for France, leaving behind hundreds of sick. He arrived at Brest on 23 November with the epidemic completely out of control. Typhus spread to Brest itself, killing 5,000 civilians, as well as to the surrounding area (and ships sent to Rochefort brought it there, too). Nearly half of the 12,000 officers and crewmen who had sailed to Canada died from disease (including Revest), a blow to the French navy as serious as the loss of a great battle.[18]

At a terrible price Louisbourg had been saved from attack. Several other places felt an impact from the French naval effort. An informal truce which lasted until November permitted both a British and a French fishing fleet to work off Newfoundland, for example. The sixty boats from Dunkirk nearly doubled their catch from the preceding year; when the British abrogated it, Moras ordered reprisals.[19] Quebec's fortunes also were tied to the navy. The troop reinforcements, sent in response to intelligence about the British reinforcements, proved a mixed blessing. The *Bizarre* and the *Célèbre* brought the epidemic, 200 of Berry's 1,100 officers and men dying from it. Furthermore the reinforcements depleted Quebec's limited food supplies.[20] Moras spent large sums to charter merchant shipping to bring provisions and other supplies to Canada, but du Bois de la Motte, blockaded in Louisbourg, was unable to provide protection. Some fifty ships reached Quebec, including thirteen provision ships, but about a third of these were sent by private speculators and carried nonessential items like brandy and dry goods. Other ships were captured by the British, including at least six provision ships and two of the six ships Moras hired from Abraham Gradis to bring recruits for Montcalm's battalions. Only enough food arrived between June and September to feed 8,000 soldiers for three months.[21]

Perhaps the area most affected by the Louisbourg campaign, however, was the Lake George region. Loudoun took his regulars to sea before the British colonies could finish mobilizing their troops. (Provincial regiments were disbanded over the winter and then recruited again for the next campaigning season.) Moreover Loudoun had not requested as many American troops as the previous year, and recruiting for both British and provincial regiments languished; substantial forces also were diverted to South Carolina to protect against a potential Indian attack. Nevertheless, Loudoun expected Major General Webb to assemble 7,500 provincial and British troops in order to attack Forts Carillon and St. Frédéric.[22] At the beginning of the summer, however, Webb's troops still were scattered among a number of forts in northern New York. The most northern of these, Fort William Henry on the south shore of Lake George, was particularly vulnerable.

By the end of June Vaudreuil was certain that the target of the impending British offensive was Louisbourg. Although some army officers wished to attack Nova Scotia,[23] Vaudreuil sent Montcalm with an army of 2,500 French regulars, 500 marines, 3,000–3,500 militia and volunteers, and 1,600–1,800 Indians to attack Fort William Henry. A March raid by Vaudreuil's brother had destroyed most of the British fleet on Lake George, so Montcalm was able to bring siege artillery by boat. When he opened his siege on 3 August, the British fort and a nearby fortified camp were garrisoned by fewer than 2,500 regular and provincial soldiers. Webb himself was only fifteen miles away at Fort Edward with about 4,000 men, but, in ill health and believing Montcalm's army even larger than it was, he failed to mount a rescue operation. On 9 August Fort William Henry surrendered after being offered lenient terms. Lacking food to feed his prisoners, Montcalm sent the garrison to Fort Edward on parole, thereby arousing the suspicion of his Indian allies, who feared they would be deprived of the spoils of the conquest. They attacked the column as it was departing from Fort William Henry, killing 100 to 200 prisoners and then departing for their villages with 500 captives. With most of his Indian scouts gone and lacking the means of transporting his artillery, Montcalm disregarded Vaudreuil's instructions to capture Fort Edward. Instead he leisurely dismantled Fort William Henry and then departed northward so that his militia could bring in the desperately needed harvest.[24]

The French navy's responsibilities extended to more than the protection of New France. It also bore the chief burden of protecting the islands and trade of the French West Indies. After Bauffremont sailed from St. Domingue on 4 May, the only French ship of the line in the West Indies was the recently captured *Greenwich*. Over the next two months six more ships of the line arrived. Five of these came to Martinique. The *Hardi*, 64, arrived from Rochefort on 13 May with a supply convoy and a new governor, Capitaine de vaisseau François de Beauharnais. Two months later she sailed for France, carrying Bompar, the former governor. Although almost captured off Rochefort, she escaped to Corunna and eventually made it home. On 17 May the *Saint-Michel*, 64, reached Martinique from Africa; she returned to France in the autumn. Three days later the *Intrépide*, 74, and *Opiniâtre*, 64, arrived. They came from their own mission to Africa, having already captured fifteen prizes worth 6 million livres. Soon they sailed to St. Domingue, arriving at the beginning of July. The final ship to reach Martinique was the *Alcyon*, 50, which sailed from Brest on 25 April and arrived in the West Indies by 13 June; she sailed for France with the *Saint-Michel*, but became separated and on 23 November sank with all hands after engaging two British frigates. The only ship of the line to sail directly to St. Domingue was the *Sceptre*, 74 (*en flûte*), which sailed from Brest on 16 April and arrived in late May or early June.

By then the British had assembled squadrons of half a dozen ships of the line apiece near Martinique and at Jamaica (covering St. Domingue). They did not have troops available to attack the French colonies, but they did have sufficient superiority of force to protect their own shipping and menace the French. On 21 October the four ships of the line at St. Domingue (*Intrépide*,

74, *Sceptre*, 74, *Opiniâtre*, 64, *Greenwich*, 50) fought a sharp action against a squadron comprised of the *Edinburgh*, 70, *Augusta*, 60, and *Dreadnought*, 60, which had been blockading the French colony. Although Capitaine de vaisseau Guy-François de Coëtnempren de Kersaint's French squadron suffered more casualties than the British, it inflicted enough damage to force the British back to Jamaica for repairs. Kersaint was able to sail for France on 13 November with a long-delayed convoy, leaving no French ships of the line in the West Indies.[25]

We have already mentioned that on 3 May du Bois de la Motte sailed in company with a squadron for the Indian Ocean. It comprised what once had been two separate squadrons, one (consisting of ten warships and transports) from the East India Company's port at Lorient and the other from Brest; another squadron had sailed from Lorient in late 1756. The long delay was occasioned in part by a collision that ruined Chef d'escadre d'Aché's first attempt to sail. Thereafter Moras transferred the *Superbe*, 74, and *Belliqueux*, 64, and a regiment of troops from d'Aché's squadron to du Bois de la Motte's squadron. D'Aché was left with only one ship of the line from Brest, the *Zodiaque*, 74, to accompany the *Bien-Aimé*, 58, *Centaure*, 58 (sailing *en flûte*), *Vengeur*, 54, and the other East India Company ships. Of perhaps even greater long-term importance, he brought only two battalions of the regiment of Lally to join the regiment of Lorraine, which had sailed with the earlier Lorient convoy. Meanwhile, Mitchell in Prussia had relayed to the British government Knyphausen's reports that troops were being sent to attack Madras; in response, four British ships of the line sailed on 13 March to reinforce the four stationed in India. Even with the four East India Company ships of the line sent earlier to the Indian Ocean, d'Aché could only expect to be equal to the British rather than enjoying the great superiority Machault had envisaged.[26]

The main departure from Machault's campaign plans, however, was the failure to outfit a fleet at Brest large enough to contest the British navy's dominance of the French coast. Here the French navy showed its inadequacies, in spite of Moras' attempts to follow the lead of his gifted predecessor.

DISASTER DEFERRED

Machault's hopes of controlling French coastal waters during 1757 were unrealistic. The French navy sent more than half its available ships of the line abroad; moreover, it lacked ships large enough to challenge the mighty 90- and 100-gun ships used by the British. When he became minister Moras hoped, however, that once the overseas detachments had sailed Conflans could outfit a fleet of twenty ships of the line, which at least would be a numerical match for the British.[27]

Unfortunately, the preparation of Conflans' fleet was slowed by shortages of materiel and particularly of sailors. The best he could do was to send small squadrons to sea, such as the *Entreprenant*, 74, and *Dragon*, 64, which cruised off Ireland. Even the frigates desperately needed to protect coastal convoys were affected, and French trade suffered more losses. French exports in 1757 dropped 22 percent from the previous year, although much of this was due to the war in Germany. Although imports declined by only 6 percent, imports from the French West Indies declined by more than 50 percent. Bordeaux, which conducted the greatest trade with the French colonies, was particularly hard hit. Insurance rates climbed to more than 50 percent, while the number of ships departing for the Western Hemisphere dropped to a fraction of the number in 1755. The effects on Nantes, another great colonial port, also were severe. [28]

By 16 August only half of Conflans' fleet was ready, including the *Soleil-Royal*, 80, and *Courageux*, 74, just finishing their armament. [29] On that day Moras ordered Conflans to suspend his preparations and use his sailors to man shore batteries. France had learned that Britain was preparing to attack the French coast and that even Brest might be threatened.

Moras' fears were not unrealistic. By now the British navy had recovered from a period of governmental instability, which began in early April 1757 when the king dismissed Secretary of State Pitt and Temple, the unpopular first lord of the admiralty. [30] For the next several months the navy was led by Daniel Finch, Earl of Winchilsea, who had held the position for two years during the previous war (March 1742 to December 1744). Winchilsea had done a poor job then and does not seem to have improved much; convoys were not properly assembled, and warships were kept unnecessarily in port. [31] At the beginning of July, however, Pitt and Newcastle were able to form a new coalition government to replace the Duke of Devonshire's. In the process Newcastle's friend Hardwicke received Pitt's consent to the return of Anson as first lord of the admiralty. [32] The navy quickly was reenergized, as Newcastle reported on 16 July. [33]

Pitt and Anson's first project was an attack on the French coast. The war in Germany was going badly for both Britain and Prussia (as will be discussed later). The French army, moreover, had taken possession of Ostend and Nieuport, which could be used to support an invasion of England. A landing on the French coast would serve as a diversion and might force France to recall some of its troops from Germany. Pitt's preferred objective was the great French naval base at Rochefort. A young army engineer named Robert Clerk had visited it in 1754 and reported that its fortifications were almost nonexistent. Furthermore, it was located in the area in which the underground Huguenot (French Protestant) Church was centered; Pitt unrealistically may have hoped for a religious uprising in support of the Protestant British. On 4 August the inner cabinet approved the operation, which involved a landing force of some 8,500 men (including ten of the thirty infantry battalions in England), commanded by Lieutenant General Sir John Mordaunt.[34]

In spite of George II's desire to divert the expeditionary force to Hanover, it sailed from Spithead, the roadstead of Portsmouth, on 8 September. It was escorted by a fleet of sixteen ships of the line commanded by Vice Admiral Edward Hawke. Twelve days later it arrived at the Basque Road off the mouth of the Charente River. A few miles upstream lay Rochefort, and in the roadstead were two French ships of the line, the *Prudent*, 74, and *Capricieux*, 64, waiting to escort a convoy to Brest. They fled to Rochefort, where only one ship of the line was in port, the *Florissant*, 74 (plus two ships of the line in construction). The French, expecting Brittany to be the British target, were caught completely by surprise. Only 3,000 men were garrisoned at Rochefort, and this number included only a few hundred regular soldiers. Few reinforcements were nearby except for poorly trained militia and coast guard troops; between Brittany and Bordeaux there were only seven battalions of regulars. The British thus had the chance to strike a crippling blow at an unprepared enemy. They failed to do so because the army and navy commanders did not know whether Rochefort could be captured without a siege and because they were concerned that changing weather conditions might cause the landing force to be stranded. For eleven days the great fleet and army lay off the French coast, accomplishing nothing beyond the capture of the small island of Aix. The French were able to bluff them into thinking Rochefort was well defended. The British then returned to England without attempting a landing. Substantial French reinforcements arrived only after Mordaunt and Hawke had left.

The French were extremely fortunate. There is no evidence the Huguenots would have helped the British and hence little chance the British could have remained long in Rochefort, but they could have destroyed several French ships of the line, a large quantity of naval materiel, and one of the three greatest naval dockyards in France. Conflans played no part in the outcome. On 24 September Moras ordered him to prepare ten ships of the line for sea and ordered two East India Company ships of the line at Lorient to prepare for joining the fleet. The Brest fleet was not yet ready when on 9 October Conflans was sent orders to suspend the armament because the British had left.[35]

Brest and Rochefort now turned their attention to preparing warships for New France. Six and a half weeks later du Bois de la Motte arrived with his infected ships, disrupting the preparations. The first ships for Louisbourg did not leave until the end of January 1758.

Meanwhile Moras prepared to use the fleet at Toulon to protect the French West Indies. After Revest's departure in March 1757, the Toulon fleet had been divided into several squadrons. The main one, five ships of the line under Chef d'escadre Jean-François Bertet de La Clue-Sabran, protected French commerce in the western Mediterranean. Smaller squadrons were sent to the central and eastern Mediterranean. When La Clue returned to Toulon in August, he was ordered to take seven months' worth of provisions and supplies aboard his squadron, the *Océan*, 80, *Guerrier*, 74, *Redoutable*, 74, *Content*, 64, and *Lion*, 64, to which the *Hippopotame*, 50, was added later. Moras planned to send the squadron to Martinique. The *Redoutable* and *Lion* would remain there while the others proceeded to St. Domingue. Two ships of the line carrying supplies would join them later. At the end of 1758 all the ships would rendezvous at St. Domingue and return to Toulon via Cadiz. Meanwhile Chef d'escadre Duquesne would use the remaining ships of the line of the Toulon fleet in the Mediterranean. La Clue's orders were sent on 19 September, and on 7 November he sailed (but with the new ship of the line *Centaure*, 74, replacing the *Lion*). On 30 November he was driven by a violent storm into the Spanish port of Cartagena, hundreds of miles east of the Straits of Gibraltar. He was still there at year's end.[36]

Superficially it would appear the French navy was stronger at the end of 1757 than it had been at the beginning of the year. The only ship of the line lost during the year was the *Alcyon*, 50, and it was counterbalanced by the capture of the *Greenwich* of the same rating. Four 74-gun ships of the line were launched during the first half of the year, the *Célèbre* and the *Minotaure* at Brest and the *Centaure* and *Souverain* at Toulon; in November the *Raisonnable*, 64, was launched at Rochefort. By year's end the navy had sixty-four ships of the line, although some still were in repair or needed repairs. Half a dozen more joined the *Modeste*, 64, in construction: the *Royal-Louis*, 116, and *Thésée*, 74, at Brest, the *Impétueux*, 90, at Rochefort, the *Robuste*, 74, at Lorient, and the *Protecteur*, 74, and *Fantasque*, 74, at Toulon (where the *Modeste* was being built). Another nine were ordered or named (the *Majestueux*, 114, *Indomptable*, 112, *Médiateur*, 90, *Astronome*, 74, *Cimeterre*, 74, *Union*, 74, *Altier*, 64, *Entêté*, 64, and *Résolu*, 64), although most of them later were cancelled.[37]

In spite of its increased numbers, the French navy entered 1758 greatly weakened. Six thousand irreplaceable men from du Bois de la Motte's squadron were dead or soon would be. Already there were huge differences in the number of warships Britain and France had in service, the number of sailors they mustered, and the amount of money they allocated for naval expenses. These differences would widen in coming years (although in 1759 France briefly would put more ships of the line in service by manning them with untrained sailors). What is remarkable are not the defeats and ship losses suffered by the French navy in 1758 and following years, but that they had been so long postponed. It is amazing that the French navy was able to save Louisbourg and to lose only one ship of the line during 1757 in spite of the huge disparity between French and British naval resources.

The most obvious disparity was in the number of ships in service. At the beginning of June 1757, the British navy had ninety-six ships of the line in service against only forty-two French. During the year Britain launched eleven ships of the line (as well as thirteen frigates). At year's end eighteen ships of the line were still in construction.[38]

What made it possible for Britain to make use of so many more ships was its advantage in number of sailors. The British navy mustered more than 60,000 crewmen for its ships (some 10,000 more than in 1756), in spite of growing competition from privateers and the need to provide crews for merchant ships, especially coastal shipping. The French navy mustered about 35,000, some two-thirds of them either trained sailors or petty officers.[39]

Competition from privateers proved a serious problem for the French navy, because of the difficulties it had in paying sailors. An effort was made in August to ban privateering, but it was quickly abandoned; the many prizes taken by privateers provided some financial relief for French seaports, the need to protect shipping diverted some of the British navy's attention, and the construction of large privateers in private dockyards provided the navy the chance to purchase frigates it did not have the resources to construct itself. Nevertheless, privateering added to the drain on French manpower; more than half of the 14,000 naval prisoners brought to Britain during 1757 were captured aboard privateers. There was little hope of their return, because Britain stopped the general exchange of prisoners that had been arranged at the beginning of 1757. The French navy was able to find enough crewmen to man only twenty-five ships of the line in the summer of 1758, largely because it had lost more than 8,500 crewmen captured or killed by disease in 1757 and could not find replacements.[40]

Moras also faced continuing shortages of masts, naval stores, and cannon in 1757, while British shortages were comparatively minor.[41] These difficulties were largely a result of the French navy's dire financial straits. The French government resolved the crisis with the Parlement of Paris over the second *vingtième*, and during the year it raised 136 million livres in loans, but it now had to support a war in Germany, too. Far from receiving the 66 million livres it had been promised, the French navy was authorized to spend only about 40 million livres, about half the army's budget (although probably it spent at least 20 million more than authorized). The monarchy's total income was about 575 million livres, but only about 273 million was available for general use. In comparison, the British government's income was about £8 million (equivalent to 192 million livres) while its navy spent more than £4.8 million (about 115 million livres).[42] The French navy's ability to function was based on the willingness of its suppliers to defer payment; the great Bordeaux merchant Abraham Gradis, for example, agreed to a five-year delay in payment for the supplies he sent to Canada. Canadian expenses, mostly the responsibility of the navy department, were estimated later at nearly 20 million livres in 1757, compared with 11.3 million in 1756 and 6 million in 1755; almost half of those bills were still unpaid when Canada fell in 1760. (These figures, compiled to demonstrate how expensive the defense of Canada had been, may be somewhat exaggerated, however.)[43] On 25 August Moras was replaced as controller general of finances by Jean de Boullongne, an experienced administrator (apparently in response to the wishes of the Parlement of Paris),[44] but even as naval minister, Moras' main task was finding money.

A lack of resources also threatened New France. At the end of the 1757 campaign a smallpox epidemic swept Canada and the Upper Country, striking Indians and Acadian refugees with particular severity.[45] Meanwhile the harvest was poor because of rainy weather and a shortage of workers. The supplies brought from France and the flour and salt pork captured at Fort William Henry soon were exhausted because of the need to feed soldiers, Acadian refugees, and France's Indian allies and their families, as well as the normal population. In December even soldiers began to eat horsemeat, and by the following May the daily ration of bread had been reduced to two ounces and food riots broke out.[46] Vaudreuil and Bigot were unable to provide adequately for their Indian allies, who were bitter at Montcalm for his interference with them at Fort William Henry and who blamed the French for the smallpox epidemic.[47] During 1757 the eastern branch of the Delawares made peace with Pennsylvania and resumed trading with the British and Americans.[48] Lack of supplies and deteriorating relations with Indian allies also were problems for the French authorities in Louisiana; this reduced the possibility of diversionary Indian attacks on the southern British colonies.[49] The British had failed to devote enough resources to ensure success in 1757, but there were indications during the winter of 1757–58 that they would not repeat their mistake: 2,000 recruits (drawn equally from the fifty battalions stationed in the British Isles) arrived in America in December, and they were followed three months later by nine 100-man companies as reinforcements for the Highlander regiments. Moreover, 30,000 of the some 90,000 British regulars were authorized to serve outside the British Isles during the coming year,[50] and eight of Holburne's ships of the line were ordered to winter over at Halifax so as to be on station for the beginning of the next campaign. Plans were made to establish a naval base at Halifax, an important strategic commitment. Even had du Bois de La Motte's ships been healthy, the port facilities would not have been adequate for them to remain.[51] With the

French army in New France at the limits of its resources, the navy again would have to carry the burden of its defense, but this time with severely diminished resources.

Thus far Moras had confronted his challenges with energy and resourceful-ness, promoting in April more than 250 officers, encouraging Montcalm to treat Indians and Canadians with respect, beginning an investigation of financial corruption in Canada, granting permission for Alsatian Protestants to emigrate to New France (hitherto reserved to Catholics), attempting to find ways to make use of privateer and merchant ship captains as naval officers, liberalizing the rules concerning neutral shipping to the French West Indies, urging colonial officials to act energetically, and making efforts to speed timber shipments and to keep frigates at sea for convoy protection.[52] Not all his decisions had been correct—probably it was a mistake to weaken d'Aché's squadron, for example—but his dedication was remarkable. Nevertheless, the problems he faced were beyond anyone's power to overcome indefinitely. The French navy and New France were doomed unless the war ended quickly; France lacked the sailors, ships, and money to compete with the British navy or to protect New France for much longer. The possibility of a quick end to the war, however, came tantalizingly close to realization in late 1757, as France and Austria, now allies, approached victory in Hanover and Silesia.

THE SECOND TREATY OF VERSAILLES

The discussions between Bernis and Starhemberg for an offensive alliance were given renewed impetus by the Prussian attack on Saxony and Austria. These negotiations continued in spite of the wounding of Louis XV and the dismissal of Argenson and Machault (who had taken opposite sides on the expansion of the war). The discussion remained stalemated, however, on questions such as war objectives and the proposed French subsidy. (Moreover, while Bernis was engaged in negotiations with the Parlement of Paris, Starhemberg to his dismay had to deal with the uncooperative Rouillé.)[53] In early February 1757, just at the time of the governmental reorganization, brief discussions about peace were held by the French and British ministers at The Hague, d'Affry and Yorke. Although the Dutch hoped to serve as intermediaries and thereby to reinforce their neutrality, the discussions produced only an exchange of generalities.[54] With Britain optimistic about its impending attack on New France, another campaign was inevitable; even had France returned Minorca and conceded every point at issue about the American frontier, it is doubtful Pitt and his colleagues would have abandoned the attempt to destroy French power in North

America. France did not as yet have to consider giving in; if it could conquer Hanover while Austria defeated Prussia and retook Silesia, George II and his government might yet be forced to make a peace that would preserve and perhaps even strengthen New France. The French navy and Vaudreuil helped bring France the opportunity to make such an advantageous peace by preventing the British from making further conquests in North America. The rest was up to the diplomats and the French and Austrian armies.

While diplomatic issues thus far had remained intractable, at least by early 1757 France and Austria were able to reach general agreement on military operations. As already mentioned, Austria still hoped to negotiate the neutrality of Hanover. It had been arranged that in the interim France would capture for Austria's benefit the great Prussian fortress of Wesel on the Rhine. On 11 February the comte d'Estrées was ordered to return to France from Vienna in order to assume command of the French army in Germany, for which he would be promoted to the rank of marshal of France. He left Vienna on 1 March, having negotiated four days earlier a convention regulating cooperation of the Austrian and French armies. By now it had been decided that his army would comprise 50,000 to 55,000 men, that another 60,000 would be added to it should the Austrian negotiations with Hanover fail, and that the siege of Wesel would begin about 10 May. On 5 March Maria Theresa sent secret instructions to Starhemberg that gave tacit approval to the French attack on Hanover if its neutrality could not be arranged.[55]

Meanwhile France had issues to resolve with several other European states. Perhaps the most pressing concern was Chargé d'affaires Douglas's mistake in consenting to Russia's joining the Franco-Austrian defensive alliance without making an exception for a Russian conflict with the Ottoman Empire. When news of this reached the French court on 13 February, Rouillé and the king were shocked. Rouillé had sent specific orders to Douglas that a Turkish war should be excluded from any defensive agreement with Russia, but Douglas had not had time to receive them. Rouillé also gave Estrées and Vergennes instructions that the Turks be given no pretext for menacing Austria or attacking Russia.[56] It took a personal letter from Louis XV to persuade Empress Elizabeth of Russia to ratify the treaty without the objectionable inclusion of the Turks; luckily, Elizabeth was a lifelong Francophile in spite of her country's rivalry with France.[57] It was also very fortunate that the Turks did not learn of Douglas's blunder, particularly since Sultan Osman III died in October 1757 and was succeeded by his bellicose cousin, Mustapha III.[58]

Elizabeth could afford to be generous. She had just renewed her own alliance with Maria Theresa (complete with an Austrian subsidy) as well as becoming a party to the Franco-Austrian alliance; moreover, although the alliance did not state it, she had been led to believe that Austria would accept Russia's absorbing Courland while Poland received East Prussia in compensation. She also believed that France would not interfere with Russian troops crossing Poland to attack Prussia.[59] In her enthusiasm, she even indicated her willingness to name Conti as duc de Courland and as head of the Russian army attacking Prussia. Louis, still upset at Conti, refused to grant him permission, and the offer, perhaps not seriously met, was not renewed.[60]

The Austrian and French assurances to Russia were less than sincere; Maria Theresa was as unenthusiastic about Russian expansion as Louis was about Russia sending troops into Poland and making it even more of a Russian client state. Moreover, Austria and France were not candid with each other. Austria urged French cooperation with the Russian troop movements and criticized those like Broglie who wished to obstruct them,[61] but Maria Theresa did not tell Louis about her assurances to Elizabeth. Louis in turn kept his Polish policy secret not only from Maria Theresa but even from Rouillé. When Broglie returned to Warsaw after a visit to France, he was given both official instructions of 25 April that everything be subordinated to the needs of the war and the king's secret ones of the same date to work for the liberty and independence of Poland and to prepare for the next royal election. France now supported Prince François-Xavier-Louis-Auguste of Saxony, the pro-French second son of Augustus and favorite brother of Louis' daughter-in-law. Even Rouillé and Bernis were conflicted about French goals in Poland.[62] The Russians in turn kept their intentions secret from France and made use of their access to Poland to increase their influence. Frederick II's survival ultimately depended on the disunion and mistrust of France, Austria, and Russia, which together decisively outweighed Prussia in military resources. Unlike Louis, Frederick was not torn between conflicting goals and operated largely independently of his ally George, king of England and elector of Hanover.

Russia and Austria were not France's only potential allies. The French government was extremely interested in winning the support of Sweden, a major source of naval supplies (which Britain now had begun seizing at sea).[63] Even more importantly, Sweden possessed West Pomerania, which was on the south shore of the Baltic, adjacent to the heartland of Prussia. Like France, Sweden was a guarantor of the 1648 Treaty of Westphalia, which Frederick had violated in attacking Saxony. Sweden's grievances against Prussia were long-standing, Prussia having taken part of Pomerania from her in 1720. In spite of the opposition of Queen Louisa Ulrika (Frederick II's sister), the Swedes on 21 March 1757 signed a convention with Austria and France to support moves in the Diet of the Holy Roman Empire to punish Prussia. The Swedes had been invited to join the Russian-Austrian alliance, and the Russians expressed pleasure at the new convention. The Swedes were not yet ready to join the war, but if Prussia attacked Sweden, Austria and France promised not to make peace until Sweden had regained the portion of Pomerania that it had lost in 1720.[64] Austria, however, carefully excluded France from its successful campaign within the Diet to condemn Frederick II and to create an Imperial army to act alongside the Austrian army against him. Maria Theresa's concern about French influence in Germany extended even to Saxony. It was Austria and Russia who promised Saxony the Prussian fortified city of Magdeburg as a reward for joining their alliance against Prussia. (It was Louis, however, who promised the Saxon royal family a pension during their exile from Dresden.) France did sign subsidy treaties with the electors of Bavaria and the Palatinate and the Duke of Württemberg for the use of 4,000 to 6,000 troops apiece, but all except the Palatine troops were promised to the Austrians. France also attempted vainly to prevent the Hessians from reaching an agreement to supply troops to Hanover. (The principalities of Brunswick and Saxe-Gotha also supplied troops to the electorate.)[65]

Other European states might also play a role in a German war. The French government was particularly interested in reaching an agreement with Denmark, hoping it would attack Hanover. France already was paying a subsidy to Denmark (although tardily). Now the French sought a full Danish military alliance by offering support for the Danish conquest of the Duchy of Bremen and the Principality of Verden, which had become part of Hanover in 1719. The British in turn had their own hopes of breaking up the Swedish-Danish maritime union and of replacing the French subsidy to Denmark with one of their own in exchange for the use of 8,000 to 12,000 troops and a dozen Danish ships of the line. They treated Danish shipping circumspectly and counted on the personal connection between George II and Frederick V of Denmark, who had been married to George's late daughter Louisa. The Danish king, however, did not wish to become involved in the war on either side, preferring to act as a mediator between Austria and Hanover. He had the good fortune of having one of the most astute foreign ministers in Europe, the German-born Graf Johann Hartwig Ernst von Bernstorff, to help him remain neutral.[66]

French policy toward the Netherlands had a different goal. The French were content to see the Dutch remain neutral, so they could bring naval materiel to France and supplies to the French West Indies. They assuaged Dutch fears of the French army massing near their eastern border and convinced them they need not increase the size of their own army. When French troops crossed the Dutch border en route to the Rhine in late April, France was quick to apologize and offer assurances that the mistake would not be repeated. The British, too, sought to placate the Dutch. When the Dutch complained of British privateers, the British government made it more difficult for Britons to obtain privateering commissions.[67]

To France, however, the most vital negotiations were those Austria was conducting with Hanover and those Starhemberg was conducting with France. If Hanover had not been ruled by the same person who was king of England, it probably would have been able to avoid becoming a belligerent. Even now George II was anxious for his beloved electorate to remain neutral, but British politics helped to prevent this. As already noted, the British government promised Frederick at the end of 1756 that it would form an army in Germany, using as its nucleus the twenty battalions of Hessian and Hanoverian troops returning from England. In spite of the king's hesitations, the British government grew increasingly committed to forming such an army. Parliament voted money not only for supporting the Hanoverian contingent but also for hiring 12,000 Hessians. At the end of March the king decided, on Frederick II's urging, to appoint his son the Duke of Cumberland to command the so-called Army of Observation of 40,000 Hanoverians, Hessians, and Brunswickers assembling at the River Lippe in Westphalia, slightly to the southwest of Hanover. He nevertheless resented the British government's intrusion into Hanoverian affairs, and there was a measure of revenge involved when he dismissed Pitt from office on 6 April. (Moreover, his son preferred not having to deal with Pitt.) Three weeks later, when George as elector rejected the demand of free passage for French troops to attack Magdeburg, Hanover's entry into the war was sealed.[68]

A few days later, the negotiations between France and Austria were concluded. By mid-March, when Bernis rejoined the discussions, Starhemberg had received authorization from the Austrian court to soften his terms on several points. (This authorization was granted on 5 March, the same time Marie Theresa gave tacit approval for the attack on Hanover.) Starhemberg was permitted to demand only the Austrian conquest of Silesia and Glatz as a precondition for the exchange of the Austrian Netherlands and the possessions of Duke Philip of Parma. He also could offer a partial repayment of the French subsidy if the war proved unsuccessful. (Apparently the Austrian flexibility was in response to rumors about the discussions in the Netherlands between d'Affry and Yorke.)[69] Rouillé, Austria's chief opponent in the Council of State, by now was isolated. Belle-Isle was increasingly enthusiastic about a closer Austrian alliance, and the other members were either allies of Bernis like Moras and Paulmy or were unprepared to oppose him. Bernis, overworked and exhausted, proved no match, however, for the shrewd and experienced Starhemberg, who conceded far less than Kaunitz had authorized; no provision was made for restitution of the subsidy, and the two parties agreed not to make peace until Prussia was almost completely dismembered.[70]

On 1 May, the anniversary of the first Treaty of Versailles, the new treaty was signed, as the first one had been, by Starhemberg, Bernis, and Rouillé. It transformed France into a full participant in the war against Frederick II, even though war never was declared between France and Prussia. France committed itself to providing 105,000 of its own troops in Germany, as well as paying for 6,000 troops from Württemberg and 4,000 from Bavaria. The French also promised to provide an annual subsidy to Austria of 12 million florins (30 million livres) for four years or until Silesia and Glatz were taken and to share equally in any subsidies to the king of Sweden and the elector of Saxony. The Austrians in return promised France the immediate use of Ostend and Nieuport and their good offices with Britain during peace negotiations for the French retention of Minorca and an end to restrictions on the fortification of Dunkirk. They also promised their cooperation in the next Polish election and in case of a disputed succession in Naples after the death of the king of Spain or the king of the Two Sicilies. If victory were obtained over Prussia, France would receive half a dozen border fortresses and the ports of Ostend and Nieuport, while Duke Philip of Parma would receive the remainder of the Austrian Netherlands in exchange for his Italian territories. A share in the spoils of victory would be given to Sweden, Saxony, Bavaria, and the Palatinate, if they joined the fight against Prussia; Starhemberg prudently kept the Austrian arrangements with Russia secret. The provisions of the 1756 treaty were confirmed, except insofar as they were modified by the present treaty; there continued to be a prohibition of any separate negotiations except by mutual consent.[71]

Prussia needed to be defeated not only so that France could gather what Austria had promised; any conquest of Hanover would be temporary if Prussia were left free to intervene. The fate of New France thus hinged not only upon the coming French campaign in Hanover but also upon the next campaign between the Austrians and the Prussians.

THE CONVENTION OF KLOSTERZEVEN

Even before the Second Treaty of Versailles was signed, the French began their campaign against the Prussian provinces along the Rhine. The extended negotiations between Austria and Hanover made it possible for them to commence hostilities against Prussia before the Hanoverians, still hoping for peace, could finish assembling the Army of Observation. On 25 March, five days before the Duke of Cumberland was appointed to head the Army of Observation, fighting occurred between Prussian and French troops.[72] The Prussians had just evacuated the great fortress of Wesel, sending its cannon down the Rhine to the Netherlands for shipment to the Baltic. With his main army assembling to renew the attack on Bohemia, Frederick did not wish to risk the loss of even the six-battalion garrison of the fort, particularly since the Army of Observation was not likely to send a relief force soon.[73] The Prussians did leave behind a garrison of 800 men in the lesser fortress of Geldern, well west of the Rhine, which the French placed under siege. Its capture required fifteen battalions of Estrées' army (somewhat over 10,000 men) and took three months.[74] Most of the French army, however, was free to cross the Rhine and engage the Army of Observation on the east bank.

It took almost two months for the rival armies to assemble, during which time the semblance of peace was preserved; the first skirmish did not occur until 3 May.[75] When open warfare commenced in late May, d'Estrées' Army of Westphalia with 100,000 men (110 battalions of infantry and 127 cavalry squadrons) enjoyed a roughly two to one advantage over Cumberland's Army of Observation, which now included the six battalions of Prussian troops evacuated from Wesel.[76] Estrées began his advance toward Hanover in early June, slowed less by enemy resistance than by the logistical difficulties in feeding and moving his huge army. It was not until late July that Cumberland, driven across the River Weser into the Electorate of Hanover itself, was ready to fight. Meanwhile, Estrées sent a detachment to capture the Prussian port of Emden on the North Sea. It surrendered on 2 July before a British squadron could arrive to save it. Hanover was cut off from the Netherlands and now was dependent on supplies sent via the North Sea to the Hanoverian port of Stade on the Elbe or to the independent neighboring city of Hamburg.[77]

By then Frederick had withdrawn the small Prussian contingent from the Army of Observation.[78] His campaign against the Austrians had failed. In mid-April he had invaded Bohemia with 115,000 troops. Although the Austrians had a comparable number of troops in Bohemia and Moravia, they were taken by surprise. Frederick defeated the Austrian army near Prague on 6 May, drove the survivors into the city, and began besieging it. By early June the city was under bombardment and its 45,000 soldiers and 70,000 civilians were reduced to eating horsemeat. Frederick expected the city to fall and Maria Theresa then to ask for peace.[79]

Louis XV responded to the plight of Maria Theresa with the same gallantry he had shown the parents of his Saxon daughter-in-law. Despite the misgivings of the Council of State, he ordered War Minister Paulmy to find troops for a 25,000-man relief force to be sent to Prague. Only a small portion of them could be taken from Estrées' Army of Westphalia. France was obligated by the Treaty of Versailles to send an auxiliary corps of 14,000 French and 10,000 Bavarians and Württemburgers to central Germany for joint operations with the newly raised Imperial army. As some of this corps, too, had to be taken from the Army of Westphalia, Estrées could spare few troops to help rescue Prague. Nevertheless, Marshal Richelieu, the victor at Minorca, was named on June 12 to command the relief force. Two weeks later Louis further pleased the Austrians by naming Bernis his new foreign minister after Rouillé resigned for health reasons. (Rouillé, however, did continue temporarily to attend meetings of the Council of State.) Finally, as another sign of his regard for his "sister and cousin" Maria Theresa, he appointed as ambassador to Vienna the astute and ambitious young Etienne-François de Choiseul, comte de Stainville, a protégé of Madame de Pompadour. Stainville had been serving as French minister to the Holy See, where he helped convince Pope Benedict XIV to issue a moderate encyclical on the Jansenist question.[80]

Maria Theresa reciprocated by ratifying the second Treaty of Versailles, by breaking diplomatic relations with Britain (although not declaring war), by expelling British ships from Ostend and Nieuport, and by immediately admitting French garrisons to those two ports; meanwhile the Dutch were reassured the cities were still Austrian. When they remained calm, France rewarded them by waiving customs duties on Dutch herring.[81]

The French detachment for Prague proved unnecessary. A 55,000-man Austrian relief force under Field Marshal Leopold Joseph, Graf von Daun, marched to its rescue. Frederick II, underestimating Daun's strength, moved to intercept him with a detachment of 35,000 Prussians. Daun took up a strong defensive position near the town of Kolin, fifty miles east of Prague. Frederick made a rash and poorly coordinated assault on 18 June that cost 13,000 or 14,000 casualties and ruined the Prussian offensive. His demoralized army was forced to abandon the siege of Prague, and a month later he had to evacuate Bohemia.[82]

By the end of July the Army of Observation also was in full retreat. Cumberland with 35,000 men had chosen to occupy a strong position on the east bank of the River Weser near the village of Hastenbeck where he awaited the attack of Estrées with 60,000. He failed to provide adequate forces for the defense of a steep hill on one of his flanks, however, and on 26 July Estrées captured it and rolled up Cumberland's line. A counterattack almost saved the day for Cumberland, but it came too late. Although the Army of Observation had suffered barely 1,000 casualties, its morale was destroyed. As it retreated northward toward Stade at the mouth of the Elbe in hopes of rescue by the British navy, it began to disintegrate from wholesale desertion.[83]

Ironically, on the day after the battle Estrées learned that he was being replaced by Richelieu as commander of the Army of Westphalia. The honorable and conscientious Estrées had annoyed the Austrians by the slowness of his advance, and his blunt language had made him enemies in France, particularly Joseph Paris du Verney, an elderly munitions contractor who had gained great influence with the king, Bernis, and Paulmy. (Paris du Verney's brother Jean Paris de Monmartel was the government's chief banker; the brothers were political allies of Bernis and Madame de Pompadour, the daughter of one of their former employees.) Moreover, Estrées did not realize that his chief of staff, Yves-Marie Desmaretz, comte de Maillebois, who was related by marriage to Paulmy, was using his contacts at court to undermine him. Finally, the Austrian victory at Kolin eliminated the need for another French army and left Richelieu without employment. Louis therefore decided to reinforce the Army of Westphalia and to name Richelieu as its commander. Meanwhile, the detachment for the Imperial army in central Germany was dispatched from France under the command of Madame de Pompadour's loyal supporter, the prince de Soubise. It arrived in Thuringia (100 miles southeast of Hanover) at the end of August. It contained 21,000 troops from the French army (thirty-one battalions of infantry and twenty-two squadrons of cavalry), including 8,000 detached from the Army of Westphalia, but few Bavarians or Württemburgers. Rather than serve under the command of Richelieu, Estrées chose to take leave from the army for the sake of his health. Meanwhile, Maillebois was imprisoned for his cowardice at the Battle of Hastenbeck. [84]

In spite of its unfortunate timing, the choice of Richelieu initially seemed to work well. The new commander was forceful and self-confident, even though also acquisitive and corrupt. He was able both to occupy Hanover and to pursue aggressively Cumberland's army, which finally reached the neighborhood of Stade at the beginning of September. It had no hope of British troops coming to its rescue, as Pitt, overcoming the objections of Newcastle, had sent them to Rochefort instead. [85]

Over the course of the summer the situation of the Prussian army also grew desperate. It had to contend not only with the advancing Austrians but also with an army of 100,000 Russians under the command of Field Marshal Stepan Fëdorovich Apraksin. The Russian commander delayed starting his campaign until the beginning of July because of the uncertain health of Empress Elizabeth, as he did not want to fight a war that her future successor, Crown Prince Peter, did not wish. On 5 July, however, Russian troops, assisted by the Russian navy, captured the important port of Memel, now in Lithuania, and soon began advancing on Königsberg, the chief city of East Prussia, 300 miles northeast of Berlin. [86] For many months Frederick II had been asking for a British squadron to come to the Baltic and for British troops to come to Germany, but the British government refused. Pitt was opposed, and although Newcastle feared that Frederick might make a separate peace, he also was frightened that the French occupation of Ostend and Nieuport might lead to a French invasion of England. (This fear was excessive; even though Belle-Isle was anxious to attempt an invasion, the Brest fleet was unprepared to support it.) Moreover, because the British government's attempts to win Danish support had failed, the British navy would have to fight its way into the Baltic and then face either a Russian fleet of seventeen ships of the line or a Swedish fleet of eleven ships of the line escorting troops across the Baltic. Britain had no desire to risk war with Austria, Russia, or Sweden, and hence it rejected the Prussian request for a Baltic squadron. It was partly to mollify Frederick, who also continued to urge a diversionary attack on the French coast, that it launched its unsuccessful attack on Rochefort.[87] (It also tried to avoid disputes with Spain in hopes of winning Spanish help in recapturing Minorca.)[88]

With the British unwilling to provide assistance and the main Prussian army tied down in Silesia, the Prussians were forced to depend on whatever forces they could find to stop Apraksin's advance. On 30 August Field Marshal Hans von Lehwaldt attacked the advancing Russian troops at Gross Jägersdorf, thirty miles east of Königsberg. His 25,000 men were beaten by 55,000 Russians, but instead of following up the victory Apraksin chose to retreat, and his army soon lost all its coherence and discipline. The news of Gross Jägersdorf, however, helped embolden Sweden to enter the war. On 22 September the Swedish government signed a supplemental treaty with France and Austria by which it agreed to provide 20,000 to 25,000 troops to attack Prussian Pomerania (and in November it became an ally of Russia). The Swedes sent an army of 20,000 men toward the vital port of Stettin at the mouth of the Oder, only seventy-five miles north of Berlin.[89] Meanwhile, the new Imperial army was gathering near Saxony, 200 miles southwest of the Prussian capital, and the Austrians were advancing in Silesia, 150 miles to its southeast. Frederick sought to at least rid himself of the French, trying in vain to bribe Madame de Pompadour and to initiate negotiations with France; the writer Voltaire also tried to arrange a Franco-Prussian peace.[90] Frederick's only hope now lay in battle.

Even that hope seemed gone for Hanover. For the British government the defeat at Hastenbeck was less of a humiliation than were the failures at Rochefort, Louisbourg, and Fort William Henry. No British troops had been involved, and the British government had no direct responsibility for Hanoverian affairs. Indeed, until it sent troops it had no real leverage with the king, who not only kept Hanoverian affairs separate from British but considered British diplomacy his own prerogative.[91] For George II, however, the defeat was a source of great shame. It was not only Hanoverian troops who had failed but also his favorite son. He asked Austria to mediate between Hanover and France, but Maria Theresa was not interested. He told both Newcastle and Frederick that he believed the electorate would have to make a separate peace regardless of its effect on the Prussian war effort.[92] Secretly, he moved to do so. On 11 August he sent instructions to Cumberland to make whatever peace he could, although a few days later he changed his mind and forbad his son from agreeing to disarm the Army of Observation.[93] Meanwhile, the British government, unaware of George's instructions to his son, told Frederick II that *Great Britain* would not make a separate peace, would continue to provide financial support for the Army of Observation, and, if possible, would send a squadron to the Elbe (a move to which the inner cabinet agreed on 5 September).[94]

Ironically, the seemingly doomed Army of Observation escaped destruction much as did the garrison of Rochefort. Richelieu, not realizing the terrible condition of the Army of Observation, was afraid to risk his own exhausted and increasingly undisciplined army by besieging in difficult terrain an enemy that could receive supplies and reinforcements via Stade.[95] Moreover, he realized that his supply lines were overextended. He was anxious to establish winter quarters at Halberstadt, 100 miles to the southeast, a site suggested to him by Paris du Verney; this would put him halfway between Hanover and Soubise's army. He anticipated the war would last another year. By using the Halberstadt region for winter quarters he would be ready at the start of the next campaigning season to besiege the nearby great Prussian fortress of Magdeburg, only eighty miles west of Berlin; the Austrians wanted him to attack it now, but he lacked horses or oxen to move his artillery.[96] It thus was concern for his army which seems to have led him on 23 August to ask French Minister Plenipotentiary Jean-François Ogier d'Enonville in Copenhagen about the possibility of Danish mediation with Cumberland, who had just written him proposing a suspension of arms.[97]

George II, as elector of Hanover, also had asked for Danish mediation. On 11 June France and Denmark had signed a convention by which France promised not to invade the duchies of Bremen and Verden (which were Hanoverian possessions) as long as they remained essentially demilitarized. Now that Hanover itself had been conquered by France, both opposing armies had entered the Duchy of Bremen, which adjoined both Denmark and the independent city of Bremen. The Danish government, fearful of being dragged into the conflict,[98] therefore agreed to act as a mediator and sent a representative to help draft terms for ending hostilities. On 8 September Cumberland signed a convention by which ten battalions of Hanoverian infantry and twenty-eight squadrons of Hanoverian cavalry would be interned at Stade, while the remainder of the Hanoverians would be interned on the east bank of the Elbe; they promised not to commit any acts of hostility during the time the convention was in effect (which was left vague) but would neither be treated as prisoners of war nor disarmed. Meanwhile, Richelieu would continue to occupy most of Hanover, prisoners of war would be exchanged, and the Hessians and Brunswickers would be free to return home. On 10 September Richelieu, at his headquarters at Klosterzeven, thirty miles south of Stade, signed the convention.[99]

George II, disregarding the initial latitude he had given Cumberland to make an agreement, ordered his son back to England in disgrace and treated him there with the kind of cruelty Frederick had shown to his younger brother August Wilhelm when he proved a military failure. Cumberland responded by resigning as commander of the Army of Observation and captain general of the British army. (Cumberland's chief of staff, the experienced Sir John Ligonier, became commander in chief of the British army, but had direct responsibility only for its forces in Great Britain.) [100] Richelieu, on the other hand, escaped punishment from Louis XV for exceeding his instructions, which had given him no latitude to negotiate with the British or Prussians; indeed, while he was signing the Convention of Klosterzeven, orders were on the way forbidding him to negotiate with Cumberland. Although the initial French reaction was positive, Bernis became outraged at Richelieu and Ogier. As a war hero and member of the highest nobility, Richelieu, however, had little to fear from the king.

Richelieu not only had failed to destroy the Army of Observation but also, because of the vagueness of the convention, had left it free to claim an excuse to rejoin the war should circumstances change. [101] Thus the fate of Hanover and with it the future of New France were left in the hands of the Austrian army. If it could destroy the Prussian army, the Army of Observation would not dare resume operations; if, however, the Austrians failed, all the French gains in Hanover and the grand strategy for saving the French empire would be at risk.

ROSSBACH, LEUTHEN, AND THEIR CONSEQUENCES

Soon after Richelieu signed the Convention of Klosterzeven, his exhausted army began its two-week march southeast to Halberstadt. He took 40,000 men and left behind a small body of infantry and cavalry to watch the Army of Observation. France and Austria at least could take some consolation that the approach of another army toward Prussia tied down a Prussian force of 7,000 men (six infantry battalions and eleven cavalry squadrons) under the command of Prince Ferdinand of Brunswick, a Prussian lieutenant general.[102] By now what was left of Prussia was almost completely surrounded by the Swedes from the north, the Imperial army from the southwest, the Austrians from the southeast, and now the French from the west (although Richelieu was really interested for the time being only in resting his army and did not plan to besiege Magdeburg until the next campaigning season). Only the northeast flank was unmenaced, thanks to the Russian retreat, but even after the Russian departure Frederick's forces were only about half the combined size of the various enemy armies on his borders. At the end of September he admitted to one of his ministers that Prussia would need miracles to survive.[103]

Even Berlin was not safe. On 16 October a 3,500-man Austrian raiding party entered the city and held it for ransom before being chased away. Fortunately for Frederick II, however, the 100,000-man main Austrian army commanded by Maria Theresa's brother-in-law Prince Charles and by Field Marshal Daun concentrated on reconquering Silesia rather than attacking the center of Prussia. By moving east into Silesia, the Austrians separated themselves from the Imperial, French, and Swedish armies. This gave Frederick a little time to deal with his other enemies.[104] Richelieu also helped relieve some of the pressure. Although he refused Frederick's offer of working with him as a peacemaker,[105] he on his own authority proposed to Ferdinand of Brunswick a temporary armistice. Although not ratified, it essentially relieved the Prussians of the threat of Richelieu's army. Richelieu went into winter quarters, detaching 12,000 more men (twenty infantry battalions and eighteen cavalry squadrons) to join Soubise's forces operating with the Imperial army. These reinforcements were without tents or supplies, and many were barefoot.[106] After their arrival Soubise's army and the Imperial army under the command of Josef Maria Friedrich Wilhelm, Prince von Sachsen-Hildburghausen, began advancing toward the Saxon city of Leipzig.

On 26 October, as Frederick II was preparing an attempt to save the besieged Silesian fortress of Schweidnitz (now Swidnica, Poland), he learned of their advance. He seized the opportunity to rid himself of this threat. The 10,000 Imperial troops, drawn from some 200 German principalities, were untrained, and Hildburghausen was unqualified. The 30,000 French troops accompanying them were undisciplined, and Soubise, although personally conscientious, honorable, kindly, and brave, was indecisive and timid as an army commander. Frederick personally led 22,000 of his best troops to intercept them. Soubise and Hildburghausen halted their offensive and seemed likely to escape; indeed, when Frederick inadvertently exposed himself to a French sniper, a French general, the duc de Crillon-Mahon, spared him. On 5 November, however, Soubise and Hildburghausen came to believe the Prussians were retreating and decided to attack.[107] Frederick surprised them near the village of Rossbach as they were marching, attacked before they could deploy in battle formation, and shattered their armies, inflicting 10,000 casualties at a cost of only 550.[108]

So spectacular a victory created a sensation throughout Europe. In the Netherlands the comte d'Affry, the French minister, called the battle insignificant, but George II's daughter Anne, the widow of the late Prince William IV of

Orange, was so overjoyed that she ordered a fireworks display.[109] Paris was correspondingly downcast by the humiliation inflicted on a French army.[110] The effect of the battle was particularly important in London, where a string of humiliations (Hastenbeck, Louisbourg, Fort William Henry, Rochefort, Klosterzeven) had shaken the confidence of the government and had increased the discontent of the public, already in a dangerous mood because of high grain prices from the preceding year's bad harvest and the unpopular new militia act. Hardwicke and Newcastle had even discussed making overtures to France through Madame de Pompadour.[111]

After the news of Rossbach, British spirits revived. George II had never ratified the Convention of Klosterzeven (as elector of Hanover), and now he was ready to break it should circumstances permit. If so, Pitt and the inner cabinet were willing to ask Parliament to pay for the Army of Observation. They already had convinced Frederick II to let Prince Ferdinand of Brunswick take leave from the Prussian army to replace Cumberland, although Frederick had doubts about Ferdinand's decisiveness.[112] France ratified the convention, but it was doomed. Disagreements broke out over the implementation of the vague agreement, and on 28 November Ferdinand, recently arrived at Stade, informed Richelieu of his intention to abrogate the convention and resume hostilities. This spoiled French and Austrian attempts to convince the Duke of Brunswick (Ferdinand's brother as well as Frederick II's brother-in-law) and the landgraf of Hesse-Cassel to withdraw their contingents from the Army of Observation or even to switch sides.[113]

Ferdinand's decision was extremely rash. At that moment the main Prussian army was in the gravest possible danger in Silesia. Had it been destroyed, as seemed almost inevitable, the Army of Observation surely would have disintegrated in panic. For all of its psychological importance (including its long-term effects on the self-confidence of the French army), the Battle of Rossbach was of only minor *strategic* importance; indeed, by disappearing to the west into Saxony, Frederick helped cause a potential disaster in Silesia. The fate of the Prussian army there was of far greater immediate strategic significance than a relatively meaningless victory over a ragtag army that posed little threat. The November battles in Silesia have largely been forgotten because Prussia miraculously escaped their consequence; had this not happened, Rossbach would be remembered chiefly as a foolhardy diversion of Prussian resources.

The first of the Austrian victories in Silesia was the capture on 14 November of the great fortress of Schweidnitz with 180 cannon and 6,000 prisoners. (Bernis told Stainville that this was ample repayment for Rossbach.) Eight days later Breslau, the fortified capital of Silesia defended by an army of 28,000 Prussians, was assaulted by 83,000 Austrians. After a desperate struggle costing nearly 10,000 Prussian casualties, the defense lines were breached and most of the Prussian army had to retreat across the Oder River. Soon afterwards the city and its remaining garrison of 4,000 troops surrendered. What was left of the nearby Prussian army disintegrated, its commander, the Duke of Bevern, preferring being captured by the Austrians to the anger of Frederick, who had threatened to execute him if he failed. Unless Breslau were immediately re-captured, the entire Prussian army in Silesia, lacking secure winter quarters, might fall apart. Frederick gathered all the troops he could and with 39,000 men rushed to assault the city. Amazingly the Austrians threw away the advantage of their entrenchments near Breslau that Frederick would have had to assault. They marched out of them with 50,000 or 55,000 soldiers to protect their line of communications, not expecting a battle. At the end of their first day's march they occupied a weak defensive position near the village of Leuthen ten miles to the northwest. On 5 December Frederick struck their exposed left flank and rolled up their army, inflicting 23,000 casualties at a cost of only 6,400. By the end of the year the Austrian army was in full retreat, Breslau and 18,000 Austrian prisoners were in Prussian hands, and Schweidnitz was the only remaining Austrian stronghold in Silesia.[114] Frederick, who earlier had exchanged letters and poems with Voltaire about suicide,[115] had won one of the most important battles of the eighteenth century. Schweidnitz would change hands three more times, but Breslau escaped further capture for the remainder of the war; the one great opportunity for Austria's regaining Silesia and France's saving Canada ended on the battlefield of Leuthen. As Bernis realized, there now was little foreseeable hope of a negotiated settlement to the war.[116]

The French offensive in Hanover had succeeded, but that success now was in danger of reversal. By December Richelieu's once-great army of 100,000 men had been reduced to 30,000 effectives. (Soubise, now in winter quarters with the remnants of his army, had even fewer; Bernis had wished to merge his army with Richelieu's, but Madame de Pompadour had interceded on Soubise's behalf.)[117] His new opponent, Ferdinand, advanced southward from Stade some seventy-five miles, but Richelieu's courage and professional skill brought the attack to a halt and saved the French army. Both armies now entered winter quarters, and the long campaign finally ended with France still in possession of most of the Electorate of Hanover. The Swedes meanwhile retreated to the Baltic coast, leaving Pomerania to the exactions of the Prussian army.

France had hoped to make the Hanoverians pay for the French occupation (as the Saxons and the inhabitants of Swedish Pomerania did for Prussian oc-cupation), but the French generals did not fear their king as the Prussians did theirs. Instead of the 16 million livres expected from the occupation of Hanover and the Prussian territories around Wesel, Halberstadt, and Cleves, the French treasury received only 4 million. Part of the shortfall resulted from the decency and compassion not entirely absent from the occupation force, but most of the money was embezzled by Richelieu and his generals and by the agents of Paris du Verney; even Bigot's padded bills in Canada were less blatant. Richelieu now resigned his command and returned to Paris to enjoy the enormous fortune he had made.[118]

Britain now prepared to renew both its attack on New France and the war in Germany. Although as yet unwilling to commit British troops in Germany as Frederick wished, the British government was ready to finance the rebuilding of both the Army of Observation and the Prussian army. Frederick II had requested a subsidy for 1758 of 4 million thalers, which was equivalent roughly to £670,000 or 16 million livres.[119] In his December address opening the new session of Parliament, George II called for financial assistance for Prussia. Holdernesse on 22 December 1757 sent Mitchell a draft treaty providing Prussia the 4 million thalers in exchange for Prussian commitments to make no separate peace and to provide some troops for the Army of Observation.[120]

In comparison France was poorly prepared for the extended war in Germany and North America that now was inevitable. Bernis described Louis as saddened but not dismayed by the news of Leuthen, after which he reasserted to Starhemberg his commitment to the alliance. A large loan subscribed at the end of the year temporarily eased the French financial crisis, but, ominously, France was already in arrears for her subsidy payment to Austria while Austria was in arrears for her 3 million florin annual subsidy to Russia (which France refused to provide directly).[121] Now that it was unlikely the French conquest of Hanover would force Britain to make a compromise peace, the protection of New France rested on the small garrisons in Louisbourg and Canada and on the French navy, gravely weakened by the typhus epidemic that had carried away so many irreplaceable sailors. On the edge of victory in the autumn of 1757, France soon was on the edge of disaster.

5

1758
A Year of Desperation

LOUISBOURG LOST, CANADA AGAIN SPARED

The terrible news from Silesia did not alter the French navy's mission. Despite shortages of sailors and money, it had to defend French trade and France's overseas possessions from the North Atlantic to the Indian Ocean. Moras again planned to send as many ships as possible to defend Louisbourg and to spend whatever funds he could find to resupply Canada. A memoir from the end of 1757 listed a dozen ships of the line, five frigates, and two armed supply ships to be sent to New France by the end of March. [1] All other theaters of war, even India where France still remained on the offensive, were subordinated to preserving Canada in the hope that somehow events in Europe would force France's enemies to the peace table.

On 14 February Moras wrote to promise the governor of Louisbourg, Capitaine de vaisseau Augustin de Boschenry de Drucour, two battalions of reinforcements. [2] He also made an enormous effort to match the ships and supplies sent the previous year to Louisbourg and Canada. By the end of June he had sent or attempted to send to North America sixteen ships of the line plus the East India Company ship of the line *Brillant*, 54; this was almost as many as the eighteen ships of the line sent by early May 1757. The British, however, with much larger resources from which to draw, were able not only to match but to drastically increase their own commitment to North America. By early summer they concentrated twenty-three ships of the line near Louisbourg, as compared with sixteen early in the previous summer. [3] This alone would have made it difficult to save Louisbourg again, but unlike 1757, a sizable portion of the French ships never reached their destination.

Machault and Moras in 1757 had been able to send their ships in three major squadrons, which arrived safely in Louisbourg within a few weeks of each other.

The terrible shortage of sailors in early 1758 led Moras to send his ships individually or in small groups as soon as they were ready, before their crews deserted or became ill. Consequently his ships of the line departed in ten separate sailings spread over five months:

(1) At the beginning of the year the *Aigle*, 50, sailed from Rochefort *en flûte*, carrying supplies. She delivered them safely at Louisbourg and then returned to France, arriving at Brest by 20 February. (Another convoy with the frigates *Frippone* and *Heroïne* and four provisions ships left Rochefort for Canada about the same time but was intercepted by the British and forced to turn back.)

(2) On 31 January the *Magnifique*, 74, and *Amphion*, 50, sailed from Brest. The *Amphion*, disabled by storms, returned to Brest in April. The *Magnifique* reached Louisbourg at the end of March, but could not enter because of ice. With most of her crew ill from typhus she returned to Europe, putting into Corunna in May and not reaching Brest until 11 November. Her subsequent career was virtually unrivaled, as she participated in six battles over the next twenty-five years before she finally was shipwrecked off Boston.

(3) The *Prudent*, 74, and *Raisonnable*, 64, sailed from Rochefort on 9 March, escorting a convoy of five navy supply ships and two chartered merchant ships. The *Prudent* reached Louisbourg on 24 April. Her captain, Jean-Antoine Charry, marquis des Gouttes, became commandant of the entire squadron that eventually assembled there, as he was the senior capitaine de vaisseau by date of rank. The *Prudent* was sunk during the British siege. The convoy also arrived safely, but the *Raisonnable* did not. She was forced by bad weather into Port Louis, near Lorient, and while trying to reach Brest she was captured by the British on 29 May.

(4) The *Apollon*, 50, sailed from Rochefort on 13 March *en flûte*, carrying supplies. She joined the *Prudent* and shared her fate.

(5) Capitaine de vaisseau Beaussier de l'Isle, who had brought Montcalm to Canada in 1756, commanded a squadron that left Brest on 4 April. It consisted of the *Entreprenant*, 74, *Bienfaisant*, 64, *Capricieux*, 64, and *Célèbre*, 64, the last three *en flûte* carrying a battalion of the regiment of Volontaires Etrangers (recruited by the army from prisoners of war). This squadron arrived on 28 April. The *Bienfaisant* eventually was captured, and the other ships of the line were destroyed.

(6) On 21 April the *Bizarre*, 64, and two accompanying frigates sailed from Brest. The frigates arrived safely, but the *Bizarre* became separated, and when she arrived on 1 June she found a British fleet off Louisbourg. Therefore she went instead to Quebec. She returned safely to France in the autumn, traveling for part of the way with du Chaffault's squadron (for which see below) and capturing a dozen prizes during the passage, including a British frigate.

(7) The East India Company ship of the line *Brillant*, 54, also returned safely. She sailed from Lorient in April, reached Louisbourg on 28 May, and departed before the British could trap her in the port.

(8) A second detachment of troops, a battalion from the regiment of Cambis, was sent from Rochefort on 2 May aboard the *Belliqueux*, 64, *Hardi*, 64, and *Sphinx*, 64, all *en flûte*. (Their departure was delayed by a skirmish with Hawke off Rochefort in early April.) They were accompanied by the *Dragon*, 64. The squadron was commanded by Capitaine de vaisseau Louis-Charles, comte du Chaffault de Besné. Avoiding the British fleet, he landed his troops at St. Ann's Bay, fifty miles northwest of Louisbourg, on 10 June and went to Quebec, arriving on the 29th. He sailed for France in mid-September, briefly encountered a British squadron returning from Louisbourg on 27 October, and reached Brest on 12 November. All his ships of the line arrived safely except for the *Belliqueux*, which had been disabled during a storm and which finally was captured by the *Antelope*, 50, off Bristol without firing a shot; her captain was cashiered from the navy.

(9) On 11 May the *Formidable*, 80, sailed from Brest carrying a recently promoted *chef d'escadre*, Charles de Courbon-Blénac, as the intended squadron commander for Louisbourg. (The *Raisonnable*, trapped at Port Louis, had been intended to accompany her.) When he arrived at Louisbourg, Blénac, too, found the entrance blockaded. The *Formidable* returned immediately to Brest, arriving on 26 June. Blénac then replaced du Guay as Brest port commandant.

(10) Finally, the *Aigle*, which had made an earlier voyage to Louisbourg with supplies, sailed *en flûte* for Quebec from Brest on 28 June. She was shipwrecked at the Strait of Belle-Isle, the dangerous northern passage to the St. Lawrence, on 8 August. Only a small amount of flour was salvaged from her cargo.[4]

In contrast, the British, drawing most of their strength from ships and men already in North America, needed to send only a single squadron, nine ships of the line under Boscawen, and two new battalions, those of the 15th and 58th regiments. After an eleven-week voyage, Boscawen reached Halifax on 9 May, where twelve other battalions were added to the assault force, one from the 1st, two from the 60th, and those of the 17th, 22nd, 28th, 35th, 40th, 45th, 47th, 48th, and 78th regiments. Leaving the 43rd regiment to protect Nova Scotia, he sailed for Louisbourg on 28 May.[5] Accompanying him was the military commander for the expedition, Acting Major General Jeffrey Amherst, who had served with Cumberland in Germany.

Unlike 1757, the British had overwhelming naval superiority as well as military superiority. The ships joining at Halifax gave Boscawen twenty-three ships of the line against the six of des Gouttes. Amherst had 14,000 troops, almost all regulars, against Drucour's 2,400 regulars (from the battalions of Artois,

Bourgogne, Volontaires Etrangers, and Cambis), 1,000 marines (in twenty-four companies), 400 militia, and 120 artillerymen. (Eventually des Gouttes put almost all of his 3,500 sailors ashore and, excepting those who were ill, they, too, participated in the defense.) Louisbourg was designed to withstand a siege of eight weeks; with its crumbling and overextended fortifications and subject to cannon fire from nearby high ground, it could hope only to delay the methodical and cautious Amherst long enough that he could not proceed to Quebec. Drucour accomplished this. The British established a beachhead on Isle Royale on 8 June, but did not capture the fort until 26 July. Des Gouttes' squadron played a part in the defense by keeping the British out of the harbor and thereby preventing an attack on the weak seaside portion of the fortress. It was only when the last of des Gouttes' ships were boarded in a surprise attack under cover of fog by sailors in small boats that Drucour judged his situation hopeless. The naval commanders on both sides acted timidly, des Gouttes repeatedly requesting Drucour's permission in order to save his ships, and Boscawen refusing to engage closely the guns of the fortress and des Gouttes' squadron. Drucour's garrison subsequently was sent to England as prisoners of war, and the civilian population of Louisbourg was transported to France; des Gouttes was cashiered.[6]

Amherst and Brigadier General James Wolfe, the subordinate who had commanded the dangerous 8 June landing, were prepared to proceed to Quebec, even after learning on 31 July that no help would be forthcoming from the British and American forces in the Lake Champlain region. Boscawen resisted, however, as he lacked river pilots and was short of provisions and materiel like cables and anchors. In early August Amherst gave up the idea. He settled for taking possession of Isle St. Jean (Prince Edward Island) which was included in Louisbourg's surrender terms. He expelled to France its 4,600 or 4,700 civilian residents (many of them refugees from the earlier expulsion of Acadians), and pillaged defenseless fishing villages along the Gulf of St. Lawrence.[7]

The most surprising aspect of the North American campaign of 1758 was not the fall of Louisbourg but the successful defense of the Canadian heartland against a separate British attack from the Lake Champlain area. The French defense of Lake Champlain, or indeed of Canada in general, would have been impossible had it not been for Moras' massive effort to charter ships for bringing provisions; he sent so much food that the court's chief administrator at Bordeaux, the royal provincial intendant, feared shortages in southwestern France. Between the middle of May and the end of June the near starvation conditions at Quebec finally lifted with the arrival of ships bringing flour, salt beef, salt pork, and other provisions. Many of these ships came from three convoys of about a dozen ships apiece dispatched from Bordeaux between 28 March and 2

May under the escort of the navy frigates *Sirène* and *Galatée* and two privateers. Other ships sailed from Spain or from Bayonne under Spanish colors; Moras even encouraged the Spaniards to fish off Newfoundland in order to provide an excuse for both Spanish and French ships under the Spanish flag to come to North America. Some ships, too, brought cod and flour from Louisbourg. Finally, du Chaffault appeared, bringing more provisions ships with him. The expense was enormous, and losses were extremely heavy. The Bordeaux merchant Abraham Gradis, for example, sent supplies and 200 recruits on eight ships of his own and six he had chartered, and although most arrived safely in Canada, only one made it back to France. Nonetheless, Vaudreuil was liberated from worrying about food riots and could devise strategy against the British.[8]

His task was more difficult than in 1757. Even after the huge commitment of troops to Louisbourg, the British still had 9,000 regulars in nine battalions (two of the 60th, plus the 27th, 42nd, 44th, 46th, 55th, 77th, and 80th) and some independent companies against fewer than 4,000 French regulars in eight depleted battalions.[9] Moreover, responding to Pitt's offer to reimburse most of their expenses, the British American colonies raised about 20,000 provincial troops, 7,000 of them in Massachusetts alone (compared with only 1,800 raised in Massachusetts the preceding year). Moreover, the British had the use of Indian allies, including 450 to 700 Cherokees. Exclusive of Louisbourg and Nova Scotia they could call on some 30,000 men, roughly triple the number of men Vaudreuil could collect from his regulars, marines, militia, and Indian allies. (This does not count the 1,200 French effectives in Louisiana.) Only 470 Indians served with Montcalm and only 15 of them arrived in time for the battle described below.[10]

As in past years, however, Vaudreuil quickly moved to take the offensive. Over Montcalm's objections he ordered Lévis to take a force of 400 regulars, 400 marines, and 1,700 Indians and militia from Montreal to the headwaters of the Mohawk River, in order to intimidate the Iroquois. From there they would sweep the Mohawk River as far as Schenectady, threatening the British line of communications between the Hudson River and Lake George. This area was defended by 2,000–3,000 troops, mostly provincials. Montcalm with the rest of the regulars would defend Fort Carillon.[11]

Meanwhile the British planned to take all of New France, including Louisiana, during 1758. After capturing Louisbourg, Amherst was expected to proceed to Quebec, while Major General James Abercromby advanced up the Lake Champlain corridor to Montreal and Quebec with most of the remaining British regulars and about 15,000 provincial troops. Meanwhile, a small force of regulars and 5,000 provincials commanded by Acting Brigadier General John Forbes was ordered to capture Fort Duquesne. Forbes used the 77th Highlanders and four companies of the 6oth, a total of 1,600 regulars; except for a part of the 8oth used on the frontier, all the other regulars were with Amherst or Abercromby or at Nova Scotia. The final part of the plan was an expedition to seize Louisiana.[12]

Fortunately for Vaudreuil and Canada, the British made two serious mistakes. First, as in previous years, they moved too slowly. The now-discredited Loudoun had learned enough from his mistakes to recommend speed over brute force. He advocated attacking Fort Carillon and Fort St. Frédéric before the snow in Quebec melted and Vaudreuil could send reinforcements. This was not done. Although Pitt urged the colonial governors to have their troops at Lake George by 1 May, the British were unable to advance until two months later (partly because of shortages of wagons and boats), giving Montcalm just enough time for his defense.[13] The second mistake was the appointment of Abercromby on 30 December 1757 to succeed Loudoun. Ligonier, the commander of the British army, lacked his predecessor Cumberland's authority over North American operations; although he made recommendations for the choice of senior commanders, real power was held by the king and the inner cabinet. They accepted his recommendations of Amherst and Forbes, but disregarded him in appointing Abercromby commander in chief in North America (although without authority over Amherst's attack on Louisbourg or Forbes's on Fort Duquesne). Amherst, overcautious, cruel, and bigoted toward Indians, was a mediocre choice. The amiable but slow-witted Abercromby, who moreover was not in good health, proved even worse.[14]

The French won the race to Fort Carillon by a narrow margin. On 30 June Montcalm arrived with the last of his 3,100 regulars, and over the next week several hundred Canadian marines and militia reinforced him. With the danger on Lake Champlain mounting, Vaudreuil on 30 June cancelled Lévis' independent operation and ordered him to reinforce Fort Carillon. He arrived on the night of 7–8 July with an advance contingent of 400 regulars, having marched day and night. Vaudreuil's brother, the chevalier de Vaudreuil, proceeding more slowly, was still en route with 3,000 additional marines, militia, and Indians. Abercromby's huge army of 6,300 regulars and 9,000 provincials sailed down Lake George on 5 July and disembarked the next morning. On the morning of 8 July he approached Fort Carillon only to discover that Montcalm, believing the fort vulnerable to siege, hastily had constructed an eight-foot-high log barrier along a ridge overlooking it and had placed behind it all but one battalion of his regulars. Montcalm had not had time, however, to occupy the 750-foot Rattlesnake Hill (later called Mt. Defiance), a mile to the south, which commanded both the fort and the log barrier; by merely dragging cannon to its summit, Major General John Burgoyne forced the Americans in 1777 to abandon Fort

Ticonderoga, built on the same site as Fort Carillon. In contrast, Abercromby, fearing the arrival of French reinforcements, failed to wait for his artillery, which could have enfiladed the French fieldworks. Instead he ordered an advance that escaped from his control and developed into a frontal assault by his infantry before his artillery could be positioned. Montcalm's fieldworks proved too strong for such an unsupported attack; seven separate assaults failed before Abercromby's army retreated in disorder, suffering almost 2,000 casualties to Montcalm's 400.[15]

Montcalm's miraculous victory saved Quebec and Montreal from attack, although there was little chance of following it up. Vaudreuil badgered Montcalm to make use of his reinforcements, but Montcalm realized that with the militia having to return in mid-August for the harvest he was short of both time and numbers. He restricted himself to raiding the British supply lines to Lake George. At the end of the campaign the British retreated from Lake George, sinking their boats in hopes of raising them for use when they returned the following spring.[16]

Once again victory added to the tension between Vaudreuil and Montcalm, who criticized the militia's performance during the battle and the late arrival of allied Indian warriors. Some French officers even considered the chevalier de Vaudreuil's failure to arrive in time to be deliberate. Furthermore, a Canadian relief column failed to reach Louisbourg, casting further discredit on the militia. The growing distrust would have terrible consequences in the following year's campaign.[17]

Of more immediate concern, the campaign elsewhere in Canada went horribly. During the stalemate after Abercromby's defeat, Lieutenant Colonel John Bradstreet used 200 small boats to bring 3,000 provincial troops along the Mohawk River route to Lake Ontario (probably with the complicity of the Iroquois). They then evaded the nine French warships guarding the lake and surprised the vital French supply post of Fort Frontenac at its northeast corner. Before Vaudreuil could send reinforcements, Bradstreet captured or destroyed what he estimated was 800,000 livres worth of irreplaceable Indian goods.[18] Overcoming even greater logistical difficulties (and his abandonment by Indian allies whom he had mishandled) Forbes finally was able to reach Fort Duquesne at the end of November. The remaining 200 or 300 starving members of the garrison blew up the fort and retreated fifty miles north to Fort Machault. The British quickly built a temporary fort on the site, Mercer's Fort, before beginning the far grander Fort Pitt in 1759.[19]

France's entire Indian alliance system in the Upper Country was crumbling; the various tribes in it faced the danger of starvation and had little choice but to switch allies. As a warning of this, thirteen Indian nations reached a peace agreement with Pennsylvania authorities at an October meeting at Easton (which the British immediately violated by not removing their troops from western Pennsylvania).[20] Montcalm urged the French government to abandon the western forts as a drain on military resources, to send him reinforcements, and to permit him to draft 3,000 militiamen into the regulars and marines. Such a course of action might at least have saved expenses, which later were estimated at nearly 28 million livres for the year. Vaudreuil, however, was unwilling to give up Fort Niagara, the Upper Country, or the independence of his militia. Montcalm sent army commissioner André Doreil and his aide-de-camp Louis-Antoine de Bougainville to France to argue his case, while Vaudreuil sent his own representative, Jean-Hugues Péan, administrator of the city of Quebec. Péan unsuccessfully urged the government to rebuild Fort Frontenac, and to promote Montcalm and recall him to France, leaving the affable Lévis in command. In contrast, Bougainville, who arrived in December, had some influence on strategy, as we shall see in the next chapter. There was little hope, however, of saving Canada. With the British in the Gulf of St. Lawrence, it was extremely difficult to send supplies; moreover, another bad harvest brought the renewed danger of mass starvation. With people already dying of malnutrition at the beginning of winter, it was pointless to think of sending reinforcements.[21]

Pitt, Anson, and their colleagues meanwhile prepared to bring overwhelming force against Canada in 1759. Newcastle, who had been forced to borrow £5 million to meet the expenses of 1758 and faced difficulty raising more, was ready to exchange Louisbourg for Minorca and make peace. His colleagues would not consider the idea, and they were supported by the king, whose desire to continue the war probably was based on the hope not only of recovering his possessions in Germany but even of adding to them. The inner cabinet ordered ten ships of the line to remain in North America for the winter; in the spring they would be so heavily reinforced that the French navy would not dare contest the coming British attack on Quebec and the Canadian heartland.[22]

THE FRENCH NAVY'S OTHER COMMITMENTS

The losses of the French navy in attempting to save Louisbourg were not the only ones it suffered in 1758. During the year it lost thirteen ships of the line, nine of which had sailed or had attempted to sail to North America, and decommissioned a fourteenth, the poorly built *Algonquin*, 72. In compensation it launched two ships of the line at Toulon, the *Robuste*, 74, and *Fantasque*, 64, and in November purchased two ships of the line from the East India Company, the *Brillant* (which had returned from Louisbourg) and *Solitaire*, each of which subsequently carried 64 cannons. By the end of the year it had only fifty-four ships of the line, plus six in construction: the *Royal-Louis*, 116, *Impétueux*, 90, *Protecteur*, 74, *Thésée*, 74, *Altier*, 64, and *Modeste*, 64, of which only one, the *Altier*, was started during the year. In 1758, the British began seven or eight ships of the line, continued construction on eight, launched ten, and captured four.[23]

The navy's problem was more than its shrinking number of ships. During 1758 it was able to keep in commission fewer than half of the ships of the line it did have. On 1 June, for example, it had in service only twenty-five of the sixty still on its books, leaving it outnumbered by the British by more than four to one; the previous year forty-two of its sixty-three were in service on 1 June.[24]

A major reason for the French navy's inability to make use of even its limited number of warships was its lack of sailors; in addition to losses from the epidemic in Brest and Rochefort, British warships and privateers continued to drain the available pool of sailors by capturing French warships, merchant ships, and privateers. Almost 9,000 prisoners were taken to England during 1758; of these almost 4,000 were petty officers or trained sailors. These numbers do not include the more than 3,000 naval crewmen captured at Louisbourg or those brought to American prisons by the growing number of privateers at New York and other American ports. By the end of 1758 the number of Frenchmen held prisoner in England approached 20,000, while there were only about 3,000 Britons in French prisons.[25] There was little the French navy could do to find trained crewmen for its warships; conscription in the ports and coastal areas brought only untrained men and boys, while intermittent embargoes on privateering were ineffective. Moreover, merchant shipping and privateering were facing shortages themselves, as demonstrated by the huge wages paid to merchant sailors and by the declining number of privateers. In contrast, the number of crewmen in the British navy rose to 70,000.[26]

The navy faced numerous other problems. Death or retirement had deprived it of such excellent admirals as La Galissonnière and du Bois de la Motte. Their replacements (such as des Gouttes) frequently seemed more concerned with the well-being of their squadrons than the needs of their country. (It should be noted, though, that the development of wider loyalties was a gradual process for the British navy, too.)[27] Leadership was increasingly deficient at lower levels as well; the odds that the navy faced began to shake its confidence, and some ship captains, like that of the ironically named *Belliqueux*, showed little appetite for combat. The navy, moreover, lacked more than officers and sailors. French naval construction and operations were hampered by continuing shortages of cannon and naval materiel, but the most pervasive problem facing the navy was the monarchy's financial difficulties. With payments in arrears to dockyard workers, sailors, and suppliers, the navy could not operate at full strength even in the Mediterranean, which was unaffected by the typhus epidemic at the beginning of the year. Sailors at Toulon deserted not only to Italy but even to British privateers and warships.[28]

In theory the French government's financial position improved slightly in 1758. Unrestricted ordinary revenues and extraordinary revenues (counting both grants and loans) increased by about 60 million livres over the previous year's, thanks largely to an advance from the Farmers General, a forced loan from government officeholders, and a grant from the clergy arranged by Bernis. The war in Germany ate up a good share of the money, however. The navy was authorized slightly more than 42 million livres, an increase of about 3 million livres over the previous year, while the army was authorized to spend an extra 15 million livres, raising its total to almost 100 million livres. Actually, the navy seems to have had less money to spend on current expenses than in 1757, forcing it to borrow money from local chambers of commerce, like that of Marseilles. By the middle of 1758 it was more than 42 million livres in debt (and eventually would be presented bills for substantial extra expenses incurred in Canada).

The future looked even more threatening. The naval debt continued to grow. Naval and colonial expenses for the year were estimated later at 55 million livres, but this probably excludes a sizable share of the Canadian debts. (British naval expenditures were far greater, reaching nearly £5 million, equivalent to about 120 million livres.) Moreover the French monarchy's ability to sustain its credit was coming into doubt. The 132.2 million livres that it raised in general loans during 1758 were almost 4 million less than the amount borrowed during 1757, and Bernis was greatly concerned about the credit of the great financier Paris de Monmartel on whom the monarchy had become dependent.[29]

Given the disparity of resources, it is hardly surprising that French warships were captured or destroyed. These losses commenced even before the disastrous Louisbourg campaign. During the first two months of 1758, two ships of the line were lost returning from the West Indies and another two en route there. As noted in the previous chapter, Capitaine de vaisseau Kersaint left St. Domingue for France in November 1757 with four ships of the line and a convoy. As he approached the French coast in early January, a winter storm scattered his forty-one-ship convoy. Only fifteen of the ships reached France or Spain by the end of February. Moreover, the *Greenwich*, 50, ran aground on a small island off the entrance to the roadstead of Brest and was destroyed. The captain of the *Opiniâtre*, 64, wounded in the October battle in the West Indies, was put ashore as soon as his ship reached the roadstead of Brest. In his absence, insufficient attention was paid to the ship's anchors. When the weather worsened, they failed to hold. The *Opiniâtre* drifted onto rocks and was destroyed.[30]

Storms also were indirectly responsible for the loss of two ships of the line in February. A storm had driven Chef d'escadre La Clue into the Spanish port of Cartagena before he could reach the Straits of Gibraltar en route to the West Indies. With the winds continuing foul he decided to await assistance from Toulon before attempting to run the Straits. Duquesne, commanding the Mediterranean fleet in La Clue's absence, decided to await the arrival of the *Orphée*, 64, *Triton*, 64, and *Fier*, 50, from Malta before sailing himself. It was not until 9 January 1758 that they appeared, needing repairs. (They had been trapped for months, until a British squadron off Malta was driven away by bad weather.) Meanwhile Duquesne learned that a valuable British convoy was leaving Leghorn. On 13 January he sent the *Souverain*, 74, and *Lion*, 64, to intercept it. Although they failed, they did reach Cartagena and join La Clue. On 14 February Duquesne finally sailed himself with the *Foudroyant*, 80, *Orphée*, 64, and *Oriflamme*, 50. He had a quick passage, but as he attempted to enter the Spanish port, a sudden storm blew him back into the Mediterranean and into the path of fifteen British ships of the line coming from Gibraltar. They captured Duquesne's two larger ships on 28 February. La Clue gave up his attempt to sail to the West Indies and returned to Toulon at the end of April, taking command of the port.[31] Short of funds and sailors, the fleet at Toulon accomplished little the remainder of the year beyond sending the *Souverain* and *Lion* to Minorca and the *Triton*, 64, to Malta and the eastern Mediterranean. In January 1759 a convoy escorted by several frigates brought desperately needed provisions to Minorca just before the British fleet reappeared.[32]

Moras did not have enough sailors to send another squadron to the Caribbean, but he did send two ships of the line. The *Palmier*, 74, sailed from Brest on 6 March with a convoy for St. Domingue and returned with another convoy at the end of the year. The *Florissant*, 74, sailed from Rochefort for Martinique on 2 May in company with du Chaffault; she was still there at year's end, but badly needing repair, nearly having been captured in a 3 November engagement against the *Buckingham*, 70. (The navy also sent the *Achille*, 64, and two frigates to intercept British trade in the South Atlantic; they sailed from Brest on 14 October.) With Britain's ten ships of the line in the Caribbean acting almost unopposed, the British were virtually able to eliminate French shipping. They even blockaded the Dutch island (and smuggling center) of St. Eustatius; luckily for the French West Indies the huge profits in smuggling attracted ships from Britain's North American colonies to the Caribbean. They particularly frequented the port of Monte Christi in Spanish Santo Domingo (now the Dominican Republic), until in 1760 the British blockaded it in disregard of Spanish neutrality. The French colonies escaped starvation, but by 1758 French trade with the Western Hemisphere was barely a tenth of what it had been in 1754, while French imports in general were a third of what they had been. Overall, French trade declined to its lowest level since 1737.[33]

The unprotected French West Indies escaped invasion largely because British attention was focused on North America and on the French slave trading region of west Africa, whose capture had been planned but postponed. In April 1758 a squadron of two British ships of the line helped capture Fort St. Louis, near the mouth of the Senegal River. At the end of the following December a squadron of five British ships of the line and 700 soldiers took the island of Gorée (defended by 250 French soldiers and 400 native troops) 100 miles to its south. Soon thereafter the British took the nearby Gambia River region, which furnished not only slaves but also gum arabic for silk manufacture.[34]

The respite for the French West Indies was temporary. Pitt hoped to capture Martinique to exchange for Minorca, leaving Britain free to keep her conquests in North America and George II free to make territorial gains for Hanover. On 12 November 1758 eight British ships of the line and an expeditionary force of 6,000 men (six expanded battalions) under the command of Major General Peregrine Thomas Hopson sailed to join British forces already in the West Indies. They reached Barbados on 3 January 1759.[35]

In contrast to North America and the Caribbean, the French navy sent a larger squadron to the Indian Ocean in 1758 than did the British. The *Minotaure*, 74, *Actif*, 64, and *Illustre*, 64, sailed from Brest on 9 March under the orders of the *Minotaure*'s captain, Michel-Joseph Froger de l'Eguille. The East India Company also sent another ship of the line, the *Fortuné*, 54, which sailed from Lorient on 7 March, the day after the *Grafton*, 70, and *Sunderland*, 60, sailed for India from England.[36] The Indian Ocean already was an active theater of war. In November 1756 news of the outbreak of war had reached India, ending a twenty-two-month truce between the British and French East India Companies. The initial phase of the new war took place in Bengal on the northeast coast. In early 1757 Robert Clive, the deputy governor of Fort St. David (100 miles south of Madras) captured the French trading post of Chandernagore, just upriver of Calcutta. (Clive recently had recaptured the company trading post at Calcutta from Suraj-ud-daula, the Newab of Bengal.) A British squadron of three ships of the line played a major role in these victories, although the *Kent*, 70, was badly damaged and later decommissioned. (Another ship of the line had become separated en route to Bengal.)

In June 1757 Clive won the Battle of Plassey over Suraj-ud-daula, who thereafter was murdered. The British replaced him with a puppet ruler and drove the French from their last posts in Bengal. On the day after Plassey, however, the French seized the British coastal trading post of Masulipatam, 600 miles southwest of Calcutta and 250 miles northeast of Fort St. George at Madras, the center of British power along the Carnatic coast of southeast India.[37] Thereafter Franco-British fighting was centered largely in the Carnatic.

At the end of April 1758, d'Aché's nine ships of the line (eight of which were East India Company ships) arrived at Pondicherry, the chief post of the French East India Company, ninety miles south of Madras. To reinforce the East India Company's troops he brought an expeditionary force of four battalions, commanded by Lieutenant General Thomas Arthur Lally, baron de Tollendal, the son of an Irish émigré. D'Aché refused, however, to assist Lally-Tollendal to attack immediately Fort St. George. Instead Lally-Tollendal and his 3,500 European and 3,000 native troops captured and razed Fort St. David, just south of Pondicherry. As long as Madras was in British hands, however, no victory was decisive. D'Aché meanwhile fought bloody but indecisive battles on 29 April and 3 August against Vice Admiral George Pocock, commander of the British Indian Ocean fleet of seven ships of the line, losing one of his company ships, the *Bien-Aimé*, 58, during the former. At the beginning of September, with the monsoon season beginning, d'Aché ignored Lally-Tollendal's pleas for assistance and sailed for the Mascarene Islands.

Lally-Tollendal thereafter decided to besiege Fort St. George even without naval assistance. At the end of November 1758, he marched on Madras with 3,200 European and 4,000 native troops. British regulars had begun joining the company and native troops at Madras, however, and the fort was well prepared for a siege. Both of the French commanders had betrayed severe character flaws during the campaign. Lally-Tollendal showed himself to be arrogant and racist, while d'Aché, although brave and a good tactician, was stubborn, overly cautious, and unable to look beyond the needs of his fleet.[38]

By the time Lally-Tollendal began his siege of Madras, there had been two changes of naval ministers in France. Moras, exhausted and overwhelmed by his terrible responsibilities, wished to resign from the naval ministry and to retire from the Council of State. At the end of May 1758, with virtually all of his ships for North America and the Caribbean having sailed, his request was granted and he was given a large pension in recognition of his courageous efforts. The position of naval minister was offered to Conflans. He declined it, although he accepted what he considered a far greater honor, that of being named marshal of France, a rank usually given to senior army officers. On 31 May the post of naval minister was accepted by Lieutenant General of the Fleet Massiac, the port commandant at Toulon to whom Moras frequently had turned for advice. Massiac was given a deputy minister, Intendant-général de la marine et des colonies Sébastien-François-Ange Lenormant de Mézy, one of the navy department's eight undersecretaries (premiers commis), who had enjoyed great influence under Rouillé, Machault, and Moras.[39]

Massiac served only until 31 October (at which time Lenormant de Mézy retired from office, too). Thus the experiment of having an admiral serve as naval minister proved unsuccessful. The seventy-one-year-old Massiac, although willing to take measures to reduce the naval debts and to continue the liberal trade policies of his predecessors, was too loyal to tradition and to his fellow admirals to accept the panaceas offered by Bernis to cut costs. His position was weakened not only by his political inexperience but also by his not having a seat on the Council of State, where he could defend himself. He also was harmed by the tactlessness of Lenormant de Mézy, who not only alienated Bernis but so insulted the invaluable Abraham Gradis (to whom the navy owed 2.7 million livres) that he did not send supplies to Canada in 1759, although his nephew Moïse did send a ship from Spain. Unable to defend himself, the honorable and well-meaning Massiac became a scapegoat for the navy's failures.[40]

The most obvious of these failures in the summer of 1758 was the navy's inability to contest new British landings along the Atlantic coast. Although the typhus epidemic brought from Louisbourg abated in March, virtually all the sailors at Brest and Rochefort had already been used to man the ships sent to North America and the Caribbean. No attempt was made to outfit anything larger than a frigate for protection of the coast or French trade; orders were sent to prepare five ships of the line at Rochefort (*Glorieux*, 74, *Dauphin-Royal*, 70, *Inflexible*, 64, *Saint-Michel*, 64, and *Warwick*, 64) for possible manning, but they were not put in service.

Without a fleet or even a squadron to oppose them, the British were free to attack virtually anywhere. Answering the pleas of Frederick II and Ferdinand of Brunswick for diversionary attacks, they were far more active than in 1757, when the attack on Rochefort miscarried. On 1 June Anson himself led a fleet of twenty-six ships to the French coast, escorting thirty-two transports with a landing force of 10,000 men (including fifteen infantry battalions). The British were unable to capture the great Breton privateering port of St. Malo, but they destroyed millions of livres worth of privateers and merchant ships. A second expedition captured Cherbourg on 7 August; before reembarking a week later, the British pillaged the city, doing millions of livres damage. In September another expedition returned to St. Malo, but this time local defense forces under the command of Emmanuel-Armand de Vignerod du Plessis de Richelieu, duc d'Aiguillon, the commandant of Brittany, put up a greater resistance. They were able to capture several hundred British soldiers as they reembarked at the little port of St. Cast. Although the victory reinvigorated French patriotism and caused the British to abandon future raids, the navy gained none of the credit, as the French army had taken over the defense of virtually the entire Breton coast.[41] British squadrons continued to cruise off the French coast; they, along with privateers, brought French coastal shipping almost to a halt.[42]

Before leaving office Massiac began planning the distribution of the navy's forces for the campaign of 1759. In addition to four ships of the line in the Indian Ocean and the *Achille* in the South Atlantic, he hoped to outfit twenty-one ships at Brest (provided he could find 10,000 crewmen) and twelve at Toulon. He also intended to send six to Canada and eight to the West Indies. The most urgent task was outfitting the squadron for the West Indies. Massiac selected eight ships of the line (*Courageux*, 74, *Défenseur*, 74, *Diadème*, 74, *Hector*, 74, *Protée*, 64, *Sage*, 64, *Vaillant*, 64, and *Amphion*, 50) and named Chef d'escadre Bompar to command them. In spite of shortages of money and materiel, the squadron was ready by early December, but bad weather kept it from sailing until 21 January 1759, already dangerously far behind the British squadron that had arrived at Barbados several weeks earlier.[43]

Shortly after preparing his plans for 1759, Massiac was forced from office. His successor was an outsider, Nicolas-René Berryer, who as lieutenant général de police of Paris had been the city's chief administrator. According to Bernis, he was selected on the recommendation of Madame de Pompadour, who did not like him personally but was grateful for his attention to her personal security.[44] Berryer had the advantage of already being a minister of state, although thus far he had been admitted only to discussions about internal affairs and finances.[45] Taciturn and upright like Machault, he lacked his great predecessor's gift for strategy and his rapport with senior naval officers. Suspicious, bad-tempered, and caring nothing about popularity, he was the perfect person for the thankless job of reducing the navy's expenses. Eventually that was the task given him, but initially his chief responsibility was the same as Machault's, Moras', and Massiac's, that of using the navy's limited resources to protect the French overseas empire. To do so he needed every available sailor. His 15 November orders to Bompar stressed taking care of the health and well-being of his crews.[46] By now the army, too, had been placed under the control of a strong administrator, after spending much of 1758 fighting on the defensive.

ON THE DEFENSIVE IN GERMANY

The energetic attempts of the naval ministry to save Canada contrast markedly with the lack of concern shown by the army ministry at the beginning of 1758. After the December 1757 offensive of Duke Ferdinand of Brunswick's Army of Observation came to an end, War Minister Paulmy and the French high command considered the French Army of Westphalia safe until the spring.

They even proposed sending its dozen most depleted infantry battalions and its thirty weakest cavalry squadrons to France for refitting, plus sending thirty-three battalions of infantry and twenty-two squadrons of cavalry to central Germany to reinforce Soubise. In the spring Soubise would proceed to Bohemia while the Army of Westphalia would undertake another offensive in northern Germany. The government was even confident enough to reject Prussian peace feelers.[47]

The Army of Westphalia, however, was merely a shell of the great army which had crossed the Rhine nine months earlier. Richelieu and his fellow generals had defrauded their own soldiers of much of their pay,[48] and many soldiers were sick, hungry, or ill-clothed. Even had the army been confident and healthy, it was dangerously overextended. Richelieu's replacement, Lieutenant General Louis de Bourbon-Condé, comte de Clermont, arrived at Hanover on 14 February, shortly after Richelieu left for Paris. Clermont had served with Marshal Saxe and was a distant cousin of the king, a member of the French Academy, and the abbot of the Paris abbey of Saint-Germain des Près. (He had received papal permission to serve in the French army.) The army ministry hoped that a general of such astonishing credentials would enjoy the moral authority needed to restore the discipline which the gifted but corrupt Richelieu had undermined. To his horror Clermont discovered that his army of 75,000 had only 30,000 effectives. On 18 February he announced plans for a strategic withdrawal.[49] That very day Ferdinand's Army of Observation, recently reinforced by a large detachment of Prussian cavalry, began a surprise winter attack on the center of the French defense line. In only six weeks his 35,000-man army advanced some 200 miles to the southwest. In their panic, the French left behind their sick, as well as mountains of supplies. At a cost of 200 casualties Ferdinand inflicted 15,000 French casualties, mostly prisoners. By early April the armies of both Clermont and Soubise were on the west bank of the Rhine, leaving behind only the garrisons of Wesel and a few other east bank forts. Ferdinand was rewarded by Frederick II with a promotion to full general of infantry in the Prussian army (and at the end of the year was promoted to field marshal).[50] The British navy even helped in the rout. A squadron of two frigates and two smaller vessels prompted the evacuation of the Prussian North Sea port of Emden, which had been occupied by a French and Austrian garrison.[51]

This humiliating retreat showed how badly the French army had deteriorated since the victories of Saxe only ten years earlier. The genius of Saxe had masked the gradual decline of an army which, basking in past victories, had failed to modernize. Paulmy had little choice but to resign, pleading ill health as an excuse. The obvious choice as his successor was Marshal of France Belle-Isle. Not only was he the most celebrated living French general, but he also was a member of the Council of State and was acceptable to Bernis, Madame de Pompadour, Paris de Monmartel, Paris du Verney, and the Austrians. He had to be coaxed to take the post, as even the highest of governmental positions was considered unworthy of so distinguished a member of the titled nobility or of one of France's dozen highest-ranking military officers. Conflans declined the naval ministry as beneath his dignity; Belle-Isle's consent to accepting the army ministry was obtained by naming one of his protégés as his chief of staff and another as chief of staff to Clermont. He assumed office on 3 March.[52]

Although seventy-three years old and in fragile health, Belle-Isle soon was working fourteen- or fifteen-hour days in an attempt to both repair and modernize Clermont's shattered army. Unable for financial reasons to raise new regiments, he hoped to increase the army, now renamed the Army of the Lower Rhine, to 80,000 men by incorporating French militia into undersized French battalions and by adding Saxon and Württemberger battalions. Meanwhile he sought to reduce the number of generals attached to the army by organizing it into permanent brigades and divisions, thereby making the army more professional and dispensing with some of its huge baggage train. He also took steps to improve the pay and rations of its soldiers.[53]

Court politics prevented Belle-Isle from having a free hand, particularly in the choice of generals, and Clermont was far from pleased with what he regarded as Belle-Isle's interference. The main problem facing the new minister was the shortage of time at his disposal. On the night of 1/2 June, several weeks before Clermont was ready to resume operations, Ferdinand launched another surprise attack. His plan, approved by Frederick II, was even bolder than the one of February. Using a bridge of boats constructed "accidentally" on Dutch soil, he crossed the Rhine with 40,000 troops. He intended to sweep south along the west bank, driving the Army of the Lower Rhine across the Meuse, forcing France's German allies out of the war, and isolating the French garrisons of Wesel and the other east bank fortresses. Because of British objections, Ferdinand did not intend to enter the Austrian Netherlands, although Holdernesse did extend permission for him to send patrols to obtain money and supplies.[54] (The French for their part sent troops to Antwerp and elsewhere to help protect the Austrian Netherlands.)[55]

Initially, Ferdinand met with great success. In panic, Clermont retreated to the south. When he finally halted and offered resistance, Ferdinand, with 33,000 men, attacked and defeated his 45,000 men at the Battle of Crefeld on 23 June, inflicting 8,000 casualties on the French. They included Belle-Isle's only son, who was mortally wounded during the battle.[56] After his defeat Clermont retreated to Cologne, twenty-five miles to the south. Wesel to the north continued to hold out, but on 7 July the great fortified city of Düsseldorf surrendered after a token resistance. Nonetheless, as Belle-Isle saw, Ferdinand's campaign plan was fatally flawed. The further south he advanced, the further he removed himself from his only bridge across the Rhine and the greater was his danger. With almost his entire army on the west bank of the Rhine, he had no way of preventing a French army on the east bank from cutting his supply lines and stranding him. Should that happen, Ferdinand's army would be in danger of capture and Hanover then would be helpless. Soubise's 30,000-man army had been scheduled to march toward Bohemia at the end of June, Louis considering it a matter of personal honor to send it there. Maria Theresa now released Louis from the obligation. [57] Soubise marched north, and on 23 July his 7,000-man advance guard, commanded by Victor-François, duc de Broglie, won a minor battle over 6,000 Hessians at Sandershausen, near Cassel. [58]

Meanwhile, Clermont was forced to resign. His army was offered to Estrées, but the former commander refused it, citing health reasons. Fearing that the army's generals would resign rather than serve under a formerly junior officer, the king appointed Clermont's most senior subordinate, Louis-Georges-Erasme, marquis de Contades, as interim commander until Estrées' health recovered. [59] Although the Army of the Lower Rhine, reinforced to 50,000 men, now outnumbered Ferdinand's, Contades was far too slow and cautious to make use of the opportunity. When Ferdinand learned of the Battle of Sandershausen, he realized his danger and managed to escape the trap, retreating across the Rhine in mid-August. Contades pursued him and spent three months on the east bank, before recrossing to enter winter quarters. The only significant action was the Battle of Lütterberg on 10 October, in which Soubise's Army of the Main (named after a German river) defeated a detachment of Ferdinand's army. [60] Briefly, Hanover appeared in danger, but Soubise soon entered winter quarters in Hesse, 100 miles south of the city of Hanover. Both he and Contades were promoted to marshal of France. Neither of them deserved the honor for such mediocre accomplishments. [61]

In several ways the campaign, conducted at enormous expense and ending in stalemate, was a major setback for France. It may have protected the French coast, as the French government threatened to burn Hanoverian cities if the British burned any French one. [62] On the other hand, it added to the financial strains of the monarchy, it brought no victory to counterbalance the loss of Louisbourg, it contributed nothing to the war against Prussia, and it produced a major change in Britain's attitude toward involvement in the war in Germany. In late 1757 and early 1758 Frederick II had asked Britain not only to provide him with a subsidy and to send a squadron to the Baltic but also to send British troops to Ferdinand's army. [63] Pitt was willing to provide Prussia a 4 million thaler subsidy (equivalent to £670,000 or to 16 million livres), which also would provide political cover for financing Ferdinand's army. He realized, though, that direct help to Prussia would be unpopular. He told Parliament in his usual exaggerated style that he would not permit a drop of British blood to be lost in the ocean of gore in Germany; indeed, Britain expected Prussia to provide the Army of Observation with infantry as well as cavalry while Britain sent nothing.[64]

On 11 April 1758 Great Britain signed a formal convention with Frederick II. In exchange for Prussia's agreeing not to make a separate peace during the next twelve months, Britain would do the same and would provide the subsidy. In an accompanying declaration George II agreed to furnish a British garrison for Emden, raid the French coast, intervene diplomatically with Sweden and Russia (in lieu of sending a squadron to the Baltic), and maintain Ferdinand's army at 55,000 men (of which Parliament would pay for 50,000 and Hanover for 5,000).[65]

This division of responsibility gradually shifted. After the first expedition to the coast of France returned to England at the beginning of July, Pitt agreed to send 6,000 British infantry and 3,000 cavalry (six battalions and fourteen squadrons) to join Ferdinand's army. Earlier, Newcastle and the king had wanted to attack the French garrison at Ostend or Nieuport in spite of the risk of war with Austria; to forestall this, Pitt had agreed to sending cavalry to Ferdinand. When news of the Battle of Crefeld arrived, increasing Ferdinand's popularity, Pitt quickly agreed to include infantry. Three of the infantry battalions for the new force were taken from the expeditionary force that had just raided St. Malo. The command of the British contingent was given to the former commander and second-in-command of the St. Malo expedition, Lieutenant General Charles Spencer, Duke of Marlborough (a grandson of the Queen Anne's general) and Major General Lord George Sackville. Pitt's sudden change of mind shocked his political allies, the king's heir, Prince George, and those associated with him; Pitt would be punished during the next reign for abandoning his friends.[66]

Marlborough's force arrived too late to assist Ferdinand. It reached Emden, the nearest port to the front, on 3 August (just as the second expedition was sailing to attack France). By the time it joined Ferdinand on 21 August, he had recrossed the Rhine. Thus it saw little action during the campaign. Marlborough died of dysentery on 20 October, leaving Sackville in command. Ferdinand appealed in vain for British reinforcements, but in compensation Parliament was prepared not only to renew the subsidy arrangement with Prussia but also to spend £2 million on Ferdinand's army. Parliament hoped Ferdinand would have 75,000 men for the next campaign and that he would not only protect Hanover but also cover Prussia's western flank.[67]

The Prussian campaign of 1758 mirrored Ferdinand's, a promising early offensive followed by great danger from an enemy with superior numbers. It opened well, the great fortress of Schweidnitz with its garrison of 5,000 Austrians surrendering on 18 April after only a ten-day siege. Instead of proceeding southwest into Bohemia, Frederick decided to strike southeast into Moravia with 55,000 men. His objective was the great fortress of Olmütz (now Olomouc in the Czech Republic), which was closer to Vienna than was Prague. The Prussians constructed siege lines and on 31 May opened their bombardment.

After a brief period of panic, Maria Theresa and her government responded bravely to the new invasion, even though Ferdinand's new offensive soon precluded any hope of French help. The Austrian army was being rebuilt to its 1757 strength of 200,000 infantry and 45,000 cavalry (including some troops fit only for garrison duty), enough to outnumber the Prussians; one modern expert estimates that in 1758 the Austrians were able to put 150,000 men in the field and their allies Russia and Sweden another 100,000, against only 135,000 Prussians.[68] The fortress of Olmütz was in good repair and had a strong garrison of 7,500 to 8,500 men. Maria Theresa sent Field Marshal Daun with an army of 40,000 men to menace Frederick's line of communication with Silesia. Daun was too cautious to be lured into battle with the stronger Prussian army. The siege went slowly, and Frederick's supplies dwindled. At the end of June the Austrians intercepted a vital provisions convoy, destroying thousands of wagons. Frederick had no choice but to abandon the siege. He conducted a skillful retreat and was back in Silesia in late July.[69] His campaign had been yet another example of the difficulties of conducting a broad strategic offensive, as had been shown already by the failure of the Prussians in Bohemia, the Austrians in Silesia, the French in Hanover, the Russians in East Prussia, and the British in North America (and was being shown by Ferdinand's campaign across the Rhine); only with a limited objective like Minorca, Louisbourg, Oswego, Fort William Henry, or the Saxon army's camp near Dresden had offensives been successful.

Defeat in Moravia exposed Frederick again to the attack of an enemy coalition, although this year he did not have to worry about the French. Reluctantly, he had to make use of the subsidy provided by the British government. He also asked Ferdinand to return the Prussian cavalry regiments serving with the Army of Observation (which Ferdinand delayed sending to him).[70] The most immediate threat came from a 60,000-man Russian army which had reached the Oder River, only fifty miles from Berlin. On 25 August Frederick's 37,000 men fought 43,000 Russians at Zorndorf. In one of the most savage battles of the century, more than 40 percent of the Russians and 30 percent of the Prussians were killed, wounded, or captured. A week later the Russians, short of supplies, retreated. In September a Swedish army penetrated to within forty miles of Berlin, but like the Russians it was hampered by logistical difficulties and lack of siege artillery; it retreated to the Baltic in November. Saxony, defended by Frederick's younger brother Prince Henry and 25,000–30,000 soldiers, was menaced by Daun, who was supported by an Imperial army. With the Russians in retreat and the Swedes only a minor threat, Frederick spent the final months of 1758 defending Dresden and Leipzig in Saxony and the endangered fortress of Neisse in Silesia. He did suffer a serious defeat, however, at the Battle of Hochkirch on 14 October, when Daun attacked his exposed position and inflicted 9,000 casualties, including the death of Frederick's best infantry commander.[71] The campaign ended with the Austrians and Prussians in much the same position as when it began, except for the Prussian recapture of Schweidnitz. The Russians, however, occupied Königsberg and the rest of East Prussia without resistance. They remained for the duration of the war, ruling mildly in order to win the population's loyalty.[72] (Ironically, half of the area, including its capital, today is Russian.)

Although the remainder of Prussia had survived a second perilous campaign, many of the best generals and troops of the Prussian army had not. Frederick henceforth would be unable to undertake offensives into Bohemia or Moravia. Moreover, he had become almost as dependent on Britain for money to hire new troops as was Ferdinand. In October he had to ask Britain to renew its subsidy agreement for another year; two months later, the British government agreed.[73]

By now, France's financial condition was hardly better than Prussia's and it had no one to which to turn; indeed, its allies were dependent on France. The war in Europe from which France had hoped for a quick victory had become a seemingly endless war of attrition financed by loans and expedients. For Bernis the only escape seemed to be a negotiated settlement; as early as January 1758, he claimed that he was thinking night and day about how to make peace with Britain.[74] Peace, however, proved as elusive as military victory.

THE DISMISSAL OF BERNIS

Bernis realized that before France could negotiate with Britain, he had to convince Maria Theresa to accept a negotiated settlement with Prussia. For a number of reasons Louis XV was not prepared to make any move toward a British peace without her approval. His vanity and sense of honor were involved. He also did not want to anger Madame de Pompadour, who had been won over by Maria Theresa and had become a zealous supporter of the alliance.[75] Moreover, he had promised his daughter and son-in-law, the duc and duchesse of Parma, that he would fight ten years if necessary to acquire the Austrian Netherlands for them.[76] Elementary prudence, too, dictated preserving the Austrian alliance. If

France made peace with Britain, Austria might make peace with Prussia and then try to capture Lorraine instead of Silesia, a frightening prospect given the poor condition of the French army and the lack of a Marshal de Saxe to lead it. It would best serve French interests if Austria could dictate peace to Prussia, permitting the exchange of the Austrian Netherlands for Parma. Even a compromise Austro-Prussian peace was desirable, though, as it might panic the British government into a quick peace treaty with France or at least might cause the withdrawal of Prussian cavalry from Ferdinand's army.

The problem, as the French ambassador to Austria, Stainville, warned Bernis, was that Maria Theresa called Frederick II a monster and argued that there could be no stable peace as long as he was strong enough to threaten it.[77] Bernis had no chance of convincing her to abandon hope of reclaiming her rightful possession of Silesia and in the process crippling Prussia. Eventually she lost heart, but in 1758 she was still optimistic of victory and regarded with contempt Bernis' desperate appeals for peace. Her ally Elizabeth of Russia was equally implacable in her hatred of Frederick.

Bernis' Austrian policy during 1758 was wildly inconsistent, his baleful warnings alternating with assurances of Louis' unshakable loyalty to Maria Theresa and the alliance.[78] Maria Theresa showed remarkable tolerance, either from fear of a total withdrawal of French support or from pity for the well-intentioned but ineffectual Louis, with his weak foreign minister, quarrelling generals, and seemingly hopeless army. She permitted him to withdraw Soubise's army for use against Ferdinand and offered to accept a reduction in the French subsidy if France would make the payments it already had missed, the subsidy being 12.75 million livres in arrears by 1 June 1758.[79]

In contrast to Austria, Prussia was anxious for peace. Frederick II urged the British to negotiate with France, was willing to discuss Spanish mediation of his war with Austria, and hoped the Turks would go to war with Russia (although an Arab revolt ended that possibility).[80] He was not so rash, however, as to risk his alliance with Britain, which provided him the money to rebuild his army, covered his western flank by supporting Hanover, and, through Pitt, offered him reassurances that Prussia would not lose a foot of territory when peace was made.[81] In his folly Bernis suggested to Stainville that France might offer Frederick a Caribbean island if he would make peace, but when Bernis actually made overtures about returning Wesel to Prussia, Frederick refused to discuss them. (At least Frederick refused to declare war on France unless Britain declared war on Austria, which Newcastle rejected.)[82] Bernis even made abortive peace feelers to Hanover and to Great Britain, using for the latter the Danish envoy in London (at the suggestion of Denmark). These hopeless attempts at a separate peace violated the terms of the Franco-Austrian Treaties of Versailles and could not be kept secret from the Austrians, who worked to undermine them.[83]

Bernis was not much more successful in finding help to make war. The Dutch did not become open enemies of France as he had feared; like the Danes and Spanish they hoped to act as peacemakers.[84] On the other hand, although continuing to ship masts and naval materiel to France, they offered little help in supplying the French colonies and made little resistance when the British blockaded St. Eustatius. Dutch boatmen even helped Ferdinand build his Rhine bridge on Dutch territory and only on French prodding did the Dutch government conduct an inquiry.[85]

The Danish government was similarly passive when the British intercepted trade with its Caribbean islands of St. Croix and St. Thomas, which like St. Eustatius were smuggling points to the French West Indies. Bernis discussed with one of his ambassadors the idea of proposing a league of the neutral maritime powers, but the Danish navy would not cooperate with the Dutch to protect neutral trade or even send any ships to join the seventeen Russian and five Swedish ships of the line protecting Baltic shipping.[86] British fears that the Danish navy might assist France to invade Britain were groundless, although the Danes did sign a 4 May 1758 convention by which France agreed to loan the Danes 6 million livres in order to arm 24,000 men to threaten Hanover. The Danes, however, were only interested in mobilizing an army because of the threat posed by Crown Prince Peter of Russia, who was also Duke of Holstein in northern Germany. He lay claim to parts of Schleswig and Holstein that had been Danish for half a century and rejected offers of two small Danish enclaves in Germany, the counties of Oldenburg and Delmenhorst, in exchange for surrendering his claims. France for its part could not afford to pay the money promised to Denmark and delayed ratifying the treaty.[87]

Bernis also hoped for support, at least diplomatic, from Spain. Spanish relations with Britain were deteriorating because of Spanish trade with the French West Indies and because of illegal British timbercutting settlements in Spanish Central America. Although Louis wrote personally to his cousin Ferdinand VI to ask for assistance, it was to no avail. Spain was of little help except as a source of loans (10 million livres in 1758 and another 4 million in 1759). Moreover, it ceased to participate in international affairs after Ferdinand VI became permanently incapacitated following the death of his beloved wife, Maria Magdalena Barbara, on 27 August 1758.[88]

France was so discredited that even Bavaria, a French client state, sought to find a patron more militarily respectable and financially reliable.[89] Relations with Sweden and Russia, too, were not fully satisfactory. The Swedes still were faithful allies, not even permitting a British envoy to enter their country,[90] but their navy was small and their army hopelessly obsolete. Russia was more powerful, but Franco-Russian cooperation was difficult because of their long-standing rivalry, particularly in Poland. Relations with Russia became less strained when the comte de Broglie was recalled from Warsaw in February 1758 and he entered military service. The "Secret du Roi" was left in Tercier's hands and was largely ineffectual. A new minister plenipotentiary, François-Just-Charles, marquis de Monteil, was sent to Poland with orders to maintain tranquility by any means possible. Douglas had been replaced in Russia by a regular ambassador, Paul-François de Galuccio, marquis de l'Hôpital, who was an advocate of abandoning all pretense of helping the Poles maintain their independence. Bernis, however, did make efforts (behind Austria's back) to keep the Russians out of Danzig, whose pro-Prussian inhabitants interfered with the passage of grain to the Russian army. The Russian military performance during 1758 was vastly improved, and their high command did make some attempts (with mixed success) to keep their troops in Poland under control, but this did not seem to bring peace closer. When Bernis inquired about the Russians' willingness to make peace, they replied they would be satisfied only with dictating it from Berlin. (A new British envoy, Robert Keith, sent to St. Petersburg in hopes of arranging a peace between Russia and Prussia, also was rebuffed.) The Russians in turn pressed France to join the Austro-Russian alliance, which was too anti-Turkish for French wishes, although Louis XV chose to give an equivocal response.[91]

Unable to make peace, Bernis was aware of his inadequacy to direct the French war effort. He told Stainville and Madame de Pompadour that the king needed a first minister or even someone with dictatorial powers. He did not want such a responsibility himself and suggested Belle-Isle, but Madame de Pompadour, aware of Louis' aversion to the idea of a first minister and fearing a threat to her influence, did not convey the suggestion to the king.[92] Meanwhile, Bernis remained the most influential member of the Council of State, although as its composition changed, his dominance was reduced. After 29 June Moras, Paulmy, and Rouillé (who was in poor health) ceased to attend. Two days later Puyzieulx resumed attendance in spite of his ill health, and Berryer and Estrées joined, although, as already noted, Berryer did not yet participate in discussions of foreign policy. (Meetings were attended also by Belle-Isle, Saint-Florentin, and the dauphin.)[93]

During the autumn Bernis expended much of his political capital in an attempt to cut royal expenses. The king was too tenderhearted and fearful of criticism to cut pensions or his household staff, and Belle-Isle was powerful enough to protect the war ministry's budget. This left the navy, as Massiac was not a member of the Council of State and hence lacked influence. In spite of his objections, a commission of five magistrates, called the Fontanieu Commission (after the name of its chairman), was established on 18 October to rule on the legitimacy of the navy department's debts. This further undermined the navy's credit.[94]

Bernis, who loved power but hated responsibility, finally inadvertently brought to an end the uncertainty about his position, which was undermining his own health as well as the French war effort. At the beginning of 1758 he was informed that Pope Benedict XIV intended to name him a cardinal. This represented an enormous potential increase in his status and power—the great government leaders Richelieu, Mazarin, Dubois, and Fleury had been cardinals—and required the consent of the rulers of the three most powerful Catholic states, France, Austria, and Spain. This was obtained, and although Benedict died on 3 May 1758, Bernis learned at the beginning of August that the new pope, Clement XIII, would honor the appointment. Bernis was so eager to become a cardinal that he conceived the idea of Louis appointing Stainville foreign minister, while Bernis remained on the Council of State, continued to see foreign ambassadors, and directed French judicial and clerical affairs. Stainville had earned Bernis' gratitude by securing Austrian consent to his clerical promotion, he was well respected by the Austrian court, and he was a protégé of Madame de Pompadour, who had secured him his prior diplomatic appointments and undoubtedly played a part in his obtaining his new promotion. (Once in office he took care to dine frequently with her.) On 25 August Stainville was given the title of duc de Choiseul, and in early October the king consented to his being appointed foreign minister. At the same time Bernis' appointment as cardinal was announced by the pope. Louis informed Maria Theresa and her husband, Francis, of the change of ministers on 2 November, and five days later Bernis announced his resignation to the members of the French diplomatic corps. The news was not made public until 1 December, however, so that Bernis could finish financial discussions with the Parlement of Paris and the Assembly of the Clergy.[95]

Bernis had made a grave miscalculation. The king did not like having political arrangements forced upon him, and Madame de Pompadour no longer trusted Bernis. Moreover, Bernis had misjudged Choiseul, who was proud, ambitious, and a ruthless practitioner of court politics. Choiseul even had betrayed his own cousin, Charlotte-Rosalie de Romanet, comtesse de Choiseul-Beaupré (who had wished to become the king's acknowledged mistress) in order to gain Madame de Pompadour's trust and obtain his first diplomatic post. Furthermore, Choiseul disagreed strongly and openly with Bernis' defeatism and thereby gained the king's respect.[96] Choiseul arrived at Versailles on 29 November, took up his duties as foreign minister four days later, and joined the Council of State on 10 December. Foolishly, Bernis planned a great banquet to celebrate his great coup, but on 13 December as he was meeting with Starhemberg he received orders from the king to leave the court within two days for an abbey of his choice.[97] Bernis' banishment from public life was not permanent; he was ordained a priest in 1760, became archbishop of Albi in 1764, and was appointed French minister to the Holy See in 1769. He thereafter spent more than twenty years serving France in the Papal States, a diplomatic post more in line with his abilities.[98] Choiseul, who began his diplomatic career in Rome, meanwhile would spend a dozen years as Louis' chief minister in all but name. He began by changing the direction of both foreign policy and war strategy.

6

1759
The Annus Horribilis

NEW ARRANGEMENTS WITH AUSTRIA AND PLANS TO INVADE BRITAIN

Like William Pitt and Frederick II, Choiseul was arrogant, astute, ruthless, manipulative, sarcastic, and charismatic.[1] He was single-minded in pursuing an honorable peace, but enormously flexible and creative in the means he chose. Technically he was not a chief minister, because Louis XV insisted on being his own chief minister. He enjoyed, however, greater power in the Council of the State than Pitt did in the inner cabinet, partly because Newcastle as first lord of the treasury was prime minister, albeit not fully in the modern understanding of the title.[2] Choiseul, moreover, did not have to depend as did Pitt on his popularity with the public, because he enjoyed a firm base at court in the friendship of Madame de Pompadour and the trust of Louis XV and because he did not have to worry about elections. This was fortunate, as the French public distrusted Choiseul, whom it believed too pro-Austrian, even though in the last war he had fought against the Austrians in Bohemia, Italy, and the Austrian Netherlands.[3]

Bernis had told Choiseul on 20 August that his task would be to avert France's destruction by making peace.[4] Bernis misjudged Louis XV, who told him on 9 October that no one wished peace more than he did, but he wished one that was solid and not dishonorable.[5] In exiling Bernis, Louis rejected the policy of making peace at any price and demonstrated a new resoluteness, perhaps because of the recent French victories in Germany, perhaps because he had begun to recover from the trauma of Damiens' attack. Choiseul, as the king knew, felt the same way. On 2 December Choiseul told Starhemberg that he disagreed completely with Bernis about making peace now; thoughts of it should be put aside so the French government could occupy itself with finding the means to wage war.[6] Quickly he moved to end the peace feelers with Britain that the Danes had arranged.[7] As he told his ambassador to the Netherlands, it was necessary to the dignity of the monarchy that the war be pursued with vigor and firmness, rather than pursuing vague and hazardous schemes of peace.[8] Only thus could Britain be forced to accept reasonable peace terms. As Choiseul told his old friend Danish foreign minister Bernstorff, this would require patience and firmness; he boasted that he would not change his mind even if the British captured Brittany and Normandy.[9]

Choiseul criticized not only the fruitless peace initiatives of 1758 but also the attempt to defeat Britain through capturing Hanover. He claimed that France's concentration on Germany had led it to neglect its own interests, particularly the defense of its colonies and commerce, for those of its allies, in which France was concerned only indirectly.[10] Choiseul was prone to making sweeping statements to emphasize a point, and his comments on the importance of colonies and commerce[11] have led some historians to see his ministry as beginning to widen the concerns of French diplomacy or even to turn away from Europe.[12] This is untrue. Choiseul made such comments when he wished to win support for the war against Britain, but his views on French security did not differ from those of his predecessors or from those of Louis XV. Colonies contributed to French prosperity, prestige, and power. Moreover, the king's honor and reputation demanded his defending them. France's security, however, rested chiefly upon the defense of its borders, and this defense necessitated having European allies. Although Choiseul complained of France's sacrifices on behalf of its allies, he emphasized France's loyalty to them and pledged that Louis would not make a separate peace.[13]

Choiseul realized, though, that France needed to reduce its financial commitments to Austria. During his tenure in Vienna he repeatedly had argued that France could no longer afford the subsidy to Austria dictated by the 1757 Second Treaty of Versailles. Bernis agreed and gave him the responsibility of negotiating new arrangements, sending him the draft of a new convention on 19 October 1758. Choiseul was successful. When he returned to Paris, he brought a revised draft by which the Austrians agreed to a reduction, provided France consented to abrogate the 1757 treaty. This would deprive France of its share in the fruits of victory if Prussia was defeated. Even worse, Louis' daughter Duchess Marie-Louise-Elizabeth and her husband, Duke Philip, would have to remain in Parma rather than become rulers of the southern Netherlands, although the Austrians were willing to make a significant concession to them. Given Ferdinand VI's failing health, it was likely that his half-brother Charles soon would leave Naples to succeed him, Philip would claim the Kingdom of the Two Sicilies, and if he were successful, Philip's territories in northern Italy would revert to Austria. Under certain conditions Maria Theresa was willing to cede to a male heir of Philip her rights to Parma, should Philip leave.

(Philip and Marie-Louise-Elisabeth had two daughters, Marie-Isabelle-Louise-Antoinette and Marie-Louise-Thérèse, and a son, Ferdinand-Marie-Philippe-Louis.) Maria Theresa also promised the marriage of her eldest son, Grand Duke Joseph, to Philip and Marie-Louise-Elizabeth's elder daughter (and hence Louis XV's granddaughter), Marie-Isabelle. Also she would release France from the obligation to continue the war until Silesia and Glatz were captured and would lighten France's financial burden. If, however, Austria captured Silesia and Glatz, France would receive only two fortified cities in the Austrian Netherlands, Chimay and Beaumont.[14]

The negotiations for a new arrangement were handled directly by Starhemberg and Choiseul, as France was represented in Vienna only by a chargé d'affaires for the first half of 1759. Starhemberg was a superb negotiator, and he was in a strong position. Choiseul was reduced to haggling over details such as the exchange rate between livres and florins. Agreement was reached on 30 March on two treaties. The first of these, predated to 30 December 1758 and usually called the Third Treaty of Versailles, renewed the Austro-French defensive treaty of 1756 in perpetuity. France agreed to provide a financial subsidy rather than an auxiliary corps and to field its own army of 100,000 troops in Germany. France promised that any treaty with George II as king or elector would specify he would provide no help to Prussia. Austria in turn promised that any treaty made with Prussia would specify Frederick would not help Britain. France could continue to station troops in Ostend and Nieuport during the war; Louis turned down any minor territorial concessions in the Austrian Netherlands as beneath his dignity. The treaty also waived Austria's rights to Parma and its dependencies Piacenza and Guastalla in favor of Philip's present and future male heirs and promised that Austria and France would work in concert with Parma and Naples to resolve the Neapolitan succession dispute between Philip and his brother Charles. (Russia joined this treaty on 7 March 1760 and Sweden on 17 September 1760.)

A second and more secret treaty, predated to 31 December 1758, annulled the Austro-French offensive treaty of 1757, thereby releasing France from the obligation of having to continue the war until Austria gained Silesia and Glatz. France agreed to pay a reduced subsidy of 288,000 florins (720,000 livres) per month, of which 38,000 florins a month would be deferred until after the war; the old subsidy had been 1 million florins per month. At war's end, however, France would also have to pay the 7.5 million florins (18.75 million livres) that now was in arrears from that prior subsidy. (During the entire war, France provided subsidies to Austria of 20–25 million florins, equivalent to 50–62.5 million livres, the lower figure being comparable to the amount France gave or loaned the United States during the following war.) France also agreed to provide a subsidy to Denmark that eventually was fixed at 2 million livres per year. Austria in turn promised to use its good offices with Britain to end the restrictions on the French use of Dunkirk. At Louis' request, it extended the rights of inheritance in Parma to Duke Philip's female heirs; in return Austria would be released from any obligations to compensate the king of Sardinia for *his* claims to Piacenza (claims that eventually were resolved by a cash settlement).[15]

Thanks to the new arrangements with Austria and other economies, Choiseul was able to cut the foreign ministry's expenses in 1759 to approximately 25 million livres, including 19 million livres in foreign subsidies. In theory this saved more than 25 million livres, although in practice France had not been meeting her obligations.[16] The major purpose of reducing France's commitments to her allies was to make it financially possible for her to regain the strategic initiative. She hoped thereby to force Britain to negotiate a compromise settlement as soon as possible. The financial savings from reducing French subsidies were far exceeded by the enormous expenses of Choiseul's attempt to end the war quickly. The means he chose was the invasion of Britain.

In December 1757, he had proposed to the Austrians the idea of threatening such an invasion. Once he was foreign minister he began almost immediately to prepare such an attack. His goal was to destroy the British government's credit, an idea suggested as early as 1755 by Etienne de Silhouette.[17] In late January 1759, Choiseul began discussions with Sweden (and thereafter with Russia) about their participating in the invasion. Over the next half year the invasion plan went through several revisions, Choiseul's ingenuity and flexibility being almost boundless (although his ability to recognize limitations was not). Belle-Isle and, probably to a lesser extent, Berryer participated in the planning. Somewhat schematizing a succession of plans that tend to blend together, they seem to have evolved in the following manner. Initially, Choiseul planned that as diversionary attacks France would land troops in Ireland while Sweden and Russia sent 12,000 troops apiece from the Swedish port of Gothenburg to Scotland, supposedly only a 24- to 30-hour voyage in good weather. Then Conflans' fleet would sail up the English Channel, escorting an army of 50,000 men to invade England.

When Empress Elizabeth of Russia showed no interest in going to war with Britain, Choiseul and his colleagues dropped plans for the Irish diversion. Now they planned that 10,000 troops from Ostend would land in eastern Scotland in August, followed in October by the Swedes. (Sweden was promised the island of Tobago as its reward.) Then the main French army would sail from Dunkirk, Calais, and Boulogne to land at Dover. A force of privateers would provide a diversion; later it was decided it would carry a small landing party to Ireland.

In May the embarkation point for the force attacking Scotland was shifted to Brittany and its command was given to Aiguillon, the victor over the British at St. Cast. Choiseul decided that no formal engagements would be made with Prince Charles Edward of the House of Stuart, the son of the "Jacobite" claimant to the British throne, as Choiseul did not trust his discretion or intelligence. The "Young Pretender" had led the dramatic attempt of 1745–46 to restore the Stuarts, but he was intoxicated when he met with Choiseul on 7 February 1759. To the Dutch, ancient enemies of the Stuarts, Choiseul described the idea of a restoration as useless, dangerous, and perhaps ridiculous, but he kept Stuart participation in Scotland as an option. [18]

By the end of July, Aiguillon's sailing date was fixed for 10 September so he could have time to undertake the siege of Edinburgh before the start of winter. His landing force was increased in August to 20,000 men, and four ships of the line (later six) were selected as his escort. The following month, as the sailing date approached, it was decided he should land on the west coast of Scotland where supplies were more abundant; the Swedes would land on the east coast in November. Conflans' Brest fleet would escort Aiguillon's forces only a brief distance before returning to the English Channel to cover the landing of 20,000 men in England rather than accompanying Aiguillon to the landing site and then sailing north of Scotland to the North Sea. [19]

These plans ignored the lack of means to accomplish them. The Swedes, already reluctant to participate, were so short of money that they were unable even to collect troops at Gothenburg. Choiseul also failed to convince Spain to send a fleet to Brest or, as a diversion, to the Caribbean. [20] A major portion of his plan involved the construction of 225 to 275 hundred-foot-long flatboats with a crew of 12 to carry troops to England, with a dozen 130-foot-long shallow-draft warships called prames with a crew of 150 to provide close escort. Although 27 million livres was allocated to this project, the first of the prames was not launched until late December. [21] Perhaps the most serious difficulty, however, was the poor quality of the fleet at Brest. By enormous effort Conflans was able to put into service twenty-one ships of the line (out of the forty-seven used by the entire French navy), but to man them properly would have required 12,870 crewmen, including 7,080 trained sailors and petty officers. Instead, Conflans had to use untrained sailors, such as coast guard troops. His fleet began entering the roadstead of Brest on 30 May. [22]

The British navy gave Conflans no opportunities to train his crews. The British government had numerous sources of intelligence; the king and Newcastle even possessed private sources of information that they were reluctant to share. Choiseul, however, made little attempt to hide the massive preparations for invasion, perhaps hoping the British would weaken the forces they were sending to Canada. Although the always anxious Newcastle was frightened, Pitt was so contemptuous of the French armed forces that it was 9 May before the inner cabinet finally began to take countermeasures.[23] Great efforts, however, had already been made to increase the number of British crewmen to 75,000, which permitted the manning of enough ships to blockade Brest; briefly during the second half of the year 80,000 crewmen were mustered. By 21 May Hawke was en route to the French coast with 23 of the British navy's 111 ships of the line.[24] Meanwhile the British concentrated the 30,000 regular troops that were available to repulse an invasion. Soldiers serving on board warships were put ashore, the militia took over guarding French prisoners, and a mobile force of six battalions was assembled at the Isle of Wight with transports ready to take them where they were needed.[25] The young Prince of Wales volunteered his services, but his grandfather did not accept (although he did permit one of his younger grandsons to serve as a midshipman aboard HMS *Hero*).[26]

In previous years an early arrival of a British fleet off the French coast had meant a subsequent early departure, as crews weakened from scurvy and other illnesses. Under the threat of invasion, the British took extraordinary measures to keep a fleet constantly off Brest. Hawke's crews escaped scurvy because he was sent a continual supply of cattle and sheep for slaughter, as well as beer and a variety of fresh vegetables and fruits (cabbages, turnips, carrots, onions, potatoes, and apples, and even lemons and oranges purchased from passing Spanish merchant ships).[27] Hawke kept the hulls of his ships clean by rotating back to port the thirty or so ships of the line at his disposal. He thus was able to maintain a slight superiority of numbers over the twenty-one ships of the line trapped at Brest. Moreover, he established an inshore squadron commanded by Commodore Augustus Hervey immediately off the entrances to the road-stead, thereby restricting the arrival of supplies and preventing any of Conflans' ships from leaving (including the ones intended to escort Aiguillon). The admiralty had enough ships left over to protect the Downs (near the mouth of the Thames) and to blockade Dunkirk and Le Havre; on 4–5 July a squadron of five ships of the line bombarded the latter port, which was the main construction site for the landing barges. At the end of August Hawke was able to detach a squadron to watch the French coast between Lorient and Nantes where the transports for Aiguillon finally were being assembled. This squadron chased the transports into Quiberon Bay on the south coast of Brittany (100 miles southeast of Brest), although it was unable to enter their protected anchorage.[28]

The best hope of freeing Conflans was sending the French Mediterranean fleet to Brest. From February to June, Toulon and the adjoining coast was block-aded by the British Mediterranean fleet. (Ironically, this paralyzed the shipping of Marseilles and thereby helped French naval recruiting.) At the end of June the British fleet, now commanded by Boscawen, had to return to Gibraltar to obtain fresh water and food; Boscawen had only fifteen ships of the line and dared not divide his fleet. [29] On 5 August La Clue sailed from Toulon with a dozen ships of the line and three frigates. During the night of 17–18 August he passed through the Strait of Gibraltar, sailing in two columns which became separated in the darkness. The British had been careful to patrol the Strait, and Boscawen immediately sailed in pursuit. Unfortunately La Clue and his captains had been given orders that were not to be opened until after they passed the Straits, making it impossible to decide in advance what to do in such a case. The captain of the *Fantasque*, 64, the senior officer of the weaker column, learned upon opening his orders that he had the option of taking refuge in the Spanish port of Cadiz instead of proceeding directly to Brest. He did so in order to escape Boscawen, taking with him the *Lion*, 64, *Triton*, 64, *Fier*, 50, *Oriflamme*, 50, and the three frigates. Boscawen elected to pursue the stronger column of seven ships of the line. The *Centaure*, 74, attempted to hold off the British fleet and put up a courageous fight before being captured, but she bought only a day's grace for La Clue. The *Guerrier*, 74, and *Souverain*, 74, escaped and eventually reached Rochefort. The remaining ships of the line sought refuge in Portuguese waters under the guns of the fort of Lagos. Disregarding Portuguese neutrality, Boscawen exchanged fire with the fort, captured the *Téméraire*, 74, and *Modeste*, 64, and burned La Clue's flagship, the *Océan*, 80, and the *Redoutable*, 74.

After the victory Boscawen split his fleet. Half of it returned to Cadiz to blockade the remaining French ships, which were joined on 28 September by the *Florissant*, 74, from Martinique. The *Florissant*, in poor condition, eventually had to be condemned. The other ships outwaited the British and were freed from the blockade when stormy weather appeared, returning to Toulon in January 1760. Boscawen meanwhile brought seven of the line back to England with two of the prizes, arriving on 25 September. Rather than adding to Conflans' strength, the attempt to reinforce Brest merely added to Hawke's— five of Boscawen's ships were with Hawke when Conflans in desperation finally sailed. [30] Britain ultimately had to pay a price for Boscawen again disregarding the rules of neutrality (as he had done off Newfoundland in 1755). Portugal became entangled against her wishes in the diplomacy of the Franco-British war and eventually became a reluctant participant in the war itself, creating a new and expensive commitment for a weary Britain. For the moment, however, Boscawen performed Hawke a great service.

La Clue's defeat should have caused the French government to abandon the attempt to invade Britain, which had become, if it had not always been, virtually impossible. The French government did not take this reasonable step, however. Instead, on 15 September it sent the commander of the proposed escorting squadron orders for where to take Aiguillon's army: the west coast of Scotland or, if this was impossible, the east coast of Scotland, or, if Scotland was too dangerous, the coast of Ireland. The orders admitted that Hawke was soon expected to receive reinforcements from the Mediterranean, giving him twenty ships of the line to match Conflans plus another fifteen to watch the coasts of Ireland and Scotland.[31] There was an element of unreality to the orders, as the French escorting squadron was still trapped at Brest with the rest of Conflans' fleet. The French government's willingness to consider subjecting a squadron and army to such risks was a sign of frustration. By the beginning of the autumn Conflans' fleet and Aiguillon's army represented its last hope, however faint, of salvaging a year of defeat. France had suffered severe reverses in the West Indies, in Germany, and, as it soon would learn, in Canada and India. To see why France was unwilling to give up the attempt to invade Britain, it is necessary to look at the other campaigns of 1759.

THE CARIBBEAN AND THE CARNATIC

In the West Indies, as in North America, the British always faced time pressure. In Canada the approach of winter ended every campaign. In the eastern Caribbean the inevitable onset of rainy weather in late March or early April adversely affected military operations. Wetter conditions increased the number of mosquitoes and hence yellow fever and malaria. Even in drier months, disease could destroy an army arriving from Europe. It took little time for disease to attack the army Major General Hopson brought to the West Indies at the end of 1758. During the ten days that he waited at Barbados for stragglers from his troop convoy, some 1,500 soldiers became incapacitated.[32] He sailed for Martinique on 13 January 1759. Three days later he landed some 4,500 or 5,000 troops near the entrance to the harbor of Fort Royal, the main French base. He seemingly had an overwhelming advantage, seven battalions of regulars against only 250 regulars and a few thousand militia. Commodore John Moore commanded ten ships of the line, while the French had only the damaged *Florissant*, which took refuge under the guns of the citadel. Nevertheless, the British attack failed. The citadel of Fort Royal was situated high enough over the water that Moore's guns could not demolish it, and there was no nearby landing place. Hopson believed it would be too difficult to haul siege artillery several miles over difficult terrain and called off the attack.[33] Governor Beauharnais had succeeded in bluffing the British; supplies had not arrived in months, and slaves were dying of malnutrition. (Soon after the British left, he threw open trade with the island to ships of all nations. For this he was applauded by Berryer, whose sympathies lay more with colonists than with French merchants.)[34] Had Hopson persisted, resistance soon would have collapsed. The British reconnoitered nearby St. Pierre, the main commercial port of Martinique, judged it too difficult to attack, and departed.[35]

Hopson and Moore were willing to abandon their attack because a seemingly easier target was available. Some 75 miles north of Fort Royal was another valuable French sugar-producing colony, Guadeloupe, separated from Martinique by the neutral island of Dominica. Although Guadeloupe seldom was used as a naval base because its main port, Basse-Terre, was relatively unsheltered, it had numerous small harbors and was a major privateering center. (There were a phenomenal number of captures in the Caribbean because prisoners were exchanged.)[36] Moreover, Guadeloupe was only 60 miles by sea from English Harbor, Antigua, a major British naval base, and only 120 miles from the Dutch smuggling center of St. Eustatius, which Moore wished to blockade.[37] The British quickly arrived from Martinique, and on 23 January Moore bombarded the citadel at Basse-Terre into near ruin. The following day Hopson landed his troops and seized the town and its fort with virtually no opposition. He failed, however, to seize an undefended redoubt in the hills above it, the Donkey's Back (*Le Dos d'âne*). This gave Governor Nadau du Treil a rallying point for his 250 regulars and 3,000 militia. He soon occupied the virtually impregnable position with more than 1,000 militia. Hopson was trapped in the town below, as this portion of the island was too heavily wooded and hilly to permit him to outflank the French. For a month he did little except watch the number of his troops dwindle from disease, until he himself died on 27 February. He was succeeded by the far more vigorous Major General John Barrington, the younger brother of the British secretary at war. On 7 March Barrington embarked 2,000 of his remaining 2,500 effectives and sailed the 40 miles to Fort Louis, a small fort on the flatter northeastern portion of Guadeloupe. (Fort Louis, whose site now is in Guadeloupe's capital city, Pointe-à-Pitre, already had been captured by a small troop detachment and two ships of the line.) Using frigates and small ships from Moore's fleet, Barrington was able to capture the adjacent coast and then work his way south toward Basse-Terre, outflanking each militia detachment which tried to contest him. By late April he had reached the region of Capesterre, the wealthiest part of the island. Faced with the destruction of their property, the local planters convinced Nadau de Treil's troop commander to sign a capitulation on 25 April.[38]

As he was doing this, Chef d'escadre Bompar was en route to Fort Louis with a squadron of nine ships of the line. Bompar finally had sailed from France on 21 January. On 8 March he reached Fort Royal, Martinique, where he added the *Florissant* to his squadron and armed fully the two of his ships of the line previously *en flûte*. It took seven weeks, however, for Governor Beauharnais to collect supplies and assemble volunteers to save Guadeloupe. Bompar may not have done everything possible to hurry him, hoping himself for the arrival of four more ships of the line promised by Berryer. It was not until 23 April that he sailed, escorting a makeshift convoy carrying 600–800 volunteer soldiers. He eluded the British by sailing along the seldom used east coast of Dominica and arrived undetected off Fort Louis on 27 April. Moore's thirteen ships of the line were still trapped by wind near his anchorage at Prince Rupert Bay on the west coast of Dominica. Bompar and Beauharnais now had a splendid opportunity to repudiate the capitulation and trap Barrington, whose army by now was barely larger than their expeditionary force. Beauharnais, however, was too timid to attack Fort Louis and landed his troops several miles away. Bompar feared the arrival of Moore, while Nadau de Treil was afraid of resuming hostilities. He claimed to be bound by the capitulation and signed a formal surrender. Bompar and Beauharnais reembarked their troops and returned to Martinique. Leaving behind the *Florissant* and the *Vaillant*, Bompar sailed for St. Domingue, via the French-held neutral island of Grenada, on 6 June (bringing Beauharnais with him) and from there to Brest. He arrived on 7 November while it was momentarily clear, Hawke having returned to England to escape a strong westerly storm.[39]

Barrington proved himself one of the finest generals in the British army, but he was very fortunate to have had such inept opponents. Subsequently, Beauharnais was relieved of his command, and Nadau de Treil was sentenced to prison; Bompar escaped formal punishment but was not given another command until after the death of Berryer.

The British were unable to follow up their victory. In March, Pitt, probably on the advice of Anson, sent orders to Hopson and Moore to capture the strategic island of St. Lucia, south of Martinique (which Bompar had occupied in 1755), once their present operations were complete. Barrington did not have enough troops to risk this. He and Moore restricted themselves to occupying the smaller islands surrounding Guadeloupe (Désiderade, Petite Terre, Marie Galante, and the Saintes). Retaining the 4th, 63rd, and 65th regiments, he then sent three regiments (the 3rd, 61st, and 64th) back to England, one (the 38th) back to Antigua, and one to North America (a battalion of the 42nd regiment, which had been sent as a reinforcement to Hopson); some soldiers of the 3rd, 61st, and 64th accompanied the 42nd to North America, swelling the latter detachment to 1,200 men.

Anson had wanted Moore's squadron to return to England to help protect against invasion, but Pitt, more confident, limited the recall to three ships of the line. Moore, however, having a very large homeward-bound convoy to protect, brought back eight ships of the line as an escort; only one, the *Burford*, 70, participated in Hawke's climactic battle against Conflans, and the departure of so many British warships assisted the revival of privateering at Martinique.[40] Trade between the remaining French West Indies and Europe remained very small, however, and Bordeaux and other French Atlantic ports continued to suffer, the British blockade of the Atlantic coast of France contributing to their problems. Overall, French exports and imports remained depressed, although slightly improved over 1758.[41] The British presence in French coastal waters was so stifling to French maritime activity that the number of prisoners taken by the British dropped significantly and French privateering in Europe declined in spite of the boom year enjoyed by British trade.[42]

During the last war, the French had found some compensation for the loss of Louisbourg by the capture of Madras. When news of Lally-Tollendal's impending siege of Madras reached France in the spring of 1759, hopes arose that history would repeat itself.[43] France had sent substantial naval reinforcements to the Indian Ocean, which should have given d'Aché a slight naval superiority. The arrival of Froger de l'Ergueille's three ships of the line at the Mascarene Islands in October 1758 compounded a dire shortage of supplies, however, and forced d'Aché to send most of his fleet to the Dutch colony at the Cape of Good Hope for replenishment. With no French naval help, the siege of Madras was abandoned in late February 1759. The British used frigates and transport ships to supply the garrison by sea, and Lally-Tollendal did not have enough cannon for the siege. (In April, moreover, the British recaptured Masulipatam.)

It was not until August 1759 that d'Aché reappeared off the coast of India with seven Company and four regular navy ships of the line. His fleet was able to fight off nine British ships of the line in a 10 September battle and to bring reinforcements, money, and supplies to Pondicherry, despite extremely heavy casualties. In spite of the pleas of Lally-Tollendal, d'Aché decided to return with his damaged fleet almost immediately to the Mascarenes; like des Gouttes and Bompar, his primary concern was the safety of his ships. Lally-Tollendal thus lost his final chance to regain the initiative; in November the British at Madras, having received reinforcements in ships and troops, opened an offensive in the Carnatic. Lally-Tollendal would have to save Pondicherry and the other French posts in the region without naval assistance. On 27–28 January 1760 a great typhoon struck the Mascarene Islands and crippled d'Aché's fleet, except for the *Condé*, 50, commanded by Charles-Henri, comte d'Estaing. She and the *Expedition*, 18, had sailed for the entrance to the Persian Gulf on 1 September, capturing several British East India Company ships during their passage.[44]

The welcome news that the siege of Madras had been lifted reached an anxious London on 12 October.[45] Although the campaign in Germany had gone well for the British, there was still great concern in England about Conflans and about the transports assembled in Brittany. Moreover, the news which thus far had arrived from Canada cast great doubt on the success of a great attack on Quebec. Over the next six weeks all the British fears would be lifted, making 1759 for them an "annus mirabilis" or "wonderful year" (and conversely making it for France—to borrow an expression used by Queen Elizabeth II to describe a recent year of travail for the British royal family—an "annus horribilis").

THE ASSAULT ON CANADA

At the beginning of 1759 the French government had reason for optimism about Bompar's cruise and Lally-Tollendal's operations, making their failures all the more disappointing. In contrast, the prospects for New France were poor at best, given the overwhelming British military and naval preponderance in North America. The French government, however, did not abandon hope. Montcalm's representative Bougainville arrived at court on 20 December 1758. Over the next weeks he presented Belle-Isle, Berryer, Choiseul, and others more than a dozen memoirs written by Montcalm, Vaudreuil, Lévis, and himself.[46] He was well received, even by Berryer (who scorned Vaudreuil's representative, Péan). Bougainville described Berryer as upright, tough, and good, but with his customary bluntness Berryer told Bougainville that when one's house was on fire, one could not worry about the stables. This piece of black humor should not be interpreted to mean that France did not care about its colonies. Ferdinand's crossing of the Rhine had threatened not only France but also the French strategy of gaining an equivalent to trade for the restoration of Canadian territory; conversely, it was only in Europe that a French victory could save New France. Until then, France could only buy time. Berryer and Belle-Isle wrote Vaudreuil and Montcalm of the importance of preserving a foothold to assist the French government during peace negotiations. Although Choiseul was pessimistic about the chances of resisting the British onslaught, even he was unwilling for Montcalm to abandon Canada and retreat to Louisiana. French plans were based on slowing the British advance, so as to prevent them from conquering all of Canada in a single campaign.[47]

The strategic choices made by the Council of State were realistic and grounded in common sense. It chose not to send anything larger than a frigate to Canada, as the Brest fleet was needed for defending the coast and later for the so-called *expédition particulière*, the invasion of Britain. (No decision was made as yet on what to do with the fleet at Toulon.)[48] This at least saved the navy from losing any ships of the line; moreover, shallower draft warships like frigates proved more useful for defending Quebec. It rejected for financial reasons Bougainville's suggestion of a diversionary attack on North or South

Carolina. Wisely, it decided not to compound Canada's food shortages by sending any more battalions of regulars; Vaudreuil later claimed that including Indians and refugees he had 90,000 people to feed. It did attempt, though, to honor Bougainville's requests for munitions, engineers, artillerymen, and 1,000 recruits for the infantry battalions already in Canada. Accepting Montcalm's arguments about strategy, it ordered Vaudreuil to concentrate his forces in the region of Quebec and Montreal. Although tempted to replace Montcalm with Lévis (as Vaudreuil wished), it eventually decided that Montcalm was indispensable, given his tactical skills and reputation; he was promoted to lieutenant general, Lévis to maréchal de camp, and Bougainville to colonel. It also decided, in spite of Bougainville's warnings, not to replace Intendant Bigot. Vaudreuil was ordered to consult Montcalm on administrative matters and to leave him in control of tactical decisions unless all of the Canadian militia was involved in a climactic battle.[49]

The French government also attempted to send whatever help it could. It tried to obtain Dutch help in provisioning Canada, but was unsuccessful because, in contrast to the West Indies, it was impossible to disguise from the British the destination of the ships involved. It was able, however, to charter private ships to carry provisions. On 22 March, for example, a convoy of seventeen merchant ships and privateer frigates left Bordeaux with 350 recruits, as well as flour, wine, brandy, lard, and gunpowder, which had been assembled by the agents of Purveyor General of Canada Joseph-Michel Cadet. The largest of the frigates, the *Machault*, 26, and its captain, Lieutenant de frégate Jacques Kanon, an auxiliary officer in the French navy, played a heroic role in defending Quebec and returned safely to France. Between 13 March and 25 March the French navy frigates *Atalante*, 34, and *Pomone*, 30, and the supply ship *Pic* sailed for Canada from Brest or Rochefort.

The first of Kanon's ships, the privateer frigate *Chézine*, 22, on which Bougainville had embarked, reached Quebec on 13 May. Over the next eleven days the three French navy vessels, most of Kanon's convoy, and several ships sailing independently arrived safely, bringing to an end the winter's famine. Acting Capitaine de brûlot Jean Vauquelin of the *Atalante* became senior naval officer at Quebec. The French government incurred some 30 million livres in expenses in defending Canada in 1759, about 2 million more than in 1758 (although a majority of its bills never were reimbursed), as well as spending over 20 million in 1760.[50]

The British government was faced with an entirely different challenge, how best to make use of the overwhelming forces at its command. In a series of letters written on behalf of the inner cabinet between 29 December 1758 and 10 February 1759, Pitt outlined for Amherst his role in the coming campaign. He was ordered to detach troops to Louisbourg to meet warships and transports arriving from Britain. With his remaining troops he could either descend the St. Lawrence from Lake Ontario toward Montreal and Quebec or march down the Lake George and Lake Champlain corridor toward them. He should reestablish the fortifications at Oswego and either rebuild Fort Duquesne or construct a replacement. He was encouraged to attack Fort Niagara and was authorized at his discretion and that of the senior naval commander to invade Louisiana at the end of the campaign.[51]

Montcalm and Bougainville estimated that they would have to fight 60,000 British and British Americans with only 10,000 or 11,000 men.[52] They underestimated their own numbers and exaggerated the enemy's strength. The British army needed to provide 30,000 regulars for home defense, 20,000 for Germany, and 13,000 for the West Indies, India, Gibraltar, and Africa; it planned to reinforce its existing twenty-four battalions of regulars in North America (at full strength about 25,000 men, including some independent companies) by only 1,000 or 2,000 troops, which would come from the Caribbean. Ten battalions were intended for a direct assault on Quebec via the St. Lawrence, while three would be left at Louisbourg. Amherst, operating independently, would have six and a half battalions to attack Canada, two and a half for use in the Lake Ontario region, one to complete the conquest of the French forts near Lake Erie, and one for garrison duty. Pitt hoped that the colonies from Pennsylvania to South Carolina could match their previous year's contribution and that New Jersey, New York, and the four New England colonies could raise 20,000 men to serve with Amherst. Even if the colonies from Pennsylvania to South Carolina raised several thousand men, the British and provincial regiments would total at most only about 50,000 men, alongside which perhaps 1,000 Indians might serve.[53]

This still would give the British a large advantage in numbers. At the beginning of the campaign Montcalm had only about 3,600 regulars, even including 500–600 militia in training that were intended to fill out his eight regular battalions. In addition, some 1,200 to 1,500 marines were still available and Montcalm hoped for 5,000 or 6,000 militiamen (although if every man could be mobilized as Berryer ordered, perhaps 12,000 or more militiamen would be available). Few Indians could be expected to come all the way to Montreal or Quebec, but Vaudreuil hoped that if the French retreat was not too precipitate, a couple of thousand might be available to help defend Fort Niagara and the other frontier posts. In spite of the friction between their commanders, the French and Canadians could be counted upon to fight for what by now was a common home, French soldiers being billeted with Canadian families and not infrequently marrying Canadian women. In fact the French defense was aided by a turnout of Canadian militia in excess of Montcalm's expectations. Perhaps as many as 10,000 militiamen eventually participated in the defense of Quebec, some as young as twelve and as old as eighty-five (although only those between sixteen and sixty were expected to serve).[54]

In contrast, the number of British and American soldiers fell short of expectations. Amherst did receive an expanded battalion of the 42nd regiment from Guadeloupe, which reached New York on 15 July before being sent to Albany, but the twenty-four battalions already in North America were more than 5,000 men under strength; the British recruits intended as replacements for attrition were used instead to strengthen Hopson's regiments. The Americans, too, fell slightly short of expectations. Although the northern colonies came close to their quotas and played a useful role in the campaign, recruiting in Pennsylvania and the colonies south of it was undercut by the capture of Fort Duquesne and the decline of Indian warfare. Virginia, for example, raised one regiment instead of two. In all, fewer than 20,000 Americans served in provincial regiments. The total number of British and American troops, counting allied Indians, numbered only about 40,000.[55]

Even more important than the shortfall in British and American troops was the inability of the British to make the best use of their advantage in numbers. The overly cautious Amherst did not succeed in reaching Quebec or even Montreal. Acting Major General James Wolfe, selected to command the expedition against the Canadian capital, was far bolder than Amherst, but he was inexperienced at commanding a large army. Moreover, he had learned his profession during the savage suppression of the Scottish revolt of 1745–46 and acted with similar cruelty in Canada, helping inadvertently to mobilize Canadian resistance.[56] As a result Wolfe was outnumbered in spite of the overall British superiority in numbers in North America. Fortunately for the British, its fleet in North America was better led than was its army. Boscawen apparently turned down the North American command in favor of serving in the Mediterranean,[57] and it was given to one of the greatest admirals of the century, Vice Admiral Charles Saunders, whose selflessness and professional ability were indispensable to the ultimate British victory at Quebec.

Wolfe and Saunders sailed from England in mid-February and arrived at Halifax on 30 April. They discovered that Rear Admiral Philip Durell, commanding the ten ships of the line left to winter there, had not accomplished his instructions to blockade the mouth of the St. Lawrence. Durell sailed a few days later, but Kanon's convoy and the warships from Brest and Rochefort entered the river before he could close it to shipping. Saunders could not yet join him because the portion of his fleet which was escorting the transports for the expedition had not yet arrived. The regiments for the expedition (the 15th,

28th, 35th, 43rd, 47th, 48th, 58th, 78th, two battalions of the 60th, three grenadier companies, and six companies of American rangers) were so under strength that Wolfe had only 8,500 troops, instead of the anticipated 12,000. Wolfe and Saunders proceeded from Halifax to Louisbourg in mid-May, but it was only on 6 June that they sailed for Quebec, leaving the 22nd, 40th, and 45th (minus their grenadier companies) to garrison Louisbourg.[58]

Kanon brought not only provisions but vital intelligence, a copy of Amherst's campaign plans that had been captured aboard a British prize. Vaudreuil and Montcalm were surprised to learn that the British planned to sail up the St. Lawrence to attack Quebec. They had expected them to use the Lake George–Lake Champlain corridor for their main attack. Vaudreuil, believing the British would not risk navigating the dangerous St. Lawrence, even had ignored Montcalm's suggestion to place cannon at strategic locations downstream. Vaudreuil and Montcalm now brought troops from Montreal and began preparations to defend sites where the British could land. Five of the eight battalions of regulars (La Sarre, Béarn, Guyenne, Languedoc, Roussillon) were used to defend Quebec itself, while the remaining three (La Reine and the two battalions of Berry) were used to protect the Lake Champlain corridor. Montcalm and Vaudreuil had agreed to defend Fort Niagara, but it would have to depend almost entirely on militia, marines, and Indians; if not attacked, Vaudreuil authorized these troops to counterattack up the Allegheny valley toward Mercer's Fort, the temporary British fort at the forks of the Ohio.[59]

Captain Pierre Pouchot, the commandant of Fort Niagara, shared the views of Vaudreuil about seizing the initiative. On 1 June he detached more than half his 1,300-man garrison to march the 175 miles southwest to Fort Machault, 60 miles north of Mercer's Fort; there they planned to rendezvous with militia and Indians from the Upper Country before attacking the British. Had the attack been successful, it might have caused Amherst to divert troops and might have restored some of the lost French prestige among the Indians. The gamble failed, however. Pouchot's scouts just missed discovering a 5,000-man force under Brigadier General John Prideaux marching toward the site of Fort Oswego, 120 miles east of Fort Niagara. (It included the 44th and 46th regiments, part of a battalion of the 60th, and provincial troops.) As in 1758, the Iroquois failed to warn the French of an approaching British force; indeed, more than half of their 1,800 warriors eventually joined the British. Prideaux reached the shores of Lake Ontario on 27 June, and five days later he embarked almost 3,000 men on small boats for the dangerous voyage to Niagara. The French had two small warships on the lake, the *Outaouaise*, 10, and *Iroquoise*, 10, but the *Outaouaise* was disabled by a storm, and the *Iroquoise* failed to detect the British during their four-day voyage. Pouchot, outnumbered by six to one, summoned help from

Fort Machault, but the relief force was intercepted a mile south of Fort Niagara and defeated. On the following day, 25 July, Pouchot surrendered. Meanwhile, an attack by 1,200 Indians, marines, and militia on the troops left by Prideaux at Oswego also failed.[60]

These defeats had serious consequences. Amherst sent 3,500 British and provincial troops to attack Fort Machault and two forts to its north; the French abandoned all three forts as well as Fort Rouillé on the north shore of Lake Ontario (at the site of today's Toronto). Fort Detroit, the major French post in the Upper Country, now was isolated, as the small stockade at Sandusky was the only French outpost left on Lake Erie. Such Indian nations as the Delawares, Shawnees, Wynandots, Ottawas, Miamis, Potawatomis, and Ojibwas made truces with the British. Furthermore, a war along the South Carolina border began too late to help Quebec.

Vaudreuil and Montcalm now had to send Lévis with 800 troops (including 100 regulars) to build a fort at the entrance to the St. Lawrence river to protect against a British attack downriver against Montreal. Luckily the new British commander, Brigadier General Thomas Gage (Prideaux having been killed during the siege of Fort Niagara), was even more timid than Amherst and refused all orders to advance. Montcalm, however, was deprived of key troops and the advice of his brilliant second-in-command during the culminating period of the British attack on Quebec.[61]

Amherst should have been able to take Montreal himself. The forces directly under his command consisted of 11,000 men, half of them regulars from the 1st, 17th, 27th, 55th, 77th, and 80th regiments; he outnumbered his opponent, Brigadier François-Charles de Bourlamaque, by more than three to one. Bourlamaque's orders were changed after Vaudreuil and Montcalm learned of the impending attack on Quebec. Instead of turning back Amherst, he merely had to delay him until a new fort could be constructed on the Isle-aux-Noix in the Richelieu River, eight miles north of where it flowed from Lake Champlain. After making a token defense, Bourlamaque abandoned Fort Carillon and then, even before it was attacked, Fort St. Frédéric. By the beginning of August, Amherst seemingly was prepared to move down Lake Champlain and the Richelieu to take Montreal and possibly even reinforce Wolfe at Quebec. He was unwilling to march the final eighty miles to the Isle-aux-Noix, however, as he feared an Indian ambush or, if Wolfe failed, a counterattack from a reinforced Bourlamaque. He could not use the lake because at its northern end there were four small French warships carrying eight to ten cannon apiece. He therefore halted his advance until he could complete his own squadron. On 12 October the new British warships trapped the French squadron, which then was scuttled. Amherst already had embarked his army on small boats, but bad weather arrived and he feared that Bourlamaque would be reinforced. He soon ordered his troops to return and then to enter winter quarters.[62]

Amherst's obsession with protecting his own troops gravely endangered those of Wolfe, who with little help from Amherst had to contend with the vast majority of Vaudreuil's and Montcalm's forces. Even a demonstration against Montreal would have greatly assisted Wolfe. Vaudreuil and Montcalm were able to make an exceptionally effective resistance in spite of the fact that they had only six and a half weeks between learning of the impending attack and the arrival of Wolfe and Saunders. Reluctantly they had to accept the fact that they could not prevent the passage upriver of Saunders's huge fleet of twenty-two ships of the line and its convoy of transports carrying Wolfe's troops; at the most dangerous part of the river for navigation, the "Traverse" thirty miles downstream of Quebec, the river was too wide for cannon to be effective, and it was too late to establish batteries elsewhere. They also realized that they could not depend on the defenses of the city itself. Although the city was fortified and had some 250 cannon, its defenses were designed chiefly against a naval attack. On the other hand, it was situated on a high cliff above the river and offered substantial geographical advantages, which Vaudreuil and Montcalm were able to exploit.

They made three key decisions. On 26 May, they decided to keep most of their food and gunpowder aboard the newly arrived supply ships and to send them and the frigates sixty miles upstream beyond the Richelieu rapids of the St. Lawrence (not to be confused with the Richelieu River). These rapids were navigable under the right wind and tidal conditions by such shallow draft ships, but they were too dangerous for Saunders's larger ships of the line.[63] The French decision was risky. If Saunders and Wolfe could push past the defenses of the city and disembark British troops upriver, they might sever its supply lines and starve the city into surrender; on the other hand, if all the supplies were stored in Quebec, then Montreal would be left helpless should Quebec surrender.[64] The second and third decisions were made by Montcalm, to whom Vaudreuil delegated tactical questions. In the face of impending British naval superiority, Montcalm wisely decided to evacuate both the right or southern bank of the St. Lawrence opposite the city and the Isle d'Orléans downstream (east) of it. Faced with the decision of how much of the left bank to defend, he was convinced by Lévis to base his left or eastern flank not on the St. Charles River immediately adjoining the city but on the Montmorency River, which flowed into the St. Lawrence about eight miles downstream. (The Montmorency could not be entered from the St. Lawrence because of the high cliffs over which it poured in a great waterfall.)[65] Montcalm's ability to defend such extensive lines was made possible by the large number of militia who rushed to the city's defense. With his 6,000 militia (eventually rising to perhaps as many as 10,000), 2,200 regulars, 1,200 marines, 1,200 disembarked sailors, and 700–800 Indians, Montcalm's forces outnumbered Wolfe's 8,500-man army.[66]

By 26 June most of Saunders's 22 ships of the line, 24 smaller warships, and 120 to 140 transports and supply ships had passed the Traverse and anchored off the Isle d'Orléans. Blessed by favorable winds, it had taken him less than three weeks to sail up the St. Lawrence in spite of the river's current and the considerable navigational challenges.[67] During the next few weeks the British fleet fended off an attack by French fireships[68] and covered landings on the Isle d'Orléans, on the right bank of the St. Lawrence opposite the city, and briefly on the bank of the Montmorency opposite Montcalm's flank defenses. Its greatest accomplishment came on 18–19 July, when the *Sutherland*, 50, three smaller warships, and three transports sailed upriver past the guns of Quebec. Vauquelin's squadron of frigates waited too long to attack them and had to abandon the attempt. The British now controlled the river on both sides of the city and could land troops to threaten the French supply lines.[69]

Wolfe was slow to take advantage of the opportunity, partly because unfavorable wind conditions prevented Saunders from sending more ships upstream to transport troops. Instead, on 31 July he made a costly frontal assault on Montcalm's defense line at the Montmorency, suffering 450 casualties. He then devoted most of August to bombarding the city and to conducting a campaign of terror in the countryside that left perhaps 8,000 people homeless. Although about 1,500 of Montcalm's militiamen deserted during the campaign, many of them no doubt to protect their families, the French defense lines remained intact. By the end of the month, time was becoming a factor. With the arrival of autumn, the British had to begin thinking about the coming onset of winter, which would force the British navy to leave the ice-choked St. Lawrence and the British army to enter winter quarters. Eventually Wolfe's three brigadier generals convinced him to shift his attack upstream (west) of the city, where the French did not have formal defense lines. Instead they depended on a mobile force of about 2,000–3,000 troops commanded by Bougainville to repulse a British landing. Several hundred of these men were used by Bougainville to guard the paths up the cliffs that ran along the river for fifteen miles upstream. Wolfe hoped to land west of the cliffs and cut the French supply lines, but bad weather spoiled his plans. He finally decided to risk an attack on the night of 12–13 September up the 175-foot-high cliffs onto the plateau called the Plains of Abraham that adjoined the city itself.[70]

Wolfe's army already had suffered 850 casualties as well as more than 1,000 ill, and he had detached 1,600 troops to destroy French settlements,[71] leaving him only 4,800 men to make the attack. He chose as his landing site the Anse au

Foulon, a cove only two miles upstream from the city walls. By now Montcalm was so overconfident that he had written Lévis to discuss winter quarters.[72] A landing feigned by Saunders downstream of the city diverted French attention, and the 100 sentries covering the path up the cliffs from the cove were not alert. Wolfe's entire landing party was able to reach the Plains of Abraham with barely any casualties. It soon was in grave danger, however. Montcalm interposed some 2,200 regulars and at least that many marines, militia, and Indians between Wolfe and the city. He also summoned Bougainville to his assistance. By mid-morning of 13 September Wolfe had been able to bring only one usable cannon up the steep path from the cove, his troops had little cover, and Montcalm occupied higher ground several hundred yards away. Had Montcalm waited for Bougainville, he might have been able to surround and destroy Wolfe's entire landing party, which had no safe way to retreat. His experience of Canada had left Montcalm little confidence in the steadfastness of Canadian militia, however, and, perhaps fearing the arrival of more British, his patience gave way. At 10 a.m. he ordered an attack, which the British were able to repulse easily, although Wolfe was mortally wounded. Montcalm's troops retreated to their camp on the other side of the city, but Montcalm himself was shot during the retreat and, also mortally wounded, carried into Quebec. The British suffered about 650 casualties during the battle, and the French and Canadians lost 1,400 or 1,500, including two regimental commanders.[73]

Vaudreuil wanted to continue the fight, but Montcalm's surviving regimental commanders decided to retreat immediately to Montreal, before the British cut their escape route. No attempt was even made to send food to the 2,000-man garrison of Quebec. By 15 September the French army had reached the Jacques Cartier River, thirty miles southwest of the city. Two days later Lévis, summoned by Vaudreuil, arrived to take command. Reenergized by its popular and trusted new commander, it turned around and marched toward Quebec. It was too late. Short of food and intimidated by the British, the garrison had surrendered on the 18th. Lévis retreated again to the Jacques Cartier River and entered winter quarters, as did the 7,000-man British garrison of Quebec.[74]

For the British navy, too, the campaign had come to an end. Saunders began sending his fleet back to England (except for five ships of the line sent to Halifax), he himself sailing on 18 October. On 25 November, with the British fleet reduced to two small warships (for fear of ice), Kanon passed the batteries of Quebec with the *Machault* and five other vessels en route to France. Aboard the *Machault* was François-Marc-Antoine Le Mercier, the former artillery commander at Quebec, who carried messages from Vaudreuil and Lévis, including an appeal for 10,000 reinforcements to help recapture Quebec.[75]

Lévis' hopes to reverse the results of 1759 proved futile. The French navy was no longer able to lend any assistance, and the British had overwhelming military superiority in North America. The courageous defense of Quebec, for all its drama, did little more than buy a year's grace for Montreal, as France was unable to take advantage diplomatically of the respite. Even had Vaudreuil and Montcalm repulsed Wolfe, it is likely much or all of Canada would have fallen during 1760. The fate of New France continued to be dependent primarily on events in Europe. Not until well into 1760 did these begin to offer any hope that the tide of British victory was ebbing.

CONTINENTAL WAR AND DIPLOMACY

The campaign of 1758 in Germany had begun with a great French defeat when Ferdinand attacked before the French were ready. A similar catastrophe almost occurred during the early months of 1759. Ferdinand again attacked before the normal campaigning season in hopes of catching the French unprepared. The two French armies in Germany had established winter quarters some 150 miles apart. The larger, Contades' Army of the Lower Rhine with 66,000 men, was based on the lower Rhine around Wesel. To the southeast was Soubise's 31,000-man Army of the Main, with its headquarters at the independent city-state of Frankfurt am Main, occupied by the French at the beginning of the year. On 18 February Soubise was named to the Council of State and rather reluctantly left active military service to return to Paris.[76] (He soon was placated by being named commander of the main force for the cross-Channel invasion.) The Army of the Main was placed in the far more competent hands of the duc de Broglie. This proved very fortunate because at the beginning of April Ferdinand marched against it with a strike force of 27,000 men (about a third of his army), hoping to destroy it or at least drive it across the Rhine before Contades was able to assemble the Army of the Lower Rhine and come to its rescue. Had he been successful, the already weak self-confidence of the French army would have been shattered and Contades likely would have had to abandon hope of any offensive campaign in Germany.

Broglie established a defense line at Bergen, just north of Frankfurt with its huge supply depots. On 13 April Ferdinand attacked, but was beaten. He retreated eighty miles north to Cassel, Broglie making little effort to pursue him. Fighting tapered off until forage was available for cavalry and transport animals, but now it was Ferdinand whose confidence was shaken. He had lost not only a great opportunity to cripple or destroy Broglie's army but also the initiative in Germany. Contades could prepare for the campaign knowing there was little likelihood Ferdinand could launch another attack.[77]

On 10 June the French launched their own offensive. They switched the bulk of their forces to the Main, but used both of their armies in conjunction, attacking Ferdinand from both the south and west, repeatedly outflanking him and pushing him north. Within a month the French had advanced virtually to the borders of Hanover. On 10 July they surprised and captured the important fortress of Minden, seventy-five miles north of Cassel. The French were now at the edge of the great North German plain, extending all the way to Prussia, but during their advance they had bypassed two major fortresses, Münster, sixty miles west of Minden and Lippstadt, fifty miles to its south. Prudently, Contades, who had taken control of both armies now that they had joined forces, paused while detachments besieged the two fortresses in succession. Münster was captured on 25 July. With 90,000 men, about half of whom were at Minden, Contades now outnumbered Ferdinand by two to one and needed only to wait until Lippstadt fell to resume his march. His chief problem was his long and exposed supply line, which Ferdinand menaced. Against his better judgment, however, Contades let himself be lured into attacking Ferdinand prematurely on 1 August. The movement of his 44,000 men was badly coordinated, and Ferdinand's 37,000 British and Germans were able to counterattack, inflicting 7,000 casualties and driving the French back into Minden. Only Ferdinand's slowness in pursuit prevented even more serious losses as the French retreated most of the way to Frankfurt. Fortunately for them, Ferdinand was forced to divert forces to recapture Münster, which did not fall until 22 November.

At the beginning of November Contades resigned command of the French army in Germany. He was relieved by Broglie, as Estrées again refused to take command. Before entering winter quarters, Broglie was even able briefly to retake the offensive as Ferdinand weakened his army to send reinforcements to Prussia. For his fine work during the campaign, Broglie was rewarded by being promoted to marshal of France, even though he and his family were on bad terms with Belle-Isle. Although he had managed to restore the army's health and morale, the campaign ended in stalemate without territory lost or gained, a disappointing result given how promising the situation had looked in July. The French had suffered a bloody and embarrassing defeat at Minden, Hanover had escaped occupation, and although 20,000 British troops now were tied down in Germany, Britain still had enough soldiers to defend itself and conduct successful campaigns in North America and the West Indies.[78]

Choiseul's diplomatic efforts on the continent also were unsuccessful. We have already seen how he failed to obtain Swedish or Russian help for his invasion of Britain. He was equally unsuccessful at obtaining the cooperation of Denmark and the Netherlands against Britain in spite of efforts which included exempting Danish herring from French import duties. The British government was adamantly against conceding the right of either the Danes or the Dutch to trade with the French West Indies and continued to intercept their ships. On the other hand the British needed access to the Amsterdam loan market and did not want an open break. Thus the government took care to defuse the threat of war by privately encouraging the admiralty courts to release Dutch and Danish prizes, by restricting the number of privateers, by hanging a few privateersmen as pirates (as it had done earlier to placate the Spaniards), by carrying on discussions with a team of Dutch negotiators, and even by looking the other way as Danish ships traded with Brest.[79] The Dutch and Danes also did not push matters too far. The Dutch navy escorted convoys to the Caribbean, and the Dutch East India Company helped d'Aché's fleet at the Cape of Good Hope and even became involved in hostilities in Bengal. Both the Dutch and the Danish discouraged trade with the French West Indies, however, and although the Danes fitted out a fleet to escort trade, it never left Copenhagen. Bernstorff even volunteered the good offices of Frederick V as a peacemaker, although Britain rejected the offer and the Danes soon lost interest.[80]

Britain also avoided any serious confrontation with Spain by returning some ships illegally seized and by issuing some restrictions on privateering activities. Until the death of Ferdinand VI on 10 August 1759, the leaderless Spanish government was incapable of anything beyond making protests to Britain. It could not even outfit a fleet to send to the Caribbean, although it did provide shelter at Cadiz for the remnants of La Clue's fleet and continued to loan money to the French government through Louis XV's new court banker, Jean-Joseph de Laborde.[81]

Ferdinand's successor was his half brother, Charles of the Two Sicilies. Charles, who became Charles III of Spain, presented both problems and opportunities to France. Charles wished one of his sons rather than his brother Philip to receive his former kingdom. Previously this would have interfered with the right of the Austrians to inherit Parma upon the move of Philip to Naples. By their treaties with France, however, the Austrians had surrendered their rights to inherit Parma, giving them little reason to care whether Philip inherited the Kingdom of the Two Sicilies. Moreover, they had no desire to risk adding Charles to their enemies. On 3 October they signed a treaty with Charles which permitted Charles's son Ferdinand to become king of the Two Sicilies and which reconfirmed the right of Philip's son Ferdinand to inherit Parma. Thus, to the disappointment of Frederick II of Prussia, war was averted in Italy, although Louis XV's daughter and son-in-law, Marie-Louise-Elizabeth and Philip, who earlier in the year had lost any chance of exchanging Parma for

Brussels, now lost their chance of gaining the throne of Naples.[82] This resolution of the Italian succession question eventually proved crucial to France, as it made possible Spain's entry into the war as a French ally.

A second problem proved more difficult. Charles was devoted to his wife, Maria Amelia, a former Saxon princess who was the sister of Maria Josepha, the wife of the dauphin of France. She was furious at France because Maria Theresa had broken off the engagement of her eldest son, Joseph, to Charles and Maria Amelia's daughter, Princess Maria Josepha, so he could marry instead Princess Marie-Isabelle-Louise-Antoinette of Parma (who was Maria Amelia's niece by marriage). Louis XV did not commit such an insult to his cousin Charles lightly; he regarded the marriage of his granddaughter to Maria Theresa's son as vital to the perpetuation of the Austrian-French alliance and was concerned at the delay of the wedding, now planned for the winter of 1759–60. This was no excuse in the eyes of the new Spanish queen, whose rejected daughter never did marry; she insisted the new Spanish royal family travel from Naples to Barcelona by sea rather than by land so they could not meet Louis XV at Lyons, as the French king wished.[83] Meanwhile, the future bride's mother, Marie-Louise-Elizabeth of Parma, who was on an extended visit to the French court, continued to work on her daughter's behalf.

On balance, however, the change of kings seemed to present great opportunities to France. Charles was energetic and forceful, he reportedly felt great loyalty to the House of Bourbon and hence might be sympathetic to his first cousin Louis, and he hated Britain, which had insulted him during the War of the Austrian Succession by threatening to bombard Naples.[84] He also was concerned that the war might spread to Spain and its empire in the Western Hemisphere, which, as he soon learned, was almost defenseless. Even while still king of the Two Sicilies, he warned the British against attacking St. Domingue, which adjoined Spanish Santo Domingo. The British offered reassurances that they had no such intentions, but Charles realized that as long as the war continued the Spanish empire was in danger. In late August Prince Albertini Giovanni Battista San Severino, the representative in London of the Kingdom of the Two Sicilies, informed Pitt of Charles's desire to act as mediator between Britain and France, but received a noncommittal response.[85] Choiseul, however, was ready for assistance in making peace; as early as July Choiseul had confided to both Ambassador to Russia L'Hôpital and Danish foreign minister Bernstorff about France's eagerness to make peace.[86] On 7 September Choiseul forwarded Louis' acceptance of Spanish mediation to Pierre-Paul, marquis d'Ossun, the French representative at Naples who at Charles's request was being sent to replace the marquis d'Aubeterre as ambassador to Spain. Choiseul warned of the British danger to the Spanish empire and urged Spain to back its mediation with force. [87] Choiseul spelled out to Ossun the terms France was prepared to accept: France would return Minorca, dismantle the fortifications of Louisbourg, withdraw its troops from Germany including Wesel and the Prussian territories, not insist on the return of the merchant ships seized in 1755, and accept Spanish mediation of the Ohio and Acadian borders. (On 23 September Choiseul wrote Bernstorff he would concede on the Ohio border and let Britain appoint an arbiter for the Acadian.) [88] In return, France expected Britain to return all its conquests, to abandon its rights to supervise Dunkirk, and to disband Ferdinand's army. Both parties could provide financial assistance to their allies, and Britain could send troops to help Prussia if France could send troops to Bohemia.

Upon receiving the French acceptance of his mediation, Charles sent orders to make a formal offer of mediation to Britain; in the interim, San Severino had conducted another unsatisfactory meeting with Pitt. The British did not reply to Charles's offer until after news of Quebec's capture arrived in mid-October (news that, according to Ossun, Charles said turned his blood to ice). Newcastle continued to believe Britain should make peace, but his influence in the inner cabinet had waned. Pitt, less eager than ever to end the war, told San Severino that it was not yet time to think of peace. When San Severino warned him of possible Spanish intervention, Pitt softened his tone, responding that Britain did not intend to keep all its conquests and would make a reasonable peace. He also promised that George William Hervey, Earl of Bristol, the new British minister in Spain, would pursue discussions. According to Newcastle, Pitt was willing to exchange Quebec, Louisbourg, and Guadeloupe, but insisted that Britain keep its other conquests in America, as well as those made in Africa. [89]

Although Choiseul had begun to think of peace, the major task of his diplomacy still was that of conducting war. It was only by France's invading Britain or seizing Hanover (or by Austria and Russia's driving Britain's ally Prussia from the war) that France might hope to save something in North America and obtain reasonable peace terms.

France's key ally still was Austria. In June, Louis appointed as ambassador to Maria Theresa's court the duc de Choiseul's cousin, César-Gabriel de Choiseul-Chevigny, comte de Choiseul. Gracious, self-confident, and prudent, the comte de Choiseul proved a superb choice for the post his cousin had occupied so brilliantly (although when he later became foreign minister Starhemberg found him proud and stubborn). [90] Given the results of Minden, however, the comte was not in a position to offer military cooperation in Germany. France still needed to fight Ferdinand of Brunswick rather than help the Austrian and Imperial armies against Prussia. [91]

France's lack of cooperation hindered the effort against Frederick II, whose army barely survived the year. Able to put barely 130,000 men in the field and outnumbered two to one by the armies of Russia, Austria, the Holy Roman Empire, and Sweden,[92] Frederick remained on the strategic defensive throughout the year as his enemies attacked from the north, east, and south. On three occasions, however, the Prussians launched tactical offensives and suffered serious defeats.

The first of these occurred on 23 July, a month after the beginning of the campaign. Frederick, who was holding Field Marshal Daun's Austrian army in check along the border of Bohemia and Silesia, ordered Lieutenant General Carl Heinrich von Wedell to attack the Russians approaching the Oder River, 100 miles to the north. At the Battle of Paltzig, 28,000 Prussians were repulsed by 40,000 Russians commanded by General Petr Semenovich Saltykov; Wedell's army suffered 8,000 casualties.

Saltykov then occupied Frankfurt an der Oder and was reinforced by a detachment of 20,000 Austrian troops sent down the valley of the Neisse River (along what today is the border between Germany and Poland). Frederick in turn led a detachment from his army to join the remnants of Wedell's forces. On 12 August Frederick with 50,000 men attacked 80,000 Russians and Austrians at Kunersdorf, just east of the Oder. This battle was extraordinarily bloody, costing the Prussians nearly 20,000 casualties and the Austro-Russian army more than 15,000. Frederick narrowly escaped being killed or captured, and his army disintegrated. For a brief time the city of Berlin, only fifty miles to the west, lay exposed to capture, but the victorious enemy army was exhausted and Saltykov was unwilling to risk a third battle. Frederick was given time to rebuild his army, and eventually the Russians and Austrians retreated before entering winter quarters.

Meanwhile, however, a mixed Imperial and Austrian army captured Dresden on 4 September. Daun moved the bulk of his forces from Silesia to Saxony in order to protect it. Frederick followed him and sent a 15,000-man detachment to cut his supply lines. Daun, abandoning his usual caution, moved quickly to trap the detachment. On 19 November at the Saxon town of Maxen, virtually the entire Prussian detachment surrendered. Frederick called for assistance from Ferdinand of Brunswick, who sent 12,000 men, thereby allowing Broglie to regain the initiative. The campaign finally ended with the strength of the Prussian army cut in half and Frederick's reputation for invincibility shattered.[93]

The pressure placed on the Prussians by the Austrian and Russian armies offered an opportunity for the Swedish army operating north of Berlin, but it failed to take advantage of it. The Swedish navy did somewhat better. In March Sweden and Russia signed a convention specifying that the Russians would provide a fleet of fifteen ships of the line in the Baltic while the Swedes provided ten. The one naval action of the year, however, was conducted by galleys and oared ships, a Swedish squadron defeating a Prussian squadron off Stettin, the Prussian port at the mouth of the Oder.[94]

While the campaign of 1759 harmed the reputations of the Prussian, French, and Swedish armies, it did little to improve the reputation of the Austrian army, which for most of the campaign operated sluggishly. Even Ferdinand's army performed poorly except for the Battle of Minden. The most impressive performance was that of Saltykov's Russians, but this created a variety of diplomatic problems. Empress Elizabeth rightfully grew suspicious that the Austrians intended to have Russia carry the burden of the fighting while enjoying none of the rewards of success. She volunteered to accede to the Third Treaty of Versailles, but to France's great discomfort she demanded that Austria and France guarantee her accession of East Prussia at the peace.[95]

Russia's increased assertiveness and military competence frightened Denmark even more than it did France, given Grand Duke Peter's continued unwillingness to accept Danish territorial offers in exchange for dropping his claims to Schleswig and Holstein; during 1759 Soltykov's army had been only 200 miles from the disputed territory.[96] Bernstorff's careful cultivation of neutrality kept Denmark out of the war, but left it dangerously isolated. With French support the Danes sought an alliance with Sweden but were rebuffed, as Sweden was beginning to search hesitantly for a way out of the war.[97] The Turks, too, were frightened of Russia, but Prussian attempts to make an alliance with them failed, in part because Britain, who did not wish to alienate Russia, refused to participate.[98] The state most directly affected by Saltykov's advance to the Oder, however, was Poland, which the Russians used as a staging area. The Poles were helpless to offer any resistance, in spite of the efforts of the "Secret du Roi" to rally them.

The "Secret du Roi" suffered its own problems. Tercier, its leader, lost his post as premier commis as the result of an intrigue by Madame de Pompadour and Tercier's fellow premiers commis, La Ville and Bussy. They exploited the fact that Tercier, while acting as royal censor, had permitted publication of a book considered heretical. The comte de Broglie resumed command of the "Secret" with Tercier as his adjunct, but he was on active military service with his brother the duc de Broglie and hence was unable to devote full attention to it.[99] He continued, however, to argue that the Russians could not be trusted. Against Broglie's advice, Louis sent a letter drafted by Tercier to Empress Elizabeth on behalf of the Poles, but she indignantly denied abridging Polish independence.[100] Although the "Secret" continued to exist, reminding the king of his opposition to Russian expansionism, its influence on French policy was marginal until after the end of the war. In 1760, however, it did send to Poland a new agent, Pierre-Michel Hennin, the secretary of the new French minister in Warsaw, former minister of war Paulmy. Hennin worked on behalf of the future royal candidacy of Prince François-Xavier-Louis-Auguste, who, using his title as comte de Lusace, presently was serving in the duc de Broglie's army.[101]

Choiseul, too, was aware of the Russian threat to those he called France's true allies: Denmark, the Ottoman Empire, and Sweden. Choiseul had no hope of being able to protect Poland, though, and did not have Paulmy encourage Polish resistance to Russia. While wishing to preserve the independence of Danzig, he pressured the city's magistrates to respect Russian interests. Given France's military and financial condition, there was little Choiseul could do to help Eastern Europe. France's official reply of 1 February 1760 to the Russian request to join the Third Treaty of Versailles treated the question of Russian territorial compensation as being exclusively an Austrian concern. [102] For the moment Choiseul was more concerned about the effect of a Prussian defeat on the balance of power. Underestimating Elizabeth's hatred of Frederick II, he expressed the hope to Ambassador L'Hôpital that she might act as a moderating influence on Maria Theresa and arrange peace in eastern Europe. (Oddly enough, the British and even Frederick himself also had illusions about the possibility of a reconciliation between Elizabeth and Frederick.) Such fantasizing was a sign of weakness. France had no way of pressuring Austria except the withdrawal of its subsidy, and it dared not even consider that. Choiseul was reduced to grumbling that he envied Cardinals Richelieu and Mazarin, who had fought the Habsburgs. [103] Russia and Austria, however, still offered at least indirect help against a danger even worse than the loss of France's influence in eastern Europe. Britain began to threaten France's very existence as a naval and colonial power, and Britain's only vulnerability was its commitments in Germany. The extent of France's danger became even more apparent as the terrible year of 1759 came to a conclusion so catastrophic that even the usually fearless Choiseul was shaken.

FINANCIAL CRISIS, NAVAL DISASTER, AND THE KING'S PERSONAL LOSS

The capture of Quebec came as a great shock to France. Choiseul, who had hoped to panic British investors by invading England, now saw the tables turned. The French government's credit already was badly stretched by a third year of heavy borrowing, more than 95 million livres in loans during 1759 plus 72 million livres in advances from the Farmers General. In three years it had borrowed about 365 million livres (exclusive of advances), a sum larger than the government's net tax revenues in 1759, which were only around 300 million livres (out of 620 million livres in total income, including overhead). Even so, it took a 24 million livre grant from the clergy and 8 million in additional fees on officeholders for the government to meet the roughly 500 million livres of expenses for the year; once again many payments were deferred because current income was needed to pay creditors' bills from past years.[104] The army department's budget for 1759 was 152 million livres, and the navy department's was about 57 million (although not all of it was actually provided). But it appears the army overspent its budget by about 17 million livres and the navy by even more (and this probably includes little of the navy department's Canadian expenses).[105]

The navy spent perhaps 30 million livres in the attempt to invade Britain, most of it for constructing flatboats and prames. Court banker Jean-Joseph de Laborde estimated 30 million was spent just on flatboats, which subsequently were used for transporting timber. Beaujon, Goosens, and Company, a consortium of bankers assembled by Jean Paris de Monmartel, which was involved in constructing landing craft, issued almost 27 million livres worth of bills of exchange during the first eight months of the year. Meanwhile Toulon and other naval ports continued to lay off dockyard workers.[106] The British spent at a comparable pace. British army expenses in North America were more than £1 million (equivalent to more than 24 million livres), and total spending on the army and navy (exclusive of perhaps £1.5 million or £2 million for foreign troops and subsidies) was more than £11.7 million divided roughly equally. Total government expenditures were just under £15.4 million and tax income about £8.1 million.[107] Newcastle faced a temporary shortage of funds in the summer of 1759 and had even greater difficulties in the spring of 1760, but basically the British government's credit was still sound, in part because of the string of British victories. Newcastle thus did not have to pay more than 4 percent interest.[108]

Undoubtedly, part of the reason the French navy could indulge in its lavish spending was the support of Berryer and Choiseul in the Council of State. It also was treated sympathetically by the controller general's department. On 4 March Boullongne was replaced as controller general by Etienne de Silhouette, a former member of the Canadian border commission who had been involved in secret negotiations with Britain in 1755. Silhouette, who joined the Council of State on 19 July, was a strong supporter both of the invasion and of taking whatever steps were necessary to save Canada.[109] He proved a mixed blessing for the navy, however, as he was partly to blame for the worsening of the financial crisis, which in later years had severe effects on naval budgets.

Politically naïve, Silhouette attempted to impose further taxes without consulting the Parlement of Paris, thereby arousing opposition and endangering the government's credit. When news of the loss of Quebec arrived on 15 October, the government quickly found itself unable to raise the money to pay its creditors, themselves now pressed to pay their own debts. Berryer immediately declared a moratorium on payments of Canadian bills of exchange (some dating from as long ago as 1755). Eventually 53 million of the 90 million livres in unpaid bills were rejected, and Bigot and his associates were fined and imprisoned. An appeal to Spain for a large loan was unsuccessful; Charles III reported his treasury empty. In November Beaujon, Goosens, and Company declared bankruptcy, and Laborde, the chief financier of the army and foreign ministry, narrowly escaped having to do the same. Silhouette, the target of mockery (including the use of his name to describe an outline without substance), was fired on 21 November. His replacement was the more politically astute Henry-Léonard-Jean-Baptiste Bertin, a protégé of Madame de Pompadour who had replaced Berryer as lieutenant général de police of Paris. (Bertin did not join the Council of State, however, until 6 November 1762.)

Louis XV's response to the crisis was courageous. Like Louis XIV in a similar crisis in 1709, he ordered the royal plate (silver and gold serving pieces) sent to the mint to be melted for specie, an example followed by the aristocracy and institutions like the French East India Company. Although wonderfully theatrical, this did not bring the crisis to an end; indeed, it frightened potential lenders. The government, however, gained time by suspending payments on its debts and by protecting its contractors like Beaujon, Goosens, and Company from prosecution.[110]

Even Choiseul seems to have been frightened by the military and economic reverses. On 29 October he reported to Ossun the suspension of debt payments, the sending of the royal plate to the mint, and the disappearance of credit. He warned that under the present circumstances France was no longer a commercial or even a military power and that if France were crushed Spain would become a British tributary state like Portugal. He admitted confidentially that France was dependent on peace even if it were disadvantageous and that France needed both financial and diplomatic assistance from Spain.[111] On the same day he privately warned his cousin in Vienna that France might have to make a separate peace with Britain, although it would continue to fulfill its financial obligations to Austria. In the official dispatch that accompanied his warnings, he said that even though France had accepted Spanish mediation, Conflans intended to risk a naval battle to escort Aiguillon's troops to Scotland. Should Conflans fail, France would attempt a winter campaign in Germany.[112] He wrote Ossun on 18 November that if Spain entered the war France would be unable to help and that Spain could not count on Sweden, Denmark, or Holland either; he preferred Charles as a mediator rather than an ally. *After* the war he wished to make a defensive alliance with Spain.[113]

Six days later Choiseul reported more bad news to Ossun: Conflans' fleet had suffered terrible losses in a naval battle.[114] Conflans was largely responsible for the battle. With the defeat of La Clue, the effort to invade Britain should have been abandoned and, quite likely, eventually would have been. Conflans, however, had spent the campaigning seasons of 1756, 1757, and 1759 (no fleet being outfitted at Brest in 1758) without leaving port, and such a humiliation was too much for him to contemplate. On 3 October he wrote Berryer proposing to sail from Brest and, if the odds were favorable, to seek out and attack Hawke. In any case he would proceed to Quiberon Bay on the south coast of Brittany and destroy the British squadron blockading the transports for the Scotland expedition. He feared that his remaining in port would dishonor France and embolden the British. He asked for orders leaving him the option of sailing. Eleven days later Louis issued them.[115]

Conflans was exceptionally courageous, but the Council of State should never have authorized him to undertake what was little better than a suicide mission. He had little chance of evading Hawke and, should Hawke find him, no chance whatsoever of defeating him. Conflans did, however, have a few pieces of good fortune. On 15 October a diversionary force of the *Blonde*, 32, three privateer frigates, and two smaller ships escaped from Dunkirk, carrying 1,200 soldiers to raid Ireland. Commanded by the famous privateer captain François Thurot, it eventually landed 600 troops near Belfast, although they spent only four days ashore. On their way back to France three of the ships were captured and Thurot was killed.[116] Meanwhile, on 5 November the *Achille*, 64, *Sirène*, 30, and *Zéphir*, 30, arrived at Brest from a yearlong voyage to the South Atlantic during which only the kindness of the Dutch at the Cape of Good Hope and the Portuguese in Brazil saved their crews from perishing of scurvy.[117] Two days later Bompar arrived from the Caribbean with seven ships of the line, the strong westerly winds that brought him having forced Hawke away in order to keep his ships off of a lee shore.[118] There was no question of adding any of these ships, needing cleaning and repairs, to Conflans' fleet, but he was able to add some veteran sailors and petty officers to his untrained crews, paying them a bonus. By now Conflans realized Hawke would outnumber him,[119] but it was too late for him to change his mind without humiliating himself.

On 14 November Conflans sailed from Brest with his entire fleet of twenty-one ships of the line. On the same day, reinforced, replenished, and forewarned of Conflans' intention to sail, Hawke himself sailed from his anchorage at Torbay, England, with twenty-three ships of the line, including a 100-gun ship and three 90's.[120] It took Hawke only six days to figure out Conflans' destination and sail there, arriving in the approaches to Quiberon just in time to save from capture the four British 50-gun ships blockading the sixty transports in the bay. Astonished at being intercepted, Conflans fled into Quiberon Bay, while the *Formidable*, 80, sacrificed herself in an attempt to hold off the British fleet (as the *Centaure* had done off Gibraltar). In spite of heavy winds and strong seas, Hawke's entire fleet followed Conflans into the bay, an act of extraordinary seamanship and courage. There it fought the disordered and outnumbered French fleet until nightfall forced it to anchor. The seas were so rough that the *Thésée*, 74, and the *Superbe*, 70, capsized during the battle with enormous loss of life. In the aftermath of the battle, the *Soleil-Royal*, 80, and *Héros*, 74, ran aground and subsequently were burned. The *Glorieux*, 74, *Robuste*, 74, *Brillant*, 64, *Dragon*, 64, *Eveillé*, 64, *Inflexible*, 64, and *Sphinx*, 64, managed to escape by sailing up the Vilaine River, which empties into the eastern portion of Quiberon Bay. The remaining nine French ships of the line fled out of the bay and reached Rochefort safely, except for the *Juste*, 70, which was shipwrecked off the mouth of the Loire. Saved, too, were the transports, which were in the protected Golfe du Morbihan at the western edge of the great bay and hence out of British reach. The only British losses were the *Resolution*, 74, and *Essex*, 64, which ran aground.[121] Hawke's fleet remained in the bay after the battle to prevent the escape of the ships in the Morbihan and Vilaine and soon received fresh ships to replace its damaged ones. On 25 November the French finally abandoned the attempt to invade Britain, too late to save the six ships of the line they had lost or the lives of some 2,500 officers and men. Further losses were prevented when the captains of the ships in the Vilaine refused Berryer's orders to return to Brest in spite of the British fleet in Quiberon Bay; the senior captain was imprisoned for two years as a result, and the others were relieved of their commands.[122]

The British capped their year of triumph by a diplomatic coup designed to prevent any outside interference with their gathering the fruits of their victories and adding further ones. They were concerned by the deterioration of relations with Spain, were under pressure from Prussia to convene a peace conference, and had learned that Frederick II had sought Spanish assistance to make peace. The British government therefore moved to forestall Spanish mediation or intervention, as well as to placate Frederick. On 25 November Prince Louis of Brunswick-Wolfenbüttel, brother of Ferdinand of Brunswick and the highest ranking officer in the Dutch army, brought the Austrian, French, and Russian ministers at The Hague a joint British-Prussian offer to submit their disputes to a peace congress.[123] (Britain also renewed its subsidy agreement with Prussia on 7 December.)[124]

For Louis XV this year of catastrophe ended with a terrible personal blow. Reporting on his mission to France, Kaunitz had remarked on how much time Louis spent with his children and called him the most tender of fathers. Now, at this moment of crisis, Louis' eldest and favorite daughter, Duchess Marie-

Louise-Elisabeth, contracted smallpox. On the sixth day of her illness, December 6, Louis' beloved "Babette" died of the disease that would kill her eldest daughter in 1763, her husband in 1765, and her father in 1774.[125] Louis XV was not the first French monarch to face military disaster and personal loss. In 1709, Louis XIV had seen victorious enemy armies at his borders, his navy disarmed, his finances shattered, his country facing famine. Over the next five years he saw the deaths of his son, two of his three grandsons, a beloved granddaughter-in-law, and the elder of his two great-grandsons. Nevertheless he courageously refused to make a dishonorable peace. Eventually, French victories and its enemies' exhaustion made possible a peace settlement that preserved most of France's power and prestige.[126] Now, half a century later, the younger of the mighty king's great-grandsons faced similar dangers and would have to find the courage to resist making peace until Britain was ready to compromise.

7

1760
Adversity and Revival

DISCUSSIONS AT THE HAGUE

French resolve was tested by the British and Prussian invitation of 25 November 1759 to send plenipotentiaries to a peace congress. Choiseul appears to have been surprised and puzzled. Suspicious of British intentions and sincerity, Choiseul responded cautiously; as he told Martin Hübner, a Danish agent being sent to England to discuss the seizure of Danish ships, he believed that Pitt did not really want peace, which would be his political ruin.[1] Given the recent defeat of Conflans and near French governmental bankruptcy, France hardly could close the door to a serious discussion of peace, but Choiseul also wished to save the Spanish mediation and to protect France's relations with Austria.[2] To accomplish all these goals he made use of a formula that had appeared in the instructions he had given to his cousin upon leaving for Vienna and that he repeated in a letter to Voltaire: France was involved in two wars, one against Britain in which none of the other powers of Europe was involved, the other between Austria and Prussia in which France was only an auxiliary of Austria.[3] Thus when Choiseul responded to Prince Louis on behalf of Louis XV he rejected submitting the Franco-British war to a peace conference because France already had accepted Spanish mediation and because none of the other European powers was involved in the war. On the other hand, he expressed a desire to see an end to the war on the continent and promised to consult France's allies about a conference to discuss it. He then drafted and submitted to Austria and Russia a joint declaration accepting in principle a European peace congress provided that the Franco-British war not be discussed and that the rulers of Sweden and Saxony-Poland be invited, too. This also was a way of gaining time to sound out Britain. It was certain that Maria Theresa and Elizabeth would not agree quickly on a response, if for no other reason than the length of time required for communicating between Vienna and St. Petersburg.[4]

At the beginning of January 1760, Choiseul drafted on the king's behalf a set of peace terms for Charles III to communicate to Britain under the pretext they had been written by Spain. These betrayed no signs of France's difficulties and offered few concessions. France was willing to accept the territorial settlement in North America that Mirepoix had forwarded on 8 March 1755 (i.e., the French counterproposal of 19 February 1755) and would agree to a mutual exchange of conquests, returning Minorca in exchange for Guadeloupe, Louisbourg, Quebec, Senegal, and Gorée. India would be restored to its condition as of 26 December 1754, and the neutral islands of the Caribbean would be divided, St. Vincent and Tobago going to Britain, Dominica and St. Lucia to France. There would be an armistice in Germany (leaving France in control of Wesel and the surrounding Prussian territory), and France and Britain would provide neither troops nor munitions to their allies. Although, as we shall see, Spain did not forward these proposals, they demonstrate Louis and Choiseul's firmness. On the other hand, the French leaders did not delude themselves about France's difficulties. When Starhemberg objected to the proposals (which Choiseul told him had been drafted at Spain's request), Choiseul admitted that France could not sustain the war for more than another year without Spanish help.[5]

On 1 February Charles received Britain's refusal to accept Spanish mediation until France responded to Britain and Prussia's offer of a general peace congress.[6] With Spanish involvement in the discussions stalled, Choiseul warmed to the idea of negotiating directly with Britain through their respective representatives at The Hague, d'Affry and Sir Joseph Yorke. Choiseul may have been influenced by reports from d'Affry that Yorke desired peace,[7] particularly since Yorke was the son of the Earl of Hardwicke, Newcastle's friend and fellow moderate. On 15 February d'Affry reported that Yorke was ready to forward any French proposals. Nine days later Choiseul responded that France would accept direct negotiations, about which it would keep Spain informed.[8]

These discussions were doomed from the start unless the French government was prepared to accept Britain's retention of her conquests, which as yet it was unready to do. Conversely, British public opinion was not prepared to accept the surrender of Britain's gains. Neither was Pitt, who was attentive to public opinion and considered France an inveterate enemy of Britain. The previous October he had expressed to San Severino a willingness to offer moderate terms, but the string of British victories changed his attitude; in December he told Felix de Abreu y Bertodano, the Spanish envoy to the British court, that the British would make use of the means God had given them to secure themselves in the future from the insults and infidelity of the French.[9] Henceforth, the future of France as a naval and colonial power would be in peril.

Given Pitt's intransigence, why had Britain approached France about nego-tiations? It seems the inner cabinet was responding to what it believed was a peace feeler from the French government. Soon after Pitt's comments to de Abreu, the British government received a peace feeler from Aiguillon relayed by Commodore Richard Howe at Quiberon. Almost certainly Aiguillon was acting without Choiseul's approval; Choiseul, who had served in battle with him, considered him a coward and hardly would have chosen him to initiate discussions. Although the initiative did not produce any direct results, it helped prepare the way for the inner cabinet to overrule Pitt and authorize Yorke's ap-proach to d'Affry. Other factors also were involved in the British initiative. Yorke reported that d'Affry had hinted at France's willingness to conduct discussions, Newcastle was worried about finances, and the news from Prussia was threat-ening. Ambassador Mitchell, Ferdinand, and even Frederick II himself were pessimistic about the Prussian army's being able to survive another campaign. Although Frederick was unwilling to give up any Prussian territory, he was ready to evacuate Saxony to obtain peace.

The British government decided to go ahead with discussions, but Pitt suc-cessfully insisted that the Prussians be included, fearing that if a separate agree-ment was made without them Parliament would cease its subsidy. (Pitt also may have hoped to use Prussia to destroy the negotiation.) On 25 January Holdernesse authorized Yorke to ascertain whether France was willing to con-duct separate negotiations with Britain and Prussia and, if so, to transmit any French proposals. It was in response to these instructions that Yorke delivered the message reported by d'Affry on 15 February. In March, Newcastle assured Knyphausen in writing that Prussia would be included.[10]

The Hague discussions thus were grounded in reciprocal British and French misunderstanding about the other party's readiness for serious negotiations, a misunderstanding to which Aiguillon, Yorke, and d'Affry all seem to have con-tributed. The British decision to include Frederick II in the discussions added another difficulty to those already present; there was no chance he would agree to an arrangement that did not include the French evacuation of his territories, but without Austrian permission, France could not agree to evacuate them. The French government had no desire to retain them; Choiseul already had told Bernstorff that France was willing to withdraw from Prussian territory.[11] It had no reason to want Austria to gain them, either. Choiseul apparently believed that to turn over permanently the fortress of Wesel and the surrounding territory to Austria would diminish French security, as he was uncertain of the permanency of the Franco-Austrian alliance and fearful of the growth of Austrian power.[12]

Moreover, such a transfer would disrupt the religious balance of Germany and arouse the opposition of the Protestant states of the Holy Roman Empire. Ultimately their return to Prussia was the best solution from the French standpoint, but to surrender them to Austria's enemy in advance of a general settlement without the prior approval of Maria Theresa would mean the destruction of the Franco-Austrian alliance and would put French security in peril.

France rejected conducting separate negotiations with Prussia for the same reason. With British approval, Frederick II tried to open such discussions, using the bailli René-François de Froulay, the representative at Versailles of the Knights of Malta. Choiseul rebuffed Froulay, but his reply was courteous and even hinted that France would help Prussia obtain peace. This was a sharp contrast to the prior exchange of insults between Frederick and Choiseul when Voltaire, the least inconspicuous of possible mediators, had tried to act as a peacemaker; Choiseul even had dared to mock Frederick's poetry. As Choiseul told Ossun, France had no interest in seeing Prussia crushed by Austria and the balance of power in Germany destroyed. Frederick, however, was unwilling to trust France as a mediator with Austria, particularly because France still held Wesel and other Prussian territory along the Rhine; once France rejected separate negotiations, Frederick viewed the Franco-British discussions with great suspicion. He no doubt realized that the British ran little risk in betraying him, given his financial weakness and the presence of a large British-Hanoverian army in Germany.[13]

Choiseul took great care to make sure Austria did not have similar suspicions of France. After the Prussian defeats at Kunersdorf and Maxen, final victory over Frederick appeared close. The Austrians already had been displeased by prospects of Spanish mediation, although this displeasure probably was based partially on Austrian suspicions of Spain and of Charles III, a former enemy. Choiseul communicated promptly with Starhemberg about the British-Prussian proposal, which the Austrians accepted only because they believed that without an armistice it was harmless. To sooth Austrian sensibilities about France's conducting negotiations with Britain prior to a general congress, Choiseul hinted that in the event of peace with Britain France would increase her subsidy so that Frederick II could be defeated. Choiseul had some success. Kaunitz, who had drafted his own response to the British-Prussian proposal, deferred to Choiseul's counterproposal excluding Franco-British issues from the peace congress.[14]

Empress Elizabeth of Russia was as anxious as was Maria Theresa to finish the dismemberment of Prussia, rejecting the British-Prussian declaration, which was personally delivered to her by the British ambassador, Sir Robert Keith.[15] Eventually she agreed to a joint counterdeclaration after lengthy discussions over the wording. She was able to use the impending peace congress to pressure a reluctant Austria into a new alliance treaty and convention signed in March by which the two powers agreed not to make peace without each other. In secret articles Russia was promised East Prussia if Austria obtained Silesia and Glatz, and Grand Duke Peter was promised support for his claims in Schleswig and Holstein. Choiseul, who had left the subject of Russian compensation to Maria Theresa, was not informed about the secret articles, and France subsequently chose not to accede to the other portions. Choiseul, whose chief concern seems to have been preserving France's relations with the Ottoman Empire, sent Auguste Le Tonnelier, baron de Breteuil, to serve as Ambassador L'Hôpital's adjutant. He hoped Breteuil would win the support of Grand Duke Peter's wife, Catherine, and possibly even become her lover. Breteuil also had instructions from the "Secret du Roi" to help the Poles. His mission was a failure, although when L'Hôpital returned to France for health reasons in mid-1761, Breteuil became his successor.[16]

The discussions between d'Affry and Yorke thus faced insuperable obstacles. These discussions began with a meeting in d'Affry's coach on the evening of 4 March 1760 and continued thereafter on a daily basis.[17] From the very beginning Yorke's insistence on the inclusion of a Franco-Prussian agreement as part of a settlement with Britain created a deadlock. The French made several attempts to break the impasse. Besides promising that *after* an agreement with Britain they would intervene with Austria on Prussia's behalf, they offered to include Hanover, Hesse, and Brunswick in the Franco-British agreement (leaving French forces occupying only the Prussian territories) and thereafter to work for a general peace. They failed to win over George II, who was little disposed toward peace unless Hanover made territorial gains; his professions of wishing a just and honorable peace were the work of Hardwicke and did not reflect the king's actual feelings.[18]

Choiseul also volunteered to send an envoy to Britain to discuss American issues. After his initial choice, Jacques O'Dunne, was rejected as being a Jacobite (a supporter of the Stuarts), he chose Lieutenant General Antoine de Ricouart, comte d'Hérouville de Claye. Meanwhile, on 3 April d'Affry finally was able to present Yorke a joint counterdeclaration of France, Austria, and Russia accepting a peace congress and proposing the German city of Augsburg as the site.[19] No further progress toward a congress was made, however, largely because negotiations for a preliminary Franco-British agreement soon collapsed. On 25 April the inner cabinet instructed Yorke to inform d'Affry that, although Hérouville was an acceptable choice as an envoy, there was no point in his coming to England, the inclusion of Prussia being a *sine qua non* which France had not accepted. Ten days later Yorke so informed d'Affry, who informally terminated the discussions. Thereafter the French ambassador took leave and returned to France. Choiseul maintained the pretense that the talks were only suspended so as not to be blamed for their failure and in order to facilitate the French government's attempts to borrow money.

The failure of the discussions exposed France to grave danger. According to Hardwicke, Pitt believed the way to obtain a general peace was to so crush France that in her desperation she would coerce her allies into making peace, too.[20] For his part, Choiseul continued to argue as he had since the beginning of his ministry that either the tide of war would turn or even without military victories French endurance would bring a successful peace; he would make similar comments in 1761.[21] From Choiseul's perspective the failed negotiations at least had accomplished one thing. Austria had accepted the principle of separate French discussions with Britain; this would make future peace talks easier.[22] On the other hand, he was disappointed in Charles III of Spain and in Charles's ministers, particularly foreign minister Ricardo Wall. The new king arrived in Madrid on 9 December 1759. His bellicosity changed as soon as he learned of the poor condition of the Spanish army, navy, colonial defenses, and finances.[23] Even after Britain rebuffed Spanish mediation, Choiseul attempted to involve Charles in peace negotiations, stressing the importance of Frederick's not being totally abased, which would affect the balance of power in Italy as well as Germany. Charles expressed his sympathy for France and his support for the discussions at The Hague, even assigning an observer, Pablo Jerónimo Grimaldi y Pallavicini, marquis de Grimaldi, the Spanish minister to the United Provinces of the Netherlands. No longer, though, did he speak of mediation with its implied threat of force; instead he proposed offering his good offices to the belligerents. Foreign Minister Wall reassured British Ambassador Bristol of Spain's good intentions and said that the mention of Spanish mediation in the French-Austrian-Russian counterdeclaration was on French insistence, not Spanish. Charles even refused Choiseul's request that he present the French peace terms as if coming from Spain, in spite of earlier assurances he would do so. Instead he decided to transmit another offer of his good offices by a new ambassador to George II, who did not even reach England until after the end of the discussions at The Hague. Choiseul did not despair of eventual Spanish assistance, but it was obvious that for the moment Charles was unprepared to help France, even though he called France Spain's natural and necessary ally.[24]

With the failure to achieve a negotiated settlement with Britain, France faced a war of attrition. The strategy of invading England had failed miserably, and what was left of New France was indefensible. Of necessity, France would have to return to her former strategy of attacking the one vulnerable possession of George II, his electorate of Hanover. In doing so Louis XV dared not cut the budget of the French army, no matter how shaky his credit. Initially the army was assigned only 120 million livres, but in March Belle-Isle was able to win the approval of the Council of State for additional funds (rather than its spending extra money on the navy). During 1760 the army was authorized to spend about 150 million livres, almost equal to what was appropriated in 1759. Doubtless it actually spent more, as Choiseul claimed the war in Germany alone was costing 150 million a year.[25] Such massive spending was possible only because Bertin, the astute new controller general, was able to borrow 130 million livres in general loans and win the approval of the Parlement of Paris for more than 100 million livres in tax increases by limiting their duration. Extraordinary revenue increased by almost 30 million livres over that of 1759, even though the government's total income slightly declined.

In spite of Bertin's success, the maintenance of the government's credit hinged on reduction of its expenses, so that it could begin to repay its creditors. It was the French navy which suffered the most severe cuts. The army's budget needed to be maintained, it was politically dangerous to make major cuts in domestic expenses, and only limited savings could be made by reducing foreign subsidies. (Payments to Sweden were reduced and payments to Denmark were suspended, with overall spending on subsidies dropping from about 19 million livres in 1759 to between 13 million and 15.5 million in 1760, including nearly 9 million to Austria.) Berryer did not have the social prestige to carry weight in the Council of State; moreover, Conflans' humiliating defeat had brought the navy into disrepute.[26] Thus, in spite of the continuing need to defend the French West Indies, Berryer had to cut spending drastically and largely demobilize the navy.

THE FRENCH NAVY'S REDUCED BUDGET

In 1759 the French navy department's budget had been almost 57 million livres. For 1760 Berryer requested 40 million livres, but was authorized to spend only 30 million. This eventually was reduced to about 23.7 million; moreover, more than half was needed to pay bills from previous years.[27] The faithful Berryer, who had offered his resignation, was left to bear the blame for implementing the cuts, which, to his concern, fell particularly hard on dockyard workers. Moreover, no officers were promoted to flag rank in 1759 or 1760, and the number of officers in general began a steady decline; by war's end the number of *capitaines de vaisseau* had dropped by a third. Supposedly Berger even refused to pay for food for the cats used to protect the dockyards from rodents.[28] As terrible as were the sacrifices made by the navy, the budget cuts helped to preserve the army's budget and, as we shall see, this ultimately helped prevent the British from imposing a draconian peace that would have severely damaged France's subsequent ability to compete with Britain as a naval and colonial power. It should be noted, too, that this hardly was the first occasion France had to curtail naval operations to concentrate its resources on the army, so the reduction hardly was unprecedented. Indeed, the Old Régime French navy never fought more than five campaigns against the British in any war before hostilities ended or drastic cutbacks were made.

The near cessation of naval operations, moreover, did help to slow the terrible hemorrhage of sailors, as only 4,000 prisoners were captured by the British navy and privateers during the year (although this low number was also in part a result of the reduced condition of French trade and the small number of privateers).[29] It also stemmed the drain of the navy's warships. By the end of 1759 the navy had been reduced to forty-seven ships of the line, a decline of seven during the year. (La Clue lost five and Conflans six, while only three, the *Royal-Louis*, 116, *Thésée*, 74, and *Modeste*, 64, were launched, and one, the East India Company ship *Orient*, 80, was purchased.) Only the *Sagittaire*, 50, joined the *Impétueux*, 90, *Protecteur*, 74, and *Altier*, 64, in construction. During 1760, the navy actually increased in size. Only two ships of the line were lost, both irreparably damaged by January storms, the *Illustre*, 64, by the Indian Ocean typhoon discussed in the previous chapter (although she was not formally condemned until October) and the *Inflexible*, 64, by an Atlantic gale that struck the ships trapped in the Vilaine. Only the *Protecteur* and *Altier* were launched during the year (and only one ship of the line was begun, the *Entêté*, 64), but the navy was able to purchase four other ships of the line for a bargain price of 500,000 livres apiece. After La Clue's defeat, Charles-Louis Merle, comte de Beauchamps, the French ambassador at Lisbon, suggested purchasing two large Genoese ships (presently in port there) that could carry 64 cannon apiece. During 1760 the French government purchased four such ships from their Genoese owner, the *Sainte-Anne*, *Notre-Dame-de-Rosaire*, *Vierge-de-Santé*, and *Saint-François-de-Paule*. Ultimately these ships, although of recent construction, did not prove very durable as they were constructed of fir rather than oak; Machault had rejected them in 1755. They were first used to carry supplies, but then served as regular ships of the line for a relatively brief period, the last of them being taken out of service in 1772.[30]

The dockyard at Toulon was particularly productive. Not only were the two new ships of the line launched there, but it also built a magnificent model of a 64-gun ship of the line for Louis XV's bereaved nine-year-old grandson, Prince Ferdinand of Parma, whom the king had never seen (and to whom he continued to send presents and advice).[31]

The main effect of the budget cuts was on naval operations. As in 1758 no fleet was outfitted at Brest or Rochefort; fortunately, the British did not make any landings on the French coast. The British navy, however, continued to interrupt French shipping and to prevent the return to Brest of the ships of the line trapped in the Vilaine. Their captains held a conference on 30 April and 1 May. On their recommendation Berryer decided that sailing jointly would be too risky. Instead, he ordered the ships to sail at night, two at a time, in order to elude the British squadron in Quiberon Bay. He appointed two promising junior officers, Lieutenants de vaisseau Charles-Henry-Louis d'Arsac de Ternay (who had devised the escape plan) and Jean-Charles, comte d'Hector, to command the first two, the *Brillant*, 64, and *Dragon*, 64, and temporarily disarmed the others. For months they awaited the right combination of a moonless night, high tides, and a favorable wind, but it had not yet occurred at year's end.[32]

The French also were fortunate that the British did not send troops to attack Martinique. In January 1760 Pitt drafted orders for Amherst to send 8,000 troops to the West Indies at the beginning of the following autumn, but apparently did not send them.[33] Berryer wished to send a dozen ships of the line to Martinique (which Choiseul expected to be attacked), but this would have cost 12 million livres. Although the Council of State spent most of March 1760 debating the matter, the money was spent on the army instead. Even plans to send the *Magnifique*, 74, and *Intrépide*, 74, to Martinique were stillborn, although a squadron of three frigates did take 200 grenadiers there (the *Fleur-de-Lys*, 30, *Sirène*, 30, and *Valeur*, 20, all three of which were captured or destroyed by year's end). Meanwhile, the *Diadème*, 74, sailed from Brest for St. Domingue in May, but she was chased by the British into Corunna and did not arrive until 17 November; after spending six weeks at St. Domingue she returned to Brest. The *Vaillant*, 64, which had been left in the West Indies by Bompar, thus was the only ship on station during the summer of 1759; she returned to Lorient in the autumn, arriving in November. French trade with the Western Hemisphere reached its lowest point during the war (and French trade in general diminished), although privateering at Martinique flourished; Commodore James Douglas, commanding the British Leeward Islands fleet, reported on 4 July that forty-seven privateers were at sea and others in port.[34]

The French navy was able to mount a cruise of four ships of the line to the central and eastern Mediterranean for convoying shipping, but only because the chamber of commerce of Marseilles loaned the navy most of the money to outfit the squadron.[35] The navy was able to accomplish less in the Indian Ocean. D'Aché's fleet might have been able to provide some help to Lally-Tollendal in India, even though the January typhoon had disabled most of its ships, had not orders arrived in June to remain at the Mascarenes to protect against an anticipated British invasion. Thus Lally-Tollendal was forced to fight the British with the assistance of only two East India Company frigates. This proved fatal. On 22 January 1760 he was badly beaten at the Battle of Wandiwash, forty miles northwest of Pondicherry. Demoralized, he watched passively as the British gradually captured French outposts. By the end of the summer Pondicherry itself was surrounded by land and blockaded by sea. On 8 December a force of four British battalions began siege works, as Lally-Tollendal waited vainly for the arrival of a French fleet. Not even a typhoon that struck the British fleet could save him; on 15 January 1761 he and his 1,400 starving troops surrendered. Within months the few remaining French East India Company posts surrendered as well.[36] In compensation, the squadron of Estaing that raided the Persian Gulf in 1759 temporarily captured several British posts in Sumatra before returning to the Mascarenes in April 1761. Five months later Estaing sailed for France on an East India Company ship.[37]

The Mascarene Islands were poorly defended, although on 10 July the regiment of Cambrésis (containing one battalion) arrived at the island of Ile de France and was retained there rather than proceeding to India as had been planned. The islands, nevertheless, almost certainly would have fallen had the British invaded. The inner cabinet considered sending an expeditionary force from England, but setbacks suffered by the British army in Germany forced postponement of the operation and it was never undertaken.[38] Unfortunately for France the success of its armies in Germany came too late to save what was left of French Canada.

THE END OF FRENCH CANADA

When Lévis and Vaudreuil sent Le Mercier to France after the fall of Quebec, Lévis estimated that his forces for the next campaign would include 2,400 regulars, 1,100 or 1,200 marines, and possibly 1,000 or 2,000 Indians. He asked for reinforcements of 6,000 regulars and 4,000 recruits for the eight existing regular battalions so that Quebec could be recaptured, but he warned that unless help were sent, France could not count on the survival of Montreal past the end of May.[39] The *Machault* reached Brest on 23 December, and soon after the beginning of 1760 Le Mercier presented to the French court Lévis and Vaudreuil's appeal. Le Mercier also submitted his own memorandum urging that troops and supplies be sent by the end of February so they could arrive at the St. Lawrence before the British. If so, an attack on Quebec could be made in May.[40]

Sending a substantial number of troops on so desperate a mission was out of the question as they would have to risk interception by the British squadron at Halifax. It also was impossible to send the supplies requested by Le Mercier, which the navy department estimated would cost 8 million livres. Berryer was unable even to obtain private financing for sending a squadron to Canada as a privateering venture. Nonetheless he did the best he could, refitting the *Machault* and at considerable expense sending her and five supply ships from Bordeaux; the *Machault* alone cost more than 100,000 livres, although Berryer cut his expenses by permitting all the ships to carry some private cargo. The tiny convoy, carrying supplies and 400 recruits, was intercepted by a British squadron soon after its 10 April sailing, and only the *Machault* and two other ships escaped. They reached the mouth of the St. Lawrence on 14 May, only to discover that the British had arrived a week earlier and were now upriver. They sailed instead to the Baie des Chaleurs on the opposite side of the Gaspé Peninsula and sent a messenger overland to Montreal with news of their arrival.[41]

The death of the chronically pessimistic Montcalm at least had brought unity between the commanding officers in Canada. Vaudreuil and Lévis reacted to their peril with a common energy, enthusiasm, and spirit of cooperation. They decided not to wait for reinforcements before attempting to recapture the fortified city of Quebec. Lévis rebuilt his army by joining 2,200 militia to his eight battalions of regulars and to the two battalions into which his marine companies now were combined. Rather than intermingling militia and regulars as Montcalm had done, he kept the militia together as companies of attached light infantry with their own Canadian officers, three companies serving with each of the ten battalions. By the end of the winter his reconstituted army had approximately 6,000 men in regular battalions, plus other militia (including 200 cavalry) and a few hundred Indians. Establishing a detachment at Cap-Rouge, less than ten miles from Quebec, he was able to maintain a loose blockade of the city.[42]

Brigadier General James Murray, left in command of the 7,000-man British garrison, saw his troops ravaged by scurvy and other diseases. By late April 1760, some 700 of the garrison were dead and almost 3,000 ill.[43]

As soon as the St. Lawrence was free of ice, Lévis brought his main body of troops from Montreal under the escort of Vauquelin's two remaining frigates, the *Pomone* and *Atalante*, landing at Pointe-aux-Trembles (twenty miles from the city) on 24 April. Four days later, as Lévis' 7,000 men approached, Murray attacked them at Ste. Foy, just north of the site of Montcalm's battle of the previous September. As with most battles of the war, the advantage lay with the troops on the defensive. The difference in casualties was not great. Murray's 3,900 men suffered more than 1,000 killed, wounded, or captured, while Lévis lost 850 of the 3,900 French and Canadians who participated in the battle. Murray, however, was forced to retreat to the city with his army as demoralized as

Montcalm's had been. Had Lévis attempted to storm the city's fortifications in the immediate aftermath of the battle he might have succeeded, but instead he mounted a siege, giving Murray the opportunity to restore discipline. Lévis was outnumbered in cannon, having only twenty light field pieces he had captured on the battlefield, while Murray could bring sixty cannon to bear on the advancing siege works; the French also were desperately short of gunpowder. Moreover, Murray had spent the winter improving the city's fortifications and soon before the battle he had expelled its civilian population. Lévis, faced with some of the same difficulties as Lally-Tollendal had encountered at Madras, could only hope for the arrival of the arms, supplies, and men requested by Le Mercier.[44]

It was Murray, however, who received assistance. On the evening of 15 May Commodore Robert Swanton arrived from England with the *Vanguard*, 70, and *Diane*, 32. They joined the *Lowestoff*, 28, which had sailed with them and had arrived a few days earlier. The following day the *Diane* and *Lowestoff* engaged Vauquelin's frigates, capturing the *Atalante* and driving the *Pomone* aground. Lévis now had no way of bringing supplies by small boats without their being intercepted. He had to lift the siege and abandon his irreplaceable cannon. During the night of 16–17 May he began his retreat toward Montreal. On the 18th the five ships of the line Saunders had left to winter at Halifax arrived at Quebec. Over the next six weeks more British warships arrived; by 1 June there were a dozen ships of the line in North America and another five on the way. Three of these ships of the line, the *Fame*, 74, *Dorsetshire*, 70, and *Achilles*, 60, convoyed workers to Louisbourg to demolish the fortifications. They were available when the *Machault*'s squadron from Bordeaux was discovered hiding in the little Restigouche River, which flows into the Baie des Chaleurs. On 8 July they came and destroyed it.[45]

Lévis later told Berryer that had a single French frigate arrived before Swanton did, he could have recaptured Quebec.[46] This seems unlikely, and even had Lévis retaken the city he would have had great difficulty holding it. Montreal, his source of supplies, was no longer protected by the forts of Lake Champlain; once Montreal fell, his army at Quebec could have been starved into surrender.

Once the siege of Quebec had been lifted, French Canada was doomed. Against ten French battalions the British had twenty-five battalions of regulars from the previous year and three newly raised battalions of light infantry (the one-battalion 90th regiment and the two-battalion 95th) plus 16,000 to 18,000 provincial troops (somewhat short of Pitt's request) and nearly 1,000 Indians. In all, there were some 45,000 officers and men.[47] Lévis could no longer count on help from the militia, now so demoralized that even those serving in regular and marine battalions began deserting. (The British helped prompt desertions by burning the homes of militiamen who did not desert and sparing the homes of those who did.) The frontier was quiet except for a Cherokee war against South Carolina, which required sending 1,300 regulars and 700 Virginia provincial troops to Charles Town (and 2,200 regulars again in 1761).[48] Only the tiny newly built forts at the Ile-aux-Noix and at the outlet of Lake Ontario prevented the British from marching down the Richelieu and St. Lawrence valleys to Montreal, which had no natural defenses.

The conquest of the remainder of Canada should have required little time once the siege of Quebec was broken, but the British commander in North America was the timid Amherst, whom Pitt left free to devise his own strategy. Amherst's final campaign against the French was so complex and time-consuming that he was unable thereafter to send troops to the Caribbean or to attack Mobile or New Orleans as Pitt had hoped.[49] It resembled the end game of a poor chess player bringing every piece into action against an opponent with nothing left but a few pawns rather than quickly moving to checkmate. Amherst's plan involved the simultaneous convergence of three separate columns at Montreal. It took sixteen weeks from the lifting of the siege of Quebec to accomplish.

Although Montreal was less than 50 miles from the northern end of Lake Champlain, Amherst decided to concentrate his largest body of troops at Oswego, some 200 miles from Montreal. He took personal command of this force and of the squadron built at Niagara to seize command of Lake Ontario from the *Iroquoise* and *Outaouaise*. It was not until mid-July that the last British warship was launched and Amherst's army of almost 11,000 men was assembled. On 10 August his army departed from Oswego in small boats, under the escort of two new 18-gun warships as well as smaller ships. To block his passage down the St. Lawrence, the French had built a small fort, Fort Lévis, in the middle of the river 100 miles upstream of Montreal. Ably commanded by Capt. Pierre Pouchot, the former commander of Fort Niagara, its 250 men and 35 cannon (supported by the two 10-gun French warships) managed to delay Amherst for a week before the *Outaouaise* was captured, the *Iroquoise* scuttled, and the fort bombarded into surrender. Between Fort Lévis and Montreal were a series of dangerous rapids. Rather than disembarking his troops, Amherst, fearing Indian attack, left them aboard his small boats to run the rapids. Eighty men were drowned. His army finally reached Montreal on 6 September.[50]

It is difficult to believe this huge expedition was necessary. Vaudreuil and Lévis did not divert a significant number of troops to oppose it. The main body of French troops contested the passage of the other two British columns, which reached Montreal at the same time as did Amherst. The British, moreover, had little reason to fear Lévis escaping to Detroit or the Illinois country as long as Fort Niagara was adequately garrisoned. Instead some of Amherst's troops might have been used to bolster the column of Brigadier General William Haviland at Lake Champlain, leaving the remainder for use in the Gulf of Mexico or the Caribbean. Haviland's force of 3,400 men departed by boat from the newly constructed Fort Crown Point (adjacent to Fort St. Frédéric) on Lake Champlain on 11 August. Four days later it reached a small French fort at the Isle-aux-Noix in the Richelieu River, defended by Bougainville with 1,500 men, the schooner *Vigilante*, 10, and a few smaller ships. Haviland was delayed for two weeks until Bougainville, out of provisions, evacuated the fort and retreated toward Montreal. Other French forts along the Richelieu valley were abandoned without a fight. Haviland met little resistance on his march to the south bank of the St. Lawrence opposite Montreal, which he reached on 5 September.[51]

The smallest of the three British columns, the 2,200 men brought 150 miles upriver from Quebec by General Murray, was the first, however, to arrive at Montreal. His troops came on forty transports, escorted by two frigates and a number of smaller ships. They landed only to terrorize villages along the river into surrender. Their major challenge was passing through the small Richelieu rapids of the St. Lawrence. Once past them they had an easy voyage, as Lévis did not have cannon on shore or warships on the river to contest their passage. Murray sailed past the main French defenses at Trois Rivières without difficulty and, reinforced by two battalions from Louisbourg, reached the Montreal area on 27 August, where he paused to await the other two columns.[52]

Once Amherst and Haviland arrived, the British had 17,000 men to oppose Lévis' army of barely 2,000, which was shrinking daily from desertions. When Vaudreuil asked for surrender terms, Amherst refused to grant honors of war because of prior Indian atrocities. Lévis was so outraged that he wished to continue fighting, but Vaudreuil, wishing to avert further suffering, overruled him and on 8 September surrendered all of Canada but not the Illinois country and the rest of Louisiana. Some 2,000 disarmed regulars and marines, many of them married to Canadian women, were permitted to remain.[53] Later in 1760 the British took possession of Trois Rivières, Fort Sandusky, Fort Detroit, and an Acadian settlement on the Restigouche. The following year they occupied Fort Michilimackinac in the straits between Lake Huron and Lake Michigan. Some 200 French soldiers from Fort Detroit, however, managed to march for more than seven months to reach New Orleans.[54]

The British conquest of Canada had unfortunate consequences, even for the conquerors. The process of modernizing the administration of the British Empire sooner or later would have disrupted Great Britain's hitherto relatively amicable relations with its North American colonies, but the Canadian conquest greatly speeded the process. The retention of a large British army in North America, the attempts of the British government to make the American colonies pay for the troops, the preservation of the governmental institutions of Canada, and finally the inclusion of the Upper Country within Canada's borders aroused American suspicions and helped lead to the American Revolution.[55]

For the losers the results were even worse. The conquest of Canada ended the balance of power in North America upon which some degree of Indian independence was dependent. Within a short time, it proved a disaster even for such Indian allies of Great Britain as the Iroquois. Amherst and his superiors in Britain quickly violated their promises to the Indians. Upon learning that the terms of the peace treaty meant the French would not be returning to the Upper Country, the Indian peoples along the British frontier rose in revolt. In spite of their new unity, their usual military prowess, and Amherst's incompetence, the Indians failed to capture Fort Pitt or Fort Detroit because they lacked the capacity for a European-style siege. The war of 1763–64, commonly called by the name of the Indian leader Pontiac, was only partially a British victory, but it began an irreversible process which led to the loss of the lands and liberty of the tribes of the Upper Country. For them the fall of French Canada was a tragedy of unprecedented dimensions.[56]

For the French inhabitants of Canada, too, the end of New France was tragic. The British did not have the resources to rule directly so large and distant a province. They gradually left to the clergy and large landowners a share in the governing of Canada, but took over its trade and in the process helped change the character of its people and its society. The adventurous and relatively egalitarian world of the *voyageurs* slowly lost its collective self-confidence and spirit of initiative as it assumed the conservative values of landowners and priests. Perhaps this would have occurred even without the British conquest, and certainly one may prefer the orderly and peaceable Québécois of the nineteenth century to their violent ancestors. The tragedy is that we shall never know what the people and their society would have become had they had the opportunity to evolve on their own (even though that prospect was unlikely, given Canada's small population and weak economy).[57] It should be noted, however, that not all French Canadians remained passive in the face of British restrictions on their political freedom. In 1837 the "Patriots" of the Richelieu River valley finally rose in a valiant but doomed revolt.[58]

For France itself the fall of Canada was a terrible warning more than a significant loss in itself, since Canada was a financial and military drain on the resources of the mother country. France was in danger of losing her other colonies in the Western Hemisphere and, of equal importance, faced the threat that Britain would retain a monopoly of the Newfoundland and St. Lawrence fisheries upon the signing of peace. Pitt, who hitherto had been willing to consider exchanging Louisbourg or even Canada, now insisted that France be excluded from the fisheries.[59] Without both the sugar colonies of the Caribbean and a share in the North Atlantic fisheries, France would lose the means of training enough sailors to rebuild itself as a great naval and colonial power. With the future of the French navy at stake, its one hope, ironically enough, was the French army.

THE REVIVAL OF THE FRENCH ARMY IN GERMANY

The campaign of 1760 completed the destruction of French power in North America and India. The British were optimistic that 1760 also would see Ferdinand's army follow up the victory at Minden by driving the French from Germany. During the late spring and summer, the British government sent some 10,000 soldiers to reinforce Ferdinand and hired 3,000 more Hessians. Ferdinand was able to put into the field an army of 80,000 men, including 22,000 Britons and 24,500 Hessians. To facilitate this, Parliament created six new infantry regiments, two regiments of dragoons, and at least twenty independent companies of infantry. This increased the number of British troops paid by Parliament to approximately 100,000, plus 65,000 foreign troops and 27,000 militia. (Also there were 12,000 troops paid by the Irish Parliament and troops raised by Britain's American colonies.) This was enormously expensive. Compared to 1759, British army expenditures rose by £2.5 million (to £8.25 million, equivalent to almost 200 million livres) while spending on the navy dropped by about 10 percent (to less than £5.5 million); total government expenditures were nearly £18 million, half of the money being borrowed.[60]

Pitt, once an opponent of continental involvements, wished Ferdinand to take the offensive and hence took an active part in the sending of what Newcastle called the "glorious reinforcement." Given Pitt's extreme sensitivity to public opinion, this was a sign of how popular in the aftermath of Minden the German war had become.[61] Although this support was wide, it was not deep. The public, including those relative few who elected the House of Commons, expected results from such a major and expensive effort. Pitt, for his part, seems to have accepted the fact that defeating France in North America would not be sufficient to force the French to accept peace terms dictated by Britain. Ferdinand would have to deprive the French of any hope that by conquering Hanover or by retaining the Prussian territories along the Rhine they could obtain easier peace terms.

British optimism was grounded not only on the increased strength of Ferdinand's army but also upon the wretched performance of Contades' army at Minden. Contades' replacement, the duc de Broglie, who had demonstrated his competence on the battlefield at Bergen, now showed himself also a superb administrator. Building on the reforms introduced by Belle-Isle, he reorganized his army by combining its regiments and squadrons into infantry and cavalry divisions and by forming light infantry companies like those of Lévis in Canada; he also maintained greater secrecy about the army's movements and was attentive to the well-being of his soldiers. He was rude and tactless to his fellow generals and even to Belle-Isle, who disliked both him and his brother, the comte de Broglie, but Choiseul and Madame de Pompadour protected him. In spite of disliking Broglie, Belle-Isle by great efforts managed to increase his army to 150,000 men, of which some 20,000 were garrison troops, leaving 130,000 available for use in the field.[62]

Broglie was ordered to advance north into Hesse and thus toward Hanover, rather than east toward Saxony, which would have risked subordinating his army to the Austrian war against Frederick.[63] He was able to begin his campaign in late June before Ferdinand was ready to undertake the offensive himself. He quickly forced the British and Germans to retreat. On 10 July Broglie won the first battle of the campaign at Korbach (twenty-five miles west of the Hessian capital of Cassel), during which Ferdinand's nephew and brilliant subordinate, Karl Wilhelm Ferdinand, Hereditary Prince (Erbprinz) of Brunswick-Wolfenbüttel, was slightly wounded; in response the British added three elite guards battalions to the "glorious reinforcement." As Broglie continued his advance, one of his wings was beaten at Warburg (twenty miles northeast of Korbach) on 31 July, but on the same day other of his troops captured Cassel. Broglie had advanced fifty miles from his starting point and was at the southern border of the electorate of Hanover, but logistical problems brought his advance to an end. Ferdinand, however, did not have enough troops to recapture Cassel, and the British government was unwilling to send him further reinforcements.[64]

Ferdinand now devised a daring plan not only to break the stalemate but also to drive the French army across the Rhine. In great secrecy he collected a 24,000-man striking force for his nephew. On 23 September it began a rapid 120-mile march west to the great fortress of Wesel, which was garrisoned by only 1,500 French troops. Broglie, caught by surprise, reacted far too slowly to save the fortress, but by good fortune a new interim commander for the Lower Rhine, Belle-Isle's young nephew Lieutenant General Charles-Eugène-Gabriel de La Croix, marquis de Castries, arrived on 2 October at Cologne, fifty miles south of Wesel. Some 12,000 men (eighteen battalions of infantry and a few squadrons of cavalry) were en route from Flanders, Normandy, and Brittany to join him, the British posing no menace at the moment to the French coast. When they arrived, Castries rushed to save Wesel. The Hereditary Prince had sent part of his army across the Rhine to complete its encirclement. Castries sent 600 men on boats past the enemy to join the garrison, while he followed with his main body. Before he could reach it, the Hereditary Prince attacked him. Before dawn on 16 October he launched a surprise assault on Castries' army, which was encamped near the convent of Clostercamp (or Kloster Kamp), ten miles southwest of Wesel. Castries had sent out numerous patrols, however, and was able to detect the attackers. By the narrowest of margins the British and Germans were defeated in the ensuing battle, Castries suffering 2,800 casualties among the 7,000 troops which participated, while the Hereditary Prince suffered 1,600 casualties to his 7,500 men. The Hereditary Prince subsequently withdrew across the Rhine, abandoned his siege, and retreated to rejoin his uncle's main force, ending the campaign of 1760.

Although small in scale, Clostercamp was one of the most important battles of not only the war but the entire century. Ricardo Wall, the astute Spanish foreign minister, believed the loss of Wesel would have forced the French to withdraw their entire army across the Rhine. It certainly would have threatened all the French supply lines north of Frankfurt and would virtually have eliminated all possibility of the French capturing Hanover. Without hope of putting pressure on Britain it is hard to see how the French could have avoided accepting British terms that would have ended France's participation in the Newfoundland fisheries. Thus she would have had little possibility of rebuilding a navy strong enough to challenge the British. Without the French victory at Clostercamp there is little chance there would have been a victory such as Yorktown twenty-one years later. There also were personal connections between the two battles. Two of Castries' subordinates were Lieutenant General Philippe-Henri, marquis de Ségur, who was wounded and captured at the beginning of the battle, and Brigadier of Infantry Jean-Baptiste-Donatien de Vimeur, comte de Rochambeau, a regimental commander and one of Clostercarp's greatest heroes. Rochambeau commanded French forces at Yorktown, while Castries was naval minister and Ségur army minister.[65]

It was not only Britain that hoped in vain to bring the war to a successful conclusion during 1760. The victory of Daun at Maxen at the end of 1759 had led Maria Theresa to expect the Prussian army soon would be destroyed, and even Frederick feared this would happen. In spite of the terrible losses of the previous year, however, Frederick gradually was able to rebuild the Prussian army in numbers if not in quality. He still was badly outnumbered. During 1760 he had to fight about 230,000 Austrians, Imperial troops, Russians, and Swedes with only 100,000 to 110,000 men.[66] While the Prussian army was slightly smaller, Maria Theresa's was a few thousand larger: 155,000 infantry (including garrison troops) and 47,500 cavalry.[67]

The campaign began well for the Austrians. While Frederick II was watching

Daun in Saxony and his brother Prince Henry was watching the Russians along the eastern border of Prussia, the Austrians enjoyed a large superiority of numbers in Silesia. During June and July the Austrian army in Silesia enjoyed great success under its commander, Lieutenant General Gideon Ernst, Freiherr von Loudon (born Gideon Ernst Laudon), who the previous year had commanded the Austrian contingent at the Battle of Kunersdorf. Loudon destroyed a small Prussian army at Landeshut and captured the fortress of Glatz, adjoining Silesia. Only the arrival of Prince Henry at the beginning of August prevented him from capturing Breslau. Meanwhile Frederick unsuccessfully besieged Dresden. After failing, he shocked Europe by spitefully destroying the Elector of Saxony's beautiful gardens at nearby Pirna.

Frederick now took his army to Silesia where he was followed by Daun, while 60,000 Russians approached from the north. Frederick had placed himself in terrible peril. Daun, for all his caution, had attacked him successfully at Hochkirch in 1758, and another such victory could have been fatal to the Prussian army, given the difficulties of retreat through the mountainous terrain in which it was operating. By the slimmest of margins, however, Frederick managed to escape. At first light on 15 August, Daun's 90,000 Austrians attacked Frederick's 30,000-man army near the Silesian village of Leignitz. (The Russians had sent 25,000 men to join Daun, but they did not arrive in time to participate.) During the night, however, Frederick had abandoned most of his lines to concentrate his forces on his left wing. Thus more than two-thirds of the Austrian army did not share in the fighting. The 25,000-man Austrian right wing, commanded by Loudon, found themselves attacking the entire Prussian army and were defeated before the rest of the Austrian army could join them. Daun did not renew the fighting, and Frederick was able to retreat to safety, joining his army with Prince Henry's and occupying an impregnable position in the mountains. The Russians, who had played little part in the campaign, fearing that they would have to bear the brunt of the fighting as they had in 1759, soon retreated. Before leaving, however, they helped participate with the Austrians in an October raid on Berlin, which they occupied for four days before the arrival of a relief force; the occupiers did little damage to the city, the Russian commander having been bribed by the Prussians. The Russians also participated with the Swedes in a siege of the Prussian fortified port of Kolberg (now Kołobrzeg, Poland), twenty-five miles northeast of the estuary of the Oder. The siege failed, in spite of the participation of twenty-one Russian and six Swedish ships of the line.

The final portion of the campaign took place in Saxony, to which Daun and Frederick brought most of their troops following the relief of Berlin. On 27 September Imperial troops captured the city of Torgau in northern Saxony, only seventy-five miles south of Berlin. Frederick moved to recapture it and Daun to defend it. On 3 November the two adversaries fought their last great battle. The Prussians by the slimmest of margins dislodged the Austrians from their defensive position and forced them to evacuate Torgau. About a third of the 48,000 participating Prussians and 30 percent of the 52,000 or 53,000 participating Austrians were killed, wounded, or captured. The campaign ended with the two opponents in much the same position as it began, except for the Austrian capture of Glatz.[68] As a result Maria Theresa lost much of her appetite for continuing a war whose objectives were beginning to seem unobtainable. In September Austria had responded negatively to Choiseul's complaints that the situation of the French treasury, commerce, and colonies required making peace. (Austria's official response was delayed, however, until the following month by the celebration of the long-deferred marriage of Joseph and Isabelle of Parma.) After the defeat of Torgau, the Austrian attitude toward peace negotiations changed dramatically. Maria Theresa finally accepted them in principle. On 11 December the comte de Choiseul told his cousin that he believed both Maria Theresa and Kaunitz sincerely wanted peace.[69]

The British public also lost much of its appetite for the war in Germany as the result of the campaign of 1760. Blame for Ferdinand's failure and debate about continuing the effort affected the unity of the inner cabinet and undermined British diplomacy. By the autumn Pitt was warning that unless Ferdinand won a decisive victory he would no longer support the German war; he was bluffing, but as usual his attitudes were a good gauge of the public mood. Pitt also was angry at Frederick II for this unwillingness to consider any territorial concessions to make peace. Frederick's popularity had also begun to decline among the public, although it enjoyed a brief revival after Torgau.[70]

During the autumn of 1760 two important developments further undermined the British war effort in Germany and helped lay the groundwork for the peace discussions of 1761–62. On 25 October George II died suddenly from a stroke at the age of seventy-six. He had been the bulwark of Britain's commitment to defend Hanover, and his support had been invaluable to Newcastle's government. He was succeeded by his twenty-two-year-old grandson, who became George III. The new king hated Pitt, did not support the German war, was indifferent to the fate of Frederick II, and took little interest in the Electorate of Hanover to whose rule he also succeeded. However, he did want to play a more important part in British political life than had his grandfather, and he placed great trust in the advice of his tutor, John Stuart, Earl of Bute, a wealthy Scottish nobleman of good intentions but limited political experience. George promptly named Bute to the ceremonial post of Groom of the Stole and gave him access to the inner cabinet, although Bute declined Holdernesse's position of secretary of state for the northern department. Newcastle's position as first lord of the treasury and Pitt's as secretary of state for the southern department were safe for the moment, as the king subsequently issued the customary orders for government officials to remain in their posts for the first six months of his reign. The king's continuing support of Newcastle and Pitt was far from assured, though. A few months before his accession he had told Bute he wanted him as first lord of the treasury. The king's views were of great importance, particularly in diplomacy, decisions concerning which were subject to royal approval.[71]

A second ominous development was the publication on 15 November of an anonymous pamphlet entitled *Considerations on the Present German War*, which criticized the British effort in Germany as an unnecessary diversion from the colonial and naval war. This pamphlet, written by a wool merchant named Israel Mauduit, soon become extremely popular, five editions being published within the next three months. Once the identity of its author was known, he became a figure of some influence.[72]

The year 1760 not only marked a turning point in British public opinion about the war but also revealed some of Pitt's limitations as a military strategist and a diplomatist. We have already noted the excessive latitude he gave Amherst, who took so long to capture Canada that he was unable to attack Louisiana or send troops to the West Indies. Pitt, with somewhat more justification, left the same latitude to Ferdinand, doing little more than encouraging him to take the offensive. Pitt's one real strategic contribution was his revival of the idea of mounting operations against the French coast. When at the beginning of October 1760 he heard that 15,000 reinforcements were being sent to Germany (Castries' force), he proposed to the inner cabinet seizing the island of Belle Isle in the Bay of Biscay. This thirty-three-square-mile island was located fifteen miles southwest of Quiberon, was near Lorient, Nantes, and other French ports, and could provide a support point for a British fleet and troops to menace the French coast. Not only might it force the French to divert soldiers from Germany, but it also might act as an equivalent for Minorca during future peace negotiations. Strategically it suffered many of the same drawbacks as the Channel Islands off the coast of Brittany and Normandy; without control of the sea it was defenseless, it was rather superfluous to whoever did control the sea, and it was inferior to the Channel Islands of Jersey and Guernsey as a base for privateers.

Although only Newcastle was opposed to attacking Belle Isle, the proposed naval commander, Captain Augustus Keppel, expressed concern about landing sites. Hawke, based at Quiberon, was ordered to take soundings, but the admiral was concerned chiefly about destroying the French ships of the line in the Vilaine and preferred to seize a peninsula along Quiberon Bay. When he sent Anson a report questioning the practicality of capturing Belle Isle, George II announced his opposition, effectively vetoing Pitt's plan. Pitt, outraged at Hawke, raised the plan again on 11 November, the day of George II's funeral, and won the inner cabinet's approval. Keppel was ordered to cover the landing of 9,000 men with five ships of the line, and Hawke was ordered to provide another eight. By the beginning of December the troops were embarked aboard transports, but the weather was too bad for them to sail, and on 11 December the operation was postponed indefinitely. It was far too late in the year for such an attack, but had it been made in the late summer or early autumn, Castries might have been deprived of some of his troops during the critical battle of Clostercamp.[73]

Pitt's most serious mistake during 1760 was in diplomacy. At the end of May a new Spanish ambassador, Joaquín Atanasio Pignatelli de Aragón y Moncayo, conde de Fuentes, presented his credentials to the British court. Fuentes' primary mission was not mediation of the Franco-British war but obtaining satisfaction for Spanish grievances against Britain and improving relations between the two countries. Charles III distrusted and disliked the British, but, realizing Spain's military weaknesses, he was willing enough to conduct serious negotiations to send an ambassador of the highest social standing (thereby greatly discomforting France). Such negotiations promised to be more difficult for Britain than resolving the conflicts with Denmark or the Netherlands over British seizures of their ships, which could be resolved by implicit compromises. Fuentes, for example, demanded a share for Spain in the Newfoundland fisheries, basing his claim on former usage and rights, as provided for by the Treaty of Utrecht.

The most important of his demands, however, was negotiable. One of the longest standing irritants to Spain were the British settlements of dubious legality along the Caribbean coast of central America. These settlements provided both a semi-legal trade in the exportation of logwood (which was used as a source of dye for woolen fabric) and a forbidden smuggling trade in the exportation of mahogany and importation of British trade goods. Fuentes offered a guaranteed supply of logwood in exchange for abandoning the settlements, but Pitt and his colleagues were unwilling to risk the public's criticism for abandoning British interests. Pitt, moreover, was contemptuous of Spain and angry that it dared to threaten Britain by letting it be known France had been given a copy of its grievances. He criticized Fuentes and informed Wall he would never permit Spain a share in the fisheries, the nursery of sailors for the British navy. The British government delayed making a formal response, however, until early 1761. By then it had lost its best chance to placate Charles III and avoid adding Spain to Britain's enemies. Such an opportunity would not come again, in large part because of the death on 27 September 1760 of Queen Maria Amelia of Spain, who had used her considerable influence with her husband on behalf of a policy of peace. By the end of the year, as Ossun reported, Charles wished to reestablish relations with Britain on the basis of equality, including perfect commercial reciprocity, an objective that would require a major transformation of British attitudes.[74]

Spain's adoption of a more forceful policy toward Britain necessarily would have to be a gradual process. On 28 November Ossun reported that Charles III agreed with Choiseul about the dangers of British naval hegemony but was restrained by the weakness of Spanish colonial defenses, the lack of supplies in the naval arsenals, and the poor condition of the navy's ships.[75] Choiseul, outraged at Portuguese assistance to Britain, recalled French ambassador Beauchamps and volunteered French help to Spain in conquering Portugal and Portuguese Brazil. Ossun did not forward the offer, however, believing that in spite of his own disputes with Portugal regarding colonial boundaries in South America Charles would be displeased by it because his sister María Ana Victoria was queen of Portugal.[76] There were, however, encouraging signs that in the coming year Spain would adopt a more aggressive diplomacy. Wall became more critical of the British, and Charles asked Louis' approval to shift the energetic (and supposedly sympathetic) Grimaldi from The Hague to Versailles.[77] Moreover, efforts were made to repair the deficiencies of the Spanish navy; Ossun described Naval Minister Julián de Arriaga as timid and lacking initiative, but honest and scrupulous in following orders.[78]

The change of Spanish policy would have a great impact on both diplomacy and war strategy by the end of 1761. In the interim, however, France's hopes of eventually breaking British resistance to a compromise peace were still dependent on events in Germany. The victories of Broglie and Castries had demonstrated the worth of the reforms instituted by War Minister Belle-Isle. The new year soon would test whether France could maintain the strategic initiative there.

1761
Saving the Navy's Future

PRESERVING THE INITIATIVE IN GERMANY

On 26 January 1761 War Minister Belle-Isle died. The following day Louis XV, in another display of resolve, named Choiseul as his replacement.[1] Choiseul kept the foreign ministry as well, and with the death of his only rival in the Council of State he became even more powerful. (The council was reduced to six active members: Choiseul, Berryer, Soubise, Estrées, Puyzieulx, and Saint-Florentin, plus the dauphin.) The king, however, did not appoint him first minister.

The choice of Choiseul to head the army was important not because it brought any major policy changes but rather because it preserved continuity; late in 1760 Choiseul told a prominent general that it was only by the war in Germany that one could wear down and humble Britain.[2] The king's approval of this policy was demonstrated by an increase in the army's budget of almost 20 million livres (to nearly 170 million for 1761) while the navy was promised only an extra 6.5 million (to about 30 million). This proved overly optimistic; had it not been for a supplemental grant made in June to protect Martinique, naval funding for the year would have been reduced by 8.5 million, and in fact not all of the authorized funds were delivered.[3] The government raised only 80 million livres in loans compared with 130 million during 1760, although increased tax revenues made up part of the shortfall, as Bertin and Choiseul's policy of accommodation weakened the resistance of the Parlement of Paris. Choiseul conceded victory to the Parlement of Besançon which had engaged in an extended dispute with the king and he was ready to betray the Society of Jesus (or Jesuits), a religious order which was the chief opponent of the Jansenists. The Parlement of Paris wished to expel the Jesuits from France, but in August 1761, the king forced it to accept a year's truce. Meanwhile the Parlement offered little resistance to royal edicts extending a third *vingtieme* and doubling another tax, the *capitation*, until the end of 1763. Moreover, Court Banker Laborde was able to borrow specie from Spain. France also saved some 3 million livres by suspending its subsidy to Denmark and reducing its subsidies to Sweden and to its German allies.[4]

Although the French army was the chief budget priority, money was not a guarantee of success. The army was dependent on its military bases east of the Rhine and north of the Main. Ferdinand, who had come close to forcing the French back across the Rhine in the autumn of 1760 as he had in February 1758, decided to try again. In February 1761, he began another surprise offensive against the French army which was dispersed in winter quarters. The duc de Broglie's army was in better condition and was far better led than in earlier years. Although some of Ferdinand's units advanced 100 miles south and reached the Main, the French did not panic. Half a dozen French posts held out, including the main post at Cassel, commanded by the comte de Broglie. An early thaw rendered roads impassable, disrupting Ferdinand's advance. By the middle of March the duc de Broglie had some 40,000 troops available and was able to counterattack Ferdinand's 30,000. On 31 March and 1 April the last units of the British-German army recrossed the Diemel River northwest of Cassel, from where they had begun their offensive, and reentered their winter quarters.[5]

The failure of Ferdinand's campaign and the subsequent recriminations helped undermine the unity of the British inner cabinet. Ferdinand blamed the British commissariat for his defeat, and when an investigation was held, Pitt placed the blame on Newcastle, who as first lord of the treasury was responsible for the commissariat (and who, as we shall see later, had antagonized Pitt).[6] Moreover, although the British public generally continued to support the war against France,[7] it began to turn against the war in Germany. The hostilities in Germany were a major part of the enormous expenses of the 120,000-man British army, whose expenditures for 1761 were almost £10 million (equivalent to 240 million livres) while subsidies to Ferdinand and Frederick II's armies added another £2 million; at the end of the year, Newcastle claimed that the war in Germany alone was costing £6 million to £7 million annually, including £3 million for provisions. (In comparison, British naval expeditions in 1761 were about £6 million.)[8] What made the expense so intolerable was the seeming endlessness of the fighting in Germany. Ferdinand was unable to regain the initiative until 1762, by which time the British public no longer cared about defending Hanover and driving the French from Hesse-Cassel.

In spite of the massive expenses paid by Parliament, Ferdinand's army of 60,000 Germans and 18,000 British was badly outnumbered once campaigning resumed in the summer of 1761. The French were able to field two full armies, one of 65,000 under the duc de Broglie in Hesse and central Germany and another of 95,000 under Soubise along the Rhine.[9] Broglie and Soubise had orders from Choiseul to operate independently, but they joined forces in July when Ferdinand advanced into Westphalia to attack Soubise's approaching army. With a courage approaching foolhardiness, Ferdinand refused to retreat. On 15 July Soubise and Broglie attacked him near the village of Vellinghausen with more than 90,000 men against his 65,000. The day's fighting was inconclusive, and that night Ferdinand shifted most of his army to the flank opposing Broglie. When he counterattacked the next morning, Soubise was slow to support Broglie, and the entire French army had to retreat.[10] At the cost of 1,500 casualties (against between 3,000 and 5,000 French casualties) Ferdinand escaped the trap, but in the long run this may not have been to Britain's advantage. The destruction of Ferdinand's army might have forced Britain to accept much the same peace terms it accepted a year later, sparing a huge amount of bloodshed and expense.

For all the importance of what might have been, the Battle of Vellinghausen did not shift the strategic initiative. Ferdinand did not pursue the French, and they soon retook the offensive. Soubise loaned 30,000 of his troops to Broglie, who eventually was reinforced by another 10,000 men under the command of Lévis, released from parole by the British. On several occasions Broglie was able to advance to the northeast and enter Hanoverian territory, even sending a detachment as far as Brunswick (east of Hanover) in October. Each time, however, Ferdinand was able to force him to retreat by menacing his supply lines. Ferdinand admitted, though, that every year since 1758 the quality of French soldiers in Germany had improved.[11] The campaign ended in stalemate, with no more major battles and no further territory gained or lost, but the French still occupied Cassel and menaced Hanover. The British government thus remained trapped in its interminable and increasingly unpopular commitment in western Germany.[12]

Unfortunately for the British government, Ferdinand's inability to win more victories was not offset by any victories of Frederick II, who also was losing his former popularity with the British public. Indeed, 1761 was, as 1759 had been, a year of Prussian defeats. The campaign began with 100,000–120,000 Prussian field troops facing 130,000–145,000 Austrians and 85,000 Russians; never, as Frederick told one of his sisters, had he had greater risks to run.[13] Nevertheless he was still unprepared to make any territorial concessions to gain peace.[14]

Until the autumn the campaign went better than Frederick expected. Field Marshal Daun, who was pessimistic that anything could be accomplished, was unable to advance against the outnumbered Prussian army in Saxony because of supply shortages. Meanwhile Frederick was able to construct a fortified camp near Schweidnitz in the mountainous terrain of Silesia, where his 55,000 men defied Loudon's 70,000 Austrians and Field Marshal Aleksandr Buturlin's 50,000 Russians; Loudon wished to attack, but Buturlin refused. Meanwhile the 15,000-man Swedish army and 15,000-man Imperial army accomplished little. In September most of the Russian army began its annual retreat into Poland to enter winter quarters, but Buturlin left 20,000 men with Loudon. Frederick now left his camp in hopes of cutting Loudon's supply lines and forcing him to retreat, too. On the morning of 1 October, however, Loudon's Austro-Russian army surprised and carried by assault the great fortress of Schweidnitz, capturing several thousand men and obtaining a base only 25 miles from Breslau and 200 miles from Berlin. This permitted the Austrians to winter in Silesia.

Before the campaign ended, however, Prussia suffered another terrible blow. A separate Russian army, aided by a fleet of eighteen Russian and six Swedish ships of the line, besieged the Baltic fortress of Kolberg, which was defended by 18,000 Prussians. By the end of November the Russian army had grown to 35,000 or 40,000 men. The Prussians soon began to evacuate the doomed fortress, which was captured on 16 December, giving the Russians a base only 50 miles from Stettin and 125 miles from Berlin.[15]

Frederick's line of defenses had been cracked twice, and his army, too weak to take the offensive or even to protect its major fortresses, had been humiliated. The Prussian king was reduced to flights of fancy, hoping that a Dutch fleet would help him recapture Kolberg, that the Turks would ally with him, or that the Tartars of southern Russia would attack their enemy, Empress Elizabeth.[16]

The Austrians, however, had their own problems. The leaders of the army had lost confidence, while the resolve of the Austrian government had been shaken by its growing financial difficulties. Chancellor Kaunitz was willing to settle for the acquisition of Glatz and the return of Saxony to its rightful ruler. Even the capture of Schweidnitz was insufficient to arrest the progressive decline of Austria's ability and will to wage war. At the end of the year the Austrians were forced for financial reasons to reduce each infantry regiment by two companies, decreasing the strength of their army by almost an eighth.[17]

Nevertheless, at the end of 1761 Prussia seemed doomed. Unlike the similar situation of 1757, the British public largely had lost interest in Frederick's fate. Tired of the war in Germany, Britain's attention turned toward a new enemy, Spain, which was drawn into the hostilities between Britain and France after peace negotiations failed.

The occupation of Cassel gave France a bargaining chip for negotiating with Britain. It was vital to France, however, to preserve its alliance with Austria. Thus, the Franco-British peace negotiations of 1761 were preceded by several months of discussions between France and Austria. Although at the end of 1760 Austria had indicated its willingness for peace talks, Kaunitz argued that discussions between France and Britain should take place as part of the proposed peace congress at Augsburg. Choiseul feared that this would complicate and delay a French agreement with Britain. Fortunately the previous year's conversation at The Hague had set a precedent for separate discussions. Finally, Austria and Russia agreed that France could conduct separate and direct discussions for an armistice with Britain prior to the convening of the general peace congress.[18] Russia not only consented to the new arrangements but was even willing to assist France directly, thereby improving relations at no cost to itself. Elizabeth accepted a plan proposed by Choiseul to make use of Prince Alexander Mikhailovich Golitsyn, the Russian minister in London, who had been passing intelligence to d'Affry.[19] On 31 March 1761 Golitsyn presented Pitt with an invitation to Britain from Louis XV and the rulers of Sweden, Saxony, Russia, and Austria to attend a peace congress at Augsburg, a personal letter to Pitt from Choiseul proposing separate Franco-British preliminary discussions, and a memoir suggesting the basis on which to negotiate.

The timing of the presentation was opportune. On the same day, Ferdinand's winter offensive ended in failure. Six days earlier Pitt's dominance over his fellow cabinet ministers had suffered its first blow, when George III's mentor, the Earl of Bute, assumed the post of secretary of state for the northern department in place of the Earl of Holdernesse, whom George had called "Pitt's footman." Bute's appointment was made at the suggestion of Newcastle in an attempt to ingratiate himself with the king. Newcastle had been given the idea by the Sardinian envoy to the British court, Francesco Giuseppe, conte di Viry, although perhaps Viry was acting at Bute's bidding or even the king's. Viry, used in the past as an intermediary with Spain and Austria, had a reputation for acumen, gentility, prudence, and modesty. Newcastle acted behind Pitt's back and with knowledge of Pitt's contempt for Bute. He thereby doomed their political partnership, which had served Britain so well.[20] Pitt was able to take revenge by blaming Newcastle for the failure of Ferdinand's offensive, but as their relationship deteriorated, Bute had the chance to influence the balance of power in the inner cabinet.

The rivalry between Pitt and Newcastle involved policy as well as power, further dividing the inner cabinet. Previously, Newcastle had deferred to his successful and popular colleague's desires for a decisive peace, in spite of his own chronic pessimism and his wishes for a quick settlement. Now, although he continued to support the war in Germany, Newcastle was ready to oppose Pitt's views on acceptable peace terms with France. The unity of the inner cabinet was further fractured by the entry into the inner cabinet of a new member without portfolio who had his own policy views. The enormously wealthy John Russell, Duke of Bedford, who served as first lord of the admiralty during the previous war and recently had been lord lieutenant of Ireland, favored a compromise peace and opposed the war in Germany.[21] Bute seems to have wished for peace but had no fixed agenda for reaching it; according to Viry, Bute had a good heart and was a man of honor, but he wished to govern without having a real hand for it. For the moment he supported Pitt, who continued to bully his colleagues into giving him free rein over diplomacy. Bute promised Newcastle, Hardwicke, and the Duke of Devonshire, the former first lord of the treasury, however, that if they felt Pitt's policies were excessive, he would withdraw his support for them.[22]

As secretary of state for the northern department Bute was responsible for negotiations with Prussia. Frederick II had come to see a separate Franco-British agreement as useful, provided the terms were acceptable and Britain continued to support him against Austria. Recently he had named his price for consenting to such an agreement. France must specify not only that it would evacuate Wesel and the western Prussian provinces but also that it would provide no subsidies to any of his enemies (although it would be acceptable for France to provide 24,000 auxiliary troops to Austria). Britain must facilitate the transfer of 30,000 troops from Ferdinand's army into his own (which Frederick long had desired) and must provide him 5 million crowns (£837,000) to pay for them, as well as continuing its annual subsidy of 4 million crowns. The inner cabinet considered these terms outrageous; luckily for Bute, discussions with Prussia were suspended while Britain explored the terms France was prepared to offer.[23]

The British hardly could refuse to make such an exploration, as the memoir sent by Choiseul was written in such reasonable terms that Newcastle told Devonshire that it could form the basis of a good peace, possibly as early as the summer.[24] Basically it offered an agreement on the basis of *uti possidetis*, that is, that Britain and France would retain whatever conquests they held at the end of hostilities. It suggested that the *uti possidetis* should become effective on 1 May in Europe, on 1 July in America and the Caribbean, and on 1 September in the Indian Ocean. Devonshire and others, however, were suspicious of such a generous offer, as France had captured from Britain only Minorca, while losing possessions in India and Africa as well as Louisbourg, Canada, and Guadeloupe. Pitt quickly perceived that the memoir said nothing of French conquests in Germany such as Cassel, Wesel, and Geldern. (Kaunitz was confused by this when the comte de Choiseul gave him a copy of the memoir.) This ambiguity provided France a way of testing the British government's loyalties while it avoided giving Britain an excuse to refuse negotiations.[25]

Britain's reply was cautious and formal. On 8 April Pitt sent Choiseul a letter and memoir accepting the invitation to negotiate both at Augsburg and directly, announcing Britain would receive a representative designated by Louis, and suggesting the possibility of delaying the *uti possidetis* by having it correspond to when the treaty was signed. Eleven days later Choiseul responded, designating the comte de Choiseul as the French representative at Augsburg and Premier Commis François de Bussy as the French representative to Britain. He insisted that the British either accept the French dates for the *uti possidetis* or negotiate an exchange of territory. He also invited Britain to send a representative to the French court. On 28 April Pitt sent a passport for Bussy and announced that Britain would be represented at Augsburg by Ambassador Yorke, by David Murray, Viscount Stormont, its minister in Warsaw, and by Charles Wyndham, Earl of Egremont, a member of the House of Lords. Britain would send to Paris Hans Stanley, a member of the House of Commons and former member of the Board of Admiralty. A week later Choiseul sent a passport for Stanley and letter of introduction for Bussy, while expressing his regrets that he could not come to London himself.

The drafting of instructions for Stanley and for Bussy took a good portion of May. Bussy aroused British suspicions by being late for a meeting at Calais with Stanley as the two passed in transit, but after a brief delay caused by bad weather in the Channel both reached their posts. Bussy held his first meeting with Pitt on 3 June and Stanley his first meeting with Choiseul on 7 June; finally after two months of preparation, serious negotiations were ready to begin. The congress at Augsburg, proposed for July, was postponed until after Britain and France reached agreement (and was never held, giving the Austrians and Russians the chance to capture Schweidnitz and Kolberg).[26]

Three serious obstacles soon faced the Franco-British negotiations: the shortcomings of the two diplomatic representatives, France's resentment at Britain's attempts to better its negotiating position by military conquests during the early phase of discussions, and Pitt's insistence on France abandoning its rights to fish off Newfoundland and in the Gulf of St. Lawrence, a concession that would have crippled France's future ability to compete with Britain as a naval power.

Neither in social status nor in ability were Bussy and Stanley of the first rank. Choiseul and the British inner cabinet did not trust each other; each wanted the other to make the first move and wished to be certain its negotiator would undertake no initiative on his own. The sixty-two-year-old Bussy was not of noble birth and had a reputation for being corruptible; the British had bought his services during his 1740–44 mission to London. He had been approached by the British in 1759, although without success, and, at the suggestion of Pitt's brother-in-law Earl Temple, another unsuccessful attempt was made now. Although he was regarded at the French foreign ministry as an office tyrant, he, according to Choiseul, feared Pitt and was not anxious to undertake the mission. He was informed of the peace terms France wished and was instructed to obtain Britain's terms in writing, but he was forbidden to reciprocate. Although he eventually got along with Pitt better than he had expected, he was distrusted by the British and served mostly to deliver messages from Choiseul.[27]

Whereas Bussy was rather old for such a mission, Stanley, born about 1720, was of an appropriate age but inexperienced in diplomacy. He volunteered for the assignment and was given it when Temple turned it down. His instructions were even more limiting than were Bussy's. The inner cabinet was divided on what to do about the French occupation of Hesse and fearful of the public, so Stanley was forbidden to propose virtually anything himself and was ordered to refer any French proposals to London, where the inner cabinet expected the serious discussions to be held. Their expectations proved wrong; when serious discussions began at the French court, Stanley played a more important role than had been envisaged. Although cultured, fluent in French, and well intentioned, Stanley proved a poor choice for the mission. Vain and opinionated, he was all too ready to offer advice to the inner cabinet, but his knowledge was often faulty and his judgment poor.[28]

Even before Bussy and Stanley arrived at their posts, Louis XV's suspicions of the British government were deepened and his anger was aroused by their attempts to conquer Belle Isle, off the French coast. A landing force was en route from England at the time that Golitsyn presented the French proposals. Rather than calling Choiseul's bluff on the *uti possidetis*, Britain stalled until after the island was captured on 8 June. Belle Isle added a difficult issue to the discussions. Louis wished its return without compensation; at most he was prepared to offer concessions on the status of Dunkirk. (The day before the surrender of Belle Isle, the British captured the island of Dominica in the Caribbean, and that too would have posed an obstacle to peace had not the negotiations largely failed before news of it reached London on 20 July; meanwhile, unknown to the French, Pitt also tried to accelerate a planned attack on Martinique.)[29]

The most serious obstacle to the success of the negotiations, however, was Pitt's insistence on blocking French access to the North American fisheries. No other issue was as contentious. France never seriously considered retaining Minorca while, in spite of an extensive lobbying campaign in England by the proponents of keeping Guadeloupe, the inner cabinet put up little resistance to returning it (partly because planters on the British sugar islands feared the economic competition if it were kept). Berryer, some veterans of the Canadian campaigns like Bourlamaque, and the chambers of commerce of the French ports were opposed to letting Britain keep Canada; Choiseul, however, did not contest the issue, apparently realizing its hopelessness. (Neither the British government nor its constituents were prepared to return it, even in exchange for the economically much more valuable Guadeloupe, which in any case France was unwilling to offer.) India and Africa caused little difficulties during the discussions, and although Britain feared France might wish to retain Ostend and Nieuport, the French government had neither the power nor the inclination to do so. The issue of the British right to prevent the fortification of Dunkirk was capable of resolution provided that Britain offered some sort of compromise, so that Louis XV could save face. Even the question of the French conquests in Germany could have been resolved had the British promptly accepted French fishing rights off Newfoundland and in the Gulf of St. Lawrence. France had no desire to keep any of its German gains and, as we shall see, was even willing to risk the Austrian alliance by returning the Prussian provinces along the Rhine. The issue of the fisheries, as both Pitt and Choiseul realized, was central because it involved not only French prestige and the prosperity of ports like St. Malo and Granville but also France's future as a naval power.[30]

There was no disagreement in Britain that the fisheries were more valuable economically than was Canada. Moreover, the inner cabinet did not challenge Pitt's views on their importance in training a considerable share of the sailors on which the French navy depended; the real question was whether to risk the failure of the negotiations in order to insist upon Britain's retaining its newly acquired monopoly of them. In 1763, after the British government of which he was no longer a member had conceded the French a share, Pitt complained that Britain had surrendered the opportunity to force upon France a peace from which it would have taken her a century to recover. He felt the same in 1761, telling George III that he would rather give up the use of his right arm than sign a peace giving France access to the fisheries. (Pitt was entitled to such rhetoric, as gout recently had prevented him from using that arm.) He was unsuccessful in convincing his colleagues to present a British monopoly of the fisheries as an ultimatum before the negotiations began, but, as we shall see, he subsequently was able to prevail, at least for a time, in the inner cabinet. In part this was because the public, particularly in London, realized that the return of the fisheries would permit France to rebuild its navy.[31] Pitt's continued dominance, as Bussy recognized, was based on his popularity with the public (a popularity reinforced by the capture of Belle Isle) and the lack of organized opposition against him.[32]

With the British adamant on preventing France a share in the fishery, the negotiations presented Louis XV with one of the most serious choices he had ever faced. He could choose to surrender the fisheries and consequently the hope of challenging Britain as a naval and colonial power for many future decades. If he did not do so, however, he would have to continue a war which had undermined his popularity and forced him to concede more power to the Parlements. Choiseul wrote Ossun on 7 July that France needed peace to over-come the internal problems that fatigued the king and made his life bitter.[33] Moreover, continued war would mean not only the certainty of substantial further expense and loss of life but also the strong likelihood of further de-feats and humiliation. The responsibility was his, not Choiseul's. He had not despaired after the disasters of 1759 and had not rushed to make concessions during the discussions at The Hague, but the continuing crisis would require of him courage, self-confidence, and strength of will comparable to that of the fabled warrior Choiseul. Louis had surrendered all of France's conquests in 1748 in order to make peace, but those conquests were not vital to France; moreover, peace had brought France a considerable indirect gain in the balance of power by weakening its rival Austria. In contrast, a peace dictated by Pitt would bring shame and would permanently weaken France, but at least it also would bring a cessation of the disastrous war. Louis' choice of whether to give in to the British demands would test him both as a person and as a king.

FRANCE LOSES PEACE BUT GAINS ANOTHER ALLY

Louis XV and Choiseul did not take long to use their only bargaining chip, the French army's occupation of western Germany. On 17 June, ten days after his first meeting with Stanley, Choiseul dropped the idea of a peace based on the *uti possidetis* and dictated to Stanley a set of peace terms based on the exchange of conquests. France would return Minorca and accept the loss of Canada, provided Britain returned Isle Royale. France would agree to demilitarize the island by completing the demolition of the fortress of Louisbourg, and would use it only as a support for the French portion of the cod fishery. The boundary between British Canada and French Louisiana would be established along the headland dividing the rivers which flowed into the Great Lakes from those which flowed into the Ohio and Mississippi rivers. France would let Britain regulate matters in the East Indies, but expected the return of the island of Gorée off the coast of Senegal, as well as Guadeloupe and its surrounding islands. Although he did not put it in writing, Choiseul told Stanley that the king would abandon his conquests in Germany and implied that this would include Wesel and the Prussian provinces along the Rhine. He either told Stanley or let it be understood that this offer was contingent on the disbanding of Ferdinand's army. He refused to offer additional compensation for Belle Isle, telling Stanley that Britain could keep it if she wished.[34]

When he reported Choiseul's proposals to Pitt, Stanley offered his opinion that they were only an opening gambit. This was a fatal misunderstanding. The king and Choiseul were taking a terrible risk in even hinting that France would return Wesel and the Prussian provinces. Starhemberg had warned Choiseul that Austria would never consent to France's returning the Prussian provinces in order to gain a separate peace with Britain, and Choiseul well realized that if Austria came to doubt France's good faith it could again become, in Choiseul's words, France's cruelest enemy.[35] Choiseul asked Stanley and the British government to maintain extreme secrecy about the peace terms, telling Stanley (inaccurately) that Bussy would not be informed of them. The king and Choiseul not only were risking the French alliance with Austria but, as we shall see, were willing to abandon the possibility of an alliance with Spain, if a quick settlement could be obtained. Stanley did not understand that if such sweeping concessions were not accepted immediately, they would not be offered again.

The inner cabinet had made its own offer to Bussy on 16 June, after it learned of the capture of Belle Isle. It proposed a two-month delay in the *uti possidetis* in order to accommodate the British success and to permit Britain to make gains in the Caribbean: 1 July for Europe, 1 September for the Western Hemisphere, and 1 November for the Indian Ocean, these dates being contingent upon a definitive treaty being signed by 1 August. Pitt told Bussy that Britain did not wish to retain Belle Isle but expected compensation and that Britain would not return French merchant ships captured before the formal declaration of war. He had already told Bussy, although he was not speaking for his colleagues, that France should not expect compensation for its conquests in Germany, as Britain took less interest in Hanover since the death of George II.[36]

On 24 June the inner cabinet debated the French offer to Stanley, which superceded the British offer and in effect ended the discussion on the basis of the *uti possidetis*. It left to Pitt the drafting of a reply. Pitt's reply offered no reciprocal concessions, demanding all of Canada and the Ohio country and insisting on "some great and important compensation" if France wished fishing rights off Newfoundland. It also demanded that Britain retain Gorée as well as Senegal, and it raised issues Choiseul had not, insisting on the demolition of the fortifications of Dunkirk and the acceptance of the harsh terms of the Treaty of Utrecht concerning the port. It also insisted the French evacuate the British settlement of Bencoolen (Bengkulu) on Sumatra (which Estaing had captured), as well as Ostend and Nieuport in the Austrian Netherlands. The "neutral" Caribbean islands of St. Lucia, St. Vincent, Dominica, and Tobago were to be left neutral or divided between Britain and France. Stanley was told that the British terms on Canada, Africa, Sumatra, Minorca, Germany, and the neutral islands was to be considered nonnegotiable.[37]

Pitt had wanted to go even further by demanding France abandon its claims to any fishing rights as a precondition of continuing the discussions. This, however, met opposition within the inner cabinet led by the wealthy and opin-ionated Bedford, who according to Newcastle was the only member immune to Pitt's bullying. Bedford had already criticized the seizure of Belle Isle and warned that demanding the fisheries would endanger France's position as a naval power and thereby alarm the rest of Europe; he even questioned the re-tention of Canada, fearing it would be too large to administer and would reduce the dependency of the American colonists on Great Britain. (These fears were shared by Hardwicke and others and conversely were later cited by Choiseul in defense of the peace, although probably this was merely sour grapes.)[38] Sup-ported by Newcastle, Bedford now urged the acceptance of Choiseul's generous terms and repeated his criticism of Pitt's position on the fishery. The astute Hardwicke recognized Choiseul's offer as an ultimatum, and even the inexperi-enced Bute recognized that France had made substantial concessions. Most of the inner cabinet was willing to accept the return of French fishing rights off Newfoundland (but not in the Gulf of St. Lawrence) in exchange for France's accepting increased restrictions on Dunkirk, but Bute, holding the balance of power, supported at least making an effort to gain the fishing monopoly that Pitt desired. On 26 June the inner cabinet agreed to let France suggest compensation for the fishing rights, a compromise favoring Pitt that so angered Bedford that thereafter he attended its meetings only irregularly. It also approved Pitt's reply to Choiseul and sent it to Stanley.[39]

Choiseul received the reply on 29 June. He immediately offered Stanley reas-surances of France's desire for peace, telling him that France had no intention of keeping Ostend or Nieuport or of contesting British retention of Canada. He said that France would be willing to accept another slaving post in Africa instead of Gorée and a smaller island than Isle Royale as a shelter (*abri*) for the fishing fleet. He advised, however, that increasing the restrictions on Dunkirk would offend French honor and lead to continual disputes. He no longer offered to evacuate Wesel, and he warned that if the war continued France would find new allies. He described the fishery as his obsession (*folie*). On the basis of this conversation Stanley warned Pitt of a possible French alliance with Spain and advised him that France would not relinquish its fishing rights if an army were in the heart of France. In his own report to Bussy, Choiseul emphasized the importance of the fishery and France's readiness to continue the war in order to regain access to it and to secure a shelter for its fishing fleet. As Choiseul told the Council of State on 1 August, the fishery was worth more than Canada and Louisiana combined. He also instructed Bussy to ascertain how strongly Pitt felt about Senegal and Dunkirk.[40]

The next two weeks were critical to the fate of the negotiations and the future of the French navy. Louis XV proved his courage. There is no indication he wavered in his support of Choiseul's position on the fishery; neither he nor Choiseul was willing to compromise the navy's future as long as France could continue fighting. Moreover, the king was unprepared a second time to risk the Austrian alliance by offering the return of Wesel. Had the French continued to wait, it is possible the British eventually would have given in; on 15 July Bute told Newcastle, Hardwicke, and Devonshire that he favored giving France fishing rights and a refuge, a substitute for Gorée, and the more liberal provisions of the Treaty of Aix-la-Chapelle concerning Dunkirk.[41]

On that same day, however, Choiseul, unwilling to wait further for the British to change their minds, gave Stanley an official response to the British proposals of 26 June which sharply contrasted with the prior French position. Ironically, the Battle of Vellinghausen also began on 15 July; perhaps, as Hardwicke suspected, France's delay in responding was based on hope of good news from Germany. Choiseul also sent a copy of the response to Bussy; in his covering letter he wrote that henceforth France would view the negotiations not as a way to make peace but as a means to prevent further attacks on the French coast until after the end of the campaigning season. Thus, rather than breaking off discussions, Choiseul continued them to buy time, hoping to gain two months.

The new French terms were as uncompromising as those Pitt had offered. No longer did France suggest the possibility of a substitute for Isle Royale as a support for the fishing fleet or a substitute for Senegal or Gorée as a slave station. France would abandon its conquests in Hesse, but not Wesel and the Prussian provinces along the Rhine, as they now belonged to Austria. If peace were made, France would provide no troops to Maria Theresa, but Ferdinand's army could provide no troops for Frederick. The British were offered Tobago, but the important island of St. Lucia would become French; St. Vincent and Dominica would remain neutral. Even more fatal to the hope of a quick peace were two accompanying notes that demonstrated that France was now chiefly concerned with her present and potential military allies. One, responding to the concerns of Starhemberg, indicated that Maria Theresa would consent to a separate peace only if she retained the Prussian provinces and recommended that Britain accept these terms (that would have required Britain to abandon its alliance with Prussia). The other, which Pitt refused to receive when Bussy presented it to him (and later described as an "enormity"), proposed that Spain be invited to guarantee the treaty and said that France regarded British satisfaction of Spanish grievances as essential to a lasting peace. The timing of when to present the note on the Spanish grievances had been left to Spanish Ambassador Fuentes, who asked that it be presented simultaneously with the French reply. There could have been no worse moment for expecting British concessions. On 23 July Bussy presented the French reply (which the inner cabinet already had received from Stanley). At almost the same time, news reached Britain of the capture of Pondicherry and Dominica and of Ferdinand's victory at Vellinghausen.[42]

Two days after Bussy's presentation, the inner cabinet forwarded to Stanley a set of ultimata drafted by Pitt, demanding France evacuate Ostend, Nieuport, and all of Germany, offering to consider French fishing rights only if the fortifications of Dunkirk were demolished, and not even mentioning a port for the fishing fleet. Without the authorization of his colleagues, Pitt even told Bussy it would take even more than the destruction of the fortifications for Britain to concede fishing rights.[43] Choiseul described these terms to Starhemberg as indecent, unacceptable, and insolent; he wrote Ossun that they resembled the laws dictated by a conqueror rather than terms of peace and that the king was revolted by Pitt's response. In a memorandum given to Grimaldi he stressed that by refusing to receive the note about the Spanish grievances Pitt insulted Spain as well as France.[44]

By now the French government, abandoning hope of peace, was preparing to make a military alliance with Spain, which had been courting France since the beginning of the year. In early 1761, Charles III was fearful that Britain and France might make peace, leaving Spain helpless. Grimaldi, the newly arrived Spanish ambassador at Versailles, was ordered to ascertain French intentions toward Britain and to insinuate that Spain might cooperate with France in the war. Choiseul, distrusting Charles and hoping that the forthcoming French negotiations with Britain would succeed, had been planning to discuss with Spain a commercial treaty and a defensive alliance to begin *after* the end of the present war. He informed Grimaldi of his plans to open negotiations with Britain and inquired whether Spain was prepared to fight against Britain in case the Franco-British negotiations failed. Grimaldi admitted he did not know Charles's intentions.

At the beginning of March Choiseul suggested to Grimaldi that France and Spain conclude an offensive and defensive alliance, but his proposals were vague about when the alliance would take effect. (He also told Ossun that negotiating a commercial treaty would be complex and could come later.) On 31 March Wall sent Grimaldi a draft proposal for an alliance but ordered him to present it as unofficial. Choiseul, however, was outraged by the Spanish proposal, which did not offer any Spanish commitment to France until after the war was over. (Charles III feared becoming involved in the war in Germany.) Moreover, Spain expected the French government to make British satisfaction of Spanish grievances part of France's own peace negotiations and also, under certain conditions, to transfer Minorca to Spain. At the end of April, Spain resumed discussions with Britain, which had expressed willingness to discuss abandoning its settlements in Central America if guaranteed a supply of logwood.[45]

French distrust of Spain was reflected in the instructions given Bussy before his departure. He was warned that Fuentes might try to undermine his negotiations and was told that the French negotiations with Spain were subordinate to obtaining peace with Britain. In the Council of State, Puyzieulx, Berryer, and Estées were openly opposed to concluding an agreement with Spain, because it would risk the peacemaking. Nevertheless, on 2 June the French government submitted to Spain its own draft for a treaty which, on Louis' personal insistence, was called a Family Compact (*pacte de famille*). It would be a defensive alliance and guarantee of territory that would come into effect only after the war had been concluded. It would be open to the Bourbon rulers of Naples and Parma as well as those of France and Spain; thus it became known as the Third Family Compact. (The two earlier compacts were concluded in 1733 and 1743.) France also proposed a separate secret convention committing Spain to enter the present war by 1 May 1762 if France and Britain had not already made peace; it also promised French assistance to Spain in obtaining satisfaction of its grievances. The treaty and convention apparently were insurance against the failure of the upcoming Bussy and Stanley negotiations; British acceptance of the French offer of 17 June certainly would have ended Choiseul's discussions with Grimaldi.[46]

Charles III and his ministers received the French proposals with obvious enthusiasm, sending their own proposals on 22 June. Grimaldi was ready to sign immediately, but several issues proved contentious, particularly the French desire that the terms of the Family Compact apply to all wars, including those in Europe, and the Spanish desire to limit it to colonial wars. A compromise eventually was reached by which any future attack on France would be covered, but not an attack upon a French ally or client state. By 15 July the only remaining issue to be solved was Charles's concern about whose ambassadors would take diplomatic precedence. Choiseul's long-standing distrust of Wall even abated; on 7 July he asked Ossun to present him his compliments and noted they had served together during the Italian campaign of 1744. The disputes with Spain gave France the opportunity of waiting for Britain to offer better terms than those of 26 June; by the middle of July with the British negotiations stalled and the Family Compact and convention almost ready for signature, it was Louis XV who decided to introduce the Spanish grievances into Bussy's discussions and to leave to Fuentes the timing of their presentation, pleasing the Spaniards but infuriating Pitt.[47]

The British government already was furious at Spain. By intercepting Grimaldi's correspondence with Fuentes, it knew as early as the beginning of March about his discussions with Choiseul. Bussy had raised the issue of Spain's claims to the four neutral islands of the Caribbean during his discussions with Pitt, which the British regarded as an unacceptable intrusion. (Later, as part of the Family Compact, the Spaniards reluctantly renounced their claim to the islands, a long-standing irritant in Franco-Spanish relations.) The negotiations with Fuentes finally pushed Pitt beyond his endurance. He told Fuentes that Britain would rather give Spain the Tower of London than the right to fish off Newfoundland.[48]

By the end of July, French government was ready to sign the treaties with Spain; on 30 July Choiseul not only informed Ossun of the insulting British ultimata of the 25th but also instructed him to tell Charles III that Louis regarded the treaty as already signed. Choiseul promised that as soon as Spain declared war on Britain France would permit Spain to garrison Minorca, as Charles had requested. (The Spaniards lacked the troops to do so, however.) Also France would discuss Louisiana, which in July 1760 Charles had expressed interest in obtaining by exchange. (At the time Choiseul had ordered Ossun to evade discussion.) Grimaldi was given the same memoir.[49]

It is clear that the decision to reject the British terms and ally with Spain was made by the king himself; what is less clear is the source of Louis' courage. Although the latest war news was the defeat at Vellinghausen and the loss of Pondicherry and Dominica, the king's position within France had been strengthened. Stanley noted the monarchy's improved financial prospects; perhaps Louis was emboldened by his victory over the Parlement of Paris in extending the duration of his wartime tax increases. Perhaps, too, some of Choiseul's courage rubbed off on his master. Stanley commented that the king and his foreign minister were inseparable and that the influence of Madame de Pompadour had declined.[50]

On the other hand, Choiseul seems to have been less wholehearted than was the king about making an alliance with Spain and abandoning the negotiations. While admitting the necessity of this policy, he continued to express his preference for peace if it could be obtained honorably. In particular, he seems to have been more hesitant than the king about presenting the memoir supporting the Spanish grievances. After the decision had been made to sign the Family Compact and convention, he even instructed Bussy that if the British accepted

France's terms he should work with Pitt on how France could evade its obligations to Spain. Noting Choiseul's earlier comments to Grimaldi about wishing for peace, Wall feared that France was using Spain in order to get better terms from Britain while Charles III complained that Bussy merely had recommended Britain remedy the Spanish grievances instead of presenting them specifically as a French demand.[51]

Louis XV, however, was as anxious to complete work on the Family Compact and secret convention as was his cousin Charles. He even agreed to promise in the secret convention that France would not make peace until Charles was content with the peace terms (an article first proposed by the Spanish government in May).[52] Meanwhile Charles satisfied French wishes by testifying to the British that Bussy had acted with his approval and consent in presenting the Spanish grievances.[53] Choiseul and Grimaldi had been granted full powers by their monarchs to sign the two agreements;[54] they did so on August 15.

The Family Compact declared that in the future any enemy of either France or Spain would be the enemy of both. If either was attacked, the other would provide the assistance of twelve ships of the line, six frigates, 18,000 infantry, and 6,000 cavalry. Neither party would make a separate truce or peace, except for the case of Germany, where France, unlike Spain, had obligations stemming from the 1648 Treaty of Westphalia. Subjects or ships of one power would enjoy certain rights in the other's territory equivalent to those of the other's subjects or ships. The rulers of Parma and Naples were invited to join the treaty, which they eventually did, reserving the right to remain neutral during the present war. France and Spain later pledged to procure an indemnity to the king of Sardinia so he would drop his claims to Piacenza.[55]

The accompanying secret convention provided that Spain would declare war on Britain on 1 May 1762 if a peace had not already been concluded by France and Britain. If Spain were attacked by Britain before that date, France would provide assistance. France also would include Spain's complaints in its negotiations with Britain and would not reach a peace agreement or sign an armistice until Charles was satisfied. The French would attempt to procure Minorca for Spain at the peace, and in the interim the Spaniards could occupy the island, as Choiseul had promised. Spain's cession of her rights to the four neutral islands of the Caribbean would be revealed only if necessary. Portugal would be pressured to join the agreement, an article first suggested not by Ossun or Choiseul but by Wall, who convinced Charles that Portugal was a British satellite. (Not only did Britain dominate Portuguese trade but Portuguese Brazil was a smuggling point for British goods into Spanish South America, and Charles feared that the Portuguese colony of Sacramento, today's Uruguay, would also become so.)[56]

At Spanish insistence, the negotiations had been kept secret from Starhemberg, who was informed of the Family Compact only on the day it was signed, not given a copy for three months, and not told at all of the secret convention. To deceive Austria, the convention was redated and signed again in early 1762 (after hostilities between Spain and Britain had begun) as though it were the original.[57]

The signing of the treaties had an instant effect on French relations with Spain. They were welcomed by Charles, who ratified them immediately, expressed his desire to honor Choiseul by making him a member of the Order of the Golden Fleece (which Choiseul postponed accepting in order to protect the secrecy of the negotiations), and wrote personally to his "Good Brother and Cousin" Louis to express his satisfaction.[58]

French negotiations with Britain continued, however, until the middle of September.[59] In spite of their apparent artificiality, they proved extremely important. They further disrupted the unity of the inner cabinet and helped lead to the downfall of Pitt. Surprisingly, moreover, they also narrowed the gap between Britain and France on the fishery question, which, although too late for 1761, greatly facilitated the negotiations of peace in 1762.

On 5 August Choiseul sent Bussy France's response to the British ultimata of 25 July. France insisted on fishing rights in the Gulf of St. Lawrence and off Newfoundland, demanded the return of the merchant ships captured by Britain before the declaration of war, and refused to return the Prussian provinces unless Austria consented. It did express a willingness to accept an island smaller than Isle Royale (such as Isle St. Jean), to evacuate Hesse, Hanover, Ostend, and Nieuport, to make concessions on Dunkirk, to give only financial assistance to Austria provided Britain did the same with Prussia, and to permit Britain to retain Belle Isle if France could retain Minorca. It also accepted in principle Britain's demand for a buffer zone between Louisiana and the British colonies. (Choiseul sent a detailed proposal five days later calling for a buffer zone between the watershed of Hudson Bay and the mouth of the Perdido River, adjoining Spanish Florida, thereby leaving France the three western Great Lakes and significant territory east of the Mississippi, including Fort Toulouse and Mobile Bay.) Choiseul also sent Bussy a personal note asserting France's right to interest itself in the affairs of Spain. Bussy was instructed to leave England if Pitt and his colleagues finally proved unyielding, although Choiseul seems to have wished the doomed negotiations to continue for several more weeks.[60]

The French proposal and Choiseul's note were presented by Bussy on 10 August. They provoked a series of acrimonious discussions in the inner cabinet, lasting from 13 August to 24 August. Pitt wished to terminate the negotiations, but a peace party led by the Dukes of Newcastle, Devonshire, and Bedford mistakenly believed that only the fishery issue prevented a settlement (even though an intercepted dispatch indicated Choiseul's negotiations were a sham). Gradually the peace party was able to persuade both the king and their colleagues in the inner cabinet, including Bute, even though Bute said that without the fishery Britain would gain nothing from the war. Pitt was unsuccessful in the debate largely because he had alienated the other members of the inner cabinet by his imperious conduct toward them and by his intemperate language toward the French. Finally he had to consent to the decision to offer France a share in both fisheries, the right to dry fish on a part of the Newfoundland coast, the tiny island of St. Pierre off Newfoundland as a refuge for their fishing fleet, and the more liberal 1748 treaty provisions regarding Dunkirk. The inner cabinet did agree that the buffer zone for Louisiana which France had suggested should be greatly reduced in size and that Britain should be given both more territory and control of the Indian tribes within the buffer zone. This offer was sent on 27 August as a final ultimatum.[61]

Had the French government been in a position to pursue this offer, perhaps it could have made peace in 1761. On the other hand, the inner cabinet was reluctant at the time to make further concessions, particularly about Germany. The negotiations thus would have taken many more months and would have required France to abandon the Spanish alliance. Such speculations are purely academic. France had hardened its position on returning the Prussian provinces and had just made an alliance with Spain, so the British offer was too little and too late.

The French government did not seriously consider the offer. Choiseul was concerned now with how he could end the negotiations in the way which would most harm the British government's ability to raise money. On 15 September Bussy presented French terms that were likely to force Britain to break off discussions: a better refuge for the fishing fleet, a division of control over the Indian tribes in the North American buffer zone, a slaving station in Africa, and the restitution of French merchant ships captured before the declaration of war. Meanwhile Stanley had reported that France had promised Spain to support her grievances. Pitt and his colleagues responded by immediately recalling Stanley, Newcastle alone dissenting. On 20 September Choiseul gave Stanley his passports to return home. (Stanley blamed Madame de Pompadour for the failure of the negotiations.) Bussy already had held his last discussion with Pitt and was preparing his own return.[62]

Two days later Choiseul told Ossun that the negotiations were broken absolutely and that it was time to make campaign plans and prepare for a wider war.[63] The break in the negotiations was clear-cut, but it proved to be only temporary. The peace negotiations of 1761, surprisingly enough, had a dual nature.

Looked at in isolation they were a tragic failure which resulted in the expansion of the war and the loss of many thousand more lives. On the other hand, if seen from a longer perspective, the negotiations were not without benefit. It took only a few months until they were resumed and the ground gained toward a compromise, particularly on the fisheries, was not lost. The British concessions proved irreversible, in large part because such concessions continued to be necessary in order to end a war in Germany of which Britain had grown weary, whatever enthusiasm it might have for fighting a colonial war against France and Spain. If Louis could stay firm, he not only could have peace, as France so much needed, but he could also win back France's share in the fisheries and save the future of France as a naval power.

SPAIN ENTERS THE WAR

The decision to recall Stanley did not end the dissensions within the inner cabinet. At the same 15 September meeting as it reached that decision, Pitt proposed to his colleagues that Britain capture without warning the annual treasure fleet bringing gold and silver from the Western Hemisphere to Spain. He had learned from an intercepted letter of Grimaldi that a Spanish squadron was preparing to meet it (news confirmed by Stanley); if the British fleet at Gibraltar could arrive first, it could administer a blow to Spain even more damaging than the one delivered to France in 1755. Grimaldi's letter also revealed that Spain had signed a treaty with France, which Pitt believed indicated that war was imminent.[64]

Pitt was eager to begin a war with Spain that presented the opportunity to make more colonial conquests and to crush another rival navy.[65] Pitt's colleagues, however, did not believe the intercepted letter proved that Spain intended war. They wished to wait until Stanley returned from France and could be questioned. For them a war with Spain presented a variety of financial, diplomatic, and military difficulties. Newcastle's concerns about raising money led him to oppose breaking off discussions with France, let alone declaring war against Spain. Alarmist though he generally was, he was not alone in his fears; the price of government securities dropped because of the prospect of a Spanish war (a development closely watched by Bussy and Choiseul). As we shall see, such a war required additional troops and sailors to counter the Spanish navy and to protect Portugal from Spanish invasion; it also, as the inner cabinet feared, disrupted British trade, thereby reducing government revenue. Increased expenses and lower revenues strained the government's credit and worsened the national debt, which by the end of 1762 reached more than £125 million (equivalent to 3 billion livres), almost double what it had been at the beginning of the war, more than a dozen times the government's annual revenue, and almost 30 percent higher than Louis XV's debt. Although the government was able to borrow the necessary funds, it had to pay higher interest rates than in the past.[66]

The expansion of the war also threatened the alliance with Prussia and the continuation of British attempts to protect Hanover. The British government thus far had taken steps to allay Frederick's suspicions of its loyalty to the alliance. It backed down when Frederick objected to Pitt's pressuring him to offer concessions, it refused French demands that Ferdinand's army not be allowed to help Prussia in case of a Franco-British peace, and it protested Bussy's note on behalf of Austria on the grounds that Britain's obligations to Prussia were a matter of national honor. Nevertheless, George III was anxious to end the war in Germany to save money and, at least according to Newcastle, even Pitt was willing to abandon the war if the king insisted. Ominously, Bute predicted to Newcastle that Britain could not afford simultaneous wars in Germany and Spain. For Newcastle, however, Germany in the long run was critical to British security, because it kept France from concentrating her resources on the navy; even for his colleagues who were less committed to the German war, the consequences of adding new military and naval responsibilities required serious consideration.[67]

Perhaps the main question facing the inner cabinet, however, was whether Britain had the necessary military and naval reserves to face an additional enemy. Ligonier believed the British army would have to be expanded by 10,000 men. His estimate of the size of the Spanish army was not inaccurate (on paper it consisted of about 90,000 men), but he greatly exaggerated its readiness and effectiveness.[68] The inner cabinet's more serious concern, however, was the Spanish navy. Pitt argued that it posed no real threat, and his contempt for it was widely shared, but not by Anson, who had long been concerned about the Spaniards.[69] In spite of his personal heroism and great professional competence, Anson, like Newcastle, was prone to alarmism. He had overestimated the danger of invasion in 1756 and sent too few ships to Byng. In 1761 he again overreacted. Although he estimated the present strength of the Spanish navy at only forty ships of the line (about half a dozen fewer than Spain actually had), he was concerned that the ships of the British Mediterranean fleet were too fouled by marine growth to properly watch the Spanish ports. He was also worried because the British navy had fewer ships of the line available than in the previous two years. On 1 June only ninety-nine ships of the line were in commission, a dozen fewer than on the same date in 1759 and 1760. In early August three new ships of the line, two older ones, and a captured French one entered service.

But Anson reported in mid-September that the navy had only 106 of the line available and that it would take until the end of October to get another 6 ships ready.

There were several reasons for the temporary decline in strength: Anson's prior overconfidence, a decline in ship construction (at the beginning of the year, sixteen ships of the line were in construction, but only four of these had been started in 1760), and a shortage of sailors in home ports that was not noticed until May. In fact, though, Anson's concerns were groundless; the French navy was still largely demobilized except for fourteen ships of the line fitting at Brest, Rochefort, and the Vilaine, while the Spanish navy was short of sailors and materiel and hence unprepared to fight. Even had the Spaniards been ready, the British navy could have met the danger, although the margin was small. There were no French ships of the line in commission at Toulon, and the seventeen or so Spanish ships of the line at Cadiz only slightly outnumbered Admiral Charles Saunders's Mediterranean fleet, which could be reinforced from England and could use nearby Gibraltar as a base. Further north Commodore Augustus Keppel had twenty-eight ships of the line in the Bay of Biscay and English Channel watching Brest and Rochefort; his force was large enough that it could have detached a small squadron to watch the seven Spanish ships of the line at Ferrol on the northwest coast of Spain. The British even had a slight numerical superiority in the Caribbean over fourteen Spanish and one French ship of the line; Jamaica, most in danger, could have been reinforced from the British islands like Antigua to windward of it.[70]

With so much at stake and so much uncertain (including even Choiseul's feelings about peace),[71] it is hardly surprising that Pitt's proposal destroyed whatever unity remained within the inner cabinet. After an acrimonious discussion on 18 September, both those favoring and those opposing the expansion of the war tried to win the help of the king. Pitt was unsuccessful at winning any support for his plan in the inner cabinet except from his brother-in-law Earl Temple, the keeper of the privy seal. At a meeting of the inner cabinet on 2 October, shortly after Stanley's return from France, Pitt announced he could not accept the decision of his colleagues to refrain from attacking Spain. Three days later he resigned as secretary of state and left the inner cabinet, followed shortly by Temple; his colleagues seem to have been shocked and disconcerted about having to bear the responsibility and dangers of directing the war without him. The king, for all his dislike of Pitt, treated him courteously.[72]

His motives for resigning and the influence of his emotions upon his decision remain unclear.[73] His action led to only two immediate personnel changes. Temple's younger brother George Grenville assumed Pitt's role as the government's spokesman and leader in the House of Commons, while the Earl of

Egremont (the former minister designate to the abortive Congress of Augsburg) became secretary of state for the southern department. Both of these men were supporters of Bute and joined him, Newcastle, and Hardwicke as the government's decision makers. The distribution of power did not promise to be permanent, however, as Bute told Grenville that Newcastle was a "crazy old man."[74]

During the inner cabinet's debate, Wall and Grimaldi insisted that Bussy's memoir on Spain's behalf had not been intended to offend Britain and that Spain, wishing only a solid peace, was not arming for war.[75] They were successful at buying time for most of the treasure fleet to reach Cadiz on 12 September (although the last straggler from the convoy did not arrive until the end of the following month); unfortunately for Britain, Ambassador Bristol failed to give warning of Spain's intentions.[76]

Upon Pitt's resignation, the initial desire of the inner cabinet seems to have been maintaining continuity. Bute immediately wrote Ambassador Mitchell in Prussia that no changes in policy would be made.[77] When the issue of the German war came up in the newly elected House of Commons on 13 November, Pitt opposed recalling British troops in terms that even Newcastle could not have surpassed, claiming America had been captured in Germany. Bute, however, did not defend the German war, and Grenville during the following month attributed the fall of Canada instead to France's shortage of sailors. Although Parliament eventually approved the continuation of subsidies for Ferdinand's army, the German war continued to be the subject of hostile pamphlets and parliamentary criticism, as Ferdinand failed to prevent Broglie's raids and Frederick II lost Schweidnitz.[78]

Militarily, the inner cabinet attempted to maintain continuity as well. Britain planned to put additional pressure on France by capturing Martinique. The attack had been in gestation since the beginning of 1761, when it had been chosen as a target instead of Louisiana. Pitt sent orders to Amherst to send an expeditionary force of 8,000 men that would make the assault in late September or early October, once the hurricane season had ended. He promised to send transports to New York; in the interim he hoped the first 2,000 men could be sent to Guadeloupe in order to capture Dominica and possibly St. Lucia before the summer hurricane season began. He also sent orders to the British governors in North America to raise two-thirds of the previous year's troop quota in order to protect the frontier and free British regulars for service in the Caribbean; Amherst hoped to raise 15,000 provincial troops and to find 4,000 recruits in America for his regular battalions (seven colonies complied, raising about 9,200 provincial troops).[79]

When negotiations with Choiseul began in March, Pitt took action to accelerate the attack. He ordered Amherst to add to the expeditionary force whatever men could be spared and to use whatever transports were available. Amherst already had selected 2,000 troops for the West Indies. In early June the British captured Dominica, although the troop commander, Andrew, Baron Rollo, chose not to proceed to St. Lucia, which recently had been reinforced from Martinique. The following month Pitt told Amherst that the transports for the expedition, delayed so they could be used for attacking Belle Isle, were ready to depart (although the king refused Pitt's request that they bring 2,000 troops from the garrison of the newly captured island). Part of the squadron at Halifax was ordered to New York as an escort to the Caribbean. The inner cabinet, responding to Pitt's threats of resignation, finally agreed in mid-September to add four battalions from Belle Isle (totaling 2,600 men) to the expedition, plus ordering half a dozen ships of the line under Rear Admiral George Rodney to escort them. By the end of the year Rodney and Major General Robert Monckton, the military commander, had assembled seventeen ships of the line and some 13,000 troops at Barbados. The twenty-one battalions there included eleven battalions (with 7,600 men) from North America. They sailed for Martinique on 5 January 1762.[80]

The new government did break continuity by softening its policy toward Spain. It asked politely about Spain's new treaty commitments to France and offered to evacuate the British settlements in central America once Spain had guaranteed a supply of logwood. It was not until 28 October, however, that Egremont instructed Ambassador Bristol about the new policy.[81] Anson already had sent reinforcements to Saunders, who reported twelve Spanish ships of the line at Cadiz and wished to attack them. Bristol's negotiations lasted so long, however, that when the discussions failed, Saunders could only blockade the port.[82]

Soon after dispatching Egremont's instructions to Bristol, the British government received a 2 November report from Bristol of a conversation with Wall in which the Spanish foreign minister admitted the existence of the Family Compact and accused Britain of wishing to ruin France so it could seize Spain's possessions.[83] The arrival of this report on 14 November caught the British by surprise, as hitherto Wall and Fuentes had indicated a willingness to compromise. Egremont, Bute, and Grenville, fearing Pitt's criticism if they appeared weak, prepared orders for Bristol to demand a categorical answer about Spain's intentions. If none were forthcoming, he was ordered to treat this as a declaration of war and depart for Lisbon without taking leave.[84] Meanwhile Bute moved immediately to open negotiations with Prussia for increasing British financial support. In exchange, Frederick would be expected to accept Britain's right to make a separate peace without prior consultation.[85] Bute also sent peace feelers to Choiseul, making use of Sardinian envoy Viry and informing only George III. On 8 December, Choiseul accepted the mediation of Viry and his counterpart at Versailles, Sardinian ambassador Roberto Ignazio, Marquis Solaro di Breglio, bailli of the Order of Malta. On Bute's behalf, Viry suggested as a basis for discussion the British ultimata of 25 July and the French of 5 August. Louis, however, expected better terms now that Pitt was out of office and Spain was ready to enter the war. Choiseul was pessimistic that any British government would dare offer them, but he claimed that France had the means to continue fighting for another two or three years to obtain them. Discussions thus were at a very preliminary stage when Bute and his colleagues received dire news from Spain.[86]

Charles III reacted with outrage to Bristol's demands, treating them as derogatory to his honor. Wall gave Bristol permission to leave, but made it impossible for him to communicate with his court or with Saunders at Gibraltar. Not until he reached the Portuguese border on 26 December could he send a report. Meanwhile the Spanish government ordered all British ships in Spanish ports embargoed (apparently most escaped, and the others were exchanged for embargoed Spanish ships). British goods were sequestered and British citizens expelled; Spain ordered the temporary embargo of other ships so as to prevent news from leaking. Orders were sent to the Western Hemisphere to attack the British, and Fuentes was instructed to return to Spain.[87]

The Spanish government's attempts to delay news of Bristol's departure were only partly successful. The news reached Lisbon, where it was relayed by the British minister. On 24–26 December the British government sent its own orders to initiate hostilities, and on 2 January 1762 George III publicly announced his intention to make war on Spain. It was not, however, until 4 January, too late to be useful, that Saunders learned that finally he was free to open hostilities.[88] The Spanish navy was now ready to join the French, and with hope restored of success at sea, the French navy received a new naval minister, Choiseul himself, and prepared to resume activity.

CHOISEUL BECOMES NAVAL MINISTER

For the French navy, 1761 was another year of humiliations, chief among them its failure to prevent the capture of Belle Isle. The attack on the island had been canceled at the end of 1760, but early in 1761 the British government learned that Grimaldi was conducting negotiations with Choiseul. The inner cabinet had been planning to send a squadron and expeditionary force to capture the Mascarene Islands in the Indian Ocean. The threat of a French alliance with

Spain made so distant an operation too dangerous. The idea of attacking Belle Isle became more attractive because the troops and ships would only have to go to the Bay of Biscay, close enough to England to be available in case of emergency. Moreover, the inner cabinet saw Belle Isle as a useful bargaining chip should peace negotiations resume. Thus the Belle Isle expedition was revived.[89]

On 29 March, just two days before Golitsyn delivered Choiseul's proposals, an expeditionary force of twelve battalions (about 7,000 men) sailed from the roadstead of Portsmouth under the escort of eleven ships of the line. The French knew from the British reconnaissance of Belle Isle that the island was endangered and had spent the winter improving its defenses. The island's 4,000-man garrison actually repelled the first British landing on 8 April. Two weeks later the British were successful at putting troops ashore but it took six and a half weeks and considerable naval and military reinforcements before the island's citadel was captured on 8 June. (In the process the British had to divert transports from New York, delaying the attack on Martinique by several months.) The French navy planned an attempt to save the island. On 29 April Berryer ordered the armament of six ships of the line from Brest (the *Défenseur*, 74, *Diadème*, 74 [replaced on 13 May by the *Protée*, 64], *Hector*, 74, *Palmier*, 74, *Brillant*, 64, and *Dragon*, 64, the last two of which finally had escaped from the Vilaine on the night of 6–7 January),[90] six from Rochefort (*Guerrier*, 74, *Intrépide*, 74, *Magnifique*, 74, *Souverain*, 74, *Solitaire*, 64, and *Saint-Michel*, 60), and two from the Vilaine (*Eveillé*, 64, and *Sphinx*, 64, the latter eventually replaced by the *Robuste*, 74); he also planned to arm two frigates, a dozen prames, a dozen gunboats, and fifty-four flat boats.

A month later Berryer prepared plans for subsequent operations, which included sending the dozen ships of the line from Brest and Rochefort to recapture Guadeloupe. The only ship of the line to reach sea before December, however, was the *Saint-Michel*, which cruised for prizes off Ireland and later went as far as the Azores with a convoy; the British had too many ships and the French too few sailors and too little materiel and supplies for an attempt to be made to save Belle Isle or to recapture it. Moreover, a British squadron arrived near Rochefort, preventing its ships from joining the ones at Brest.[91] For Britain, however, the conquest of Belle Isle had few military benefits, as Bedford, a former first lord of the admiralty, astutely had predicted. No further operations could be mounted against the French coast, and valuable British troops had to be used to garrison it.[92]

The failure to save Belle Isle was not the only humiliation suffered by the French navy. Short of funds, Berryer even had to sell some naval materiel. Lack of pay drove sailors into privateering; most of the 9,000 men taken prisoner in 1761 were captured aboard privateers. In May, Berryer tried unsuccessfully to disarm privateers in order to provide naval crews and prevent incidents from disrupting the peace talks. Some sailors found work on merchant ships. There was an increase of trade with the West Indies, particularly from Bordeaux, even though the navy was able to send only one ship of the line to the Caribbean in 1761. The *Courageux*, 74, and two frigates brought 500 troops to Martinique. To save money the *Courageux* carried some private trade goods. She was captured off Portugal while returning, the Portuguese with their usual kindness to Frenchmen caring for the wounded brought ashore.[93] The navy did not even fit out any ships of the line at Toulon, although as a goodwill gesture France purchased at Malta a Turkish ship of the line that had been seized by Christian slaves and sent it under escort of a frigate to Constantinople.[94]

Unable to make use of its ships, the navy loaned nine ships of the line to private contractors for privateering ventures or to carry supplies while *en flûte*. Only three had any success: the *Protée*, 64, which cruised for prizes and returned in March, the *Vaillant*, 64, loaned to the East India Company, which sailed to India and arrived safely, and the *Sage*, 64, which sailed to St. Domingue and returned with eight prizes taken off New England. Two, the *Notre-Dame-de-Rosaire*, 64, and *Vierge-de-Santé*, 64, had to return to Toulon after nearly being captured. The remaining four, the *Achille*, 64, *Sainte-Anne*, 64, *Warwick*, 64, and *Oriflamme*, 50, were taken by the British.[95] With the loss of five ships of the line and the formal condemnation of the *Florissant*, the navy was reduced to forty-six of the line by the end of the year. Only one ship of the line was launched during 1761, the *Sagittaire*, 50, and one begun, the *Cimeterre*, 74.[96]

With the impending entry of Spain into the war, however, the navy's fortunes showed promise of improvement. Berryer already had largely relinquished direction of naval operations to Choiseul while he concentrated on holding down expenses. On 13 October, as Spain prepared to enter the war, Choiseul took over direct control. Berryer, in ill health, resigned and, at the suggestion of Madame de Pompadour, was honored for his integrity and faithfulness by being made keeper of the royal seals. (He died the following August.) In spite of Choiseul's previous criticism of the navy, it now had a spokesman of unrivaled power and influence. He retained his post as army minister, thereby reducing competition between the two services. He did, however, relinquish formal direction of the foreign ministry to his cousin, the comte de Choiseul, although he retained direct control over relations with Spain (and the other Bourbon states, Parma and Naples), further centralizing direction of the war against Britain. The comte had left Vienna in May preparatory to the proposed Congress of Augsburg and joined the Council of State on 27 August.[97] He was replaced in Vienna by two successive chargés d'affaires, Claude-Pierre-Maximilien Radix de Sainte-Foy (who soon joined Bussy and La Ville as a *premier commis*) and

Conrad-Alexandre Gérard, and then by an inexperienced minister plenipotentiary, Louis-Marie-Florent, comte de Châtelet-Lomont.[98]

There were several encouraging developments within the first few months of Choiseul's tenure as naval minister. In November, Ternay and Hector, now commanding the *Robuste* and *Eveillé*, escaped from the Vilaine to Corunna and then to Brest.[99] Froger de l'Eguille arrived at Brest with the *Minotaure*, 74, *Zodiaque*, 74, and *Actif*, 64, on 31 January 1762 after a five-month passage from the Ile de Bourbon. (This squadron had been sent orders in February 1761, to return home, leaving defense of the Mascarenes to East India Company ships; d'Aché returned to France in advance on an East India Company frigate.)[100] Most importantly, the president of the Estates of Languedoc proposed in November that the province donate an 80-gun ship of the line to the French navy. The motion was approved by acclamation, and soon other provincial estates, groups of government officials, city governments, and other corporate bodies and individuals also offered donations. Although not all the subscriptions were successful, enough money was raised to build seventeen ships of the line. Moreover, 16 million livres was pledged for the general use of the navy, permitting the royal treasury to assign the navy 14 million livres more in 1762 than in the previous year. Contributions were all the more welcome as virtually nothing was obtained from foreign loans in 1762. The government needed another advance from the Farmers General, while both the army, with its 190 million livre budget, and the navy with its 30 million received advances from Laborde. Because of timber shortages, not all the ships could be started immediately, so Choiseul also was able to borrow from the contributions to finance current naval operations.

Three ships of the line already were in construction: the *Impéteux*, 90, renamed *Ville-de-Paris*, the *Cimeterre*, 74, renamed *Citoyen*, and the *Entêté*, 64, renamed *Orion* and later *Union*. The keels of nine were laid in 1762: *Languedoc*, 80, *Saint-Esprit*, 80, *Bourgogne*, 74, *Diligent*, 74, *Six-Corps*, 74, *Zélé*, 74, *Union* (later *Provence*), 64, *Bordelaise*, 56, and *Ferme*, 56. The last five were begun after the war: *Bretagne*, 100, *Marseillais*, 74, *Artésien*, 64, *Flamand*, 56, and *Utile*, 56. The *Diligent* and *Six-Corps* were launched in 1762 and the other fifteen by the end of 1766.[101] Choiseul had prepared the way by a brilliant piece of public relations, publishing the diplomatic correspondence from the peace discussions accompanied by his own commentary so as to demonstrate Britain's bad faith, much as Louis XIV had done in 1709. Although such a gesture had a limited effect on the general public, it had a substantial impact upon the wealthy and influential; Voltaire, for example, praised it and said he would like to see it printed by 100 ships of the line and delivered to Madras or Boston. Choiseul did send copies to d'Affry to distribute in England and to various diplomats to distribute in the countries to which they were accredited. Ironically, Choiseul may also have helped to smooth subsequent negotiations as well; not realizing discussions soon would be resumed, he apparently had recommended concessions in the 5 August French ultimatum primarily for the sake of their publication. [102] As naval minister, however, Choiseul's two most immediate concerns were the protection of the West Indies and the development of a war strategy to make use of Spain's impending entry into the war.

The urgency of the first of these was apparent by Bussy's warnings that Martinique likely would be attacked. [103] Luckily, Choiseul could build upon work already in progress. The fleet being outfitted to save Belle Isle and then to recapture Guadeloupe already had been shifted to the more prosaic task of reinforcing the remaining French islands. The six ships of the line at Brest were supplemented by the *Duc-de-Bourgogne*, 80, and the squadron was placed under the command of Chef d'escadre Courbon-Blénac, the port commandant of Brest; it was ordered to take two battalions to St. Domingue. The six at Rochefort were supplemented by the *Orient*, 80, *Tonnant*, 80, and *Northumberland*, 70, and placed under the command of Chef d'escadre Morel d'Aubigny, the port commandant of Rochefort; they were ordered to take three battalions to Martinique. Given the threat to Martinique, Blénac's squadron was ordered to stop there before proceeding to St. Dominigue and to disembark some or all of its troops, now increased to 4,000 officers and men. Both squadrons were delayed, however. The Brest squadron, which had planned to sail in October, did not leave until December, and it was forced by weather to return to port, while the Rochefort squadron, planned for about 20 December, was not yet ready. The only reinforcements to leave for the West Indies during late 1761 were 850 troops who left Bordeaux for St. Domingue on four of Abraham Gradis's merchant ships on 29 November and 3 December; they arrived safely in January. [104] (Early in 1762, six merchant ships and a battalion of troops were sent to Louisiana, but only two ships and 300 troops arrived). [105]

By the end of 1761, plans for Blénac and Aubigny's squadrons had been expanded. Choiseul hoped the Spanish and French navies would help force Britain to make peace. For this he needed Spain to begin hostilities against Britain. Waiting for Spain proved frustrating. The secret convention did not require Spain to enter the war until 1 May 1762. On 17 September 1761 Ossun reported that Spain, wishing more time to prepare for war, planned to negotiate with Britain until December. Repeatedly but unsuccessfully Choiseul urged Spain to commence hostilities sooner; moreover, he was unable to obtain more than a small increase in the monthly loans Laborde was receiving from Spain, in spite of his offer to give Louisiana to Charles III in exchange for a major loan or for an immediate Spanish declaration of war against Britain.

At least, however, Spain was moving closer to war with Portugal, even though their South American border disputes had been resolved. Ossun reported on 17 September that Spain was applying diplomatic pressure on Portugal to join the Family Compact; although optimistic, Spain was prepared to use force if the negotiations failed. Spanish optimism soon vanished. By November Spain was preparing to invade Portugal with an army of 30,000 men, much to the delight of Choiseul, who announced to Ossun on 15 November that France was sending Jacques O'Dunne to Lisbon as minister plenipotentiary in order to help Spain put pressure on Portugal; he would stop in Madrid to coordinate plans. Choiseul, however, hoped diplomacy would fail, believing it would be to the mutual benefit of Spain and France to have Portugal as an enemy to be plundered, a sentiment that Ossun said was shared by Charles III. Choiseul even told Starhemberg that he wished that those who would not join the fight against Britain would be regarded as enemies; he told Ossun, however, that the Netherlands were not the same as Portugal (undoubtedly remembering they still helped supply the French West Indies as well as bringing naval materiel to French ports). He added, though, that if the next campaign was unsuccessful France would consider attacking them, too, as Charles had suggested.[106]

As relations deteriorated between Spain and Portugal, Choiseul made plans for how to conduct the war once Spain openly began hostilities. On 25 November he sent Ossun detailed war plans. France was willing to subordinate the war in Germany to a direct war on Britain and its client state Portugal; France planned to reduce its army in Germany to 130,000 men, making any new conquests doubtful. Choiseul volunteered on behalf of the king to participate in a Spanish attack on Jamaica and promised to assemble an army of 30,000 men in the area of Dunkirk and Calais for a new attempt to invade England. He suggested that as a feint Spain threaten an invasion of the British Isles by assembling troops in Galicia.[107] Meanwhile, Spain formalized arrangements for its colonial governors to assist the French. Some officials, like those in Santo Domingo who sent food to neighboring St. Dominique, were more cooperative than others, particularly in Havana.[108]

The news that Spain had broken off discussions with Britain brought further offers of cooperation from Choiseul. On 25 December he told Ossun that, although it was now too close to the rainy season to plan an immediate attack on Jamaica, he would do all he could to help the Brest and Rochefort squadrons reach the West Indies where they could cooperate with Spain. He offered to use ten ships of the line from Toulon to help Charles's son defend Sicily, to form a corps of 15,000 men in the provinces of Provence and Dauphiné adjoining the possessions of the king of Sardinia so as to keep him from taking Piacenza by force (as Charles feared), to send troops to relieve the Spaniards being used to attack Portugal, and even to help in an attack on Gibraltar. Ominously, however,

Ossun warned that the Spanish army probably would not be ready to attack Portugal by the planned date of 1 March (assuming negotiations failed); of equal concern he reported on 28 December the arrival of a British squadron at Lisbon. Unknown to France, Bute had just promised Portuguese ambassador Martinho de Melo e Castro an expeditionary force of 6,000 British troops to help defend Portugal. With the help of the British, Portugal would not prove as defenseless as Spain had assumed.[109]

Meanwhile, Choiseul and the comte de Choiseul could not neglect eastern Europe. In his commentary to his documentary history of the peace negotiations, the duc de Choiseul stressed France's fidelity to its alliance with Austria,[110] and he tried to soothe the suspicions of Starhemberg and the Austrians about both the Franco-British peace discussions and France's relations with Austria's old rival Spain; although he did not reveal the existence of the secret Franco-Spanish convention, he did suggest that Spain wished an alliance with Austria.[111] Relations with Austria became somewhat less complicated once French negotiations with Britain ended. France now was concerned only that its allies pursue the war as vigorously as it did. The comte de Choiseul assured the Austrians that, if necessary, France could fight for another two or three years.[112]

In spite of the capture of Schweidnitz and Kolberg, the military and diplomatic situation in eastern Europe was precarious at year's end. As we have seen, financial difficulties caused Austria to reduce the size of its army. In spite of French bribes and the French subsidy, Sweden was preparing to leave the war, while the Turks were cold toward France. Terrified by Crown Prince Peter of Russia, the Danes threatened an alliance with Prussia if he refused to relent, but instead he increased his demands. The Poles wanted closer relations with France and had even sent an emissary to revive the idea of the prince de Conti's candidacy for their throne, but Louis XV rejected the idea. The duc de Choiseul's fears that somehow Britain and Spain might reconcile had proved groundless, but his fears that either Austria or Russia might drop out of the war were not without foundation. In spite of their victories, the Russians too were weary of the war. Only Empress Elizabeth was willing to press on until Frederick was crushed, and her health had grown so weak that she no longer appeared in public.[113] Not only the fate of Prussia was dependent upon her; Choiseul's plans for pressuring Britain into a compromise peace soon were complicated by developments in St. Petersburg.

9

1762
Military Failures, Diplomatic Success

Empress Elizabeth's illness, perhaps cancer, proved to be terminal; she died on 5 January 1762 (or, according to the Russian calendar, 25 December 1761). No one knew what to expect of her nephew, the Grand Duke, who now became Emperor Peter III. In spite of his professed admiration for Frederick II, Peter had never met him, and even the Prussian ruler was unsure of Peter's intentions. All France could do was hope for the best and take care not to displease him.[1]

Peter's admiration of Prussia was not disinterested. Like Maria Theresa's son Joseph, who became ruler of Austria nineteen years later, he wished to model his state after Prussia so as to better compete in the European balance of power. He intended to make Russia more economically progressive but also more centralized and militarily efficient. He hoped to use Prussia to further his designs on Schleswig and Holstein, which were not a sentimental folly but rather a bold extension of Russia's expansion westward. If successful, Russia would become a major power in Germany and, by reducing Denmark to dependency, would dominate the Baltic.[2]

He quickly moved to reconcile with Prussia, while making obvious his hatred of France, the only other power to whom the Danes could turn for assistance. He ordered the Russian army in the area of Kolberg to cease offensive operations and the Russian auxiliary corps serving with the Austrians in Silesia to return to the main army. He also dismissed all Frenchmen in Russian service and, more seriously for France, prevented Golitsyn's designated successor, Baron Heinrich von Gross, from replacing him at The Hague. (Gross was a major intelligence source for France who already had been promised 50,000 livres per year.) Peter's friendliness to British envoy Robert Murray Keith contrasted sharply with his insults to Breteuil and the new Austrian ambassador, Florimond-Claude-

Charles, Graf Mercy d'Argenteau. Perhaps most important, he refused to receive a subsidy payment from Austria, announcing the end of the Austrian alliance.[3]

Frederick II was quick to respond to the change of rulers. While continuing his negotiations with the Tartars and Turks, he now sought to turn them against the Austrians rather than the Russians. He released all Russian prisoners of war and named Colonel Bernhard von der Goltz as Prussian minister to the Russian court in order to negotiate a peace settlement. Goltz was given secret orders to agree to Prussian neutrality in case of a war between Russia and Denmark.[4] On 23 February, while Goltz still was traveling to St. Petersburg, Peter sent declarations to his nominal allies France, Sweden, and Austria, announcing that for the sake of peace Russia was renouncing its conquests and urging them to do the same. Three weeks later he signed a two-month armistice with Prussia, promising to return all the Prussian territory that Russia had conquered and offering to negotiate an offensive and defensive alliance. Frederick II, who by now had lost faith in his alliance with Britain, gave Goltz permission to sign whatever treaty Peter proposed. On 24 March the 20,000-man Russian auxiliary corps in Silesia began marching toward the Oder.[5]

The negotiation of a formal peace treaty was largely a formality; it was signed on 5 May. The Russians returned East Prussia and the portion of Pomerania that they had held, and by a secret article both parties pledged to work toward an alliance. As France suspected, Frederick was not enthusiastic about going to war with Denmark and was concerned about Peter gaining territory in northern Germany. Outweighing this, however, was his need for Russian help against Austria. Even before signing an alliance, he promised the Russians an auxiliary corps of 20,000 men for use against Denmark. Meanwhile, Sweden, which had signed an armistice with Prussia in April, signed a peace treaty on 22 May, both parties returning their conquests.[6]

The Danes, although careful to give Peter no excuse for war, refused to surrender to his demands and mobilized an army to resist him. They found as little international support as the Czechoslovakian government did in 1938. The Austrians refused to become involved, denying even a French request for aid in providing Denmark financial assistance. The British crown, like the French, was a guarantor of Schleswig by a 1720 treaty, and Britain did not want to see Denmark driven into French arms or Russia gain power in Germany and the Baltic Sea. It was too dependent, however, on Russian naval supplies to offer more than neutrality. France, Denmark's supposed protector, was no more helpful, hoping Britain would rescue the Danes. Bernstorff sent his nephew to Versailles to obtain the 6 million livres the French government was in arrears for its subsidy payments, but all that Choiseul could promise was 600,000 livres by year's end. The comte de Choiseul, realizing that Breteuil's situation was hopeless, sent him orders to depart from Russia for Stockholm in order to replace Ambassador Havrincourt; after Breteuil was banished from the Russian court over a breach of protocol, he demanded his passports and then left St. Petersburg on 25 June.[7]

Six days earlier Goltz had signed a twenty-year treaty of friendship and alliance with Russia. It contained secret clauses by which Peter guaranteed Frederick's possession of Silesia and Glatz, in return for which Frederick guaranteed Peter's possession of Schleswig and electoral Holstein. The Russian auxiliary corps that had served with the Austrians joined with the Prussian army and began sending raiding parties into Bohemia. On 4 July a Russian fleet of eight ships of the line sailed from Kolberg. The Danes briefly occupied Hamburg in order to force its bankers to loan money to them, and on 13 July a Danish fleet of fourteen ships of the line sailed from Copenhagen. (The rival navies had twenty-five or thirty ships of the line apiece.) Peter treated the Danish occupation of Hamburg as an act of war and prepared to leave St. Petersburg to join the army. While Sweden was able to maintain its neutrality, Frederick II seemingly had little choice but to permit the Russians to march through Prussia to attack Denmark; he offered his mediation, but the terms were too pro-Russian. Denmark rejected them and mobilized for war.[8]

In preparing for a war that he alone desired, Peter misjudged his freedom of action. He was neither unsophisticated nor irrational, but he was arrogant and overconfident. His political reforms angered influential members of the Russian Church and aristocracy. Even more dangerous for him, he alienated the Russian army by returning its conquests from Prussia and disregarding its traditions. Perhaps most dangerous of all, he continued to threaten and insult his wife, Catherine, who was more ruthless, courageous, and politically skilled than he realized. Disregarding Frederick's warnings about leaving Russia before he was formally crowned emperor, Peter announced he would leave for Germany at the end of July. On 9 July (or 28 June by the Russian calendar) elite regiments of the Russian army seized St. Petersburg and proclaimed Catherine empress. Peter soon was arrested and forced to abdicate; two weeks later he was murdered by his captors.[9]

Although Catherine II does not seem to have ordered the killing, she did not punish the killers. On the other hand she treated her late husband's friends and followers mildly, and violence ceased. This caution and moderation marked her domestic and foreign policy in general during the initial part of her reign. She announced she would honor the peace treaty with Prussia, but not the treaty of alliance, as she wished to live in peace with all her neighbors. She evacuated her troops from East Prussia and Silesia and offered to mediate a general peace, but, to her regret, Russia played no direct role in either the French and Spanish negotiations with Britain or the Austria negotiations with Prussia. Undoubtedly her policy of neutrality was wise, given the exhaustion of the Russian treasury and her need to secure her hold on the throne.[10]

Catherine II's foreign policy doomed the Prussian attempts to persuade the Tartars and Turks to participate in the war. Frederick had hoped to use them to terrorize Hungary, forcing the Austrians to detach troops from Silesia and Saxony, but without the possibility of Russian support his prospective allies chose to remain neutral, having no real grounds to quarrel with Austria.[11]

Frederick, thrown on his own resources, concentrated on recapturing Schweidnitz. The commander of the Russian auxiliary corps delayed his departure long enough to help Frederick drive off Daun and surround the fortress in late July, but capturing it required a nine-week siege. On 9 October, however, Schweidnitz and its 10,000-man garrison surrendered. Three weeks later Prince Henry won a battle in Saxony, ending an Austrian advance north of Dresden. Before going into winter quarters he launched raids against the central German principalities allied with Austria. The Austrians gave up hope of regaining Silesia, but at the end of 1762 they still held Glatz and Dresden, while the French still held Wesel and the Prussian provinces along the Rhine.[12]

For Spain, as for Austria, the campaign of 1762 brought little but defeat and disappointment. It was not for want of effort. Charles III spent almost a third of his 1762 budget on the navy, outfitting forty-seven ships of the line. He also expanded his army to 141 battalions of infantry and 71 squadrons of cavalry, which on paper totaled almost 110,000 troops, although actually they were 30,000 men under strength.[13] Consistently, however, Charles overestimated the abilities of his forces to overcome the enemy and surmount logistical difficulties.

Nowhere was Spanish overconfidence and inexperience more apparent than in the Portuguese campaign. On 15 February Ossun reported to Choiseul that because of shortages of artillery the invasion could not begin before 1 April. Partly because of bad weather and logistical difficulties, however, it did not begin until 30 April, several months later than Choiseul wished and Charles III intended. This at least gave Charles the opportunity to soothe his conscience, or, as Ossun called it, his good heart. In private life a man of exceptional decency and honor, he, unlike Choiseul, had moral reservations about attacking Portugal. He decided to give his brother-in-law Joseph I a chance to demonstrate that Portugal was not a satellite of Great Britain by closing Portuguese ports to British shipping and by permitting Spain to occupy Portugal's fortifications. He sent to Lisbon a Spanish minister, José Terrero, who was accompanied by O'Dunne; they arrived on 10 February. Although Terrero was ordered to give Joseph only four days to respond, Charles hesitated to break off discussions because of Joseph's obvious desire for peace. The negotiations proved unsuccessful because ultimately Joseph was unwilling to break with Britain, but it was not until the last week of April that Terrero and O'Dunne left Lisbon. (Portugal declared war on France and Spain in May, while France declared war on Portugal on 20 June.)[14]

In spite of the delay, Spain should have had little difficulty overcoming the Portuguese army, which had barely 10,000 effectives and whose quality O'Dunne described as pitiful. Against them the Spaniards deployed more than 40,000 troops (plus a dozen French battalions or around 8,000 men which arrived in midcampaign). Portugal was saved by the arrival of 6,000 British troops between May and July, by Spain's logistical difficulties in fighting a war in a backward country with difficult terrain, and, above all, by poor Spanish strategy. Rather than simply sending his army up the valley of the Tagus River to Lisbon, Charles decided to invade the mountainous northern part of Portugal. Supposedly this was because he believed the Tagus valley could not be forced, but perhaps this choice also was designed to spare his sister from humiliation by giving Portugal a chance to surrender before Lisbon was occupied. The poorly trained and inexperienced Spanish army was overwhelmed by the difficult terrain and never reached its objective, the coastal city of Oporto. In mid-campaign the army was ordered south to the Tagus, but first it had to besiege the border fortress of Almeida. On 25 August, after the arrival of French reinforcements, the Spaniards procured its surrender, their only important military victory. By the time the army reached the Tagus, it was on the verge of collapse from disease and exhaustion. Meanwhile the British and Portuguese had established a defensive position downriver at Abrantes. After a few skirmishes, the Spaniards retreated across the Spanish border. The outcome of the campaign helped the cause of peace by dampening Charles's ardor for war; had the Spanish invasion been successful it might have complicated the peace negotiations, although, as the historian Richard Pares astutely comments, Britain likely would have captured something to exchange for Portugal. Ossum predicted that if Spain conquered Portugal, it would offer Portugal and Oran in exchange for Gibraltar.[15]

The British campaign in the West Indies inflicted another defeat on Spain, as well as defeats on France. Martinique, which had been so difficult to attack in 1759, was conquered with relative ease in 1762. The French had eight battalions of militia but only 700 regular infantry and 300 marines, too few to resist 13,000 invaders. The British landed near Fort Royal on 16 January, captured its fortress on 3 February, and accepted the surrender of the entire island on 13 February.[16] The British proceeded to capture St. Lucia on 25 February and Grenada on 4 March. Rear Admiral George Rodney, disregarding orders to keep his fleet concentrated, then sent Commodore James Douglas with nine ships of the line to reinforce the seven ships of the line stationed at Jamaica, which Rodney believed threatened. Once there, Douglas detached seven ships of the line to blockade St. Domingue, where a French squadron had arrived.[17]

Meanwhile, Britain was preparing to attack Cuba, the most valuable Spanish possession in the Caribbean. The plans, drafted by Anson, were approved by the inner cabinet on 6 January. Five ships of the line under Admiral George Pocock, who had performed superbly in India, were ordered to escort four battalions from England to take over the garrisoning of Martinique, which the British expected to capture before they arrived. The same troops used for its conquest would be used to capture Havana. Pocock was appointed commander of the naval forces for the operation, while the land forces were led by Lieutenant General George Keppel, Earl of Albemarle (brother of Commodore Augustus Keppel, who served under Pocock's command).

Pocock sailed on 6 March, but when he arrived at Barbados on 20 April, he found most of Rodney's squadron dispersed. Pocock picked up four additional ships of the line and the 11,000–12,000 troops for the Cuban invasion and sailed from Martinique on 6 May. Between Cuba and St. Dominigue he met an additional sixteen ships of the line, including those that had been blockading the French colony. He then sailed via the dangerous and seldom used Old Bahama Channel along the northern coast of Cuba to Havana. His arrival on 6 June took the Spaniards by complete surprise, and an immediate attack would have captured the city. Unfortunately for the British, an audacious plan had been entrusted to a cautious and conventional general, as it had been at Rochefort and Guadeloupe. Instead of a direct attack on Havana, Albemarle began a regular siege of the fortress, El Morro, protecting its eastern side. El Morro was brilliantly defended and did not surrender until 30 July. Fortunately for the British, the onset of yellow fever was somewhat delayed, so that part of the invasion force was still usable. Moreover, at the end of July and beginning of August, the British received 3,250 reinforcements from North America, somewhat more than half of whom were provincial troops from New York, New Jersey, Rhode Island, and Connecticut. With their help Albemarle finally captured Havana on 12 August, along with nine Spanish ships of the line (including two awaiting commissioning); another three Spanish ships of the line were scuttled to block the entrance to the harbor. Barely a quarter of the 2,300 Spanish regulars who had led the defense of Havana were left when it surrendered.

Choiseul later claimed that the defenders of Cuba had saved St. Domingue. It is difficult to predict if Albemarle would have attempted another invasion had he captured Cuba more quickly (or whether Amherst would have captured Louisiana if his troops had not been needed by Albemarle), but the long siege, like that of Louisbourg in 1758 or Quebec in 1759, made further operations impossible. By mid-October some 5,300 British and American soldiers were dead, all but 600 of them from disease.[18]

The Spaniards suffered the loss of another colonial possession, although news of it did not reach Europe until after a peace agreement and thus it had to be returned to Spain. On 7 October the weakly defended city of Manila surrendered to a force of several thousand troops, including a battalion of regulars, and eight ships of the line sent from India; the rest of Luzon and the islands subordinate to it were included in the surrender terms.[19] Only in South America was Spain successful, capturing the Portuguese colony of Sacramento along with twenty-six British merchant ships and repulsing an attack of British privateers and Portuguese troops against Buenos Aires on the opposite shore of the Rio de la Plata.[20]

Choiseul wrote Ossun in confidence on 20 October 1762 that had he known before what he knew now he would not have proposed to Louis XV that Spain enter the war. Choiseul apparently did not realize how critical was the Spanish war in leading the British to negotiate seriously with France. It increased British expenses and the national debt; moreover, the disruption of trade caused by the extension of the hostilities to Spain and the Spanish Empire adversely affected the British economy, helping to cause a 13 percent drop in British exports and an increase in unemployment. Both fiscal and economic factors had political consequences; by increasing public disenchantment they reinforced the British government's willingness to offer moderate terms to France in order to escape a war which had grown insupportably large, expensive, and unpopular. Nonetheless, one can understand Choiseul's disappointment. The Spanish army had failed miserably in Portugal, and the Spanish navy had performed no better. At the beginning of 1761 Ossun had reported that in case of war Spain planned to use the navy as a fleet in being in order to tie down the British navy rather than risking it to combat, leaving privateers to conduct operations at sea. In effect, this largely was what had happened, as the Spanish navy offered no challenge to the British fleet at Havana or Manila. In European waters, too, it proved too weak to risk fighting the British, even in cooperation with the French navy, whose performance during 1762 was little better than the Spanish.[21]

At the beginning of the year, the navy's most important mission was the defense of Martinique. The Brest squadron of Blénac and the Rochefort squadron of Morel d'Aubigny were still in port, however, when Rodney arrived in the West Indies. On 24 January 1762 Blénac finally sailed from Brest with his seven ships of the line (*Duc-de-Bourgogne*, 80, *Défenseur*, 74, *Diadème*, 74 [which had replaced the *Palmier*, 74], *Hector*, 74, *Brillant*, 64, *Dragon*, 64, and *Protée*, 64), when the British squadron blockading Brest was blown off station. He reached Martinique on 7 March, three weeks too late to save the island. He was able to deceive the British, however, and sail unimpeded to St. Domingue with the 5,500 troops he had brought. When he arrived there ten days later, the *Dragon* ran aground, the only ship of the line lost by the French navy during 1762. Blénac disembarked his troops in order to protect the colony, rather than using them to make an attack on Jamaica, and volunteered the service of his squadron to help protect Cuba. The Spanish officials at Havana rejected his offer, and once Douglas's squadron of seven ships of the line arrived in April to blockade him, the opportunity was lost. The French squadron thus accomplished little during the remainder of the campaign. A council of war between army and navy officials held on 11 May decided to do nothing until British intentions were clear. By the time the British landed in Cuba, many of the troops Blénac had brought were dead or sick from tropical diseases. Although no longer blockaded, he restricted himself to sending detachments from his squadron on short cruises, the most useful of which was one in which the *Diadème, Brillant,* and a frigate captured five transports off the Bahamas bringing troops from North America for Cuba. Finally, Blénac brought 600 troops from Spanish Santo Domingo to Santiago de Cuba, 500 miles southeast of Havana, only to find the Cuban capital already had surrendered. In June, one of his ships, the *Protée,* encountered a British squadron while she was returning to port and fled for safety to France, arriving at Brest on 9 July; his remaining five ships of the line sailed for Brest in mid-September. By the time they reached France, an armistice had been signed.[22]

The Rochefort squadron did not attempt to sail for the West Indies. Instead it formed a key element in a plan to invade England to which Spain and France agreed in late April upon the urging of Charles III. It faced a serious problem, however. A British squadron of a dozen ships of the line was in the roadstead of Rochefort (near the Ile d'Aix) and the 74's of the French squadron drew too much water to pass from the Charente River into the roadstead unless their cannon were temporarily disembarked. Thus the British had to be driven away before Morel d'Aubigny's ships could leave the safety of the Charente.

The plan to rescue the blockaded squadron and invade England had several components. First, it was planned to send enough ships of the line from Cadiz to reinforce the squadron at Ferrol to eighteen or twenty ships of the line. This then would make a fleet large enough to challenge the British off Brest. Once the Spanish fleet reached Brest, it would be reinforced by several French ships of the line. Then the combined fleet would sail to Rochefort to form a force large enough to escort 30,000 troops from Dunkirk and Calais to invade England. If, however, the Brest contingent could escape earlier, it would proceed to Ferrol and then accompany the Spaniards to Rochefort. The Spanish government set a target date of 1 October for the Ferrol squadron to sail.

Not even the first stage of the plan was accomplished. It was very risky to send ships from Cadiz to Ferrol, as the British had enough ships to blockade simultaneously French and Spanish ports from Brest to Cadiz and still convoy troops to Portugal. Moreover, the news arriving from the Caribbean meant that every available Spanish ship might soon be needed in the Western Hemisphere; the Spanish government was paralyzed by fear for its other colonies. By the end of July the troops for invading England were ordered to Germany, and Choiseul gave up the idea of invading England.[23]

Choiseul now came up with a new plan. He ordered the arming at Brest of a squadron consisting of the *Royal-Louis*, 116, *Minotaure*, 74, *Palmier*, 74, *Sceptre*, 74, *Zodiaque*, 74, *Protée*, 64, and *Sage*, 64 (to which the *Actif*, 64, was later added). These would escort 5,000 troops under the command of the comte d'Estaing to Brazil to attack Bahia and Rio de Janeiro (which half a century earlier had been captured by a French squadron); although he was an army officer, Estaing, who had acquired naval experience during his cruise to the Persian Gulf and Sumatra, secretly was given the naval rank of chef d'escadre. (In the War of American Independence he commanded both fleets and landing parties.) Before the squadron could sail, however, the Franco-British armistice was signed.[24] Also canceled were plans, long under consideration, for the recapture of Senegal.[25]

Because the main French squadrons at Brest and Rochefort were blockaded, the accomplishments of the French navy during 1762 were few. The Mediterranean was left free so that the British could blockade Cadiz, so Bompar, commanding at Toulon, was able to sail with ten ships of the line. The navy, however, did not want to risk sending them through the Straits of Gibraltar where they might be intercepted by Saunders with a fleet twice their size. Instead two were sent to the eastern Mediterranean, one to Italy, and the rest to Malta.[26] Meanwhile, on 8 May Ternay escaped from Brest with the *Robuste*, 74, and *Eveillé*, 64, taking 600 troops on a raid against Newfoundland. He captured the weakly defended port of St. John's on 27 June and captured or sank over 400 British fishing boats and other vessels. Choiseul was so encouraged by these results that he hoped Ternay could hold his conquest. He therefore sent Ternay a frigate and a privateer with supplies and reinforcements. Before they could reach him, two British ships of the line and 1,500 troops arrived at Newfoundland from Halifax. Ternay quickly sailed for France, expecting the British squadron would soon be reinforced. On 18 September the French post at St. John's surrendered; two days later three more ships of the line arrived from England. Ternay was chased into Corunna during this return voyage, and he, too, did not reach Brest until after the end of hostilities. Already there were the last two ships from the Vilaine, the *Glorieux*, 74, and *Sphinx*, 64, brought by Ternay's friend Hector.[27]

Once again the main burden of France's war against Britain was carried by the army in Germany. As already mentioned, Choiseul had not expected it to be able to accomplish much because of its reduced size. It suffered two further blows before the campaign began. First, the defection of Russia virtually doomed any hopes that Ferdinand would be distracted by attacks on the Prussian heartland. Second, the French army lost its commander. Choiseul had lost confidence in the duc de Broglie after the unsuccessful campaign of 1761, but he had no one to replace him. He gave Broglie permission to discuss with the king the results of the campaign, but when Broglie arrived at court in January 1762, he was imprudent enough to criticize Choiseul and to assign the blame for the defeat at Vellinghausen to Soubise, who was among the highest ranks of the nobility, a protégé of Madame de Pompadour, and a member of the Council of State. Moreover, in spite of his failings as a general, Soubise was generally liked and respected for his admirable qualities as a person. On 18 February, the king, outraged at Broglie's impertinence, ordered him and his brother, the head of the "Secret du Roi," to retire to their estates. The comte de Broglie directed the "Secret" while he was in exile, but it continued to decline in effectiveness. Command of the main French army was offered to Estrées, who again declined for reasons of health. He agreed, however, to go to Germany to direct strategy while Soubise commanded the day-to-day operations of the army.[28]

This division of command was highly risky, particularly since the French left 30,000 men on the lower Rhine. This meant that in spite of reductions in British army expenditures, Estrées and Soubise were outnumbered by Ferdinand, 95,000 against 80,000.[29] They occupied what appeared to be a strong position north of Cassel, but on 24 June Ferdinand surprised and defeated them at the Battle of Wilhelmsthal. For the next two months the French were forced to retreat until the arrival of the army from the Rhine enabled them to stabilize the front at the Ohm River, halfway between Cassel and their key base at Frankfurt, roughly the point at which Broglie began the offensive of 1760. In the process the garrison at Cassel was cut off from the main army and, after mid-October, besieged. What was absolutely critical to the peace negotiations, however, is that Estrées and Soubise avoided a second major defeat and kept their army intact. Thus France had something to offer, its withdrawal from Germany, in exchange for British concessions; indeed, the French won their share of the skirmishes that occurred during the summer and early fall. In order that the final negotiations not be complicated by a sudden change in Germany, it was very important that the 5,300-man garrison of Cassel avoid surrendering. It held out until 1 November, too late for the news of its capture to arrive before an armistice and preliminary peace agreement were signed at Paris.[30]

The campaign of 1762 generally was undramatic and inglorious, an affair not of great battles but of tedious sieges like those of Schweidnitz, Havana, and Cassel, which were intended to improve bargaining positions during the peace process. The war ended not because of a great victory but because all the participants were exhausted and ready to make peace. Because France had persevered, particularly in Germany, she was able to engage in the final discussions not as a humiliated suppliant but as a full participant able to make demands with something to offer in exchange.

THE SEARCH FOR PEACE RESUMES

The outbreak of war between Spain and Britain temporarily interrupted Bute's attempt to resume negotiations with Choiseul, using the Sardinian diplomats Viry and Solaro as intermediaries. Early in 1762, however, Bute sent word to Choiseul that Spanish issues such as logwood cutting and prizes could be handled simultaneously with the Franco-British discussions and need pose no obstacle to a settlement. Choiseul, optimistic about the impact of Spain on the fortunes of the war, responded coldly. He insisted in a 23 January letter and during a 25 January discussion with Solaro that Britain should be the first to make specific offers. He also told Grimaldi that he would not negotiate with Britain without Spanish concurrence. Solaro's 1 February letter to Viry reporting these developments was delayed in transit, however, and it was late February before the British government made another attempt to contact Choiseul.[31] Meanwhile Bute and the inner cabinet became involved in a new diplomatic initiative directed toward France's ally Austria.

This initiative was not in the service of peace but directed against France and Spain. It was the idea of either Newcastle or George III, who shared in the general enthusiasm engendered by the beginning of hostilities against Spain and who desired to change the policies of the grandfather whom he had hated, George II. Under the king's impulse (or at least with his enthusiastic consent) the British government attempted to switch allies by jettisoning the Prussian alliance in favor of an alliance with Austria. On 24 December 1761 the king suggested to Bute that Britain send a fleet to help Maria Theresa conquer Naples.[32] Soon thereafter the British government attempted a *rapprochement* with Austria.[33]

There was a superficial logic to the plan. Prussia seemed close to defeat. For decades, Austria and Spain had been rivals in Italy, and France had signed the Family Compact without consulting Austria. Could not the British make use of Austrian resentment against France to induce Maria Theresa to break with her ally? Then might not the Austrians be convinced to attack the Spanish possessions in Italy with the help of the British navy? Finally, might not the old alliance system of Britain, the Netherlands, Austria, and Sardinia be revived to counter the aggression of the House of Bourbon as it last had done in the 1740s? Newcastle, who had never fully rejected the Old System in his heart in spite of the Diplomatic Revolution, went along with the idea (or possibly even suggested it), provided that an Austro-Prussian peace be concluded first, and that Bute also give his support. Prince Louis of Brunswick was selected as an intermediary, and both he and Ambassador Yorke were enthusiastic. On 26 January Prince Louis broached the idea to Thaddäus, Freiherr von Reischach, the Austrian envoy at The Hague.

The initiative was doomed from the beginning. There was no possibility of its precondition being met, Frederick II's agreeing to make peace with Austria. Although news of Elizabeth's death had not yet arrived, the Prussian king had not given up hope of rescue by the Turks and Tartars, and he was prepared to commit suicide before accepting responsibility for the surrender of Prussian territory.[34] Furthermore the Austrians did not welcome the proposal. Kaunitz believed it a trick. He feared that if he showed any interest, the British would leak it to Louis XV in order to poison French-Austrian relations. Thus he refused to discuss it and kept it secret from France.[35] Henceforth George III left diplomacy to Bute and gave him unreserved support, so the initiative did make some contribution to eventual peace.

A leading contemporary scholar of Bute suggests that he consented to the overture in hopes it would fail and would thereby provide him with an argument for withdrawing the 20,000-man British contingent from Ferdinand's army.[36] In any case, the news of Elizabeth's death caused Bute to rethink his attitude about the German war. Hitherto he and the king had favored ending the British military involvement in order to save money and permit Britain to concentrate on fighting Spain. Newcastle agreed that Britain could not continue the war more than another year, but he and Devonshire feared that without British troops Ferdinand would be defeated and France would have another 150,000 troops with which to intimidate the Dutch and possibly even invade England.[37] Now, with France and Austria about to lose the support of Russia, Bute's hopes revived and he agreed to support a final campaign in Germany, Newcastle assuring him the necessary £5 million could be found. When the Duke of Bedford disregarded his wishes and introduced a motion in the House of Lords on 5 February to withdraw the British contingent, Bute used a procedural motion to defeat it. The king, however, continued to talk of withdrawing the troops, and it was not until the middle of April that Bute decided definitively to support a final campaign in Germany.[38] The belief that Britain could not long continue the war in Germany gave Bute a powerful motive to do whatever was necessary to make peace with France.

The news from Russia also affected the British subsidy to Frederick II. Until the end of January Bute had been willing to pay another year's subsidy of £670,000 (4 million crowns) but not to renew the subsidy treaty itself because Frederick insisted on retaining its requirement for Britain to consult Prussia before making a peace treaty. The British government then learned of Peter III's accession. On 6 February Bute was imprudent enough to tell Russian minister Golitsyn, who was departing for St. Petersburg, that he hoped Frederick II would make peace. Soon even Newcastle had reservations about continuing to subsidize Prussia, given the growing indications that Russia was changing allegiances; it took Hardwicke's warnings about Britain's potential diplomatic isolation to maintain his support for the subsidy. The inner cabinet decided, however, that it would not be paid unless Britain were certain that Frederick would use the changed diplomatic situation to make peace rather than expand the war. When no assurances were forthcoming, the inner cabinet decided on 30 April to suspend the subsidy. Bute even accused Frederick of enmity toward Britain. When Parliament adjourned for the summer without taking further action, the alliance with Prussia effectively was terminated.[39]

Frederick II more than returned Bute's animosity. In a letter to Knyphausen and Michell intercepted by the British secret service, he called Bute a madman. His rage increased when Peter gave him an exaggerated account of Bute's conversation with Golitsyn and when he learned in April of the British overture to Austria. By then he had abandoned hope of a new subsidy. By increased expropriations from occupied territories, currency debasement, and loans, Frederick was able to do without it, assisted of course by the improving prospects of the war. (The former subsidy had accounted for only 20 percent of his income.) He refused British involvement in his peace negotiations with Austria, although, as we shall see, he accepted British help in arranging the return of the territory occupied by France. After the war he made no attempt to resurrect the alliance with Britain, instead signing a defensive alliance with Russia in April 1764. His animosity was directed at Bute and his supporters rather than at the British people, however, and the change of alliances was dictated by diplomatic logic rather than emotion. Although the end of Britain's alliance with Prussia was inevitable, given the British government's retreat from a commitment to Hanover, Bute's handling of the affair was clumsy and the British government's penny-pinching was dangerous; by withdrawing its subsidy, the British government weakened Frederick's ability to resist Peter's designs in Germany, which were a menace to Hanover, Prussia, and the entire Baltic region. The British approach to Austria was particularly misguided; it reinforced Frederick's sense of isolation and reinforced his need to support Peter's plans, knowing that Russian goodwill was dependent on Prussian compliance.[40]

The British government's handling of Peter was no better. Its Austrian initiative angered him as well as Frederick. It then insulted him by sending a special agent named Thomas Wroughton to St. Petersburg with £100,000 for bribes. Its chief sin in Peter's eyes, however, was that of not supporting his plans to coerce Denmark.[41] Britain was very fortunate that Catherine's coup prevented the outbreak of a new war. After Catherine became empress, the British government made plans for a postwar alliance with Russia.[42] These plans failed in the face of Britain's reluctance either to admit she needed allies or to spend the money for a subsidy for Russia; instead, Catherine allied with Prussia. Subsequent British attempts met increased Russian demands, and Britain was left in a diplomatic isolation that lasted through the War for American Independence.[43] (The same combination of overconfidence and worry about money led to Britain's attempting to make the American colonists pay for British troops, helping lead to that war.)

The deterioration of relations with Prussia and the failure to improve relations with Russia made it all the more imperative for Britain to make peace with France and Spain. While the inner cabinet pondered the Prussian subsidy and the change of rulers in Russia, Bute moved to restart the negotiations with France. Having as yet no news of the French response to the letters he had sent at the beginning of the year, he needed an excuse to contact Choiseul. He found one in the capture off Brittany on 27 December 1761 of the East India Company frigate *Boullogne*, aboard which was the comte d'Estaing. The comte faced imprisonment for violating parole after being captured in India in December 1758. His family asked Solaro for help, and Solaro contacted Viry. On 22 February Secretary of State Egremont informed Choiseul that Estaing was being sent to Calais to rejoin his family. In response Choiseul wrote Egremont on 7 March, expressing not only gratitude for the gesture of goodwill but also Louis' desire for the friendship of George III.[44] With this encouragement Egremont began to draft peace terms to send to Choiseul.

What had caused the shift in French attitudes during the six weeks since Choiseul had spoken so coldly to Solaro? Obviously, the foreign news was threatening: Peter's accession and hostility, the delays in the Spanish attack on Portugal, the possibility that Austria might be defeated or even forced to leave the war. There were domestic reasons, too, for seeking an end to the war. A new crisis with the Parlements was likely. On the day after Choiseul's letter to Egremont, the king issued an edict attempting to reform and thus protect the Society of Jesus, the religious order that was despised by the Jansenists and threatened by the Parlements.[45] Finally, Choiseul appears to have come to believe that Bute's wish to negotiate was sincere.

During the next few weeks Egremont prepared specific peace terms offering France a number of concessions, including a division of the neutral islands by which France would receive St. Lucia, the most strategically important of them. The news of the British capture of Martinique, however, caused Bute to reconsider. He consulted the inner cabinet, which on 29 March concurred with his recommendation to propose instead conducting discussions on the basis of the 1761 ultimata. It also agreed to approach the Spanish court through the Sardinian ambassador at Madrid. Consequently a royal declaration was sent to Choiseul on 8 April suggesting an exchange of ministers, along with letters from Egremont to Choiseul granting Estaing unconditional freedom, from Bute to Viry expressing his desire for peace, and from Viry to Solaro leaving to France the choice of whether to appoint ministers at the present time. A week later the comte de Choiseul wrote Egremont accepting the British offer, but suggesting that France and Britain exchange memoirs so as to establish preliminary terms before sending ministers. The French also told Solaro that they wished to continue his services and those of Viry until a preliminary agreement was reached. They asked that the discussions be kept secret, with no Britons except the king, Bute, and Egremont to be informed. They conceded that Canada was lost and asked only for what they had requested the previous summer plus the return of Martinique; its return and that of Guadeloupe were not negotiable, as the duc de Choiseul told Ossun. By now the Choiseuls had learned that Sweden was prepared to sign an armistice with Prussia; the duc de Choiseul feared that a general peace would be made in Germany without French participation or at best with consent imposed on France. This seems to have been the final blow to French hopes of gaining better peace terms than those for which they asked in 1761.[46]

The initial phase of negotiations proved complex, requiring more than three months of exchanging proposals through Viry and Solaro. Not until the end of July could thought be given to the exchange of ministers for the final phase of discussions. The difficulties, particularly for Britain, were political as well as diplomatic. Bute faced serious constraints on his ability to make concessions. He and George III wished to make personnel changes in Britain that would strengthen the king's position in relation to Parliament, changes that could be made only after the end of the war. They had no desire to delay them by continuing the war in order to force France to surrender its vital interests such as access to the fisheries or possession of Martinique and Guadeloupe; moreover, both of them hated the war in Germany and realized that the war in general was expensive and growing increasingly unpopular. Bute's colleagues in the inner cabinet, however, did not share his political views and were less prepared to make concessions to France. The inner cabinet debated for a week after the French response was received on 21 April. The question of retaining Guadeloupe was raised again. Bute and his supporter Egremont were forced to compromise with Grenville and the more bellicose members of the inner cabinet. On 30 April (the same meeting at which the subsidy to Prussia was suspended), the inner cabinet decided to offer the French fishing rights off Newfoundland and in the Gulf of St. Lawrence, the island of Miquelon as a refuge for the fishing fleet, the return of Guadeloupe, Martinique, and Gorée, the more liberal terms of the Treaty of Aix-la-Chapelle regarding Dunkirk, and the exchange of Belle Isle for Minorca. Britain also would consider French proposals about India. On the other hand, the inner cabinet insisted on all of Louisiana east of the Mississippi and not only the neutral islands of St. Lucia, Dominica, St. Vincent, and Tobago but also Grenada and the Grenadines.[47]

Bute was only a secretary of state as Pitt had been and hence was limited in his ability to sway his colleagues. He now moved to strengthen his political position. He and Newcastle long had disagreed on a number of policy matters, and recently Newcastle had challenged Bute by reverting to his former support of a subsidy for Frederick II as well as full funding for Ferdinand's army. Having arranged the bulk of the loans for the year, Newcastle had become expendable as first lord of the treasury. By assuming that office, Bute would become prime minister. When Newcastle recommended asking for an additional £2 million for the wars in Germany and Portugal as soon as Parliament returned from its recess, Bute had an opportunity to force him from office. He used information provided by Samuel Martin, secretary of the Board of Treasury, to argue against the request. Betrayed by a subordinate and challenged on treasury matters, Newcastle felt his honor at stake. He resigned on 26 May, three weeks after announcing his intention to do so. Bute became first lord of the treasury and prime minister, but was forced to appoint George Grenville his successor as secretary of state for the northern department. Grenville was not known for moderation; he argued that by reducing expenses in Germany Britain could pressure France and Spain into making peace.[48]

Bute was forced to fill another position when Anson died on 6 June. As a stopgap measure (or so Newcastle referred to it), the position of first lord of the admiralty was given to the Earl of Halifax, the former head of the Board of Trade and presently lord lieutenant of Ireland. Halifax was in ill health, but the year's naval operations were already set, and his appointment had little effect on the conduct of the war.[49]

The duc and comte de Choiseul were generally pleased at the terms offered by Britain, but they, too, had constraints on their freedom of action. They had no rivals in the Council of State, as Estrées and Soubise were in Germany and the only other active members were the sickly Puyzieulx and the ineffectual Saint-Florentin; Choiseul's rival, Controller General Bertin, did not join the council until 6 November. On the other hand, as Solaro pointed out to Viry, they were forced to consider public opinion when formulating terms.[50] They were concerned when Newcastle resigned, fearing the return of Pitt; Choiseul told Solaro that he would rather be a galley slave than negotiate again with him. Reassured by Viry that Bute was in no political danger, the Choiseuls and Louis XV continued the negotiations, but they trusted only Bute (believing he, too, feared Pitt's return), Egremont, and George III; George in turn wrote to Bute that the duc de Choiseul was a man of honor.[51]

During the preliminary negotiations of May, June, and July,[52] the French were forced to concede possession of the island of Dominica, to abandon plans for a corridor several miles wide along the east bank of the Mississippi, and to give up hope of recovering trading rights in Senegal (although ultimately France did procure the return of the notorious slaving station of Gorée, whose financial value the British did not realize).[53] On three issues, however, France needed to be satisfied before some degree of consensus on the perimeters of an agreement could be reached and France and Britain could exchange ministers for final discussions.

One of the issues was the fisheries. The Choiseuls asked for the island of St. Pierre as well as Miquelon, the right to dry cod in designated areas along the shore of Newfoundland before taking it to Europe, and the limitation of British rights to inspect St. Pierre and Miquelon. Although these topics were the last to be resolved during the final discussions, there was room for compromise, and they did not delay the conclusion of the preliminary talks.

A more difficult issue was the boundary of Louisiana.[54] Bute considered it important to have the Mississippi as a boundary between the British possessions and French Louisiana so as to avoid the interminable disputes which followed the peace of 1748. He had little knowledge, however, of either the commercial prospects of the Mississippi valley or of its geography. He therefore made the mistake of accepting the border proposed by the duc de Choiseul, which ran along the supposed easternmost channel of the Mississippi through Lake Pontchartrain, a channel that did not exist. (Choiseul also claimed that New Orleans was on an island rather than on the east bank of the Mississippi.) Bute compounded his mistake by not informing Egremont and subsequently engaging in an elaborate series of subterfuges to deceive him. For his part Choiseul had to use his own subterfuges to disguise from Spain his giving the British access to the mouth of the Mississippi and, worse still, the port of Mobile on the Gulf of Mexico (which Spain strongly opposed surrendering because of the possibility it could be used for smuggling). Ultimately, however, this issue also could be resolved because Choiseul was willing to permit the British to navigate the real channel of the Mississippi as long as they did not control either of its banks from New Orleans to the Gulf. He realized that without them the British had no way of enforcing their rights.

The most dangerous of the disputes about peace terms involved the island of St. Lucia. This was the most important of the neutral islands, both economically and strategically (because of its proximity to Martinique). Nonetheless, it was not as critical to the future of the French navy as were the Newfoundland and St. Lawrence fisheries. Although Martinique and Guadeloupe were vital to French trade and hence the navy, St. Lucia was not, and its loss would pose only hypothetical dangers to the neighboring islands.[55] (St. Lucia's capture by Britain in 1778 did not lead to the fall of any other French islands, although as a base for a British squadron it did interfere with French trade and privateering.) Egremont was prepared to give it to France until the news of Martinique arrived. Thereafter if Martinique and Guadeloupe were to be returned, it was necessary to make concessions to public opinion (and also to Egremont's and Bute's opponents in the inner cabinet). Similar motives probably were a factor in French diplomacy. The duc de Choiseul, well aware of the public fury at the terms of the Treaty of Aix-la-Chapelle, likely was afraid of surrendering St. Lucia (senior naval officers being likely to lead the complaints). He certainly took care to avoid arousing public opinion; partly for fear of the public he eventually was willing to sacrifice the Society of Jesus to the Parlements.[56]

Whatever their reasons, the Choiseuls treated the return of St. Lucia as nonnegotiable. Bute and George III, who were willing to return the far more valuable Guadeloupe and Martinique, were not prepared to risk the peace for it. At a 26 July meeting, the remainder of the inner cabinet under the leadership of Grenville resisted, and it took the king's help for Bute to overcome their opposition. Their concurrence in giving up St. Lucia was conditional, however, on France's giving assurances she would provide no further assistance to Spain (particularly in Portugal) should the Spanish government refuse to make peace with Britain.[57] On the same day that this decision was reached, 28 July, the inner cabinet confirmed the choice of the Duke of Bedford to conduct final negotiations in Paris. Although Grenville, Newcastle, and Hardwicke criticized the choice, nobody else was more likely to win the trust of the French government. Bedford, with his wealth, social standing, and record of supporting peace, was a great contrast to Stanley, the preceding year's British representative.[58]

Before final negotiations could begin, however, another set of problems had to be resolved. Britain, having abandoned its alliance with Prussia, had relative freedom to make its own terms, although it could not avoid discussing the fates of Portugal, Cassel, and the Prussian provinces occupied by France. France, however, was vitally concerned with maintaining its alliances with Austria and Spain. For Britain and France to make peace, they would have to resolve the questions of Germany and Spain, as well as the details of their own agreement.

THE BEST PEACE POSSIBLE

France had to consider its allies while making peace. Austria was a lesser problem than was Spain, because France no longer had the obligation to gain Maria Theresa's consent in order to make a preliminary agreement with Britain. Afraid, however, that Maria Theresa might make a separate peace, the Choiseuls did not inform Starhemberg about their own negotiations until mid-May, when apparently they grew worried that news might leak. Starhemberg and Kaunitz were astonished when the Choiseuls suddenly admitted what they had so long denied, but Austria gave its permission for France to continue the negotiations.

The issue of Wesel and the Prussian provinces occupied by France became a subject of contention during the Franco-British discussions. The Third Treaty of Versailles specified that they were to be governed by Austrian commissioners, even though they were occupied by France. Austria had taken an interest in them ever since France captured them; for example, it had used a Dutch passport to send grain to Wesel.[59] The French government insisted that until a general peace was signed, French or Austrian garrisons should remain, whereas the British argued that to accept this would mean disposing of Prussian territory without Frederick's permission. Bute and Egremont flirted, however, with the idea of having a neutral power like Bavaria or Cologne take over the occupation.

Acting on a suggestion of Viry's, the French offered the British a choice of a joint British and French occupation or of simply including the territory in a general mutual evacuation of Germany. At the end of July the inner cabinet agreed to the latter. As the Prussian provinces were close to the Austrian Netherlands, it seemed that Austrian troops could quickly occupy the area. This did not bother Bute, who told Bedford he was willing to see the Austrians do so, but Frederick was outraged at what he perceived as a new British betrayal and insisted that a British treaty with France include their restitution to Prussia. (Bedford subsequently was ordered to obtain this.) To add to the damage, the British government also made a commitment that Ferdinand's army would not provide troops for Frederick in return for a French pledge that they would provide no direct military assistance to Maria Theresa. These issues were not fully resolved until after the preliminary agreement between Britain and France, but they were not a major obstacle to peace; France had no enthusiasm for aiding Austria and sought only how to avoid blame for failure to fulfill its obligations, while Britain acted only to avoid shame.[60]

France could not afford to treat Spain so cavalierly. On 17 April Grimaldi was informed of the opening of negotiations and given copies of the diplomatic correspondence with Britain, although Spain was not informed of the discussions held before the release of Estaing. France continued thereafter to provide

Spain with copies of its correspondence with the British government. Louis XV asked Charles III's permission to continue discussions, stressing France's need for peace and the likelihood that Britain would not offer better terms than at present. The French recommended, however, that the information be kept secret from Austria, as there already was a danger that Maria Theresa would make a separate peace.[61]

Charles gave his permission, but reserved the right to conduct separate negotiations himself. The timing of the French request was unfortunate, as the attack on Portugal was about to begin. Moreover, Charles was worried not only that France would accept disadvantageous terms, particularly in North America, but also that the French negotiations might cause Austria to break the alliance and take revenge by attacking the Bourbon states in Italy. Ossun said Charles was more concerned with the slightest risk to the possessions of his son Ferdinand, the king of the Two Sicilies, than he was to the loss of the Indies. The Spanish king also was worried by the use of diplomats from Sardinia, another traditional Bourbon rival in Italy. Choiseul sent reassurances that Louis would not make peace without the satisfaction as well as the consent of his cousin Charles, claiming that for France the Family Compact was a thousand times more important than Canada. He also sought to lessen Spanish fears of Austria. Had it not been for Charles's October 1759 treaty with Austria about the succession question, it is difficult to imagine how France could have maintained the simultaneous alliances with Austria and Spain necessary to put pressure on Britain in both Germany and Portugal. This pressure was the means by which France secured reasonable peace terms.[62]

The negotiations between Spain and Britain went poorly. The inner cabinet on 27 April expressed a willingness to compromise about the logwood cutting settlements in Honduras, but not about Spanish claims about prizes seized by the British or claims to fishing rights off Newfoundland (on both of which issues Choiseul secretly admitted the British were correct). Spain accepted Choiseul's suggestion that Grimaldi handle its negotiations with Britain, but Charles III refused to make any concessions and opposed any French concessions that might affect Spain; as we have seen, the Choiseuls hid from him those they made concerning Louisiana. Bute was willing to postpone further negotiations with Spain until an agreement was made with France, but his colleagues were concerned about the fate of Portugal. Unless France could convince Spain to make peace, Bedford was ordered to insist that France break the Family Compact as a precondition of a British-French agreement. Meanwhile, the British kept discussions with Spain alive by pretending that Grimaldi's refusal to consider concessions was unofficial.[63]

Before France and Britain exchanged ministers for the final negotiations,

Louis XV insisted on receiving his cousin's permission. His reasons were personal as well as diplomatic. The previous year Charles had volunteered to bring an army to France if Louis needed assistance against his domestic enemies and had called Louis not only the head of the House of Bourbon but also his best friend; Choiseul now spoke to Ossun of Louis' love for Charles. The French king wrote a personal letter to his cousin and entrusted O'Dunne to carry it to the Spanish court (apparently at the suggestion of Puyzieulx). It was not until nearly the end of August that Louis received Charles's consent and the final negotiations could begin. Charles again entrusted his negotiations to Grimaldi, who conducted them with Bedford at Versailles. Grimaldi was given permission to concede provisional logwood cutting rights in Honduras if the British demolished their illegal settlements. As in 1762 France elected to conduct simultaneous discussions at the British and French courts. They named as their minister to the British court someone whose social prestige was equivalent to Bedford's, Choiseul and Madame de Pompadour's old friend, the duc de Nivernais, who had been selected in 1756 for the final attempt to avert war with Prussia. Nivernais was far more urbane than Bussy, although something of a dilettante, and he proved equal to his responsibilities, but, as in 1761, the major negotiations occurred at Versailles.[64]

Nivernais was instructed to obtain, if possible, an Indian buffer state on the east bank of the Mississippi and to try to restrict British navigation of the river to downstream traffic because of Spanish fears of contraband. (He failed on both counts and Britain obtained all of Louisiana east of the Mississippi, except for the "island" of New Orleans.) Although an alliance with Britain would be an infallible way of ensuring peace to Europe, said his instructions, it was probably a chimera; he should work, however, to establish friendship with Britain and to make the terms of peace clear enough to prevent future disputes. Bute, too, expressed hope for an alliance, but he also seems to have regarded the minimizing of disputes as the only goal attainable.[65]

Nivernais sailed from Calais on 11 September after a meeting with Bedford, who was en route to Paris, just as Bussy had met with Stanley before the beginning of their missions. He was accompanied to England by two secretaries, François-Michel Durand and Charles-Geneviève-Louise-Auguste-André-Timothée, chevalier d'Eon de Beaumont, who, unknown to Nivernais, were agents of the "Secret du Roi"; this was the beginning of the secret diplomacy's evolution to being an anti-British as well as an anti-Russian organization.[66] Although Nivernais was welcomed cordially by George III upon his arrival at court, his reports to the Choiseuls were sobering: Bute and Egremont were politically isolated, were terrified of making further concessions and, like George, were obsessed with making peace before Parliament reconvened in November.

He predicted that if the treaty were not finished before Parliament reconvened, Pitt would return to power. He said that the British public was unimpressed by the Spanish capture of the fortress of Almeida and assumed that Britain easily could capture Spanish colonies. Given Bute's reluctance to negotiate, Nivernais was reduced to quibbling over details; when he presented a revised draft treaty on 24 September, the British government treated the changes as a breach of trust.[67]

Bute's political weakness severely hampered Bedford's negotiations as well. The comte de Choiseul described Bedford as a good man, polite and well-intentioned, but somewhat limited and overly scrupulous about following his instructions. He had been instructed to obtain clear conditions concerning the Louisiana border and a common right to navigate the Mississippi. Moreover, he was forbidden to sign a separate peace unless France committed itself to withholding aid from Spain. Before he arrived in France, Egremont added a new limitation on his powers, specifying that George III had to approve peace preliminaries before Bedford could sign them. Bedford was highly insulted by having his hands tied; even the few minor concessions he offered were criticized by the inner cabinet. Reduced to playing the role of an intermediary like Solaro and Viry, he transmitted to England a copy of the same draft treaty that was presented by Nivernais.[68]

His discussions with Grimaldi went no better. To his dismay Bedford learned that the Choiseuls had not told Grimaldi about their concessions concerning the borders of Louisiana. The Spanish minister also had not been informed that Spain could not expect compensation for the portion of Portugal it occupied whereas the British expected compensation if they captured Havana. The Choiseuls asked Bedford not to discuss these subjects. Even on the subjects they could discuss, Bedford found it difficult to negotiate with Grimaldi, whose arrogance and rudeness infuriated even Choiseul and Solaro. As Ossun had predicted, the most contentious topic was Charles III's opposition to renewing Spain's commercial treaties with Britain as part of a peace settlement. Regarding them as unfair and exploitative, Charles wished no more than a six-month renewal while new relations were negotiated. Bedford and Grimaldi were convinced by the Choiseuls to propose to their governments a one-year renewal, but the British government rejected it. Fearful that the chances for peace were disappearing, the duc de Choiseul appealed to Charles to make whatever concessions were needed, but he promised that France would not make peace if Spain insisted on continuing the war. He also said that Louis XV was ready to evacuate the rest of Louisiana if it would further the peace, as it had no decent port and cost 800,000 livres a year without giving any return.[69]

What broke the impasse was the arrival at the end of September of the news that Havana had been captured, news that both Choiseul and Bute claimed they had not expected.[70] Bute, who was far from pleased with this development, would have been willing to return Havana without compensation, but only the king agreed with him. In the face of public enthusiasm about the news, even Egremont joined Grenville in opposing Bute. George III and Bute now acted with considerable courage and political adroitness. (As Choiseul said to Ossun, it took as much courage in Britain to make peace as to make war.) They waited to call a meeting of the inner cabinet until reactions subsided and, as Nivernais urged, postponed the convening of Parliament until 25 November. Bute rid himself of Grenville by pressuring him into exchanging posts with Halifax, the first lord of the admiralty, who became secretary of state for the northern department on 14 October and thereafter served Bute loyally. (Grenville, a former member of the Board of Admiralty, served until the following April, when he replaced Bute as prime minister.) With Grenville no longer his co-secretary of state, the opportunistic Egremont resumed his support of Bute. Grenville's other responsibility, that of leading the government's supporters in the House of Commons, was given to the adroit army paymaster general, Henry Fox (who had declined the position given to Halifax).[71]

With Bute reascendant, the inner cabinet acquiesced in a revised set of instructions that were sent to Bedford on 26 October, the most important of which concerned his negotiations with Grimaldi. Britain was willing to destroy its fortifications in Honduras if Spain accepted British logwood cutting and settlements in central America, desisted from its claims to a share in the fisheries and compensation for prizes taken by the British, agreed to unconditional renewal of existing commercial treaties, and returned all the territory conquered from Portugal in Europe and South America. Britain would return Havana and any territory subsequently captured, but Spain would have to give Britain either Florida or Puerto Rico. Bedford was given some freedom to negotiate final details, but Richard Rigby, an associate of Fox as well as Bedford, was sent to Versailles to stiffen his resolve.[72]

The news of Havana reached Paris on 3 October, four days after its arrival in London. On the same day the duc de Choiseul learned from Ossun that Charles III had said that if France was satisfied with British terms he would not prolong the war for his own interests. Choiseul took this as authorization to dictate terms to Grimaldi.[73] He and Ossun almost wasted their opportunity, however. Choiseul commented to Ossun on the danger facing Spain's other colonies, and a week later Ossun presented Choiseul's warnings tactlessly to Charles, who responded by declaring with bravado that he had never slept more soundly than after hearing the news of Havana. He claimed that Spain still had great resources with which to continue the war if Bedford changed his terms, and he expressed a willingness to lose all his possessions in the Western Hemisphere if necessary. Fortunately, on 9 October Louis XV took an action to tie Charles's hands so he could not refuse to make peace. Having learned from Bedford that the British would not accept New Orleans and the remaining French portion of Louisiana in exchange for Havana, he formally offered them to Spain in compensation for whatever territory Spain lost as a result of the peace settlement. He also volunteered to send his ten-year-old granddaughter Marie-Louise-Thérèse of Parma to live in Spain and become the future bride of one of Charles's sons. (She did marry the eldest, the future Charles IV, a cousin of hers, in September 1765, and became notorious for infidelity after becoming Queen Maria Luísa.) In an accompanying note, the duc de Choiseul suggested confidentially and unofficially to Ossun that although an immediate peace was essential to France and Spain, they could use it to rebuild their navies so as to resume the war in five years, this time taking Britain by surprise. Such a suggestion was possible only because the Newfoundland fisheries had been saved. Choiseul had told Ossun a few months earlier that in spite of the loss of Canada, French power and wealth could be restored by reestablishing its navy. In his official covering letter for Louis' offer, Choiseul offered to break off the French negotiations with Britain if Charles III wished and warned Ossun not to try to influence Charles's decision.[74]

In the long run, France's giving the rest of Louisiana to Spain helped French diplomacy by making France less menacing to the British colonies in America. This facilitated the French alliance with the Americans after they declared their independence in 1776. There is no indication, however, that France's offer to Spain was motivated by any desire other than winning Spain's agreement to making peace. Charles III attempted to evade accepting Louisiana, but Louis XV pressed the offer, continuing to place on his cousin the responsibility for making peace or war (and also reminding him that France could do little to prevent Britain from capturing more Spanish colonies). Meanwhile, on 15 October Choiseul informed Ossun that Britain would ask for Puerto Rico, part of Yucatan, or Florida in exchange for Havana. This advance information was possible because Bute and Egremont had the good sense to leak the terms through Viry to Nivernais before they were approved by the inner cabinet (although it dropped the potential exchange of Yucatan). Because Britain was gaining Mobile from France as a port on the Gulf of Mexico, Spain could no longer prevent British smuggling, and thus Florida became expendable; although its eastern coast was a valuable privateering center, the entire colony had only a few thousand colonists and could not even feed itself. The acquisition of New Orleans at least would compensate for the loss of Mobile. Moreover, the portion of Louisiana west of the Mississippi would form a valuable buffer for Mexico and eliminate a long-standing border dispute with France over the western boundary of the French colony. After Ossun informed the Spaniards on 22 October that they would be able to exchange Florida for Havana, Charles ordered Grimaldi to sign the peace treaty.[75]

The final negotiations of Bedford with the Choiseuls and Grimaldi began on 31 October. The Choiseuls had reason to hurry: Parliament was due to reconvene in a few weeks and at any time the news might arrive that Cassel had fallen. Keeping Grimaldi's instructions secret, they were able to play on Bedford's concerns about Spain's coming to terms. They were assisted by Bute's having leaked to them without the knowledge of the inner cabinet the subjects on which Bedford was free to compromise. They and Grimaldi were able to expand the area in central America in which Britain would be forbidden to construct fortifications, and they also obtained a waiver of Britain's right to inspect St. Pierre and Miquelon and secured a considerable reduction in the coastal areas closed to French fishing. On 3 November at the royal chateau of Fontainbleau, the Choiseuls, Grimaldi, and Bedford signed an armistice and provisional peace treaty. The previous day the comte de Choiseul had been named duc de Praslin; his cousin, already a duc, was rewarded by being made a peer of France. [76] Grimaldi secretly signed on 3 November an agreement to accept Louisiana, which Charles finally ratified later in the month; the British did not learn of it until the following January.[77]

The English public used the preliminary agreement as a reason to pillory the unpopular Scotsman Bute, but Parliament ratified it in December. Although Pitt criticized it for returning most of Britain's conquests and thereby permitting France to rebuild her navy, he refused to cooperate with Newcastle in blocking it. [78] Several issues needed to be resolved before a final peace treaty could be signed, however.

The most important of these related to Germany. While there had been no disagreement about France and Britain evacuating Germany and ceasing subsidies to Austria and Prussia, Bedford had accepted two French suggestions favorable to Austria. By the first France had agreed to evacuate Wesel and the Prussian territories after a "reasonable interval." This would allow the French to control the timing so as to favor an Austrian occupation (and France quietly signed an agreement to leave supplies in Wesel for Austrian use). By the second, France was permitted to pay the back installments of her subsidy to Maria Theresa. France had been too clever for her own good. Frederick II began forming a corps to contest control of the area, using the Prussian troops who had been serving with Ferdinand. The French government did not want a new war to begin in western Germany and agreed to a suggestion of Halifax's which also won Frederick's approval. In exchange for the return of the Prussian provinces, Prussia would agree to treat the Austrian Netherlands as neutral; the small German states allied to Austria, terrorized by the raids of Prince Henry, would be treated similarly.[79]

The other changes were less drastic. The British East India Company was dissatisfied with the preliminary terms regarding India, so they were changed. The French also agreed not to fortify the mouth of the Mississippi, to fill in a drainage ditch at Dunkirk, and to recognize the Protestant succession in Britain. The British agreed to return the munitions captured in Havana. Once all these changes were made, the final treaty was signed in Paris on 10 February 1763.[80] The Franco-British agreement on Germany quickly became moot. Maria Theresa was unwilling to continue the war to preserve her conquest of Glatz, which she had disparaged as being of little importance. In exchange for its return, Frederick was willing to evacuate Saxony and to recognize the rights of the Grand Duke Joseph to succeed his father as Holy Roman Emperor. (This right was solemnized by his selection as King of the Romans, virtually a German equivalent to being Prince of Wales.) A Prusso-Austrian peace treaty was signed at the Silesia hunting lodge of Hubertusburg on 15 February, returning Austria and Prussia to their prewar condition and ending Maria Theresa's dream of recovering Silesia; Frederick signed an agreement with Elector Augustus of Saxony the same day.[81] Maria Theresa's dream had cost the lives of 125,000 Austrian soldiers and 160,000 or 180,000 Prussian soldiers. Russian losses must have been comparable, while civilian deaths may have outnumbered military ones.[82]

The French merchant community was disappointed in the treaty, but the French and Spanish governments were relieved by the limited extent of their losses. The comte de Choiseul was confirmed in his prediction that, although the peace would not be brilliant, it would not be as bad as one might expect. Louis XV described it as neither good nor glorious but as the best possible under the circumstances. He deserves much of the credit that this was so; the duc de Choiseul said that when the news of the fall of Havana arrived, it was only he and the king who did not lose courage.[83]

France's ability to continue to compete as a naval power had been saved, above all, by Louis' and his ministers' perseverance in wearing down British resistance by the wars in Germany and, later, Portugal, just as Louis XIV's persistence had worn down British resistance fifty years earlier. It was a policy that was extraordinarily expensive in financial terms, as the army in Germany contributed a major share of the enormous costs of the war. It was enormously costly in human terms as well. Without mechanisms to adjudicate disputes or protect security, eighteenth-century European states were forced to conduct international relations largely by warfare.[84] Louis XV was tenderhearted and sentimental, but he bears a share of the responsibility for the Austro-Prussian war, as well as being complicit in the unprovoked Spanish attack on Portugal and responsible for the unprovoked French attack on Hanover. The civilians of Portugal and western Germany became victims of his and his cousin Charles's desire to protect themselves from the consequences of an unwanted conflict in the woods of Pennsylvania. During the next two centuries, the routine cruelty of Louis XIV and Louis XV's armies in Germany would be repaid many times over in France by German armies of even greater cruelty.[85]

10

Epilogue
Toward a New War, 1763–1774

At the beginning of 1763 France possessed 47 ships of the line, some of which were in need of repairs, and Spain 37, whereas the British had 111.[1] If the Bourbons were to seek revenge in another war, they would need not only to match the number of British ships of the line but to surpass it, given Britain's advantage in giant 90- and 100-gun ships, her pool of experienced and confident sailors and officers, and her veteran commanders. The British attempted to maintain 80 ships of the line in condition to serve. Louis set a goal of 80 ships of the line for the French navy and expected Spain to provide 60; the duc de Choiseul hoped they would be ready in four or five years.[2]

France had a head start because of the ships of the line donated during 1762, of which only two had been launched by the end of the year. During the first four years after the Treaty of Paris the French navy launched the other fifteen donated ships, purchased the *Vengeur*, 64, and rebuilt the *Conquérant*, 74, *Palmier*, 74, and *Zodiaque*, 74.[3] Choiseul complained to Ossun in 1762 that he worked eight hours a day on naval matters and was convinced the navy needed a complete overhaul. In March 1765 he issued a comprehensive reform and codification of naval regulations.[4] He also made a major effort to fill the dockyards with the naval materiel necessary for building, repairing, and maintaining the fleet. The number of masts rose from 1,576 in 1763 to 4,341 in 1766 and the amount of wood for constructing hulls from 497,322 cubic feet to 697,000 cubic feet, while the amount of hemp and number of anchors also increased.[5]

As naval minister, Choiseul also was responsible for France's remaining colonies. He unsuccessfully tried to circumvent the Treaty of Paris by reestablishing control over the posts France had lost in the region of the Senegal and Gambia rivers of western Africa.[6] In the West Indies, the heart of the remaining

French Empire, he replaced commanders, gave Guadeloupe its own governor general, and attempted to strengthen military authority. He also made an unsuccessful attempt to colonize French Guiana on the northern coast of South America. Perhaps most importantly he loosened mercantilistic restrictions on trade between France and the West Indies so as to balance more fairly the needs of West Indian planters and the merchants of the French ports. His efforts had mixed results, but they did demonstrate a commitment to strengthening the colonies economically and militarily.[7]

France would stand a better chance of defending her colonies and of taking the offense in a future war if the British army and navy were tied down by a revolt in North America. In 1765 Choiseul predicted an eventual American revolution, although he told Louis XV that they probably would not see it themselves.[8] He sent a Lieutenant Pontleroy to the British colonies to gather intelligence. The results were sufficiently encouraging for him to send a more senior observer, Acting Lieutenant Colonel Johann de Kalb, who a decade later became a major general in the Continental army. By the time de Kalb returned to France in 1768, however, Choiseul seems to have given up any hope of an impending rebellion, an opinion shared by de Kalb.[9]

By this time Choiseul seems also to have abandoned hope of a war of revenge in the near future. The improved relations between Britain and her American colonies during the Rockingham administration of 1765–66 may have had an effect on his thinking, but by the end of 1766 several other factors also seem to have inhibited thoughts of an early war. The first factor was the difficulty of sustaining the French navy's building program until the goal of 80 ships of the line was reached, given the king's waning interest and the continuing weakness of royal finances. The navy still had not paid all its debts from the war, and the government had difficulty increasing its revenues.[10] Second, the Spanish navy's rebuilding program, the necessary corollary to the French, began very slowly. During the first four years of peace Spain launched only eight ships of the line.[11] It would be several more years before Spain possessed the 60 ships of the line upon which France counted. Third, Choiseul's attention seems to have been increasingly diverted by France's declining influence in eastern Europe. After Augustus III of Poland died in October 1763, France was unable to prevent the election to the Polish throne of a Russian-backed candidate, Empress Catherine II's former lover Stanislas Poniatowski.[12] Catherine and her new ally Frederick II of Prussia were not satisfied, however, and promptly demanded that Poland protect the rights of the country's Protestant and Orthodox Catholic religious minorities. If the Polish Diet could be bullied into such a concession and into recognizing Catherine and Frederick as protectors of Poland's religious minorities, Poland effectively would lose its remaining independence and France her pretense of influence in Polish affairs. France's influence in Sweden and Denmark was rapidly declining, too. In April 1766 Choiseul turned over the naval ministry to his cousin the duc de Praslin and resumed direct control over foreign affairs; however important to him may have been preparing for war against Britain, the problems of the continent demanded his immediate attention.[13]

After Choiseul left office, the naval budget was reduced. This had an impact on the royal dockyards. Although wood for construction continued to arrive, the number of masts and amount of hemp and sailcloth began to decline.[14]

Ironically, Choiseul's new tenure as foreign minister was marked by a colonial conflict. Charles III was outraged when he learned the British had sent a small squadron and landing party to one of the Falkland Islands, off the Spanish portion of South America. Choiseul counseled moderation, telling Spain in September 1766, that France would need another eighteen months to prepare for war. Within a few months he postponed until 1769 the projected time at which France would be ready. Meanwhile the French naval ministry gave a guarded reaction to a detailed Spanish plan of war.[15] The Spanish government soon was distracted by internal political issues, and the Falkland Island crisis was deferred for several years. When it finally occurred in 1770 the French navy still was not ready to fight. Its program of ship construction had been drastically reduced after 1766 and did not revive until after Louis XV's death in 1774. From 1766 through 1774 it launched only eleven ships of the line, the *Couronne*, 80, *Actif*, 74, *Bien-Aimé*, 74, *César*, 74, *Victoire*, 74, *Alexandre*, 64, *Brillant*, 64, *Eveillé*, 64, *Protée*, 64, *Roland*, 64, and *Solitaire*, 64. (It also purchased the *Actionnaire*, 64, *Indien*, 64, and *Mars*, 64, from the bankrupt East India Company.)[16] This did not equal the seventeen ships of the line that were lost or retired from service between the beginning of 1763 and the end of 1774 (the *Royal-Louis*, 116, *Couronne*, 74, *Défenseur*, 74, *Actif*, 64, *Altier*, 64, *Aventurier* [ex-*Saint-François-de-Paule*], 64, an earlier *Brillant*, 64, *Content*, 64, an earlier *Eveillé*, 64, *Hasard* [ex-*Notre-Dame-de-Rosaire*], 64, *Mars*, 64, an earlier *Protée*, 64, *Rencontre* [ex-*Vierge-de-Santé*], 64, *Sage*, 64, an earlier *Solitaire*, 64, *Ferme*, 56, and *Utile*, 56). Thus, only sixty ships of the line were available on 1 January 1775. This was only thirteen more than on 1 January 1763 and only three more than on 1 January 1755.[17]

During his second tenure as foreign minister, Choiseul enjoyed one clear victory, the leasing from the Republic of Genoa of the island of Corsica, which proved a permanent acquisition. In spite of the British public's outrage, the weak government of the ailing Pitt, now Earl of Chatham, and the inexperienced Augustus Henry Fitzroy, Duke of Grafton, protested but did nothing more.[18] This victory was overshadowed, however, by disastrous defeats for

France's friends in eastern Europe. In March 1768 the Poles rebelled against their government in response to the rights recently given to religious minorities. Six months later the Turks, with French encouragement, went to war against the Russians.[19] Chosieul had badly misjudged the situation. Logistical and financial difficulties prevented France from sending more than limited financial aid and a few volunteers to help the Polish rebels. The relatively modern Russian army was called into Poland, and it proved more than a match for both the Poles and the Turks. Aided by the British, the Russians even were able to send a fleet from the Baltic via Britain to the Aegean Sea, where in 1770 it annihilated a Turkish fleet.[20] France's entire system of client states in eastern European now was threatened and her impotence in foreign affairs revealed to all.

Choiseul's position at the French court also was weakening. It is possible he at least flirted with the idea that a war with Britain would restore his power. In 1770 the conflict over the Falklands became acute when the Spanish commander at Buenos Aires sent a squadron to the British post at Port Egmont and expelled the garrison. Choiseul's diplomatic correspondence with Ossun was ambiguous about France's plans and the king was left in doubt about Choiseul's intentions. Facing renewed struggles with the parlements, Louis XV wished peace at any price and extracted a promise from Choiseul that he would do his utmost to preserve it. In December 1770, his suspicions that Choiseul was pursuing a separate policy led to the downfall of the foreign minister. War was averted when Charles III apologized to George III for the insult given Britain. In exchange, Frederick, Lord North, the British prime minister, secretly promised that Britain quietly would evacuate the islands later.[21]

Choiseul's downfall also brought down his cousin, Naval Minister Praslin. After a short interval Pierre-Etienne Bourgeois de Boynes, the former president of the Parlement of Besançon and supporter of the king whom Chosieul had betrayed, became naval minister.[22] During his three years in office, supplies of masts, wood for construction, and other naval materiel declined drastically.[23] With its rebuilding program stalled and its dockyards depleted of supplies, the navy apparently was not very formidable when he left office in 1774. Nevertheless it had hidden strengths and in several areas was superior to the navy of twenty years earlier. First, its ships of the line on average were somewhat larger. At the end of 1774, 32 of its 60 ships of the line carried 74 or more guns (increasingly the measure of a true ship of the line), whereas only 25 of the 57 ships of the line at the beginning of 1755 had carried that many guns. More importantly, thanks to the great expansion of colonial trade and fishing since the end of the Seven Years' War,[24] it could draw on a larger pool of sailors and hence man more ships. Here, France's saving of her access to the Newfoundland and St. Lawrence fisheries was crucial; the sailors they trained made the difference of perhaps a dozen ships of the line. (The fisheries trained roughly a third of the navy's sailors. If half of these could not have found alternate maritime employment, the navy would have lost a sixth of the crews of the 63–73 ships of the line it used in the War of American Independence.)[25] The balance of opposing naval forces in the War for American Independence was so close that a dozen ships of the line were enough to make a crucial difference. More likely, however, France would not have risked involvement in the war had the navy been weakened by the loss of the fishery. Finally, the navy could look for help from the Spanish navy, which had grown almost as large as the French; from 1767 through 1774 it launched 22 ships of the line.[26] The French navy had received Spanish help during the Seven Years' War only after it had been fatally weakened; if it could find earlier help, it might hope for different results, even though the British launched 52 ships of the line between 1 January 1763 and 1 January 1775 and ended the period with 106 ships of the line.[27]

In 1774 the possibility that the French navy might soon see combat, however, was unlikely. What transformed the situation was the death of Louis XV and the accession to the foreign ministry of a former member of the "Secret du Roi" who put into practice the policies of the "Secret," including striking at Russia through Great Britain.

THE "SECRET DU ROI" AND THE AMERICAN REVOLUTION

The unsuccessful revolt of the Poles against the Russians was especially painful for the "Secret du Roi." France had been liberated from her contradictory policies in Poland when the Russian alliance ceased in 1762. Nevertheless, France subsequently made little attempt to rebuild a French party among the Poles because of the sorry state of French finances and because of Choiseul's belief that such a policy would be futile. After the death of Augustus III in 1763, France made only a token effort to contest the election of Stanislas Poniatowski, the Russian candidate, as his successor. Indeed both the official and the secret diplomacy engaged in discussions with him. The "Secret du Roi," however, did make some feeble efforts on behalf of rival candidates such as Prince Xavier of Saxony and the Polish magnate Grand-General Jan Klemens Branicki, thereby alienating the Russians and their Polish clients.[28]

With the annihilation of French hopes in Poland, the secret diplomacy had lost its original reason for being. It was saved from disbandment by its development of a new program (and by Louis XV's continuing love of intrigue). This program seems to have been the creation of Nivernais' assistant François-Michel Durand, a former chargé d'affaires in London and The Hague, a former minister plenipotentiary in Warsaw, and still a major figure in the "Secret du Roi." Durand, an enthusiast for a war of revenge against Britain, won the comte de Broglie's support for using the secret diplomatic service to reconnoiter possible landing sites along the English coast and to draft invasion plans. Theoretically this may have been too risky a project for the regular French diplomatic mission at the British court; in practice, however, it proved too large for the "Secret du Roi" to handle alone. Broglie shared his plans with Choiseul (without revealing the existence of the secret diplomacy), and the naval ministry participated in the reconnaissance as well as surveying French ports for possible use. In spite of some duplication of effort, detailed invasion plans were drafted, but this work proved meaningless in face of Louis XV's growing reluctance for war. After 1770 the plans were shelved; nine years later, when an invasion was attempted, Broglie's advice was ignored in favor of far less grandiose plans.[29]

The peaceful resolution of the Falkland Islands crisis did seem to promise an opportunity for the "Secret du Roi" to end its isolation. Choiseul's position as foreign minister was left vacant for almost six months while his duties were performed reluctantly by Saint-Florentin. Broglie, still head of the secret diplomacy, was widely perceived as the leading candidate for the office. The king wished peace in order to concentrate on his struggle with the parlements, however, and Broglie's recklessness made him too dangerous. In June 1771, the king finally selected the duc d'Aiguillon, the hero of St. Cast and a leading opponent of the parlements while in Brittany, but with little experience in foreign affairs and hence unlikely to risk war.[30]

Aiguillon inherited an almost hopeless situation in eastern Europe. Both the Polish rebellion and the Turkish war against Russia that Choiseul had encouraged were going very badly. French diplomacy had been paralyzed by the Falkland Islands crisis and the subsequent vacancy at the foreign ministry. Meanwhile, Frederick II of Prussia had been laying plans to take advantage of the Polish and Turkish collapse. The Russian triumphs were so extensive that they threatened either to disrupt the balance of power in eastern Europe or to lead to a Russo-Austrian war that would involve Prussia as an ally of Russia. Frederick sought to avert such a war and simultaneously to eliminate the Polish corridor that separated East Prussia from the major portion of his domains in Germany. He plotted to convince Empress Catherine II to limit her gains against the Turks in favor of seizing a major portion of Poland, while permitting Austria and Russia to do the same. Although this would preserve the balance of power, it would be detrimental in the long run to both Russia, for whom Poland was by now a virtually helpless client state, and Austria, for whom Poland was a useful buffer against both Prussia and Russia. Nevertheless the Russians did not wish a wider war, and Austria, which could not be certain of French help, feared coming to the aid of the Poles and Turks; moreover, both of the empresses were greedy. France was left contemptuously in ignorance of the Austro-Prusso-Russian negotiations, which led in 1772 to the three great eastern powers taking 29 percent of Poland's territory and 35 percent of her population.[31]

The partition of Poland shook France's system of client states. A series of armistices gave only a temporary respite to the Turks; war with Russia resumed in 1773 and ended the following year with Catherine taking little territory but gaining the opportunity subsequently to protect the rights of Orthodox Catholics in the Ottoman Empire, the same wedge she had used to cripple Polish independence. Sweden, dominated by its corrupt and factionalized legislature, the Diet, also seemed doomed to become a Russian satellite. Previously France had financed the Hats, one of the two political parties in the Diet, while Russia and Britain had financed the rival Caps. Rejecting this sterile and expensive competition, France supported a successful coup d'état in August 1772 by Sweden's young king, Gustavus III.[32] When Gustavus promptly ended the independence and power of the Diet, Catherine threatened intervention on behalf of Swedish liberty, a liberty which, like that of the Polish Diet, had kept its country helpless to oppose Russia. Aiguillon now turned for help to Britain, whose relations with Russia had cooled since the partition of Poland. George III, Prime Minister North, and Secretary of State William Henry Zuylestein, Earl of Rochford, were willing to listen to Aiguillon's proposals and even to entertain a secret emissary he sent, but they were afraid to defy the English public's Francophobia. Instead they humiliated France by forcing her to suspend the mobilization of a fleet in the Mediterranean with which Aiguillon had hoped to threaten the Russians. Although Catherine's behavior may have been moderated by widespread rumors of a Franco-British *rapprochement*, Sweden was saved chiefly because Russian attention was diverted by renewed difficulties with the Turks.[33] Meanwhile Britain inadvertently was preparing a chance for France to take revenge; by coincidence, just as the Swedish crisis was ebbing, Parliament passed the Tea Act, oblivious to the danger it posed to Britain's relations with her colonies in America.

During this period of humiliation and failure, the "Secret du Roi" came to an ignominious end. At one time it had enlisted some of the most talented and visionary members of the French diplomatic service, men dedicated to France's role as protector of the weak states of Europe from predatory powers such as Russia and Prussia. By now, though, even Broglie urged its disbandment. Increasingly its ranks had become filled with adventurers like the chevalier d'Eon de Beaumont, director of the secret diplomacy in England, who blackmailed his own government. Its chief function had become that of protecting itself from exposure and the king from embarrassment, a task which would have been impossible had it not recruited the talented lieutenant général de police of Paris, Antoine-Raymond-Gualbert-Gabriel de Sartine. Finally in April 1774, the king learned that the intelligence service of Austria long since had gained access to the correspondence of the secret diplomacy. He was saved from further humiliation only by his death from smallpox the following month.[34]

Although France was weakened abroad, Louis' final years had been spent strengthening the monarchy's position within France by reducing its debts, streamlining the administration of its finances, and replacing the parlements with a more tractable court system. His reforms, although unpopular, did stabilize the budget; moreover, although his successor restored the parlements, their will to resist the king had been weakened; they gave relatively little trouble to the ministers who had to finance the war that France entered four years later.[35] Louis XV thus was in two major respects an architect of American independence: first, by saving the fisheries and hence the French navy, and second, by smoothing the work of financing the French participation in the American Revolution (although it is most unlikely he would have agreed to this participation).

His successor was his nineteen-year-old grandson, who became Louis XVI. (The young king's father, the dauphin, had died in 1765.) The new king, who dismissed all of his grandfather's senior ministers, disbanded the "Secret du Roi" and seized its files. Although Broglie subsequently was cleared of any wrongdoing, he was left in retirement, and the secret diplomatic service that he had headed disappeared, leaving an unbroken record of failure. By one of the great ironies of eighteenth-century diplomacy, however, the history of the secret diplomacy did not end with its dissolution; instead, the "Secret du Roi" soon became dominant at the French foreign ministry. Its functionaries and fellow travelers took direction of official French diplomacy and used it to implement their policies. The most consequential result of these policies was France's decision to become involved in the American Revolution, a decision reflecting not Choiseul's plans for revenge but the secret diplomacy's program for restoring France's position in the European balance of power.

This astonishing triumph was to a large degree the result of a power vacuum at the center of the French government. Louis XVI was idealistic. He was concerned chiefly with French domestic reform and uninterested in war, but he also was inexperienced and naïve. His choice of a chief adviser was the French naval minister during the War of the Austrian Succession, the aged comte de Maurepas, who seems to have been more concerned with maintaining his own power than in implementing any program of his own. The former agents of the secret diplomacy were able to win his acquiescence in their plans by supporting his primacy in the Council of State. Into the policymaking vacuum left by Louis and Maurepas moved a group of former agents and supporters of the "Secret du Roi" led by Louis' choice as foreign minister, the comte (formerly chevalier) de Vergennes.[36]

In an essay first published in 1883, the great diplomatic historian Albert Sorel wrote of the selection of Vergennes, "It was the coming to power and the striking revenge of the secret diplomacy."[37] Most of Vergennes' career had been spent combating the Russians. Between 1755 and 1769 he served as France's diplomatic representative in Constantinople, while also reporting to the "Secret du Roi" on Russian activities in eastern Europe. Choiseul fired him for insufficient zeal in encouraging the Turks to go to war against Russia, but Broglie then saved his career by recommending him to Aiguillon for the critical post of ambassador to Sweden. While in Stockholm he saw the Russian and British ministers cooperate in funding the Cap Party, assisted Gustavus III's coup d'état, and witnessed Britain's foiling of France's attempts to protect Sweden from Russia. He acquired a reputation for extreme caution, a reputation that seems to have helped him secure higher office from a king who wished no foreign adventures and from a de facto chief minister who wished no rivals. Vergennes, however, was anxious to reverse France's decline in the balance of power by following the program propounded by the "Secret du Roi." That program consisted of supporting as best as possible the weaker states of central and eastern Europe, avoiding French territorial expansion, reducing France's dependence on Austria, supporting the balance of power in Germany, weakening Russia's backer Britain and, above all, blocking the expansion of Russia. One of Vergennes' closest colleagues later testified that Vergennes did not wish to crush Britain, but only to weaken it enough to restore French prestige. Vergennes hoped that if Britain no longer was able to treat France with contempt, the two states might even cooperate as they had in the time of Cardinal Fleury, which both Vergennes and Maurepas considered a golden age.[38] Unlike his rival Choiseul, Vergennes seems to have seen Britain not principally as a colonial rival but as a former ally turned opponent.

When Vergennes arrived at the foreign ministry he found willing collaborators in the two *premiers commis* he inherited from Aiguillon, both of whom, although not members of the secret diplomacy, had been involved in Polish affairs. Conrad-Alexandre Gérard, now chiefly remembered as the first French minister in Philadelphia, had on two occasions served as chargé d'affaires in Vienna and in July 1765 had undertaken a secret mission to meet with Grand-General Branicki.[39] His fellow *premier commis* was his younger brother Joseph-Mathias Gérard, who as diplomatic resident and consul at Danzig from 1768 to 1774 incurred the animosity of Frederick II for fanning the city's resistance to absorption by Prussia. He also had translated into French Theophilus Lindsey's 1773 satire on the despoiling of Poland, *The Polish Partition, Illustrated in Seven Dramatic Dialogues*.[40] When the elder Gérard went to Philadelphia, Vergennes named as his replacement an old friend from the "Secret du Roi," Pierre-Michel Hennin, whose personal qualities earned the praise of the comte de Broglie, Voltaire, and Thomas Jefferson. During his diplomatic career he had been expelled from Dresden by the Prussians and from Warsaw by the Russians.[41]

In addition to Vergennes and Hennin, other former members of the "Secret du Roi" served in important positions. Breteuil, also formerly the minister to Russia, served as French ambassador to Austria before becoming the secretary of state for household affairs in 1783. Gabriel de Sartine was promoted to naval minister in 1774 and cooperated with Vergennes in clearing Broglie's name and liquidating the affairs of the notorious chevalier d'Eon.[42]

Vergennes was successful in maneuvering Louis XVI into a war against Britain he did not wish. Although that war procured American independence, it did not destroy Britain's domination of American trade. Moreover, Vergennes was no more successful than Puyzieulx and Aiguillon had been in reestablishing better relations with Britain; indeed, the war made his task far more difficult because it increased the British public's hatred and suspicion of France. Finally, the war worsened the monarchy's financial difficulties. In 1753 the government's debts had been about 1.36 billion livres. By 1764 they were about 2.325 billion livres. By 1787 they were some 5 billion livres, and 40 percent of the French royal budget was being consumed by the increasingly futile attempt to meet interest payments. The War of the Austrian Succession, Seven Years' War, and War for American Independence played the major part in this wreck of the monarchy's finances, collectively costing perhaps 3.5 billion livres (perhaps a third of it coming from the Seven Years' War).[43] This was less than the £245 million (equivalent to 5.8 billion livres) Britain spent on those wars,[44] but the British government, paying lower interest rates, was able to manage its debts. Louis XVI could not. After a final burst of spending failed to prove that the monarchy's credit was still sound, he was forced in 1787 to call an Assembly of Notables and, after that failed, the Estates General. What happened thereafter was not foreordained, but the monarchy needed a king far more self-confident and politically astute than Louis XVI to avoid the fate of the established church and the system of noble privilege with which it had become intertwined. Made vulnerable by the costs of the wars of Louis XV and Louis XVI, the French monarchy itself became their final victim.

Appendixes

The number immediately after a ship name represents the number of cannon it theoretically carried.

A number in parentheses gives the year a ship was launched.

A number after "capt." gives the year a foreign-built ship was captured.

A number after "pur." indicates the year a ship was purchased.

Appendix A

French Ships of the Line, 1 January 1744

Not included are three ships in construction (*Invincible*, 74, *Magnanime*, 74, *Vigilant*, 64) and three 50-gun ships classified as heavy frigates (*Auguste, Jason, Rubis*). For further information consult Demerliac, *La Marine de Louis XV*. Ships marked with an asterisk (*) subsequently were removed from service. Ships marked with 1 were used in the first attempt to invade England. Ships marked with 2 fought in the Battle of Toulon.

Tonnant, 80 (1743)
Dauphin-Royal, 74 (1738)[1]
Duc-d'Orléans, 74 (1722)[2]
Espérance, 74 (1724)[2]
Ferme, 74 (1723)[2]
Juste, 74 (1725)[1]
Neptune, 74 (1723)[1]
Saint-Esprit, 74 (1726)[2]
Saint-Philippe, 74 (1722)
Sceptre, 74 (1720)
Superbe, 74 (1738)[1]
Terrible, 74 (1739)[2]
Lys, 72 (1706)[1]
Grafton, 70 (1700, capt. 1707)
Alcide, 64 (1743)
Ardent, 64 (1723)
Borée, 64 (1734)[2]
Eclatante, 64 (1721)[1]
Elisabeth, 64 (1722)[1]

Eole, 64 (1733)[2]
Fleuron, 64 (1730)[1]
Léopard, 64 (1727)
Mars, 64 (1740)[1]
Saint-Louis, 64 (1723)[1]
Saint-Michel, 64 (1741)[1]
Serieux, 64 (1740)[2]
Solide, 64 (1722)[2]
Trident, 64 (1742)[2]
Content, 60 (1717)[1]
Heureux, 60 (1730)[2]
Mercure, 60 (1696)[1]
Toulouse, 60 (1714)[2]
Triton, 60 (1728)[1]
Brillant, 56 (1724)
Alcyon, 50 (1726)[2]
Apollon, 50 (1740)[1]
Diamant, 50 (1733)[2]
Tigre, 50 (1724)[2]

Appendix B

French Ships of the Line, 1 January 1749

Ships marked with an asterisk were unfit for further service. Years of launching are given only for those ships listed for the first time. Five ships were launched during the war but became war losses (*Invincible*, 74, *Magnanime*, 74, *Monarque*, 74, *Fougueux*, 64, *Vigilant*, 64); the *Severn*, 50, was captured but subsequently was recaptured by the British.

Tonnant, 80
Conquérant, 74 (1746)
Dauphin-Royal, 74
*Duc-d'Orléans, 74
Espérance, 74
Ferme, 74
Intrépide, 74 (1747)
Juste, 74
*Saint-Esprit, 74
Sceptre, 74 (1747)
Superbe, 74
Northumberland, 70 (1743, capt. 1744)
Achille, 64 (1747)
Alcide, 64
Content, 64 (1747)
Dragon, 64 (1747)
*Elisabeth, 64

Léopard, 64
Lys, 64 (1746)
Protée, 64 (1748)
Saint-Michel, 64
*Solide, 64
Triton, 64 (1747)
Fier, 60 (1745)
*Heureux, 60
Saint-Laurent, 60 (1748)
*Toulouse, 60
Alcyon, 50
Apollon, 50
Arc-en-Ciel, 50 (1745)
*Caribou, 50 (1744)
Oriflamme, 50 (1744)
Tigre, 50

Appendix C

French Ships of the Line and Frigates, 1 January 1755

The *Ferme*, 74, is listed, although subsequently it was judged unfit for service and was never sailed again. The *Conquérant*, 74, although judged fit for service, needed repairs and was not used during the war. An asterisk indicates ships decommissioned or lost before 1 January 1763.

FRENCH SHIPS OF THE LINE

Duc-de-Bourgogne, 80 (1751)
Formidable, 80 (1751)
Foudroyant, 80 (1750)
Soleil-Royal, 80 (1749)
Tonnant, 80
Conquérant, 74
Courageux, 74 (1753)
Couronne, 74 (1749)
Dauphin-Royal, 74
Défenseur, 74 (1754)
Entreprenant, 74 (1751)
Espérance, 74
Ferme, 74
Florissant, 74 (1750)
Guerrier, 74 (1753)
Héros, 74 (1752)
Intrépide, 74
Juste, 74
Magnifique, 74 (1749)
Palmier, 74 (1752)
Prudent, 74 (1753)

Redoutable, 74 (1752)
Sceptre, 74
Superbe, 74
Téméraire, 74 (1749)
Algonquin, 72 (1753)
Northumberland, 70
Achille, 64
Actif, 64 (1752)
Alcide, 64
Bienfaisant, 64 (1754)
Bizarre, 64 (1751)
Capricieux, 64 (1753)
Content, 64 (1747)
Dragon, 64
Eveillé, 64 (1752)
Hardi, 64 (1750)
Hercule, 64 (1749)
Illustre, 64 (1750)
Inflexible, 64 (1752)
Léopard, 64
Lion, 64 (1751)
Lys, 64
Opiniâtre, 64 (1750)

Orphée, 64 (1749)

Protée, 64

Sage, 64 (1751)

Saint-Michel, 64

Triton, 64

Fier, 60

Aigle, 50 (1750)

Alcyon, 50

Amphion, 50 (1749)

Apollon, 50

Arc-en-Ciel, 50

Hippopotame, 50 (1749)

Oriflamme, 50

FRENCH FRIGATES

Aquilon, 40 (1733)

Junon, 40 (1747)

Atalante, 34 (1741)

Améthyste, 30 (1754)

Comète, 30 (1752)

Favorite, 30 (1747)

Fleur-de-Lys, 30 (1754)

Pomone, 30 (1749)

Rose, 30 (1752)

Sirène, 30 (1744)

Zéphir, 30 (1754)

Diane, 28 (1741)

Emeraude, 28 (1744)

Hermione, 28 (1749)

Flore, 26 (1728)

Duc-de-Cumberland, 24 (capt. 1744)

Fidèle, 24 (1748)

Frippone, 24 (1747)

Galatée, 24 (1744)

Gracieuse, 24 (1750)

Héroïne, 24 (1752)

Mutine, 24 (1744)

Nymphe, 24 (1752)

Thetis, 24 (1751)

Topaze, 24 (1750)

Valeur, 20 (1754)

Appendix D

Order of Battle, 1 June 1755

BRITAIN (61)

Home Waters

Prince, 90
Ramillies, 90
Royal Anne, 90
Saint George, 90
Barfleur, 80
Prince George, 80
Culloden, 74
Bedford, 70
Buckingham, 70
Captain, 70
Elizabeth, 70
Essex, 70
Monmouth, 70
Nassau, 70
Orford, 70
Prince Frederick, 70
Revenge, 70
Vanguard, 70
Lancaster, 66
Ipswich, 64
Trident, 64
Kingston, 60
Medway, 60
Warwick, 60
Weymouth, 60

York, 60
Eagle, 58
Windsor, 58
Antelope, 50
Colchester, 50
Falmouth, 50
Greenwich, 50
Newcastle, 50
Rochester, 50
Winchester, 50

Off Newfoundland

Monarch, 74
Torbay, 74
Northumberland, 70
Somerset, 70
Fougueux, 64
Mars, 64
Anson, 60
Dunkirk, 60
Nottingham, 60
Defiance, 58
Litchfield, 50

Chesapeake Bay

Centurion, 50
Norwich, 50

En Route to North America

Terrible, 74
Chichester, 70
Edinburgh, 70
Grafton, 70
Yarmouth, 70
Augusta, 60

Indian Ocean

Kent, 70
Cumberland, 66

Tiger, 60
Salisbury, 50

Mediterranean

Deptford, 50

Jamaica

Severn, 50

Leeward Islands

Advice, 50

FRANCE (21)

Ships marked with an asterisk were *en flûte*, temporarily carrying a reduced number of cannon.

Atlantic Ports

Formidable, 80
Héros, 74
Palmier, 74
Eveillé, 64
Inflexible, 64
Aigle, 50

En Route to North America

*Dauphin-Royal, 74
*Défenseur, 74
Entreprenant, 74
*Espérance, 74

*Algonquin, 72
Actif, 64
Alcide, 64
Bizarre, 64
*Illustre, 64
*Léopard, 64
*Lys, 64
*Opiniâtre, 64
*Apollon, 50

West Indies

Saint-Michel, 64
*Arc-en-Ciel, 50

Appendix E

Order of Battle, 1 June 1756

BRITAIN (88)

Home Waters

Royal George, 100
Royal Sovereign, 100
Duke, 90
Namur, 90
Prince, 90
Princess Royal, 90
Royal Anne, 90
Saint George, 90
Barfleur, 80
Cambridge, 80
Newark, 80
Invincible, 74
Magnanime, 74
Monarch, 74
Terrible, 74
Torbay, 74
Bedford, 70
Chichester, 70
Edinburgh, 70
Elizabeth, 70
Essex, 70
Monmouth, 70
Northumberland, 70
Orford, 70
Prince Frederick, 70

Somerset, 70
Sterling Castle, 70
Swiftsure, 70
Vanguard, 70
Yarmouth, 70
Devonshire, 66
Alcide, 64
Augusta, 60
Dunkirk, 60
Jersey, 60
Medway, 60
Saint Albans, 60
Weymouth, 60
York, 60
Eagle, 58
Tilbury, 58
Windsor, 58
Antelope, 50
Colchester, 50
Falkland, 50
Falmouth, 50
Harwich, 50
Newcastle, 50
Oxford, 50
Rochester, 50
Sutherland, 50

En Route to England

Severn, 50

Mediterranean

Ramillies, 90
Culloden, 74
Buckingham, 70
Captain, 70
Revenge, 70
Lancaster, 66
Intrepid, 64
Trident, 64
Kingston, 60
Defiance, 58
Princess Louisa, 58
Deptford, 50
Portland, 50

En Route to Mediterranean

Prince George, 80
Hampton Court, 70
Ipswich, 70
Nassau, 70
Isis, 50

North America

Fougueux, 64
Centurion, 50

Litchfield, 50
Norwich, 50

En Route to North America

Grafton, 70
Nottingham, 60

Leeward Islands

Anson, 60
Bristol, 50
Winchester, 50

Jamaica

Dreadnought, 60
Princess Mary, 60
Greenwich, 50

Indian Ocean

Kent, 70
Cumberland, 66
Tiger, 60
Salisbury, 50

En Route to Africa

Assistance, 50

En Route to South Atlantic

Hampshire, 50

FRANCE (33)

Not including the East India Company ship of the line *Duc-d'Orléans* 54, en route to the Indian Ocean. Ships marked with an asterisk were *en flûte*, temporarily carrying a reduced number of cannon.

Atlantic Ports

Soleil-Royal, 80
Tonnant, 80
Dauphin-Royal, 74
Défenseur, 74
Juste, 74
Superbe, 74
Bienfaisant, 64
Capricieux, 64
Eveillé, 64
Inflexible, 64
Sphinx, 64

Mediterranean

Foudroyant, 80
Couronne, 74
Guerrier, 74
Redoutable, 74
Téméraire, 74
Content, 64
Lion, 64

Orphée, 64
Sage, 64
Triton, 64
Fier, 50
Hippopotame, 50

West Indies

Courageux, 74
Prudent, 74
Protée, 64
Warwick, 60
Aigle, 50
Amphion, 50

North America

*Héros, 74
*Illustre, 64
*Léopard, 64

En Route to North America

*Arc-en-Ciel, 50

Appendix F

Order of Battle, 1 June 1757

BRITAIN (96)

Home Waters

Royal George, 100
Royal Sovereign, 100
Duke, 90
Namur, 90
Neptune, 90
Princess Royal, 90
Ramillies, 90
Royal Anne, 90
Union, 90
Royal William, 84
Barfleur, 80
Cambridge, 80
Prince George, 80
Princess Amelia, 80
Dublin, 74
Magnanime, 74
Torbay, 74
Buckingham, 70
Burford, 70
Chichester, 70
Essex, 70
Prince Frederick, 70
Somerset, 70
Devonshire, 66
Lancaster, 66

Alcide, 64
Fougueux, 64
Trident, 64
Achilles, 60
America, 60
Dunkirk, 60
Medway, 60
Prince of orange, 60
York, 60
Eagle, 58
Windsor, 58
Antelope, 50
Falkland, 50
Falmouth, 50
Guernsey, 50
Hampshire, 50
Harwich, 50
Isis, 50
Norwich, 50
Preston, 50
Rochester, 50

En Route to England

Jersey, 60

Mediterranean

Prince, 90

Saint George, 90
Culloden, 74
Monarch, 74
Berwick, 70
Hampton Court, 70
Monmouth, 70
Revenge, 70
Saint Albans, 60
Princess Louisa, 58
Portland, 50

En Route to Mediterranean

Swiftsure, 70

North America

Nottingham, 60
Sutherland, 50

En Route to North America

Newark, 80
Invincible, 74
Terrible, 74
Bedford, 70
Captain, 70
Grafton, 70
Nassau, 70
Northumberland, 70
Orford, 70
Kingston, 60
Defiance, 58
Sunderland, 58
Tilbury, 58
Centurion, 50

Leeward Islands

Buckingham, 70
Sterling Castle, 70
Trident, 64
Anson, 60
Bristol, 50
Winchester, 50

Jamaica

Marlborough, 80
Edinburgh, 70
Augusta, 60
Dreadnought, 60
Princess Mary, 60
Assistance, 50

India

Cumberland, 66
Tiger, 60
Salisbury, 50

En Route to India

Elizabeth, 70
Yarmouth, 70
Weymouth, 60
Newcastle, 50

Africa

Litchfield, 50

South Atlantic

Colchester, 50

FRANCE (42)

Not including the East India Company ships of the line *Comte-de-Provence*, 58, *Duc-de-Bourgogne*, 54, *Duc-d'Orléans*, 54, and *Saint-Louis*, 54 (Indian Ocean), *Bien-Aimé*, 58, *Centaure*, 58, and *Vengeur*, 54 (en route to Indian Ocean). Ships marked with an asterisk were *en flûte*, temporarily carrying a reduced number of cannon.

Atlantic Ports

Entreprenant, 74
Florissant, 74
Palmier, 74
Prudent, 74
Capricieux, 64
Dragon, 64
Warwick, 64
Apollon, 50

Mediterranean

Océan, 80
Guerrier, 74
Redoutable, 74
Content, 64
Lion, 64
Orphée, 64
Triton, 64
Fier, 50

North America

Tonnant, 80
Défenseur, 74
Diadème, 74
Eveillé, 64
Inflexible, 64

En Route to North America

Duc-de-Bourgogne, 80

Formidable, 80
Glorieux, 74
Hector, 74
Héros, 74
Dauphin-Royal, 70
Superbe, 70
Achille, 64
Belliqueux, 64
Bizarre, 64
Célèbre, 64
Sage, 64
Vaillant, 64

West Indies

Intrépide, 74
Hardi, 64
Opiniâtre, 64
Saint-Michel, 64
Greenwich, 50

En Route to West Indies

*Sceptre, 74
Alcyon, 50

En Route to Indian Ocean

Zodiaque, 74

Appendix G

Order of Battle, 1 June 1758

BRITAIN (104)

Home Waters

Royal George, 100
Royal Sovereign, 100
Duke, 90
Neptune, 90
Princess Royal, 90
Ramillies, 90
Royal Anne, 90
Union, 90
Barfleur, 80
Newark, 80
Lenox, 74
Magnanime, 74
Norfolk, 74
Shrewsbury, 74
Torbay, 74
Warspight, 74
Chichester, 70
Conqueror, 70
Dorsetshire, 70
Alcide, 64
Duke of Aquitaine, 64
Essex, 64
Fougueux, 64
Sterling Castle, 64
Achilles, 60

America, 60
Dunkirk, 60
Intrepid, 60
Medway, 60
Rippon, 60
Windsor, 58
Antelope, 50
Chatham, 50
Deptford, 50
Falmouth, 50
Hampshire, 50
Isis, 50
Norwich, 50
Portland, 50
Rochester, 50
Winchester, 50

En Route to England

Nassau, 64
Revenge, 64
Montague, 60
Falkland, 50
Litchfield, 50

Mediterranean

Prince, 90
Saint George, 90

Culloden, 74
Monarch, 74
Swiftsure, 70
Berwick, 64
Hampton Court, 64
Monmouth, 64
Jersey, 60
Saint Albans, 60
Princess Louisa, 58
Guernsey, 50
Preston, 50

North America

Namur, 90
Royal William, 84
Princess Amelia, 80
Dublin, 74
Terrible, 74
Burford, 70
Northumberland, 70
Orford, 70
Somerset, 70
Vanguard, 70
Devonshire, 66
Lancaster, 66
Bedford, 64
Captain, 64
Prince Frederick, 64
Kingston, 60
Nottingham, 60
Pembroke, 60
Prince of Orange, 60
York, 60
Defiance, 58
Centurion, 50
Sutherland, 50

Leeward Islands

Cambridge, 80
Buckingham, 70
Trident, 64
Bristol, 50

Jamaica

Marlborough, 80
Edinburgh, 64
Augusta, 60
Dreadnought, 60
Princess Mary, 60
Assistance, 50

En Route to Jamaica

Eagle, 58
Harwich, 50

Indian Ocean

Elizabeth, 70
Yarmouth, 70
Tiger, 60
Weymouth, 60
Cumberland, 58
Newcastle, 50
Salisbury, 50

En Route to Indian Ocean

Grafton, 70
Sunderland, 58

South Atlantic

Colchester, 50

FRANCE (25)

Not counting East India Company ships of the line *Brillant*, 54 (North America), *Comte-de-Provence*, 58, *Vengeur*, 54, *Condé*, 50, *Duc-de-Bourgogne*, 50, *Duc-d'Orléans*, 50, *Moras*, 50, *Saint-Louis*, 50 (Indian Ocean), *Centaure*, 58 (disarmed to provide crews for other ships in Indian Ocean), and *Fortuné*, 54 (en route to Indian Ocean). Note that the armament of East India Company ships changed periodically; the *Condé* and *Moras*, for example, had been 44-gun heavy frigates. Ships marked with an asterisk were *en flûte*, temporarily carrying a reduced number of cannon.

Atlantic Ports

*Aigle, 50

Spanish Ports

Magnifique, 74

Mediterranean

Centaure, 74
Guerrier, 74
Souverain, 74
Triton, 64
Fier, 50

North America

Entreprenant, 74
Prudent, 74
*Belliqueux, 64
*Bienfaisant, 64
*Bizarre, 64
*Capricieux, 64
*Célèbre, 64

Dragon, 64
*Hardi, 64
*Sphinx, 64
*Apollon, 50

En Route to North America

Formidable, 80

West Indies

Palmier, 74

En Route to West Indies

Florissant, 74

Indian Ocean

Zodiaque, 74

En Route to Indian Ocean

Minotaure, 74
Actif, 64
Illustre, 64

Appendix H

Order of Battle, 1 June 1759

BRITAIN (111)

Home Waters

Royal George, 100
Duke, 90
Princess Royal, 90
Ramillies, 90
Royal Anne, 90
Sandwich, 90
Union, 90
Fame, 74
Hercules, 74
Hero, 74
Magnanime, 74
Mars, 74
Resolution, 74
Torbay, 74
Chichester, 70
Dorsetshire, 70
Temple, 70
Belliqueux, 64
Bienfaisant, 64
Essex, 64
Monmouth, 64
Revenge, 64
Achilles, 60
Anson, 60
Dunkirk, 60

Firm, 60
Kingston, 60
Montague, 60
Nottingham, 60
Defiance, 58
Windsor, 58
Antelope, 50
Chatham, 50
Colchester, 50
Deptford, 50
Isis, 50
Norwich, 50
Rochester, 50

En Route to England

Falkland, 50
Preston, 50

Mediterranean

Namur, 90
Prince, 90
Newark, 80
Culloden, 74
Warspight, 74
Conqueror, 70
Swiftsure, 70
America, 60

Edgar, 60
Intrepid, 60
Jersey, 60
Saint Albans, 60
Princess Louisa, 58
Guernsey, 50
Portland, 50

North America

Neptune, 90
Royal William, 84
Princess Amelia, 80
Dublin, 74
Shrewsbury, 74
Terrible, 74
Northumberland, 70
Orford, 70
Somerset, 70
Vanguard, 70
Devonshire, 66
Alcide, 64
Bedford, 64
Captain, 64
Prince Frederick, 64
Sterling Castle, 64
Trident, 64
Medway, 60
Pembroke, 60
Prince of Orange, 60
Centurion, 50
Sutherland, 50

Leeward Islands

Saint George, 90
Cambridge, 80
Norfolk, 74
Buckingham, 70

Burford, 70
Lancaster, 66
Berwick, 64
Nassau, 64
Raisonnable, 64
Lion, 60
Panther, 60
Rippon, 60
Bristol, 50
Hampshire, 50
Winchester, 50

Jamaica

Marlborough, 80
Edinburgh, 64
Augusta, 60
Dreadnought, 60
Assistance, 50
Harwich, 50

Indian Ocean

Elisabeth, 70
Grafton, 70
Yarmouth, 70
Tiger, 60
Weymouth, 60
Cumberland, 58
Sunderland, 58
Newcastle, 50
Salisbury, 50

En Route to Indian Ocean

Lenox, 74
Duke of Aquitaine, 64
York, 60
Falmouth, 50

FRANCE (47)

Not including the East India Company ships of the line *Comte-de-Provence*, 74, *Centaure*, 68, *Fortuné*, 64, *Vengeur*, 64, *Duc-de-Bourgogne*, 54, *Duc-d'Orléans*, 54, and *Saint-Louis*, 54 (Indian Ocean), *Condé*, 50, and *Moras*, 50 (disarmed for lack of crewmen).

Atlantic Ports

Formidable, 80
Orient, 80
Soleil-Royal, 80
Tonnant, 80
Glorieux, 74
Héros, 74
Intrépide, 74
Magnifique, 74
Robuste, 74
Thésée, 74
Dauphin-Royal, 70
Juste, 70
Northumberland, 70
Superbe, 70
Bizarre, 64
Brillant, 64
Dragon, 64
Eveillé, 64
Inflexible, 64
Solitaire, 64
Sphinx, 64

Mediterranean

Océan, 80
Centaure, 74
Guerrier, 74
Redoutable, 74

Souverain, 74
Téméraire, 74
Fantasque, 64
Lion, 64
Modeste, 64
Triton, 64
Fier, 50
Oriflamme, 50

West Indies

Courageux, 74
Défenseur, 74
Diadème, 74
Florissant, 74
Hector, 74
Protée, 64
Sage, 64
Vaillant, 64
Amphion, 50

Indian Ocean

Minotaure, 74
Zodiaque, 74
Actif, 64
Illustre, 64

South Atlantic

Achille, 64

Appendix I

Order of Battle, 1 June 1760

BRITAIN (111)

Home Waters

Royal George, 100
Duke, 90
Namur, 90
Prince, 90
Princess Royal, 90
Royal Anne, 90
Saint George, 90
Sandwich, 90
Union, 90
Royal William, 84
Barfleur, 80
Newark, 80
Princess Amelia, 80
Royal Sovereign, 80
Bellona, 74
Centaur, 74
Culloden, 74
Dragon, 74
Hercules, 74
Hero, 74
Magnanime, 74
Mars, 74
Monarch, 74
Shrewsbury, 74
Thunderer, 74

Torbay, 74
Valiant, 74
Warspight, 74
Burford, 70
Chichester, 70
Conqueror, 70
Orford, 70
Swiftsure, 70
Bedford, 64
Modeste, 64
Monmouth, 64
Prince Frederick, 64
Sterling Castle, 64
Anson, 60
Edgar, 60
Intrepid, 60
Nottingham, 60
Princess Mary, 60
Saint Florentine, 60
Defiance, 58
Centurion, 50
Chatham, 50
Deptford, 50
Isis, 50
Portland, 50

En Route to England

Marlborough, 80

Berwick, 64
Windsor, 58

En Route to the Mediterranean

Neptune, 90
Somerset, 70
Dunkirk, 60
Firm, 60
Jersey, 60
Guernsey, 50
Preston, 50

North America

Fame, 74
Dorsetshire, 70
Northumberland, 70
Vanguard, 70
Alcide, 64
Trident, 64
Achilles, 60
Kingston, 60
Pembroke, 60
Prince of Orange, 60
Falkland, 50
Rochester, 50

En Route to North America

Devonshire, 66
Antelope, 50
Norwich, 50
Sutherland, 50
Winchester, 50

Leeward Islands

Dublin, 74
Buckingham, 70
Temple, 70
Lancaster, 66
Belliqueux, 64

Bienfaisant, 64
Nassau, 64
Raisonnable, 64
Lion, 60

En Route to Leeward Islands

Foudroyant, 80
Montague, 60

Jamaica

Cambridge, 80
Edinburgh, 64
Dreadnought, 60
Hampshire, 50
Harwich, 50

Indian Ocean

Lenox, 74
Grafton, 70
Duke of Aquitaine, 64
Elizabeth, 64
Tiger, 60
Weymouth, 60
York, 60
Sunderland, 58
Falmouth, 50
Newcastle, 50
Salisbury, 50

En Route to the Indian Ocean

Norfolk, 74
America, 60
Medway, 60
Panther, 60

South Atlantic

Yarmouth, 64
Rippon, 60
Colchester, 50

FRANCE (14)

Not including the East India Company ships of the line *Condé*, 50 (Sumatra) or *Vengeur*, 54 (Cape of Good Hope or Indian Ocean). The remainder of the East India Company ships in the Indian Ocean (as well as the *Illustre*, 64) were out of service as a result of damage suffered in the typhoon of 27–28 January 1760.

Atlantic Ports

Glorieux, 74
Robuste, 74
Brillant, 64
Dragon, 64
Eveillé, 64

Spanish Ports

Diadème, 74

Mediterranean

Fantasque, 64

Lion, 64
Fier, 50
Hippopotame, 50

West Indies

Vaillant, 64

Indian Ocean

Minotaure, 74
Zodiaque, 74
Actif, 64

Appendix J

Order of Battle, 1 June 1761

BRITAIN (99)

Home Waters

Royal George, 100
Duke, 90
Namur, 90
Ocean, 90
Prince, 90
Princess Royal, 90
Sandwich, 90
Union, 90
Royal William, 84
Newark, 80
Princess Amelia, 80
Royal Sovereign, 80
Arrogant, 74
Bellona, 74
Dragon, 74
Fame, 74
Hero, 74
Magnanime, 74
Mars, 74
Superb, 74
Temeraire, 74
Torbay, 74
Valiant, 74
Warspight, 74
Buckingham, 70

Burford, 70
Chichester, 70
Dorsetshire, 70
Orford, 70
Swiftsure, 70
Vanguard, 70
Marlborough, 68
Alcide, 64
Essex, 64
Hampton Court, 64
Modeste, 64
Monmouth, 64
Nassau, 64
Prince Frederick, 64
Trident, 64
Achilles, 60
Edgar, 60
Intrepid, 60
Nottingham, 60
Prince of Orange, 60
Rippon, 60
Saint Florentine, 60
Windsor, 58
Guernsey, 50
Winchester, 50

Mediterranean

Neptune, 90

Hercules, 74
Shrewsbury, 74
Thunderer, 74
Somerset, 70
Anson, 60
Dunkirk, 60
Firm, 60
Jersey, 60
Isis, 50
Preston, 50

En Route to Portugal

Bedford, 64

North America

Northumberland, 70
Devonshire, 66
Norwich, 50
Rochester, 50

En Route to North America

Antelope, 50
Assistance, 50

Leeward Islands

Foudroyant, 80
Culloden, 74
Dublin, 74
Temple, 70
Lancaster, 66
Belliqueux, 64

Bienfaisant, 64
Raisonnable, 64
Sterling Castle, 64
Montague, 60
Falkland, 50
Sutherland, 50

Jamaica

Cambridge, 80
Centaur, 74
Pembroke, 60
Defiance, 58
Centurion, 50
Hampshire, 50

Indian Ocean

Lenox, 74
Norfolk, 74
Grafton, 70
Elizabeth, 64
America, 60
Medway, 60
Panther, 60
Weymouth, 60
York, 60
Chatham, 50
Falmouth, 50

South Atlantic

Lion, 60
Portland, 50

FRANCE (17)

Not including the following ships of the line being used by private contractors or the East India Company: *Achille*, 64 (La Corunna), **Notre-Dame-de-Rosaire*, 64, **Vierge-de-Santé*, 64 (Mediterranean), *Sage*, 64, **Sainte-Anne*, 64 (West Indies), *Vaillant*, 64 (en route to Indian Ocean). Ships marked with an asterisk were *en flûte*, temporarily carrying a reduced number of cannon.

Atlantic Ports

Défenseur, 74
Guerrier, 74
Hector, 74
Intrépide, 74
Magnifique, 74
Palmier, 74
Protée, 74
Robuste, 74

Souverain, 74
Brillant, 64
Dragon, 64
Eveillé, 64
Solitaire, 64
Saint-Michel, 60

West Indies

*Courageux, 74

Indian Ocean

All of the East India Company ships of the line in the Indian Ocean (and the *Zodiaque*, 74) were in repair or disarmed for coastal defense.

Minotaure, 74

Actif, 64

Appendix K

Order of Battle, 1 June 1762

BRITAIN (110)

Home Waters

Royal George, 100
Duke, 90
Ocean, 90
Prince, 90
Princess Royal, 90
Sandwich, 90
Union, 90
Royal William, 84
Princess Amelia, 80
Royal Sovereign, 80
Bellona, 74
Cornwall, 74
Fame, 74
Hero, 74
Kent, 74
Magnanime, 74
Mars, 74
Shrewsbury, 74
Superb, 74
Torbay, 74
Buckingham, 70
Burford, 70
Swiftsure, 70
Lancaster, 66
Bedford, 64

Captain, 64
Essex, 64
Monmouth, 64
Nassau, 64
Prince Frederick, 64
Revenge, 64
Saint Ann, 64
Trident, 64
Achilles, 60
Dreadnought, 60
Prince of Orange, 60
Princess Mary, 60
Saint Florentine, 60
Saint George, 52
Antelope, 50
Guernsey, 50
Portland, 50

En Route to England

York, 60

Mediterranean and Approaches

Neptune, 90
Newark, 80
Arrogant, 74
Hercules, 74
Thunderer, 74

Warspight, 74
Chichester, 70
Dorsetshire, 70
Somerset, 70
Africa, 64
Belliqueux, 64
Bienfaisant, 64
Anson, 60
Dunkirk, 60
Firm, 60
Jersey, 60
Montague, 60
Windsor, 58
Isis, 50
Preston, 50

En route to the Mediterranean or Portugal

Blenheim, 90
Lion, 60

North America

Northumberland, 70
Intrepid, 60

Leeward Islands

Foudroyant, 80
Vanguard, 70
Modeste, 64
Falkland, 50
Norwich, 50
Rochester, 50

En Route to Cuba

Namur, 90
Cambridge, 80
Centaur, 74
Culloden, 74
Dragon, 74

Dublin, 74
Temeraire, 74
Valiant, 74
Orford, 70
Temple, 70
Marlborough, 68
Devonshire, 66
Alcide, 64
Belleisle, 64
Hampton Court, 64
Sterling Castle, 64
Edgar, 60
Nottingham, 60
Pembroke, 60
Rippon, 60
Defiance, 58
Deptford, 50
Hampshire, 50

Jamaica

Centurion, 50
Sutherland, 50

En Route to Jamaica

Winchester, 50

Indian Ocean

Lenox, 74
Norfolk, 74
Grafton, 70
Elizabeth, 64
America, 60
Medway, 60
Panther, 60
Weymouth, 60
Chatham, 50
Falmouth, 50

South Atlantic

Assistance, 50

PORTUGAL (9)

List kindly provided by Professor Jan Glete, University of Stockholm.

Home Waters

Nuestra Señora do Monte do Carmo, 74
Nuestra Señora Madre de Deus e S. José,
  64
S. José e Neustra Señora des Mercês, 64
Nuestra Señora do Livramento e S. José,
  60(?)
Nuestra Señora da Natividade, 50

En Route to South America

Nuestra Señora de Ajuda e S. Pedro de
  Alcântara, 68
Nuestra Señora da Assunçâo, 64

Indian Ocean

Nuestra Señora des Necessidades, 70
Nuestra Señora do Vencimento e S. José,
  58

FRANCE (27)

Not including East India Company ships of the line *Comte-de-Provence*, 74, *Comte-d'Artois*, 64, *Fortuné*, 64, *Vaillant*, 64, *Vengeur*, 64 (Indian Ocean).

Atlantic Ports

Orient, 80
Tonnant, 80
Guerrier, 74
Intrépide, 74
Magnifique, 74
Souverain, 74
Northumberland, 70
Solitaire, 64
Saint-Michel, 60

Mediterranean

Couronne, 74
Protecteur, 74
Altier, 64
Content, 64
Fantasque, 64

Lion, 64
Saint-François-de-Paule, 64
Triton, 64
Hippopotame, 50
Sagittaire, 50

En Route to Newfoundland

Robuste, 74
Eveillé, 64

West Indies

Duc-de-Bourgogne, 80
Défenseur, 74
Diadème, 74
Hector, 74
Brillant, 64
Protée, 64

SPAIN (47)

Cadiz

Fenix, 80
Rayo, 80
Aquilas, 74
Magnanimo, 74
Africa, 70
Princesa, 70
Triufante, 70
Constante, 68
España, 68
Hector, 68
Hercules, 68
Dragon, 60
Septentrion, 60

Ferrol

Brillante, 74
Gallardo, 74
Guerrero, 74 (possibly at Cadiz)
Principe, 74
Victorioso, 74
Diligente, 70
Oriente, 70
Poderoso, 70
Soberbio, 70
Campion, 60

Mediterranean

Atalante, 74
Glorioso, 74
Terrible, 74
Astuto, 58

Caribbean

Aquilón, 70
Arrogante, 70
Dichoso, 70
Firme, 70
Galicia, 70
Infante, 70
Monarca, 70
Neptuno, 70
Reina, 70
Serio, 70
Soberano, 70
Tigre, 70
Tridente, 70
Vencedor, 70
América, 60
Asia, 60
Castilla, 60
Europa, 60
Conquestador, 58

Pacific Coast of South America

Peruano, 50

Appendix L

French Ships of the Line and Frigates, 1 January 1763

FRENCH SHIPS OF THE LINE

Royal-Louis, 116 (1759)
Duc-de-Bourgogne, 80
Orient, 80 (1756, pur. 1759)
Tonnant, 80
Conquérant, 74
Couronne, 74
Défenseur, 74
Diadème, 74 (1756)
Diligent, 74 (1762)
Glorieux, 74 (1756)
Guerrier, 74
Hector, 74 (1755)
Intrépide, 74 (1759)
Magnifique, 74
Minotaure, 74 (1757)
Palmier, 74
Protecteur, 74 (1760)
Robuste, 74 (1758)
Sceptre, 74
Six-Corps, 74 (1762)
Souverain, 74 (1757)
Zodiaque, 74 (1756)
Dauphin-Royal, 70
Northumberland, 70

Actif, 64
Altier, 64 (1760)
Bizarre, 64
Brillant, 64 (1757, pur. 1758)
Content, 64
Eveillé, 64
Fantasque, 64 (1758)
Hardi, 64
Hasard, 64 (1757, pur. 1760; ex-Notre-
    Dame-de-Rosaire)
Lion, 64
Protée, 64
Rencontre, 64 (1759, pur. 1760; ex-Vierge-
    de-Santé)
Saint-François-de-Paule, 64 (1759, pur.
    1760; later Aventurier)
Sage, 64
Solitaire, 64 (1758)
Sphinx, 64 (1755)
Triton, 64
Vaillant, 64 (1755)
Saint-Michel, 60
Amphion, 50
Fier, 50
Hippopotame, 50
Sagittaire, 50 (1761)

FRENCH FRIGATES

Losses between 1 January 1755 and 31 December 1762 consisted of forty-seven frigates: the twenty-one frigates listed in appendix C with an asterisk plus five frigates captured from the British (*Victoire*, 40 [1757], *Tigre*, 36 [1758], *Hussar*, 28 [1762], *Deal Castle*, 24 [1758], *Winchelsea*, 22 [1758]) and twenty-one frigates launched or purchased in French ports during this period (*Danaé*, 40 [1756], *Abénakise*, 36 [1756], *Aréthuse*, 36 [1757], *Harmonie*, 34 [1757], *Bellone*, 32 [1757], *Blonde*, 32 [1755], *Bouffone*, 32 [1758], *Brune*, 32 [1755], *Felicité*, 32 [1756], *Folle*, 32 [1761], *Vestale*, 32 [1756], *Concorde*, 30 [1755], *Hermine*, 30 [1757], *Minerve*, 30 [1756], *Oiseau*, 30 [1757], *Opale*, 30 [1757], *Sauvage*, 30 [1756], *Echo*, 28 [1757], *Terpsichore*, 28 [1758], *Guirland*, 26 [1761], and *Zenobie*, 24 [1759]). For a list of French frigates in 1774 see Dull, *French Navy and American Independence*, 356.

Hébé, 40 (1757)

Aigrette, 32 (1756)

Améthyste, 32 (on loan to private contractor)

Diligente, 32 (1756, pur. 1761)

Licorne, 32 (1755)

Malicieuse, 32 (1758)

Heroïne, 30

Thetis, 30

Chimère, 28 (1758)

Fortune, 26 (1756, pur. 1762)

Pleïade, 26 (1755)

Gracieuse, 24

Topaze, 24

Biche, 22 (capt. 1762)

Etourdie, 20 (1761)

Notes

1. 1748–1754—AN UNEASY PEACE

1. Richard Lodge, *Studies in Eighteenth-Century Diplomacy, 1740–1748* (London: John Murray, 1930), 410–11; Reed Browning, *The Duke of Newcastle* (New Haven: Yale University Press, 1975), 159.

2. An able study of Franco-British tensions is Jeremy Black, *Natural and Necessary Enemies: Anglo-French Relations in the Eighteenth Century* (London: Gerald Duckworth, 1986).

3. Examples include Jean Meyer and John Bromley, "The Second Hundred Years' War (1689–1815)," in Douglas Johnson, François Crouzet, and François Bédarida, eds., *Britain and France: Ten Centuries* (Folkestone, Eng.: William Dawson and Sons, 1980), 139–72, and François Crouzet, "The Second Hundred Years' War: Some Reflections," *French History* 10 (1996): 432–50.

4. See especially Max Savelle, "The American Balance of Power and European Diplomacy, 1713–78," in Richard B. Morris, ed., *The Era of the American Revolution: Studies Inscribed to Evarts Boutell Greene* (New York: Columbia University Press, 1939), 140–69, although even Savelle treats this development as gradual.

5. See Jacob M. Price, "Who Cared about the Colonies? The Impact of the Thirteen Colonies on British Society and Politics, circa 1714–1775," in Bernard Bailyn and Philip D. Morgan, eds., *Strangers within the Realm: Cultural Margins of the First British Empire* (Chapel Hill: University of North Carolina Press, 1991), 395–436; Jack P. Greene, "'A Posture of Hostility': A Reconsideration of Some Aspects of the Origins of the American Revolution," *Proceedings of the American Antiquarian Society*, n.s., 87 (1977): 27–68.

6. Jeremy Black, "British Neutrality in the War of the Polish Succession, 1733–1735," *International History Review* 8 (1986): 358–59.

7. Pierre Henri Boulle, "The French Colonies and the Reform of Their Administration During and Following the Seven Years' War" (Ph.D. diss., University of California, Berkeley, 1968), 320–31, discusses the deficiencies of the Canadian economy. For the importance of tobacco from British North America to the French economy, see Jacob M.

Price, *France and the Chesapeake: A History of the French Tobacco Monopoly, 1674–1791, and of Its Relationship to the British and American Tobacco Trades,* 2 vols. (Ann Arbor: University of Michigan Press, 1973).

8. Browning, *Duke of Newcastle,* 207.

9. French Foreign Ministry Archives, Political Correspondence, Britain (Angleterre), volume 438, fiches 280–84, Antoine-Louis Rouillé, the French foreign minister, to Gaston-Charles-Pierre de Lévis de Lamogne, marquis de Mirepoix, the French ambassador to the British court, March 17, 1755. I will follow a simplified format for footnotes from French and British archival sources, giving the series (by country for documents from the French foreign ministry archives, by letters and numbers for naval documents from the French National Archives, by either "State Papers" and country or "Admiralty" for documents from the Public Record Office) followed by volume and page (or fiche) numbers. Rouillé's letter is quoted by Richard Waddington, *Louis XV et le renversement des alliances: Préliminaires de la guerre de Sept Ans, 1754–1756* (Paris: Firmin-Didot, 1896), 82–83, and Theodore Calvin Pease, ed., *Anglo-French Boundary Disputes in the West, 1749–1763* (Springfield: Illinois State Historical Library, 1936), 159–64.

10. See the astute comments of Daniel Baugh in "Great Britain's 'Blue-Water' Policy, 1689–1815," *International History Review* 10 (1988): 46.

11. Crouzet, "Second Hundred Years War," 443; C. I. Hamilton, *Anglo-French Naval Rivalry, 1840–1870* (Oxford: Clarendon Press, 1993); Jan Glete, *Navies and Nations: Warships, Navies, and State Building in Europe and America, 1500–1860,* 2 vols. (Stockholm: Almqvist and Wiksell International, 1933), 2:428.

12. Black, "British Neutrality," 357.

13. For the Franco-British alliance, see Ragnhild Hatton, *Diplomatic Relations between Great Britain and the Dutch Republic, 1714–1721* (London: East and West, 1950) and *George I* (New Haven: Yale University Press, 2001); Jeremy Black, *British Foreign Policy in the Age of Walpole* (Atlantic Highlands NJ: Humanities Press, 1985) and "French Foreign Policy in the Age of Fleury Reassessed," *English Historical Review* 103 (1988): 359–84; Arthur McCandless Wilson, *French Foreign Policy during the Administration of Cardinal Fleury, 1726–1743: A Study in Diplomacy and Commercial Development* (Cambridge: Harvard University Press; London: Humphrey Milford, Oxford University Press, 1936).

14. See Jeremy Black, *The Collapse of the Anglo-French Alliance, 1727–1731* (Gloucester, Eng.: A. Sutton; New York: St. Martin's Press, 1987) and "British Neutrality," 345–66.

15. Wilson, *French Foreign Policy,* 321–27; Georges Lacour-Gayet, *La Marine militaire sous le règne de Louis XV,* rev. ed. (Paris: Honoré Champion, 1910), 137–38; Richard Harding, *Amphibious Warfare in the Eighteenth Century: The British Expedition to the West Indies, 1740–1742* (Woodbridge, Eng., and Rochester: Boydell Press for the Royal Historical Society, 1991), 91–93; Richard Dean Bourland Jr., "Maurepas and the Administration of the French Navy on the Eve of the War of the Austrian Succession (1737–1742)" (Ph.D. diss., University of Notre Dame, South Bend, Ind., 1978), 321–432.

16. Peter B. Campbell, *Power and Politics in Old Regime France, 1720–1745* (London: Routledge, 1996), 166–71.

17. For the ensuing war, see Lodge, *Studies in Eighteenth-Century Diplomacy;* M. S.

Anderson, *The War of the Austrian Succession, 1740–1748* (London: Longman, 1995); Reed Browning, *The War of the Austrian Succession* (New York: St. Martin's Press, 1993); Jeremy Black, *America or Europe? British Foreign Policy, 1739–63* (London and Bristol, Pa.: UCL Press, 1998); Rohan Butler, *Choiseul*, vol. 1, *Father and Son, 1719–1754* (Oxford: Clarendon Press, 1980); [Jacques-Victor-] Albert, duc de Broglie, *Frédéric II et Marie-Thérèse, d'après des documents nouveaux, 1740–1742*, 2 vols. (Paris: Calmann Lévy, 1883); *Frédéric II et Louis XV, d'après des documents nouveaux, 1742–1744*, 2 vols. (Paris: Calmann Lévy, 1885); *Marie-Thérèse impératrice, 1744–1746*, 2 vols. (Paris: Calmann Lévy, 1888); *Maurice de Saxe et le marquis d'Argenson*, 2 vols. (Paris: Calmann Lévy, 1891) and *La Paix de Aix-la-Chapelle* (Paris: Calmann Lévy, 1892).

18. Jean Colin, *Louis XV et les Jacobites: Le Projet de débarqement en Angleterre, 1743–44* (Paris: R. Chapelot, 1901); John S. Gibson, *Ships of the '45: The Rescue of the Young Pretender* (London: Hutchinson, 1967); Eveline Cruickshanks, *Political Untouchables: The Tories and the '45* (London: Gerald Duckworth, 1979); Julian S. Corbett, *Some Principles of Maritime Strategy* (London: Longsmans, Green, 1911), 247–53; Frank Edward McLynn, *France and the Jacobite Rising of 1745* (Edinburgh: Edinburgh University Press, 1981); Christopher Duffy, *The '45* (London: Cassell, 2003).

19. Gerhard Ritter, *Frederick the Great: A Historical Profile*, trans. Peter Paret (Berkeley: University of California Press, 1968), 93.

20. P. G. M. Dickson, *Finance and Government under Maria Theresia, 1740–1780*, 2 vols. (Oxford: Clarendon Press, 1987), 1:19–40; Richard Waddington, *La Guerre de Sept Ans: Histoire diplomatique et militaire*, 5 vols. (Paris: Firmin-Didot, 1899–1914), 1:3; Christopher Duffy, *The Austrian Army in the Seven Years' War*, vol. 1, *Instrument of War* (Rosemont, Ill.: Emperor's Press, 2000), 34; H. J. Habakkuk, "Population, Commerce, and Economic Ideas," in Albert Goodwin, *The New Cambridge Modern History*, vol. 8, *The American and French Revolutions, 1763–93* (Cambridge: Cambridge University Press, 1965), 714–15.

21. Waddington, *Louis XV*, 132; Carl William Eldon, *England's Subsidy Policy toward the Continent during the Seven Years' War* (Philadelphia: Graduate School of the University of Pennsylvania, 1938), 1–2.

22. Robert Pick, *Empress Maria Theresa: The Earlier Years, 1717–1757* (New York: Harper and Row, 1966), 202–7; Lothar Schilling, *Kaunitz und des Renversement des Alliances: Studien zur aussenpolitik Konzeption Wenzel Anton von Kaunitz* (Berlin: Duncker and Humblot, 1994), 145–59; Reed Browning, "The British Orientation of Austrian Foreign Policy, 1749–1754," *Central European History* 1 (1968): 299–323; William J. McGill, "The Roots of Policy: Kaunitz in Vienna and Versailles, 1749–1753," *Journal of Modern History* 43 (1971): 228–44; Max Braubach, *Versailles und Wien von Ludwig XIV bis Kaunitz: Die Vorstadien der diplomatischen Revolution im 18 Jahrhundert* (Bonn: Ludwig Röhrscheid, 1952), 417–23.

23. James C. Riley, "French Finances, 1727–1768," *Journal of Modern History* 59 (1987): 224–25.

24. Jeffrey W. Merrick, *The Desacrilization of the French Monarchy in the Eighteenth Century* (Baton Rouge: Louisiana State University Press, 1990), 72–77.

25. Butler, *Choiseul*, 806–8.

26. John L. Sutton, *The King's Honor and the King's Cardinal: The War of the Polish Succession* (Lexington: University Press of Kentucky, 1980), 183–84.

27. Michel Antoine and Didier Ozanam, "Le Secret du roi et la Russie jusqu'à la morte de la czarine Elisabeth en 1762," *Annuaire-Bulletin de la Société de l'histoire de France* 86 (1954–55): 69–93.

28. David Bayne Horn, *Sir Charles Hanbury Williams and European Diplomacy (1747–58)* (London: G. G. Harrap, 1930), 18–27, 38.

29. For the "Secret du Roi," see Didier Ozanam and Michel Antoine, eds., *Correspondance secrète du comte de Broglie avec Louis XV (1756–1774)*, 2 vols. (Paris: C. Klincksieck, 1956–61); [Paul-] Edgard Boutaric, ed., *Correspondance secrète inédite de Louis XV sur la politique étrangère avec le comte de Broglie, Tercier, etc.*, 2 vols. (Paris: Henri Plon, 1866); [Jacques-Victor-] Albert, duc de Broglie, *The King's Secret: Being the Secret Correspondence of Louis XV with His Diplomatic Agents, from 1752 to 1774*, 2 vols. (London: Cassell, Petter and Galpin, 1879).

30. Max Savelle, *The Origins of American Diplomacy: The International History of Angloamerica, 1492–1763* (New York: Macmillan; London: Collier-Macmillan, 1967), 140–45, 274–79, 321–54, 372–85, 419–22; Sir Richard Lodge, ed., *The Private Correspondence of Sir Benjamin Keene, K. B.* (Cambridge: Cambridge University Press, 1933) and "Sir Benjamin Keene, K. B.: A Study in Anglo-Spanish Relations," *Transactions of the Royal Historical Society*, 4th ser., 15 (1932): 1–43.

31. Lodge, *Studies in Eighteenth-Century Diplomacy*, 359–60.

32. Black, *Natural and Necessary Enemies*, 37–38, 51–54, and *America or Europe?* 62–66, 69; Butler, *Choiseul*, 912.

33. Jack M. Sosin, "Louisbourg and the Peace of Aix-la-Chapelle, 1748," *William and Mary Quarterly*, 3rd ser., 14 (1957): 516–35.

34. H. M. Scott, "'The True Principles of the Revolution': The Duke of Newcastle and the Idea of the Old System," in Jeremy Black, ed., *Knights Errant and True Englishmen: British Foreign Policy, 1660–1800* (Edinburgh: John Donald, 1989), 55–91; Reed Browning, "The Duke of Newcastle and the Imperial Election Plan, 1749–1754," *Journal of British Studies* 7 (1967): 28–47; David Bayne Horn, "The Cabinet Controversy on Subsidy Treaties in Time of Peace, 1749–50," *English Historical Review* 45 (1930): 463–66 and "The Origins of the Proposed Election of a King of the Romans, 1748–1750," *English Historical Review* 42 (1927): 361–70.

35. Pease, *Boundary Disputes*, xxvi–xxvii, Newcastle to his friend Philip Yorke, Earl of Hardwicke, 25 August 1749; T. R. Clayton, "The Duke of Newcastle, the Earl of Halifax, and the American Origins of the Seven Years' War," *Historical Journal* 24 (1981): 575; Philip C. Yorke, *The Life and Correspondence of Philip Yorke, Earl of Hardwicke, Lord High Chancellor of Great Britain*, 3 vols. (Cambridge: Cambridge University Press, 1913), 2:23, Newcastle to Hardwicke, 2 September 1749.

36. Glete, *Navies and Nations*, 1:220–22; Geoffrey Symcox, *The Crisis of French Sea Power, 1688–1697: From the Guerre d'Escadre to the Guerre de Course* (The Hague: M. Nijhoff, 1974); Daniel Dessert, *La Royale: Vaisseaux et marins du Roi-Soleil* (Paris: Fayard,

1996). For a more positive view, see Patrick Villiers, *Marine royale, corsaires et trafic dans l'Atlantique de Louis XIV à Louis XVI*, 2 vols. (Dunkirk: Société Dunkerquoise d'Histoire et d'Archéologie, 1991), 1:17–200.

37. For a brief introduction to the Nine Years' War of 1688–97 and the War of the Spanish Succession of 1701–14, see John B. Wolf, *Louis XIV* (New York: W. W. Norton, 1968), 426–595, and John A. Lynn, *The Wars of Louis XIV* (London: Longman, 1999), 191–360. For the British navy during this period, see John Ehrman, *The Navy in the War of William III, 1689–1697: Its State and Direction* (Cambridge: Cambridge University Press, 1953); J. H. Owen, *War at Sea under Queen Anne, 1702–1708* (Cambridge: Cambridge University Press, 1938); John Hattendorf, *England in the War of the Spanish Succession: A Study in the English View and Conduct of Grand Strategy, 1701–1713* (New York: Garland, 1987).

38. J. Meirat, "Le Siège de Toulon en 1707," *Neptunia*, no. 71 (Autumn 1963): 2–9; Fernand Braudel, *The Identity of France*, vol. 1, *History and Environment*, trans. Siân Reynolds (London: Collins, 1988), 351–72.

39. The number of 1715 ships of the line is based on counting the warships of the first to third rates in a list of warships in B⁵3 (mostly unpaginated); Glete, *Navies and Nations*, 1:220–21; 2:576; Alain Demerliac, *La Marine de Louis XV: Nomenclature des navires français de 1715 à 1774* (Nice: Editions Omega, 1995), 19–24, and *La Marine de Louis XIV: Nomenclature des vaisseaux du Roi-Soleil de 1661 à 1715* (Nice: Editions Omega, 1992), 11–19, 22–29.

40. James C. Riley, *The Seven Years War and the Old Regime in France: The Economic and Financial Toll* (Princeton NJ: Princeton University Press, 1986), 162–68.

41. Demerliac, *La Marine de Louis XV*, 35, 37, 42–43, 48–50; Glete, *Navies and Nations*, 1:260. My interpretation differs from that of Jacques Bertier and Françoise Vergneault, "Traitment graphique d'une information: Les Marines royales de France et de Grande-Bretagne (1697–1747)," *Annales: Economies-sociétés-civilisations* 22 (1967): 991–1004. See also Villiers, *Marine royale*, 1:212–16.

42. Demerliac, *La Marine de Louis XV*, 43, 49, 50.

43. Demerliac, *La Marine de Louis XV*, 35, 37–38, 43, 50.

44. They are listed in appendix A.

45. Glete, *Navies and Nations*, 1:269; 2:629; John Robert McNeill, *Atlantic Empires of France and Spain: Louisbourg and Havana, 1700–1763* (Chapel Hill: University of North Carolina Press, 1985), 69; C. de Saint Hubert, "Ships of the Line of the Spanish Navy (1714–1825)," *Warship* 10 (1986): 129–33.

46. Based on the lists in Admiralty Series 8, vols. 24–26. See also Richard Middleton, "Naval Administration in the Age of Pitt and Anson, 1755–1763," in Jeremy Black and Philip Woodfine, eds., *The British Navy and the Use of Naval Power in the Eighteenth Century* (Atlantic Highlands NJ: Humanities Press International, 1989), 112.

47. Georges Lacour-Gayet, *La Marine militaire de la France sous le règne de Louis XV*, rev. ed. (Paris: Honoré Champion, 1910), 145–220; Ch. Chabaud-Arnault, "Etudes historiques sur la marine militaire de France," *Revue maritime* 111 (1891): 86–131.

48. Appendix A; Lacour-Gayet, *La Marine militaire*, 164–67; Colin, *Louis XV*; Sir

Herbert W. Richmond, *The Navy in the War of 1739–48*, 3 vols. (Cambridge: Cambridge University Press, 1920), 2:66–85.

49. The best introduction to the battle is John Creswell, *British Admirals of the Eighteenth Century: Tactics in Battle* (London: George Allen and Unwin, 1972), 62–80. See also Appendix A and Richmond, *Navy*, 2:1–57.

50. See James Pritchard, *Anatomy of a Naval Disaster: The 1746 French Naval Expedition to North America* (Montreal: McGill-Queen's University Press, 1995).

51. Lacour-Gayet, *La Marine militaire*, 203–19; Richmond, *Navy*, 3:178–225.

52. Lacour-Gayet, *La Marine militaire*, 179–88; William Laird Clowes, *The Royal Navy: A History from the Earliest Times to the Present*, 7 vols. (Boston: Little, Brown; London: Sampson Low, Marston and Co., 1897–1903), 3:124–28.

53. See appendix B; Johann Gustav Droysen et al., eds., *Politische Correspondenz Friedrich's des Grossen*, 47 vols. and supp. to date (Berlin: Alexander Duncker and other publishers, 1879–), 6:74–75; E. J. B. Rathery, ed., *Journal et mémoires du marquis d'Argenson*, 9 vols. (Paris: Mme. Veuve Jules Renouard, 1859–1867), 5:202; T. J. A. Le Goff, "Le Impact des prises effectuées par les anglais sur la capacité en hommes de la marine française au XVIII ᵉ siècle," in Martine Acerra, José Marino, and Jean Meyer, eds., *Les Marines de guerre européennes XVII–XVIII siècles* (Paris: Presses de l'Université de Paris-Sorbonne, 1985), 106.

54. McLynn, *France and the Jacobite Rising*, 67. See also Catherine M. Desbarats, "France in North America: The Net Burden of Empire during the First Half of the Eighteenth Century," *French History* 11 (1997): 22–23.

55. Chabaud-Arnault, "Etudes historiques," *Revue maritime* 110 (1891): 56; Demerliac, *La Marine de Louis XV*, 35.

56. Richmond, *Navy*, 3:251–52; Harding, *Amphibious Warfare*.

57. N. A. M. Rodger, *The Wooden World: An Anatomy of the Georgian Navy* (London: Collins, 1986), 30–31, 301–2, and *The Insatiable Earl: A Life of John Montagu, 4th Earl of Sandwich, 1718–1792* (New York: W. W. Norton, 1994), 20–39, 55–68; Middleton, "Naval Administration," in Black and Woodfine, *British Navy*, 109–27. For Bedford, see chapter 8, section 2.

58. James Pritchard, *Louis XV's Navy, 1748–1762: A Study of Organization and Administration* (Montreal: McGill-Queen's University Press, 1987), 6–7. The Council of State will be discussed at the beginning of chapter 2. For Maurepas and his rivals, see McLynn, *France and the Jacobite Rising*, 35–56.

59. Pritchard, *Louis XV's Navy*, 7–8; Lacour-Gayet, *La Marine militaire*, 224–26.

60. See appendix C; not included there is the *Orignal*, 60, which was wrecked upon launching in 1750; Demerliac, *La Marine de Louis XV*, 35–36, 38–39, 44–45, 49, 51; Pritchard, *Louis XV's Navy*, 130–31, 137; St. Hubert, "Ships of the Line of the Spanish Navy," 133–34, 208–9; David Lyon, comp., *The Sailing Navy List: All the Ships of the Royal Navy Built, Purchased, and Captured, 1688–1860* (London: Conway Maritime Press, 1993), 40–41, 44, 47, 72–73, 75–76; Brian Lavery, *The Ship of the Line*, vol. 1, *The Development of the Battlefleet, 1650–1850* (Annapolis: Naval Institute Press; London: Conway Maritime Press, 1983), 171–74.

61. Pritchard, *Louis XV's Navy*, 137–40; Jean Delmas et al., *Histoire militaire de la France*, vol. 2, *De 1715 à 1871* (Paris: Presses universitaires de France, 1992), 181; Paul W. Bamford, *Privilege and Profit: A Business Family in Eighteenth-Century France* (Philadelphia: University of Pennsylvania Press, 1988), 51; James Pritchard, "Fir Trees, Financiers, and the French Navy during the 1750's," *Canadian Journal of History* 23 (1988): 347.

62. Pritchard, *Louis XV's Navy*, 143–53, 216, 218; Pritchard, "Fir Trees," 348.

63. Michel Antoine, comp., *Le Gouvernement et l'administration sous Louis XV: Dictionnaire biographique* (Paris: Editions du centre national de la recherche scientifique, 1978), 17, 213–14.

64. Pritchard, *Louis XV's Navy*, 8–9; see also Butler, *Choiseul*, 1:1061–62.

65. Such was the assessment of the Earl of Albemarle, the able British ambassador: Waddington, *Louis XV*, 57; see also Rathery, *Journal d'Argenson*, 5:475, 8:385.

66. For an introduction to New France, see William J. Eccles, *France in America* (New York: Harper and Row, 1972).

67. James A. Henretta, *"Salutary Neglect": Colonial Administration under the Duke of Newcastle* (Princeton: Princeton University Press, 1972), 331–44.

68. Pease, *Boundary Disputes*, 337–38; McNeill, *Atlantic Empires*, 138–41; R. Cole Harris, ed., *Historical Atlas of Canada*, vol. 1, *From the Beginnings to 1800* (Toronto: University of Toronto Press, 1987), plates 21 and 25; J. S. McLennan, *Louisbourg from Its Foundation to Its Fall, 1713–1758* (London: Macmillan, 1918), 218–20, 226, 395; Pierre H. Boulle, "Patterns of French Colonial Trade and the Seven Years' War," *Histoire sociale–Social History* 7 (1974): 67–70; B. A. Balcom, *The Cod Fishery of Isle Royale, 1713–58* ([Ottawa]: National Historic Parks and Sites Branch, Parks Canada, Environment Canada, 1984); Christopher Moore, "The Other Louisbourg: Trade and Merchant Enterprise in Ile Royale, 1713–58," *Histoire sociale-Social History* 12 (1979): 79–96.

69. Jean-François Brière, "Pêche et politique à Terre-Neuve au XVIIIe siècle: La France veritable gagnante du traité d'Utrecht?" *Canadian Historical Review* 64 (1983): 168–87 and *La Pêche française en Amérique du Nord au XVIIIe siècle* (Saint-Laurent, Quebec: Fides, 1990), 223. See also McNeill, *Atlantic Empires*, 82, 93, 107, 138; T. J. A. Le Goff, "Offre et productivité de la main-d'oeuvre dans les armements français au XVIIIe siècle," *Histoire, économie et société* 2 (1983): 459, 462, 467, and "The Labour Market for Sailors in France," in Paul van Royen, Jaap Bruijn, and Jan Lucassen, eds., *"Those Emblems of Hell"? European Sailors and the Maritime Labour Market, 1570–1870* (St. John's, Newfoundland: International Maritime History Association, 1997), 300; Charles de la Morandière, *Histoire de la pêche française de la morue dans l'Amérique septentrionale*, 2 vols. (Paris: G. P. Maisonneuve et Larose, 1962), 2:999.

70. McNeill, *Atlantic Empires*, 18–26; Savelle, *Origins of American Diplomacy*, 238–50.

71. McNeill, *Atlantic Empires*, 81–86, 92–97; Desbarats, "France in North America," 11; Frederick J. Thorpe, *Remparts lointains: La Politique française des travaux publics à Terre-Neuve et à l'île Royale, 1695–1758* (Ottawa: Editions de l'Université d'Ottawa, 1980); Bruce W. Fry, *"An Appearance of Strength": The Fortifications of Louisbourg*, 2 vols. (Ottawa:

Historical Parks and Sites Branch, Parks Canada, Environment Canada, 1984), 1:53–56; Robert Emmet Wall Jr., "Louisbourg, 1745," *New England Quarterly* 37 (1964): 64–83.

72. Savelle, *Origins of American Diplomacy*, 362–72.

73. Julian Gwyn, "The Royal Navy in North America, 1713–1776," in Black and Woodfine, *British Navy*, 130–34.

74. McLennan, *Louisbourg*, 128–67; John A. Schutz, *William Shirley: King's Governor of Massachusetts* (Chapel Hill: University of North Carolina Press, 1961), 79–100; George A. Rawlyk, *Yankees at Louisbourg* (Orono: University of Maine Press, 1967); Julian Gwyn, ed., *The Royal Navy and North America: The Warren Papers, 1736–1752* (London: Navy Records Society, 1973), and *An Admiral for America: Sir Peter Warren, Vice Admiral of the Red, 1703–1752* (Gainesville: University Press of Florida, 2004), 75–99.

75. Henretta, *"Salutary Neglect,"* 279–82; Gwyn, "Royal Navy," in Black and Woodfine, *Britain's Navy*, 136; Richmond, *Navy*, 3:3–6, 23–32; Arthur H. Buffington, "The Canada Expedition of 1746: Its Relation to British Politics," *American Historical Review* 45 (1939–40): 552–80.

76. Schutz, *William Shirley*, 158–66; Savelle, *Origins of American Diplomacy*, 386–95; Lawrence Henry Gipson, *The British Empire before the American Revolution*, 15 vols. (Caldwell, Idaho: Caxton [vols. 1–3] and New York: Alfred A. Knopf [vols. 4–15], 1936–70), 5:298–328; Enid Robbie, *The Forgotten Commissioner: Sir William Mildmay and the Anglo-French Commission of 1750–1755* (East Lansing: Michigan State University Press, 2003).

77. Jean-Pierre Guicciardi and Philippe Bonnet, eds., *Mémoires du duc de Choiseul* (Paris: Mercure de France, 1982), 152–53.

78. W. J. Eccles, *Essays on New France* (Toronto: Oxford University Press, 1987), 110; [Jacques-Victor-] Albert, duc de Broglie, *L'Alliance autrichienne* (Paris: Calmann Lévy, 1895), 85–87. Canada's meager economic returns and increasing costs are discussed in Eccles, *Essays on New France*, 120–21, and Lucien Schöne, "La politique de la France au XVIIIᵉ siècle à l'égard des ses colonies," *Revue coloniale*, n.s., 6 (1906): 95–96.

79. Douglas Edward Leach gives examples in *Arms for Empire: A Military History of the British Colonies in North America, 1607–1763* (New York: Macmillan; London: Collier-Macmillan, 1973), 243–48.

80. Greene, "Posture of Hostility," 33–36.

81. Waddington, *Louis XV*, 9–17, 54–55; Max Savelle, *The Diplomatic History of the Canadian Boundary, 1749–1763* (New Haven: Yale University Press; Toronto: Ryerson Press; London: Oxford University Press, 1940), 27–31.

82. Harris, *Historical Atlas*, plates 39–41; Michael N. McConnell, *A Country Between: The Upper Ohio Valley and Its People, 1724–1774* (Lincoln: University of Nebraska Press, 1992), 5–60.

83. McConnell, *A Country Between*, 61–88, 98–108; Richard White, *The Middle Ground: Indians, Empires, and Republics in the Great Lakes Region, 1650–1815* (Cambridge: Cambridge University Press, 1991), 186–242; Francis Jennings, *Empire of Fortune: Crown, Colonies, and Tribes in the Seven Years' War in America* (New York: W. W. Norton, 1988), 24–57; Fred Anderson, *Crucible of War: The Seven Years' War and the Fate of Empire in*

British North America, 1754–1766 (New York: Alfred A. Knopf, 2000), 22–32; Joseph L. Peyser, *On the Eve of the Conquest: The Chevalier de Raymond's Critique of New France in 1754* (East Lansing: Michigan State University Press; Mackinac Island: Mackinac State Historic Parks, 1997), 18–24; Charles Morse Stotz, *Outposts of the War for Empire: The French and English in Western Pennsylvania: Their Armies, Their Forts, Their People, 1749– 1764* (Pittsburgh: University of Pittsburgh Press for the Historical Society of Western Pennsylvania, 1985), 72–79. For the career of Ange, marquis Duquesne-Menneville, see Michel Vergé-Franceschi, *Les Officiers généraux de la marine royale (1715–1774): Origines- conditions-services,* 7 vols. (Paris: Librairie de l'Inde, 1990), 1:68–69; 3:956–58, 965–69, and Francess G. Halpenny, ed., *Dictionary of Canadian Biography,* vol. 4, *1771 to 1800* (Toronto: University of Toronto Press; Les Presses de l'Université Laval, 1979), 255– 58.

84. E. B. O'Callaghan et al., eds, *Documents Relative to the Colonial History of the State of New-York,* 15 vols. (Albany: Weed, Parson, 1853–87), 10:220–32, 242–45; Roland Lamontagne, *Aperçu structural du Canada au XVIIIᵉ siècle* (Montreal: Leméac, 1964), 43–44, 93–112, and "La Galissonnière et ses conceptions coloniales d'après le 'Mémoire sur les colonies de la France dans l'Amérique septentrionale' (Decembre 1750)," *Revue d'histoire de l'Amérique française* 15 (1961–62): 163–70. For La Galissonnière see Francess G. Halpenny, ed., *Dictionary of Canadian Biography,* vol. 3, *1741 to 1770* (Toronto: University of Toronto Press; Les Presses de l'Université Laval, 1974), 26–32; Vergé-Franceschi, *Les Officiers généraux,* 1:30; 3:1311–22.

85. Gipson, *British Empire,* 4:190–224, 269–75; McConnell, *A Country Between,* 89–98; John Richard Alden, *Robert Dinwiddie, Servant of the Crown* (Charlottesville: University Press of Virginia, 1973), 40–45; Kenneth P. Bailey, *The Ohio Company of Virginia and the Westward Movement, 1748–1792: A Chapter in the History of the Colonial Frontier* (Glendale, Calif.: Arthur H. Clark, 1939), 17–31, 147–59.

86. Gipson, *British Empire,* 4:293–310; 6:20–43; Stotz, *Outposts,* 14–15, 80–87; Ander- son, *Crucible of War,* 5–7, 46–65; Douglas S. Freeman, *George Washington: A Biography,* vol. 1, *Young Washington* (New York: Charles Scribner's Sons, 1948), 327–411; W. W. Abbot et al., eds., *The Papers of George Washington: Colonial Series,* 10 vols. (Charlottesville: University Press of Virginia, 1983–95), 1:63–173; Harry M. Ward, *Major General Adam Stephen and the Cause of American Liberty* (Charlottesville: University Press of Virginia, 1989), 6–13; David A. Bell, "Jumonville's Death: War Propaganda and National Identity in Eighteenth-Century France," in Colin Jones and Dror Wahrman, eds., *The Age of Cultural Revolution: Britain and France, 1750–1820* (Berkeley: University of California Press, 2002), 33–61.

87. For the diplomacy of the crisis, see Waddington, *Louis XV,* 56–95; Savelle, *Ori- gins of American Diplomacy,* 399–419; Clayton, "Newcastle," 571–603; Patrice Louis-René Higonnet, "The Origins of the Seven Years' War," *Journal of Modern History* 40 (1968): 57–90.

88. Savelle, *Origins of American Diplomacy,* 279–87, 356–62, 390–95.

89. Leach, *Arms for Empire,* 244–46.

90. Braddock's instructions are given in O'Callaghan, *Documents,* 6:920–22, and in

Stanley McCrory Pargellis, ed., *Military Affairs in North America, 1748–1765: Selected Documents from the Cumberland Papers in Windsor Castle* (New York: Century, 1936), 45–48. For the British strategy and its political background, see Clayton, "Newcastle," 590–97; Browning, *Duke of Newcastle*, 206–13; J. C. D. Clark, *The Dynamics of Change: The Crisis of the 1750s and English Party Systems* (Cambridge: Cambridge University Press, 1982), 99–105; Dominick Graham, "The Planning of the Beauséjour Operation and the Approaches to War in 1755," *New England Quarterly* 41 (1968): 555–61; Thad W. Riker, "The Politics behind Braddock's Expedition," *American Historical Review* 13 (1907–8): 742–52.

91. Waddington, *Louis XV*, 75n; Higonnet, "Origins," 94–95.

2. 1755—COUNTERING THE BRITISH ASSAULT

1. Newcastle to Ambassador to France William Anne Keppel, Earl of Albemarle, 5 September 1754, in Pease, *Boundary Disputes*, 50–52.

2. See, for examples, Waddington, *La Guerre*, 5:181, 210–11.

3. For the character of George II (1683–1760), see Charles P. Chenevix Trench, *George II* (London: Allen Lane, 1973), 39–40, 145, 299–301; J. C. D. Clark, ed., *The Memoirs and Speeches of James, 2nd Earl Waldegrave, 1742–1763* (Cambridge: Cambridge University Press, 1988), 146–48; Aubry Newman, *The World Turned Inside Out: New Views on George II: An Inaugural Lecture Delivered in the University of Leicester 10 October 1987* (Leicester, Eng.: History Department, University of Leicester, 1988). A recent sensitive biography of Frederick is Donald Fraser, *Frederick the Great: King of Prussia* (London: Allen Lane, 2000).

4. Jules Flammermont, *Rapport à M. le ministre de l'instruction publique sur les correspondances des agents diplomatiques étrangères en France avant la Révolution conservées dans les archives de Berlin, Dresden, Genève, Turin, Gênes, Florence, Naples, Simancas, Lisbonne, Londres, La Haye et Vienne* (Paris: Imprimerie Nationale, 1896), 26; Frédéric Masson, ed., *Mémoires et lettres de François-Joachim de Pierre, Cardinal de Bernis (1715–1758)*, 2 vols. (Paris: E. Plon, 1878), 2:198, 216–17. For Fleury's influence, see Ozanam and Antoine, *Correspondance de Broglie*, 1:xiii; Campbell, *Power and Politics*, 131. Michel Antoine has written the best biography of Louis to date, *Louis XV* (Paris: Fayard, 1989).

5. McLynn, *France and the Jacobite Rising*, 35–56.

6. For the aged Tencin, see Jean Sareil, *Les Tencin: Histoire d'une famille au dix-huitième siécle d'après de nombreux documents inédits* (Geneva: Droz, 1969), 400–401.

7. Ozanam and Antoine, *Correspondance de Broglie*, 1:xxvii–xxviii; Rathery, *Journal d'Argenson*, 8:382.

8. Flammermont, *Rapport*, 27–28. For the great esteem enjoyed by Puyzieulx, see Butler, *Choiseul*, 1:892.

9. Butler, *Choiseul*, 391–92; Camille Rousset, ed., *Correspondance de Louis XV et du maréchal de Noailles*, 2 vols. (Paris: Didier, 1907), 1:11–26; 2:377–78.

10. Clayton, "Newcastle," 589.

11. Bourland, "Maurepas," 450–64; Campbell, *Power and Politics*, 143; John Hardman, *French Politics, 1774–1789: From the Accession of Louis XVI to the Fall of the Bastille* (London: Longman, 1995), 29–31.

12. Antoine, *Louis XV*, 614; Flammermont, *Rapport*, 30–31; Waddington, *Louis XV*, 57; Pritchard, *Louis XV's Navy*, 8–9.

13. Flammermont, *Rapport*, 29–30. There is a recent biography of him, Yves Combeau, *Le Comte d'Argenson (1696–1764): Ministre de Louis XV* (Paris: Ecole des Chartes, 1999).

14. Rathery, *Journal d'Argenson*, 8:387–88, 408; Flammermont, *Rapport*, 31; Antoine, *Louis XV*, 703; Higonnet, "Origins," 69.

15. L. Jay Oliva, *Misalliance: A Study of French Policy in Russia during the Seven Years' War* (New York: New York University Press, 1964), 27.

16. Rathery, *Journal d'Argenson*, 9:144; Masson, *Mémoires et lettres de Bernis*, 2:111–12.

17. Droysen, *Politische Correspondenz*, 11:267n, 292–93n, 409–10n; 12:69–70n.

18. Antoine, *Louis XV*, 498; Guicciardi and Bonnet, *Mémoires de Choiseul*, 95.

19. Pritchard, *Louis XV's Navy*, 7.

20. Dodo Heinrich, Freiherr von Knyphausen to Frederick II, 24 February 1755, Droysen, *Politische Correspondenz*, 11:77–78n; Jean-Pierre Samoyault, *Les Bureaux du secrétariat d'état des affaires étrangères sous Louis XV: Administration, personnel* (Paris: A. Pedone, 1971), 54–55.

21. Samoyault, *Les Bureaux*, 49–50, 53, 88, 278; Rathery, *Journal d'Argenson*, 9:29; Eveline Cruickshanks, "101 Secret Agent," *History Today* 19 (1969): 273–76; Philip Woodfine, *Britannia's Glories: The Walpole Ministry and the 1739 War with Spain* (Woodbridge, Eng.: Boydell Press for the Royal Historical Society, 1998), 37–39.

22. Samoyault, *Les Bureaux*, 47–49, 295–95; Waddington, *Louis XV*, 64; Higonnet, "Origins," 75, 83; Clayton, "Newcastle," 599n; Rathery, *Journal d'Argenson*, 8:396.

23. Guicciardi and Bonnet, *Mémoires de Choiseul*, 112.

24. Samoyault, *Les Bureaux*, 51, 307; Ozanam and Antoine, *Correspondance de Broglie*, 1:xxix, 12n; Didier Ozanam, "La Disgrace d'un premier commis: Tercier et l'Affair De L'Esprit (1758–1759)," *Bibliothèque de l'Ecole de chartes* 113 (1955): 141–43.

25. Droysen, *Politische Correspondenz*, 11:102; Philippe Bonnet, ed., *Mémoires du Cardinal de Bernis* (Paris: Mercure de France, 1980), 134; Waddington, *Louis XV*, 64–65, 111; Robbie, *Forgotten Commissioner*, 165.

26. Britain 438: 13, Mirepoix to Rouillé, 9 January 1755; Pease, *Boundary Disputes*, 60–83; Paul Vaucher, ed., *Recueil des instructions données aux ambassadeurs et ministres de France depuis les traités de Westphalie jusqu'à la révolution française*, vol. 25, part 2, *Angleterre, tome troisième (1698–1791)* (Paris: Editions du Centre national de la recherche scientifique, 1969), 333, 360–62n.

27. B⁴68: 3–5, 10; Jacques Aman, *Une Campagne navale méconnue à la veille de la guerre de Sept Ans: L'Escadre de Brest en 1755* (Vincennes, France: Service historique de la marine, 1986), 1–3. The ships are listed in my appendix D. For the three naval commanders, see Vergé-Franceschi, *Les Officiers généraux*, 1:52, 97–98, 110–11, 258–60, 266–71; 3:1422–29; 4:1596–1603; Halpenny, *Dictionary of Canadian Biography*, 3:92–93; Hubert Granier, "Le

Vice-Admiral Emmanuel-Auguste de Cahideuc, comte du Bois de la Motte (1683–1764)," *Marins et océans* 3 (1992): 72–84. For Dieskau's experience in small unit or irregular warfare, see Martin L. Nicolai, "A Different Kind of Courage: The French Military and the Canadian Irregular Soldier during the Seven Years' War," *Canadian Historical Review* 70 (1989): 55, 61; Peter E. Russell, "Redcoats in the Wilderness: British Officers and Irregular Warfare in Europe and America, 1740 to 1760," *William and Mary Quarterly*, 3rd ser., 35 (1978): 633–34.

28. Britain 438: 37, Rouillé to Mirepoix, 20 January 1755; State Papers 78 (France) 250:82.

29. Habakkuk, "Population," in Goodwin, *New Cambridge Modern History*, 8:714; J. N. Biraben, "Le Peuplement du Canada français," *Annales de démographie historique* 1 (1966): 124; J. F. Bosher, *The Canada Merchants, 1713–1763* (Oxford: Clarendon Press; New York: Oxford University Press, 1987), 12; Marc Egnal, *New World Economies: The Growth of the Thirteen Colonies and Early Canada* (New York: Oxford University Press, 1998), 164; Hubert Charbonneau, Bertrand Desjardins, Jacques Légaré, and Hubert Denis, "The Population of the St. Lawrence Valley, 1608–1760," in Michael R. Haines and Richard K. Steckel, eds., *A Population History of North America* (New York: Cambridge University Press, 2000), 104. For Braddock's regiments, see Stephen Brumwell, *Redcoats: The British Soldier and War in the Americas* (New York: Cambridge University Press, 2002), 12n.

30. O'Callaghan, *Documents*, 10:270.

31. Droysen, *Politische Correspondenz*, 11:27n, Knyphausen to Frederick II, 3 January 1755.

32. Droysen, *Politische Correspondenz*, 11:77–78n, Knyphausen to Frederick II, 24 February 1755.

33. Britain 438: 15–36, Mirepoix to Rouillé, 16 and 17 January 1755 with enclosures. Extracts of these documents and an English translation are printed in Pease, *Boundary Disputes*, 86–98. Copies of the initial memoirs exchanged between Mirepoix and Robinson are in State Papers Series 78 (France) 250: 45–47.

34. Pease, *Boundary Disputes*, 85–86.

35. McConnell, *A Country Between*, 58–59, 77; Jennings, *Empire of Fortune*, 32; Anderson, *Crucible of War*, 12–32; Arnold Toynbee, Fred L. Israel, and Emanuel Chill, eds., *Major Peace Treaties of Modern History, 1648–1967*, 4 vols. (New York: McGraw-Hill, 1967), 1:210.

36. Clayton, "Newcastle," 571–603.

37. Britain 438: 38–53, Mirepoix to Rouillé, 23 January 1755 with enclosures including Robinson's memoir of 22 January; Pease, *Boundary Disputes*, 99–101.

38. Sir Julian S. Corbett, *England in the Seven Years' War: A Study in Combined Strategy*, 2nd ed., 2 vols. (London: Longmans, Green, 1918), 1:37, quoting Newcastle to Keene, 27 January 1755. See also Waddington, *Louis XV*, 78.

39. Britain 438: 81–97, Rouillé to Mirepoix, 3 February 1755 with enclosures; the memoir given to Robinson is also in State Papers 78 (France), 250: 73–75. See also Pease, *Boundary Disputes*, 102–8.

40. Waddington, *Louis XV*, 64.

41. Britain 438: 114–31, Mirepoix to Rouillé, 10 February 1755 with enclosures; Pease, *Boundary Disputes*, 109–11. See also Robinson's comments quoted in Black, *America or Europe?*, 77.

42. Evan Charteris, *William Augustus, Duke of Cumberland and the Seven Years' War* (London: Hutchinson, 1925), quoting Cumberland to Robinson, 11 February 1755.

43. Britain 438: 154–85, Rouillé to Mirepoix, 19 February with enclosures; State Papers 78 (France) 250: 105–8; Pease, *Boundary Disputes*, 116–135 and map facing 150.

44. Clayton, "Newcastle," 598–601.

45. Britain 438: 253–66, Mirepoix to Rouillé, 8 March 1755 with enclosures; State Papers 250 (France) 78: 116–23; Pease, *Boundary Disputes*, 148–55.

46. Britain 438: 280–86, Rouillé to Mirepoix, 17 March 1755.

47. The remaining discussions are documented in Britain 438: 297–452; Britain 439: 2–270; State Papers 78 (France) 250: 124–326.

48. Corbett, *England in the Seven Years' War*, 1:40–41; Rodger, *Wooden World*, 145; Stephen F. Gradish, *The Manning of the British Navy during the Seven Years' War* (London: Royal Historical Society, 1980), 30–32, 71–73; Nicholas Tracy, *Navies, Deterrence, and American Independence: Britain and Seapower in the 1760s and 1770s* (Vancouver: University of British Columbia Press, 1988), 29, 84–85, 162.

49. Higonnet, "Origins," 81.

50. Corbett, *England in the Seven Years' War*, 1:41–45; Clayton, "Duke of Newcastle," 602; Clark, *Dynamics of Change*, 158. See appendix D for the ships in Boscawen's squadron, which are listed there as "Off Newfoundland."

51. Schutz, *William Shirley*, 155–58; Freeman, *Washington*, 2:11, 15n, 46–50; Pargellis, *Military Affairs*, 81–95; Robert Alonzo Brock, ed., *The Official Records of Robert Dinwiddie, Lieutenant-Governor of the Colony of Virginia, 1751–1758*, 2 vols. (Richmond: Virginia Historical Society, 1883–84), 1:495–528, 2:1–19; Charles Hamilton, ed., *Braddock's Defeat: The Journal of Captain Robert Cholmley's Batman, the Journal of a British Officer, [and] Halkett's Orderly Book* (Norman: University of Oklahoma Press, 1959), 9n, 17, 40.

52. O'Callaghan, *Documents*, 10:275–78, 280–81, Machault to Duquesne, 17 February and 17 March 1755.

53. Pritchard, *Louis XV's Navy*, 9. For Bompar see Vergé-Franceschi, *Les Officiers généraux*, 1:44–45; 2:840–53; 5:2567.

54. Aman, *Une Campagne navale méconnue*, 3n.

55. Aman, *Une Campagne navale méconnue*, 6–10; Rathery, *Journal d'Argenson*, 8:468, 471–77, 9:2, 4; Pitchard, "Fir Trees," 349; T. J. A. Le Goff, "Problèmes de recrutement de la marine française pendant la Guerre de Sept Ans," *Revue historique* 238 (January–June 1990): 222–23.

56. White, *Middle Ground*, 208–9; Halpenny, *Dictionary of Canadian Biography*, 4:662–74; Roger Michalon, "Vaudreuil et Montcalm: Les Hommes, leurs relations, influence de ces relations sur la conduite de la guerre, 1756–1759," in Jean Delmas et al., eds., *Conflits de sociétés au Canada français pendant la guerre de Sept Ans et leur influence sur les operations: Colloque international de histoire militaire, Ottawa, 19–27 août 1978*

(Vincennes, France: Service historique de la armée de terre, 1978), 51–54; Guy Frégault, *Le Grand Marquis, Pierre de Rigaud de Vaudreuil, et la Louisiane* (Montreal: Fides, 1952).

57. Guy Frégault, *François Bigot: Administrateur français*, 2 vols. (Montreal: Institut d'histoire de l'Amérique française, 1948) is the standard biography. Vaudreuil praised Bigot's abilities in a 28 October 1755 letter to Machault: Abbé Henri-Raymond Casgrain, ed., *Extraits des archives des ministères de la marine et de la guerre à Paris. Canada, correspondance général: MM. Duquesne et Vaudreuil, gouverneurs généraux, 1755–1760* (Quebec: L.-J. Demers et frère, 1890), 69–70. For a defense of Bigot, see Bosher, *Canada Merchants*, 69, 87.

58. O'Callaghan, *Documents*, 10, 290–94, Instructions for Vaudreuil, 1 April 1755. See also Casgrain, *Extraits des archives*, 31–34.

59. Britain 439: 22–23, Rouillé to Mirepoix, 2 May 1755.

60. Sweden 228: 521, Rouillé to Louis de Cardevac, marquis d'Havrincourt, 21 May 1755; Aman, *Une Campagne navale méconnue*, 10–12, 186–87.

61. The voyages of the three French squadrons are documented in $B^4$68; an eyewitness account is given in Charles Coste, ed., *Aventures militaires au XVIIIe siècle d'après les mémoires de Jean-Baptiste d'Aleyrac* (Paris: Berger-Levrault, 1935), 16–22.

62. See appendix D; Corbett, *England in the Seven Years' War*, 1:45, 47–49, 56; Gipson, *British Empire*, 6:110–17; Casgrain, *Extraits des archives*, 35–36, 107–10, Vaudreuil to Machault, 27 June and 30 October 1755; David Bonner-Smith, ed., *The Barrington Papers: Selected from the Letters and Papers of Admiral the Hon. Samuel Barrington*, 2 vols. (London: Navy Records Society, 1937–41), 1:114; Jean G. P. Blanchet, ed., *Collection des manuscrits contenant lettres, mémoires et autres documents relatifs à la Nouvelle-France*, 4 vols. (Quebec: A. Coté, 1883–85), 3:543, Périer de Salvert to Machault, 6 July 1755; Peter H. Kemp, "Boscawen's Letters to His Wife, 1755–1756," in Christopher Lloyd, ed., *The Naval Miscellany*, vol. 4 (London: Navy Records Society, 1952), 190–93, Boscawen to Anson, 21 June 1755.

63. Corbett, *England in the Seven Years' War*, 1:49, 58, the latter citation quoting Hardwicke to Newcastle, 14 July 1755.

64. Casgrain, *Extraits des archives*, 14–17; Halpenny, *Dictionary of Canadian Biography*, 4:562–64; Ronald D. Martin, "Confrontation at the Monongahela: Climax of the French Drive into the Upper Ohio Region," *Pennsylvania History* 37 (1970): 148–49; Dan L. Thrapp, ed., *Encyclopedia of Frontier Biography*, 4 vols. (Glendale, Calif.: Arthur H. Clark, 1988–94), 2:812.

65. Pargellis, *Military Affairs*, 131–32; Paul E. Kopperman, *Braddock at the Monongahela* (Pittsburgh: University of Pittsburgh Press, 1977); Robert L. Yaple, "Braddock's Defeat: The Theories and a Reconsideration," *Journal of the Society for Army Historical Research* 46 (1968): 194–201.

66. Graham, "Planning," 551–66; Abbé Henri-Raymond Casgrain, ed., *Collection des manuscrits du maréchal de Lévis*, 12 vols. (Montreal: C.-D. Beauchemin et fils; Quebec: L. J. Demers et frère, 1889–1895), 11:7–51; John Clarence Webster, *The Forts of Chignecto: A Study of Eighteenth-Century Conflict between France and Great Britain in Acadia* (Shediac, New Brunswick: privately printed, 1930), 38–45, 49–84, 110–16; C. P. Stacey, *Quebec, 1759:*

The Siege and the Battle (Toronto: Macmillan, 1959), 130; George A. Rawlyk, *Nova Scotia's Massachusetts: A Study of Massachusetts–Nova Scotia Relations, 1630 to 1784* (Montreal: McGill-Queen's University Press, 1973), 202–13.

67. Jennings, *Empire of Fortune*, 159, 164–66, 189–94; O'Callaghan, *Documents*, 10:410–12, 423; White, *Middle Ground*, 242–45; Freeman, *Washington*, 2:104–32; Anthony F. C. Wallace, *King of the Delawares: Teedyuscung, 1700–1763* (Philadelphia: University of Pennsylvania Press, 1949), 70–83; Guy Frégault, *Canada: The War of the Conquest*, trans. Margaret M. Cameron (Toronto: Oxford University Press, 1969), 99.

68. Schutz, *William Shirley*, 193–98; Stanley McCrory Pargellis, *Military Affairs*, 81–84 and *Lord Loudoun in North America* (New Haven: Yale University Press; London: Humphrey Milford, Oxford University Press, 1933), 31–33.

69. William J. Eccles, "The French Forces in North America during the Seven Years' War," in Halpenny, *Dictionary of Canadian Biography*, 3:xvii–xix; Eccles, *France in America*, 183; Thomas Chapais, *Le Marquis de Montcalm (1712–1759)* (Quebec: J.-P. Garneau, 1911), 81–82.

70. Blanchet, *Collection des manuscrits*, 3:548–51, Vaudreuil to Dieskau, 15 August 1755; Frégault, *Canada*, 101–6; O'Callaghan, *Documents*, 10:311–12, 340–41; Ian Steele, *Betrayals: Fort William Henry and the "Massacre"* (New York: Oxford University Press, 1990), 43–44.

71. Blanchet, *Collection des manuscrits*, 3:555–65; Gipson, *British Empire*, 6:168–74; Wyllis E. Wright, *Colonel Ephraim Williams: A Documentary Life* (Pittsfield MA: Berkshire County Historical Society, 1970), 127–49; D. Peter MacLeod, "Microbes and Muskets: Smallpox and the Participation of the Amerindian Allies of New France in the Seven Years' War," *Ethnohistory* 39 (1992): 47.

72. Steele, *Betrayals*, 55–65; Russell P. Bellico, *Sails and Steam in the Mountains: A Maritime and Military History of Lake George and Lake Champlain* (Fleischmanns NY: Purple Mountain Press, 1992), 33, 36–37.

73. Schutz, *William Shirley*, 204–15; Alan Rogers, *Empire and Liberty: American Resistance to British Authority, 1755–1763* (Berkeley: University of California Press, 1974), 25–30.

74. For the British American contribution during the first few years of war, see Pargellis, *Lord Loudoun*, 109; Gipson, *British Empire*, 6:181; Fred Anderson, *A People's Army: Massachusetts Soldiers and Society in the Seven Years' War* (Chapel Hill: University of North Carolina Press, 1984), 59–60n; Harold E. Selesky, *War and Society in Colonial Connecticut* (New Haven: Yale University Press, 1990), 112, 168; James Titus, *The Old Dominion at War: Society, Politics, and Warfare in Late Colonial Virginia* (Columbia: University of South Carolina Press, 1990), 63, 103, 122.

75. Robert C. Newbold, *The Albany Congress and Plan of Union of 1754* (New York: Vantage, 1955); Alison Gilbert Olson, "The British Government and Colonial Union, 1754," *William and Mary Quarterly*, 3rd ser., 17 (1960): 22–34.

76. Graham, "Planning," 565, quoting Newcastle to Hardwicke, 26 August 1755.

77. Charteris, *Cumberland*, 29–30, 194; Sir John W. Fortescue, *A History of the British Army*, vol. 2, *First Part—To the Close of the Seven Years' War*, vol. II, 2nd ed. (London: Macmillan, 1910), 267, 294; H. C. B. Rogers, *The British Army of the Eighteenth Century*

(London: George Allen and Unwin, 1977), 23–25; John Brooke, ed., *Horace Walpole: Memoirs of King George II*, 3 vols. (New Haven: Yale University Press, 1985), 2:85–90.

78. Stephen B. Baxter, "The Conduct of the Seven Years' War," in Stephen B. Baxter, ed., *England's Rise to Greatness, 1660–1763* (Berkeley: University of California Press, 1983), 347n.

79. Frégault, *Canada*, 74.

80. Charles Henry Lincoln, ed., *Correspondence of William Shirley, Governor of Massachusetts and Military Commander in America, 1731–1760*, 2 vols. (New York: Macmillan, 1912), 2:350–54; Nathanael Bouton, ed., *Provincial Papers of New Hampshire*, vol. 6, *Documents and Records Relating to the Province of New-Hampshire from 1749 to 1763* (Manchester N H: James H. Campbell, 1872), 463–67.

81. Pargellis, *Lord Loudoun*, 37–39.

82. Frégault, *Canada*, 164–200; Jennings, *Empire of Fortune*, 179–82; Harris, *Historical Atlas*, plate 30; Gipson, *British Empire*, 6:243–344; Biraben, "Le Peuplement," 124; Geoffrey Plank, *An Unsettled Conquest: The British Campaign against the Peoples of Acadia* (Philadelphia: University of Pennsylvania Press, 2001), 140–57; Naomi E. S. Griffiths, "The Acadians," in Halpenny, *Dictionary of Canadian Biography*, 4:xvii–xxxi, and *The Contexts of Acadian History, 1686–1784* (Montreal: McGill-Queen's University Press, 1992), 89–90.

83. White, *Middle Ground*, 158–59, 166–68; Halpenny, *Dictionary of Canadian Biography*, 4:663; Frégault, *Bigot*, 2:119.

84. Boulle, "French Colonies," 193–240; John J. McCusker, *Rum and the American Revolution: The Rum Trade and the Balance of Payments of the Thirteen Continental Colonies*, 2 vols. (New York: Garland, 1989), 2:666–67, 707–8; Ruggiero Romano, "Documenti e prime considerazioni intorno alla 'balance du commerce' della Francia dal 1716 al 1780," in *Studii in onore di Armando Sapori*, 2 vols. (Milan: Instituto Editoriale Cisalpino, 1957), 2:1291.

85. See appendix D; Jacques Aman, *Une Campagne navale méconnue*, 147–50; Richard Pares, *War and Trade in the West Indies, 1739–1763* (Oxford: Clarendon Press, 1936), 314; *London Evening Post*, 20–22 January 1756.

86. Aman, *Une Campagne navale méconnue* provides a brilliant analysis of Machault's strategy. For Lenormant de Mézy, see Pritchard, *Louis XV's Navy*, 7, 34.

87. Aman, *Une Campagne navale méconnue*, 18–23, 174–79.

88. Aman, *Une Campagne navale méconnue*, 12–13; Vergé-Franceschi, *Les Officiers généraux*, 1:65–66, 4:1831–34, 1838; Lacour-Gayet, *La Marine militaire*, 186.

89. Aman, *Une Campagne navale méconnue*, 28–41.

90. Britain 438: 250–51, Mirepox to Rouillé, 15 July 1755; Rathery, *Journal d'Argenson*, 8:44; Charteris, *Cumberland*, 168.

91. Britain 438: 65–72, Mirepoix to Rouillé, 10 May 1755.

92. Waddington, *Louis XV*, 167–68.

93. Britain 438: 255–56, Rouillé to Mirepoix, 18 July 1755; Waddington, *Louis XV*, 101–4.

94. Britain 438: 268–70; Aman, *Une Campagne navale méconnue*, 48–49.

95. Waddington, *Louis XV*, 190; Rathery, *Journal d'Argenson* 9:51; Droysen, *Politische Correspondenz*, 11:113–14n, 115, 266–67; L.-E. Dussieux and E. Soulié, eds., *Mémoires du*

duc de Luynes sur la cour de Louis XV (1735–1758), 17 vols. (Paris: Firmin Didot frères, fils, & c.i.e., 1860–65), 14:207–8, 211; John Debrett, ed., *The History, Debates, and Proceedings of Both Houses of Parliament of Great Britain from the Year 1743 to the Year 1774*, 7 vols. (London: J. Debrett, 1792), 3:292–388.

96. Aman, *Une Campagne navale méconnue*, 43–47, 61–63, 89–114, 181–84, 189.

97. Such was the analysis of Knyphausen: Droysen, *Politische Correspondenz*, 11:240–42n, Knyphausen to Frederick II, 24 July 1755.

98. Waddington, *Louis XV*, 132, 155–70, 294–95; Rathery, *Journal d'Argenson*, 9:46–48, 77, 93; Droysen, *Politische Correspondenz*, 11:267n; Dussieux and Soulié, *Mémoires de Luynes*, 14:202–3; Rousset, *Correspondance de Noailles*, 2:369–409; Combeau, *Argenson*, ix, 181–82; Philippe Bonnet, ed., *Mémoires du Cardinal de Bernis* (Paris: Mercure de France, 1980), 137–38; John Charles Batzel, "Austria and the First Three Treaties of Versailles, 1755–1758" (Ph.D. diss., Brown University, 1974), 57–60, 70–72; Alice Clare Carter, *The Dutch Republic in Europe in the Seven Years' War* (London: Macmillan, 1971), 38–39; Emmanuel-Henri, vicomte de Grouchy and Paul Cottin, eds., *Journal inédite du duc de Croij, 1718–1784*, 4 vols. (Paris: Ernest Flammarion, 1906–7), 1:306–8.

99. L. G. Wickham Legg, ed., *British Diplomatic Instructions, 1689–1789*, vol. 7, *France, part IV, 1745–1789* (London: Royal Historical Society, 1934), 52, Secretary of State Robinson to Chargé d'affaires Ruvigny de Cosne, 22 July 1755.

100. Corbett, *England in the Seven Years' War*, 1:50–53, 59–62, 69; Charteris, *Cumberland*, 157–72; Waddington, *Louis XV*, 102–3; Aman, *Une Campagne navale méconnue*, 79; Gipson, *British Empire*, 6:377; Clark, *Waldegrave*, 69; Ruddock F. Mackay, ed., *The Hawke Papers: A Selection, 1743–1771* (Aldershot, Eng.: Scolar Press for the Navy Records Society, 1990), 125.

101. Corbett, *England in the Seven Years' War*, 1:70–72; Aman, *Une Campagne navale méconnue*, 65–66, 83; Charteris, *Cumberland*, 174; Dussieux and Soulié, *Mémoires de Luynes*, 14:213, 233, 270; Rathery, *Journal d'Argenson*, 9:56–58; Villiers, *Marine royale*, 2:445–47; Albert Waddington, ed., *Recueil des instructions données aux ambassadeurs et ministres de France depuis les traités de Westphalie jusqu'à la révolution française*, vol. 16, *Prusse* (Paris: Félix Alcan, 1901), 453, Instructions for Louis-Jules-Barbon Mancini-Mazarini, duc de Nivernais, Minister Plenipotentiary to Prussia, 12 November 1755.

102. Yorke, *Hardwicke*, 2:258, discusses the decision not to declare war.

103. Villiers, *Marine royale*, 2:453; Le Goff, "Problèmes de recrutement," 231–32, and "L'Impact des prises," in Acerra et al., *Les Marines de guerre*, 106, 110; Patrick Villers, "Commerce coloniale, traite de noirs et cabotage dans les ports du Ponant pendant la guerre de Sept Ans," *Centre de recherches sur l'histoire du monde Atlantique-enquêtes et documents* 17 (1990): 25–31; [Barthélemy-François-Joseph Mouffle d'Angerville], *Vie privée de Louis XV, ou principaux evenémens, particularitiés et anecdotes de son règne*, 4 vols. (London: John Peter Lyton, 1781), 3:48–49, 250–65. For losses suffered by various French ports, see B^{3}526: 223; B^{3}527: 183–204; Hervé, vicomte du Halgouet, *Nantes: Ses Relations commerciales avec les îles d'Amérique au XVIIIe siècle; ses armateurs* (Rennes: Oberthur, 1939), 76; Jean Meyer, *L'Armement nantais dans la deuxième moitié du XVIIIe*

siècle (Paris: SEVPEN., 1969): 379–83; Henri Malo, *Les Dernières Corsaires: Dunkerque (1715–1815)* (Paris: Emile-Paul frères, 1922), 45.

104. Aman, *Une Campagne navale méconnue*, 126–44; Gipson, *British Empire*, 6:119–26; Clowes, *Royal Navy*, 3:141, 289–90; Bonner-Smith, *Barrington Papers*, 1:141–45.

105. Eldon, *Subsidy Policy*, 1, 12–14, 26–35; Carter, *Dutch Republic*, 38–39; Waddington, *Louis XV*, 144n; Browning, *Duke of Newcastle*, 220; Clive Parry, comp., *The Consolidated Treaty Series*, 243 vols. (Dobbs Ferry NY: Oceana Publications, 1969–86), 40: 259–67; Sir Reginald Savory, *His Britannic Majesty's Army in Germany during the Seven Years' War* (Oxford: Clarendon Press, 1966), 4–5, 450–54; John Childs, *Armies and Warfare in Europe, 1648–1789* (Manchester, Eng.: Manchester University Press, 1982), 42.

106. Th. [Carel Hendrik Theodoor] Bussemaker, ed., *Archives, ou correspondance inédite de la maison d'Orange-Nassau. Quatrième série*, 4 vols. (Leiden: A. W. Sijthoff, 1908–14), 2:471, Newcastle to Count William Bentinck, 11 March 1755.

107. Corbett, *England in the Seven Years' War*, 1:22–23; Herbert H. Kaplan, *Russia and the Outbreak of the Seven Years' War* (Berkeley: University of California Press, 1968), 17.

108. Austria 261:151; Waddington, *Louis XV*, 246; Childs, *Armies and Warfare in Europe*, 42; Rathery, *Journal d'Argenson*, 9:180; André Corvisier, *L'Armée française de la fin du XVIIe siècle au ministère de Choiseul: Le Soldat*, 2 vols. (Paris: Presses universitaires de France, 1964), 1:154, 158; Lee Kennett, *The French Armies in the Seven Years' War: A Study in Military Organization and Administration* (Durham: Duke University Press, 1967), 77, 80; Christopher Duffy, *The Military Experience in the Age of Reason* (New York: Routledge and Kegan Paul, 1987), 62, 93, 117, 121.

109. Russia 54: 336; Kaplan, *Russia*, 56–57; Childs, *Armies and Warfare in Europe*, 42; Dickson, *Maria Theresia*, 2:348, 353, 356.

110. Waddington, *Louis XV*, 129–48; Eldon, *Subsidy Policy*, 11–21; Broglie, *L'Alliance autrichienne*, 133–50; Batzel, "Austria," 49–50, 57–58, 61–63; Alfred, Ritter von Arneth, *Geschichte Maria Theresia's* (10 vols, Vienna: Wilhelm Braumüller, 1863–79), 4:372–81; Uriel Dann, *Hanover and Great Britain, 1740–1760: Diplomacy and Survival* (Leicester: Leicester University Press, 1991), 90–93.

111. Parry, *Consolidated Treaty Series*, 40:269–83; Waddington, *Louis XV*, 129–30, 134; Kaplan, *Russia*, 25–33; Browning, *Duke of Newcastle*, 220; Horn, *Williams*, 178–205.

112. Kaplan, *Russia*, 31–32; Horn, *Williams*, 221. For Elizabeth, see Evgeny V. Anisimov, *Empress Elizabeth: Her Reign and Her Russia, 1741–1761*, trans. John T. Alexander (Gulf Breeze FL.: Academic International Press, 1995).

113. Kaplan, *Russia*, 18–19. See also Browning, *Duke of Newcastle*, 229–30.

114. Patrick Francis Doran, *Andrew Mitchell and Anglo-Prussian Diplomatic Relations during the Seven Years War* (New York: Garland, 1986), 22–23, which quotes Newcastle to Secretary of State Holdernesse, 6 June 1755.

115. Dann, *Hanover and Britain*, 93–95; Doran, *Andrew Mitchell*, 24; Droysen, *Politische Correspondenz*, 11:191–425; David Bayne Horn, "The Duke of Newcastle and the Origins of the Diplomatic Revolution," in J. H. Elliot and H. G. Koenigsberger, eds., *The Diversity of History: Essays in Honor of Sir Herbert Butterfield* (Ithaca NY: Cornell University Press, 1970), 262; Clark, *Dynamics of Change*, 174–75.

116. Parry, *Consolidated Treaty Series*, 40: 291–99; Droysen, *Politische Correspondenz*, 12:12–16; Doran, *Andrew Mitchell*, 20–31; Waddington, *Louis XV*, 197–221; David Bayne Horn, *Williams*, 210–11, and "The Diplomatic Revolution" in J. O. Lindsay, ed., *The New Cambridge Modern History*, vol. 7, *The Old Regime, 1713–1763* (Cambridge: Cambridge University Press, 1963), 447.

117. Droysen, *Politische Correspondenz*, 11:230–32, 240–45, Frederick to Dodo Heinrich, Baron von Knyphausen, 2 and 9 August 1755; Waddington, *Louis XV*, 163, 172–74; Walter L. Dorn, *Competition for Empire, 1740–1763* (New York: Harper Brothers, 1940), 304–5.

118. Droysen, *Politische Correspondenz*, 11:143–45, Knyphausen to Frederick II, 25 April 1755, Frederick II to Knyphausen, 6 May 1755. For the Franco-Prussian disagreement over Hanover, see Broglie, *L'Alliance autrichienne*, 104–16.

119. Waddington, *Louis XV*, 165; Droysen, *Politische Correspondenz*, 11:173; Rathery, *Journal d'Argenson*, 8:12; André-Louis-Waldemar-Alphée, marquis de Sinéty, *Vie du maréchal de Lowendal*, 2 vols. (Paris: Bachelin-Deflorenne, 1867–68), 2:287.

120. Broglie, *L'Alliance autrichienne*, 120–32, 229–30, 240–47; Waddington, *Louis XV*, 167n, 172–94, 239–49, and *Recueil*, 16:443–70, Instructions for Nivernais, 12–13 November 1755. For contrasting views of Nivernais' abilities, compare Waddington, *Louis XV*, 255, 264, 280, with Broglie, *L'Alliance autrichienne*, 266–68.

121. Droysen, *Politische Correspondenz*, 11:397–98, 408–10, Frederick II to Duke Karl of Brunswick, 24 November 1755, Knyphausen to Frederick II, 17 November 1755, Frederick II to Knyphausen, 2 December 1755; Waddington, *Louis XV*, 192–96; Broglie, *L'Alliance autrichienne*, 188–89, 214–21, 232–38.

122. Waddington, *Louis XV*, 278–79.

123. Droysen, *Politische Correspondenz*, 11:227–28, 244, 373, 380–82n.

124. For Bernis' account of the 1755 negotiations, see Bonnet, *Mémoires de Bernis*, 130–54. They are discussed from an Austrian perspective in Batzel, "Austria," 90–103.

125. Waddington, *Louis XV*, 116–25.

126. Léon Cahen, "Les Mémoires du Cardinal de Bernis et les débuts de la guerre de Sept ans," *Revue d'histoire moderne et contemporaine* 12 (1909): 73–99, is a brilliant critique to which I am much indebted.

127. Batzel, "Austria," 105–7; Waddington, *Louis XV*, 284–303; Broglie, *L'Alliance autrichienne*, 179–228; Horn, "Diplomatic Revolution," in Lindsay, *New Cambridge Modern History*, 7:451.

128. Waddington, *Louis XV et le renversement des alliances*, 246–48; [Clara Adèle Luce Herpin], *Un Petit-nevue de Mazarin: Louis Mancini-Mazarini, duc de Nivernais*, 7th ed. (Paris: Calmann Lévy, 1899), 352.

129. Carter, *Dutch Republic in Europe*, 50–53; P. Coquelle, *L'Alliance franco-hollandaise contre l'Angleterre, 1735–1788, d'après les documents inédits du ministère des affaires étrangères* (Paris: Plon-Nourrit, 1902), 58–61; Louis André and Emile Bourgeois, eds., *Recueil des instructions données aux ambassadeurs et ministres de France depuis les traités de Westphalie jusqu'à la révolution française*, vol. 23, *Holland, tome troisième, 1730–1788* (Paris: E. de Boccard, 1924), 227–29, 237–63.

130. Pierre Duparc, ed., *Recueil des instructions données aux ambassadeurs et ministres*

de France depuis les traités de Westphalie jusqu'à la révolution française, vol. 29, *Turquie* (Paris: Editions de Centre national de la recherche scientifique, 1969), 388–421; Orville T. Murphy, *Charles Gravier, Comte de Vergennes: French Diplomacy in the Age of Revolution, 1719–1787* (Albany: State University of New York Press, 1982), 55–87; Louis Bonneville de Marsangy, *Le Chevalier de Vergennes: Son Ambassade à Constantinople*, 2 vols. (Paris: E. Plon, Nourrit, 1894), 1:196–225, 251–82, 389–93; W. Konopczynski, "La Deuxième Mission du comte de Broglie: Un Supplèment aux 'Instructions de Pologne' (1755–1756)," *Revue d'histoire diplomatique* 21 (1907): 495–98.

131. Droysen, *Politische Correspondenz*, 11:282, Frederick II to Knyphausen, 30 August 1755.

132. Konopczynski, "La Deuxième mission du comte de Broglie," 495–508; Waddington, *Louis XV*, 180–81; Droysen, *Politische Correspondenz*, 11:168–69, 288, 357, 432; Ozanam and Antoine, *Correspondance de Broglie*, 1:xxxv–xxxvii; Albert Sorel, *Essais d'histoire et de critique*, 4th ed., (Paris: Plon-Nourrit, 1913), 172; Horn, *Williams*.

133. Oliva, *Misalliance*, 12–22.

134. Batzel, "Austria," 112–15.

135. Rathery, *Journal d'Argenson*, 9:123; Bonnet, *Mémoires de Bernis*, 159–60; Waddington, *Louis XV*, 185–87, 236–37, 251–53, 263, 274; Corbett, *England in the Seven Years' War*, 1:83; Robbie, *Forgotten Commissioner*, 211–12; Droysen, *Politische Correspondenz*, 12:35–38, 142–43, 194, 199–200, 203–8, 274n, 335, 343–47; Price, *France and the Chesapeake*, 1:577–78; *Gentleman's Magazine* 26 (1756): 38; Black, *America or Europe?* 20, 187; Clark, *Dynamics of Change*, 190–95; Lodge, *Correspondence of Keene*, 459–60, 463; William Cobbett and Thomas C. Hansard, eds., *The Parliamentary History of England from the Earliest Period to the Year 1803*, 36 vols. (London: T. C. Hansard, 1806–20), 15:527–29; Max Savelle, "Diplomatic Preliminaries of the Seven Years' War in America," *Canadian Historical Review* 20 (1939): 33–35; marquis de Valori, ed., *Mémoires des négociations du marquis de Valori, ambassadeur de France à la cour de Berlin*, 2 vols. (Paris: Firmin Didot père et fils, 1820), 2:30–38.

136. B⁴93:34; Pritchard, *Louis XV's Navy*, 187, 215–22; Didier Neuville, ed., *Etat sommaire des archives de la marine antérieures à la Révolution* (Paris: L. Baudouin, 1898), 616–17; Henri Legohérel, *Les Trésoriers généraux de la marine, 1517–1788* (Paris: Cujas, 1965), 177–86; Claude C. Sturgill, "The French Army's Budget in the Eighteenth Century: A Retreat from Loyalty," in David G. Troyansky, Alfred Cismaru, and Norwood Andrews Jr., eds., *The French Revolution in Culture and Society* (Westport CT: Greenwood Press, 1991), 132.

137. Joël Félix, *Finances et politique au siècle des Lumières: Le ministère L'Averdy, 1763–1768* (Paris: Comité pour l'histoire économique et financière de la France, 1999), 42; see also Riley, "French Finances," 223–27, 232, and *Seven Years War*, 56–64, 140–41, 147–49; Peter Mathias and Patrick O'Brien, "Taxation in Britain and France, 1715–1810: A Comparison of the Social and Economic Incidence of Taxes Collected for the Central Government," *Journal of European Economic History* 5 (1976): 604; Michel Morineau, "Budgets de l'état et gestion des finances royales en France au dix-huitième siècle," *Revue historique* 264 (July–December 1980): 314; Marcel Marion, *Histoire financière de la France*

depuis 1715, 6 vols. (Paris: A. Rousseau, 1914–31), 1:180–81; Yves-René Durand, *Les Fermiers Généraux au XVIIIᵉ siècle* (Paris: Presses universitaires de France, 1971), 57.

138. Riley, *Seven Years War*, 109–10.

139. Mathias and O'Brien, "Taxation," 605; Clark, *Dynamics of Change*, 149; John Brewer, *The Sinews of Power: War, Money, and the English State, 1688–1783* (New York: Alfred A. Knopf, 1989), 90, 115; B. R. Mitchell and Phyllis Deane, eds., *Abstract of British Historical Statistics* (Cambridge: Cambridge University Press, 1962), 386–87; John J. Mc-Cusker, *Money and Exchange in Europe and America, 1600–1775: A Handbook* (Chapel Hill: University of North Carolina Press, 1978), 35, 97; Kathryn Norberg, "The French Fiscal Crisis of 1788 and the Financial Origins of the Revolution of 1789," in Philip T. Hoffman and Kathryn Norberg, eds., *Financial Crises, Liberty, and Representative Government, 1450–1789* (Stanford, Calif.: Stanford University Press, 1994), 252–98.

140. Pritchard, *Louis XV's Navy*, 192; Rathery, *Journal d'Argenson*, 9:102–3.

141. See appendix C; B⁴68: 17; B¹66: 11; Waddington, *Louis XV*, 245; Aman, *Une Campagne navale méconnue*, 23–24.

142. Glete, *Navies and Nations*, 1:268; Lyon, *Sailing Navy List*, 62–63, 66–67, 73, 76–77; Lavery, *Ship of the Line*, 96–97, 173–76; Middleton, "Naval Administration," in Black and Woodfine, *British Navy*, 112; Rodger, *Wooden World*, 149; Robert Beatson, *Naval and Military Memoirs of Great Britain, from 1727 to 1783*, 6 vols. (London: Longman, Hurst, Rees and Orme, 1804), 3:95–97; Dwight E. Robinson, "Secret of British Power in the Age of Sail: Admiralty Records of the Coasting Fleet," *American Neptune* 52 (1992): 5–21; Peter Earle, "English Sailors, 1570–1775," in Van Royen et al., *"Those Emblems of Hell"?*, 76–78; David J. Starkey, "War and the Market for Seafarers in Britain, 1736–1792," in Lewis R. Fisher and Helge W. Nordvik, eds., *Shipping and Trade, 1750–1950: Essays in International Maritime Economic History* (Pontefract, Eng.: Lofthouse, 1990), 40–41.

143. Le Goff, "Problèmes de recrutement," 207–11, 222–24, and "Labour Market," in Van Royen et al., *"Those Emblems of Hell"?*, 300; Jacques Captier, *Etude historique et économique sur l'inscription maritime* (Paris: Bussière, Giard et Brière, 1907); Pritchard, *Louis XV's Navy*, 74.

144. Jean Boudriot, "Les Compagnies franches de la marine," *Neptunia*, no. 120 (winter 1975): 24–32; W. J. Eccles, "The French Forces in America during the Seven Years' War," in Halpenny, *Dictionary of Canadian Biography*, 3:xvii.

145. Pritchard, *Louis XV's Navy*, 56, and "The French Naval Officer Corps during the Seven Years' War," in *New Aspects of Naval History: Selected Papers from the 5th Naval History Symposium* (Baltimore: Nautical and Aviation Publishing Company of America, 1985), 62.

146. Vergé-Francheschi, *Les Officiers généraux*, 1:32–33, 38–39; 2:880, 886–92; 5:2338–47; 7:44.

147. Sweden 229: 32–33, 95–100, 136, 181, 236, 335; Pritchard, *Louis XV's Navy*, 152–53, and "Fir Trees," 349; Chabaud-Arnault, "Etudes historiques," *Revue maritime* 114 (1892): 67–68.

148. Pritchard, *Louis XV's Navy*, 153–55; Aman, *Une Campagne naval méconnue*, 140–41; Emile Garnault, *Le Commerce rochelais au XVIIIᵉ siècle d'après les documents com-*

posant les anciennes archives de la chambre de commerce de la Rochelle, vol. 4, *Marine et colonies de 1749 au traité de paix de 1763* (Paris: Augustin Challamel; La Rochelle: E. Martin, 1898), 118–19.

149. B^{2}351:102, 117, 191, 199; B^{4}68: 18.

150. B^{4}68: 19. These ships sailed in early 1756 (see the following chapter); meanwhile, dispatches and emergency supplies were sent to the West Indies and Canada by individual warships: Aman, *Une Campagne navale méconnue*, 139–40, 151; Maurice Dupont, *D'Entrecosteaux: Rien que la mer, un peu de gloire* (Paris: Editions maritimes et d'outrmer, 1983), 30–37.

151. Aman, *Une Campagne navale méconnue*, 150; O'Callaghan, *Documents*, 10:385–87; Frégault, *Bigot*, 2:122.

152. Rathery, *Journal d'Argenson*, 9:167–68; Waddington, *Louis XV*, 237.

3. 1756—FRANCE TAKES THE OFFENSIVE

1. Corbett, *England in the Seven Years' War*, 1:103.

2. Bonnet, *Mémoires de Bernis*, 161; Rathery, *Journal d'Argenson*, 9:159–60, 193, 195, 224–25; Dussieux and Soulié, *Mémoires de Luynes*, 15:148–49; H. Binet, "La Guerre des côtes en Bretagne au XVIIIe siècle: Le Commandement du duc d'Aiguillon en Bretagne au début de la Guerre de Sept Ans (1756)," *Annales de Bretagne* 26 (1910–11): 321; Edmund-Jean-François Barbier, *Chronique de la régence et du règne de Louis XV (1718–1763); ou, Journal de Barbier*, 8 vols. (Paris: Charpentier, 1857), 6:277; Dudley Pope, *At Twelve Mr. Byng Was Shot* (Philadelphia: J. B. Lippincott, 1962), 68–69, 98–99.

3. Corbett, *England in the Seven Years' War*, 1:85–92; Droysen, *Politische Correspondenz*, 11:450–52; York, *Hardwicke*, 2:285–87; Pope, *Byng*, 63; Gradish, *Manning*, 35; Ruddock F. Mackay, *Admiral Hawke* (Oxford: Clarendon Press, 1965), 136.

4. Gradish, *Manning*, 32–34, 37–38, 42. The number of crewmen mustered reached about 50,000 during the summer of 1756, about 20,000 more than the previous summer: Gradish, *Manning*, 42; Lloyd, *British Seaman*, 287; Neal, "Interpreting Power and Profit," 22.

5. Hubert Cole, *First Gentleman of the Bedchamber: The Life of Louis-François-Armand, maréchal duc de Richelieu* (New York: Viking Press, 1965), 195–98.

6. B^{3}529: 32–86; B^{4}69: 216; B^{4}70: 13, 34; Le Goff, "Problèmes de recrutement," 210–11; Pritchard, *Louis XV's Navy*, 80, 153; Lacour-Gayet, *La Marine militaire*, 276–77, 504–13; Boulle, "French Colonies," 93n; Vincent-Félix Brun, *Guerres maritimes de la France: Port de Toulon, ses armements, son administration depuis son origine jusqu'à nos jours*, 2 vols. (Paris: Henri Plon, 1861), 1:382–87; Edouard-Louis-Maxime Guillon, *Port-Mahon: La France à Minorque sous Louis XV (1756–1763) d'après les documents inédits des archives de France et des Baléares* (Paris: Ernest Leroux, 1894), 11–18.

7. B^{4}70: 3–10, 38–44.

8. Pope, *Byng*, 66–89, 101–2, 114–18, 131–32, 163, 249, 273, 341; Gradish, *Manning*, 35–40; Corbett, *England in the Seven Years' War*, 1:97–98, 102–3, 134; Yorke, *Hardwicke*, 2:285–86;

Waddington, *Louis XV*, 443; Debrett, *Debates of Parliament*, 3:297–388; Lodge, "Keene," 34; Mackay, *Hawke Papers*, 129–30; Beatson, *Naval and Military Memoirs*, 1:464n; Giles Stephen Holland Fox-Strangways, Earl of Ilchester, *Henry Fox, First Lord Holland, His Family and Relations*, 2 vols. (London: J. Murray, 1920), 1:324; David Erskine, ed., *Augustus Hervey's Journal: Being the Intimate Account of the Life of a Captain in the Royal Navy Ashore and Afloat, 1746–1759* (London: William Kimber, 1953), 203, 213. The fullest collection of documents for the preparation and operations of Byng's squadron is Sir Herbert W. Richmond, ed., *Papers Relating to the Loss of Minorca in 1756* (London: Navy Records Society, 1913).

9. La Galissonnière's operations are documented in B^{4}70 and B^{4}71. For the battle, see also Clowes, *Royal Navy*, 3:151n; Pope, *Byng*, 136–57, 253–71, 286–93; Creswell, *British Admirals*, 94–104; William Cuthbert Brian Tunstall, *Naval Warfare in the Age of Sail: The Evolution of Fighting Tactics, 1650–1815*, ed. Nicolas Tracy (Annapolis: Naval Institute Press, 1990), 107–11. For the decision to return to Gibraltar and Byng's subsequent punishment, see Pope, *Byng*, 158–62, 180, 236–337, 347–50; Gradish, *Manning*, 134; Corbett, *England in the Seven Years' War*, 1:124–28, 132–34; Margarette Lincoln, *Representing the Royal Navy: British Sea Power, 1750–1815* (Aldershott, Eng. and Burlington, Vt.: Ashgate, 2002), 46–53; Donald J. Greene, ed., *Samuel Johnson: Political Writings* (New Haven: Yale University Press, 1977), 249.

10. B^{4}69: 116–18 and passim; Guillon, *Port-Mahon*, 43–49, 54–60, 65–70; Waddington, *Louis XV*, 454–60; Raoul de Cisternes, *La Campagne de Minorque d'après le journal du commandeur de Glandevez et de nombreuses lettres inédites* (Paris: Calmann Lévy, 1899), 356–61; [Philippe-Henri, Comte de Grimoard, ed.], *Correspondance particulière et historique du maréchal duc de Richelieu en 1756, 1757 et 1758, avec M. Paris du Verney, conseiller d'état*, 2 vols. (London and Paris: Buisson, 1789), 2:43–338; Desmond Gregory, *Minorca, the Illusory Prize: A History of the British Occupations of Minorca between 1708 and 1802* (Rutherford NJ: Farleigh Dickinson University Press; London and Toronto: Associated University Presses, 1990), 158–78; Charles-Pierre-Victor, comte Pajol, *Les Guerres sous Louis XV*, 7 vols. (Paris: Firmin-Didot, 1881–91), 6:1–28.

11. B^{2}354: 157; Britain 440: 214–16, 221–27, and B^{4}72: 5–8, rough draft and printed version of the French declaration of war; Pope, *Byng*, 99–100, 104; Corbett, *England in the Seven Years' War*, 1:128–29; Cisternes, *Minorque*, 351–54; Fortescue, *British Army*, 299; Charteris, *Cumberland*, 197; Bonner-Smith, *Barrington Papers*, 1:152–55.

12. Pope, *Byng*, 163, 166, 168–70, 177, 352; Mackay, *Hawke Papers*, 138–42, and *Admiral Hawke*, 147–49; Corbett, *England in the Seven Years' War*, 1:129–32; Guillon, *Port-Mahon*, 60; W. S. Lewis et al., eds., *The Yale Edition of Horace Walpole's Correspondence*, 48 vols. (New Haven: Yale University Press; Oxford: Oxford University Press, 1937–83), 20:559–62.

13. B^{2}354: 167, 174, 176, 250, 342; Mackay, *Admiral Hawke*, 149–51; Le Goff, "Problèmes de recrutement," 210–11; Brun, *Port de Toulon*, 1:390–92; Paul Walden Bamford, *Forests and French Sea Power, 1660–1789* (Toronto: University of Toronto Press, 1956), 64.

14. B^{2}354: 461; B^{3}529: 32–86, 99; for Massiac see Vergé-Franceschi, *Les Officiers généraux*, 1:99–100; 2:538–45; 7:403–4; Antoine, *Le Gouvernement*, 178.

15. Barbier, *Chronique*, 6:332–34; Broglie, *L'Alliance autrichienne*, 380–82.

16. Pope, *Byng*, 173, 189–90; Waddington, *Louis XV*, 356–57; Doran, *Andrew Mitchell*, 84; Browning, *Duke of Newcastle*, 241.

17. Pope, *Byng*, 180–83, 189–90, 202, 309–11; Browning, *Duke of Newcastle*, 243; Clark, *Dynamics of Change*, 235–36.

18. Pargellis, *Lord Loudoun*, 39–41, 47, 61–67, 105; Fortescue, *British Army*, 2:302; Lincoln, *Correspondence of Shirley*, 2:393–95; Brock, *Records of Dinwiddie*, 2:367–68; Leach, *Arms for Empire*, 383; Freeman, *Washington*, 2:166–69; Schutz, *William Shirley*, 232–50; Gipson, *British Empire*, 6:180–92; Daniel J. Beattie, "The Adaption of the British Army to Wilderness Warfare, 1755–1763," in Maarten Ultee, ed., *Adapting to Conditions: War and Society in the Eighteenth Century* (University: University of Alabama Press, 1986), 71–72; William Hand Browne, ed., *Correspondence of Governor Horatio Sharpe*, vol. 1, *1753–57* (Baltimore: Maryland Historical Society, 1888), 380.

19. Pargellis, *Loudoun*, 42–44; Beattie, "Adaption" in Ultee, *Adapting*, 62–65; Russell, "Redcoats," 645.

20. Michalon, "Vaudreuil et Montcalm" in Delmas, *Conflits*, 61–90; Casgrain, *Collection des manuscrits*, 3:39–43; Halpenny, *Dictionary of Canadian Biography*, 3:84–87, 458–69, 4:477–82.

21. Halpenny, *Dictionary of Canadian Biography*, 4:660–62; Michalon, "Vaudreuil et Montcalm," in Delmas, *Conflits*, 94–96; Frégault, *Canada*, 124; Eccles, *Essays on New France*, 206–7n.

22. B ³528: 231 (pagination for Brest); B ⁴73:23–84, 93–105, 124; Casgrain, *Collection des manuscrits*, 7:111–12; Aman, *Une Campagne navale méconnue*, 155–56; Halpenny, *Dictionary of Canadian Biography* 3:54–55; Lacour-Gayet, *La Marine militaire*, 382–83; Pritchard, *Louis XV's Navy*, 134; Edward P. Hamilton, ed., *Adventure in the Wilderness: The American Journals of Louis Antoine de Bougainville, 1756–1760* (Norman: University of Oklahoma Press, 1964), 4; Louis-Guillaume Parscau du Plessis, "Journal d'une campagne au Canada à bord de *la Sauvage* (mars-juillet 1756)," *Rapport de l'archiviste de la province de Québec* 9 (1928–29): 211–26; Pierre Héliot, "La Campagne du régiment de la Sarre au Canada (1756–1760)," *Revue d'histoire de l'Amérique française* 3 (1949–50): 518–19.

23. O'Callaghan, *Documents*, 10:413–19, Montcalm to d'Argenson and Machault, 12 June 1756.

24. MacLeod, "Microbes and Muskets," 47–48; O'Callaghan, *Documents*, 10:410–13, 423, 435–38; Jennings, *Empire of Fortune*, 189–95, 214, 262–63; McConnell, *A Country Between*, 121–28; Waddington, *La Guerre*, 1:242; Wallace, *Teedyuscung*, 87; Matthew C. Ward, "Fighting the 'Old Women': Indian Strategy on the Virginia and Pennsylvania Frontier, 1754, 1758," *Virginia Magazine of History and Biography* 103 (1995): 297–320, and *Breaking the Backcountry: The Seven Years' War in Virginia and Pennsylvania* (Pittsburgh: University of Pittsburgh Press, 2003); C. A. Weslanger, *The Delaware Indians: A History* (New Brunswick NJ: Rutgers University Press, 1972), 231. For British recruiting in the American colonies, see Pargellis, *Lord Loudoun*, 104–9, 111.

25. Lincoln, *Correspondence of Shirley* 2:370–73, 433–38; Brock, *Records of Dinwiddie*, 2:346–48; Anderson, *People's Army*, 59n, 226; Selesky, *War and Society*, 168; Bouton, *New Hampshire*, 6:463–67; Gary B. Nash, *The Urban Crucible: Social Change, Political Con-*

sciousness, and the Origins of the American Revolution (Cambridge: Harvard University Press, 1979), 242.

26. Lincoln, *Correspondence of Shirley*, 2:388–91, 415–16; Stotz, *Outposts*, 101–5; Abbot et al., *Papers of George Washington*, 2:316–17; 3:243–46, 322–23n; 4:10, 82; William A. Hunter, *Forts on the Pennsylvania Frontier, 1753–1758* (Harrisburg: Pennsylvania Historical and Museum Commission, 1960); J. Bennett Nolan, *General Benjamin Franklin: The Military Career of a Philosopher* (Philadelphia: University of Pennsylvania Press; London: Humphrey Milford, Oxford University Press, 1936), 66–80; Leonard W. Labaree et al., eds. *The Papers of Benjamin Franklin*, 37 vols. to date (New Haven: Yale University Press, 1959–), 6:366–67, 380–82; Louis M. Waddell, "Defending the Long Perimeter: Forts on the Pennsylvania, Maryland, and Virginia Frontier, 1755–1765," *Pennsylvania History* 62 (1995): 171–95; Louis Koontz, *The Virginia Frontier, 1754–1763* (Baltimore: Johns Hopkins University Press, 1925), 111–48; John Richard Alden, *John Stuart and the Southern Colonial Frontier: A Study of Indian Relations, Trade, and Land Problems in the Southern Wilderness, 1754–1775* (Ann Arbor: University of Michigan Press; London: Humphrey Milford, Oxford University Press, 1944), 47–60; David H. Corkran, *The Cherokee Frontier: Conflict and Survival, 1740–62* (Norman: University of Oklahoma Press, 1962), 66–104; P. M. Hamer, "Anglo-French Rivalry in the Cherokee Country, 1754–1757," *North Carolina Historical Review* 2 (1925): 303–22.

27. Hunter, *Forts*, 383–94, 405–10; Waddell, "Long Perimeter," 187, 194n; Leach, *Arms for Empire*, 389–91; O'Callahan, *Documents*, 10:396–97, 403–5, 411–12; Halpenny, *Dictionary of Canadian Biography*, 4:146; Harris, *Historical Atlas*, plate 42; Titus, *Old Dominion*, 95–96; Ward, *Stephen*, 35–36; D. Peter MacLeod, *The Canadian Iroquois and the Seven Years' War* (Toronto: Dundurn Press, 1996), 23–33; Matthew C. Ward, " 'The European Method of Warring Is Not Practiced Here': The Failure of British Military Policy in the Ohio Valley, 1755–1759," *War in History* 4 (1997): 258–59; Gilbert Hagerty, *Massacre at Fort Bull: The Léry Expedition against Oneida Carry* (Providence: Mowbray, 1971); Milton W. Hamilton, *Sir William Johnson, Colonial American, 1715–1763* (Port Washington NY: Kennikat Press, 1976), 208.

28. Jennings, *Empire of Fortune*, 162, 290–92; Leach, *Arms for Empire*, 381–82, 409–10n; William G. Godfrey, *Pursuit of Profit and Preferment in Colonial North America: John Bradstreet's Quest* (Waterloo, Ont.: Wilfrid Laurier University Press, 1982), 76–87.

29. Lincoln, *Correspondence of Shirley*, 2:453–60; Gipson, *British Empire*, 6:192, 199, 204; Steele, *Betrayals*, 68.

30. Casgrain, *Collection des manuscrits*, 1:45–75; 2:19–107; Hamilton, *Adventure in the Wilderness*, 13; Frégault, *Canada*, 126.

31. O'Callaghan, *Documents*, 10:433–85, 520–23; Casgrain, *Collection des manuscrits*, 7:85–110; Frégault, *Canada*, 125–42; Pargellis, *Lord Loudoun*, 148–52, 158–59; Jennings, *Empire of Fortune*, 292–94; Gipson, *British Empire*, 6:192–202; Leach, *Arms for Empire*, 384–87; Steele, *Betrayals*, 79; Harris, *Historical Atlas*, plate 42; Pargellis, *Military Affairs*, 187–221; MacLeod, *Canadian Iroquois*, 79–94; Brian Leigh Dunnigan, ed., *Memoirs on the Late War in North America between France and England by Pierre Pouchot*, trans. Michael Cardy (Youngstown NY: Old Fort Niagara Association, 1994), 90–92, 104; Charles-Nicolas

Gabriel, *Le Maréchal de camp Desandrouins, 1729–1792: Guerre du Canada, 1756–1760; Guerre de l'indépendance américaine, 1780–1782* (Verdun: Renvé-Lallemant, 1887), 36–65; D. Peter MacLeod, "The French Siege of Oswego in 1756: Inland Naval Warfare in North America," *American Neptune* 49 (1989): 262–71, and "The Canadians against the French: The Struggle for Control of the Expedition to Oswego in 1756," *Ontario History* 80 (1988): 143–57; W. L. Greene, "The Capture of Oswego by Montcalm in 1756: A Study in Naval Power," *Transactions of the Royal Society of Canada*, 3rd ser., 8 (1914–15): 193–214; Jean-Guillaume-Charles de Plantavit de Margon, chevalier de La Pause, "Mémoire et observations sur mon voyage en Canada," *Rapport de l'archiviste de la province de Québec* 12 (1931–32): 26–27.

32. Hamilton, *Adventure in the Wilderness*, 28–42; Waddington, *La Guerre*, 1:234; Steele, *Betrayals*, 66–73; Anderson, *People's Army*, 173–79; Pargellis, *Lord Loudoun*, 90–97, 187–210; Gipson, *British Empire*, 6:204–8; Rogers, *Empire and Liberty*, 75–87, 110–11.

33. Michalon, "Vaudreuil and Montcalm," in Delmas, *Conflits*, 98–101; O'Callahan, *Documents*, 10:471–75; Nicolai, "Different Kind of Courage," 61–62.

34. O'Callaghan, *Documents*, 10:401–6, 414; Hamilton, *Adventure in the Wilderness*, 5–6; Jean de Maupassant, *Un Grand Armateur de Bordeaux, Abraham Gradis (1699?-1780)* (Bordeaux: Ferret, 1917), 58; Jacques Mathieu, "La Balance commerciale: Nouvelle-France-Antilles au XVIIIe siècle," *Revue d'histoire de l'Amérique française* 25 (1971–72): 473, 493, and *Le Commerce entre la Nouvelle-France et les Antilles au XVIIIe siècle* (Montreal: Fides, 1981), 164–65, 225, 227. James Pritchard, "The Pattern of French Colonial Shipping to Canada before 1760," *Revue française d'histoire d'outre-mer* 63 (1976): 189–210, provides a very useful compilation of trade statistics throughout the war.

35. O'Callaghan, *Documents*, 10:491; Eccles, *Essays on New France*, 92–93; Waddington, *La Guerre*, 1:242–43; Wallace, *Teedyuscung*, 98–99, 114; Leach, *Arms for Empire*, 392–93; Jennings, *Empire of Fortune*, 271–80; Dunnigan, *Memoirs by Pierre Pouchot*, 108–9; White, *Middle Ground*, 246; Frégault, *Bigot*, 2:164–70; Jean Elizabeth Lunn, "Agriculture and War in Canada, 1740–1760," *Canadian Historical Review* 16 (1935): 131–33; Jane T. Merritt, *At the Crossroads: Indians and Empires on a Mid-Atlantic Frontier* (Chapel Hill: University of North Carolina Press, 2003), 198–227.

36. Clark, *Dynamics of Change*, 261–96; Richard Middleton, *The Bells of Victory: The Pitt-Newcastle Ministry and the Conduct of the Seven Years' War, 1757–1762* (London: Cambridge University Press, 1985), 5–7.

37. Richard Middleton, "Pitt, Anson, and the Admiralty, 1756–1761," *History*, n.s., 55 (1970): 190–93; Peter Douglas Brown, *William Pitt, Earl of Chatham, the Great Commoner* (London: George Allen and Unwin, 1978), 140.

38. Middleton, *Bells of Victory*, 9–10; Pargellis, *Military Affairs*, 235–36, 262–63 and *Lord Loudoun*, 211, 228–32; Fortescue, *British Army*, 2:305–6; Doran, *Andrew Mitchell*, 115–16; Rogers, *British Army*, 23–25; Charteris, *Cumberland*, 205, 267n; Gertrude Selwyn Kimball, ed., *Correspondence of William Pitt When Secretary of State with Colonial Governors and Military and Naval Commissioners in America*, 2 vols. (New York: Macmillan, 1906), 1:1–2, 15; William Stanhope Taylor and John Henry Pringle, eds., *Correspondence of William Pitt, Earl of Chatham*, 4 vols. (London: John Murray, 1838–40), 1:206–7. For the raising of

the Highland regiments, see Corbett, *England in the Seven Years' War*, 1:142n; E. M. Lloyd, "The Raising of the Highland Regiments in 1757," *English Historical Review* 17 (1902): 466–69.

39. Yorke, *Hardwicke*, 2:261–67; Taylor and Pringle, *Correspondence of Chatham*, 1:257–62; John R. Western, *The English Militia in the Eighteenth Century: The Story of a Political Issue, 1660–1802* (London: Routledge and Kegan Paul; Toronto: University of Toronto Press, 1965), 127–41; Stanley Ayling, *The Elder Pitt, Earl of Chatham* (London: Collins, 1976), 176, 190; Eliga H. Gould, *The Persistence of Empire: British Political Culture in the Age of the American Revolution* (Chapel Hill: University of North Carolina Press, 2000), 83–98.

40. O'Callaghan, *Documents*, 10:496–99; Hamilton, *Adventure in the Wilderness*, 69.

41. $B^2$353: 34 (pagination for Rochefort); $B^3$528: 211; $B^4$73: 127–44; Clowes, *Royal Navy*, 3:290–91; Mouffle d'Angerville, *Vie privée*, 3:75; Christian Buchet, *La Lutte pour l'espace caraïbe et la facade de l'Amérique centrale et du sud (1672–1763)*, 2 vols. (Paris: Librairie de l'Inde, 1991), 1:372–73. For d'Aubigny, see Vergé-Franceschi, *Les Officers généraux*, 1:104; 3:1157–63.

42. $B^4$73:155–78; Buchet, *La Lutte*, 1:374; Pares, *War and Trade*, 267–68. For Périer, see Vergé-Franceschi, *Les Officiers généraux*, 1:110, 256–58, 263–66.

43. Pares, *War and Trade*, 361–70; Boulle, "French Colonies," 98–99.

44. Parry, *Consolidated Treaty Series*, 40:387–400; Corbett, *England in the Seven Years' War*, 1:144; [Jean-Baptiste-] Gaétan de Raxis de Flassan, *Histoire générale et raisonnée de la diplomatie française, ou de la politique de la France, depuis la fondation de la monarchie jusqu'à la fin du règne de Louis XVI*, 2nd ed., 7 vols. (Paris and Strasburg: Treuttel et Würtz, 1811), 6:67–71, 586.

45. $B^2$354: 266–67, 296, 304: $B^3$529: 112; $B^3$530: 320–21; $B^4$72: 273–74; Brun, *Port de Toulon*, 1:390–92.

46. $B^2$358: 98 (pagination for Brest); $B^4$72: 63–64. Eleven are listed in appendix E; the twelfth, the *Apollon*, 50, entered the roadstead of Brest in July.

47. Vergé-Franceschi, *Les Officiers généraux*, 1:57–58; 5:2323–24, 2328; Clowes, *Royal Navy*, 3:122, 274–75.

48. $B^2$353:52–54 (pagination for Brest); $B^4$72: 63–64; B^{53}unpaginated, list of frigates; Mackay, *Admiral Hawke*, 140–43, and *Hawke Papers*, 129–33; Clowes, *Royal Navy*, 3:291; Vergé-Franceschi, *Les Officiers généraux*, 5:2562; Garnault, *Le Commerce rochelais*, 136–37; Meyer, *L'Armament nantais*, 379–83; Richard Middleton, "British Naval Strategy, 1755–1762: The Western Squadron," *Mariner's Mirror* 75 (1989): 352–55. David J. Starkey, *British Privateering Enterprise in the Eighteenth Century* (Exeter: University of Exeter Press, 1990), 178.

49. Boulle, "French Colonies," 96–97n; Villiers, "Commerce coloniale," 35–38, and *Marine royale*, 1:390, 2:451, 454, 456, 460–63; Le Goff, "Problèmes de recrutement," 210n; Riley, *Seven Years War*, 109–10; Halgouet, *Nantes*, 76; Romano, "Balance du commerce," 2:1274, 1291; Paul Butel, "La Guerre maritime vue de Bordeaux et de Saint-Domingue au XVIIIe siècle," in France, Service historique de la marine, *Guerres et paix, 1660–1815: Journées Franco-anglaises d'histoire de la marine organisées par la service historique de la*

marine à la Corderie royale de Rochefort les 20, 21 et 22 mars 1986 (Vincennes: Service historique de la marine, 1987), 299, 303–4; Pierre Dardel, *Navires et marchandises dans les ports de Rouen et du Havre au XVIIIᵉ siècle* (Paris: SEVPEN, 1963), 257, 548–51, 560, 645.

50. B³527: 42; B³532: 101–13; Boulle, "French Colonies," 94n.

51. Butel, "La Guerre maritime," 305–6; Boulle, "French Colonies," 94–96; Villiers, "Commerce coloniale," 43, and *Marine royale*, 1:348–75; Garnault, *Le Commerce rochelais*, 4:126–32; Malo, *Les Dernières Corsaires*, 62–64; Le Goff, "Labour Market" in Van Royen et al., *"Those Emblems of Hell"?*, 306–7, 310; Patrick Crowhurst, " 'Guerre de course' et 'privateering': Vers un étude comparatif," in France, Service historique de la marine, *Guerres et paix*, 311–22, and *The Defence of British Trade, 1689–1815* (Folkestone, Eng.: William Dawson and Sons, 1977), 20, 26–32; P. Thomas-Lacroix, "La Guerre de course dans les ports des Amirautés de Vannes et de Lorient, 1744–1783," *Mémoires de la sociétés d'histoire et d'archéologie de Bretagne* 26 (1946): 208; Richard Harding, *Seapower and Naval Warfare, 1650–1830* (London: UCL Press, 1999), 209; Raymond de Bertrand, "Le Port et le commerce maritime de Dunkerque au XVIIIᵉ siècle," *Mémoires de la Société dunkerquoise pour l'encouragement des sciences, des lettres et des arts* 9 (1862–64): 314–16.

52. B¹66: 111; Demerliac, *La Marine de Louis XV*, 36, 39–40, 44, 46; Lavery, *Ship of the Line*, 173–77; Lyon, *Sailing Navy List*, 67, 73, 76, 82–84, 85–86, 89–90; Daniel A. Baugh, "The Politics of British Naval Failure, 1775–1777," *American Neptune* 52 (1992): 242–43.

53. B³353: 60; B⁵3: unpaginated, memoir of 23 October 1756; Sweden 231: 242, 341–42; Sweden 237: 122, 216; Holland 502: 154, 397; Holland 504: 11; Carter, *Dutch Republic*, 91–97; Waddington, *La Guerre*, 3:425–26; Pritchard, *Louis XV's Navy*, 153–54; Lacour-Gayet, *La Marine militaire*, 315–17. For the difficulties caused the French navy by the British interruption of trade with the Baltic, see Rathery, *Journal d'Argenson*, 9:296; Pritchard, "Fir Trees," 337–54.

54. James Pritchard, "The French Navy, 1748–1762: Problems and Perspectives," in Robert William Love et al., eds., *Changing Interpretations and New Sources in Naval History: Papers from the Third United States Naval Academy History Symposium* (New York: Garland, 1980), 147; Paul Walden Bamford, *Forests and French Sea Power, 1660–1789* (Toronto: University of Toronto Press, 1956), 74.

55. Vergé-Franceschi, *Les Officiers généraux*, 1:112–14; 3:1055–64; 5:2561; 7:443.

56. Vergé-Franceschi, *Les Officiers généraux*, 7:444–46; Dussieux and Soulié, *Mémoires de Luynes*, 16:35; Rodger, *Wooden World*, 16; Beatson, *Naval and Military Memoirs*, 1:446–47; Pritchard, *Louis XV's Navy*, 56, and "French Naval Officers Corps," 66n.

57. Le Goff, "Problèmes de recrutement," 231–32; Pritchard, "French Navy," in Love, *Changing Interpretations*, 147.

58. B³527: 267–68; B⁴94: 34; Pritchard, *Louis XV's Navy*, 215–22; Legohérel, *Les Trésoriers généraux*, chart facing 180; Neuville, *État sommaire*, 616–17; Mackay, *Admiral Hawke*, 305.

59. Droysen, *Politische Correspondenz*, 13:29, Knyphausen to Frederick II, 25 June 1756. For the *vingtième* (one-twentieth) tax, see Michael Kwass, *Privilege and the Politics of Taxation in Eighteenth-Century France: Liberté, Egalité, Fiscalité* (Cambridge: Cambridge University Press, 2000), 32–47, 67–68.

60. Marion, *Histoire Financière*, 1:180–83; Rathery, *Journal d'Argenson*, 9:286, 288, 328, 350–51, 369; Bonnet, *Mémoires de Bernis*, 139–40; Kwass, *Privilege*, 160–61; Julian Swann, *Politics and the Parlement of Paris under Louis XV, 1754–1774* (Cambridge: Cambridge University Press, 1995), 86–133, 160–82; Dale E. Van Kley, *The Damiens Affair and the Unraveling of the Ancien Régime, 1750–1770* (Princeton: Princeton University Press, 1984), 56–57, 85–86, 99–165; Jean Egret, *Louis XV et l'opposition parliamentaire, 1715–1774* (Paris: Armand Colin, 1970), 76–80.

61. Machault's plans are discussed in B^{2}353, B^{4}72 and B^{4}73, and B^{5}3; see also B^{4}75: 4–5.

62. B^{2}352: 1; B^{3}526: 60–65; Crowhurst, *Defence of British Trade*, 229–30; Jean Boudriot, *Compagnie des Indes, 1720–1770: Vaisseaux, hommes, voyages, commerce*, 2 vols. (Paris: Jean Boudriot, 1983), 1:18–129, 2: passim; Philippe Haudrère, "La Flotte de la compagnie française des Indes durant les conflits maritimes du milieu du XVIIIe siècle," in Acerra et al., *Les Marines de guerre*, 272–73 and *La Compagnie française des Indes au XVIIIe siècle (1719–1795)*, 4 vols. (Paris: Librairie de l'Inde, 1989), 2:487–538, 4:1227–53.

63. B^{4}73: 212–60. For d'Aché see Vérge-Franceschi, *Les Officiers généraux*, 1:20–23; 3:1070–77; 7:444–45.

64. B^{4}73: 3–17.

65. B^{4}77: 3–49.

66. Tibulle Hamont, *La fin d'un empire français aux Indes sous Louis XV: Lally-Tollendal d'après des documents inédits* (Paris: E. Plon, Nourrit, 1887), 59–72.

67. Bonnet, *Mémoires de Bernis*, 187–90; Waddington, *La Guerre*, 1:70, 93–95.

68. Waddington, *Louis XV*, 275–76 (quoting from Newcastle to the Hanoverian minister, Freiherr Gerlach Adolf von Münchhausen, 13 February 1756 and to Joseph Yorke, 23 March 1756); Horn, *Williams*, 211–12 (quoting from Newcastle to Count William Bentinck, 10 February 1756).

69. Waddington, *Louis XV*, 226–29, 347–48; Carter, *Dutch Republic*, 17–21, 50–63; Bussemaker, *Archives*, 3:9–10, 27, 32, 56, 69–70, 85; Richard Pares, *Colonial Blockade and Neutral Rights, 1739–1763* (Oxford: Clarendon Press, 1938), 243–45.

70. Savory, *His Britannic Majesty's Army*, 5; *London Evening Post*, issues of 20–22 May 1756 and 25–27 May 1756; Dann, *Hanover and Britain*, 96; Charteris, *Cumberland*, 203; Cobbett and Hansard, *Parliamentary History*, 15: 700–701; Clark, *Dynamics of Change*, 234–36.

71. Yorke, *Hardwicke*, 2:261; Gould, *Persistence of Empire*, 50–52.

72. Waddington, *Louis XV*, 343–44; Arneth, *Geschichte Maria Theresia's*, 4:456; Kaplan, *Russia*, 72–73.

73. Waddington, *Louis XV*, 221, 313; Droysen, *Politische Correspondenz*, 12:71n, 93n–96n, 105–6n, Knyphausen to Frederick II, 23 January, 30 January, and 2 February 1756; Broglie, *L'Alliance autrichienne*, 288, 314.

74. Droysen, *Politische Correspondenz*, 12:72–73, 93–99, 162–65, Frederick II to Knyphausen, 3 February, 10 February, and 2 March 1756; Waddington, *Louis XV*, 252–59, 313; Broglie, *L'Alliance autrichienne*, 319–20.

75. For the Nivernais and Valory negotiations, see Waddington, *Louis XV*, 249–83,

316; Broglie, *L'Alliance autrichienne*, 266–83, 311–29; Droysen, *Politische Correspondenz*, 12:162–65, 180, Frederick II to Knyphausen, 2 and 9 March 1756; Doran, *Andrew Mitchell*, 40; Rathery, *Journal d'Argenson*, 9:200; Herpin, *Nivernais*, 365–99; Waddington, *Recueil*, 16:472–74; Valori, *Mémoires de Valori*, 1:302–14; 2:1–216.

76. Droysen, *Politische Correspondenz*, 12:117–18, 162–65, Frederick II to Knyphausen, 16 February and 2 March 1756; Waddington, *Louis XV*, 268–69.

77. Droysen, *Politische Correspondenz*, 12:118–19n, Knyphausen to Frederick II, 8 February 1756; Waddington, *Louis XV*, 267–68 and *La Guerre*, 3:449–50; Bonnet, *Mémoires de Bernis*, 164–65.

78. The negotiations are discussed by Waddington, *Louis XV*, 301–32; Broglie, *L'Alliance autrichienne*, 330–415; Arneth, *Geschichte Maria Theresia's*, 4:462–72; Batzel, "Austria," 112–39, 542–43; Cahen, "Les Mémoires de Bernis," 73–99. For Aubeterre and Bernis, see Austria 255: 246–54; Bonnet, *Mémoires de Bernis*, 176–78; Didier Ozanam, ed., *Receuil des instructins données aux ambassadeurs et ministres de France depuis les traités de Westphalie jusqu'à la revolution française*, vol. 27, *Espagne, tome quatrième, volume complimentaire* (Paris: Editions du Centre de la recherché scientifique, 1960), 80.

79. For her 4 March instructions to Starhemberg on the subject, see Batzel, "Austria," 125.

80. Rathery, *Journal d'Argenson*, 9:216, 219, 222–23, 225, 232, 249; Grouchy and Cottin, *Journal de Croÿ*, 1:346–49. Antoine, *Le Gouvernement*, 201; Bonnet, *Memoires de Bernis*, 176–78.

81. Van Kley, *Damiens Affair*, 145; Rathery, *Journal d'Argenson*, 9:241–42, 247, 267, 287, 290; Antoine, *Le Gouvernement*, 26, 225. On 2 May Starhemberg sent Kaunitz an account of the final negotiations: Gustav Berthold Volz and George Küntzel, eds., *Preussische und Osterreichische Acten zur Vorgeschichte des Siebenjährigen Krieges* (Leipzig: S. Hirzel, 1899), 330–37. See also Starhemberg to Kaunitz, 17 April, ibid., 305–10.

82. The neutrality convention and treaty are reproduced in Parry, *Consolidated Treaty Series*, 40:331–34, 335–49 and analyzed in Waddington, *Louis XV*, 333–71. See also Valori, *Mémoires de Valori*, 2:54–68.

83. Waddington, *Louis XV*, 338; Broglie, *L'Alliance autrichienne*, 378–80, 388.

84. Bonnet, *Mémoires de Bernis*, 171.

85. Bonnet, *Mémoires de Bernis*, 174.

86. Volz and Küntzel, *Acten*, 338–41; Broglie, *L'Alliance autrichienne*, 450–55.

87. Bonnet, *Mémoires de Bernis*, 184; Waddington, *Louis XV*, 464, 469, 477, and *La Guerre*, 1:70, 76–77.

88. Droysen, *Politische Correspondenz*, 12:322–23, Frederick II to Dodo Heinrich, Baron von Knyphausen, 11 May 1756; Waddington, *Louis XV*, 358, 480; Broglie, *L'Alliance autrichienne*, 399.

89. Waddington, *Louis XV*, 343–46; Broglie, *L'Alliance autrichienne*, 395–97; Arneth, *Geschichte Maria Theresia's*, 4:457.

90. Droysen, *Politische Correspondenz*, 12:435–36, Secretary of State Graf Karl Wilhelm Finck von Finckenstein to Frederick II, 19 June 1756; Savelle, *Origins of American Diplomacy*, 440–41; Corbett, *England in the Seven Years' War*, 1:144–45; Pares, *Colonial*

Blockade, 286–87; Glete, *Navies and Nations*, 1:269; Lodge, "Keene," 36–37; Bonner-Smith, *Barrington Papers*, 1:147.

91. Holland 491: 192–93; Pares, *Colonial Blockade*, 249–51, 293–301; Carter, *Dutch Republic*, 66–83, 88, 98, 104–5, 112–17; Parry, *Consolidated Treaty Series*, 40:373–85; Gunner Lind, "The Making of the Neutrality Convention of 1756: France and Her Scandinavian Allies," *Scandinavian Journal of History* 8 (1983): 171–92; Michael Roberts, *The Age of Liberty: Sweden, 1719–1772* (New York: Cambridge University Press, 1986), 178–82; Pierre Muret, *La Préponderance anglaise (1713–1763)*, 3rd ed. (Paris: Presses universitaires de France, 1949), 509; Roger Charles Anderson, *Naval Wars in the Baltic, 1522–1850*, rev. ed. (London: Francis Edwards, 1969), 223.

92. Russia 52: 82–90, 106–13; Browning, *War of the Austrian Succession*, 272; Kaplan, *Russia*, 36–79, 84–85, 93–98, 112, 115–17; Waddington, *Louis XV*, 350–55, 486–87, and *La Guerre*, 1:197–201; Broglie, *L'Alliance autrichienne*, 356–59; Parry, *Consolidated Treaty Series*, 40:437–50; Oliva, *Misalliance*, 31–33; Glete, *Navies and Nations*, 1:302; 2:654; Duffy, *Austrian Army*, 122; Horn, *Williams*, 221–76; Sir Herbert Butterfield, *The Reconstruction of an Historical Episode: The History of the Enquiry into the Origins of the Seven Years' War* (Glasgow: Jackson, Son, 1951), 31–38. For the exchange rate between florins and livres, see Waddington, *La Guerre*, 3:452.

93. Bonnet, *Mémoires de Bernis*, 179.

94. The initial phase of the negotiations (May to August 1756) is discussed in Bonnet, *Mémoires de Bernis*, 179–80; Waddington, *Louis XV*, 337–39, 462–76, 519–20; Batzel, "Austria," 152–91; Volz and Küntzel, *Acten*, 344–54, 360–66, 384–92, 396–410, 413–19, 422–23, 434, 438–39, 442–53, 466, 476–81, 484–93, 502–9, 512–44, 549–56, 566–71. For the ongoing Franco-Austrian dispute about an attack on Hanover, see Batzel, "Austria," 213–14, 218, 226, 235–36.

95. Pick, *Maria Theresa*, 263; Dickson, *Maria Theresia*, 2:37, 101.

96. Anthony Hull, *Charles III and the Revival of Spain* (Washington: University Press of America, 1981), 84–85.

97. Broglie, *L'Alliance autrichienne*, 360–61, 392–93; Waddington, *Louis XV*, 468–69, 522–24; Droysen, *Politische Correspondenz*, 9:328–29; 12:195; Karl W. Schweizer, *Frederick the Great, William Pitt, and Lord Bute: The Anglo-Prussian Alliance, 1756–1763* (New York: Garland, 1991), 16.

98. Droysen, *Politische Correspondenz*, 12:380, 426–46; 13:97–100, 114; Waddington, *Louis XV*, 480–84, 493; Doran, *Andrew Mitchell*, 58–60, 66, 93n.

99. Corbett, *England in the Seven Years' War*, 1:146; Droysen, *Politische Correspondenz*, 12:399–400; Doran, Andrew Mitchell, 73–74; Kaplan, Russia, 82.

100. Corbett, *England in the Seven Years' War*, 1:146–48; Droysen, *Politische Correspondenz*, 13:26, 34–35, 95–100, 123, 188, 240–42, 247; Doran, *Andrew Mitchell*, 58–99; Waddington, *Louis XV*, 485–91; Horn, *Williams*, 238–39, 284.

101. Droysen, *Politische Correspondenz*, 12:329; Dorn, *Competition for Empire*, 303–4.

102. Droysen, *Politische Correspondenz*, 13:130–34 and passim; Butterfield, *Reconstruc-*

tion, 9–12, 22–23; Bonnet, *Mémoires de Bernis*, 181; Broglie, *L'Alliance autrichienne*, 406–7; Valori, *Mémoires de Valori*, 2:100–101, 121–27.

103. Waddington, *Louis XV*, 498, 504–5 and *La Guerre*, 1:4–44; Dickson, *Maria Theresia*, 2:356; Christopher Duffy, *Frederick the Great: A Military Life* (London: Routledge and Kegan Paul, 1985), 84–110.

104. Droysen, *Politische Correspondenz*, 13:424–25, Knyphausen to Frederick II, 10 September 1756.

105. Waddington, *Louis XV*, 520, and *La Guerre*, 1:14, 45–49, 56–57, 117–18, 168; Droysen, *Politische Correspondenz*, 13:293–94, 424–25, 433–35, 496, 503–4, 581–82; 14:6–7; Valori, *Mémoires de Valori*, 1:313–14; 2:210–15, 349–59; Bonnet, *Mémoires de Bernis*, 191.

106. Schweizer, *Anglo-Prussian Alliance*, 41; Doran, *Andrew Mitchell*, 101; Dann, *Hanover and Britain*, 105.

107. Droysen, *Politische Correspondenz*, 13:124–25, 191–94, 578–79; 14:56–60, 63–66, 117–23, 133–34; Doran, *Andrew Mitchell*, 62, 80–81, 88, 100–101, 116–20; Corbett, *England in the Seven Years' War*, 1:147–48, 153–56; Waddington, *Louis XV*, 490–91, and *La Guerre*, 1:157–73; Jeremy Black, "Naval Power and British Foreign Policy in the Age of Pitt the Elder," in Black and Woodfine, *British Navy*, 100.

108. Schweizer, *Anglo-Prussian Alliance*, 69n; Doran, *Andrew Mitchell*, 112, 120–24; Clark, *Dynamics of Change*, 302–3, 310; Middleton, *Bells of Victory*, 10.

109. Austria 256: 60–475; Austria 256 ^bis^: passim; Austria 257: 3; Holland 491: 407–10; Bonnet, *Mémoires de Bernis*, 183–93, 214; Waddington, *La Guerre*, 1:60–106; Dann, *Hanover and Great Britain*, 104–8; Batzel, "Austria," 212–67, 305, 563–615; Dussieux and Soulié, *Mémoires de Luynes*, 15:233; Pajol, *Les Guerres*, 4:49–50; Albert Sorel, ed., *Recueil des instruction données aux ambassadeurs et ministres de France depuis les traités de Westphalie jusqu'à la révolution française*, vol. 1, *Autriche* (Paris: Félix Alcan, 1884), 338–53.

110. Dann, *Hanover and Britain*, 108; Waddington, *La Guerre*, 1:179; Batzel, "Austria," 265.

111. Russia 52:37–59, Douglas to Rouillé, 26 January 1757; Kaplan, *Russia*, 62–64, 76–78, 94–119; Oliva, *Misalliance*, 29–57; Waddington, *La Guerre*, 1:14–15, 63–64, 81–82, 99–100, 111–18, 197–200; Horn, *Williams*, 266–67, 275–76; Ozanam and Antoine, *Correspondance de Broglie*, 1:xl–xliii, 1–5; Boutaric, *Correspondance secrète de Louis XV*, 1:212–14; Flammermont, *Rapport*, 171–72; Antoine, *Louis XV*, 728; Van Kley, *Damiens Affair*, 64–65, 143–47; Alfred Rambaud, ed., *Recueil des instructions données aux ambassadeurs et ministres de France depuis les traités de Westphalie jusqu'à la révolution française*, vol. 9, *Russie, tome deuxième* (Paris: Félix Alcan, 1890), 18–27.

4. 1757—TO THE EDGE OF VICTORY

1. Swann, *Politics and the Parlement of Paris*, 110, 124.

2. Swann, *Politics and the Parlement of Paris*, 91–92, 125–33, 160–82; Van Kley, *Damiens Affair*, 145–52.

3. Van Kley, *Damiens Affair*, 3–13; Grouchy and Cottin, *Journal de Croÿ*, 1:364–66.

4. Swann, *Politics and the Parlement of Paris*, 142–43; Van Kley, *Damiens Affair*, 152–53; Bonnet, *Mémoires de Bernis*, 217, 225–26.

5. John D. Woodbridge, *Revolt in Prerevolutionary France: The Prince de Conti's Conspiracy against Louis XV, 1755–1757* (Baltimore: Johns Hopkins University Press, 1995), 135; Francis Thackeray, *A History of the Right Honourable William Pitt, Earl of Chatham*, 2 vols. (London: C. and J. Rivington, 1827), 1:521–22.

6. Waddington, *La Guerre*, 1:135–36; Brooke, *Walpole Memoirs*, 2:198.

7. Swann, *Politics and the Parlement of Paris*, 144–50; Van Kley, *Damiens Affair*, 153–55; Bonnet, *Mémoires de Bernis*, 203–12; Egret, *Louis XV*, 85–86; Merrick, *Desacrilization*, 96–104.

8. Waddington, *La Guerre*, 1:141–44; Bonnet, *Mémoires de Bernis*, 225–26; Van Kley, *Damiens Affair*, 152–53; Swann, *Politics and the Parlement of Paris*, 142–43; Antoine, *Louis XV*, 721–23; Combeau, *Argenson*, 187–90; Pritchard, *Louis XV's Navy*, 68.

9. Bonnet, *Mémoires de Bernis*, 225; Pritchard, *Louis XV's Navy*, 10–11; Chabaud-Arnault, "Etudes historiques," *Revue maritime* 114 (1892): 483; Lacour-Gayet, *La Marine militaire*, 241; Maupassant, *Gradis*, 66, 241.

10. Waddington, *La Guerre*, 1:144; Antoine, *Le Gouvernement*, 249.

11. Bonnet, *Mémoires de Bernis*, 220; Dussieux and Soulié, *Mémoires de Luynes*, 15:373. For a contemporary appraisal of the dauphin by the Saxon minister at the French court, see Flammermont, *Rapport*, 175. See also Grouchy and Cottin, *Journal de Croij*, 1:434.

12. Pargellis, *Lord Loudoun*, 109–10; Arthur G. Doughty, ed., *A Historical Journal of the Campaigns in North America for the Years 1757, 1758, 1759, and 1760 by Captain John Knox*, 3 vols. (Toronto: Champlain Society, 1914–16), 1:15–17; Brumwell, *Redcoats*, 20.

13. For a critical view of Holburne, see Erskine, *Hervey's Journal*, 248.

14. See appendix F; Doughty, *Historical Journal*, 1:19–49; Pargellis, *Lord Loudoun*, 230–43, 265–67, and *Military Affairs*, 317–27, 343–79, 387–94; Kimball, *Correspondence of Pitt*, 1:14–22, 34–51, 69–80; Middleton, *Bells of Victory*, 11–12; Gipson, *British Empire*, 7:91–95, 102–3, 108–14, 148; Nash, *Urban Crucible*, 239; McLennan, *Louisbourg*, 204; Hamilton, *Adventure in the Wilderness*, 140; Jeremy Black, *Pitt the Elder* (Cambridge: Cambridge University Press, 1992), 172–73; Jesse Lemisch, "Jack Tar in the Streets: Merchant Seamen in the Politics of Revolutionary America," *Willam and Mary Quarterly*, 3rd ser., 25 (1968): 383.

15. B^{4}75: 11; B^{4}76: 98–99, 108, 110, 114, 130–31; Clowes, *Royal Navy*, 3:294; Corbett, *England in the Seven Years' War*, 1:359–60; *London Evening Post*, 1–3 February 1757; Middleton, "British Naval Strategy," 355. For Bauffremont, see Vergé-Franceschi, *Les Officiers généraux*, 1:32–33; 5:2338–47.

16. B^{2}357: 1, 10, 31; B^{3}536: 53; Clowes, *Royal Navy*, 3:169–70; Lacour-Gayet, *La Marine militaire*, 383; Chabaud-Arnault, "Etudes historiques," *Revue maritime* 114 (1892): 487. For Revest see Halpenny, *Dictionary of Canadian Biography*, 3:93.

17. B^{2}353: 44; B^{4}75: 4–5.

18. B^{3}354: 20; B^{4}74: 117–18; B^{4}75: 4–5; B^{4}76: passim; B^{4}78: 44, 129–35 (and also some information in B^{2}356 and 358); Middleton, "British Naval Strategy," 355–56; Clowes, *Royal Navy*, 3:168–69, 172; Doughty, *Historical Journal*, 1:100–101; Kimball, *Correspondence of*

Pitt, 1:84–85; Pargellis, *Lord Loudoun*, 238; Waddington, *La Guerre*, 1:252–56; Le Goff, "Problèmes de recrutement," 219–20, 222, 226–27; Pritchard, *Louis XV's Navy*, 83–84; Brun, *Port de Toulon*, 1:394; Jean-Pierre Goubert, *Malades et médecins en Bretagne, 1770–1790* (Paris: C. Klincksieck, 1974), 332–37; Prosper-Jean Levot, *Histoire de la ville et du port de Brest*, vol. 2, *Le Port depuis 1681* (Paris: Bachelin-Deflorenne, 1865), 114–39; O. Troude, *Batailles navales de la France*, vol. 1 (Paris: Challamel ainé, 1867), 343–44.

19. Bertrand, "Dunkerque," 323–25.

20. $B^4$76: 198–99; Waddington, *La Guerre*, 1:271–72; Hamilton, *Adventure in the Wilderness*, 115, 138–39, 181–83; Blanchet, *Collection des manuscrits*, 4:83–85; Casgrain, *Collection des manuscrits*, 3:67–71; 7:304–5; Gilles Archambault, "La Question des vivres au Canada au cours de l'hiver 1757–1758," *Revue d'histoire de l'Amérique française* 21 (1967–68): 20; William J. Eccles, *The Canadian Frontier, 1534–1760*, rev. ed. (Albuquerque: University of New Mexico Press, 1983), 176.

21. Hamilton, *Adventure in the Wilderness*, 113, 116, 185; Casgrain, *Collection des manuscrits*, 6:59; 7:212, 216, 304; Archambault, "La Question des vivres," 36–37; Gipson, *British Empire*, 7:106n; Garnault, *Le Commerce rochelais*, 154–56; O'Callaghan, *Documents*, 10:666–67; Maupassant, *Gradis*, 59–64, 176–80; Bosher, *Canada Merchants*, 149–50, 180; Edouard Ducéré, *Histoire maritime de Bayonne: Les Corsairs sous l'ancien régime* (Bayonne, France: E. Hourquet, 1895), 255; François Caron, *La Guerre incomprise; ou, les raisons d'un échec (capitulation de Louisbourg, 1758)* (Vincennes, France: Service historique de la marine, 1983), 236.

22. Pargellis, *Military Affairs*, 370–72, Loudoun to Webb, 20 June 1757; Pargellis, *Lord Loudoun*, 211–27, 245n; Gipson, *British Empire*, 7:31–45, 96–99, 141–47; Nash, *Urban Crucible*, 242; Kimball, *Correspondence of Pitt*, 1:3–6; O'Callaghan, *Documents*, 7:216; Anderson, *People's Army*, 13, 59n; Selesky, *War and Society*, 108–10, 168; Titus, *Old Dominion*, 90, 102–7; Ward, *Stephen*, 42–47; Rogers, *Empire and Liberty*, 47; Douglas Edward Leach, *Roots of Conflict: British Armed Forces and Colonial Americans, 1677–1763* (Chapel Hill: University of North Carolina Press, 1986), 93–94; Hayes Baker-Crothers, *Virginia and the French and Indian War* (Chicago: University of Chicago Press, 1928), 115–25.

23. Hamilton, *Adventure in the Wilderness*, 88; Casgrain, *Collection des manuscrits*, 2:148–50; 7:162–63; Archambault, "La Question des vivres," 20–22.

24. The Fort William Henry campaign is the subject of an excellent book, Steele, *Betrayals*, which largely exonerates Montcalm from the charges of complicity in the massacre. See also Hamilton, *Adventure in the Wilderness*, 85–87, 112, 119, 122–79; Blanchet, *Collection des manuscrits*, 4:89–93, 100–125; Casgrain, *Collection des manuscrits*, 1:88–103; 2:109–35; 5:163–92; 7:151–54, 223–307; O'Callaghan, *Documents*, 10:542–625; Pargellis, *Lord Loudoun*, 235, 243–51; Gipson, *British Empire* 7:62–89; Selesky, *War and Society*, 110; Michalon, "Vaudreuil et Montcalm," in Delmas, *Conflits*, 105–6, 133–35; La Pause, "Mémoire," 54–55; Chapais, *Montcalm*, 217–18; Bellico, *Sails and Steam*, 39–57; James Sullivan et al., eds., *The Papers of Sir William Johnson*, 14 vols. (Albany: University of the State of New York, 1921–65), 2:728–30; Abbé Henri-Raymond Casgrain, *Guerre du Canada, 1756–1760: Montcalm et Lévis*, 2 vols. (Quebec: L.-J. Demers et frère, 1891), 2:449–51.

25. B^{2}356: 275; B^{4}75: 11; B^{4}76: 3, 198–99; B^{4}77: 3–49, 102; B^{4}96: 34, 47; Clowes, *Royal Navy*, 3:164–66, 297; Corbett, *England in the Seven Years' War*, 1:363–69; Bonner-Smith, *Barrington Papers*, 1:170–71, 185–93. For Kersaint, see Lacour-Gayet, *La Marine militaire*, 525n.

26. B^{4}75: 11; B^{4}76: 200, 203; B^{4}77: 133–82, 282–88; Corbett, *England in the Seven Years' War*, 1:340; Hamont, *Lally-Tollendal*, 73; Taylor and Pringle, *Correspondence of Chatham*, 1:206–9, Mitchell to Holdernesse, 9 December 1756; Ayling, *Pitt*, 139; Jacques Michel, *La Vie aventureuse et mouvementée de Charles-Henri, comte d'Estaing* ([Paris]: privately printed, 1976), 28–29. See also appendix F.

27. For the distribution of the French navy, see appendix F.

28. Vergé-Franceschi, *Les Officiers généraux*, 5:2325; Riley, *Seven Years War*, 109–10; Romano, "Balance du commerce," 2:1274, 1291; Boulle, "French Colonies," 96–97n; Villiers, "Commerce coloniale," 35, and *Marine royale*, 2:451–54, 463; Garnault, *Le Commerce rochelais*, 4:157–59; Butel, "La Guerre maritime," in France, Service historique de la marine, *Guerres et paix*, 299; Halgouet, *Nantes*, 76.

29. B^{4}75: 9–10.

30. Clark, *Dynamics of Change*, 302–6, 310–11, 327–28, 354–59, and *Waldegrave*, 188–95.

31. Clark, *Waldegrave*, 195–96; Erskine, *Hervey's Journal*, 244; Richmond, *Navy*, 1:196, 224–25; 2:145. For the workings of the British convoy system, see R. P. Crowhurst, "The Admiralty and the Convoy System in the Seven Years' War," *Mariner's Mirror* 57 (1971): 163–73.

32. Clark, *Waldegrave*, 196–211, and *Dynamics of Change*, 353–447; Baxter, "Conduct," in Baxter, *England's Rise*, 334–35, 340; Browning, *Duke of Newcastle*, 256–61; Middleton, "Pitt," 190–92.

33. Newcastle to Mitchell, 16 July 1757, quoted in Corbett, *England in the Seven Years' War*, 1:179.

34. Middleton, *Bells of Victory*, 26–31; Woodbridge, *Revolt*, 97–105; William Kent Hackmann, "English Military Expeditions to the Coast of France, 1757–1761" (Ph.D. diss., University of Michigan, Ann Arbor, 1969), 18–33; Rex Whitworth, *Field Marshal Lord Ligonier: A Study of the British Army, 1702–1770* (Oxford: Clarendon Press, 1958), 212.

35. Holland 495: 243, Bernis to d'Affry, 15 September 1757; B^{2}356: 1–80, 211–43; B^{3}552: 106–11; B^{4}74: 88–111; B^{4}75: 9–10, 41–43; B^{5}7: 8; Hackmann, "English Military Expeditions," 34–74; Lacour-Gayet, *La Marine militaire*, 317–18, 327–32; Corbett, *England in the Seven Years' War*, 1:200–222; Boulle, "French Colonies," 110–11; Garnault, *Le Commerce rochelais*, 167; Dussieux and Soulié, *Mémoires de Luynes*, 16: 146–47; Waddington, *La Guerre*, 1:462; Harding, *Amphibious Warfare*, 181–82; Mouffle d'Angerville, *Vie privée*, 3:323–25; Mackay, *Admiral Hawke*, 159–78, 184–85 and *Hawke Papers*, 149–88; William Kent Hackmann, "The British Raid on Rochefort, 1757," *Mariner's Mirror* 64 (1978), 263–75; E. R. Adair, "The Military Reputation of Major-General James Wolfe," in Canadian Historical Association, *Report of the Annual Meeting Held at Ottawa, May 26–27, 1936* (Toronto: University of Toronto Press, 1936), 13.

36. B^{2}357: 221 and passim; B^{3}535 and B^{3}536: passim; B^{4}75: 56, 108–30; B^{4}77: 121–22, 127; Brun, *Port de Toulon*, 1:394–403. See also appendix F. For La Clue see Vergé-

Franceschi, *Les Officiers généraux*, 1:38–39; 2:880, 886–92. For the activities of the British Mediterrranean fleet during 1757, see Erskine, *Hervey's Journal*, 246–67.

37. B¹66: unpaginated, memoir of 22 May 1757; G 49: 46; Pritchard, *Louis XV's Navy*, 132–33; Demerliac, *La Marine de Louis XV*, 35, 40, 46.

38. For the number of ships of the line in service, see appendix F, and for British naval construction, see Lyon, *Sailing Navy List*, 62–63, 66–67, 73, 76–77, 82–83, 85, 90; Lavery, *Ship of the Line*, 173–77.

39. Gradish, *Manning*, 42; Le Goff, "Problèmes de recrutement," 212, 223, 225; Lloyd, *British Seaman*, 287–88; Rodger, *Wooden World*, 149, 178; Starkey, "War and the Market for Seamen," 32, 40; Robinson, "Secret of British Power," 5–21; Baugh, *British Naval Administration*, 205; Larry Neal, "Interpreting Power and Profit in Economic History: A Case Study of the Seven Years War," *Journal of Economic History* 37 (1977): 22, 26.

40. Pritchard, *Louis XV's Navy*, 80–81, 135; T. J. A. Le Goff, "Problèmes de recrutement," 212, 218–21, 225, 231–32; Ducéré, *Bayonne*, 269, 278–87, 297–98; Crowhurst, *Defence of British Trade*, 20, 29, 32; Neal, "Interpreting Power and Profit," 29; Starkey, *British Privateering Enterprise*, 178; Pierre Vignes, *L'Armament en course à Bayonne de 1744 à 1783* (Bordeaux: Imprimerie Bière, 1942), 34–35; John Dobson, *Chronological Annals of the War: From Its Beginning to the Present Time* (Oxford: Clarendon Press, 1763), 33–44; Isaac Schomberg, *The Naval Chronology; or, An Historical Summary of Naval and Maritime Events from the Time of the Romans to the Treaty of Peace of Amiens*, 5 vols. (London: T. Egerton, 1815), 5:29–32; John Entick et al., *The General History of the Late War: Containing Its Rise, Progress and Event, in Europe, Asia, Africa, and America*, 5 vols. (London: Edward Dilly and John Millan, 1763–64), 3:33.

41. Pritchard, *Louis XV's Navy*, 154, 175; Middleton, *Bells of Victory*, 127; James Pritchard, "Fir Trees," 351.

42. Riley, *Seven Years War*, 137, 140–41; Pritchard, *Louis XV's Navy*, 193–94, 215–22; Mackay, *Admiral Hawke*, 305; Legohérel, *Les Trésoriers généraux*, chart facing 180; Neuville, *Etat sommaire*, 616–17; Sturgill, "French Army's Budget," 131;Mitchell and Deane, *Abstract*, 387, 390; Félix, *L'Averdy*, 42; Chris Cook and John Stevenson, comps., *British Historical Facts, 1688–1760* (London: Macmillan, 1988), 173. A table listing French loans from 1747 to 1788 is in François R. Velde and David R. Weir, "The Financial Market and Government Debt Policy in France, 1746–1793," *Journal of Economic History* 52 (1992): 20.

43. Schöne, "La Politique de la France," 96; Boulle, "French Colonies," 101; Maupassant, *Gradis*, 65; Frégault, *Bigot*, 2:225; Michel Allard, *La Nouvelle France* (Montreal: Guérin, 1976), 67; André Coté,*Joseph-Michel Câdet, 1717–1781: Négociant et munitionnaire du roi en Nouvelle-France* (Sillery, Canada: Septentrion; Paris: Christian, 1998), table 20.

44. Pritchard, *Louis XV's Navy*, 10, 194. For Boullongne, see Antoine, *Le Gouvernement*, 48–49, and Amédée, Vicomte de Caix de Saint-Aymour, *Une Famille d'artistes et des financiers au XVIIIe et XVIIIe siècles: Les Boullongne* (Paris: Henri Laurens, 1919), 63–86, 117–39.

45. Casgrain, *Collection des manuscrits*, 7:322; Hamilton, *Adventure in the Wilderness*, 192; MacLeod, "Microbes and Muskets," 49; Steele, *Betrayals*, 132, 135, 143.

46. Casgrain, *Collection des manuscrits*, 1:118–19; 6:63–65, 92–93; 7:323; Hamilton, *Ad-*

venture in the Wilderness, 140, 175–77, 181, 187–88; Waddington, *La Guerre*, 1:273–75; 2:372–73; Frégault, *Bigot*, 2:220, 231–36; O'Callaghan, *Documents*, 10:584–86, 666–67, 686; Dunnigan, *Memoirs by Pouchot*, 133–34, 163n, 164n; Archambault, "La Question des vivres," 17–32; Lunn, "Agriculture and War," 131–32; Arthur G. Doughty, ed., "Montcalm's Correspondence," in *Report of the Public Archives of Canada for the Year 1929* (Ottawa: F. A. Acland, 1930), 63.

47. Steele, *Betrayals*, 132; MacLeod, "Microbes and Muskets," 50; White, *Middle Ground*, 245–47; McConnell, *A Country Between*, 128–29.

48. O'Callaghan, *Documents*, 7:280–321; Jennings, *Empire of Fortune*, 337, 342–47; Wallace, *Teedyuscung*, 162.

49. Alden, *Stuart*, 52–53, 61–62, 94–95; Dunbar Rowland, A. G. Sanders, and Patricia Kay Galloway, eds., *Mississippi Provincial Archives*, vol. 5, *French Dominion, 1749–1763* (Baton Rouge: Louisiana State University Press, 1984), 180–90; David H. Corkran, *Cherokee Frontier*, 100–141, and *The Creek Frontier, 1540–1783* (Norman: University of Oklahoma Press, 1967), 174–92.

50. Pargellis, *Military Affairs*, 383; Fortescue, *British Army*, 2:320; Kimball, *Correspondence of Pitt*, 1:209; Rogers, *British Army*, 25; Richard Middleton, "A Reinforcement for North America, Summer 1757," *Bulletin of the Institute of Historical Research* 41 (1968): 58–72.

51. Pritchard, *Louis XV's Navy*, 95; Middleton, *Bells of Victory*, 50; Kimball, *Correspondence of Pitt*, 1:89–90, 110–11, 125–26; Gwyn, "Royal Navy" in Black and Woodfine, *British Navy*, 139–40.

52. Boulle, "French Colonies," 110–22; Garnault, *Le Commerce rochelais*, 4:159, 166–67; Dussieux and Soulié, *Mémoires de Luynes*, 16:35; Roger Michalon, "Vaudreuil et Montcalm" in Delmas, *Conflits*, 106–7; Chabaud-Arnault, "Etudes historiques," *Revue maritime* 114 (1892): 483–85; Pares, *War and Trade*, 371–73; Bamford, *Forests and French Sea Power*, 63; Jacques Aman, *Les Officiers bleus dans la marine française au XVIIIᵉ siècle* (Geneva: Droz, 1976), 85–86.

53. Waddington, *La Guerre*, 1:146, 150. For Starhemberg's contempt for Rouillé see, for example, Batzel, "Austria," 184–85.

54. Waddington, *La Guerre*, 1:149n; Savelle, *Origins of American Diplomacy*, 446; Doran, *Andrew Mitchell*, 124; Bonnet, *Mémoires de Bernis*, 187.

55. Austria 256 bis: 373–74, Louis XV to Emperor Francis I, 11 February 1757; Austria 256 bis: 438, 449–53, Estrées to Rouillé, 27 February 1757 with enclosed convention of 25 February; Austria 257: 3, Chargé d'affaires Ratte to Rouillé, 2 March 1757; Holland 493: 407–10, memoir of Marshal Belle-Isle, 18 February 1757; Waddington, *La Guerre*, 1:104.

56. Russia 51: 91, Rouillé to Douglas, 20 November 1756; Russia 52: 129–34, Rouillé to Douglas, 16 February 1757; Russia 52: 155–77, Douglas to Rouillé, 26 February 1757 (new style); Oliva, *Misalliance*, 54–55, 59; Boutaric, *Correspondance secrète de Louis XV*, 1:217; Sorel, *Recueil*, 1:348; Marsangy, *Vergennes*, 2:38–43; Murphy, *Vergennes*, 103–8.

57. Russia 52: 215, 262–63, 324, 342–43; Waddington, *La Guerre*, 1:121–23; Oliva, *Misalliance*, 59–61; Sorel, *Essais d'histoire et de critique*, 183–207; Albert Vandal, *Louis XV et Elisabeth de Russie: Etude sur les relations de la France et de la Russie au dix-huitième siècle*

d'après les archives du Ministère des affaires étrangères, 3rd ed. (Paris: E. Plon, Nourrit, 1896), 300–302.

58. Marsangy, *Vergennes*, 2:12–17, 24–25, 34–37, 48; Murphy, *Vergennes*, 118.

59. Arneth, *Geschichte Maria Theresia's*, 5:54–71; Horn, *Williams*, 273–77; Batzel, "Austria," 273.

60. Oliva, *Misalliance*, 61–63; Boutaric, *Correspondance secrète de Louis XV*, 1:217–18, 222–24.

61. Waddington, *La Guerre*, 1:63, 81–82, 99–100; Batzel, "Austria," 253–54, 267–69.

62. Russia 53: 238; Oliva, *Misalliance*, 66; Batzel, "Austria" 175, 267–69; Waddington, *La Guerre*, 1:118–20; Ozanam and Antoine, *Correspondance de Broglie*, 1:xliii–xlvi, 5–12, 26–27, 35–38; Boutaric, *Correspondance secréte de Louis XV*, 1:85, 216, 220–21, 227; Louis Farges, ed., *Recueil des instruction données aux ambassadeurs et ministres de France depuis les traités de Westphalie jusqu'à la révolution française*, vol. 5, *Poland, tome second (1729–1794)* (Paris: Félix Alcan, 1888), 190–95.

63. H. S. K. Kent, *War and Trade in Northern Seas: Anglo-Scandinavian Economic Relations in the Mid-Eighteenth Century* (Cambridge: Cambridge University Press, 1973), 131, 137–39.

64. Sweden 232: 137–40, 145–47, 151–53, 233; Russia 52: 316, Douglas to Rouillé, 21 April 1757; Waddington, *La Guerre*, 1:80, 202–4; Oliva, *Misalliance*, 73–75; Parry, *Consolidated Treaty Series*, 31:127–47; 40:445–46, 457–73.

65. For the functioning of the Imperial Army and the competition for influence in Germany, see Waddington, *La Guerre*, 1:146–47, 173–75, 210–14; Bonnet, *Mémoires de Bernis*, 186; Eldon, *Subsidy Policy*, 88–91, 161; Savory, *His Britannic Majesty's Army*, 9–10, 449, 452–57; Pajol, *Les Guerres*, 4:54; John G. Gagliardo, *Reich and Nation: The Holy Roman Empire as Idea and Reality, 1763–1806* (Bloomington: Indiana University Press, 1980), 35–39; André Lebon, ed., *Recueil des instructions données aux ambassadeurs et ministres de France depuis les traités de Westphalie jusqu'à la révolution française*, vol. 7, *Bavière, Palatinat, Deux-Ponts* (Paris: Félix Alcan, 1889), 319n, 325–63, 469.

66. Waddington, *La Guerre*, 1:152, 205; Eldon, *Subsidy Policy*, 87–88, 94–95; Kent, *War and Trade*, 131–32, 142; Doran, *Andrew Mitchell*, 120, 129; Brooke, *Walpole Memoirs*, 2:255; Edouard-Marie, comte de Barthélemy, *Histoire des relations de la France et du Danemarck sous le ministère du comte de Bernstorff, 1751–1770* (Copenhagen: Jørgensen, 1887), 86–92; James Frederick Chance, ed., *British Diplomatic Instructions, 1689–1789*, vol. 3, *Denmark* (London: Royal Historical Society, 1926), 160–61.

67. Carter, *Dutch Republic*, 71, 110–12, 118–21, 147–48; Coquelle, *L'Alliance franco-hollandaise*, 74–77; Pares, *War and Trade*, 376–84; Bamford, *Forests and French Sea Power*, 64; Pajol, *Les Guerres*, 4:53.

68. Savory, *His Britannic Majesty's Army*, 9–13; Waddington, *La Guerre*, 1:184–96; Doran, *Andrew Mitchell*, 113–30; Batzel, "Austria," 281–88; Droysen, *Politische Correspondenz*, 14:380, 402–3, 501; Dann, *Hanover and Britain*, 108–9, 122; Charteris, *Cumberland*, 247.

69. Waddington, *La Guerre*, 1:148–50; Batzel, "Austria," 289–91.

70. Waddington, *La Guerre*, 1:150–51, 314; Batzel, "Austria," 292–93; Bonnet, *Mémoires de Bernis*, 228.

71. Parry, *Consolidated Treaty Series*, 41:1–44; Waddington, *La Guerre*, 1:151–56; Bonnet, *Mémoires de Bernis*, 230–31.

72. Droysen, *Politische Correspondenz*, 14:465; Savory, *His Britannic Majesty's Army*, 14.

73. Droysen, *Politische Correspondenz*, 14:63–66; Savory, *His Britannic Majesty's Army*, 13–14, 451; Coquelle, *L'Alliance franco-hollandaise*, 77–79; Waddington, *La Guerre*, 1:173, 194; Pajol, *Les Guerres*, 4:54.

74. Waddington, *La Guerre*, 1:389–90, 460; Dussieux and Soulié, *Mémoires de Luynes*, 16:46.

75. Droysen, *Politische Correspondenz*, 15:68–69, Estrées to Lieutenant General August Friedrich von Spörcken of the Army of Observation, 7 May 1757; Savory, *His Britannic Majesty's Army*, 22; Pajol, *Les Guerres*, 4:59.

76. Waddington, *La Guerre*, 1:380–81, 391; Dussieux and Soulié, *Mémoires de Luynes*, 15:398; Savory, *His Britannic Majesty's Army*, 22–24; Doran, *Andrew Mitchell*, 141–42.

77. Savory, *His Britannic Majesty's Army*, 22–28; Waddington, *La Guerre*, 1:380–426; Coquelle, *L'Alliance franco-hollandaise*, 79; Corbett, *England in the Seven Years' War*, 1:185–86.

78. Droysen, *Politische Correspondenz*, 14:238–39; Waddington, *La Guerre*, 1:412; Savory, *His Britannic Majesty's Army*, 25; Dann, *Hanover and Britain*, 110.

79. Droysen, *Politische Correspondenz*, 15:9, 14–15; Waddington, *La Guerre*, 1:280–311; Duffy, *Frederick the Great*, 111–22; Robert B. Asprey, *Frederick the Great: The Magnificent Enigma* (New York: Ticknor and Fields, 1986), 441–54.

80. Austria 258: 186, 332–53; Waddington, *La Guerre*, 1:321–27, 412–13, 447, 527–28; Dussieux and Soulié, *Mémoires de Luynes*, 16:86; Bonnet, *Mémoires de Bernis*, 231–36; Sorel, *Recueil*, 1:356–79; Van Kley, *Damiens Affair*, 143–44; Maurice, vicomte Boutry, ed., *Choiseul à Rome, 1754–1757: Lettres et mémoires inédits* (Paris: Calmann Lévy, 1895).

81. Holland 494: 322; Holland 495: 40, 52; Waddington, *La Guerre*, 1:327–28; Carter, *Dutch Republic*, 87; Coquelle, *L'Alliance franco-hollandaise*, 88, 93–102; Bussemaker, *Archives*, 3:527–29; Batzel, "Austria," 311; Lord John Russell, ed., *Correspondence of John, Fourth Duke of Bedford, Selected from the Originals at Woburn Abbey*, 3 vols. (London: Longman, Brown, Green, and Longmans, 1842–46), 2:259; Frederic Hervey et al., *The Naval History of Great Britain: From the Earliest Times to the Rising of the Parliament in 1779*, vol. 5 (London: J. Bew, 1779), 49–51.

82. Droysen, *Politische Correspondenz*, 15:84–85, 137, 159–60, 173–76; Waddington, *La Guerre*, 1:329–47; Duffy, *Frederick the Great*, 124–31; Asprey, *Frederick the Great*, 454–58.

83. Savory, *His Britannic Majesty's Army*, 28–38, 44–45; Waddington, *La Guerre*, 1:426–44.

84. Waddington, *La Guerre*, 1:396–97, 409–18, 424, 442–57, 528–29, 535–36; Bonnet, *Mémoires de Bernis*, 236–40. For the Paris brothers, see Dickson, *Maria Theresia*, 2:367–68.

85. Waddington, *La Guerre*, 1:444–45, 452–70, 478–79; Doran, *Andrew Mitchell*, 151; Dann, *Hanover and Britain*, 113; Middleton, *Bells of Victory*, 23–26; Grimoard, *Correspondance de Richelieu*, 1:29–40.

86. Russia 53: 10–11, 36–38; Waddington, *La Guerre*, 1:572–77; Oliva, *Misalliance*, 78–79; Anderson, *Naval Wars*, 223–24; Christopher Duffy, *Russia's Military Way to the West: Origins and Nature of Russian Military Power, 1700–1800* (London: Routledge and Kegan Paul, 1981), 74–76.

87. Droysen, *Politische Correspondenz*, 14:297, 305–6, 426, 446–47; 15:142–43, 161–62, 193–94, 199, 229–31, 236–37; Corbett, *England in the Seven Years' War*, 1:185, 187, 197–200; Anderson, *Naval Wars*, 223–26; Oliva, *Misalliance*, 76; Doran, *Andrew Mitchell*, 148–51; Grouchy and Cottin, *Journal de Croÿ*, 1:409–11; Hackmann, "English Military Expeditions," 24; Kent, *War and Trade*, 166; Andrew Bisset, ed., *Memoirs and Papers of Sir Andrew Mitchell, K. B., Envoy and Minister Plenipotentiary from the Court of Great Britain, to the Court of Prussia, from 1756 to 1771*, 2 vols. (London: Chapman and Hall, 1850), 1:254–65; John B. Hattendorf, R. J. B. Knight, A. W. H. Pearsall, N. A. M. Rodger, and Geoffrey Till, eds., *British Naval Documents, 1204–1960* (Aldershot, Eng.: Scolar Press for the Navy Records Society, 1993), 329–31.

88. Middleton, *Bells of Victory*, 31–33, 44; Taylor and Pringle, *Correspondence of Chatham*, 1:247–56, 263–77; Yorke, *Hardwicke*, 3:165–69; Kimball, *Correspondence of Pitt*, 1:105–6; Pares, *Colonial Blockade*, 286–88, and *War and Trade*, 561–62; Ilchester, *Fox*, 1:342; Black, *America or Europe?*, 152; Stetson Conn, *Gibraltar in British Diplomacy in the Eighteenth Century* (New Haven: Yale University Press; London: Humphrey Milford, Oxford University Press, 1942), 165–68; J. Leitch Wright Jr., *Anglo-Spanish Rivalry in North America* (Athens: University of Georgia Press, 1971), 105.

89. Russia 53: 86–89; Russia 54: 173, 211, 225, 302; Sweden 233: 27–32, 202–23; Waddington, *La Guerre*, 1:577–84; Duffy, *Russia's Military Way*, 76–81; Oliva, *Misalliance*, 79–82; Anderson, *Naval Wars in the Baltic*, 226; Parry, *Consolidated Treaty Series*, 41:101–30; A. Geffroy, ed., *Recueil des instruction données aux ambassadeurs et ministres de France depuis les traités de Westphalie jusqu'à la révolution française*, vol. 2, *Suède* (Paris: Félix Alcan, 1885), 383–400.

90. Droysen, *Politische Correspondenz*, 15:187, 218, 300–301, 338–40, 362, 377–78, 389–92; Waddington, *La Guerre*, 1:369–70, 378–79, 451, 584–93; Masson, *Mémoires et lettres de Bernis*, 2:122–25, 243–44; Sareil, *Les Tencin*, 411–13.

91. Middleton, *Bells of Victory*, 19–20.

92. Waddington, *La Guerre*, 1:479–85; Droysen, *Politische Correspondenz*, 15:317; Doran, *Andrew Mitchell*, 153; Dann, *Hanover and Great Britain*, 113–14; Chenevix Trench, *George II*, 283; see also Hardwicke to Newcastle, 7 August 1757, quoted in Black, *America or Europe?*, 24.

93. Waddington, *La Guerre*, 1:485–88, 502–3; Chenevix Trench, *George II*, 283–84; Droysen, *Politische Correspondenz*, 15:433; Charteris, *Cumberland*, 289–90; Middleton, *Bells of Victory*, 36.

94. Waddington, *La Guerre*, 1:489–90, 494–95; Doran, *Andrew Mitchell*, 151, 155–56; Middleton, *Bells of Victory*, 36; Corbett, *England in the Seven Years' War*, 1:198–99; Ayling, *Pitt*, 210.

95. Waddington, *La Guerre*, 1:465–66; Charteris, *Cumberland*, 297. Corbett, *England in the Seven Years' War*, 1:199, argues the logic of Richelieu's case.

96. Austria 260: 46–47, Bernis to Stainville, 8 November 1757; Waddington, *La Guerre*, 1:449–50, 454–55, 464, 537; Grimoard, *Correspondance de Richelieu*, 1:41–66.

97. Waddington, *La Guerre*, 1:464–67.

98. Parry, *Consolidated Treaty Series*, 41:51–56; Waddington, *La Guerre*, 1:470–72, 481; Dann, *Britain and Hanover*, 111, 113; Pajol, *Les Guerres*, 4:80–89; Barthélemy, *Histoire des relations*, 90, 96–100.

99. Waddington, *La Guerre*, 1:472–73; Grimoard, *Correspondance de Richelieu*, 1:177–86; Entick, *General History*, 2:276–80.

100. Yorke, *Hardwicke*, 3:180–81, 188; Charteris, *Cumberland*, 303–4, 310–13; Waddington, *La Guerre*, 1:499–506, 512–14; Chenevix Trench, *George II*, 284–85; Russell, *Correspondence of Bedford*, 2:275–80; Dann, *Hanover and Britain*, 115; Middleton, *Bells of Victory*, 44–46; Pargellis, *Lord Loudoun*, 340–41; Rex Whitworth, *Field Marshal Lord Ligonier: A Study of the British Army, 1702–1770* (Oxford: Clarendon Press, 1958), 226–28. For Frederick's humiliation of his brother see, for example, Droysen, *Politische Correspondenz*, 15:257–58.

101. Austria 259: 163–66, Bernis to Stainville, 12 September 1757; Austria 259: 212–15, Bernis to Ogier, 20 September 1757; Russia 54: 64; Holland 495: 524; Waddington, *La Guerre*, 1:474–75, 497, 509–12, 520; Bonnet, *Mémoires de Bernis*, 241–42, 254–55; Masson, *Mémoires et lettres de Bernis*, 2:115–16; Barthélemy, *Histoire des relations*, 98–106.

102. Savory, *His Britannic Majesty's Army*, 41; Waddington, *La Guerre*, 1:538–42; Barthélemy, *Histoire des relations*, 101; Bonnet, *Mémoires de Bernis*, 257, 260.

103. Droysen, *Politische Correspondenz*, 15:379, Frederick to Karl Wilhelm, Graf Finck von Finckenstein, 27 September 1757.

104. Waddington, *La Guerre*, 1:532–40, 544–45, 558–71, 584–88, 606–9, 746; Droysen, *Politische Correspondenz*, 15:348, 350, 403–4, 423, 435–46; Christopher Duffy, *Prussia's Glory: Rossbach and Leuthen 1757* (Chicago: Emperor's Press, 2003), 102–8.

105. Droysen, *Politische Correspondenz*, 15:336–37, 363, 369–71, 411, 429–30; Bonnet, *Mémoires de Bernis*, 241–42; Waddington, *La Guerre*, 1:584–89, 592–93, 600; Masson, *Mémoires et lettres de Bernis*, 2:122–25; Grimoard, *Correspondance de Richelieu*, 1:198–202.

106. *Politische Correspondenz*, 15:396–97, 416–19, 434–35, 443–44; Bonnet, *Mémoires de Bernis*, 261–62; Waddington, *La Guerre*, 1:535–36, 539, 555–56, 596–99, 609–10; Masson, *Mémoires et letters de Bernis*, 2:132–34; Dussieux and Soulié, *Mémoires de Luynes*, 16:240–41; Lewis, *Walpole Correspondence*, 21:158–59n.

107. Duffy, *Prussia's Glory*, 23–64; Bonnet, *Mémoires de Bernis*, 261, 264–65, 354–55; Waddington, *La Guerre*, 1:530–32, 536–38, 550–57, 609–16; Masson, *Mémoires et lettres de Bernis*, 2:134–38; Correlli Barnett, *Britain and Her Army, 1509–1970: A Military, Political, and Social Survey* (London: Allen Lane, 1970), 184; for Soubise's character, see Bonnet, *Mémoires de Bernis*, 238; Pajol, *Les Guerres*, 4:133n; Waddington, *La Guerre*, 5:212–14.

108. Duffy, *Prussia's Glory*, 65–91; Waddington, *La Guerre*, 1:617–30.

109. Holland, 496: 34–35; Holland, 497: 276–77, 293–95, 315–17; Coquelle, *L'Alliance franco-hollandaise*, 85, 89–91, 97–98, 105; Waddington, *La Guerre*, 2:428–29; Bussemaker, *Archives*, 3:487n, 491, 494, 512.

110. Barbier, *Chronique*, 6:595.

111. Waddington, *La Guerre*, 1:504–5; Middleton, *Bells of Victory*, 41; Van Kley, *Damiens Affair*, 41; Albert von Ruville, *William Pitt, Earl of Chatham*, 3 vols., trans. H. J. Chaytor and Mary Morison (London: W. Heinemann; New York: G. P. Putnam's Sons, 1907), 2:159; T. S. Ashton, *Economic Fluctuations in England, 1700–1800* (Oxford: Clarendon Press, 1959), 21.

112. Middleton, *Bells of Victory*, 36–38; Waddington, *La Guerre*, 1:501–3, 507–9, 514–20, 524–26, 655–56; Droysen, *Politische Correspondenz*, 14:132–33; 15:467; 16:15–17; Dann, *Hanover and Britain*, 109, 116.

113. Savory, *His Britannic Majesty's Army*, 47–52; Waddington, *La Guerre*, 1:507–12, 516–24, 645–58; Bonnet, *Mémoires de Bernis*, 257–58; Pajol, *Les Guerres*, 4:106; Barthélemy, *Histoire des relations*, 101; Cole, *Richelieu*, 225; Chr. [Christophe-Guillaume de] Koch, *Table des traités entre la France et les puissances étrangères depuis la paix de Westphalie jusqu'à nos jours*, 2 vols. (Basel: J. Decker; Paris: Ch. Pougens, 1802), 2:97–102.

114. Austria 260: 199; Droysen, *Politische Correspondenz*, 16:70, 78, 110, 116–17, 126–27, 133; Waddington, *La Guerre*, 1:569–72, 686–726; Duffy, *Prussia's Glory*, 95–181; Asprey, *Frederick the Great*, 473–82.

115. Theodore Besterman, ed., *The Complete Works of Voltaire: Correspondence and Related Documents (Definitive Edition)*, 51 vols. (Toronto: Toronto University Press; Geneva: Institut et Musée Voltaire [and other publishers], 1968–77), 18:127, 140–41, 152–53, 180–82, 198–99, 205–7, 248–50, 260–61.

116. Masson, *Mémoires et lettres de Bernis*, 2:159–63; Waddington, *La Guerre*, 1:732; Oliva, *Misalliance*, 82–83; Marsangy, *Vergennes*, 2:48.

117. Bonnet, *Mémoires de Bernis*, 266; Masson, *Mémoires et lettres de Bernis*, 2:148–50; Waddington, *La Guerre*, 1:638–41.

118. Waddington, *La Guerre*, 1:459, 522–23, 546–47, 596, 638–42, 657–67, 670–71, 674–81, 747; 2:53; Pajol, *Les Guerres*, 4:122–27; Savory, *His Britannic Majesty's Army*, 52–58; Duffy, *Frederick the Great*, 109–10; Masson, *Mémoires et lettres de Bernis*, 2:133; Childs, *Armies and Warfare*, 160.

119. Droysen, *Politische Correspondenz*, 15:193–94, 228–29, 278–79, 314–16, 318–19; Bisset, *Memoirs of Mitchell*, 1:256–57, 270–72.

120. Middleton, *Bells of Victory*, 47–48, 57; Droysen, *Politische Corrrespondenz*, 15:455–56, 466–67; Schweizer, *Anglo-Prussian Alliance*, 80–81; Doran, *Andrew Mitchell*, 161–65; Cobbett and Hansard, *Parliamentary History*, 15: 829–30.

121. Russia 53: 232; Masson, *Mémoires et lettres de Bernis*, 2:146, 155, 157; Waddington, *La Guerre*, 1:596, 728–32; Dickson, *Maria Theresia*, 2:183–84; Batzel, "Austria," 338.

5. 1758—A YEAR OF DESPERATION

1. B⁴75: 6. A revised list of 14 February, including ships for other destinations, is in B⁴78: 23.

2. Canada, Public Archives, *Report Concerning Canadian Archives for the Year 1905*

in Three Volumes, vol. 1 (Ottawa: S. E. Dawson, 1906), part 6, 264. For Drucour, see Halpenny, *Dictionary of Canadian Biography,* 3:71–74.

3. Compare appendixes F and G and see Clowes, *Royal Navy,* 3:182.

4. B²356: 180–97; B²358; B⁴74: 121–23; B⁴75: 6–7; B⁴76; B⁴78: 14, 18, 23; B⁴80; B⁴91:43–63; B⁴96: 227; G 49: 112–20; Canada, Public Archives, *Report,* 1: part 6, 263–67; Clowes, *Royal Navy,* 3:299; Hamilton, *Adventure in the Wilderness,* 217, 239; Casgrain, *Collection des manuscrits,* 7:469, 485; 9:30, 39; Waddington, *La Guerre,* 2:335–37, 373, 412–13; Dunnigan, *Memoirs by Pouchot,* 166; Caron, *La Guerre incomprise,* 276–98, 310–11, 319; Levot, *Brest,* 2:140; Mackay, *Hawke Papers,* 192–201; Bonner-Smith, *Barrington Papers,* 1:195–201; Crowhurst, *Defence of British Trade,* 164; Antoine Roy, ed., "Les Lettres de Doreil," *Rapport de l'archiviste de la province de Québec* 25 (1944–45): 145; Maurice Linÿer de La Barbée, *Le Chevalier de Ternay: Vie de Charles Henry Louis d'Arsac de Ternay, chef d'escadre des armées navales, 1723–1780,* 2 vols. (Grenoble: Editions des 4 seigneurs, 1972), 1:51–56. For the British squadron Chaffault encountered on his return, see Corbett, *England in the Seven Year's War,* 1:334–35; David Spinney, *Rodney* (London: George Allen and Unwin, 1969), 144.

5. Boscawen to Pitt, 10 May 1758 in Kimball, *Correspondence of Pitt,* 1:242; Doughty, *Historical Journal,* 1:162–66n.

6. For the Louisbourg campaign, see B⁴80: 58–291; Holland 498: 431–32; Waddington, *La Guerre,* 2:336–64; Corbett, *England in the Seven Years' War,* 1:313–29; Caron, *La Guerre incomprise,* 293–314; Doughty, *Historical Journal,* 1:179, 184–85, 205–59; McLennan, *Louisbourg,* 243–93, 413–16; Gipson, *British Empire,* 7:180–207; Blanchet, *Collection des manuscrits,* 4:196, 215–18; Harris, *Historical Atlas,* plate 42; John Clarence Webster, ed., *The Journal of Jeffrey Amherst: Recording the Military Career of General Amherst in America from 1758 to 1763* (Toronto: Ryerson Press; Chicago: University of Chicago Press, 1931), 50–71; J. Mackay Hitsman and C. C. J. Bond, "The Assault Landing at Louisbourg, 1758," *Canadian Historical Review* 35 (1954): 314–30.

7. Doughty, *Historical Journal,* 1:263, 266–67, 271, 275–78n; Webster, *Journal of Amherst,* 72–74, 85; McLennan, *Louisbourg,* 417–23; Corbett, *England in the Seven Years' War,* 1:330–31; Kimball, *Correspondence of Pitt,* 1:313–14, 348; Waddington, *La Guerre,* 2:364–67; Harris, *Historical Atlas,* plate 42; Frégault, *Canada,* 219–20; Adair, "Wolfe," 16–18; Black, *Pitt the Elder,* 182; Lawrence Shaw Mayo, *Jeffrey Amherst: A Biography* (London: Longmans, Green, 1916), 100; Robin Reilly, *The Rest to Fortune: The Life of Major-General James Wolfe* (London: Cassell, 1960), 191–93.

8. *London Evening Post,* issue of 27–30 May 1758; Caron, *La Guerre incomprise,* 276–77; Hamilton, *Adventure in the Wilderness,* 206–14, 277; Roy, "Les Lettres de Doreil," 134–35; Casgrain, *Collection des manuscrits,* 7:353–54, 366, 373; Frégault, *Canada,* 211; Boulle, "French Colonies," 112–13, 120n; Canada, Public Archives, *Report,* 1: part 6, 259, 271–72; Maupassant, *Gradis,* 67–74; Gabriel, *Desandrouins,* 144–45; La Pause, "Mémoire," 79; J. F. Bosher, *Canada Merchants,* 14–15, 95–96, 145, 175–76, 180, *Business and Religion in the Age of New France, 1600–1760: Twenty-two Studies* (Toronto: Canadian Scholars Press, 1974), 474–75, 483, and "Financing the French Navy in the Seven Years War: Beaujon, Goosens et Compagnie in 1759," *Business History* 28, no. 3 (July 1986): 130n.

9. Delmas, "Rapport de synthèse," in Delmas, *Conflits*, 4; Doughty, *Historical Journal*, 1:162–66n (which, however, fails to list the 80th).

10. Waddington, *La Guerre*, 2:368; Kimball, *Correspondence of Pitt*, 1:136–43, 203–4; 2:132; Pargellis, *Lord Loudoun*, 352–53; Anderson, *People's Army*, 13, 16, 59–60n; MacLeod, "Microbes and Muskets," 45, 51; Rowland et al., *Mississippi Archives*, 5:188–90; Gregory Evans Dowd, "'Indian Friends': Gift Giving and the Cherokee-British Alliance in the Seven Years' War," in Andrew R. L. Cayton and Fredrika Teute, eds., *Contact Points: American Frontiers from the Mohawk Valley to the Mississippi, 1750–1830* (Chapel Hill: University of North Carolina Press, 1998), 150; Baron Marc Villiers du Terrage, *Les Derniers Années de la Louisiane française: Le Chevalier de Kerlérec, d'Abbadie, Aubry, Laussat* (Paris: Librairie orientale et américaine, 1904), 88.

11. Casgrain, *Collection des manuscrits*, 1:129–30; 4:25–32; 7:364, 376; O'Callaghan, *Documents*, 10:719; Michalon, "Vaudreuil et Montcalm" in Delmas, *Conflits*, 110–13; Chapais, *Montcalm*, 392–97; Waddington, *La Guerre*, 2:370; Gipson, *British Empire*, 7:217n.

12. Kimball, *Correspondence of Pitt*, 1:143–51, 170–71, 202–3; Corbett, *England in the Seven Years' War*, 1:306–7; Gipson, *British Empire*, 7:177; Middleton, *Bells of Victory*, 53–55; Whitworth, *Ligonier*, 236–41.

13. Pargellis, *Lord Loudoun*, 356–58; Kimball, *Correspondence of Pitt*, 1:137–38, 193–94; Middleton, *Bells of Victory*, 50–51; Pargellis, *Military Affairs*, 429–32.

14. Kimball, *Correspondence of Pitt*, 1:133–35; Gipson, *British Empire*, 7:174–75; Whitworth, *Ligonier*, 236–37, 241–42; Middleton, *Bells of Victory*, 51–55; Pargellis, *Lord Loudoun*, 337–48; Baxter, "Conduct," in Baxter, *England's Rise*, 337; Ayling, *Pitt*, 217–18. For an example of Amherst's bigotry, see Kimball, *Correspondence of Pitt*, 2:44.

15. An excellent recent account of the battle is Ian McCulloch, "'Like roaring lions breaking from their chains': The Battle of Ticonderoga, 8 July 1758," in Donald E. Graves, ed., *Fighting for Canada: Seven Battles, 1758–1945* (Toronto: Robin Bass Studio, 2000), 23–80. See also Casgrain, *Collection des manuscrits*, 1:135–38; 2:195–97; 7:384–405, 422; 11:149–74; O'Callaghan, *Documents*, 10:721–27, 732–34, 737–41, 748–50, 752–56, 762–71, 889–97; Waddington, *La Guerre*, 2:376–84; Hamilton, *Adventure in the Wilderness*, 221–40, 254; La Pause, "Mémoire," 80–83; Gipson, *British Empire*, 7:223–31; Harris, *Historical Atlas*, plate 42; Pargellis, *Lord Loudoun*, 298–99; Anderson, *Crucible of War*, 240–48; Bellico, *Sails and Steam*, 64–72, 170–71, 176; Louis-Etienne Dussieux, ed., *La Canada sous la domination française d'après les archives de la marine et de la guerre*, 3rd ed. (Paris: Victor Lecoffre, 1883), 257–69; Gabriel, comte de Maurès de Malartic, ed., *Journal des campagnes au Canada de 1755 à 1760 par le comte de Maurès de Malartic* (Paris: A. Plon, Nourrit, 1890), 183.

16. Casgrain, *Collection des manuscrits*, 7:405–10, 422–24, 435, 479; 8:50; O'Callaghan, *Documents*, 10:756–60; Waddington, *La Guerre*, 2:384–87; Hamilton, *Adventure in the Wilderness*, 235, 241–84; Gipson, *British Empire*, 7:235–36; Bellico, *Sails and Steam*, 72–85; Michalon, "Vaudreuil et Montcalm," in Delmas, *Conflits*, 113–19.

17. Casgrain, *Collection des manuscrits*, 7:336–37, 362–63, 447–48; Waddington, *La Guerre*, 2:360, 395–98; Hamilton, *Adventure in the Wilderness*, 240, 247; Michalon, "Vaudreuil et Montcalm," in Delmas, *Conflits*, 115–16; Frégault, *Canada*, 214; Nicolai, "Different

Kind of Courage," 53–54, 63; O'Callaghan, *Documents*, 10:799–83, 810; Ian K. Steele, *Guerrillas and Grenadiers: The Struggle for Canada, 1689–1760* (Toronto: Ryerson Press, 1969), 120: Fairfax Downey, *Louisbourg: Key to a Continent* (Englewood Cliffs NJ: Prentice-Hall, 1965), 175.

18. O'Callaghan, *Documents*, 10:821–30, 937; Waddington, *La Guerre*, 2:388–90; Hamilton, *Adventure in the Wilderness*, 266, 276; Gipson, *British Empire*, 7:236–46; Malartic, *Journal des campagnes*, 200; Roy, "Les Lettres de Doreil," 155–59; Frégault, *Canada*, 222–23; Pargellis, *Lord Loudoun*, 356; Anderson, *Crucible of War*, 259–66; Jennings, *Empire of Fortune*, 366; Eccles, *France in America*, 195–96; Godfrey, *Bradstreet*, 124–31; E. C. Kyte, ed., *An Impartial Account of Lieut. Col. Bradstreet's Expedition to Fort Frontenac* (Toronto: Rous and Mann, 1940); Richard Preston and Leopold Lamontagne, eds., *Royal Fort Frontenac* (Toronto: Champlain Society, 1958), 450–57; James Thomas Flexner, *Lord of the Mohawks: A Biography of Sir William Johnson* (Boston: Little, Brown, 1979), 194; Robert Malcomson, *Warships of the Great Lakes, 1754–1834* (London: Chatham, 2001), 17.

19. Gipson, *British Empire*, 7:246–86; Frégault, *Canada*, 223–24; Jennings, *Empire of Fortune*, 374–79, 384, 391, 406–11; Waddington, *La Guerre*, 2:406–9; Corkran, *Cherokee Frontier*, 142–62; Ward, *Stephen*, 48–57; Stotz, *Outposts*, 120–40; Alfred Procter James, ed., *Writings of General John Forbes Relating to His Service in North America* (Menasha, Wis.: Collegiate Press, 1938); Alfred Procter James and Charles Morse Stotz, *Drums in the Forest: Decision at the Forks / Defense in the Wilderness* (Pittsburgh: Historical Society of Western Pennsylvania, 1958), 126–40; Sylvester K. Stevens, Donald H. Kent, and Autumn L. Leonard, eds., *The Papers of Henry Bouquet*, vol. 2, *The Forbes Expedition* (Harrisburg: Pennsylvania Historical and Museum Commission, 1951); Niles Anderson, "The General Chooses a Road: The Forbes Campaign of 1758 to Capture Fort Duquesne," *Western Pennsylvania Historical Magazine* 42 (1959): 109–38, 241–58, 383–401.

20. Jennings, *Empire of Fortune*, 396–404; McConnell, *A Country Between*, 128–33; White, *Middle Ground*, 250–52; James H. Merrell, *Into the American Woods: Negotiators on the Pennsylvania Frontier* (New York: W. W. Norton, 1999), 242–82.

21. O'Callaghan, *Documents*, 10:860–63, 874–77, 897–900; Casgrain, *Collection des manuscrits*, 4:45–51; 7:463, 492; Hamilton, *Adventure in the Wilderness*, 261, 277, 296–98; Frégault, *Canada*, 211–13, 227–29; Michalon, "Vaudreuil et Montcalm," in Delmas, *Conflits*, 115–20; Preston and Lamontagne, *Fort Frontenac*, 457–63; Roy, "Les Lettres de Doreil," 153, 166–67; Waddington, *La Guerre*, 2:390, 400–403; Nicolai, "Different Kind of Courage," 65–66; Dussieux, *La Canada*, 279–81; Côté, *Cadet*, table 20; Chapais, *Montcalm*, 473–76; Frégault, *Bigot*, 2:239–40, 243; Pierre-Georges Roy, ed., "La Mission de M. de Bougainville en France en 1758–1759," *Rapport de l'archiviste de la province de Québec* 4 (1923–24): 2–4. For Doreil and Péan, see Halpenny, *Dictionary of Canadian Biography*, 3:187–89; 4:614–17.

22. *London Evening Post*, issue of 25–28 November 1758; Middleton, *Bells of Victory*, 88–90; Corbett, *England in the Seven Years' War*, 1:334, 372–74, 396; Ayling, *Pitt*, 232; Kimball, *Correspondence of Pitt*, 1:309; Reed Browning, "The Duke of Newcastle and the Financing of the Seven Years' War," *Journal of Economic History* 31 (1971): 350; Richard Pares, *The Historian's Business, and Other Essays* (Oxford: Clarendon Press, 1961), 153.

23. Demerliac, *La Marine de Louis XV*, 35–36, 38–40, 42–46, 50; Lavery, *Ship of the Line*, 174–78; Lyon, *Sailing Navy List*, 62–64, 67–68, 73, 76–77, 203–4.

24. See appendixes F and G.

25. Le Goff, "Problèmes de recrutement," 222, 231–32; Nash, *Urban Crucible*, 237; Gipson, *British Empire*, 8:68; Starkey, *British Privateering Enterprise*, 178; Olive Anderson, "The Establishment of British Supremacy at Sea and the Exchange of Naval Prisoners of War, 1689–1763," *English Historical Review* 75 (1960): 87.

26. Pritchard, *Louis XV's Navy*, 73–75, 81, 84–88; Garnault, *Le Commerce rochelais*, 4:219–21; Pares, *War and Trade*, 327–28; Le Goff, "Problèmes de recrutement," 215n, 227–29, and "The Labour Market for Sailors in France," in Van Royen et al., *"Those Emblems of Hell"?*, 309, 312; Bertrand, "Dunkerque," 326; Ducéré, *Bayonne*, 253; Crowhurst, *Defence of British Trade*, 20, 29, 32; Gradish, *Manning*, 42–45; Middleton, "Naval Administration," in Black and Woodfine, *British Navy*, 119; Lloyd, *British Seaman*, 288.

27. Rodger, *Insatiable Earl*, 31.

28. Brun, *Port de Toulon*, 1:412–13. See also Le Goff, "Problèmes de recrutement," 212–13; Pritchard, *Louis XV's Navy*, 87–88, 110–11, 122–23, 154, 175, 194–95; Marion, *Histoire financière*, 1:186.

29. Pritchard, *Louis XV's Navy*, 196–97, 215–22; Marion, *Histoire financière de la France*, 1:185–87; Riley, *Seven Years War*, 140–41, 146; Legohérel, *Les Trésoriers généraux*, chart facing 180, 206; Neuville, *Etat sommaire*, 616–17; Sturgill, "French Army's Budget," 131; Masson, *Mémoires et lettres de Bernis*, 2:201–2, 212, 232, 238–39; Bonnet, *Mémoires de Bernis*, 276–77; Pritchard, "French Navy," in Love et al., *Changing Interpretations*, 150; Mackay, *Admiral Hawke*, 305; André Dussauge, *Etudes sur la guerre de sept ans: Le Ministèe de Belle-Isle*, vol. 1, *Krefeld et Lütterberg (1758)* (Paris: L. Fournier, 1914), 210, 307n.

30. B^{2}358: 23, 27; B^{4}74: 121–23; B^{4}78: 17 (and further information in B^{4}81); Garnault, *Le Commerce rochelais*, 4:195; Caron, *La Guerre incomprise*, 263–65, 272–73.

31. B^{2}357: 167, 172, 238–41; B^{3}536: 392, 396; B^{3}540: 197; B^{3}541:193, 195, 198, 217, 223, 228; B^{4}78: 42; B^{4}79: 70–148; Brun, *Port de Toulon*, 1:395–407; Clowes, *Royal Navy*, 3:189–90; Erskine, *Hervey's Journal*, 257, 264–74; Frédéric D'Agay, "Un Episode naval de la guerre de Sept Ans," *Marins et Océans* 2 (1991): 143–71.

32. B^{3}540; B^{3}541; B^{4}78: 27, 47; B^{4}79: 206; Erskine, *Augustus Hervey's Journal*, 284; Brun, *Port de Toulon*, 1:408–10; Le Goff, "Problèmes de recrutement," 213; Guillon, *Port Mahon*, 73–74. There also is information in B^{2}360, to which I did not have access.

33. B^{2}358: 135, 138, 411, 608–9, 612; B^{2}359: 88, 101; B^{4}77: 52; B^{4}78: 23, 26, 86–102; B^{4}81:112–39; Clowes, *Royal Navy*, 3:300; Riley, *Seven Years War*, 109–10; Pares, *War and Trade*, 327–28, 360, 371–73, 384–89, 446–68, and *Colonial Blockade*, 164, 211, 255–58; Buchet, *La Lutte*, 1:383–84, 449; Butel, "La Guerre maritime," 299; Dardel, *Navires*, 560; Meyer, *L'Armement nantais*, 79–80; Romano, "Balance du Commerce," 1274, 1291; Villers, "Commerce coloniale," 35, and *Marine royale*, 2:451–56; Kimball, *Correspondence of Pitt*, 2:78–80; R. C. Anderson, ed., "The Reminiscences of Lieutenant Malmsköld," in Lloyd, *Naval Miscellany*, 259–60; Linÿer de La Barbée, *Ternay*, 1:51–52; Neil R. Stout, *The Royal Navy in America, 1760–1775: A Study of the Enforcement of British Colonial Policy in the Era of the American Revolution* (Annapolis: Naval Institute Press, 1973), 17; Théophile Malvezin,

Histoire du commerce de Bordeaux, depuis les origines, jusqu'à nos jours, vol. 3, *XVIIIe siècle* (Bordeaux: A. Bellier, 1892), 302–7.

34. Gipson, *British Empire*, 8:173–77; Middleton, *Bells of Victory*, 85; Taylor and Pringle, *Correspondence of Chatham*, 1:221–22; Ayling, *Pitt*, 153–54, 224; James L. A. Webb Jr., "The Mid-Eighteenth-Century Gum Arabic Trade and the British Capture of Saint-Louis du Sénégal, 1758," *Journal of Imperial and Commonwealth History* 25 (1997): 37–58; A. J. Marsh, "The Taking of Goree, 1758," *Mariner's Mirror* 51 (1965): 117–30; Thomas Keppel, *The Life of Augustus, Viscount Keppel, Admiral of the White and First Lord of the Admiralty in 1782–3*, 2 vols. (London: Henry Colburn, 1842), 1:269–78.

35. Gipson, *British Empire*, 8:83–87; Middleton, *Bells of Victory*, 85–87; Corbett, *England in the Seven Years' War*, 1:373–77; Waddington, *La Guerre*, 3:357; Smelser, *Campaign for the Sugar Islands*, 20–34, 188; Black, *Pitt the Elder*, 181; Whitworth, *Ligonier*, 269–71.

36. B^{4}78: 23, 86–102; B^{4}81: 275–382; Thomas-Lacroix, "La Guerre de course," 169; for Froger de l'Eguille, see Vergé-Franceschi, *Les Officiers généraux*, 1:77, 282–83.

37. Corbett, *England in the Seven Years' War*, 1:341–44; Clowes, *Royal Navy*, 3:160–64; Ayling, *Pitt*, 193–94; Gipson, *British Empire*, 8:122–36; Taylor and Pringle, *Correspondence of Chatham*, 1:206–9; S. C. Hill, ed., *Indian Record Series: Bengal in 1756–1757: A Selection of Public and Private Papers Dealing with the Affairs of the British in Bengal during the Reign of Siraj-Uddaula*, 3 vols. (London: John Murray, 1905), 2: passim; H. C. Wylly, "*Primus in Indis*": *A Life of Lieutenant-General Sir Eyre Coote, K. B.* (Oxford: Clarendon Press, 1922), 22–32, 40–53; Michael Edwardes, *The Battle of Plassey and the Conquest of Bengal* (London: Batsford, 1963), 110–16, 134–49; Ram Gopal, *How the British Occupied Bengal: A Corrected Account of the 1756–1765 Events* (New York: Asia Publishing House, 1963), 183–216; Tom Pocock, *Battle for Empire: The Very First World War, 1756–63* (London: Michael O'Mara Books, 1998), 58–83.

38. B^{4}77: 199, 212–41; B^{4}80: 141–272; Clowes, *Royal Navy*, 3:174–82; Wylly, *Coote*, 59; Gipson, *British Empire*, 8:140–53; Waddington, *La Guerre*, 3:381–96; Pocock, *Battle for Empire*, 128–37; Hamont, *Lally-Tollendal*, 76–145; Chabaud-Arnault, "Etudes historiques," *Revue maritime* 117 (1893): 596–607; Michel, *Estaing*, 33–40; Tunstall, *Naval Warfare*, 112–13. See appendix G for the rival fleets.

39. B^{4}78: 5–6; Russia 56: 250; Waddington, *La Guerre*, 2:452–53; Pritchard, *Louis XV's Navy*, 11–13, 31, 34–35; Vergé-Franceschi, *Les Officiers généraux*, 5:2325; Antoine, *Le Gouvernement*, 178; Mouffle d'Angerville, *Vie privée*, 3:150–52. For examples of Moras asking advice of Massiac, see B^{3}535: 30–32, 34–36.

40. Masson, *Mémoires et lettres de Bernis*, 2:312, 317–18, 322–23; Pritchard, "French Navy," 150, 155n, and *Louis XV's Navy*, 13–14; Boulle, "French Colonies," 117–18, 122; Lacour-Gayet, *La Marine militaire*, 244–46; Maupassant, *Gradis*, 75–79, 89.

41. B^{2}356: 151; B^{2}359: 381, 414; B^{3}552: 106–11; B^{4}74: 121–23, 207–441; B^{4}78: 23, 36, 46, 49, 217–46, 302–5; B^{5}3: unpaginated, ship lists of May (?) and 30 August 1758; French National Library, Paris, France: New Acquisitions, item 9403 (Magry collection); Middleton, *Bells of Victory*, 64–78, 81–85; Corbett, *England in the Seven Years' War*, 1:264–88, 293–304; Waddington, *La Guerre*, 3:345–53; Whitworth, *Ligonier*, 245–68; Dussauge, *Belle-Isle*, 1:410; Caron, *La Guerre incomprise*, 245–46, 289–90, 333; Hackmann, "English Military

Expeditions," 75–149; Harding, *Amphibious Warfare*, 182–84 and "Sailors and Gentlemen of Parade: Some Professional and Technical Problems Concerning the Conduct of Combined Operations in the Eighteenth Century," *Historical Journal* 32 (1989): 55; A. W. H. Pearsall, ed., "Naval Aspects of the Landings on the French Coast, 1758," in N. A. M. Rodger, ed., *The Naval Miscellany*, vol. 5 (London: George Allen and Unwin for the Navy Records Society, 1984), 207–43; Richard Middleton, "The British Coastal Expeditions to France, 1757–1758," *Journal of the Society for Army Historical Research* 71 (1993): 82–92; H. Binet, "La Défense des côtes de Bretagne au XVIIIe siècle: Etudes et documents. Ve Série: Les Descents sur les côtes de la Manche en 1758," *Revue de Bretagne*, n.s., 47 (1912): 236–53, 304–11, 352–58; 48 (1912): 5–23, 80–93; P. Loyer, "La Défense des côtes de Bretagne pendant la guerre de Sept Ans: La Bataille de Saint-Cast," *Revue maritime*, n.s., no. 156 (December 1932): 721–39, and no. 157 (January 1933): 75–98; Pierre de La Condamine, *Un Jour d'été à Saint-Cast: L'Epopée de la Bretagne* (Cohélais-Saint-Molf, France: La Bateau qui vire, 1977).

42. Garnault, *Le Commerce rochelais*, 4:187–91; Villiers, "Commerce coloniale," 36–38; Starkey, *British Privateering Enterprise*, 178; Bamford, *Forests and French Sea Power*, 64–65; Bonner-Smith, *Barrington Papers*, 1:217–33; Middleton, "British Naval Stategy," 358.

43. B^{2}359: 38, 157, 476–83; B^{4}74: 190; B^{4}78: 57–67, 103–26; B^{4}91:100–101, 193–95; B^{5}3: unpaginated, ship list of 30 August 1758; Pritchard, *Louis XV's Navy*, 88; Caron, *La Guerre incomprise*, 322–26, 337n, 342–43.

44. B^{4}78: 8; Antoine, *Le Gouvernement*, 30; Bonnet, *Mémoires de Bernis*, 285–89.

45. Austria 265: 30, Bernis to Stainville, 6 July 1758. For Berryer's selection to the Council of State, see section 4 below.

46. Caron, *La Guerre incomprise*, 274. For Berryer, see Grouchy and Cottin, *Journal de Croÿ*, 1:445; Maupassant, *Gradis*, 82; Boulle, "French Colonies," 147n.

47. Waddington, *La Guerre*, 1:735–45; 2:2; Savory, *His Britannic Majesty's Army*, 7–8; Masson, *Mémoires et lettres de Bernis*, 2:171; Droysen, *Politische Correspondenz*, 16:266–67; Pajol, *Les Guerres*, 4:215.

48. Waddington, *La Guerre*, 1:679.

49. Waddington, *La Guerre*, 1:670–71, 683; 2:1–8; Savory, *His Britannic Majesty's Army*, 56–58; Pajol, *Les Guerres*, 4:217–18.

50. Waddington, *La Guerre*, 2:6–50, 190–91; Savory, *His Britannic Majesty's Army*, 55, 59–68; Pajol, *Les Guerres*, 4:218–30; Droysen, *Politische Correspondenz*, 16:286–87, 326–27, 419n; Dussauge, *Belle-Isle*, 1:129–31.

51. *London Evening Post*, 25–28 March 1758, Commodore Charles Holmes to Secretary of the Admiralty John Clevland, 21 March 1758; Waddington, *La Guerre*, 2:48; Savory, *His Britannic Majesty's Army*, 62, 65; Pajol, *Les Guerres*, 4:227, 229; Droysen, *Politische Correspondenz*, 16:383; Corbett, *England in the Seven Years' War*, 1:247–53.

52. Waddington, *La Guerre*, 2:14, 427–28; Dussauge, *Belle-Isle*, 1:123–25; Masson, *Mémoires et lettres de Bernis*, 2:166–67, 188; Bonnet, *Mémoires de Bernis*, 279; Grouchy and Cottin, *Journal de Croÿ*, 1:422–24, 433; Antoine, *Le Gouvernement*, 26.

53. Waddington, *La Guerre*, 2:54–62, 71–72, 76; Dussauge, *Belle-Isle*, 1:160–66, 196–98,

224, 261–300, 398–410, 469; Masson, *Mémoires et lettres de Bernis*, 2:196; Kennett, *French Armies*, 30–31; Duffy, *Military Experience*, 20, 42, 62, 138, 182, 232.

54. Waddington, *La Guerre*, 1:72–74, 77–78, 120; Savory, *His Britannic Majesty's Army*, 68–72; Droysen, *Politische Correspondenz*, 16:402–3, 412–13.

55. Waddington, *La Guerre*, 2:119–20; Pajol, *Les Guerres*, 4:241; Corbett, *England in the Seven Years' War*, 1:282–83.

56. Waddington, *La Guerre*, 2:101–17; Savory, *His Britannic Majesty's Army*, 76–85.

57. Waddington, *La Guerre*, 1:735, 742–44; 2:58–60, 91–94, 431, 434–35, 439–41; Masson, *Mémoires et lettres de Bernis*, 2:173–74, 196, 235–36, 242–43, 435–36; Dussauge, *Belle-Isle*, 221.

58. Waddington, *La Guerre*, 2:135–41; Savory, *His Britannic Majesty's Army*, 95–99.

59. Sweden 235: 16; Waddington, *La Guerre*, 2:123–30; Masson, *Mémoires de Bernis*, 2:249; Bonnet, *Mémoires du Cardinal de Bernis*, 282–83; Dussauge, *Belle-Isle*, 251–54, 301–4; Kennett, *French Armies*, 17.

60. Waddington, *La Guerre de Sept Ans*, 2:172–78; Savory, *His Britannic Majesty's Army*, 104–8.

61. Accounts of the summer and autumn campaign are given in Waddington, *La Guerre*, 2:77–185; Savory, *His Britannic Majesty' Army*, 67–115; Pajol, *Les Guerres*, 4:234–326; Dussauge, *Belle-Isle*, 227–60, 301–40, 345–69.

62. Albert Sorel, *Europe and the French Revolution: The Political Traditions of the Old Regime*, trans. Alfred Cobban and J. W. Hunt (Garden City NY: Doubleday, Anchor Books, 1971), 80.

63. Droysen, *Politische Correspondenz*, 15:455, 466–67; 16:175–76; Bisset, *Memoirs of Mitchell*, 1:389–93, 399–400.

64. Brooke, *Walpole Memoirs*, 3:3.

65. Waddington, *La Guerre*, 2:195–208; Droysen, *Politische Correspondenz*, 16:160, 196–200, 276–78, 285, 293–94, 332–33, 403–4; Parry, *Consolidated Treaty Series*, 41:179–90; Yorke, *Hardwicke*, 3:129–33, 199–214, 218–29; Middleton, *Bells of Victory*, 57–63; Doran, *Andrew Mitchell*, 163–77, 212–15; Schweizer, *Anglo-Prussian Alliance*, 81–88; Eldon, *Subsidy Policy*, 109–11.

66. Waddington, *La Guerre*, 2:142; Corbett, *England in the Seven Years' War*, 1:284–89; Middleton, *Bells of Victory*, 73–78, 83; Hackmann, "English Military Expeditions," 115–19; Whitworth, *Ligonier*, 247–48; Ayling, *Pitt*, 235–36; Chenevix Trench, *George II*, 292–93.

67. Waddington, *La Guerre*, 2:142, 158, 190; Savory, *His Britannic Majesty's Army*, 94, 109, 116–17, 460–61, 465–66; Middleton, *Bells of Victory*, 77–78, 90–92, 97–98; Eldon, *Subsidy Policy*, 114–15, 121, 161–62; Debrett, *Debates of Parliament*, 3:427–30.

68. Austria 263: 68; Austria 264: 298 and passim; Duffy, *Frederick the Great*, 155; Dickson, *Maria Theresia*, 2:348–49; Bernard R. Kroener, "Die matieriellen Grundlagen öesterreichischer und preussischer Krieganstrengungen, 1756–1763," in Bernard R. Kroener, ed., *Europa in Zeitalter Freiedrichs des Grossen: Wirtschaft, Gesellschaft, Kriege* (Munich: R. Oltenbourg, 1989), 59.

69. Accounts of the Olmütz campaign include Waddington, *La Guerre*, 2:218–46, 431; Duffy, *Frederick the Great*, 155–61; Hans Delbrück, *History of the Art of War within*

the Framework of Political History, vol. 4, *The Modern Era*, trans. Walter J. Renfroe Jr. (Westport CT: Greenwood Press, 1985), 346–52.

70. Droysen, *Politische Correspondenz*, 16:276–78, 293–94; 17:25–26, 118–20, 135–36, 147–48, 166, 176, 179–80, 205, 211–12, 234–35, 246–47, 283; Doran, *Andrew Mitchell*, 221; Savory, *His Britannic Majesty's Army*, 100n.

71. Waddington, *La Guerre*, 2:250–332; Droysen, *Politische Correspondenz*, 17:191–92 and passim; Duffy, *Frederick the Great*, 161–79 and *Russia's Military Way*, 81–92; Asprey, *Frederick the Great*, 494–506; Dennis E. Showalter, *The Wars of Frederick the Great* (London: Longman, 1996), 211–30.

72. Waddington, *La Guerre*, 2:248–49; Droysen, *Politische Correspondenz*, 17:203; Duffy, *Russia's Military Way*, 82–83.

73. Droysen, *Politische Correspondenz*, 17:314, 318–19; Parry, *Consolidated Treaty Series*, 41:229–34.

74. Masson, *Mémoires et lettres de Bernis*, 2:172, Bernis to French Ambassador to Austria Stainville, 25 January 1758. See also Austria 267: 92; Batzel, "Austria," 373–74.

75. Waddington, *La Guerre*, 2:59, 472–73.

76. Masson, *Mémoires et lettres de Bernis*, 2:266, Bernis to Etienne-François, comte de Stainville and now duc de Choiseul, 4 September 1758.

77. Waddington, *La Guerre*, 1:740–41; 2:436–37, 440–41; Masson, *Mémoires et lettres de Bernis*, 2:432, 450–51.

78. Austria 263: 168, 296–97; Austria 264: 18 and passim; Austria 265: 23 and passim; Austria 266: 56–61 and passim; Holland 497: 332; Russia 56: 161–63; Sweden 234: 297–306, 457–60; Waddington, *La Guerre*, 1:732–45; 2:58–60, 92, 415–52, 459–65; Masson, *Mémoires et lettres de Bernis*, 2:163–66, 170–74, 194–96, 203–5, 207, 243, 253–55, 266–68, 276–82, 319–20, 413–71.

79. Austria 264: 18–19, 175, 214–21, 262, 286–90; Austria 265: 367–69; Waddington, *La Guerre*, 2:422–27, 440–41; Batzel, "Austria," 338, 370, 373–487, 497, 509.

80. Waddington, *La Guerre*, 2:478–80; Droysen, *Politische Correspondenz*, 17:252–53, 258–59, 263, 407–9, 415–19, 426–28; Masson, *Mémoires et lettres de Bernis*, 2:279; Marsangy, *Vergennes*, 2:50–51; Murphy, *Vergennes*, 118.

81. Droysen, *Politische Correspondenz*, 17:436–37; 18:9–10.

82. Masson, *Mémoires et lettres de Bernis*, 2:441; Droysen, *Politsche Correspondenz*, 16:256; 17:138–39; Bisset, *Memoirs of Mitchell*, 1:419–21; Doran, *Andrew Mitchell*, 170–71.

83. Batzel, "Austria," 466.

84. Holland 497: 82–89, 131–33, 276–77, 315–17, 331; Austria 264: 25–32; Waddington, *La Guerre*, 1:735; 2:201–2, 424, 428–29, 474–75; Doran, *Andrew Mitchell*, 222–23; Droysen, *Politische Correspondenz*, 17:407–9; Masson, *Mémoires et lettres de Bernis*, 2:204, 213–14; Bonnet, *Mémoires de Bernis*, 299; Coquelle, *L'Alliance franco-hollandaise*, 89–91, 104–7; Bussemaker, *Archives*, 3:487n, 494, 501–12; Barthélemy, *Histoire des relations*, 117–18, 120–21, 128–30, 162–63; [Peter August Frederik Stoud Vedel], ed., *Correspondance entre le comte Johan Hartvig Ernst Bernstorff et le duc de Choiseul, 1758–1766* (Copenhagen: Gylendal, 1871), 84–87.

85. Waddington, *La Guerre*, 1:732–33; 2:79, 83; Masson, *Mémoires et lettres de Bernis*,

2:279; Coquelle, *L'Alliance franco-hollandaise*, 99–101; Carter, *Dutch Republic*, 71–73, 104–12, 121–24, 148; Pares, *Colonial Blockade*, 180–225, 247–61; Savory, *His Britannic Majesty's Army*, 70–72; Bamford, *Forests and French Sea Power*, 64.

86. Barthélemy, *Histoire des relations*, 125; Carter, *Dutch Republic*, 71–72; Pares, *Colonial Blockade*, 279–83, and *War and Trade*, 387; Oliva, *Misalliance*, 138–39; Kent, *War and Trade*, 170–72; Anderson, *Naval Wars*, 226–27.

87. Middleton, *Bells of Victory*, 94; Baxter, "Conduct," in Baxter, *England's Rise*, 338, 347n; Waddington, *La Guerre*, 2:418–19; Barthélemy, *Histoire des relations*, 119–25, 135; Masson, *Mémoires et lettres de Bernis*, 2:243; Bonnet, *Mémoires de Bernis*, 299; Oliva, *Misalliance*, 114–17; Parry, *Consolidated Treaty Series*, 41:191–210; Eldon, *Subsidy Policy*, 111–12; Carol S. Leonard, *Reform and Regicide: The Reign of Peter III of Russia* (Bloomington: Indiana University Press, 1993), 118–19.

88. Waddington, *La Guerre*, 2:428–29, 437–38, 443, 474, 479; Masson, *Mémoires et lettres de Bernis*, 2:163, 191, 204, 449; Bonnet, *Mémoires de Bernis*, 299–300; Coquelle, *L'Alliance franco-hollandaise*, 104; Pares, *Colonial Blockade*, 286–88, 304, and *War and Trade*, 540–55; Dickson, *Maria Theresia*, 2:175–76; Gipson, *British Empire*, 8:238–44; Savelle, *Origins of American Diplomacy*, 443–45, 457 and *Diplomatic History*, 88–89; Flassan, *Histoire*, 6:265–69; Yves-René Durand, ed., "Mémoires de Jean-Joseph de Laborde, fermier général et banquier de la cour," *Annuaire-Bulletin de la Société de l'histoire de France*, no. 478 (1968–69): 84–85, 124–35, 151; Charles C. Noel, "The Crisis of 1758–1759 in Spain: Sovereignty and Power during a 'Species of Interregnum,'" in Robert Oresko, G. C. Gibbs, and H. M. Scott, eds., *Royal and Republican Sovereignty in Early Modern Europe: Essays in Memory of Ragnhild Hatton* (Cambridge: Cambridge University Press, 1997), 588–600; Jean O. McLachlan, "The Uneasy Neutrality: A Study of Anglo-Spanish Disputes over Spanish Ships Prized, 1756–1759," *Cambridge Historical Journal* 6 (1938–40): 55–77.

89. Eldon, *Subsidy Policy*, 112, 117–18.

90. Waddington, *La Guerre*, 2:424; Michael Roberts, *British Diplomacy and Swedish Politics, 1758–1773* (Minneapolis: University of Minnesota Press, 1980), 17. For Britain's attempts to gain the support of Sweden, Denmark, and the Netherlands, see Eldon, *Subsidy Policy*, 108–12.

91. Russia 56: 27; Russia 58: 232; Russia 59: 13, 19, 203–6; Oliva, *Misalliance*, 71–73, 87–88, 91–108; Masson, *Mémoires et lettres de Bernis*, 2:199, 205, 225–26; Batzel, "Austria," 447, 465; Boutaric, *Correspondance secrète de Louis XV*, 1:90, 228–30; Ozanam and Antoine, *Correspondance de Broglie*, 1:xlvii–xlix, 48n, 49–73, 77; Farges, *Recueil*, 5:203–14; Rambaud, *Recueil*, 9:32–48, 85; Waddington, *La Guerre*, 2:482–83; Duffy, *Russia's Military Way*, 82, 85; Middleton, *Bells of Victory*, 95.

92. Bonnet, *Mémoires de Bernis*, 269–70, 282, 289–90; Masson, *Mémoires et lettres de Bernis*, 2:199, 239, 244.

93. Waddington, *La Guerre*, 2:452–55; Bonnet, *Mémoires de Bernis*, 271, 287–88; Masson, *Mémoires et lettres de Bernis*, 2:247; Antoine, *Le Gouvernement*, 20, 98, 214; Dussieux and Soulié, *Mémoires de Luynes*, 16:491, 17:1.

94. Bonnet, *Mémoires de Bernis*, 289–93; Masson, *Mémoires et lettres de Bernis*, 2:216–17, 253, 299–300, 311–14, 317–20, 322–23, 327; Pritchard, *Louis XV's Navy*, 13–14, 195–96

and "French Navy," in Love, *Changing Interpretations*, 150–51; Antoine, *Louis XV*, 746; Marion, *Histoire financière*, 1:188; Bosher, *Canada Merchants*, 192–94, "Financing the French Navy," 117, and "The French Government's Motives in the *Affaire du Canada*, 1761–1763," *English Historical Review* 96 (1981): 76–77. For an outline of the career of Gaspard-Moïse de Fontanieu, see Antoine, *Le Gouvernement*, 105.

95. Austria 267: 18–20; Waddington, *La Guerre*, 2:456–58; Bonnet, *Mémoires de Bernis*, 276–77, 294–98; Masson, *Lettres et mémoires de Bernis*, 2:182–84, 191–92, 209, 218, 224–26, 252–56, 264–65, 269–70, 275–76, 281–82, 285, 287–92, 302, 321, 412; Grouchy and Cottin, *Journal de Croÿ*, 1:430–32; Swann, *Politics and the Parlement of Paris*, 153.

96. Austria 265: 50–56, 160; Waddington, *La Guerre*, 1:741; 2:438–39, 445–48; Masson, *Lettres et mémoires de Bernis*, 2:170, 232, 433–34, 443–44, 453; Antoine, *Louis XV*, 747–48; Butler, *Choiseul*, 1:930–48, 995–1000; Bonnet, *Mémoires de Bernis*, 232.

97. Austria 265: 160 and passim; Waddington, *La Guerre*, 2:465–74; Bonnet, *Mémoires de Bernis*, 297, 358n; Masson, *Mémoires et lettres de Bernis*, 2:341–47, 476–88; Grouchy and Cottin, *Journal de Croÿ*, 1:432; Antoine, *Le Gouvernement*, 70.

98. Antoine, *Le Gouvernement*, 29; Frédéric Masson, *Le Cardinal Bernis depuis son ministère, 1758–1794* (Paris: E. Plon, Nourrit, 1884).

6. 1759—THE ANNUS HORRIBILIS

1. For contrasting analyses of Choiseul's character, compare Waddington, *La Guerre*, 3:447–48; 4:483, 487–88, and Antoine, *Louis XV*, 751–52.

2. For Pitt's role in the inner cabinet, see Middleton, *Bells of Victory*, 211–13 and passim.

3. Butler, *Choiseul*, 1:296–373, 483–608, 636–711.

4. Oliva, *Misalliance*, 136. See also Masson, *Mémoires et lettres de Bernis*, 2:264–65, Bernis to Choiseul, 26 August 1758.

5. Masson, *Mémoires et lettres de Bernis*, 2:299–300.

6. Waddington, *La Guerre*, 2:468–69; Batzel, "Austria," 500.

7. Waddington, *La Guerre*, 2:474; 3:461; Vedel, *Correspondance entre Bernstorff et Choiseul*, 5–8, Choiseul to Bernstorff, 21 December 1758; Barthélemy, *Histoire des relations*, 139–40; Alfred Bourguet, *Etudes sur la politique étrangère du duc de Choiseul* (Paris: Plon-Nourrit, 1907), 6–8; Charles Giraud, ed., "Mémoire de M. de Choiseul remis au roi en 1765," *Journal des savants* 66 (1881): 173.

8. Holland 500: 11, Choiseul to d'Affry, 4 January 1759.

9. Vedel, *Correspondance entre Bernstorff et Choiseul*, 5–8, Choiseul to Bernstorff, 21 December 1758.

10. Russia 59: 119–23, memoir sent to the marquis de L'Hôpital, 19 January 1759 (quoted in Oliva, *Misalliance*, 137). See also Sorel, *Recueil*, 1:386–87.

11. See, for example, A. Morel-Fatio and H. Léonardon, eds., *Recueil des instructions données aux ambassadeurs et ministres de France depuis les traités de Westphalie jusqu'à la révolution française*, vol. 12 ᵇⁱˢ, Espagne, tome troisième (1722–93) (Paris: Félix Alcan, 1898), 349, Choiseul to Pierre-Paul, marquis d'Ossun, 7 September 1759.

12. See, for example, Max Savelle, "American Balance of Power," 160–61; and Edward Corwin, *French Policy and the American Alliance of 1778* (Princeton: Princeton University Press, 1916), 33–34.

13. Russia 59: 114, Choiseul to L'Hôpital, 11 January 1759. See also Waddington, *La Guerre*, 2:482–83.

14. Austria 264: 18, Stainville to Bernis, 1 May 1758; Austria 264: 214–21, memoir of circa 30 May 1758; Austria 266: 208–21, Bernis to Choiseul, 19 October 1758 and enclosed draft convention; Austria 267: 91–100, Choiseul's memoir on the proposed convention, 9 December 1758. For background, see Waddington, *La Guerre*, 1:736–40; 2:461–63, 468–69, 480–82; Masson, *Mémoires et lettres de Bernis*, 2:420, 426–28, 432–33, 436–38, 451, 463–65, 469–70; Batzel, "Austria," 507–10. For the Duke of Parma and his family, see Patrick Van Kerrebrouck, ed., *Nouvelle Histoire généalogique de l'august maison de France*, vol. 4, *La Maison de Bourbon, 1256–1987* (Villeneuve d'Ascq, France: privately printed, 1987), 273, 467–69.

15. Parry, *Consolidated Treaty Series*, 41:235–59, 261–68; Waddington, *La Guerre*, 3:451–54; Batzel, "Austria," 517–23; Barthélemy, *Histoire des relations*, 140–41; Vedel, *Correspondance entre Bernstorff et Choiseul*, 15–16n; Dickson, *Maria Theresia*, 2:173–74; E. James Ferguson, *The Power of the Purse: A History of American Public Finance, 1776–1790* (Chapel Hill: University of North Carolina Press, 1961), 40–41, 126–28.

16. Giraud, "Mémoire de Choiseul," 173–74; Durand, "Mémoires de Laborde," 97n.

17. Austria 260: 322; Caron, *La Guerre incomprise*, 349–51.

18. Britain 442: 136–38 and passim; Holland 495: 290–91; Sweden 237: 10–12; B⁴82: 42–112; Bourguet, *Etudes*, 86–88; Coquelle, *L'Alliance franco-hollandaise*, 117; Claude Nordmann, "Choiseul and the Last Jacobite Attempt of 1759," in Eveline Cruickshanks, ed., *Ideology and Conspiracy: Aspects of Jacobitism, 1689–1759* (Edinburgh: John Donald, 1982), 201–17; Frank Edward McLynn, *Charles Edward Stuart: A Tragedy in Many Acts* (London: Routledge, 1988), 450–53.

19. Sweden 235: 244, 322; Sweden 236: 55–62, 224–28, 328–29, 406–26, 440–45; Sweden 237: 13–28, 48–51, 89–95, 113, 155–62, 175–78, 184–91; Russia 59: 116–23, 215, 270–71; Britain 442: 174–84, 234–35; Britain, supplementary volume 12: 50–59; B⁴84: passim; B⁴86: 8–12; B⁴87: 16, 19–21, 24–25, 32–35, 41–42, 141–43, 152–57, 170, 172–76, 181–82; Nordmann, "Choiseul and the Last Jacobite Attempt," 205–10; Caron, *La Guerre incomprise*, 339–49; Lacour-Gayet, *La Marine militaire*, 341–48; Villiers, *Marine royale*, 1:294–96; Flassan, *Histoire de la diplomatie française*, 6:146–70; P. Coquelle, "Les projets de descente en Angleterre d'après les archives des affaires étrangères," *Revue d'histoire diplomatique* 15 (1901): 607–17.

20. Sweden 237: 194–96, 213–15, 229–35, 251–56, 265–67; Eldon, *Subsidy Policy*, 127; Roberts, *British Diplomacy and Swedish Politics*, 22–23; Nordmann, "Choiseul and the Last Jacobite Attempt," 207; Alfred Bourguet, *Le Duc de Choiseul et l'alliance espagnole* (Paris: Plon-Nourrit, 1906), 5–8.

21. Holland 501: 341–48, 376–77, 400–401, 407; Britain 442: 145; B¹66: 219–22; B³553: 25, 88; B⁴74: 41–50; B⁴93: 53; list in B⁵4: unpaginated; Nordmann, "Choiseul and the Last Jacobite Attempt," 202–7; Coquelle, "Les Projets de descente," 611; Villiers, *Marine royale*,

1:294; Pritchard, *Louis XV's Navy*, 135–36, 142; Demerliac, *La Marine de Louis XV*, 77–78; Grouchy and Cottin, *Journal de Croÿ*, 1:445–72; Bosher, "Financing the French Navy," 126; Bertrand, "Dunkerque," 338; Anderson, "Reminiscences of Malmsköld," in Lloyd, *Navy Miscellany*, 262.

22. B⁴87: 159–60 and passim; Waddington, *La Guerre*, 3:367; Pritchard, *Louis XV's Navy*, 75, 84; Lacour-Gayet, *La Marine militaire*, 366–67; Le Goff, "Problèmes de recrutement," 229–30. I list in appendix H the ships in the French navy in service on 1 June, but because I did not have access to B²361 and B²362, I undoubtedly have somewhat overestimated the number of ships already in commission at Brest on that date.

23. Corbett, *England in the Seven Years' War*, 2:3–18, 23; Frégault, *Canada*, 236; Baxter, "Conduct," in Baxter, *England's Rise*, 338–39; Browning, *Duke of Newcastle*, 267; Geoffrey Marcus, *Quiberon Bay* (Barre MA: Barre, 1963), 25–27.

24. Marcus, *Quiberon Bay*, 27–39; Gradish, *Manning*, 42, 48, 49; Middleton, *Bells of Victory*, 109–11, "British Naval Strategy," 360–63 and "Naval Administration," in Black and Woodfine, *British Navy*, 120–21; Mackay, *Hawke Papers*, 208–18.

25. Middleton, *Bells of Victory*, 98, 112, 118–19, 125–27, 131–34; Cobbett and Hansard, *Parliamentary History*, 15: 940; Whitworth, *Ligonier*, 282–84, 287–95; Rogers, *British Army*, 26.

26. Whitworth, *Ligonier*, 296–97; Chenevix Trench, *George II*, 294–95; Bonner-Smith, *Barrington Papers*, 1:261–62.

27. Marcus, *Quiberon Bay*, 47, 59, 64–66, 121, 124–25; Middleton, *Bells of Victory*, 121, 124–25; Hattendorf et al., *British Naval Documents*, 442; Baugh, *British Naval Administration*, 350–52; N. A. M. Rodger, "The Victualing of the British Navy during the Seven Years' War," *Bulletin du Centre d'histoire des espaces Atlantiques*, n.s., 2 (1985): 45; Michael Duffy, "The Establishment of the Western Squadron as the Linchpin of British Naval Strategy," in Michael Duffy, ed., *Parameters of British Naval Power, 1650–1850* (Exeter: University of Exeter Press, 1992), 68.

28. Marcus, *Quiberon Bay*, 39–69, 74–82, 85–104, 107–8; Mackay, *Hawke Papers*, 218–90; Middleton, "British Naval Strategy," 360–63; Corbett, *England in the Seven Years' War*, 2:16–17, 21–22, 24–30, 41–42; Lacour-Gayet, *La Marine militaire*, 350–51; Erskine, *Hervey's Journal*, 301–5; Spinney, *Rodney*, 148–63.

29. Corbett, *England in the Seven Years' War*, 2:10, 31–33; Middleton, *Bells of Victory*, 112; Le Goff, "Problèmes de recrutement," 213–14; Brun, *Port de Toulon*, 1:411–16.

30. Spain 536: 216; Portugal 90: 241, 245, 327–30; B²363: 130–31, 153–54, 157, 274–79, 285, 288; B³544: 108, 111; B³545: 344; B³548: 81; B⁴90: 119–297; B⁴91: 79, 88–91; B⁴94: 182; Marcus, *Quiberon Bay*, 82–88, 105–6, 192; Corbett, *England in the Seven Years' War*, 2:33–41, 87–88; Lacour-Gayet, *La Marine militaire*, 305–10, 514–16; Brun, *Port de Toulon*, 1:423; Mackay, *Hawke Papers*, 328–29; Caron, *La Guerre incomprise*, 361–63; Clowes, *Royal Navy*, 3:211–15; Creswell, *British Admirals*, 107–9; Tunstall, *Naval Warfare*, 114. See also appendix H.

31. B⁴87: 24–35, Orders for Capitaine de vaisseau Sébastien-François Bigot de Morogues, 15 September 1759. Aiguillon also was sent orders: Lacour-Gayet, *La Marine militaire*, 346. For a 20 September 1759 French intelligence report listing the disposition of the ships of the British Navy, see Villiers, *Marine royale*, 1:258–59.

32. Smelser, *Campaign for the Sugar Islands*, 37–38.

33. Smelser, *Campaign for the Sugar Islands*, 39–56; Gipson, *British Empire*, 8:87–94; Barreau, *Les Guerres en Guadeloupe*, 42–43; Beatson, *Naval and Military Memoirs*, 3:210.

34. Smelser, *Campaign for the Sugar Islands*, 57–59; Pares, *War and Trade*, 328–29, 385, 389; Boulle, "French Colonies," 171–86.

35. Smelser, *Campaign for the Sugar Islands*, 59–65.

36. Smelser, *Campaign for the Sugar Islands*, 75; Lacour-Gayet, *La Marine militaire*, 391; Corbett, *England in the Seven Years' War*, 1:379, 394–95; Villiers, Marine royale, 2:475.

37. Smelser, *Campaign for the Sugar Islands*, 114n; Barreau, *Les Guerres en Guadeloupe*, 74; Pares, *Colonial Blockade*, 164; Daniel Baugh, *British Naval Administration in the Age of Walpole* (Princeton: Princeton University Press, 1965), 352–55.

38. Smelser, *Campaign for the Sugar Islands*, 76–149; Barreau, *Les Guerres en Guadeloupe*, 46–88; Gipson, *British Empire*, 8:95–105; Villiers, *Marine royale*, 2:479–80; Clowes, *Royal Navy*, 3:203; Sir John W. Fortescue, "Guadeloupe, 1759," *Blackwood's Magazine* 234 (1933): 552–66. One British observer called the Capesterre region the most beautiful part of any island in the West Indies: Barreau, *Les Guerres en Guadeloupe*, 81. It still is.

39. B⁴86: 205; B⁴87: 249–50; B⁴91: 93–274 (particularly Bompar's defense of his conduct on 193–208); Smelser, *Campaign for the Sugar Islands*, 113–20, 143–47, 156, 166–67, 178–79; Barreau, *Les Guerres en Guadeloupe*, 87–88; Corbett, *England in the Seven Years' War*, 1:383–91; Waddington, *La Guerre*, 3:357; Buchet, *La Lutte*, 1:395–96; Vergé-Franceschi, *Les Officiers généraux*, 5:2567; Marcus, *Quiberon Bay*, 130–32, 138. Moore's fleet was the same as that listed in appendix H for 1 June, except for the *Nassau* and *Raisonable*, which arrived only on 31 May.

40. For the aftermath of the campaign, see Smelser, *Campaign for the Sugar Islands*, 148–61, 176–79; Barreau, *Les Guerres en Guadeloupe*, 88–89; Corbett, *England in the Seven Years' War*, 1:392–95; Boulle, "French Colonies," 151–53; Marcus, *Quiberon Bay*, 134, 192; Kimball, *Correspondence of Pitt*, 1:56–59, 66; Middleton, *Bells of Victory*, 120; Fortescue, *British Army*, 363.

41. Pares, *War and Trade*, 327–28, and *Colonial Blockade*, 164; Villiers, *Marine royale*, 2:453–56 and "Commerce coloniale," 35–38, 44n; Romano, "Balance du commerce," 1274, 1291; Dardel, *Navires*, 250, 560; Meyer, *L'Armament nantais*, 79–80; Riley, *Seven Years War*, 109–10; Malvezin, *Commerce de Bordeaux*, 3:302–7; Bamford, *Forests and French Sea Power*, 65; Starkey, *British Privateering Enterprise*, 178; Paul Butel, "La Guerre maritime," in France, Service historique de la marine, *Guerres et paix*, 299 and "Bordeaux et la Holland au XVIIIᵉ siècle: L'Exemple du négociant Pellet (1694–1772)," *Révue d'histoire économique et sociale* 45 (1967): 61, 65, 67; Robert Stein, "The French Sugar Business in the Eighteenth Century: A Quantitative Study," *Business History* 22 (1980): 10, 14; Christian Pfister-Langanay, *Ports, navires et négotiants à Dunkerque (1662–1792)* (Dunkirk: Société dunkerquoise, 1985), 446.

42. Le Goff, "Problèmes de recrutement," 231–32; Crowhurst, *Defence of British Trade*, 20, 28–32, 131, 162, 183; Mitchell and Deane, *Abstract*, 280; Ashton, *Economic Fluctuations*, 60–61.

43. Grouchy and Cottin, *Journal de Croÿ*, 1:454.

44. B⁴92: 171–307; B⁴99: 4–6; Gipson, *British Empire*, 8:152–64; Waddington, *La Guerre*, 3:395–421; Lacour-Gayet, *La Marine militaire*, 405–8; Corbett, *England in the Seven Years' War*, 2:121–26; Fortescue, *British Army*, 2:443–67; Clowes, *Royal Navy*, 3:197–201; Hamont, *Lally-Tollendal*, 149–91, 219–23; Chabaud-Arnault, "Etudes historiques," *Revue maritime* 117 (1893): 607–13; Wylly, *Coote*, 59–70; Michel, *Estaing*, 43–51; see also appendix H.

45. Lewis, *Walpole Correspondence*, 21:335–37.

46. Frégault, *Canada*, 229–30; Casgrain, *Collection des manuscrits*, 4:79–90; Roy, "La Mission de Bougainville," 6–41.

47. Casgrain, *Collection des manuscrits*, 3:103–11, 161–64, 166–70, 180–83; Hamilton, *Adventure in the Wilderness*, 323; Pease, *Boundary Disputes*, lxxviin; Grouchy and Cottin, *Journal de Croÿ*, 1:448; Canada, Public Archives, *Report*, 1, part 6, 292–93. The description of Berryer ("intègre avec fracas, dur, bon") is from Casgrain, *Collection des manuscrits*, 3:106.

48. Roy, "La Mission de Bougainville," 18–19; Casgrain, *Collection des manuscrits*, 3:161–64; Frégault, *Canada*, 229–30; Waddington, *La Guerre*, 3:255–56.

49. Casgrain, *Collection des manuscrits*, 3:103–11, 145–46, 174–77; Hamilton, *Adventure in the Wilderness*, 323–24; Waddington, *La Guerre*, 3:254–62; O'Callaghan, *Documents*, 10:906–7, 937–39, 962; Gipson, *British Empire*, 7:381–86; Stacey, *Quebec*, 20–22; Boulle, "French Colonies," 126–33; Frégault, *Canada*, 234, and *Bigot*, 2:253, 255–61.

50. B⁴91:20–44; B⁷411, unpaginated, Commissaire Astier to Massiac, 28 September 1758; Waddington, *La Guerre*, 3:259–61, 265; Frégault, *Canada*, 234–35, 240, and *Bigot*, 2:323; Boulle, "French Colonies," 101, 133, 138; Chabaud-Arnault, "Etudes historiques," *Revue maritime* 115 (1892): 613; Halpenny, *Dictionary of Canadian Biography*, 3:321–22; 4:125–26, 751–52; Côté, *Cadet*, 124–26, table 20; Butel, "La Guerre maritime," in France, Service historique de la marine, *Guerres et paix*, 299; Bosher, *Canada Merchants*, 95–99, 179, 196–97; Pritchard, "Pattern," 201; Caron, *La Guerre incomprise*, 352, 355–56; Jean de Maupassant, "Les Armateurs bordelais au XVIIIᵉ siècle: Les Deux Expéditions de Pierre Desclaux au Canada (1759 et 1760)," *Revue historique de Bordeaux* 8 (1915): 227–39; Aegidus Fauteux, "Journal du siège de Québec du 10 mai au 18 septembre 1759," *Rapport de l'archiviste de la province de Québec* 1 (1920–21): 140, 202.

51. Kimball, *Correspondence of Pitt*, 1:432–34; 2:12–14, 36–38.

52. Roy, "La Mission de Bougainville," 8–10; Waddington, *La Guerre*, 3:263; O'Callaghan, *Documents*, 10:960–62; Casgrain, *Collection des manuscrits*, 5:310–11; Blanchet, *Collection des manuscrits*, 4:223–27.

53. Kimball, *Correspondence of Pitt*, 1:414–20; Dunnigan, *Memoirs by Pierre Pouchot*, 165n; Rogers, *British Army*, 26; Smelser, *Campaign for the Sugar Islands*, 20–21; Brumwell, *Redcoats*, 33n.

54. Roy, "La Mission de Bougainville," 8–10, 29–31; Dunnigan, *Memoirs by Pierre Pouchot*, 252; William J. Eccles, "The French Forces in North America during the Seven Years' War," in Halpenny, *Dictionary of Canadian Biography*, 3:xviii, xxi; Stacey, *Quebec, 1759*, 43–44; Frégault, *Canada*, 245, and *Bigot*, 2:254–55, 284; Waddington, *La Guerre*, 4:339; Nicolai, "Different Kind of Courage," 65–67; Jean Delmas, "Rapport de synthèse," and Jean Berenger and Philippe Roy, "Relations des troupes reglées (Troupes de terre

et Troupes de marine) avec les Canadiens," in Delmas, *Conflits*, 4, 25; Abbé Georges Robitaille, *Montcalm et ses historiens: Etude critique* (Montreal: Granger frères, 1936), 102.

55. Rogers, *British Army*, 26; Gipson, *British Empire*, 7:290–328; Kimball, *Correspondence of Pitt*, 2:209–10; Middleton, *Bells of Victory*, 102–3; Anderson, *People's Army*, 13, 59n, and *Crucible of War*, 317–23, 805–6; Nash, *Urban Crucible*, 242; Selesky, *War and Society*, 115, 168; Titus, *Old Dominion at War*, 127–28; Webster, *Journal of Amherst*, 141, 327–30; John A. Schutz, *Thomas Pownall, British Defender of American Liberty: A Study of Anglo-American Relations in the Eighteenth Century* (Glendale, Calif.: Arthur H. Clark, 1951), 163–73.

56. Frégault, *Canada*, 244–45, 251–52; Stacey, *Quebec, 1759*, 47, 87–92, and "Quebec, 1759: Some New Documents," *Canadian Historical Review* 47 (1966): 351; James Thomas Findlay, *Wolfe in Scotland in the '45 and from 1749 to 1753* (London: Longman, Green, 1928).

57. Erskine, *Hervey's Journal*, 301.

58. Middleton, *Bells of Victory*, 102–7; Stacey, *Quebec*, 5–8; Kimball, *Correspondence of Pitt*, 1:433–35, 444–45; 2:92–93, 115–18; Taylor and Pringle, *Correspondence of Chatham*, 1:378–81; Doughty, *Historical Journal*, 1:306, 322–23, 333–34, 357–59; C. H. Little, ed., *Despatches of Rear-Admiral Philip Durell, 1758–1759 and Rear-Admiral Lord Colville, 1759–1761* (Halifax: Maritime Museum of Canada, 1958), 6–8.

59. Casgrain, *Collection des manuscrits*, 4:144–62; O'Callaghan, *Documents*, 10:952–56; Waddington, *La Guerre*, 3:260–61, 264; Gipson, *British Empire*, 7:382, 388–89; Stacey, *Quebec*, 25–40; Frégault, *Canada*, 241–43; Adair, "Wolfe," 21–22; Dunnigan, *Memoirs by Pierre Pouchot*, 171.

60. Dunnigan, *Memoirs by Pierre Pouchot*, 170–235, 411, 496–98, 503–28; Gipson, *British Empire*, 7:336–38, 344–57; Waddington, *La Guerre*, 3:283–88; Halpenny, *Dictionary of Canadian Biography*, 3:378–79; Jennings, *Empire of Fortune*, 415–17; McConnell, *A Country Between*, 144; Sullivan, *Papers of Johnson*, 3:27–113; Brian Leigh Dunnigan, *Siege 1759: The Campaign against Niagara* (Youngstown NY: Old Fort Niagara Association, 1986); Frank H. Severance, *An Old Frontier of France: The Niagara Region and Adjacant Lakes under French Control*, 2 vols. (New York: Dodd, Mead, 1917), 2:258–328.

61. Dunnigan, *Memoirs by Pierre Pouchot*, 236, 238–39, 374–76, and *Siege 1759*, 91; Doughty, *Historical Journal*, 2:198–200; Gipson, *British Empire*, 7:333–35, 357–60; Kimball, *Correspondence of Pitt*, 2:130–34, 196; Sullivan, *Papers of Johnson*, 3:115–18; Severance, *Old Frontier*, 2:409; Waddington, *La Guerre*, 3:283, 288; Casgrain, *Collection des manuscrits*, 1:194, 200; 8:102; Webster, *Journal of Amherst*, 171; McConnell, *A Country Between*, 130–44; White, *Middle Ground*, 249–55; Godfrey, *Bradstreet*, 147–48; Corkran, *Cherokee Frontier*, 3, 150–76, and *Creek Frontier*, 193–200; John Oliphant, *Peace and War on the Anglo-Cherokeee Frontier, 1756–63* (Baton Rouge: Louisiana State University Press, 2001), 31–112; Tom Hatley, *The Dividing Paths: Cherokees and South Carolinians through the Era of Revolution* (New York: Oxford University Press, 1993), 120–40.

62. Doughty, *Historical Journal*, 1:456–512; 2:180–82, 192–208; Webster, *Journal of Amherst*, 123–83; Kimball, *Correspondence of Pitt*, 2:186–202; Stacey, *Quebec*, 43–44; Middleton, *Bells of Victory*, 132–33; Waddington, *La Guerre*, 3:266, 289–93, 337–38; Bellico, *Sails*

and Steam, 86–113; Casgrain, *Collection des manuscrits,* 5:67–69; O'Callaghan, *Documents,* 10:1054–57; David Lee, "The Contest for Isle aux Noix, 1759–1760: A Case Study in the Fall of New France," *Vermont History* 37 (1969): 96–107.

63. Dunnigan, *Memoirs by Pierre Pouchot,* 363; Frégault, *Canada,* 245; Casgrain, *Collection des manuscrits,* 7:523–26, 528–29; Maupassant, "Les Armateurs bordelais," 314; Stacey, *Quebec,* 28–33; Beatson, *Naval and Military Memoirs,* 3:231; Thomas Mante, *The History of the Late War in North-America, and the Islands of the West-Indies, including the Campaigns of MDCCLXIII and MDCCLXIV against His Majesty's Indian Enemies* (London: W. Strahan and T. Cadell, 1772), maps on 233, 333.

64. For a critical appraisal of the decision, see Eccles, *Essays on New France,* 127.

65. Casgrain, *Collection des manuscrits,* 6:166–69; Michalon, "Vaudreuil et Montcalm," in Delmas, *Conflits,* 143. Waddington, *La Guerre,* 3:274 attributes the Montmorency decision to Vaudreuil, acting on the advice of Lévis.

66. Stacey, *Quebec,* 43–44; Michalon, "Vaudreuil et Montcalm," in Delmas, *Conflits,* 143–44; Gipson, *British Empire,* 7:391; Corbett, *England in the Seven Years' War,* 1:418–19.

67. Doughty, *Historical Journal,* 1:371–74; Stacey, *Quebec,* 49–51; Gipson, *British Empire,* 7:377–80; Edward Salmon, *Life of Admiral Sir Charles Saunders, K. B.* (London: Isaac Pitman and Sons, 1914), 103–7. For the naval dimensions of the Quebec campaign, see C. H. Little, ed., *Despatches of Vice-Admiral Charles Saunders, 1759–1760: The Naval Side of the Capture of Quebec* (Halifax: Maritime Museum of Canada, 1958).

68. Frégault, *Bigot,* 2:284; Casgrain, *Collection des manuscrits,* 7:561.

69. Stacey, *Quebec,* 51–55, 94; Corbett, *England in the Seven Years' War,* 1:422–34; Waddington, *La Guerre,* 3:279–80, 293–94.

70. Stacey, *Quebec,* 56–119, 184–91; Corbett, *England in the Seven Years' War,* 1:434–61; Waddington, *La Guerre,* 3:280–82, 293–304, 310; Adair, "Wolfe," 24–27; Doughty, *Historical Journal,* 1:374–456; 2:1–94; Casgrain, *Collection des manuscrits,* 1:180–89, 192–94; 2:227–33; 7:521–610; 8:62–105; Leach, *Arms for Empire,* 483; O'Callaghan, *Documents,* 10:1057–59; Donald W. Olson, William D. Liddle, Russell L. Doescher, Leah M. Behrends, Tammy D. Silakowski, and François-Jacques Saucier, "Perfect Tide, Ideal Moon: An Unappreciated Aspect of Wolfe's Generalship at Québec, 1759," *William and Mary Quarterly,* 3rd ser., 59 (2002): 957–74; A. Doughty and G. W. Parmalee, *The Siege of Quebec and the Battle of the Plains of Abraham,* 6 vols. (Quebec: Dussault and Proulx, 1901), vols. 4 and 5.

71. Doughty, *Historical Journal,* 2:105; Stacey, *Quebec,* 106–8.

72. Casgrain, *Collection des manuscrits,* 6:225–28. See also Eccles, *Essays on New France,* 125–27.

73. Corbett, *England in the Seven Years' War,* 1:461–71; Waddington, *La Guerre,* 3:304–16; Doughty, *Historical Journal,* 2:94–106; Casgrain, *Collection des manuscrits,* 1:205–12; 7:610–16; Michalon, "Vaudreuil et Montcalm," in Delmas, *Conflits,* 148–56; Eccles, *Essays on New France,* 129–33; Kimball, *Correspondence of Pitt,* 2:163–69; Harris, *Historical Atlas,* plate 43; Stacey, *Quebec,* 120–51, 170–78, "New Documents," and "The Anse au Foulon, 1759: Montcalm and Vaudreuil," *Canadian Historical Review* 40 (1959): 27–37.

74. Doughty, *Historical Journal,* 2:106–32; Stacey, *Quebec,* 156–60; Halpenny, *Dictio-*

nary of Canadian Biography, 4:650–53; Casgrain, *Collection des manuscrits*, 1:212–17; 7:614–16; 8:105–9; O'Callaghan, *Documents*, 10:1004–9; Waddington, *La Guerre*, 3:317–36.

75. B ^{4}91: 41; Corbett, *England in the Seven Years' War*, 1:473–74; Maupassant, "Les Armateurs bordelais," 318–19; Waddington, *La Guerre*, 3:338–41; Halpenny, *Dictionary of Canadian Biography*, 3:321–22; 4:458–61; Casgrain, *Collection des manuscrits*, 1:234; 2:239–66; Clowes, *Royal Navy*, 3:209–10; Little, *Despatches of Saunders*, 22–27; George F. G. Stanley, *New France: The Last Phase, 1744–1760* (Toronto: McClelland and Stewart, 1968), 242–43.

76. Antoine, *Le Gouvernement*, 219; Grouchy and Cottin, *Journal de Croÿ*, 1:458.

77. Waddington, *La Guerre*, 2:190–91; 3:1–18; Savory, *His Britannic Majesty's Army*, 116–39, 467–68; Corbett, *England in the Seven Years' War*, 2:14; Droysen, *Politische Correspondenz*, 17:395–96; 18:59–60; Pajol, *Les Guerres*, 4:346–62; Piers Mackesy, *The Coward of Minden: The Affair of Lord George Sackville* (London: Allen Lane, 1979), 48–56; [Jacques-Victor-Albert], duc de Broglie and Jules Vernier, eds., *Correspondance inédite de Victor-François, duc de Broglie avec le prince Xavier de Saxe, comte de Lusace, pour servir à l'histoire de la Guerre de Sept Ans (campagnes de 1759 à 1761)*, 4 vols. (Paris: Albin Michel, 1903–5), 1:1–9.

78. Waddington, *La Guerre*, 3:19–109; Pajol, *Les Guerres*, 4:363–478; Mackesy, *Coward of Minden*, 57–151; Savory, *His Britannic Majesty's Army*, 140–98; Broglie and Vernier, *Correspondance de Broglie*, 1:9–179; Grouchy and Cottin, *Journal de Croÿ*, 1:481–82, 490; Kennett, *French Armies*, 17–26; Broglie, *King's Secret*, 1:272.

79. Corbett, *England in the Seven Years' War*, 2:7–8, 28n; Barthélemy, *Histoire des relations*, 141–50; Bourguet, *Etudes*, 47–50, 63–82, 92–93; Pares, *War and Trade*, 376–87, and *Colonial Blockade*, 18, 22–23, 164, 180–225, 255–61, 270, 279–83, 287; Middleton, *Bells of Victory*, 118; Bertrand, "Dunkerque," 332; Kent, *War and Trade*, 143–44, 152–60; Carter, *Dutch Republic*, 105, 118–19, 125–28, and "How to Revise Treaties without Negotiating: Common Sense, Mutual Fears, and the Anglo-Dutch Trade Disputes of 1759," in Ragnhild Hatton and M. S. Anderson, eds., *Studies in Diplomatic History: Essays in Memory of David Bayne Horn* (London: Longman, 1970), 214–35.

80. Waddington, *La Guerre*, 3:461–63; Vedel, *Correspondance entre Bernstorff et Choiseul*, 60–63, 84–87, 95–104; Pares, *Colonial Blockade*, 260–61, 276n, 308; Kent, *War and Trade*, 157; Anderson, *Naval Wars*, 227; Eldon, *Subsidy Policy*, 125; Bourguet, *Etudes*, 97–98; Corbett, *England in the Seven Years' War*, 2:127–28; Barthélemy, *Histoire des relations*, 150, 156–57, 162–63, 169–70, and "Le Traité de Paris entre la France et l'Angleterre (1763)," *Revue des questions historiques* 43 (1888): 431–32.

81. Waddington, *La Guerre*, 3:427–30; Bourguet, *Choiseul et l'alliance espagnole*, 5–7, 26–29; Pease, *Boundary Disputes*, lxxivn; Dickson, *Maria Theresia*, 2:175–76; Flassan, *Histoire de la diplomatie française*, 6:269; McLachlan, "Uneasy Neutrality," 72–75. For Laborde see Durand, "Mémoires de Laborde," 73–162, and François d'Ormesson and Jean-Pierre Thomas, *Jean-Joseph de Laborde: Banquier de Louis XV, mécène des Lumières* (Paris: Perron, 2002).

82. Bourguet, *Choiseul et l'alliance espagnole*, 14, 22–26; Droysen, *Politische Corre-*

spondenz, 18:118–19; Parry, *Consolidated Treaty Series*, 41:335–42; Sir Charles Petrie, *King Charles III of Spain: An Enlightened Despot* (London: Constable, 1971), 65–66.

83. Austria 272: 331–32, 435; Austria 273: 56, 135, 154–55, 435; Waddington, *La Guerre*, 3:431, 459–60; Bourguet, *Choiseul et l'alliance espagnole*, 14; Lewis, *Walpole Correpondence*, 21:322–24; François Rousseau, *Règne de Charles III d'Espagne (1759–1788)*, 2 vols. (Paris: Plon-Nourrit, 1907), 1:6.

84. Spain 528: 90–91, Pierre-Paul, marquis d'Ossun to Choiseul, 31 March 1760; Waddington, *La Guerre*, 3:430–31; Bourguet, *Choiseul et l'alliance espagnole*, 16–17; Richmond, *Navy*, 1:212–15; Didier Ozanam, "Les Origines de troisième pacte de famille (1761)," *Revue d'histoire diplomatique* 75 (1961): 309–10, 315–16; Cesáreo Fernádez Duro, *Armada española desde la unión de los Reinos de Castilla y de Aragón*, 9 vols. (Madrid: Tipográfico "Succesores de Rivadeneyra," 1895–1903), 7:7.

85. Spain 529: 272, Ossun to Choiseul, 22 February 1760; Waddington, *La Guerre*, 3:431–32; Bourguet, *Choiseul et l'alliance espagnole*, 21; Ozanam, "Les Origines," 315; Pease, *Boundary Disputes*, 274–76; Thackeray, *History of Pitt*, 1:393–95, 422–23.

86. Oliva, *Misalliance*, 143, Choiseul to L'Hôpital, 8 July 1759; Vedel, *Correspondance entre Bernstorff et Choiseul*, 39–50, Choiseul to Bernstorff, 29 July 1759.

87. A. Morel-Fatio and H. Léonardon, eds., *Recueil des instructions données aux ambassadeurs et ministres de France depuis les traités de Westphalie jusqu'à la révolution française*, vol. 12bis, Espagne, tome troisième (1722–1793) (Paris: Félix Alcan, 1899), 348–53, Choiseul to Ossun, 7 September 1759. See also Savelle, *Origins of American Diplomacy*, 449–50. For Ossun's appointment, see Bourguet, *Choiseul et l'alliance espagnole*, 34; François Rousseau, *Règne de Charles III d'Espagne* (1759–1788), 2 vols. (Paris: Plon-Nourrit, 1907), 1:19.

88. Vedel, *Correspondance entre Bernstorff et Choiseul*, 73–79; Barthélemy, *Histoire des relations*, 160–61; Pease, *Boundary Disputes*, lxxvi.

89. Waddington, *La Guerre*, 3:434–36, 540; Bourguet, *Choiseul et l'alliance espagnole*, 5–7, 46–47, 60–61; Pease, *Boundary Disputes*, 266; Middleton, *Bells of Victory*, 135; Savelle, *Origins of American Diplomacy*, 449; Yorke, *Hardwicke*, 3:241–42; Thackeray, *History of Pitt*, 1:421–22; Browning, *Duke of Newcastle*, 268–69; Black, *Pitt the Elder*, 191–93; Peter D. Brown and Karl W. Schweizer, eds., *The Devonshire Diary: William Cavendish, Fourth Duke of Devonshire: Memoranda on State of Affairs, 1759–1762* (London: Royal Historical Society, 1982), 25–26; Jack M. Sosin, *Whitehall and the Wilderness: The Middle West in British Colonial Policy, 1760–1775* (Lincoln: University of Nebraska Press, 1961), 6.

90. Waddington, *La Guerre*, 3:458–59; Butler, *Choiseul*, 1:474. The comte's instructions are given in Sorel, *Receueil*, 1:382–91.

91. Waddington, *La Guerre*, 3:3–4; Kennett, *French Armies*, 40–41.

92. Waddington, *La Guerre*, 3:116–17; Duffy, *Austrian Army*, 123; Dickson, *Maria Theresia*, 2:349; Kroener, "Die materiellen Grundlagen," in Kroener, ed., *Europa in Zeitalter Friedrichs des Grossen*, 59; Olaf Groehler, *Die Kriege Friedrichs II* (Berlin: Deutscher Militärverlag, 1966), 129–31.

93. Droysen, *Politische Correspondenz*, vol. 18; Waddington, *La Guerre*, 3:115–246; Savory, *His Britannic Majesty's Army*, 199–200; Duffy, *Russia's Military Way*, 104–12, and

Frederick the Great, 179–96, 369–70; Delbrück, *History of the Art of War*, 4:354–59; Showalter, *Wars*, 236–59; Dieter Ernst Bangert, *Die russisch-österreichische militärische Zusammenarbeit im Siebenjähigen Kriege im den jahren 1758–1759* (Boppart-am-Rhein: Harald Boldt, 1971), 142–298.

94. Waddington, *La Guerre*, 3:117, 248–51; Parry, *Consolidated Treaty Series*, 41:285–305; Anderson, *Naval Wars in the Baltic*, 228–29.

95. Waddington, *La Guerre*, 3:469–70; Oliva, *Misalliance*, 147–48; Vandal, *Louis XV et Elisabeth de Russie*, 362.

96. Waddington, *La Guerre*, 3:461–62; Oliva, *Misalliance*, 160–63; Barthélemy, *Histoire des relations*, 147–48, 151–54, 157–58; Vedel, *Correspondance entre Bernstorff et Choiseul*, 25–30, 39–64.

97. Barthélemy, *Histoire des relations*, 151–54, 159–60, 163–64; Vedel, *Correspondance entre Bernstorff et Choiseul*, 41–45, 69–73; Roberts, *British Diplomacy and Swedish Politics*, 22–23.

98. Droysen, *Politische Correspondenz*, 18:241–44, 339, 342–45; Waddington, *La Guerre*, 3:113–14; Doran, *Andrew Mitchell*, 225–26; Marsangy, *Vergennes*, 2:69–84.

99. Ozanam and Antoine, *Correspondance de Broglie*, 1:xlix–li, 12n, 89–96; Boutaic, *Correspondance secrète de Louis XV*, 1:237–39; Ozanam, "La Disgrace," 140–70.

100. Ozanam and Antoine, *Correspondance de Broglie*, 1:91–92n; Antoine and Ozanam, "Le Secret du roi," 85–86.

101. Ozanam and Antoine, *Correspondance de Broglie*, 1:li–liii, 115–17, 122–23; Boutaric, *Correspondance secrète de Louis XV*, 1:240, 252–53; Vandal, *Louis XV et Elisabeth de Russie*, 353, 386–90; Oliva, *Misalliance*, 155–58, 175; Farges, *Recueil*, 5:215–29. For Xavier's service with the French army, see Pajol, *Les Guerres*, 4:309–10n; Broglie and Vernier, *Correspondance de Broglie*, passim.

102. Russia 59: 218, 222–24, 380–82; Russia 60: 59; Russia 61: 277–78, 387–90; Waddington, *La Guerre*, 3:467–70; Oliva, *Misalliance*, 141, 149–51, 155–57; Ozanam and Antoine, *Correspondance de Broglie*, 1:lii.

103. Waddington, *La Guerre*, 3:111–12, 441, 463–69; Oliva, *Misalliance*, 143; Antoine and Ozanam, "Le Secret du roi," 88–89; Vandal, *Louis XV et Elisabeth de Russie*, 357–58; Middleton, *Bells of Victory*, 95–96; Eldon, *Subsidy Policy*, 122–23; Besterman, *Voltaire*, 21:463–64 Choiseul to Voltaire, 13 July 1760.

104. Riley, *Seven Years War*, 140–41, 148, and "French Finances," 227; Félix, *L'Averdy*, 42; Waddington, *La Guerre*, 3:456; Pritchard, *Louis XV's Navy*, 219; Sturgill, "French Army's Budget," 126; Durand, "Mémoires de Laborde," 150; Marion, *Histoire financière*, 1:191.

105. Sturgill, "French Army's Budget," 126, 131; Pritchard, *Louis XV's Navy*, 215–22; Neuville, *Etat sommaire*, 616–17; Legohérel, *Les Trésoriers généraux*, chart facing 180; Caron, *La Guerre incomprise*, 394–97n.

106. Pritchard, *Louis XV's Navy*, 110–11, 142, 197–98; Durand, "Mémoires de Laborde," 151; Brun, *Port de Toulon*, 1:419–20; Bosher, "Financing the French Navy," 118–26; Frégault, *Bigot*, 2:323.

107. Eldon, *Subsidy Policy*, 161–62; Dickson, *Maria Theresia*, 2:395; Pargellis, *Loudoun*, 290; Mitchell and Deane, *Abstract*, 387, 390; Cook and Stevenson, *British Historical Facts*,

171; Mackay, *Admiral Hawke*, 305. I give preference to Mackay for naval expenditures and to Mitchell and Deane for army expenditures.

108. Waddington, *La Guerre*, 3:475–77; Middleton, *Bells of Victory*, 113–18, 153–54; Browning, "Financing of the Seven Years' War," 367, 372–75; Baxter, "Conduct," in Baxter, *England's Rise*, 340; O. A. Sherrard, *Lord Chatham: Pitt and the Seven Years' War* (London: Bodley Head, 1955), 314–17.

109. Antoine, *Le Gouvernement*, 230–31; Grouchy and Cottin, *Journal de Croÿ*, 1:456–58, 462–63, 470–71; Pease, *Boundary Disputes*, 248–65; Vaucher, *Recueil*, 25, part 2: 369; Coquelle, "Les Projets de descente," 613–14.

110. Austria 274: 138; Côté, *Cadet*, 195–255; Riley, *Seven Years War*, 149–59; Waddington, *La Guerre*, 3:456–58; Durand, "Mémoires de Laborde," 94–96, 154–57; Marion, *Histoire financière*, 1:191–98; Pritchard, *Louis XV's Navy*, 198–204; Frégault, *Bigot*, 2:323, 341–88; Barthélemy, "Le Traité de Paris," 424–25; Boulle, "French Colonies," 103n, 160–62, 521–27; Antoine, *Le Gouvernement*, 34, and *Louis XV* (Paris: Fayard, 1989), 791–92; Bosher, "Financing the French Navy," 126–28, "*Affaire du Canada*," 59–78 and *Canada Merchants*, 78, 195–97, 206–12; Swann, *Politics and the Parlement of Paris*, 183–86; Barbier, *Chronique*, 7:200; Lynn, *Wars of Louis XIV*, 327–28; Colin Jones, *The Great Nation: France from Louis XIV to Napoleon* (New York: Columbia University Press, 2002), 242.

111. Barthélemy, "Le Traité de Paris," 424–25; Bourguet, *Choiseul et l'alliance espagnole*, 41–45; Ozanam, "Les Origines," 310–11.

112. Austria 274: 132–40; Waddington, *La Guerre*, 3:444–46; Bourguet, *Etudes*, 31–35.

113. Spain 526: 58–65; Bourguet, *Choiseul et l'alliance espagnole*, 50–53. Emphasis is mine.

114. Spain 526: 74–76.

115. B^{4}85: 96–97, 188; B^{4}87: 181–86, 249–50; Waddington, *La Guerre*, 3:367–68; Lacour-Gayet, *La Marine militaire*, 349–50.

116. B^{4}90: 26–116; B^{4}94: 111–54; B^{7}413: unpaginated, Commissaire Astier to Berryer, 12 November 1759; Lacour-Gayet, *La Marine militaire*, 373–74; Waddington, *La Guerre*, 3:377–79; Middleton, *Bells of Victory*, 118; Corbett, *England in the Seven Years' War*, 2:47–48, 89–91; Russell, *Correspondence of Bedford*, 2:360–65; Malo, *Les Dernières Corsaires*, 68–69, 83–96; Beatson, *Naval and Military Memoirs*, 3:250; Whitworth, *Ligonier*, 310–11; Sir John Knox Laughton, *Studies in Naval History* (London: Longmans, Green, 1887), 342–58.

117. B^{4}86: 203–4; Portugal 91: 156–57; Holland 500: 263.

118. B^{4}86: 205; B^{4}87: 249–50; Marcus, *Quiberon Bay*, 130–32, 138.

119. B^{4}85: 205, Conflans to Aiguillon, 7 November 1759.

120. Marcus, *Quiberon Bay*, 129, 134–38, 192–93; Corbett, *England in the Seven Years' War*, 2:48–49.

121. There are numerous accounts of the battle, including Marcus, *Quiberon Bay*, 138–62, 194–95; Mackay, *Admiral Hawke*, 239–54, and *Hawke Papers*, 344–50; Creswell, *British Admirals*, 108–19; Tunstall, *Naval Warfare*, 115–17; Guy Le Moing, *La Bataille navale des "Cardinaux"* (Paris: Economica, 2003). French accounts of the battle are given in B^{4}87: 258–64, 276–77; B^{4}88: 201–19, 224–64, 280–88, 292, 296–318.

122. B⁴88: 265–72, 319; Marcus, *Quiberon Bay*, 141–42, 163–68; Lacour-Gayet, *La Marine militaire*, 365–66; Linÿer de La Barbée, *Ternay*, 1:65–70, 81–82.

123. Holland 502: 334–36, Ambassador d'Affry to Choiseul, 26 November 1759; Waddington, *La Guerre*, 2:479–80; 3:477–82, 485–89; Thackeray, *History of* Pitt, 1:421–22; Carter, *Dutch* Republic, 27–29; Middleton, *Bells of Victory*, 135–36; Droysen, *Politische Correspondenz*, 17:417–18, 426–28; 18:30–31, 291, 337–41, 432, 511–12, 592, 626–27; Doran, *Andrew Mitchell*, 229–31; Zenab Esmat Rashed, *The Peace of Paris, 1763* (Liverpool: Liverpool University Press, 1951), 31–33.

124. Eldon, *Subsidy Policy*, 115.

125. Spain 526: 180, Choiseul to Ossun, 6 December 1759; Austria 274: 368, circular letter of 9 December 1759; Philippe Amiguet, *Lettres de Louis XV à son petit-fils l'Infant Ferdinand de Parme* (Paris: Bernard Grasset, 1938), 11; Derek Beales, *Joseph II*, vol. 1, *In the Shadow of Maria Theresa, 1741–1780* (Cambridge: Cambridge University Press, 1987), 69, 77; Wenzel-Anton, Fürst Kaunitz-Ritberg, "Memoire sur la cour de France, 1752," *Revue de Paris* 11, part 4 (July/August 1904): 443.

126. Wolf, *Louis XIV*, 555–91, 610–13.

7. 1760—ADVERSITY AND REVIVAL

1. Frederik Bajer, "Les Entrevues de Martin Hübner avec le duc de Choiseul en 1759," *Revue d'histoire diplomatique* 18 (1904): 415–18. See also Giraud, "Mémoire de Choiseul," 174.

2. Austria 274: 333–34, the duc de Choiseul to the comte de Choiseul, 2 December 1759; Austria 275: 24–25, the duc de Choiseul to the comte de Choiseul, 9 January 1760. See also Holland 502: 361, Choiseul to d'Affry, 1 December 1759; Spain 526: 123–25, Choiseul to Ossun, 1 December 1759; Russia 61: 326–27, Choiseul to L'Hôpital, 2 December 1759.

3. Russia 61: 387–90, Choiseul to L'Hôpital, 14 December 1759; Spain 527: 11, Choiseul to Ossun, 6 January 1760; Arneth, *Geschichte Maria Theresia's*, 6:435; Sorel, *Recueil*, 1:386, Instructions for the comte de Choiseul, June 1759; Besterman, *Voltaire*, 21:53, Choiseul to Voltaire, 20 December 1759.

4. For the early stages of the negotiations, see Waddington, *La Guerre*, 3:489–505; Barthélemy, "Le Traité de Paris," 426–28; Coquelle, *L'Alliance franco-hollandaise*, 121–26; Bourguet, *Etudes*, 132–48, 160–62, 168; Vedel, *Correspondance entre Bernstorff et Choiseul*, 104–10.

5. Spain 527: 11–15, 19–21, Choiseul to Ossun, 6 January 1760 and enclosed "Draft of Preliminary Articles"; Austria 275: 18, the duc de Choiseul to the comte de Choiseul, 9 January 1760; Vedel, *Correspondence entre Bernstorff et Choiseul*, 117–24. Pease, *Boundary Disputes*, 267–70, 271–74, provides excerpts (with English translations) of the proposals.

6. Spain 527: 140–41, Ossun to Choiseul, 4 February 1760. See also Waddington, *La Guerre*, 3:438–39.

7. See, for example, Holland 502: 406–10, d'Affry to Choiseul, 14 December 1759.

8. Holland 503: 139–43, d'Affry to Choiseul, 15 February 1760; Holland 503: 159–62, Choiseul to d'Affry, 24 February 1760.

9. Brown and Schweizer, *Devonshire Diary*, 32–33. See also Waddington, *La Guerre*, 3:438–39; Yorke, *Hardwicke*, 3:244; Marie Peters, *Pitt and Popularity: The Patriot Minister and London Opinion during the Seven Years' War* (Oxford: Clarendon Press, 1980), 165–69.

10. State Papers 84 (Netherlands), 487: unpaginated, Holdernesse to Yorke, 25 January 1760; Waddington, *La Guerre*, 3:499–504; Brown and Schweizer, *Devonshire Diary*, 34; Taylor and Pringle, *Correspondence of Chatham*, 1:463–64; 2:26–31; Corbett, *England in the Seven Years' War*, 2:73–78; Droysen, *Politische Correspondenz*, 19:3–4, 38–40; Bisset, *Memoirs of Mitchell*, 2:124–27; Doran, *Andrew Mitchell*, 233; Butler, *Choiseul* 1:535–46; Guicciardi and Bonnet, *Mémoires de Choiseul*, 53–55.

11. Vedel, *Correspondance entre Bernstorff et Choiseul*, 73–79. See also Bajer, "Hübner," 417.

12. Waddington, *La Guerre*, 3:440–42; Roger H. Soltau, *The Duke de Choiseul: The Lothian Essay, 1908* (Oxford: B. H. Blackwell; London: Simpkin, Marshall, 1909), 60.

13. For discussions between France and Prussia, see Waddington, *La Guerre*, 3:505, 515–26; Droysen, *Politische Correspondenz*, 19:101–4, 106–12, 117–19, 129, 165, 188, 204–6, 208–9, 222–23; Bisset, *Memoirs of Mitchell*, 2:151–53; Coquelle, *L'Alliance franco-hollandaise*, 126–27; Bourguet, *Etudes*, 147–49, 154; Besterman, *Voltaire*, 21:36–40, 52–53, 94–95, 143–44, 192–94, 209–10, 225–26, 254–55, 274–77, 287–89, 322–24, 400–402, 463–64.

14. Austria 275: 17–27 and passim; Waddington, *La Guerre*, 3:442–43, 470, 489–98, 505–8; Soltau, *Choiseul*, 43, 53–54; Bourguet, *Choiseul et l'alliance espagnole*, 85–86.

15. Waddington, *La Guerre*, 494–95.

16. Russia 61: 386; Russia 62: 44–57 and passim; Russia 63: 389–401 and passim; Russia 64: 192–201, 239–40; Austria 276: 12, 198, 222, 237–38; Parry, *Consolidated Treaty Series* 41:371–99; Waddington, *La Guerre*, 4:460–64, 495–98; Oliva, *Misalliance*, 151–54, 159–63, 168–81; Vedel, *Correspondance entre Bernstorff et Choiseul*, 129, 134–208; Droysen, *Politische Correspondenz*, 19:10–11, 305–8, 396; Barthélemy, "Le Traité de Paris," 435–36, and *Histoire des relations*, 168–69, 174–204; Ozanam and Antoine, *Correspondance de Broglie*, 1:91–92n, 109–15; Boutaric, *Correspondance secrète de Louis XV*, 1:245–50, 257–61; Antoine and Ozanam, "Le Secret du Roi," 90; Vandal, *Louis XV et Elisabeth de Russie*, 369–86; Alfred Rambaud, ed., *Receuil des instructions données aux ambassadeurs et ministres de France depuis les traités de Westphalie jusqu'à la révolution française*, vol. 6, *Russie, tome second (1749–1789)* (Paris: Félix Alcan, 1890), 118–61.

17. They are documented in Holland 503: passim; Holland 504: 1–29; State Papers Series 84 (Netherlands), 487: unpaginated, beginning with Yorke to Holdernesse, 4 March 1760; State Papers Series 84 (Netherlands), 488: unpaginated, through Yorke to Holdernesse, 6 May 1760. Copies of the d'Affry-Yorke correspondence were also sent to Austria and retained in Austria 275 and Austria 276. For description and analysis, see Waddington, *La Guerre*, 3:503–5, 512–15, 526–39; Barthélemy, "Le Traité de Paris," 429–31; Coquelle, *L'Alliance franco-hollandaise*, 125–34; Bourguet, *Etudes*, 152–71.

18. Brown and Schweizer, *Devonshire Diary*, 26, 31; Yorke, *Hardwicke*, 3:241–42; Bourguet, *Etudes*, 143–46, 148–49, 152–53; Middleton, *Bells of Victory*, 147; Baxter, "Conduct,"

in Baxter, *England's Rise*, 338; R. C. Simmons and P. D. G. Thomas, eds., *Proceedings and Debates of the British Parliaments Respecting North America, 1754–1783*, 6 vols. to date (Millwood NY: Kraus International Publications, 1982–), 1:296–97.

19. Spain 528: 69, Choiseul to Ossun, 25 March 1760; Coquelle, *L'Alliance franco-hollandaise*, 124–25; Droysen, *Politische Correspondenz*, 19:81.

20. Sherrard, *Chatham*, 355.

21. Russia 59: 112, Choiseul to L'Hôpital, 11 January 1759; Vedel, *Correspondence entre Bernstorff et Choiseul*, 94–95, 132–33; Besterman, *Voltaire*, 21:94–95; Bourguet, *Etudes*, 193–95; Thackeray, *History of Pitt*, 1:525.

22. Vedel, *Correspondence entre Bernstorff et Choiseul*, 132, Choiseul to Bernstorff, 27 March 1760.

23. Spain 527: 272, Ossun to Choiseul, 22 February 1760; Spain 528: 269, 300, 367–68, Choiseul to Ossun, 20 May, 27 May, and 21 June 1760; see also Waddington, *La Guerre*, 3:439–40; Bourguet, *Choiseul et l'alliance espagnole*, 40, 46–47, 70–71, 96; Ozanam, "Les Origines," 317–19; Rousseau, *Règne de Charles III*, 1:50.

24. Spain 527: passim; Spain 528: passim; Spain 529: 29, Ossun to Choiseul, 4 July 1760; Waddington, *La Guerre*, 3:440, 508–10, 544–45; 4:420–21; Bourguet, *Choiseul et l'alliance espagnole*, 70, 87–92, 97–105; Rousseau, *Règne de Charles III*, 1:43–51; Barthélemy, "Le Traité de Paris," 426–33; Taylor and Pringle, *Correspondence of Chatham*, 2:22–23; Pease, *Boundary Disputes*, lxxxv–lxxxvi, 274–76.

25. Austria 277: 253, the duc de Choiseul to the comte de Choiseul, 9 September 1760; Sturgill, "French Army's Budget," 131; Jules-A. Tashereau, ed., "Conseils des ministres sous Louis XV," in *Revue retrospective, ou bibliothèque historique, contenant des mémoires et documents authentiques, inédits et originaux, pour servir à l'histoire proprement dite, à la biographie, à l'histoire de la littérature et des arts*, 20 vols. (Paris: H. Fournier aîné, 1833–38), 20 (3rd ser., 3), 348–51, 370–72. See also Austria 278: 88, the comte de Choiseul to the duc de Choiseul, 12 October 1760.

26. Riley, *Seven Years War*, 137, 140–41; Félix, *L'Averdy*, 42; Grouchy and Cottin, *Journal de Croÿ*, 1:491–92; Dickson, *Maria Theresia*, 2:173–74, 181–82, 396; Kwass, *Privilege*, 37, 161–79; Swann, *Politics and the Parlement of Paris*, 186–90; Marion, *Histoire financière*, 1:185–86, 198–210; Antoine, *Louis XV*, 791–92; Egret, *Louis XV*, 93–95; Durand, "Mémoires de Laborde," 97n.

27. B⁴94: 42–53, Memoir of Berryer presented to the Council of State, 6 March 1760; Pritchard, *Louis XV's Navy*, 200–201, 215–22; Legohérel, *Les Trésoriers généraux*, chart facing 180; Neuville, *Etat sommaire*, 616–17; Caron, *La Guerre incomprise*, 383–84.

28. B⁴94:42–53; Caron, *La Guerre incomprise*, 377–80, 383–87; Bamford, *Privilege and Profit*, 137–38; Brun, *Port de Toulon*, 1:438–39; Chabaud-Arnault, "Etudes historiques," *Revue maritime* 115 (1892): 404–6; Grouchy and Cottin, *Journal de Croÿ*, 1:480; Vergé-Francheshi, *Les Officiers généraux*, 7:447; Pritchard, *Louis XV's Navy*, 56, 201–2, and "French Naval Officer Corps," 62, 66n.

29. Le Goff, "Problèmes de recrutement," 232; Crowhurst, *Defence of British Trade*, 20, 29, 32; Meyer, *L'Armament nantais*, 79–80.

30. Portugal 90: 329–30, 396–98; Portugal 91: 30, 36, 49–51, 88, 103, 124–32, 163–71, 216–

17, 226–34, 243–44, 257–67, 287–88; Portugal 92: 55–58, 90–92, 126–27; B^{2}351: 108–10, 216, 229; B^{2}366: 59, 66, 205; B^{3}548: 11, 25, 47–48, 175, 187, 219; B^{3}550: 196; Demerliac, *La Marine de Louis XV*, 46–47; Brun, *Port de Toulon*, 1:423–25.

31. There is a substantial amount of correspondence concerning the model ship, including B^{2}366: 204; B^{2}369: 12, 82, 93, 109, 121; B^{3}551:307, 362–63. For Louis and his grandson, see Amiguet, *Lettres de Louis XV* (Paris: Bernard Grasset, 1938), 29–33 and passim.

32. B^{1}67: 3; B^{3}547: 279, 284–85, 294, 297, 299, 305–7; B^{3}549: 100–104; Linÿer de La Barbée, *Ternay*, 1:71–126.

33. Kimball, *Correspondence of Pitt*, 2:247–50.

34. Spain 528: 379; B^{1}67: 12–15, 18, 93; B^{2}367: 22, 139; B^{3}547: 266; B^{4}94: 43; B^{4}98: 48–84; B^{4}103: 381–82; G 49: 155; Caron, *La Guerre incomprise*, 383; Chabaud-Arnault, "Etudes historiques," *Revue maritime* 115 (1892): 619; Bourguet, *Choiseul et l'alliance espagnole*, 91–92; Buchet, *La Lutte*, 1:399, 443; Clowes, *Royal Navy*, 3:225–26, 303; Riley, *Seven Years War*, 109–10; Romano, "Balance du commerce," 1274, 1291; Villers, *Marine royale*, 2:453–56, 475 and "Commerce coloniale," 35, 38, 41–42, 44n; Pares, *War and Trade*, 386–87 and *The Historian's Business*, 156–58; Tashereau, "Conseils des ministres," 346–56; Beatson, *Naval and Military Memoirs*, 2:375–76; Troude, *Batailles navales*, 1:423–24; Malvezin, *Commerce de Bordeaux*, 3:302–7; N. A. M. Rodger, "The Douglas Papers, 1760–1762," in Rodger, *Naval Miscellany*, 253.

35. B^{2}366: 212bis–217bis and passim; B^{3}548: passim; B^{4}93: 244–418; B^{4}102: 4–7, 11–25; G 49: 147, 152–54; Brun, *Port de Toulon*, 1:425–26; Beatson, *Naval and Military Memoirs*, 2:407. See appendix I for the ships.

36. B^{4}99: 6; Chabaud-Arnault, "Etudes historiques," *Revue maritime* 115 (1892): 614; Bourguet, *Choiseul et l'alliance espagnole*, 92; Hamont, *Lally-Tollendal*, 244–69; Lacour-Gayet, *La Marine militaire*, 408; Waddington, *La Guerre*, 5:1–35; Corbett, *England in the Seven Years' War*, 2:133–35; Fortescue, *British Army*, 471–82; Wylly, *Coote*, 74–107, 382–95.

37. Holland 505: 42–47; B^{4}92: 250–307; B^{4}99: 107–13; Crowhurst, *Defence of British Trade*, 237–40; Michel, *Estaing*, 48–60.

38. Waddington, *La Guerre*, 5:23–24; Corbett, *England in the Seven Years' War*, 2:81–82, 132–40, 149–50; Beatson, *Naval and Military Memoirs*, 2:420; Whitworth, *Ligonier*, 319; Middleton, *Bells of Victory*, 166, 173, 176–77; Antoine Chelin, *Une Ile et son passé: Ile Maurice (1507–1947)* (Port Louis, Mauritius: Mauritius Print, 1973), 41, 46.

39. Casgrain, *Collection des manuscrits* 2:246–47, Lévis to Belle-Isle, 1 November 1759 (with a similar letter to Berryer). See also Waddington, *La Guerre*, 3:339–41; Stanley, *New France*, 242–43.

40. B^{4}91:41; O'Callaghan, *Documents*, 10:1065–68, Memoir of Le Mercier, 7 January 1760.

41. Waddington, *La Guerre*, 4:334, 364; Frégault, *Canada*, 270; Halpenny, *Dictionary of Canadian Biography*, 4:28, 207; Bosher, "Financing the French Army," 129 and *Canada Merchants*, 200–201; Maupassant, "Les Armateurs bordelais," 320–25; Gilles Proulx, "Le Dernier Effort de la France au Canada: Secours ou fraude?" *Revue d'histoire de l'Amérique française* 36 (1982–83): 413–26; C. H. Little, ed., *The Battle of Restigouche: The Last Naval*

Engagement between France and Britain for the Possession of Canada (Halifax: Maritime Museum of Canada, 1962), 3–6.

42. Casgrain, *Collection des manuscrits*, 1:254–57; Waddington, *La Guerre*, 4:339–41; Nicolai, "Different Kind of Courage," 71–73.

43. Waddington, *La Guerre*, 4:338; Doughty, *Historical Journal*, 2:353, 364n, 389n; Brumwell, *Redcoats*, 153n; R. H. Mahon, *Life of General the Hon. James Murray, a Builder of Canada* (London: John Murray, 1921), 219.

44. Casgrain, *Collection des manuscrits*, 1:257–82; 2:292–94, 304–8; 4:213–23; 11:219–42; O'Callaghan, *Documents*, 10:1069–89; Doughty, *Historical Journal*, 2:376–452; Waddington, *La Guerre*, 4:342–60; Stanley, *New France*, 244–49; Harris, *Historical Atlas*, plate 43; Brumwell, *Redcoats*, 256–61; La Pause, "Mémoire," 108–16.

45. Casgrain, *Collection des manuscrits*, 1:280–83; 2:311–12; 11:263–71; Doughty, *Historical Journal*, 2:425–36; 3:245–51, 360–85, 397–410; Waddington, *La Guerre*, 4:360–63; Little, *Battle of Restigouche*, 7–24; Maupassant, "Les Armateurs bordelais," 325–26; Frégault, *Canada*, 273–74; Clowes, *Royal Navy*, 3:227–28; Little, *Despatches of Durell*, 15–17, 22–23; Gilles Proulx, *Fighting at Restigouche: The Men and Vessels of 1760 in Chaleur Bay* (Ottawa: National Historic Sites, Parks Canada, 1999). For a list of the British warships in North America, see appendix I.

46. Casgrain, *Collection des manuscrits*, 2:362, Lévis to Berryer, 28 June 1760. See also Stanley, *New France*, 259; Frégault, *Canada*, 279 and *Bigot*, 2:317.

47. Harris, *Historical Atlas*, plate 42; Gipson, *British Empire*, 7:445–46; Kimball, *Correspondence of Pitt*, 2:231–37; Anderson, *People's Army*, 19, 59n and *Crucible of War*, 805–6; Selesky, *War and Society*, 168, 190; Webster, *Journal of Amherst*, 328; Gipson, *British Empire*, 7:445–46; Harrison Bird, *Battle for a Continent* (New York: Oxford University Press, 1965), 359–60.

48. Doughty, *Historical Journal*, 2:519–20; Titus, *Old Dominion*, 129–30; Webster, *Journal of Amherst*, 198; Kimball, *Correspondence of Pitt*, 2:263; Corkran, *Cherokee Frontier*, 207–15; Hatley, *Dividing Paths*, 105–40; Oliphant, *Peace and War*, 8–188; Dowd, "Gift Giving," in Cayton and Teute, *Contact Points*, 114–50.

49. Kimball, *Correspondence of Pitt*, 2:346–47, Pitt to Amherst, 24 October 1760.

50. Doughty, *Historical Journal*, 2:524–58; 3:257; Webster, *Journal of Amherst*, 227–45; Waddington, *La Guerre*, 4:377–81, 383; Dunnigan, *Memoirs by Pouchot*, 52, 173, 259–62, 271n, 281n, 286–317, 364–76, 502.

51. Waddington, *La Guerre*, 4:373–77; Gipson, *British Empire*, 7:454–57; Lee, "Isle aux Noix," 103–5; Bellico, *Sails and Steam*, 103–7.

52. Casgrain, *Collection des manuscrits*, 1:284–303; Doughty, *Historical Journal*, 2:463–522; 3:306–27; Little, *Despatches of Durell*, 23–24; Clowes, *Royal Navy*, 3:227–28; Waddington, *La Guerre*, 363, 368–73, 377; Gipson, *British Empire*, 7:457–60; Stanley, *New France*, 251–55.

53. Casgrain, *Collection des manuscrits*, 1:302–35; Doughty, *Historical Journal*, 2:558–90; Webster, *Journal of Amherst*, 245–49; Harris, *Historical Atlas*, plate 43; Waddington, *La Guerre*, 4:381–87; Jean Berenger and Philippe Roy, "Relations des troupes reglées (troupes de terres et troupes de marine) avec les Canadiens," in Delmas, *Conflits*, 25; Kimball,

Correspondence of Pitt, 2:340; Pease, *Boundary Disputes*, lxxx–lxxxi, map opposite 568; Halpenny, *Dictionary of Canadian Biography*, 3:xxii; Eccles, *France in America*, 207n and *Essays on New France*, 122.

54. Kimball, *Correspondence of Pitt*, 2:387–88, 404; Doughty, *Historical Journal*, 3:386–97, 416–21; Harris, *Historical Atlas*, plate 42; Halpenny, *Dictionary of Canadian Biography*, 4:27–29; Leach, *Arms for Empire*, 476–77; Robert Sauvageau, *Acadie: La Guerre de cent ans des Français d'Amérique aux Maritimes et en Louisiane, 1670–1769* (Paris: Berger-Levrault, 1987), 386–93; Louise P. Kellogg, ed., "La Chapelle's Remarkable Retreat through the Mississippi Valley, 1760–61," *Mississippi Valley Historical Review* 22 (1935–36): 63–81.

55. There are many superb analyses of the connection between the war against France and the American Revolution, among them Rogers, *Empire and Liberty*; John M. Murrin, "The French and Indian War, the American Revolution, and the Counterfactual Hypothesis: Reflections on Lawrence Henry Gipson and John Shy," *Reviews in American History* 1 (1973): 307–18; John Shy, *Toward Lexington: The Role of the British Army in the Coming of the American Revolution* (Princeton: Princeton University Press, 1965); Jack P. Greene, "The Seven Years' War and the American Revolution: The Causal Relationship Reconsidered," *Journal of Imperial and Commonwealth History* 8 (1979–80): 85–105, and *Understanding the American Revolution: Issues and Actors* (Charlottesville: University Press of Virginia, 1995), 52–56; John L. Bullion, "Securing the Peace: Lord Bute, the Plan for the Army, and the Origins of the American Revolution," in Karl W. Schweizer, ed., *Lord Bute: Essays in Re-Interpretation* (Leicester: Leicester University Press, 1988), 17–39.

56. Harris, *Historical Atlas*, plate 44; White, *Middle Ground*, 249–314; McConnell, *A Country Between*, 135–206; Gregory Evans Dowd, *War under Heaven: Pontiac, the Indian Nations, and the British Empire* (Baltimore: Johns Hopkins University Press, 2002).

57. Dunnigan, *Memoirs by Pouchot*, provides a wonderful account of the Canadians by a sympathetic French observer; see in particular 321–22 for his praise of Canadian women. For the social effects of the fur trade, see Bosher, *Canada Merchants*, and S. D. Clark, *The Developing Canadian Community* (Toronto: University of Toronto Press, 1962), 20–40. A succinct introduction to the immediate postwar period is Eccles, *France in America*, 208–15, 219–35. For a survey of recent work on Canadian society, see Jean-Paul Bernard, "L'Historiographie canadienne récente (1964–94) et l'histoire des peuples du Canada," *Canadian Historical Review* 76 (1995): 321–53.

58. Two recent studies of the uprising are Allen Greer, *The Patriots and the People: The Rebellion of 1837 in Rural Lower Canada* (Toronto: University of Toronto Press, 1993) and Beverly Boissery, *A Deep Sense of Wrong: The Treason, Trials, and Transportation to New South Wales of Lower Canadian Rebels after the 1838 Rebellion* (Toronto: Allen and Unwin, 1995).

59. Pease, *Boundary Disputes*, 286–87; Sosin, *Whitehall and the Wilderness*, 6–7; Yorke, *Hardwicke*, 3:313–15; Marjorie G. Reid, "Pitt's Decision to Keep Canada in 1761," in *The Canadian Historical Association Report of the Annual Meeting Held in the City of Ottawa, May 17–18, 1926* (Ottawa: Department of Public Archives, n.d.), 25.

60. Savory, *His Britannic Majesty's Army*, 202–3, 477–78; Eldon, *Subsidy Policy*, 129–30; Waddington, *La Guerre*, 4:170; Middleton, *Bells of Victory*, 150–51; Dickson, *Maria There-*

sia, 2:396; Brewer, *Sinews of Power*, 41; Mitchell and Deane, *Abstract*, 387, 390; Mathias and O'Brien, "Taxation," 605; Mackay, *Admiral Hawke*, 305; Cook and Stevenson, *British Historical Facts*, 171; Fortescue, *British Army*, 2:508–10, 529–30; Whitworth, *Ligonier*, 317.

61. Middleton, *Bells of Victory*, 147–48, 155–56; Corbett, *England in the Seven Years' War*, 2:81–85.

62. Austria 275: 363; Waddington, *La Guerre*, 3:109; 4:157–70, 236–39, 274–75, 285–86; 5:198; Savory, *His Britannic Majesty's Army*, 241–42; Grouchy and Cottin, *Journal de Croÿ*, 1:490; Nicolai, "Different Kind of Courage," 70–71; Duffy, *Military Experience*, 182, 279; Brent Nosworthy, *The Anatomy of Victory: Battle Tactics, 1689–1763* (New York: Hippocrene Books, 1990), 329–36.

63. Savory, *His Britannic Majesty's Army*, 203–4; Kennett, *French Armies*, 40.

64. Savory, *His Britannic Majesty's Army*, 207–59; Waddington, *La Guerre*, 4:171–247; Pajol, *Les Guerres*, 5:14–87.

65. Austria 278: 229–30; Spain 530: 143; State Papers Series 87 (Foreign Military Expeditions), 38: 189–90; Savory, *His Britannic Majesty's Army*, 260–83; Waddington, *La Guerre*, 4:248–87; Pajol, *Les Guerres*, 5:87–114; Cook and Stevenson, *British Historical Facts*, 167; [Jean-Baptiste-Donatien de Vimeur], comte de Rochambeau, *Mémoires militaires, historiques et politiques de Rochambeau, ancien maréchal et grand officier de la Legion d'Honneur*, 2 vols. (Paris: Fain, 1809), 1:158–63; Pierre-Marie-Maurice-Henri, marquis de Ségur, *Le Maréchal de Ségur (1724–1801) ministre de guerre sous Louis XVI* (Paris: E. Plon, Nourrit, 1895), 175–76; Thomas Lindner, *Die Peripetie des Siebenjährigen Krieges: Der Herbstfeldzug 1760 in Sachsen und der Winterfeldzug 1760/61 in Hessen* (Berlin: Duncker and Humblot, 1993), 131–57.

66. Waddington, *La Guerre*, 4:2; Droysen, *Politische Correspondenz*, 19:59, 86, 367; Duffy, *Austrian Army*, 33, 123–24; Kroener, "Die materiellen Grundlagen," in Kroener, *Europa im Zeitalter Friedrichs des Grossen*, 59.

67. Dickson, *Maria Theresia*, 2:349.

68. For the campaign of 1760, see Droysen, *Politische Correspondenz*, 19:360–607; 20:1–142; Waddington, *La Guerre*, 4:4–156; Lindner, *Die Peripetie*, 26–130; Asprey, *Frederick the Great*, 527–44; Showalter, *Wars*, 260–96; Anderson, *Naval Wars*, 229–30; Christopher Duffy, *The Army of Maria Theresa: The Armed Forces of Imperial Austria, 1740–1780* (North Pomfret VT: David and Charles, 1977), 193, 196–202, *Frederick the Great*, 196–219, and *Russia's Military Way*, 112–16.

69. Austria 277: 251–60, 331–32, 375–90; Austria 278: 7–8, 39, 113–16, 147, 465; Waddington, *La Guerre*, 4:445–60; Beales, *Joseph II*, 1:71–82; Ursula Tamussino, *Isabella von Parma, Gemahlin Josephs II* (Vienna: Osterreichischer Bundesverlag Gesellschaft, 1989), 105–26, 159–71.

70. Middleton, *Bells of Victory*, 165; Corbett, *England in the Seven Years' War*, 2:94–95; Doran, *Andrew Mitchell*, 252–54.

71. Middleton, *Bells of Victory*, 83, 170–72; Brown and Schweizer, *Devonshire Diary*, 42–48; Clark, *Waldegrave*, 213–17; Baxter, "Conduct," in Baxter, *England's Rise*, 326–43; Romney Sedgwick, ed., *Letters from George III to Lord Bute, 1756–1766* (London: Macmillan, 1939), 11, 24, 28–29, 45, 49–50; John Brooke, *King George III* (New York: McGraw-Hill,

1972), 42–89; John Brewer, *Party Ideology and Popular Politics at the Accession of George III* (New York: Cambridge University Press, 1976), 10. The role of George III in postwar British diplomacy is discussed in H. M. Scott, *British Foreign Policy in the Age of the American Revolution* (Oxford: Clarendon Press, 1990), 15–18.

72. Corbett, *England in the Seven Years' War*, 2:144–48; Doran, *Andrew Mitchell*, 253; Gipson, *British Empire*, 8:43–46; Peters, *Pitt and Popularity*, 183; Schweizer, *Anglo-Prussian Alliance*, 101–4, and "Israel Mauduit: Pamphleteering and Foreign Policy in the Age of the Elder Pitt," in Stephen Taylor, Richard Connors, and Clyve Jones, eds., *Hanoverian Britain and Empire: Essays in Memory of Philip Lawson* (Woodbridge, Eng.: Boydell Press, 1998), 198–209; [Israel Mauduit], *Considerations on the Present German War* (London: J. Wilkie, 1760); Robert J. Taylor, "Israel Mauduit," *New England Quarterly* 24 (1951): 208–30.

73. Middleton, *Bells of Victory*, 166–70, 173; Corbett, *England in the Seven Years' War*, 2:81–82, 95–104, 131–32; Hackmann, "English Military Expeditions," 155–64; Mackay, *Hawke Papers*, 370–71, and *Admiral Hawke*, 268–76; Caron, *La Guerre incomprise*, 220–21.

74. Spain 529: 129, Ossun to Choiseul, 28 July 1760; Spain 530: 394–95, Ossun to Choiseul, 29 December 1760; Brown and Schweizer, *Devonshire Diary*, 59–60; Middleton, *Bells of Victory*, 162–63; Waddington, *La Guerre*, 3:544; 4:415–18; Scott, *British Foreign Policy*, 71; Corbett, *England in the Seven Years' War*, 2:150–51; Taylor and Pringle, *Correspondence of Chatham*, 2:22–23, 46–47, 68–72; 4:69n; Thackeray, *History of Pitt*, 1:487–92; 2:486–95; Ozanam, "Les Origines," 319–21; Bourguet, *Choiseul et l'alliance espagnole*, 90–92, 103–5, 123–24, 131–33, 150–53, 168–69; Savelle, *Origins of American Diplomacy*, 452, 460–64; Parry, *Consolidated Treaty Series*, 28:334–35; Pease, *Boundary Disputes*, lxxxvi-lxxxvii; Pares, *War and Trade*, 540–55; Rousseau, *Règne de Charles III*, 1:51–53; Ayling, *Pitt*, 286–87; Rashed, *Peace of Paris*, 59–61; Allan Christelow, "Economic Background of the Anglo-Spanish War of 1762," *Journal of Modern History* 18 (1946): 25.

75. Spain 530: 241–42, 248–49. For previous French warnings about such dangers, see Spain 530: 67, 138–43, Ossun to Choiseul, 17 October and 30 October 1760; Spain 530: 194, Choiseul to Ossun, 14 November 1760.

76. Spain 530: 196–98, Choiseul to Ossun, 14 November 1760; Spain 530: 210–20, 345–52, Ossun to Choiseul, 17 November and 22 December 1760; Spain 531: 20, Choiseul to Ossun, 6 January 1761; Portugal 91: 22–23, 89, 112, 211–12, 235–36, 239–46, 254, 256, 270: Portugal 92: 33–36, 80–89, 197, 237; Bourguet, *Choiseul et l'alliance espagnole*, 161–62, 165–66, 173. For María Ana Victoria, see Kerrebrouck, *Maison de France*, 330.

77. Waddington, *La Guerre*, 4:420–26; Ozanam, "Les Origines," 312–13, 321–22; Barthélemy, "Le Traité de Paris," 430, 432–34, 437–38, 442–43; Rousseau, *Règne de Charles III*, 1:49–51, 53; Bourguet, *Choiseul et l'alliance espagnole*, 96–97, 106–22, 124–30, 133–49, 153–67, 170–73; Savelle, *Origins of American Diplomacy*, 464–65; Allan Christelow, "French Interest in the Spanish Empire during the Ministry of the Duc de Choiseul, 1759–1771," *Hispanic American Historical Review* 21 (1941): 520–21; André Soulange-Bodin, *La Diplomatie de Louis XV et le pacte de famille* (Paris: Perrin, 1894), 101, 136–47.

78. Spain 530: 295, Ossun to Choiseul, 8 December 1760. For Arriaga, see also Spain 526: 64, Ossun to Choiseul, 18 November 1759; Spain 530: 55–56, Ossun to Choiseul, 13

October 1760; State Papers Series 94 (Spain), 164: 79, Bristol to Pitt, 31 August 1761 (which is printed in Thackeray, *History of Pitt*, 1:566). For prior reports on the Spanish navy, see Spain 526: 86; Spain 527: 60, 272; Spain 529: 29; Spain 530: 16.

8. 1761—SAVING THE NAVY'S FUTURE

1. Antoine, *Le Gouvernement*, 26, 69–70.

2. Grouchy and Cottin, *Journal de Croÿ*, 1:513.

3. Sturgill, "French Army's Budget," 131; Pritchard, *Louis XV's Navy*, 201–2, 215–22; Neuville, *Etat sommaire*, 616–17; Legohérel, *Les Trésoriers généraux*, chart facing page 180; Giraud, "Mémoire de Choiseul," 179.

4. Riley, *Seven Years War*, 137–38, 140–41, 146, 148, 226–27, and "French Finances," 224–25; Dickson, *Maria Theresia*, 2:396; Antoine, *Louis XV*, 754–56, 759–61, 773–74, 793, 802; Kwass, *Privilege*, 179–81; Egret, *Louis XV*, 93–95, 140–44, 146; Durand, "Mémoires de Laborde," 96; Swann, *Politics and the Parlement of Paris*, 187–90, 198–204, 206–13, 221, and "Parlements and Political Crisis under Louis XV: The Besançon Affair, 1757–1761," *Historical Journal* 37 (1994): 824–25; Dale E. Van Kley, *The Jansenists and the Expulsion of the Jesuits from France, 1757–1765* (New Haven: Yale University Press, 1975), 82–87, 129–32; Alfred Bourguet, "Un Négotation diplomatique du duc de Choiseul relative aux Jésuites (1761–1762)," *Revue d'histoire diplomatique* 16 (1902): 161–75; Arthur S. Aiton, "The Diplomacy of the Louisiana Cession," *American Historical Review* 36 (1930–31): 706n; H. M. Scott, "Religion and Realpolitik: The Duc de Choiseul, the Bourbon Family Compact, and the Attack on the Society of Jesus, 1758–1775," *International History Review* 25 (2003): 37–62.

5. Savory, *His Britannic Majesty's Army*, 281–301; Waddington, *La Guerre*, 4:284–331; Broglie and Vernier, *Correspondance de Broglie*, 3:520–51; Pajol, *Les Guerres*, 5:138–72; Linder, *Die Peripetie*, 169–237.

6. Savory, *His Britannic Majesty's Army*, 302–8; Brown and Schweizer, *Devonshire Diary*, 93–96; Middleton, *Bells of Victory*, 180–82; Brown, *Pitt*, 234–35; Peters, *Pitt and Popularity* (Oxford: Clarendon Press, 1980), 187–88.

7. Peters, *Pitt and Popularity*, 197–98.

8. Middleton, *Bells of Victory*, 182, 206; Eldon, *Subsidy Policy*, 142, 161–62; Mitchell and Deane, *Abstract*, 390; Cook and Stevenson, *British Historical Facts*, 97; Mackay, *Admiral Hawke*, 305; Black, *America or Europe?*, 176.

9. Savory, *His Britannic Majesty's Army*, 310–11; Waddington, *La Guerre*, 5:60–61, 70; Middleton, *Bells of Victory*, 177; Doran, *Andrew Mitchell*, 251; Fortescue, *British Army*, 2:529–30.

10. Savory, *His Britannic Majesty's Army*, 320–28, 500–503, and Waddington, *La Guerre*, 5:85–121 provide full accounts of the battle.

11. Waddington, *La Guerre*, 5:198.

12. For the summer and fall campaign of 1761, see Broglier and Vernier, *Correspondance de Broglie*, 3:591–612; 4: passim; Savory, *His Britannic Majesty's Army*, 309–59;

Waddington, *La Guerre*, 5:59–197; Pajol, *Les Guerres*, 5:173–284; Fortescue, *British Army*, 2:534–43.

13. Waddington, *La Guerre*, 5:380–81; Droysen, *Politische Correspondenz*, 20:336–37, Frederick II to Princess Amelie of Prussia, 15 April 1761; Duffy, *Frederick the Great*, 219, and *Russia's Military Way*, 116; Kroener, "Die materiellen Grundlagen," in Kroener, *Europa im Zeitalter Friedrichs des Grossen*, 59.

14. Droysen, *Politische Correspondenz*, 20:323, 507–9; Bisset, *Memoirs of Mitchell*, 2:212–13.

15. Austria 281: 273, the comte de Choiseul to the duc de Choiseul, 15 February 1761; Waddington, *La Guerre*, 5:215–76; Duffy, *Frederick the Great*, 220–26, *Russia's Military Way*, 116–17, and *Army of Maria Theresa*, 202–3; Showalter, *Wars*, 300–309; Anderson, *Naval Wars*, 231; Franz A. Szabo, *Kaunitz and Enlightened Absolutism, 1753–1780* (Cambridge: Cambridge University Press, 1994), 275–77. There is a beautiful map of the siege of Kolberg in Russia 66: 259.

16. Droysen, *Politische Correspondenz*, 21:75–76, 109–10, 129–31, 144, 152–54, 156–57, 160, 168, 172–73.

17. Austria 284: 26, Minister Plenipotentiary to Austria Louis-Marie-Florent, comte de Châtelet-Lomont to the comte de Choiseul (who had become foreign minister), 2 November 1761; Austria 288: 37, Châtelet-Lomont to the comte de Choiseul, 21 April 1762; Duffy, *Austrian Army*, 105–6, 124–28; Szabo, *Kaunitz and Enlightened Absolutism*, 275–78; Dickson, *Maria Theresa*, 2:349; Waddington, *La Guerre*, 5:290.

18. Waddington, *La Guerre*, 4:459–72, 479–92; Arneth, *Geschichte Maria Theresia's*, 6:206–25; Rashed, *Peace of Paris*, 63–65.

19. Waddington, *La Guerre*, 4:459–69, 473–78, 483–90; Oliva, *Misalliance*, 180–86; Rashed, *Peace of Paris*, 63–65; Vandal, *Louis XV et Elisabeth de Russie*, 390–401; Rambaud, *Recueil*, 9:98–100, 163–78, 182; P. Coquelle, "L'Espionage en Angleterre pendant la Guerre de Sept Ans d'après des documents inédits," *Revue d'histoire diplomatique* 14 (1900): 529. Golitsyn's name is spelled in various ways, including Galitzin.

20. Waddington, *La Guerre*, 4:408–13; Brown and Schweizer, *Devonshire Diary*, 72–90; Browning, *Duke of Newcastle*, 269, 271–76; Sir Lewis Namier, *England in the Age of the American Revolution*, 2nd ed. (New York: St. Martin's Press, 1961), 163–67; Frank O'Gorman, *The Rise of Party in England: The Rockingham Whigs, 1760–82* (London: G. Allen and Unwin, 1975), 32–34. For Viry, see Britain 447: 42–43; Namier, *England*, 81–82 and passim; Clark, *Dynamics of Change*, 284; Ruville, *Pitt*, 2:395n; Flammermont, *Rapport*, 317; Lord Edmond Fitzmaurice, *Life of William, Earl of Shelburne, Afterwards First Marquess of Lansdowne*, rev. ed., 2 vols. (London: Macmillan, 1912), 1:109.

21. Brown, *Pitt*, 224–30. For appraisals of Bedford, generally negative, see Rodger, *Insatiable Earl*, 17–18; Baugh, *British Naval Administration*, 71–72; Lewis Merriam Wiggin, *The Faction of Cousins: A Political Account of the Grenvilles, 1733–1763* (New Haven: Yale University Press, 1958), 271. Some of his papers have been published in Russell, *Correspondence of Bedford*.

22. Brown and Schweizer, *Devonshire Diary*, 79, 90.

23. Brown and Schweizer, *Devonshire Diary*, 65, 76; Waddington, *La Guerre*, 4:402–

8; Droysen, *Politische Correspondenz*, 19:409; 20:63, 156–58, 162–63, 167–68, 175–78, 203–5, 217, 232–35, 283–84, 323, 632–34; Bisset, *Memoirs of Mitchell*, 2:212–13, 219–20, 223–24; Doran, *Andrew Mitchell*, 255–61; Schweizer, *Anglo-Prussian Alliance*, 106–12.

24. Rashed, *Peace of Paris*, 71.

25. For the negotiations before formal discussions began in June, see Britain 443: 62–149; State Papers Series 78 (France) 251:1–63; Brown and Schweizer, *Devonshire Diary*, 96–99; Waddington, *La Guerre*, 4:494–523; Doran, *Andrew Mitchell*, 261–65; *Parliamentary History*, 15: 1019–37; Thackeray, *History of Pitt*, 2:511–14; Bourguet, *Etudes*, 181–86; Etienne-François, duc de Choiseul-Stainville, *Mémoire historique sur la négociation de la France et de l'Angleterre, depuis le 26 mars 1761 jusqu'au 20 septembre de la même année, avec les pièces justificatives* (Paris: Imprimerie royale, 1761), 9–47.

26. Britain 443: 161–92; State Papers Series 78 (France) 251:76–88; Waddington, *La Guerre*, 4:492–93, 523–26; Thackeray, *History of Pitt*, 1:514–23.

27. Droysen, *Politische Correspondenz*, 20:371–72, 408, 416–17; Waddington, *La Guerre*, 4:512–17; Bourguet, *Etudes*, 187; Thackeray, *History of Pitt*, 2:525; Cruickshanks, "101 Secret Agent," 273–76; Samoyault, *Les Bureaux*, 88, 175–76, 278; Vaucher, *Recueil*, vol. 25, part 2: 372–84; William L. Grant, "La Mission de M. de Bussy à Londres en 1761," *Revue d'histoire diplomatique* 20 (1906): 358; Ninetta S. Jucker, ed., *The Jenkinson Papers, 1760–1766* (London: Macmillan, 1949), 1–2, 6–8. For Bussy's relations with Pitt, see Waddington, *La Guerre*, 4:527; Bourguet, *Etudes*, 199–200; Black, *Pitt the Elder*, 209–10, 215; Robitaille, *Montcalm et ses historiens*, 221–22n.

28. Britain 443: 144–45, 188–89, Bussy to Choiseul, 30 May and 11 June 1761; Waddington, *La Guerre*, 4:517–18, 521–24, 549; Thackeray, *History of Pitt*, 1:506–8; Brown and Schweizer, *Devonshire Diary*, 98–99; Taylor and Pringle, *Correspondence of Chatham*, 2:116–19; Pease, *Boundary Disputes*, xcv; Legg, *British Diplomatic Instructions*, 7:53–54; Brown, *Pitt*, 235; Soulange-Bodin, *La Diplomatie de Louis XV*, 151; George Thomas Keppel, Earl of Albemarle, ed., *Memoirs of the Marquis of Rockingham and His Contemporaries*, 2 vols. (London: Richard Bentley, 1852), 1:21–22.

29. *London Gazette*, 22 July 1761; Waddington, *La Guerre*, 4:511, 516–17; Vaucher, *Receuil*, 25, part 2: 382; Bourguet, *Etudes*, 190–91.

30. Thackeray, *Life of Pitt*, 1:541; Namier, *England*, 273–82; Frégault, *Canada*, 268–69, 290, 296–332; Garnault, *Le Commerce rochelais*, 4:308–35; Labaree, *Franklin Papers*, 9:47–100; Peters, *Pitt and Popularity*, 164–68; Sosin, *Whitehall and the Wilderness*, 9–10; Pierre-Georges Roy, ed., "Les Chambres de commerce de France et la cessation du Canada," *Rapport de l'archiviste de la province de Québec* 5 (1924–25): 199–228; William L. Grant, "Canada versus Guadeloupe: An Episode of the Seven Years' War," *American Historical Review* 17 (1911–12): 735–43.

31. Thackeray, *History of Pitt*, 1:487; Brown and Schweizer, *Devonshire Diary*, 92, 94–95; Brown, *Pitt*, 232–33; Albemarle, *Memoirs of Rockingham*, 1:23–24; Pease, *Boundary Disputes*, 288–90, 293–94; Waddington, *La Guerre*, 4:501; Schweizer, *Anglo-Prussian Alliance*, 124; Middleton, *Bells of Victory*, 188; Yorke, *Hardwicke*, 3:315–17; Corbett, *England in the Seven Years' War*, 2:156–57; Pares, *The Historian's Business*, 127; William Kent Hackmann, "George Grenville and English Politics in 1763," *Yale University Library Gazette* 64 (1990):

164; Kate Hotblack, "The Peace of Paris, 1763," *Transactions of the Royal Historical Society*, 3rd ser., 2 (1908): 244, 266, and *Chatham's Colonial Policy: A Study in the Fiscal and Economic Implications of the Colonial Policy of the Elder Pitt* (London: G. Routledge and Sons; New York: E. P. Dutton, 1917), 51.

32. Bourguet, *Etudes*, 197–98.

33. Spain 533: 35. This passage is quoted in Waddington, *La Guerre*, 4:553.

34. State Papers Series 78 (France), 251:130–34, Stanley to Pitt, 18 June with enclosure; Britain 443: 219–20, private note of Choiseul to Bussy, 19 June; Thackeray, *History of Pitt*, 1:539–43, 549–55; Waddington, *La Guerre*, 4:531–35, 546; Middleton, *Bells of Victory*, 187; Grant, "La Mission de Bussy," 359.

35. Russia 60: 277, Choiseul to L'Hôpital, 8 July 1761; Waddington, *La Guerre*, 4:511–12. See also Doran, *Andrew Mitchell*, 265.

36. Britain 443: 211–17, Bussy to Choiseul, 16 June 1761; State Papers Series 78 (France), 251:101–6, Cabinet Memoranda, 16 June 1761; Thackeray, *History of Pitt*, 2:523–24; Waddington, *La Guerre*, 4:526–27, 529; Bourguet, *Etudes*, 192–96; Rashed, *Peace of Paris*, 74–75; Jeremy Black, "The Crown, Hanover, and the Shift in British Foreign Policy in the 1760s," in Black, *Knights Errant*, 121–23; Choiseul-Stainville, *Mémoire historique*, 50–53; Arnold Schaefer, "Urkundliche Beiträge zur Geschichte des siebenjährigen Kriegs," *Forschungen zur Deutsche Geschichte* 17 (1877): 31–38.

37. State Papers Series 78 (France), 251:136, 145, 147–50, Pitt to Stanley, 26 June 1761; Thackeray, *History of Pitt*, 1:543–49.

38. Frégault, *Canada*, 293, 319–20; Sosin, *Whitehall and the Wilderness*, 13n; Murrin, "French and Indian War," 309; Eccles, *Essays on New France*, 147–48; Nancy F. Koehn, *The Power of Commerce: Economy and Governance in the First British Empire* (Ithaca: Cornell University Press, 1994), 149–83.

39. Doran, *Andrew Mitchell*, 265–66; Middleton, *Bells of Victory*, 187–88; Grant, "La Mission de Bussy," 362; Waddington, *La Guerre*, 4:537–39; Brown and Schweizer, *Devonshire Diary*, 99–100; Corbett, *England in the Seven Years' War*, 2:174–75; Schweizer, *Anglo-Prussian Alliance*, 124–25; Russell, *Correspondence of Bedford*, 3:14–17, 21–22, 25–26, 56; Pease, *Boundary Disputes*, 294–96; Bullion, "Securing the Peace," in Schweizer, *Lord Bute*, 27; Black, *America or Europe?*, 181–82; George A. Wood, *William Shirley, Governor of Massachusetts, 1741–1756* (New York: Columbia University Press; London: P. S. King and Son, 1920), 318.

40. State Papers Series 78 (France), 252: 160–63, 166–67, Stanley to Pitt, 29 June–5 July 1761; Britain 443: 324–27, Choiseul to Bussy, 4 July 1761; Thackeray, *History of Pitt*, 2:532–42; Waddington, *La Guerre*, 4:541–43, 547; Rashed, *Peace of Paris*, 85–86; Pease, *Boundary Disputes*, 337–38.

41. Brown and Schweizer, *Devonshire Diary*, 101–2.

42. State Papers Series 94 (Spain) 163: unpaginated, Pitt to Ambassador Bristol, 28 July 1761; State Papers Series 78 (France), 251:183–95, 212–13; Britain 443: 351–70; Britain 444: 8–18, 38, 48–56, 73–74; *London Gazette*, 20 July, 22 July, and 24 July; Choiseul-Stainville, *Mémoire historique*, 60–82; Schaefer, "Geschichte," 38–46; Thackeray, *History of Pitt*, 1:546–53, 557–58, 570–73; 2:542–57; Waddington, *La Guerre*, 4:544–64; Bourguet, *Etudes*,

201–8; Rashed, *Peace of Paris*, 87–91; Corbett, *England in the Seven Years' War*, 2:181–82; Pease, *Boundary Disputes*, cvii; Ozanam, "Les Origines," 332–33; Barthélemy, "Le Traité de Paris," 448–49; William James Smith, ed., *The Grenville Papers: Being the Correspondence of Richard Grenville, Earl Temple, K. G. and the Right Hon. George Grenville, Their Friends and Correspondents*, 4 vols. (London: John Murray, 1852–53), 1:376–77.

43. State Papers Series 78 (France), 251:214–20, 222–27; Britain 444: 59–72, Bussy to Choiseul, 26 July; Choiseul-Stainville, *Mémoire historique*, 83–89; Thackeray, *History of Pitt*, 2:554–60; Cobbett and Hansard, *Parliamentary History*, 15:1047–50, Pitt to Stanley, 25 July and enclosed British ultimata. See also State Papers Series 78 (France), 251:230–37, Stanley to Pitt, 30 July 1761; Smith, *Grenville Papers*, 1:380; Pease, *Boundary Disputes*, 331–35; Bourguet, *Etudes*, 210–11.

44. Spain 533: 173–75, Choiseul to Ossun, 30 July 1761; Waddington, *La Guerre*, 4:428, 560, 569–73; Grant, "La Mission de Bussy," 365; Bourguet, *Choiseul et l'alliance espagnole*, 225.

45. Spain 531: 266, Ossun to Choiseul, 17 February 1761; Spain 531: 295, 325–26, Choiseul to Ossun, 24 February and 3 March 1761; Spain 532: 7–18, Ossun to Choiseul, 3 April 1761; Spain 532: 68, Choiseul to Ossun, 21 April 1761; Spain 532: 289–303, French comments on Grimaldi's draft treaty, May 1761; Waddington, *La Guerre*, 4:417–19, 427–33; Rashed, *Peace of Paris*, 60–63, 76–78, 236–43; Ozanam, "Les Origines," 323–29; Bourguet, *Choiseul et l'alliance espagnole*, 175–205; Taylor and Pringle, *Correspondence of Chatham*, 2:92–93, 95–96; Pares, *War and Trade*, 573; Rousseau, *Règne de Charles III*, 54–56, 61–64.

46. Spain 532: 235–36, Choiseul to Ossun, 12 May 1761; Spain 532: 316–41, 342–43, draft of Family Compact and covering letter from Choiseul to Ossun, 2 June 1761; Waddington, *La Guerre*, 4:433–34; Rashed, *Peace of Paris*, 78–79; Ozanam, "Les Origines," 328–30; Bourguet, *Choiseul et l'alliance espagnole*, 205–8, 212–13; Pease, *Boundary Disputes*, xcix; Vaucher, *Recueil*, 25, part 2: 375–76.

47. Spain 532: 16–18, Ossun to Choiseul, 22 June 1761; Spain 533: 2–13, 19, 44–49, Ossun to Choiseul, 2 July, 6 July, and 13 July 1761; Spain 533: 34–37, 53–58, Choiseul to Ossun, 7 July and 14 July 1761; Spain 533: 61–110, Revised draft of Family Compact and Secret Convention, sent to Ossun, 14 July 1761; Waddington, *La Guerre*, 4:434–35, 544–45, 553–54; Ozanam, "Les Origines," 330–34; Bourguet, *Choiseul et l'alliance espagnole*, 212–22, and *Etudes*, 189; Pease, *Boundary Disputes*, civ–cv, cix; Barthélemy, "Le Traité de Paris," 447–48; Corbett, *England in the Seven Years' War*, 2:186–87; Savelle, *Origins of American Diplomacy*, 476n.

48. Spain 528: 191, Ossun to Choiseul, 24 April 1760; Spain 533: 36, Choiseul to Ossun, 7 July 1761; Spain 533: 186–90, Ossun to Choiseul, 31 July 1761; Waddington, *La Guerre*, 4:544; Ozanam, "Les Origines," 335–36; Bourguet, *Choiseul et l'alliance espagnole*, 181, and *Etudes*, 212; Rashed, *Peace of Paris*, 86–87; Savelle, *Origins of American Diplomacy*, 461; Ayling, *Pitt*, 287. Some of the intercepted Spanish correspondence is printed in Taylor and Pringle, *Correspondence of Chatham*, 2:91–93, 95–101, 105–7, 139–41.

49. Spain 529: 32, Ossun to Choiseul, 4 July 1760; Spain 529: 74, Choiseul to Ossun, 15 July 1760; Spain 533: 8–9, 122–24, Ossun to Choiseul, 2 July and 16 July 1761; Spain 533: 173–75, Choiseul to Ossun, 30 July 1761; Britain 444: 114–17, 126–28, Choiseul to Bussy,

5 August 1760; Waddington, *La Guerre*, 4:432–33, 570–72; Schaefer, "Geschichte," 46–47; Ozanam, "Les Origines," 332, 334; Bourguet, *Choiseul et l'alliance espagnole*, 210, 225–26; Rashed, *Peace of Paris*, 93; Pease, *Boundary Disputes*, 278–80, 329–31; Savelle, *Origins of American Diplomacy*, 476n; Aiton, "Diplomacy of the Louisiana Cession," 704–6, 710–11.

50. State Papers Series 78 (France), 251: 230–37, Stanley to Pitt, 30 July 1761; State Papers Series 78 (France), 252: 12–35, Stanley to Pitt, 6 August 1761; Thackeray, *History of Pitt*, 2:563, 571–89; Ozanam, "Les Origines," 334.

51. Britain 444: 145–48, Choiseul to Bussy, 10 August 1760; Spain 533: 179–94, Ossun to Choiseul, 31 July 1760; Waddington, *La Guerre*, 4:590–91, 602–3; Ozanam, "Les Origines," 332–34; Bourguet, *Choiseul et l'alliance espagnole*, 206–7, 213; Barthélemy, "Le Traité de Paris," 451–52; Rashed, *Peace of Paris*, 92–94; Pease, *Boundary Disputes*, cvi, cix, 336–41; Aiton, "Diplomacy of the Louisiana Cession," 710.

52. Britain 444: 145–48, Choiseul to Bussy, 10 August 1761; Waddington, *La Guerre*, 4:572, 593–94; Ozanam, "Les Origines," 334; Rousseau, *Règne de Charles III*, 1:62–63.

53. Ozanam, "Les Origines," 335; Bourguet, *Etudes*, 218–19, and *Choiseul et l'alliance espagnole*, 227–28.

54. Ozanam, "Les Origines," 332; Bourguet, *Choiseul et l'alliance espagnole*, 220–21; Pease, *Boundary Disputes*, cix; Corbett, *England in the Seven Years' War*, 2:187.

55. Spain 533: 270–85, Pacte de famille, 15 August 1761; Parry, *Consolidated Treaty Series*, 42:85–100, 115–17; Waddington, *La Guerre*, 4:606–9; Pares, *War and Trade*, 574; Soulange-Bodin, *La Diplomatie de Louis XV*, 164; Christelow, "French Interest," 525, 535; Louis Blart, *Les Rapports de la France et de l'Espagne après de pacte de famille, jusqu'à la fin du ministère du duc de Choiseul* (Paris: Félix Alcan, 1915), 205–13.

56. Spain 531: 34–35, Ossun to Choiseul, 12 January 1761; Spain 532: 10–13, Ossun to Choiseul, 3 April 1761; Spain 533: 174, Choiseul to Ossun, 30 July 1761; Spain 533: 290–94, Secret Convention, 15 August 1761; Parry, *Consolidated Treaty Series*, 42:133–38; Waddington, *La Guerre*, 4:609–10; Blart, *Les Rapports*, 214–17; Christelow, "Economic Background," 27. For British domination of Portuguese trade, see B^{7}412: unpaginated, report of 17 July 1759 on ships entering Lisbon harbor.

57. Austria 284: 120, the comte de Choiseul to the comte de Châtelet-Lomont, 23 November 1761; Spain 534: 266–68, Choiseul to Ossun, 8 December 1761; Waddington, *La Guerre*, 4:573–74; 5:279; Arthur S. Aiton, "A Neglected Intrigue of the Family Compact," *Hispanic American Historical Review* 11 (1931): 387–93.

58. Spain 533: 338–42, Ossun to Choiseul, 24 August 1761; Spain 533: 345, Charles III to Louis XV, 27 August 1761; Spain 533: 394–95, Choiseul to Ossun, 8 September 1761; Spain 534: 320, Bourguet, *Choiseul et l'alliance espagnole*, 231–33.

59. The 1 August–20 September phase of the negotiations is documented in Britain 444: 108–320 and State Papers Series 78 (France), 252: 4–218.

60. Britain 444: 114–17, 118–23, Choiseul to Bussy, 5 August 1761 and enclosed French ultimatum; Britain 444: 145–48, 150–59, Choiseul to Bussy, 10 August 1761 and enclosed memoir on the proposed limits of Louisiana; Choiseul-Stainville, *Mémoire historique*, 91–101, 106–8; Cobbett and Hansard, *Parliamentary History*, 15:1050–59; Thackeray, *Life of Pitt*, 1:574–75; 2:566–70; Pease, *Boundary Disputes*, cxvii–cxviii, 344–65; Waddington, *La*

Guerre, 4:575–78; Bourguet, *Etudes*, 209–10, 217–18; Rashed, *Peace of Paris*, 95. For earlier discussions about the borders of Louisiana, see Pease, *Boundary Disputes*, 314–15, 319–24, 331–35, 339; Sosin, *Whitehall and the Wilderness*, 14.

61. State Papers Series 78 (France), 252: 87–96, 98–108, Pitt to Stanley, 27 August and enclosed memorandum; Thackeray, *Life of Pitt*, 2:591–97, 604–8; Choiseul-Stainville, *Mémoire historique*, 109–25; Cobbett and Hansard, *Parliamentary History*, 15:1059–67; Pease, *Boundary Disputes*, cxix, 367–83, map opposite 568; Brown and Schweizer, *Devonshire Diary*, 100–102, 107–16; Taylor and Pringle, *Correspondence of Chatham*, 2:136; Russell, *Correspondence of Bedford*, 3:22–42; Middleton, *Bells of Victory*, 190–92; Rashed, *Peace of Paris*, 95–96, 102n; Waddington, *La Guerre*, 4:578–87; Corbett, *England in the Seven Years' War*, 2:189–94; Savelle, *Origins of American Diplomacy*, 481–83; Yorke, *Hardwicke*, 3:271–73, 317–22; Black, *America or Europe?*, 158 and *Pitt the Elder*, 214–19; Brown, *Pitt*, 237–42; William Cuthbert Brian Tunstall, *William Pitt, Earl of Chatham* (London: Hodder and Stoughton, 1938), 297–300. For eighteenth-century St. Pierre and its larger neighboring island, Miquelon, see Harris, *Historical Atlas*, plate 25; La Morandière, *Histoire de la pêche française*, 2:732–36.

62. Britain 444: 264–65, 266–72, Choiseul to Bussy, 9 September 1761 and enclosed memoir; Britain 444: 311–20, Bussy to Choiseul, 19 September 1761; State Papers Series 78 (France) 252: 215, Stanley to Choiseul, 20 September 1761; State Papers Series 78 (France) 252: 217–18, Choiseul to Stanley, 20 September 1761; Thackeray, *History of Pitt*, 2:625–26; Choiseul-Stainville, *Mémoire historique*, 126–35, 139–41; Cobbett and Hansard, *Parliamentary History*, 15:1067–73; Pease, *Boundary Disputes*, cxx, 390–97; Brown and Schweizer, *Devonshire Diary*, 118–25; Taylor and Pringle, *Correspondence of Chatham*, 2:141–44; Russell, *Correspondence of Bedford*, 3:43–46; Middleton, *Bells of Victory*, 192–93; Rashed, *Peace of Paris*, 97–99; Waddington, *La Guerre*, 4:588–98; Brown, *William Pitt*, 242–43; Bourguet, *Etudes*, 224–30; Sedgwick, *Letters to Bute*, 65.

63. Spain 533: 452–53; Barthélemy, "Le Traité de Paris," 453.

64. State Papers Series 78 (France) 252: 194, Stanley to Pitt, 8 September 1761; Taylor and Pringle, *Correspondence of Chatham*, 2:139–41, Grimaldi to Fuentes, 31 August 1761 (English translation); Thackeray, *History of Pitt*, 2:618–19.

65. Brown and Schweizer, *Devonshire Diary*, 130; Corbett, *England in the Seven Years' War*, 2:192–93; Bourguet, *Etudes*, 231; Soulange-Bodin, *La Diplomatie de Louis XV*, 155; Brown, *Pitt*, 239, 243–44.

66. Brown and Schweizer, *Devonshire Diary*, 99–100, 124, 127–28; Middleton, *Bells of Victory*, 192–94; Brewer, *Sinews of Power*, 30, 114–15; Riley, *Seven Years War*, 183; Albemarle, *Memoirs of Rockingham*, 1:25–26, 30–31; Browning, "Financing of the Seven Years' War," 352–53, 367–68; Ashton, *Economic Fluctuations*, 124–25, 187; Mitchell and Deane, *Abstract*, 387; Koehn, *Power of Commerce*, 6, 12; Bullion, "Securing the Peace," in Schweizer, *Lord Bute*, 24; Bourguet, *Etudes*, 213.

67. Taylor and Pringle, *Correspondence of Chatham*, 2:107–13; Corbett, *England in the Seven Years' War*, 2:148; Droysen, *Politische Correspondenz*, 20:480–81, 507–9; Schweizer, *Anglo-Prussian Alliance*, 129–32, 143; Waddington, *La Guerre*, 4:563, 584, 599–600; Doran, *Andrew Mitchell*, 323; Scott, "True Principles," and Black, "Crown," in Black, *Knights*

Errant, 75, 120; Browning, *Duke of Newcastle*, 262, 279–80, 284; Scott, *British Foreign Policy*, 45.

68. Spain 534: 335, Ossun to Choiseul, 28 December 1761; Brown and Schweizer, *Devonshire Diary*, 130; Middleton, *Bells of Victory*, 202; Corbett, *England in the Seven Years' War*, 2:204–5; Browning, *Duke of Newcastle*, 282; Waddington, *La Guerre*, 4:631; Yorke, *Hardwicke*, 3:278; Whitworth, *Ligonier*, 354; Petrie, *King Charles III*, 101–2.

69. Brown, *Pitt*, 243–44, 256; Soulange-Bodin, *La Diplomatie de Louis XV*, 161; Corbett, *England in the Seven Years' War*, 2:79; Bourguet, *Choiseul et l'alliance espagnole* (Paris: Plon-Nourrit, 1906), 13–14.

70. See appendix J; Spain 533: 378–79, list of Spanish warships and their locations sent Ossun by Wall, 7 September 1761; Brown and Schweizer, *Devonshire Diary*, 124, 129–30; Yorke, *Hardwicke*, 3:278; Corbett, *England in the Seven Years' War*, 2:198–99, 203; Middleton, *Bells of Victory*, 175–76, 192–93, and "Naval Administration" in Black and Woodfine, *British Navy*, 123; Bourguet, *Choiseul et l'alliance espagnole*, 176–77; Waddington, *La Guerre*, 4:612; Gradish, *Manning*, 42, 50–51; Glete, *Navies and Nations*, 1:280; Fernández Duro, *Armada española*, 7:8; Saint Hubert, "Ships of the Line of the Spanish Navy," 132–34; Lyon, *Sailing Navy List*, 62–64, 68–70, 73, 77; Jeremy Black, "Anglo-Spanish Naval Relations in the Eighteenth Century," *Mariner's Mirror* 77 (1991): 236; *London Evening Post*, issues of 24–26 February, 8–11 August, and 11–13 August 1761; David F. Marley, "Havana Surprised: Prelude to the British Invasion, 1762," *Mariner's Mirror* 78 (1992): 304n.

71. Brown and Schweizer, *Devonshire Diary*, 135–36; Taylor and Pringle, *Correspondence of Chatham*, 2:141–44; Thackeray, *History of Pitt*, 2:612, 623–24; Sedgwick, *Letters to Bute*, 65; Karl W. Schweizer, "Lord Bute and William Pitt's Resignation in 1761," *Canadian Journal of History* 8 (1973): 114–15.

72. Brown and Schweizer, *Devonshire Diary*, 118–39; Yorke, *Hardwicke*, 3:272–80, 320–35; Sedgwick, *Letters to Bute*, 63; Schweizer, "Lord Bute and Pitt's Resignation," 111–22; Smith, *Grenville Papers*, 1:386–87; W. Hunt, "Pitt's Retirement from Office, 5 Oct. 1761," *English Historical Review* 21 (1906): 119–32; H. W. V. Temperley, "Pitt's Retirement from Office, 1761," *English Historical Review* 21 (1906): 327–30.

73. For a sample of historical commentary, see Brown, *Pitt*, 251; Peters, *Pitt and Popularity*, 203–4; Brewer, *Party Ideology*, 101–3.

74. Brown and Schweizer, *Devonshire Diary*, 137, 141–42, 145; Brown, *Pitt*, 251–53; Middleton, *Bells of Victory*, 200–201; Smith, *Grenville Papers*, 1:395; Browning, *Duke of Newcastle*, 282; Namier, *England*, 294–302.

75. Brown and Schweizer, *Devonshire Diary*, 119, 141; Thackeray, *History of Pitt*, 1:579–88, Bristol to Pitt, 31 August 1761; Waddington, *La Guerre*, 4:604–5, 610–12; Rashed, *Peace of Paris*, 100; Bourguet, *Etudes*, 218–19 and "Le duc de Choiseul et l'alliance espagnole: Après le Pacte de famille," *Revue historique* 94 (1907): 14.

76. Spain 533: 234, 347–50, 430, Ossun to Choiseul, 10 August, 27 August, and 17 September 1761; Spain 534: 165, Ossun to Choiseul, 9 November 1761; Waddington, *La Guerre*, 4:610; Pease, *Boundary Disputes*, cx; John Almon, ed., *The Debates and Proceedings of the British House of Commons from 1743 to 1774*, 11 vols. (London: J. Almon, 1766–

75), 6:81–82, Bristol to Pitt, 21 September 1761; Kate Hotblack, "The Peace of Paris, 1763," *Transactions of the Royal Historical Society*, 3rd ser., 2 (1908): 264–65.

77. Schweizer, *Anglo-Prussian Alliance*, 142 and "Lord Bute and Pitt's Resignation," 118.

78. Corbett, *England in the Seven Years' War*, 2:214–15, 227–28; Schweizer, *Anglo-Prussian Alliance*, 143–46; Doran, *Andrew Mitchell*, 295–96; Eldon, *Subsidy Policy*, 141–42; Gipson, *British Empire*, 8:58–59; Black, "Crown," in Black, *Knights Errant*, 122–23; Simmons and Thomas, *Proceedings and Debates*, 1:362–63; Derek Jarrett, ed., *Horace Walpole: Memoirs of the Reign of King George the Third*, 4 vols. (New York: Yale University Press, 2000), 1:63–66, 69.

79. Corbett, *England in the Seven Years' War*, 2:142–43; Doran, *Andrew Mitchell*, 254; Middleton, *Bells of Victory*, 176–77; Kimball, *Correspondence of Pitt*, 2:344–47, 365–73, 384–87, 389–90; Selesky, *War and Society*, 168; Anderson, *People's Army*, 21, 59n and *Crucible of War*, 805–6; Jucker, *Jenkinson Papers*, 24; Webster, *Journal of Amherst*, 280.

80. Corbett, *England in the Seven Years' War*, 2:154–55, 177–78, 198–99, 209–10, 217–18; Brown and Schweizer, *Devonshire Diary*, 91, 102, 131, 134n; Kimball, *Correspondence of Pitt*, 2:403–8, 429–32, 436–44, 452–56, 469, 475–87; Brown, *Pitt*, 232, 235, 238; Gipson, *British Empire*, 8:187–91; Waddington, *La Guerre*, 4:560–61; 5:57; Thackeray, *History of Pitt*, 2:502–5, 556; Hackmann, "English Military Expeditions," 187–88; Clowes, *Royal Navy*, 3:233, 242–44; Spinney, *Rodney*, 176–81; Mante, *History of the Late War*, 352–53, 406–7; N. A. M. Rodger, ed., "The Douglas Papers, 1760–1762," in N. A. M. Rodger, ed., *The Naval Miscellany*, vol. 5 (London: George Allen and Unwin for the Navy Records Society, 1984), 264–65, 269–70; C. H. Little, ed., *The Recapture of Saint John's, Newfoundland: Despatches of Rear-Admiral Lord Colville, 1761–1762* (Halifax: Maritime Museum of Canada, 1959), 3–4, 8.

81. State Papers Series 94 (Spain) 164: 145–57, Egremont to Bristol, 28 October 1761, with enclosures; Brown and Schweizer, *Devonshire Diary*, 128, 131, 133–34, 141; Middleton, *Bells of Victory*, 202; Corbett, *England in the Seven Years' War*, 2:198, 215–16; Waddington, *La Guerre*, 4:619–21; Pares, *War and Trade*, 587; Salmon, *Saunders*, 177–83; John Almon, ed., *Debates and Proceedings of the British House of Commons from 1743 to 1774*, 11 vols. (London: J. Almon, 1766–75), 6:88–90. There also is a documentary history of Bristol's negotiations with the Spaniards in Cobbett and Hansard, *Parliamentary History*, 15:1130–1210.

82. Admiralty Series 1 (Incoming Letters) 384: unpaginated, Saunders's report of 16 December 1761; State Papers Series 94 (Spain) 164: 188; Brown and Schweizer, *Devonshire Diary*, 131; Corbett, *England in the Seven Years' War*, 2:217, 230–31; Salmon, *Saunders*, 184.

83. Almon, *Debates and Proceedings of the House of Commons*, 6:90–96; Bourguet, "Après le Pacte de famille," 11; Waddington, *La Guerre*, 4:621–22.

84. State Papers Series 94 (Spain), 222–37, Egremont to Bristol, 19 November (five letters); Almon, *Debates and Proceedings*, 6:96–102; Brown and Schweizer, *Devonshire Diary*, 141, 149; Brown, *Pitt*, 257; Ayling, *Pitt*, 287.

85. Brown and Schweizer, *Devonshire Diary*, 149n; Schweizer, *Anglo-Prussian Alliance*, 146–48; Doran, *Andrew Mitchell*, 296; Frank Spencer, "The Anglo-Prussian Breach of 1762: An Historical Revision," *History*, n.s., 41 (1956): 105.

86. Spain 534: 306, the duc de Choiseul to Ossun, 15 December 1761; Austria 284: 53, the comte de Choiseul to Châtelet-Lomont, 13 November 1761; Russia 67: 414, the comte de Choiseul to Breteuil, 21 December 1761; Brown, *Pitt*, 255, 260; Schweizer, *Anglo-Prussian Alliance*, 144, 163; Rashed, *Peace of Paris*, 113–14, 118–21; H. W. V. Temperley, "The Peace of Paris" in J. Holland Rose, A. P. Newton, and E. A. Benians, eds., *The Cambridge History of the British Empire*, vol. 1, *The Old Empire from Its Beginnings to 1783* (Cambridge: Cambridge University Press, 1929), 495.

87. State Papers Series 94 (Spain) 164: 314, Bristol to Egremont, 26 December 1761 (and for the dispatches he was unable to send, see 164: 269–301, 330–93); Spain 534: 297–98; Spain 535: 166, Ossun to Choiseul, 8 February 1762; *London Evening Post*, 9–12 January 1762; Almon, *Debates and Proceedings*, 6:104–5, 110–12, 120–43; Bourguet, "Après le Pacte de famille," 19–23; Waddington, *La Guerre*, 4:622–24; Corbett, *England in the Seven Years' War*, 2:229–30; Christelow, "Economic Background," 29–30.

88. Corbett, *England in the Seven Years' War*, 2:231–32; Little, *Recapture of Saint Johns*, 13; Almon, *Debates and Proceedings*, 6:106–9, 113–20; Jarrett, *Walpole Memoirs*, 1:86–87; Waddington, *La Guerre*, 4:625–27; Sedgwick, *Letters to Bute*, 75; *London Evening Post*, 29–31 December 1761, 31 December 1761 to 2 January 1762, 2–5 January 1762, 5–7 January 1762, 9–12 January 1762, and 21–23 January 1762.

89. Brown and Schweizer, *Devonshire Diary*, 91; Middleton, *Bells of Victory*, 180; Corbett, *England in the Seven Years' War*, 2:152–55; Hackmann, "English Military Expeditions," 164–65.

90. For the escape, see B^{2}367: 8; B^{2}368: 196; B^{4}89: 335–37, 342–72; Linÿer de La Barbée, *Ternay*, 1:126–28; Mackay, *Admiral Hawke*, 279.

91. For the Belle Isle campaign and the French response, see B^{1}67: 50–58, 68, 72–78, 98–105; B^{2}367: 68–71, 85, 120, 129, 171–72, 199–220, 506–8, 511–12, 522; B^{3}552: 93–97; B^{4}89: 51–388; B^{4}100: 56–66, 235–67; B^{4}101:4–176; Corbett, *England in the Seven Years' War*, 2:157–71; Hackmann, "English Military Expeditions," 166–82; Linÿer de La Barbée, *Ternay*, 1:131–42; Lacour-Gayet, *La Marine militaire*, 368–70; Waddington, *La Guerre*, 5:44–55; Keppel, *Keppel*, 1:302–23; Bonner-Smith, *Barrington Papers*, 1:294–315; Beatson, *Naval and Military Memoirs*, 3:332–35; Anderson, "Malmsköld," in Lloyd, *Naval Miscellany*, 262–63; Mackay, *Admiral Hawke*, 277; H. Binet, "La Défense des côtes de Bretagne au XVIIIe siècle: Etudes et documents. VIe Série: Les Anglais à Belle-Isle-en-Mer (1761–1763)," *Revue de Bretagne*, n.s., 49 (1913): 123–47, 172–76; F. J. Hebbert, "The Belle-Ile Expedition of 1761," *Journal of the Society for Army Historical Research* 64 (1986): 81–93.

92. Corbett, *England in the Seven Years' War*, 2:176–77; Hackmann, "English Military Expeditions," 185–88; Middleton, *Bells of Victory*, 189; Russell, *Correspondence of Bedford*, 3:16, 23–24; Black, *Pitt the Elder*, 208.

93. Portugal 93: 189–90, 201–2, 223, 243; Spain 533: 365–66; B^{1}67: 86, 93; B^{4}98: 33, 85–143; B^{4}103: 246, 283–85; Villiers, *Marine royale*, 2:470: Pritchard, *Louis XV's Navy*, 202; Boulle, "French Colonies," 166–67; Clowes, *Royal Navy*, 3:306–7; Le Goff, "Problèmes de recrutement," 232; Bertrand, "Dunkerque," 342–43; Bamford, *Forests and French Sea Power*, 66; Crowhurst, *Defence of British Trade*, 20, 29, 32; Durand, "Mémoirs de Laborde," 85; Caron, *La Guerre incomprise*, 265–66; Romano, "Balance du commerce," 1291; Butel,

"La Guerre maritime," 299; Villiers, "Commerce coloniale," 35 and *Marine royale*, 2:453–56; Pares, *War and Trade*, 375, 386; Malvezin, *Commerce de Bordeaux*, 3:306–7.

94. Holland 508: 66; Spain 532: 87–89, 223–24, 226–28; B^{2}369: 13, 75 (second pagination); B^{2}371:162–63, 172, 177–78; B^{3}551:92, 94, 103–4; B^{4}102: 59–91; Brun, *Port de Toulon*, 1:432–44; Demerliac, *La Marine de Louis XV*, 40; Murphy, *Vergennes*, 124–30; Flassan, *Histoire de la diplomatie française*, 6:234–56.

95. Spain 531:413; Spain 532: 222; Spain 533: 351; B^{2}367: 43, 54, 401; B^{2}369: 9, 44, 81; B^{3}548: 303–7; B^{3}551:44, 53, 84, 199; B^{3}555: 8, 18; B^{4}100: 50; B^{4}103: 15–20, 27–120, 283–85, 297–98; Villers, *Marine royale*, 2:471–72; Clowes, *Royal Navy*, 3:306; Brun, *Port de Toulon*, 1:427–31; Salmon, *Saunders*, 167–71.

96. Demerliac, *La Marine de Louis XV*, 41, 51.

97. Boulle, "French Colonies," 187–91; Pritchard, *Louis XV's Navy*, 15, 202; Linÿer de la Barbée, *Ternay*, 1:143n; Caron, *La Guerre incomprise*, 276; Antoine, *Le Gouvernement*, 30, 69–70, 211–12; Bourguet, "Après le Pacte de famille," 7.

98. Waddington, *La Guerre*, 4:559; Sorel, *Recueil*, 1:393–407, Instructions for Châtelet-Loment, 29 June 1761; Samoyault, *Les Bureaux*, 56–57, 288–89, 304n; John J. Meng, ed., *Despatches and Instructions of Conrad-Alexandre Gérard, 1778–1780* (Baltimore: Johns Hopkins University Press, 1939), 35–38; Ruth Strong Hudson, *The Minister from France: Conrad-Alexandre Gérard, 1729–1790* (Euclid, Ohio: Lutz Printing and Publishing, 1994), 21–27.

99. B^{3}553: 310; B^{4}89: 342–72; Linÿer de La Barbée, *Ternay*, 1:146–48.

100. B^{2}367: 31–32; B^{4}99:10, 14, 28 and passim; Chelin, *Ile Maurice*, 43, 45–49.

101. B^{5}4: unpaginated, various ship lists; Demerliac, *La Marine de Louis XV*, 36, 40–42, 47, 51; Pritchard, *Louis XV's Navy*, 142, 204–5, 218, 220; Lacour-Gayet, *La Marine militaire*, 415; Giraud, "Mémoire de Choiseul," 252; Durand, "Mémoires de Laborde," 96; Riley, *Seven Years War*, 140–41, 148, 226–27; Mouffle d'Angerville, *Vie privée*, 4:14–15; Garnault, *Le Commerce rochelais*, 4:292–301; Sturgill, "French Army's Budget," 131; Martine Acerra, *Rochefort et la construction naval française, 1661–1815*, 4 vols. (Paris: Librairie de l'Inde, 1993), 4:849; Edmond Dziembowski, *Un nouveau Patriotisme français, 1750–1770: La France face à la puissance anglaise à l'époque de la guerre de Sept Ans* (Oxford: Voltaire Foundation, 1998), 458–72.

102. Britain 443: 355, Choiseul to Bussy, 15 July 1761; Holland 508: 115, 128; Sweden 238: 141–70; Sweden 241:97; Austria 283: 387; Portugal 93: 271; Dziembowski, *Un nouveau Patriotisme français*, 448–50; Grouchy and Cottin, *Journal de Croÿ*, 1:512; Barthélemy, "Le Traité de Paris," 440, 454; Choiseul-Stainville, *Mémoire historique*; Besterman, *Voltaire*, 24: 69–70, Voltaire to Pierre-Michel Hennin, 26 October 1761; Rashed, *Peace of Paris*, 88, 112–13; Andrew Lossky, *Louis XIV and the French Monarchy* (New Brunswick NJ: Rutgers University Press, 1994), 272–73.

103. Britain 444: 311–20, Bussy to Choiseul, 19 September 1761.

104. B^{1}67: 134–38; B^{2}368; B^{3}552: 22–23, 477, 484; B^{4}100: 31–35; B^{4}103: 228–31, 332–52; Spain 533: 452–53, Choiseul to Ossun, 22 September 1761; Corbett, *England in the Seven Years' War*, 2:233–34; Boulle, "French Colonies," 528–29, 546; Barthélemy, "Le Traité de Paris," 453; Buchet, *La Lutte*, 1:407–8; Maupassant, *Gradis*, 105–9; C. A. Banbuck, *Histoire*

politique, économique et sociale de la Martinique sous l'Ancien Régime (1635–1789) (Paris: Marcel Rivière, 1935), 132.

105. B⁴104: 13; Spain 534: 213–14, Choiseul to Ossun, 25 November 1761; Boulle, "French Colonies," 527–28; Bourguet, "Après le Pacte de famille," 16–17; Villiers du Terrage, *Les Dernières Années*, 138–39.

106. Spain 531:51, 288, Ossun to Choiseul, 13 January and 22 February 1761; Spain 533: 320, 430–39, 443–51, 465–66, Ossun to Choiseul, 17 August, 17 September, 21 September, and 23 September 1761; Spain 533: 210, 452–53, Choiseul to Ossun, circa 31 July and 22 September 1761; Spain 534: 30–32, 44–47, 87–88, 169, 267, Choiseul to Ossun, 6 October, 13 October, 19 October 1761, 15 November 1761, and 8 December 1761; Spain 534: 22–24, 165, 171, 206, 232–33, Ossun to Choiseul, 3 October, 9 November, 16 November, 23 November, and 30 November 1761; Spain 534: 71–80, 119–25, Spanish and French memoirs of circa 15 October and circa 26 October 1761; Spain supplement 15: 235 and following, extracts of Spanish-Portuguese border convention sent by Ossun, 11 May 1761; Waddington, *La Guerre*, 4:610; 5:281; Pares, *War and Trade*, 594; Bamford, *Forests and French Sea Power*, 67; Pritchard, "Fir Trees," 352–53; Christelow, "Economic Background," 28; Aiton, "Diplomacy of the Louisiana Cession," 705–9; Bourguet, "Après le Pacte de famille," 3–15 and "Le Duc de Choiseul et l'alliance espagnole: Un Ultimatum franco-espagnole au Portugal (1761–1762)," *Revue d'histoire diplomatique* 24 (1910): 27; Amédée, Vicomte de Caix de Saint-Aymour, ed., *Recueil des instructions données aux ambassadeurs et ministres de France depuis les traités de Westphalie jusqu'à la révolution française*, vol. 3, *Portugal* (Paris: Félix Alcan, 1886), 334–37, Instructions for O'Dunne, 15 November 1761.

107. Spain 533: 452–53, Choiseul to Ossun, 22 September 1761; Spain 534: 212–17, Choiseul to Ossun, 25 November 1761; Bourguet, "Après le Pacte de famille," 16–17; Barthélemy, "Le Traité de Paris," 453; Giraud, "Mémoire de Choiseul," 252.

108. Spain 533: 367–70, Ossun to Choiseul, 6 September 1761; Aiton, "Diplomacy of the Louisiana Cession," 706n; Boulle, "French Colonies," 518, 543–44; Marley, "Havana Surprised," 303n.

109. Spain 533: 10, Ossun to Choiseul, 2 July 1761; Spain 534: 294–304, 332, Ossun to Choiseul, 14 December and 28 December 1761; Spain 534: 323–29, Choiseul to Ossun, 25 December 1761; Bourguet, "Après le Pacte de famille," 23–26 and "Un Ultimatum," 26; Corbett, *England in the Seven Years' War*, 2:310; Salmon, *Saunders*, 185–88; Browning, *Duke of Newcastle*, 284; Blart, *Les Rapports*, 35; A. D. Francis, "The Campaign in Portugal, 1762," *Journal of the Society for Army Historical Research* 59 (1981): 26.

110. See, for example, Choiseul-Stainville, *Mémoire historique*, 55.

111. For the concerns of Starhemberg and the Austrians, see Waddington, *La Guerre*, 4:555–59, 572–74; 5:279–82.

112. Austria 284: 53, the comte de Choiseul to the comte de Châtelet-Lomont, 13 November 1761; Waddington, *La Guerre*, 5:280.

113. Spain 534: 44–47, Choiseul to Ossun, 13 October 1761; Sweden 241: 43–45, 112, 126, 136, 155–60; Waddington, *La Guerre*, 5:291–93; Rashed, *Peace of Paris*, 116; Murphy, *Vergennes*, 122; Vedel, *Correspondance entre Bernstorff et Choiseul*, 216, 222, 227n, 283; Barthélemy, *Histoire des relations*, 204–24; Ozanam and Antoine, *Correspondance de*

Broglie, 1:120–26; Oliva, *Misalliance*, 188–89, 192; Roberts, *Age of Liberty*, 42–45; Leonard, *Reform and Regicide*, 118–20.

9. 1762—MILITARY FAILURES, DIPLOMATIC SUCCESS

1. Sweden 241: 257–60, the comte de Choiseul to Havrincourt, 11 February 1762; Droysen, *Politische Correspondenz*, 21:189–93; Schweizer, *Anglo-Prussian Alliance*, 197–98; Waddington, *La Guerre*, 5:293–310; Rambaud, *Recueil*, 9:192–94, Instructions for Breteuil, 9 February 1762.

2. Leonard, *Reform and Regicide* provides a balanced account of Peter's reign and a perceptive analysis of his foreign and domestic policies. The comparison to Joseph is my own.

3. Russia 68: 174 and passim; Holland 508: 65, 108, 190, 214–15, 238, 251–57; Holland 509: 211–13; Leonard, *Reform and Regicide*, 125–26; Waddington, *La Guerre*, 5:320–21; Oliva, *Misalliance*, 192; Coquelle, *L'Alliance franco-hollandaise*, 167–71; Mrs. Gillispie Smith, ed., *Memoirs and Correspondence (Official and Familiar) of Sir Robert Murray Keith, K. B.*, 2 vols. (London: Henry Colburn, 1849), 1:40–46.

4. Droysen, *Politische Correspondenz*, 21:234–36, 397–98; Schweizer, *Anglo-Prussian Alliance*, 200–206; Doran, *Andrew Mitchell*, 310–11.

5. Droysen, *Politische Correspondenz*, 21:386–87; Leonard, *Reform and Regicide*, 125; Schweizer, *Anglo-Prussian Alliance*, 268–69; Doran, *Andrew Mitchell*, 325–26; Waddington, *La Guerre*, 5:393; Parry, *Consolidated Treaty Series*, 42:139–48.

6. Sweden 241: 379–81, Prusso-Swedish Armistice Convention, 7 April 1762; Austria 286: 294, the comte de Choiseul to Châtelet-Lomont, 9 April 1762; Parry, *Consolidated Treaty Series*, 42:149–58, 163–70; Droysen, *Politische Correspondenz*, 21:319, 321–22, 367, 448–49, 451–53, 458; Leonard, *Reform and Regicide*, 128–29, 135; Schweizer, *Anglo-Prussian Alliance*, 269–71; Waddington, *La Guerre*, 5:318–19, 328–29, 393–94; Roberts, *British Diplomacy and Swedish Politics*, 27.

7. Russia 68: 290–93, 361, 398, the comte de Choiseul to Breteuil, 1 March, 14 March, and 30 March 1762; Russia 69: 128, 191, 242–43, 249–50, 291, the comte de Choiseul to Breteuil, 27 April, 23 May, 31 May, 13 June, and 28 June 1762; Russia 69: 278–79, 293, chargé d'affaires Laurent Bérenger to the comte de Choiseul, 18 June and 29 June 1762; Sweden 241: 455, the comte de Choiseul to Havrincourt, 20 May 1762; Spain 536: 332–33, the duc de Choiseul to Ossun, 12 June 1762; Schweizer, *Anglo-Prussian Alliance*, 236–37, 285; Doran, *Andrew Mitchell*, 316–17; Leonard, *Reform and Regicide*, 129, 133–34; Waddington, *La Guerre*, 5:365; Parry, *Consolidated Treaty Series*, 31:221–31; Barthélemy, *Histoire des relations*, 225–34; Karl W. Schweizer and Carol S. Leonard, "Britain, Prussia, Russia, and the Galitzin Letter: A Reassessment," *Historical Journal* 26 (1983): 552.

8. Russia 68: 267–68, Breteuil to the comte de Choiseul, 18 June 1762; Leonard, *Regicide and Reform*, 130–31, 134–37; Barthélemy, *Histoire des relations*, 229–34; Waddington, *La Guerre*, 5:336–38, 401, 406, 409; Droysen, *Politische Correspondenz*, 21:326, 346–48, 387, 409–13, 539–45, 558; 22:1–2, 26–27, 33–34; Schweizer, *Anglo-Prussian Relations*, 322–23, 330;

Duffy, *Russia's Military Way*, 123, and *Army of Maria Theresa*, 203; Anderson, *Naval Wars*, 232; Glete, *Navies and Nations*, 1:300, 302.

9. Russia 69: 293, Bérenger to the comte de Choiseul, 29 June 1762; Russia 70: 86, Lieutenant General of the Police of Paris Antoine-Raymond-Gualbert-Gabriel de Sartine to the comte de Choiseul, 30 July 1762 (reporting news of the coup); Leonard, *Reform and Regicide*, 127–28, 138–49; Smith, *Memoirs of Keith*, 1:52–58; Droysen, *Politische Correspondenz*, 21:407–9, 411–12; Waddington, *La Guerre*, 5:294–95, 305–6, 330–46, 365; Isabel de Madariaga, *Russia in the Age of Catherine the Great* (New Haven: Yale University Press, 1981), 26–32; John T. Alexander, *Catherine the Great: Life and Legend* (New York: Oxford University Press, 1989), 3–16.

10. Madariaga, *Russia*, 32, 187; Duffy, *Russia's Military Way*, 124; Waddington, *La Guerre*, 5:348–55, 359–64, 367, 372, 374; Droysen, *Politische Correspondenz*, 22:51, 96; Bisset, *Memoirs of Mitchell*, 2:324, 330.

11. Droysen, *Politische Correspondenz*, 21:152–54, 367–69, 421, 489–91; Waddington, *La Guerre*, 5:379, 393–94, 399–401; Murphy, *Vergennes*, 137–38; Marsangy, *Vergennes*, 2:195, 200.

12. Waddington, *La Guerre*, 5:357, 383–442; Duffy, *Frederick the Great*, 235–41; Showalter, *Wars*, 315–20; Asprey, *Frederick the Great*, 555–58.

13. See appendix K; Guillon, *Port-Mahon*, 107; Jacques A. Barbier, "Indies Revenue and Naval Spending: The Cost of Colonialism for the Spanish Bourbons, 1763–1805," *Jahrbuch für Geschichte von Staat, Wirtshaft, und Gesellschaft Lateinamerikas* 21 (1984): 176.

14. Spain 534: 295; Spain 535: 190 and passim; Spain 536: 8, 56, 103, 115, 139; Portugal 93: 293–476; Waddington, *La Guerre*, 5:283; Corbett, *England in the Seven Years' War*, 2:301–2; Caix de Saint-Aymour, *Recueil*, 3:338–40; Bourguet, "Un Ultimatum," 28, 35–38; Rousseau, *Règne de Charles III*, 1:73–76; *Annual Register or a View of the History, Politicks and Literature of the Year 1762* (London: R. and J. Dodsley, 1763), 203–22.

15. Portugal 93: 386, O'Dunne to Choiseul, 27 February 1762; Spain 536: 85–86, 280, Ossun to Choiseul, 19 April and 31 May 1762; Spain 537: 48–50, Choiseul to Ossun, 17 August 1762; Rousseau, *Règne de Charles III*, 76–82; Corbett, *England in the Seven Years' War*, 2:252, 296–97, 299–300, 313, 316–17, 322; Brown and Schweizer, *Devonshire Diary*, 166; Gipson, *British Empire*, 8:258–60; Francis, "Campaign in Portugal," 25–43; Pajol, *Les Guerres*, 6:128–53; Blart, *Les Rapports*, 35–36; Pares, *War and Trade*, 595 and *The Historian's Business*, 161–62. There is a superb map of the area of operations in C. V. Townshend, *The Military Life of Field Marshal George, First Marquess Townshend, 1724–1807* (London: J. Murray, 1901), facing 318.

16. Corbett, *England in the Seven Years' War*, 2:219–25; Gipson, *British Empire*, 8:191–95; Banbuck, *Histoire de la Martinique*, 132–39; Mante, *History of the Late War*, map facing 347, 354–82; Spinney, *Rodney*, 184–88; Sidney Daney, *Histoire de la Martinique depuis la colonisation jusq'en 1815*, vol. 2 (Fort Royal, Martinique: E. Ruelle, 1846), 313–39.

17. Corbett, *England in the Seven Years' War*, 2:225–26, 236–45; Spinney, *Rodney*, 188–91, 195–99, 435; Clowes, *Royal Navy*, 3:244–46; David Syrett, ed., *The Siege and Capture of Havana, 1762* (London: Navy Records Society, 1970), xvi–xvii, 72, 77, 87–88.

18. See appendix K; Corbett, 2:246–84; Mante, *History of the Late War*, 397–459; Clowes, *Royal Navy*, 3:246–50; Gipson, *British Empire*, 8:263–68, 275; Middleton, *Bells of Victory*, 204–5; McNeill, *Atlantic Empires*, 102–4; Selesky, *War and Society*, 190; Marley, "Havana Surprised," 293–305; Fernández Duro, *Armada Española*, 7:59–82; Pocock, *Battle for Empire*, 198–230; Giraud, "Mémoire de Choiseul," 175; Syrett, *Siege and Capture of Havana*, "American Provincials and the Havana Campaign of 1762," *New York History* 49 (1968): 374–90, and "The British Landing at Havana: An Example of an Eighteenth-Century Combined Operation," *Mariner's Mirror* 55 (1969): 325–31; Sonia Keppel, *Three Brothers at Havana, 1762* (Wilton, Eng.: Michael Russell, 1981); Allan J. Kuethe, *Cuba, 1753–1815: Crown, Military, and Society* (Knoxville: University of Tennessee Press, 1986), 16–20.

19. Corbett, *England in the Seven Years' War*, 2:248, 254; Fernández Duro, *Armada española*, 7:83–89; Gipson, *British Empire*, 8:275–82; Clowes, *Royal Navy*, 3:239–42; Waddington, *La Guerre*, 5:40–43; Rousseau, *Règne de Charles III*, 1:88; Nicholas P. Cushner, ed., *Documents Illustrating the British Conquest of Manila, 1762–1763* (London: Royal Historical Society, 1971); Nicholas Tracy, "The Capture of Manila, 1762," *Mariner's Mirror* 55 (1969): 311–23 and *Manila Ransomed: The British Assault on Manila in the Seven Years War* (Exeter: University of Exeter Press, 1995), 1–56.

20. Fernández Duro, *Armada española*, 7:101–5, 110–13; Gipson, *British Empire*, 8:268–69; Clowes, *Royal Navy*, 3:251–52; Rousseau, *Règne de Charles III*, 1:89–90; Petrie, *King Charles III*, 109.

21. Spain 531: 92, Ossun to Choiseul, 26 January 1761; Blart, *Les Rapports*, 42; Mitchell and Deane, *Abstract*, 280; Ashton, *Economic Fluctuations*, 76, 150–51; Peters, *Pitt and Popularity*, 257; Francis P. Renaut d'Oultre-Seille, *Le Pacte de famille et l'Amérique: La Politique coloniale franco-espagnole de 1760 à 1792* (Paris: Editions Leroux, 1922), 63–64.

22. Spain 536: 365–66; B ^{2}371:21, 38; B ^{4}103: 318–79; B ^{4}104: 17–42, 86–240; G 49: 159–60; Syrett, "American Provincials and the Havana Campaign," 386–87; Spinney, *Rodney*, 192–94; Corbett, *England in the Seven Years' War*, 2:236–37, 257; Pares, *War and Trade*, 590–93; Marley, "Havana Surprised," 297–99; Buchet, *La Lutte*, 1:409–10; 2:716; Maupassant, *Gradis*, 110–11; *London Evening Post*, 27–29 July 1762.

23. Spain 536: 24–27, 100–101, 152–57, 256–58, 294, 459–60; Spain 537: 10; B^{4}100: 235–67, 311–21, 356–81; Fernández Duro, *Armada española*, 7:53–58; Corbett, *England in the Seven Years' War*, 2:297–98, 302–23, 345; Grouchy and Cottin, *Journal de Croÿ*, 2:46–47; Mackay, *Admiral Hawke*, 283–93, and *Hawke Papers*, 379–91; Middleton, "British Naval Strategy," 366; Black, "Anglo-Spanish Naval Relations," 253; Bourguet, "Après le Pacte de famille," 16–17, 24–25.

24. Spain 535: 165–66; B ^{2}371:71–244, 697–701; B ^{3}553: 298, 304; B ^{3}554: 22, 33, 227–44; B ^{4}104: 4–9; B ^{4}105: 4–137; Buchet, *La Lutte*, 1:411–12; Boulle, "French Colonies," 539–42; Giraud, "Mémoire de Choiseul," 252; Lacour-Gayet, *La Marine militaire*, 394; Vergé-Francheschi, *Les Officiers généraux*, 7:448; Michel, *Estaing*, 62–70. For the French capture of Rio de Janeiro in September 1711, see Buchet, *La Lutte*, 1:235–36; Charles de La Roncière, *Histoire de la marine française*, 6 vols. (Paris: Plon-Nourrit, 1899–1932), 6:530–40.

25. Spain 536: 39–40; B ^{1}67: 92; B^{4}102: 141; B^{4}104: 4–9; Boulle, "French Colonies," 535.

26. See appendix K; B^{2}369: 196 (first pagination), 198–381, 453–55, 459–62 (second pagination); B^{3}555; B^{4}102: 93–125, 142–60; B^{5}4: unpaginated, paper dated 12 November 1762; Vergé-Franceschi, *Les Officiers généraux*, 2:852; Brun, *Port de Toulon*, 1:450–55.

27. B^{4}104: 4–9, 43–85; Corbett, *England in the Seven Years' War*, 2:324–25; Boulle, "French Colonies," 534–35; Mackay, *Admiral Hawke*, 285; Gipson, *British Empire*, 8:270–73; Mante, *History of the Late War*, 466–75; Lacour-Gayet, *La Marine militaire*, 372; Halpenny, *Dictionary of Canadian Biography*, 4:31; Linÿer de la Barbée, *Ternay*, 1:151–71; Little, *Recapture of St. John's*; Georges Cerbelaud Salagnac, "La Reprise de Terre-Neuve par les Français en 1762," *Revue française d'histoire d'oute-mer* 63 (1976): 211–22; Evan W. H. Fyers, "The Loss and Recapture of St. John's, Newfoundland, in 1762," *Journal of the Society for Army Historical Research* 11 (1932): 179–215.

28. Austria 286: 340–41, the comte de Choiseul to Châtelet-Lomont, 22 February 1762; Russia 68: 213–14, the comte de Choiseul to Breteuil, 22 February 1762; Waddington, *La Guerre*, 5:132, 146–47, 198–212; Grouchy and Cottin, *Journal de Croÿ*, 2:32–33; Giraud, "Mémoire de Choiseul," 180; Ozanam and Antoine, *Correspondance de Broglie*, 1:142–42; Savory, *His Britannic Majesty's Army*, 334, 362.

29. Austria 286: 151–52, the comte de Choiseul to Châtelet-Lomont, 2 February 1762; Spain 536: 30, the duc de Choiseul to Ossun, 5 April 1762; Mitchell and Deane, *Abstract*, 390; Fortescue, *British Army*, 2:556; Neal, "Interpreting Power and Profit," 34; Cook and Stevenson, *British Historical Facts*, 97; Whitworth, *Ligonier*, 373.

30. Savory, *His Britannic Majesty's Army*, 364–440; Fortescue, *British Army*, 2:556–66; Pajol, *Les Guerres*, 5:309–468.

31. Brown and Schweizer, *Devonshire Diary*, 155; Pease, *Boundary Disputes*, cxxvii–cxxviii; Savelle, *Origins of American Diplomacy*, 491; Albemarle, *Memoirs of Rockingham*, 1:97–99, Choiseul to Solaro, 23 January 1762; Schaefer, "Geschichte," 65–68, 68, Solaro to Viry, 1 February 1761 (two letters); Rashed, *Peace of Paris*, 121–26; Aiton, "Diplomacy of the Louisiana Cession," 712. For Solaro's role in the negotiations, see Schaefer, "Geschichte," 64–65, Charles Emmanuel III to Solaro, 19 December 1761; Rashed, *Peace of Paris*, 118n; Barthélemy, "Le Traité de Paris," 458n; Rousseau, *Règne de Charles III*, 1:91; Pease, *Boundary Disputes*, cxxxviii.

32. Sedgwick, *Letters to Bute*, 75; Scott, "True Principles," in Black, *Knights Errant*, 76–78, 90n; Schweizer, *Anglo-Prussian Alliance*, 171–72; Doran, *Andrew Mitchell*, 301–2; Sir Herbert Butterfield, "Review Article: British Foreign Policy, 1762–5," *Historical Journal* 6 (1963): 132.

33. The fullest account of the initiative is Schweizer, *Anglo-Prussian Alliance*, 171–81, but see also Doran, *Andrew Mitchell*, 298, 301–7; Butterfield, "Review Article," 132–33; Corbett, *England in the Seven Years' War*, 2:291; Black, "Crown," in Black, *Knights Errant*, 124.

34. Droysen, *Politische Correspondenz*, 21:165–66, Frederick II to Graf Finckenstein, 6 January 1762. Ritter, *Frederick the Great*, 124–25, takes Frederick's threat to commit suicide seriously.

35. Schweizer, *Anglo-Prussian Alliance*, 181; Waddington, *La Guerre*, 5:285–87.

36. Schweizer, *Anglo-Prussian Alliance*, 176–77.

37. Albemarle, *Memoirs of Rockingham*, 1:99–100; Brown and Schweizer, *Devonshire Diary*, 154–55; Sedgwick, *Letters to Bute*, 78–79; Doran, *Andrew Mitchell*, 323; Schweizer, *Anglo-Prussian Alliance*, 146, 169.

38. Brown and Schweizer, *Devonshire Diary*, 156–57; Doran, *Andrew Mitchell*, 321–22; Schweizer, *Anglo-Prussian Alliance*, 168–69, 219–27, 289–93; Sedgwick, *Letters to Bute*, 91, 93; Russell, *Correspondence of Bedford*, 3:72–73; Eldon, *Subsidy Policy*, 161; Clark, *Waldegrave*, 90, 295–301; Brown, *Pitt*, 262.

39. Brown and Schweizer, *Devonshire Diary*, 170; Doran, *Andrew Mitchell*, 297–98, 314–23; Schweizer, *Anglo-Prussian Alliance*, 147–58, 190–93, 235–38, 242–49, 271–93, 338–46; Sedgwick, *Letters to Bute*, 81, 86; Russell, *Correspondence of Bedford*, 3:75–77; Brown, *Pitt*, 266.

40. Duffy, *Frederick the Great*, 227; Brown and Schweizer, *Devonshire Diary*, 158–59; Doran, *Andrew Mitchell*, 300, 306–7, 318–19, 324; Schweizer, *Anglo-Prussian Alliance*, 190–96, 237–38, 254–55, 267, 272, 276–82, 297–303, 317n; Droysen, *Politische Correspondenz*, 21:209, 353–55, 438–39; 22:117, 159–60, 207–8, 221–22; Ritter, *Frederick the Great*, 125; Butterfield, "Review Article," 135; Bisset, *Memoirs of Mitchell*, 2:283–88; Schweizer and Leonard, "Galitzin Letter," 531–56; Horst Dippel, "Prussia's English Policy after the Seven Years' War," *Central European History* 4 (1971): 195–214.

41. Schweizer, *Anglo-Prussian Alliance*, 235–38, 254–55, 340; Waddington, *La Guerre*, 5:308–9, 324–25, 329–30; Butterfield, "Review Article," 134; Leonard, *Reform and Regicide*, 129, 132, 134.

42. Madariaga, *Russia*, 188–89; Scott, *British Foreign Policy*, 46–47.

43. Butterfield, "Review Article," 138–39; Scott, *British Foreign Policy*, 55–61, and "Great Britain, Poland, and the Russian Alliance, 1763–1767," *Historical Journal* 19 (1976): 53–74; Michael Roberts, *Splendid Isolation, 1763–1780* (Reading: University of Reading, 1970).

44. Britain 446: 12–13, note reporting the capture of Estaing; Spain 536: 70, Egremont to the duc de Choiseul, 22 February 1762; Britain 446: 27, the duc de Choiseul to Egremont, 7 March 1762 (also printed in Schaefer, "Geschichte," 68–69); Rousseau, *Règne de Charles III*, 90–91; Savelle, *Origins of American Diplomacy*, 491; Pease, *Boundary Disputes*, cxxix; Barthélemy, "Le Traité de Paris," 458–59; Michel, *Estaing*, 43, 60–64.

45. Spain 535: 315, the duc de Choiseul to Ossun, 16 March 1762; Van Kley, *Expulsion of the Jesuits*, 171–74 and *Damiens Affair*, 197.

46. Spain 536: 31, the duc de Choiseul to Ossun, 5 April 1762; Britain 446: 40–43, Viry to Solaro, 8 April 1762 (two letters); Britain 446: 44, Declaration of King George III, 8 April 1762; Britain 446: 45–46, Bute to Viry, 8 April 1762; Britain 446: 47–48, Egremont to the duc de Choiseul, 8 April 1762; Britain 446: 49–50, Viry to Solaro, 9 April 1762; Britain 446: 51–52, the duc de Choiseul to Egremont, April 1762; Britain 446: 53–54, the duc de Choiseul to Egremont, 14 April 1762; Britain 446: 55–60, the comte de Choiseul to Solaro, circa 15 April 1762; Britain 446: 62–65, the comte de Choiseul to Egremont, circa 20 April 1762; Sweden 241: 350–61, Havrincourt to the comte de Choiseul, 26 March 1762; Schaefer, "Geschichte," 69–72; Pease, *Boundary Disputes*, cxxix–cxxxii, 409–11, 415–17; Brown and Schweizer, *Devonshire Diary*, 161–64; Rashed, *Peace of Paris*, 131–33; Savelle, *Origins of American Diplomacy*, 491–93; Rousseau, *Règne de Charles III*, 91–92; Corbett,

England in the Seven Years' War, 2:301; Barthélemy, "Le Traité de Paris," 456; Great Britain. Historical Manuscripts Commission, *Tenth Report of the Royal Commission on Historical Manuscripts* (London: Eyre and Spottiswoode, 1885), 449–50.

47. Britain 446: 66–68, Egremont to the comte de Choiseul, 1 May 1762; Britain 446: 70–75, Egremont to Viry, 1 May 1762 (three letters); Britain 446: 76, Viry to Solaro, 4 May 1762; Schaefer, "Geschichte," 72–79; Pease, *Anglo-French Boundary Disputes*, cxxxii, 421–25; Brown and Schweizer, *Devonshire Diary*, 168–69; Rashed, *Peace of Paris*, 140–42; Savelle, *Origins of American Diplomacy*, 493–95; Corbett, *England in the Seven Years' War*, 2:332–34.

48. Schweizer, *Anglo-Prussian Alliance*, 168–69, 226–27, 286–88; Black, "Crown," in Black, *Knights Errant*, 122; Eldon, *Subsidy Policy*, 141–42; Russell, *Correspondence of Bedford*, 3:78–81; Sedgwick, *Letters to Bute*, 96; Brown and Schweizer, *Devonshire Diary*, 161–62; Middleton, *Bells of Victory*, 207–9; Namier, *England*, 313–26; O'Gorman, *Rise of Party*, 37–39; Browning, *Duke of Newcastle*, 287–88; Wiggin, *Faction of Cousins*, 263–64; Karl W. Schweizer and J. Bullion, "The Vote of Credit Controversy, 1762," *British Journal for Eighteenth-Century Studies* 15 (1992): 175–88; Philip Lawson, *George Grenville: A Political Life* (Oxford: Clarendon Press, 1984), 131–33.

49. Corbett, *England in the Seven Years' War*, 2:342; Rodger, *Insatiable Earl*, 95.

50. Pease, *Boundary Disputes*, 483–85, Solaro to Viry, 21 July 1762; Antoine, *Le Gouvernement*, 34; Swann, *Politics and the Parlement of Paris*, 218–19, 236–37.

51. Spain 536: 207–8, the duc de Choiseul to Ossun, 12 May 1762; Austria 288: 240, the comte de Choiseul to Châtelet-Lomont, 17 May 1762; Britain 446: 98–102, Viry to Solaro, 22 May 1762 (four letters); Britain 447: 42–43, undated memoir, circa 2 September 1762; Russell, *Correspondence of Bedford*, 3:81–87, the duc de Choiseul to Solaro, 13 May 1762; Pease, *Anglo-French Boundary Disputes*, cxxxv; Rashed, *Peace of Paris*, 143–45; Sedgwick, *Letters to Bute*, 115.

52. For this portion of the negotiations, see Britain 446: 77–262; Schaefer, "Geschichte," 79–85; Pease, *Boundary Disputes*, cxxxiii–cxlviii, 425–500; Rashed, *Peace of Paris*, 145–58; Savelle, *Origins of American Diplomacy*, 495–503; Boulle, "French Colonies," 548–55.

53. Boulle, "French Colonies," 549–50; Judith Blow Williams, "The Development of British Trade with West Africa, 1750 to 1850," *Political Science Quarterly* 50 (1935): 197; Ronald Hyam, "Imperial Interests and the Peace of Paris, 1763," in Ronald Hyam and Ged Martin, *Reappraisals in British Imperial History* (London: Macmillan, 1975), 37.

54. See Russell, *Correspondence of Bedford*, 3:76; Rashed, *Peace of Paris*, 147–48, 153–57, 159–60; Savelle, *Origins of American Diplomacy*, 494–503; Rousseau, *Règne de Charles III*, 1:97–98; Hyam, "Imperial Interests," 34; Sosin, *Whitehall and the Wilderness*, 19; Pease, *Anglo-French Boundary Disputes*, cxxxiii–cxxxiv, cxxxviii–cxlviii, 425–27, 430–34, 438–62, 466–69, 473–88, 496–99, 555, and "The Mississippi Boundary of 1763: A Reappraisal of Responsibility," *American Historical Review* 40 (1934–35): 278–86.

55. For the relative importance of St. Lucia, see Spain 533: 55–56, the duc de Choiseul to Ossun, 14 July 1761; Pease, *Boundary Disputes*, 427–29, 431–32; Bullion, "Securing the Peace," in Schweizer, *Lord Bute*, 30–31; Gaston Martin, *Nantes au XVIIIe siècle*, vol. 2, *L'Ere des négriers (1714–1774), d'après des documents inédits* (Paris: Félix Alcan, 1931), 283.

56. For the public's criticism of Choiseul on foreign policy issues, see Savelle, *Origins of American Diplomacy*, 484. For other explanations of Choiseul's betrayal of the Jesuits, see Van Kley, *Expulsion of the Jesuits*, 200, and Scott, "Religion and Realpolitik."

57. Britain 446: 243–51, Egremont to the comte de Choiseul and enclosed memoir, 31 July 1762; Britain 446: 252–57, Egremont to Viry, 31 July 1762; Britain 446: 258–62, Viry to Solaro, 1 August 1762; Brown and Schweizer, *Devonshire Diary*, 173–75; Pease, *Boundary Disputes*, cxxxvii–cxlvii, 461–62, 481–95; Russell, *Correspondence of Bedford*, 3:88–91; Rashed, *Peace of Paris*, 149–50, 153–58; Savelle, *Origins of American Diplomacy*, 500–503; Corbett, *England in the Seven Years' War*, 2:346–50; Sedgwick, *Letters to Bute*, 121–22, 124–29; Giles Stephen Holland Fox-Strangways, Earl of Ilchester, *Henry Fox, First Lord Holland, His Family and Relations*, 2 vols. (London: J. Murray, 1920), 2:179–80.

58. Pease, *Boundary Disputes*, cxlvi, 460; Rashed, *Peace of Paris*, 158, 167; Savelle, *Origins of American Diplomacy*, 500; Corbett, *England in the Seven Years' War*, 2:343, 348; Lawson, *George Grenville*, 137; Wiggin, *Faction of Cousins*, 271.

59. Austria 288: 239–43, 343–48, the comte de Choiseul to Châtelet-Lomont, 17 May and 31 May 1762; Holland 495: 147; Waddington, *La Guerre*, 5:284–88, 319, 322, 402; Barthélemy, "Le Traité de Paris," 461; Pease, *Boundary Disputes*, cxln; Corbett, *England in the Seven Years' War*, 2:345–46; Rashed, *Peace of Paris*, 135–37, 144–45.

60. Britain 446: 229–31, the comte de Choiseul to Egremont, 21 July 1762; Austria 290: 96–104, the comte de Choiseul to Châtelet-Lomont, 27 July 1762; Austria 290: 226, Châtelet-Lomont to the comte de Choiseul, 11 August 1762; Austria 291:88, the comte de Choiseul to Châtelet-Lomont, 20 September 1762; Rashed, *Peace of Paris*, 141–42, 147, 153–55, 158, 166; Pease, *Boundary Disputes*, cxxxn, 339, 461–63, 481–83; Corbett, *England in the Seven Years' War*, 2:345–50; Russell, *Correspondence of Bedford*, 3:89; Droysen, *Politische Correspondenz*, 22:103–4, 223, 229–32; Doran, *Andrew Mitchell*, 265, 342–52; Savelle, *Origins of American Diplomacy*, 491–92; Parry, *Consolidated Treaty Series*, 41:242–43; Soulange-Bodin, *La Diplomatie de Louis XV*, 186; Schweizer, *Anglo-Prussian Alliance*, 324–27, and "Britain, Prussia and the Prussian Territories on the Rhine, 1762–1763," *Studies in History and Politics* 4 (1985), 103–14.

61. Spain 536: 62–83, Louis XV to Grimaldi, 17 April 1762, with enclosed copies of Egremont to the duc de Choiseul, 22 February 1762 and other documents; Spain 536: 176–90, 263–70, 500–542; Rashed, *Peace of Paris*, 134, 137–38; Barthélemy, "Le Traité de Paris," 456; Pease, *Boundary Disputes*, cxxix, cxxxii; Savelle, *Origins of American Diplomacy*, 492–93; Rousseau, *Règne de Charles III*, 1:92.

62. Spain 536: 93–101, 130–38, 274–80, Ossun to the duc de Choiseul, 26 April, 2 May, and 31 May 1762; Spain 536: 167–75, 221–22, the duc de Choiseul to Ossun, 12 May and 17 May 1762; Russell, *Correspondence of Bedford*, 3:84–85, Choiseul to Solaro, 13 May 1762; Rashed, *Peace of Paris*, 138–40; Barthélemy, "Le Traité de Paris," 456–60; Aiton, "Diplomacy of the Louisiana Cession," 713–14; Bourguet, "Un Ultimatum," 30–34; Noel, "Crisis" in Oresko et al., *Royal and Republican Sovereignty*, 605–6.

63. Spain 536: 221–22, the duc de Choiseul to Ossun, 17 May 1762; Spain 537: 6–9, Ossun to the duc de Choiseul, 2 August 1762; Russell, *Correspondence of Bedford*, 3:84–85, 89; Rashed, *Peace of Paris*, 133, 140, 146, 151–54, 159–60, 163; Barthélemy, "Le Traité de Paris,"

459–65; Pease, *Boundary Discussions*, cxliv–cxlix, 463–64, 470–71, 490–96; Savelle, *Origins of American Diplomacy*, 491–503, 501–3; Corbett, *England in the Seven Years' War*, 2:331–32; Brown and Schweizer, *Devonshire Diary*, 163n, 168–69, 173–75; Gipson, *British Empire*, 8:301–3; Sedgwick, *Letters to Bute*, 125n, 127–28n; Temperley, "Peace of Paris," 497.

64. Spain 532: 417, Ossun to the duc de Choiseul, 22 June 1761; Spain 533: 120–21, Ossun to the duc de Choiseul, 16 July 1761; Spain 537: 20–22, 26–27, 48, 109–12, the duc de Choiseul to Ossun, 8 August, 9 August, 17 August, and 27 August 1762; Spain 537: 53–56, Ossun to Choiseul, 18 August 1762; Spain 537: 84–88, O'Dunne to Choiseul, 22 August 1762; Spain 537: 103–7 and Britain 446: 291–94, the comte de Choiseul to Egremont, 26 August 1762; Britain 446: 295–96, the comte de Choiseul to Solaro, 26 August 1762; Rashed, *Peace of Paris*, 160–64; Barthélemy, "Le Traité de Paris," 464–66; Pease, *Boundary Disputes*, cxlvii–cxlix; Savelle, *Origins of American Diplomacy*, 503–4; Rousseau, *Règne de Charles III*, 1:93–95; Soulange-Bodin, *La Diplomatie de Louis XV*, 169–70, 174–75; Brown and Schweizer, *Devonshire Diary*, 174, 177; Jarrett, *Walpole Memoirs*, 1:124; Russell, *Correspondence of Bedford*, 3:99n; Morel-Fatio and Léonardon, *Recueil*, 12bis: 342; Butler, *Choiseul*, 1:473, 713–14, 719, 784; Giles Stephen Holland Fox-Strangways, Earl of Ilchester, ed., *Letters to Henry Fox, Lord Holland, With a Few Addressed to His Brother Stephen, Earl of Ilchester* (London: privately printed for the Roxburghe Club, 1915), 156–57.

65. Britain 447: 3–29, Instructions for Nivernais and Observations on the Draft Treaty, 2 September 1762; Pease, *Boundary Disputes*, cxxxvi, cxxxviii; Vaucher, *Recueil*, 25[bis]: 387–404; Bullion, "Securing the Peace," in Schweizer, *Lord Bute*, 32–33.

66. Britain 447: 65–66, 66–67, 67, 69–72, Nivernais to the comte de Choiseul, 6 September, 7 September (two letters), and 9 September 1762; State Papers Series 78 (France), 253: 39–41, Bedford to Egremont, 8 September 1762; Pease, *Boundary Disputes*, 508–11; Ozanam and Antoine, *Correspondance de Broglie*, 1:lv.

67. Britain 447: 76–78, 79–82, 83–88, 123–26, 128–29, 134–37, 143–54, Nivernais to the comte de Choiseul, 14 September, 15 September, 16 September, 20 September, 22 September, 23 September, and 24 September 1762; Britain 447: 100–108, 109–20, the comte de Choiseul to Nivernais, 20 September with enclosed draft articles of peace; Spain 537: 160–68, 169–83, 184–85, the duc de Choiseul to Ossun, 20 September (two letters and enclosed draft articles); Rashed, *Peace of Paris*, 169; Barthélemy, "Le Traité de Paris," 465, 467, 469–70; Pease, *Boundary Disputes*, 516–18, 524–28; Soulange-Bodin, *La Diplomatie de Louis XV*, 180–92; Sedgwick, *Letters to Bute*, 135–41; Ilchester, *Letters to Henry Fox*, 158–59; Herpin, *Nivernais*, 491–501.

68. Britain 447: 92–99, the comte de Choiseul to Nivernais, 19 September 1762; Austria 291: 86, the comte de Choiseul to Châtelet-Lomont, 20 September 1762; State Papers Series 78 (France) 253: 1–23, Instructions for Bedford, 4 September 1762; Series 78 (France) 253: 24–28, 33–38, 42–47, Egremont to Bedford, 7 September (two letters) and 16 September 1762; Series 78 (France) 253: 58–63, 64–65, 67–75, 90–91, 94–95, 96–108, Bedford to Egremont, 15 September, 17 September, 19 September, and 21 September 1762 (two letters and enclosed French proposals); Russell, *Correspondence of Bedford*, 3:92–93, 96–117, 125–27; Rashed, *Peace of Paris*, 165–66, 168–69, 172–74; Pease, *Boundary Disputes*,

cli–cliv, 505–6, 511–13, 519–24; Sedgwick, *Letters to Bute*, 131n, 138–40n; Corbett, *England in the Seven Years' War*, 2:357–59; Doran, *Andrew Mitchell*, 351–54; Legg, *British Diplomatic Instructions*, 7:55–69; Smith, *Grenville Papers*, 1:474–76.

69. Spain 536: 98, Ossun to the duc de Choiseul, 26 April 1762; Spain 537: 2–13, Ossun to the duc de Choiseul, 2 August 1762; Spain 537: 160–68, 184–85, the duc de Choiseul to Ossun, 20 September (two letters); Spain 537: 189–90, Ossun to Wall, 27 September 1762; Russell, *Correspondence of Bedford*, 3:106–10; Rashed, *Peace of Paris*, 162–63, 167, 169–75; Pease, *Boundary Disputes*, clii–clv, 496–99, 507, 514–15, 525–28, 531–38; Barthélemy, "Le Traité de Paris," 461–62, 466–70; Rousseau, *Règne de Charles III*, 1:96–97; Corbett, *England in the Seven Years' War*, 2:341, 358; Aiton, "Diplomacy of the Louisiana Cession," 716–17; Christelow, "Economic Background," 33–35; William R. Shepherd, "The Cession of Louisiana to Spain," *Political Science Quarterly* 19 (1904): 446–47.

70. Spain 537: 185, the duc de Choiseul to Ossun, 20 September 1762; Brown and Schweizer, *Devonshire Diary*, 179n; Pease, *Boundary Disputes*, cli, 533; Herpin, *Nivernais*, 504. See also Austria 290: 346–47, the comte de Choiseul to Châtelet-Lomont, 28 August 1762.

71. Spain 536: 383–84, duc de Choiseul to Ossun, 29 June 1762; Brown and Schweizer, *Devonshire Diary*, 18, 179–86; Russell, *Correspondence of Bedford*, 3:120–21, 130–36; Sedgwick, *Letters to Bute*, 143–53; Rashed, *Peace of Paris*, 155–56, 176–78; Pease, *Boundary Disputes*, clv–clix, clxiv–clxvi; Barthélemy, "Le Traité de Paris," 470–75, 478–79; Corbett, *England in the Seven Years' War*, 2:360–61; Legg, *British Diplomatic Instructions*, 7:72–73; Herpin, *Nivernais*, 502–12; Soulange-Bodin, *La Diplomatie de Louis XV*, 192–94, 198–204; Pares, *War and Trade*, 554, 606–8; Lawson, *George Grenville*, 138–42; Wiggin, *Faction of Cousins*, 272–74.

72. State Papers Series 78 (France) 253: 161–67, 168–207, 208–15, 216–17, 218–19, 220–21, Egremont to Bedford, 26 October 1762 with various enclosures; Russell, *Correspondence of Bedford*, 3:118–19, 137–43; Legg, *British Diplomatic Instructions*, 69–72; Sedgwick, *Letters to Bute*, 151; Rashed, *Peace of Paris*, 178–80; Pease, *Boundary Disputes*, clxvi, 542–44.

73. Spain 537: 201–7, Ossun to the duc de Choiseul, 29 September 1762; Russell, *Correspondence of Bedford*, 3:120–21; Rashed, *Peace of Paris*, 175–76; Pease, *Boundary Disputes*, cliii, clix–clx; Barthélemy, "Le Traité de Paris," 470–71. For the arrival of the news in London, see Holland 511: 187 and Austria 291: 172–73.

74. Spain 536: 495, the duc de Choiseul to Ossun, 22 July 1762; Spain 537: 208–9, 215–20, 223–24, 225–26, 256–62, the duc de Choiseul to Ossun, 3 October, 9 October (three letters) and 20 October 1762; Spain 537: 221–22, Louis XV to Charles III, 9 October 1762; Spain 537: 227–30, Ossun to Choiseul, 10 October 1762; Rashed, *Peace of Paris*, 180–82; Pease, *Boundary Disputes*, clx–clxiii; Barthélemy, "Le Traité de Paris," 473–76; Rousseau, *Règne de Charles III*, 1:100–101, 104; Soulange-Bodin, *La Diplomatie de Louis XV*, 194–97; Savelle, *Origins of American Diplomacy*, 506; Blart, *Les Rapports*, 42; Richard B. Stenberg, "The Louisiana Cession and the Family Compact," *Louisiana Historical Quarterly* 19 (1936): 205, 207.

75. Britain 447: 278, 279–81, Nivernais to the comte de Choiseul, 11 October and enclosed peace terms; Spain 237: 235–37, 238–40, 241–42, 243–44, Nivernais to the comte

de Choiseul, 12 October (two letters) and 13 October 1762 (two letters, and see also Britain 447: 284–94); Spain 537: 249–50, 251, the duc de Choiseul to Ossun, 15 October 1762 and enclosure; Spain 537: 266–73, Ossun to the duc de Choiseul, 22 October 1762; Russell, *Correspondence of Bedford*, 3:120–21; Rashed, *Peace of Paris*, 182–83; Pease, *Boundary Disputes*, clxii–clxiii; Barthélemy, "Le Traité de Paris," 476–78; Soulange-Bodin, *Le Diplomatie de Louis XV*, 197–98; Rousseau, *Règne de Charles III*, 101–2; Herpin, *Nivernais*, 513; Aiton, "Diplomacy of the Louisiana Cession," 718; Shepherd, "Cession of Louisiana," 449n; Stenberg, "Louisiana Cession," 206; Hyam, "Imperial Interests" in Hyam and Martin, *Reappraisals*, 32; Wright, *Anglo-Spanish Rivalry*, 105–10; Villiers du Terrage, *Les Dernières Années*, 154; Daniel J. Weber, *The Spanish Frontier in North America* (New Haven: Yale University Press, 1992), 176–77, 198–200; Robert L. Gold, *Borderland Empires in Transition: The Triple-Nation Transfer of Florida* (Carbondale: Southern Illinois University Press; London: Feffer and Simons, 1969), 69–73; Wilbur H. Siebert, "How the Spaniards Evacuated Pensacola in 1763," *Florida Historical Quarterly* 11 (1932): 48–57 and "Spanish and French Privateering in Southern Waters, July, 1762, to March, 1763," *Georgia Historical Quarterly* 16 (1932): 163–78.

76. Britain 448, 10–11, the comte de Choiseul to Nivernais, 3 November 1762; Spain 537: 290–91, the duc de Choiseul to Ossun, 3 November 1762; Russell, *Correspondence of Bedford*, 3:121–22, 143–49; Rashed, *Peace of Paris*, 184–86; Pease, *Boundary Disputes*, clxvi–clxvii; Barthélemy, "Le Traité de Paris," 478–79; Herpin, *Nivernais*, 514; Parry, *Consolidated Treaty Series*, 42:209–38.

77. Spain 537, 292–93, Louis XV to Charles III, 3 November 1762; Parry, *Consolidated Treaty Series*, 42:239–41; Rashed, *Peace of Paris*, 193n; Pease, *Boundary Disputes*, clxiv; Soulange-Bodin, *La Diplomatie de Louis XV*, 165, 196n, 197; Aiton, "Diplomacy of the Louisiana Cession," 718–20; Shepherd, "Cession of Louisiana," 449–51; Stenberg, "Louisiana Cession," 207–8; Villiers du Terrage, *Les Dernières Années*, 155; E. Wilson Lyon, *Louisiana in French Diplomacy, 1759–1804* (Norman: University of Oklahoma Press, 1934), 28–34.

78. Russell, *Correspondence of Bedford*, 3:159–63; Sedgwick, *Letters to Bute*, 160, 166–68; Corbett, *England in the Seven Years' War*, 2:354, 363–64; Herpin, *Nivernais*, 516; Doran, *Andrew Mitchell*, 356–57; Thackeray, *History of Pitt*, 2:14–23; Simmons and Thomas, *Proceedings and Debates*, 1:412–24; O'Gorman, *Rise of Party*, 47–53; Brown, *Pitt*, 271–74.

79. Austria 291:322–27, the comte de Choiseul to Châtelet-Lomont, 6 November 1762; Brown and Schweizer, *Devonshire Diary*, 184n; Russell, *Correspondence of Bedford*, 3:90–91, 97; Legg, *British Diplomatic Instructions*, 78–79; Droysen, *Politische Correspondenz*, 22:261–62, 483–85; Rashed, *Peace of Paris*, 166, 173–74, 185, 205; Doran, *Andrew Mitchell*, 350–56, 370; Schweizer, *Anglo-Prussian Alliance*, 327–28, 333, and "Prussian Territories on the Rhine," 108–10; Soulange-Bodin, *La Diplomatie de Louis XV*, 214–19; Corbett, *England in the Seven Years' War*, 2:350, 355–57, 362–65; Duffy, *Frederick the Great*, 558; Savory, *His Britannic Majesty's Army*, 438–39; Sir Richard Lodge, *Great Britain and Prussia in the Eighteenth Century* (Oxford: Clarendon Press, 1923), 137.

80. Parry, *Consolidated Treaty Series*, 42:279–345; Russell, *Correspondence of Bedford*, 3:177–83, 190–98; Brown and Schweizer, *Devonshire Diary*, 183n; Rashed, *Peace of Paris*,

192–200; Pease, *Boundary Disputes*, clxviii–clxix, 545–68; Barthélemy, "Le Traité de Paris," 481–86; Soulange-Bodin, *La Diplomatie de Louis XV*, 219–20; Lucy Sutherland, "The East India Company and the Peace of Paris," in Aubrey Newman, ed., *Politics and Finance in the Eighteenth Century: Lucy Sutherland* (London: Hambleton Press, 1984), 165–76.

81. Austria 288: 190, Châtelet-Lomont to the comte de Choiseul, 15 May 1762; Waddington, *La Guerre*, 5:288; Duffy, *Frederick the Great*, 559; Parry, *Consolidated Treaty Series* 42:347–59, 361–86.

82. Droysen, *Politische Correspondenz*, 21:314; Duffy, *Frederick the Great*, 228–30, *Austrian Army*, 128, 358, and *Military Experience*, 309; Childs, *Armies and Warfare*, 166; Showalter, *Wars*, 322–23; Leonard, *Reform and Regicide*, 117; Scott, *Emergence of the Eastern Powers*, 73–74, 84–85.

83. Austria 290: 347, the comte de Choiseul to Châtelet Lomont, 28 August 1762; Rashed, *Peace of Paris*, 186, 206; Barthélemy, "Le Traité de Paris," 479–80; Blart, *Les Rapports*, 41–42; Boutaric, *Correspondence secréte de Louis XV*, 1:288–89, Louis XV to Tercier, 26 February 1763; Roy, "Les Chambres de commerce," 210–11, 223–25.

84. The classic critique of eighteenth-century diplomacy is Sorel, *Europe and the French Revolution*. See also Paul W. Schroeder, *The Transformation of European Politics, 1763–1848* (Oxford: Clarendon Press, 1994), 3–52.

85. For one example, see Savory, *His Britannic Majesty's Army*, 335.

10. EPILOGUE—TOWARD A NEW WAR, 1763–1774

1. The French ships of the line are listed in appendix L. The number of Spanish ships of the line is based on deducting the ten lost at Havana from the forty-seven listed in appendix K. The number of British ships of the line is computed from Lyon, *Sailing Navy List*, 40–44, 62–64, 66–69, 72–73, 75–77.

2. Giraud, ed., "Mémoire de Choiseul," 252–53; H. M. Scott, "The Importance of Bourbon Naval Reconstruction to the Strategy of Choiseul after the Seven Years' War," *International History Review* 1 (1979): 19, 33; Clive Wilkinson, "The Earl of Egmont and the Navy, 1763–66," *Mariner's Mirror* 84 (1998): 431; Raymond E. Abarca, "Classical Diplomacy and Bourbon 'Revanche' Strategy, 1763–1770," *Review of Politics* 32 (1970): 326.

3. Demerliac, *La Marine de Louis XV*, 35–36, 40–41, 47, 51.

4. Spain 537: 111, Choiseul to Ossun, 27 August 1762. For contrasting opinions of the significance of Choiseul's reforms, compare Boulle, "French Colonies," 593–97, and Pritchard, *Louis XV's Navy*, 213–14.

5. $B^5$10: unpaginated, list probably from late 1775 or early 1776 entitled "Tableau des forces navales du roi dans le courant des treize années." See also Bamford, *Forests and French Sea Power*, 33, 41–42, 61–62, 103–5, 131–33, 145–49.

6. Boulle, "French Colonies," 669–73; Tracy, *Navies*, 48–53.

7. Boulle, "French Colonies," 597–666; E. Daubigny, *Choiseul et la France d'outre-mer après le traité de Paris: Etude sur la politique coloniale au XVIIIe siècle* (Paris: Hachette, 1892); Dorothy Burne Goebel, "The 'New England Trade' and the French West Indies,

1763–1774: A Study in Trade Policies," *William and Mary Quarterly*, 3rd ser., 20 (1963): 331–72.

8. Giraud, "Mémoire de Choiseul," 178.

9. [Amblard-Marie-Raymond-Amédée], vicomte de Noailles, *Marins et soldats français en Amérique pendant la guerre de l'indépendance des Etats-Unis (1778–1783)* (Paris: Perrin, 1903), 1–14; Cornélius de Witt, *Thomas Jefferson: Etude historique sur la démocratie américaine* (Paris: Didier, 1861), 407–64; Josephine F. Pacheco, "French Secret Agents in America, 1763–1778" (Ph.D. diss., University of Chicago, 1951).

10. Legohérel, *Les Tresoriers généraux*, 207; Riley, "French Finances," 224–25.

11. Saint Hubert, "Ships of the Line of the Spanish Navy," 209.

12. H. M. Scott, "France and the Polish Throne, 1763–1764," *Slavonic and East European Review* 53 (1975): 370–88.

13. Scott, "Importance of Bourbon Naval Reconstruction," 34–35; Alexander, *Catherine the Great*, 122–28; Madariaga, *Russia*, 196–97; Roberts, *British Diplomacy and Swedish Politics*, 213–16.

14. "Tableau des forces navales"; Legohérel, *Les Trésoriers généraux*, chart facing 180. For the British naval budget in the postwar years, see Mackay, *Admiral Hawke*, 305.

15. Abarca, "Bourbon 'Revanche' Strategy," 319–31; Julius Goebel Jr., *The Struggle for the Falkland Islands: A Study in Legal and Diplomatic History* (New Haven: Yale University Press, 1927), 319–31.

16. Demerliac, *La Marine de Louis XV*, 36, 40–41, 47. See also Jean Boudriot, "Les Vaisseaux 'La Couronne' 1749 et 1766," *Neptunia*, no. 187 (September 1992): 8–17.

17. Demerliac, *La Marine de Louis XV*, 35, 38–39, 44–47, 51. The list of ships of the line in August 1774, in Jonathan R. Dull, *The French Navy and American Independence: A Study of Arms and Diplomacy, 1774–1787* (Princeton: Princeton University Press, 1975), 351, is unchanged for 1 January 1775. For the ships of the line of 1755, see appendix C.

18. Tracy, *Navies*, 62–68; Scott, *British Foreign Policy*, 115–22; Thadd E. Hall, *France and the Eighteenth-Century Corsican Question* (New York: New York University Press, 1971).

19. For a concise summary, see Herbert H. Kaplan, *The First Partition of Poland* (New York: Columbia University Press, 1962), 89–105.

20. M. S. Anderson, "Great Britain and the Russian Fleet, 1769–70," *Slavonic and East European Review* 31 (1952–53): 148–63.

21. Tracy, *Navies*, 69–99; Goebel, *Struggle for the Falkland Islands*, 271–363.

22. For de Boynes' tenure as naval minister, see Lacour-Gayet, *La Marine militaire*, 428–34, 537–46; Dull, *French Navy and American Independence*, 12–14; Joannes Tramond, "La Marine et les reformes de M. de Boynes," *Revue maritime*, n.s., 61 (1925): 153–80; Lucien Laugier, *Un Ministère réformateur sous Louis XV: Le Triumvirat (1770–1774)* (Paris: La Pensée universelle, 1975), 503–60.

23. Dull, *French Navy and American Independence*, 22–23.

24. Boulle, "French Colonies," 237–38, 311–18, 676, and "Patterns," 68; Romano, "Balance du commerce," 1291; Le Goff, "Labour Market," in Van Royen et al., *"Those Emblems of Hell"?*, 295, 297, 320; Brière, *La Pêche Française*, 100–102, 149–51, 179–81; La Morandière, *Histoire de la pêche française*, 2:843–955, 999.

25. The number was smaller during the first year of the war. See Dull, *French Navy and American Independence*, 144n, 256n, 359–76; Brière, *La Pêche française*, 223; Meyer and Bromley, "Second Hundred Years' War," 147.

26. Saint Hubert, "Ships of the Line of the Spanish Navy," 206.

27. Computed from Lyon, *Sailing Navy List*, 40, 43–44, 62–70, 72–74, 76–78.

28. Scott, "France and the Polish Throne," 370–88.

29. Ozanam and Antoine, *Correspondance de Broglie*, 1:lxiv–lxxix, 162–69, 176–77, 196–97; Lacour-Gayet, *La Marine militaire*, 458–83; Margaret Cotter Morison, "The Duc de Choiseul and the Invasion of England, 1768–1770," *Transactions of the Royal Historical Society*, 3rd ser., 4 (1910): 83–115.

30. Ozanam and Antoine, *Correspondance de Broglie*, 1:xc–xci; Laugier, *Un Ministère réformateur sous Louis XV*, 345–502.

31. Albert Sorel, *The Eastern Question in the Eighteenth Century: The Partition of Poland and the Treaty of Kainardji*, trans. F. C. Bramwell (London: Methuen, 1898); Kaplan, *First Partition of Poland*.

32. Roberts, *British Diplomacy and Swedish Politics*, 349–403.

33. Madariaga, *Russia*, 226–32; Scott, *British Foreign Policy*, 181–91; Michael Roberts, *British Diplomacy and Swedish Politics*, 370–71, 408–9, and "Great Britain and the Swedish Revolution, 1772–73," *Historical Journal* 7 (1964): 1–46.

34. For the declining years of the "Secret du Roi," see Ozanam and Antoine, *Correspondance de Broglie*, 1:lxxix–cxiii; 2: passim; Broglie, *King's Secret*, 2:369–461.

35. Eugene Nelson White, "Was There a Solution to the Ancien Régime's Financial Dilemma?" *Journal of Economic History* 49 (1989): 548–55; J. F. Bosher, *French Finances, 1770–1795: From Business to Bureaucracy* (Cambridge: Cambridge University Press, 1970), 142–65; William Doyle, "The Parlements of France and the Breakdown of the Old Régime," *French Historical Studies* 6 (1969–70): 443–46.

36. For Louis' selection of Vergennes, see Murphy, *Vergennes*, 206–7; Baron Jehan de Witte, ed., *Journal de l'abbé de Véri*, 2 vols. (Paris: Jules Tallandier, 1928–30), 1:107–8; John Hardman, *Louis XVI* (New Haven: Yale University Press, 1993), 31–32, and *French Politics, 1774–1789: From the Accession of Louis XVI to the Fall of the Bastille* (London: Longman, 1995), 22, 34–36.

37. "C'était l'avènement au pouvoir et la revanche éclatante de la diplomatie secrète": Albert Sorel, *Essais d'histoire et de critique*, 4th ed. (Paris: E. Plon, 1913), 178.

38. Archives du Ministère des affaires étrangères, Mémoires et Documents, France 446, piece 33, f. 352; de Witte, *Journal de l'abbé de Veri*, 1:96; Henri Doniol, *Politiques d'autrefois: Le Comte de Vergennes et P. M. Hennin, 1749–1787* (Paris: Armand Colin, 1898), 103–7.

39. Farges, *Recueil*, 5:249–54; Hudson, *Conrad-Alexandre Gérard*, 28–33; Meng, *Despatches and Instructions of Gérard*, 38.

40. Droysen, *Politische Correspondenz*, 33:147, 159, 163, 174, 188; 34:37, 352; 35:87–88, 375; 36:368, 376, 494; 37:59, 243; Frédéric Masson, *Le Département des affaires étrangères pendant la Révolution, 1787–1804* (Paris: E. Plon, 1877).

41. Doniol, *Politiques d'autrefois*, 16; Ozanam and Antoine, *Correspondance de Broglie*,

1:lx–lxi; Scott, "France and the Polish Throne," 381–86; Besterman, *Voltaire*, 31:308; Julian P. Boyd et al., eds., *The Papers of Thomas Jefferson*, 31 vols. to date (Princeton: Princeton University Press, 1950–), 11:96.

42. Boutaric, *Correspondance secrète de Louis XV*, 2:493–96.

43. Dull, *French Navy and American Independence*, 345–50; Riley, *Seven Years War*, 68, 138–42, 147, 178, 183–84; Bosher, *French Finances*, 23–24; Morineau, "Budgets," 314, 325; James B. Collins, *The State in Early Modern France* (Cambridge: Cambridge University Press, 1995), 227; Robert D. Harris, *Necker, Reform Statesman of the Ancien Régime* (Berkeley: University of California Press, 1979), 118–19; Frédéric Braesch, *Finances et monnaie révolutionnaire (recherches, études, et documents)*, 3 vols. (Nancy: Roumegoux, 1934–36), 2:202; James Macdonald, *A Free Nation Deep in Debt: The Financial Roots of Democracy* (New York: Farrar, Straus and Giroux, 2003), 239–53.

44. Brewer, *Sinews of Power*, 30, 39–40. For other estimates, see Macdonald, *Free Nation*, 233; Neal, "Interpreting Power and Profit," 31; Koehn, *Power of Commerce*, 5; Daniel A. Baugh, "Why Did Britain Lose Control of the Sea during the War for America?" in Black and Woodfine, *British Navy*, 159–60; Charles Wilson, "The British Isles," in Charles Wilson and Geoffrey Parker, eds., *An Introduction to the Sources of European Economic History, 1500–1800* (Ithaca NY: Cornell University Press, 1977), 132.

Bibliography

UNPUBLISHED MATERIAL

French Foreign Ministry Archives, Paris

Eighteenth-century volumes are divided into two general categories, "Political Correspondence," which concerns the day-to-day operations of the ministry, and "Memoirs
and Documents," which are miscellaneous memoranda on foreign policy issues. I have
mostly used the "Political Correspondence," which is arranged by country. I have consulted the following volumes:

Austria: Volumes 255–67, 271–78, 281–84, and 286–91.
Britain: Volumes 438–48 and supplementary volume 12.
Holland (United Provinces of the Netherlands): Volumes 491–511.
Portugal: Volumes 90–93.
Russia: Volumes 51–70.
Spain: Volumes 526–37 and supplementary volume 15.
Sweden: Volumes 228–41 and supplementary volumes 9–11.

French National Archives, Paris

The French Navy's eighteenth-century documents are kept at the French National Archives, although they are the property of the Historical Service of the Navy. My major
source was Series B (general service), which is divided into subseries, of which I used the
following:

B^1 (Decisions): Volumes 66–67.
B^2 (Orders and Dispatches): Volumes 351–54, 356–59, 363, 366–69, 371. (Intervening
volumes were unavailable to the public.)
B^3 (Letters Received): Volumes 520–55.
B^4 (Campaigns): Volumes 67–105.

B^5 (Armaments): Volumes 3–7, 10, 12.

B^7 (Foreign Countries, Commerce, and Consulates): Volumes 395–420.

I have also used Series G (Diverse Documents): Volumes 47–50 and 127–28.

Manuscript Holdings, French National Library, Paris

I used item 10764 from the French manuscripts collection, the papers of the abbé Beliardy, the French commercial representative in Madrid. From the new acquisitions portion of the French manuscripts collection I used items 9402–6, the Magry collection.

Public Record Office, Kew

This beautiful new facility just outside London contains British military, naval, and diplomatic correspondence. Of use were the following volumes:

Admiralty Series 1 (Incoming Letters): Volumes 161–62, 236–37, 307, and 384.
Admiralty Series 8 (List Books): Volumes 24–26 and 30–38.
State Papers Series 42 (State Papers Naval): Volume 116.
State Papers Series 78 (France): Volumes 250–53.
State Papers Series 84 (Netherlands): Volumes 487–88.
State Papers Series 87 (Foreign Military Expeditions): Volume 38.
State Papers Series 89 (Portugal): Volumes 54–57.
State Papers Series 94 (Spain): Volumes 163–64.

NEWSPAPERS AND OTHER CONTEMPORARY PUBLICATIONS

The *London Evening Post* was the newspaper I generally found most informative about naval matters, but I also used the *London Chronicle*, the *Gentleman's Magazine*, the *Pennsylvania Gazette*, and the *Gazette de Leyde* (the Dutch journal also known as *Nouvelles extraordinaires de divers endroits*).

PUBLISHED SOURCES

Abbot, W. W. et al., eds. *The Papers of George Washington: Colonial Series.* 10 vols. Charlottesville: University Press of Virginia, 1983–95.

Acerra, Martine. *Rochefort et la construction navale française, 1661–1815.* 4 vols. Paris: Librairie de l'Inde, 1993.

Acerra, Martine, José Marino, and Jean Meyer, eds. *Les Marines de guerre européennes XVII–XVIIIe siécles.* Paris: Presses de l'Université de Paris-Sorbonne, 1985.

Acerra, Martine, Jean-Pierre Poussou, Michel Vergé-Franceschi, and André Zysberg, eds. *Etat, marine, et société: Hommage à Jean Meyer.* Paris: Presses de l'Université de Paris-Sorbonne, 1995.

Adair, E. R. "The Military Reputation of Major-General James Wolfe." In *Canadian Historical Association, Report of the Annual Meeting Held at Ottawa, May 26–27, 1936*, 7–31. Toronto: University of Toronto Press, 1936.

Aiton, Arthur S. "The Diplomacy of the Louisiana Cession." *American Historical Review* 36 (1930–31): 701–20.

————. "A Neglected Intrigue of the Family Compact." *Hispanic American Historical Review* 11 (1931): 387–93.

Albemarle, George Thomas Keppel, Earl of, ed. *Memoirs of the Marquis of Rockingham and His Contemporaries*. 2 vols. London: Richard Bentley, 1852.

Albion, Robert Greenhalgh. *Forests and Sea Power: The Timber Problem of the Royal Navy, 1652–1862*. Cambridge: Harvard University Press, 1926.

Alden, John Richard. *John Stuart and the Southern Colonial Frontier: A Study of Indian Relations, Trade, and Land Problems in the Southern Wilderness, 1754–1775*. Ann Arbor: University of Michigan Press; London: Humphrey Milford, Oxford University Press, 1944.

————. *Robert Dinwiddie, Servant of the Crown*. Charlottesville: University Press of Virginia, 1973.

Alexander, John T. *Catherine the Great: Life and Legend*. New York: Oxford University Press, 1989.

Algrant, Christine Pevitt. *Madame de Pompadour: Mistress of France*. New York: Grove Press, 2002.

Allard, Michel. *La Nouvelle France*. Montreal: Guérin, 1976.

Almon, John, ed. *The Debates and Proceedings of the British House of Commons from 1743 to 1774*. 11 vols. London: J. Almon, 1766–75.

Aman, Jacques. *Une Campagne navale méconnue à la veille de la guerre de Sept Ans: L'Escadre de Brest en 1755*. Vincennes, France: Service historique de la marine, 1986.

————. *Les Officiers bleus dans la marine française au XVIIIᵉ siècle*. Geneva: Droz, 1976.

Amiguet, Philippe, ed. *Lettres de Louis XV à son petit-fils l'Infant Ferdinand de Parme*. Paris: Bernard Grasset, 1938.

Anderson, Fred. *Crucible of War: The Seven Years' War and the Fate of Empire in British North America, 1754–1766*. New York: Alfred A. Knopf, 2000.

————. *A People's Army: Massachusetts Soldiers and Society in the Seven Years' War*. Chapel Hill: University of North Carolina Press, 1984.

Anderson, M. S. *The War of the Austrian Succession, 1740–1748*. London: Longman, 1995.

Anderson, Niles. "The General Chooses a Road: The Forbes Campaign of 1758 to Capture Fort Duquesne." *Western Pennsylvania Historical Magazine* 42 (1959): 109–38, 241–58, 383–401.

Anderson, Olive. "The Establishment of British Supremacy at Sea and the Exchange of Naval Prisoners of War, 1689–1783." *English Historical Review* 75 (1960): 77–89.

Anderson, Roger Charles. *Naval Wars in the Baltic, 1522–1850*. Rev. ed. London: Francis Edwards, 1969.

Anisimov, Evgeny V. *Empress Elizabeth: Her Reign and Her Russia, 1741–1761*. Translated by John T. Alexander. Gulf Breeze FL: Academic International Press, 1995.

Annual Register or a View of the History, Politicks and Literature of the Year 1762. London: R. and J. Dodsley, 1763.

Antoine, Michel. *Louis XV.* Paris: Fayard, 1989.

————, comp. *Le Gouvernement et l'administration sous Louis XV: Dictionnaire biographique.* Paris: Editions du Centre national de la recherche scientifique, 1978.

Antoine, Michel, and Didier Ozanam. "Le Secret du roi et le Russie jusqu'à la morte de la czarine Elisabeth en 1762." *Annuaire-Bulletin de la Société de l'histoire de France* 86 (1954–55): 69–93.

Archambault, Gilles. "La Question des vivres au Canada au cours de l'hiver 1757–1758." *Revue d'histoire de l'Amérique française* 21 (1967–68): 16–50.

Arneth, Alfred, Ritter von. *Geschichte Maria Theresia's.* 10 vols. Vienna: Wilhelm Braumüller, 1863–79.

Arsenault, Bona. *Louisbourg, 1713–1758.* Quebec: Le Conseil de la vie française en Amérique, 1971.

Ashton, T. S. *Economic Fluctuations in England, 1700–1800.* Oxford: Clarendon Press, 1959.

Asprey, Robert B. *Frederick the Great: The Magnificent Enigma.* New York: Ticknor and Fields, 1986.

Ayling, Stanley. *The Elder Pitt, Earl of Chatham.* London: Collins, 1976.

Bailey, Kenneth P. *The Ohio Company of Virginia and the Westward Movement, 1748–1792: A Chapter in the History of the Colonial Frontier.* Glendale CA: Arthur H. Clark, 1939.

Bajer, Fredrik. "Les Entrevues de Martin Hübner avec le duc de Choiseul en 1759." *Revue d'histoire diplomatique* 18 (1904): 406–24.

Baker-Crothers, Hayes. *Virginia and the French and Indian War.* Chicago: University of Chicago Press, 1928.

Balcom, B. A. *The Cod Fishery of Isle Royale, 1713–58.* [Ottawa]: National Historic Parks and Sites Branch, Parks Canada, Environment Canada, 1984.

Bamford, Paul Walden. *Forests and French Sea Power, 1660–1789.* Toronto: University of Toronto Press, 1956.

————. *Privilege and Profit: A Business Family in Eighteenth-Century France.* Philadelphia: University of Pennsylvania Press, 1988.

Banbuck, C. A. *Histoire politique, économique et sociale de la Martinique sous l'Ancien Régime (1635–1789).* Paris: Marcel Rivière, 1935.

Bangert, Dieter Ernst. *Die russisch-österreichische militärische Zusammenarbeit im Siebenjährigen Kriege in dem jahren 1758–1759.* Boppart-am-Rhein: Harald Boldt, 1971.

Barbier, Edmund-Jean-François. *Chronique de la régence et du règne de Louis XV (1718–1763); ou Journal de Barbier.* 8 vols. Paris: Charpentier, 1857.

Barbier, Jacques A. "Indies Revenue and Naval Spending: The Cost of Colonialism for the Spanish Bourbons, 1763–1805." *Jahrbuch für Geschichte von Staat, Wirtshaft und Gesellschaft Lateinamerikas* 21 (1984): 171–88.

Barnett, Correlli. *Britain and Her Army, 1509–1970: A Military, Political and Social Survey.* London: Allen Lane, 1970.

Barreau, Jean. *Les Guerres en Guadeloupe au XVIII*ᵉ *siècle (1703, 1759 et 1794)*. Nérac, France: Imprimerie J. Owen, n.d.

Barthélemy, Edouard-Marie, comte de. *Histoire des relations de la France et du Danemarck sous le ministère du comte de Bernstorff, 1751–1770*. Copenhagen: Jørgensen et cie., 1887.

———. "Le Traité de Paris entre la France et l'Angleterre (1763)." *Revue des questions historiques* 43 (1888): 420–88.

Batzel, John Charles. "Austria and the First Three Treaties of Versailles, 1755–1758." Ph.D. diss., Brown University, 1974.

Baugh, Daniel. *British Naval Administration in the Age of Walpole*. Princeton: Princeton University Press, 1965.

———. "Great Britain's 'Blue-Water' Policy, 1689–1815." *International History Review* 10 (1988): 33–58.

———. "Withdrawing from Europe: Anglo-French Maritime Geopolitics, 1750–1800." *International History Review* 20 (1998): 1–32.

Baxter, Stephen B. "The Conduct of the Seven Years' War." In Stephen B. Baxter, ed., *England's Rise to Greatness, 1660–1763*, 323–48. Berkeley: University of California Press, 1983.

———. "The Myth of the Grand Alliance in the Eighteenth Century." In Paul R. Sellin and Stephen B. Baxter, eds., *Anglo-Dutch Cross Currents in the Seventeenth and Eighteenth Centuries*, 41–59. Los Angeles: William Andrews Clark Memorial Library, 1976.

Beales, Derek. *Joseph II*, vol. 1, *In the Shadow of Maria Theresa, 1741–1780*. New York: Cambridge University Press, 1987.

Beatson, Robert. *Naval and Military Memoirs of Great Britain, from 1727 to 1783*. 6 vols. London: Longman, Hurst, Rees and Orme, 1804.

Beaucourt, Gaston de Fresne, marquis de. "Le Caractère de Louis XV." *Revue des questions historiques* 3 (1867): 172–217; 4 (1868): 181–254.

Bell, David. "Jumonville's Death: War Propaganda and National Identity in Eighteenth-Century France." In Colin Jones and Dror Wahrman, eds., *The Age of Cultural Revolution: Britain and France, 1750–1820*, 33–61. Berkeley: University of California Press, 2002.

Bell, Whitfield J., and Leonard W. Labaree. "Franklin and the 'Wagon Affair,' 1755." *Proceedings of the American Philosophical Society* 101 (1957): 551–58.

Bellico, Russell P. *Sails and Steam in the Mountains: A Maritime and Military History of Lake George and Lake Champlain*. Fleischmanns NY: Purple Mountain Press, 1992.

Bertin, Jacques, and Françoise Vergneault. "Traitment graphique d'une information: Les Marines royales de France et de Grande-Bretagne (1697–1747)." *Annales: Economies-sociétés-civilisations* 22 (1967): 991–1004.

Bertrand, Raymond de. "Le Port et le commerce maritime de Dunkerque au XVIII ᵉ siècle." *Mémoires de la Société dunkerquoise pour l'encouragement des sciences, des lettres et des arts* 9 (1862–64): 112–407; 10 (1864–65): 69–424.

Bertsch, W. H. "The Defenses of Oswego." *Proceedings of the New York State Historical Association* 13 (1914): 108–27.

Besterman, Theodore, ed. *The Complete Works of Voltaire: Correspondence and Related*

Documents (Definitive Edition). 51 vols. Toronto: University of Toronto Press; Geneva: Institut et Musée Voltaire (and other publishers), 1968–77.

Binet, H. "La Défense des côtes de Bretagne au XVIIIe siècle: Etudes et documents. Ve Série: Les Descents sur les côtes de la Manche en 1758." *Revue de Bretagne*, n.s., 47 (1912): 236–53, 304–11, 352–58; 48 (1912): 5–23, 80–93.

———. "La Défense des côtes de Bretagne au XVIIIe siècle: Etudes et documents. VIe Série: Les Anglais à Belle-Isle-en-Mer (1761–1763)." *Revue de Bretagne*, n.s., 49 (1913): 123–47, 172–76.

———. "La Guerre des côtes en Bretagne au XVIIIe siècle: Le Commandement du duc d'Aiguillon en Bretagne au début de la Guerre de Sept Ans (1756)." *Annales de Bretagne* 26 (1910–11): 307–51.

———. "La Guerre des côtes en Bretagne au XVIIIe siècle: Saint-Malo et la région malouine après les descentes anglaises de 1758." *Annales de Bretagne* 25 (1909–10): 295–321.

Biraben, J. N. "Le Peuplement du Canada français." *Annales de démographie historique* 1 (1966): 105–38.

Bird, Harrison. *Battle for a Continent.* New York: Oxford University Press, 1965.

Bisset, Andrew, ed. *Memoirs and Papers of Sir Andrew Mitchell, K. B., Envoy and Minister Plenipotentiary from the Court of Great Britain, to the Court of Prussia, from 1756 to 1771.* 2 vols. London: Chapman and Hall, 1850.

Bittner, Ludwig et al., eds. *Repertorium der diplomatischen Vertreter aller Länder seit dem Westfälischen Frieden (1648).* 3 vols. Oldenburg and Berlin: Gerhard Stalling; Zurich: Fretz und Wasmuth; Graz and Cologne: Hermann Böhlaus Nachf., 1936–65.

Black, Jeremy. *America or Europe? British Foreign Policy, 1739–63.* London and Bristol PA: UCL Press, 1998.

———. "Anglo-Spanish Naval Relations in the Eighteenth Century." *Mariner's Mirror* 77 (1991): 235–58.

———. *British Foreign Policy in the Age of Walpole.* Atlantic Highlands NJ: Humanities Press, 1985.

———. "British Foreign Policy in the Eighteenth Century: A Survey." *Journal of British Studies* 26 (1987): 26–53.

———. "British Intelligence and the Mid-Eighteenth-Century Crisis." *Intelligence and National Security* 2 (1987): 209–29.

———. "British Neutrality in the War of the Polish Succession, 1733–1735." *International History Review* 8 (1986): 345–66.

———. "Essay and Reflection: On the 'Old System' and the 'Diplomatic Revolution' of the Eighteenth Century." *International History Review* 12 (1990): 301–23.

———. "French Foreign Policy in the Age of Fleury Reassessed." *English Historical Review* 103 (1988): 359–84.

———. *Natural and Necessary Enemies: Anglo-French Relations in the Eighteenth Century.* London: Gerald Duckworth, 1986.

———. *Pitt the Elder.* New York: Cambridge University Press, 1992.

————, ed. *Knights Errant and True Englishmen: British Foreign Policy, 1660–1800.* Edinburgh: John Donald, 1989.

Black, Jeremy, and Philip Woodfine, eds. *The British Navy and the Use of Naval Power in the Eighteenth Century.* Atlantic Highlands NJ: Humanities Press International, 1989.

Blanchet, Jean G. P., ed. *Collection des manuscrits contentant lettres, mémoires et autres documents relatifs à la Nouvelle-France.* 4 vols. Quebec: A. Coté et cie., 1883–1885.

Blart, Louis. *Les Rapports de la France et de l'Espagne après le pacte de famille, jusqu'à la fin du ministère du duc de Choiseul.* Paris: Félix Alcan, 1915.

Boislisle, Arthur-André-Gabriel Michel de, ed. *Mémoires authentiques du maréchal de Richelieu (1725–1757).* Paris: Société de l'histoire de France, 1918.

Bonnault, Claude de. "Le Canada et la conclusion de pacte de famille en 1761." *Revue d'histoire de l'Amérique française* 7 (1953–54): 341–55.

————. "Les Français de l'Ohio. Un Drame dans la prairie: L'Affaire Jumonville (1749–1754)." *Revue d'histoire de l'Amérique française* 1 (1947–48): 501–18.

Bonner-Smith, David, ed. *The Barrington Papers: Selected from the Letters and Papers of Admiral the Hon. Samuel Barrington.* 2 vols. London: Navy Records Society, 1937–41.

Bonnet, Philippe, ed. *Mémoires du Cardinal de Bernis.* Paris: Mercure de France, 1980.

Bosher, J. F. *Business and Religion in the Age of New France, 1600–1760: Twenty-two Studies.* Toronto: Canadian Scholars Press, 1994.

————. *The Canada Merchants, 1713–1763.* Oxford: Clarendon Press; New York: Oxford University Press, 1987.

————. "Financing the French Navy in the Seven Years War: Beaujon, Goossens et Compagnie in 1759." *Business History* 28, no. 3 (July 1986): 115–33.

————. "The French Government's Motives in the *Affaire du Canada*, 1761–1763." *English Historical Review* 96 (1981): 59–78.

————. "Success and Failure in Trade to New France, 1660–1760." *French Historical Studies* 15 (1987–88): 444–61.

Boudriot, Jean. *Compagnie des Indes, 1720–1770: Vaisseaux, hommes, voyages, commerce.* 2 vols. Paris: Jean Boudriot, 1983.

————. "Les Compagnies franches de la marine." *Neptunia*, no. 120 (Winter 1975): 24–32.

————. *The History of the French Frigate.* Translated by David H. Roberts. Rutherford, Eng.: Jean Boudriot Publications, 1993.

————. *The Seventy-four Gun Ship: A Practical Treatise on the Art of Naval Architecture.* Translated by David H. Roberts. 4 vols. Annapolis: Naval Institute Press, 1986–88.

————. *Les Vaisseaux de 50 à 64 canons, 1650–1850.* Paris: ANCRE, 1994.

————. *Les Vaisseaux de 74 à 120 canons: Etude historique, 1650–1850.* Paris: ANCRE, 1995.

————. "Les Vaisseaux 'La Courrone' 1749 & 1766." *Neptunia*, no. 187 (September 1992): 8–17.

Boulle, Pierre Henri. "The French Colonies and the Reform of their Administration during and following the Seven Years' War." Ph.D. diss., University of California, Berkeley, 1968.

————. "Patterns of French Colonial Trade and the Seven Years' War." *Histoire sociale-Social History* 7 (1974): 48–86.

Bourguet, Alfred. *Le Duc de Choiseul et l'alliance espagnole*. Paris: Plon-Nourrit et cie., 1906.

————. "Le Duc de Choiseul et l'alliance espagnole: Après le Pacte de famille." *Revue historique* 94 (1907): 1–27.

————. "Le Duc de Choiseul et l'alliance espagnole: Un Ultimatum franco-espagnole au Portugal (1761–1762)." *Revue d'histoire diplomatique* 24 (1910): 25–38.

————. *Etudes sur la politique étrangère du duc de Choiseul*. Paris: Plon-Nourrit et cie., 1907.

————. "Un Négotiation diplomatique du duc de Choiseul relative aux Jésuites (1761–1762)." *Revue d'histoire diplomatique* 16 (1902): 161–75.

Bourland, Richard Dean, Jr. "Maurepas and the Administration of the French Navy on the Eve of the War of the Austrian Succession (1737–1742)." Ph.D. dissertation, University of Notre Dame, South Bend IN, 1978.

Boutaric, [Paul-] Edgard, ed. *Correspondance secrète inédite de Louis XV sur la politique étrangère avec le comte de Broglie, Tercier, etc.* 2 vols. Paris: Henri Plon, 1866.

Bouton, Nathaniel, ed. *Provincial Papers of New Hampshire*, vol. 6, *Documents and Records relating to the Province of New-Hampshire from 1749 to 1763*. Manchester NH: James H. Campbell, 1872.

Boutry, Maurice, vicomte. *Choiseul à Rome, 1754–1757: Lettres et mémoires inédits*. Paris: Calmann Lévy, 1895.

Braubach, Max. *Versailles und Wien von Ludwig XIV bis Kaunitz: Die Vorstadien der diplomatischen Revolution im 18 Jahrhundert*. Bonn: Ludwig Röhrscheid, 1952.

Brebner, John Bartlet. *New England's Outpost: Acadia before the Conquest of Canada*. New York: Columbia University Press; London: P. S. King and Son, 1927.

Brecher, Frank W. *Losing a Continent: France's North American Policy, 1753–1763*. Westport CT: Greenwoood Press, 1998.

Brewer, John. *Party Ideology and Popular Politics at the Accession of George III*. New York: Cambridge University Press, 1976.

————. *The Sinews of Power: War, Money, and the English State, 1688–1783*. New York: Alfred A. Knopf, 1989.

Brière, Jean-François. "Pêche et politique à Terre-Neuve au XVIIIe siècle: La France véritable gagnante du traité d'Utrecht?" *Canadian Historical Review* 64 (1983): 168–87.

————. *La Pêche française en Amérique du Nord au XVIIIe siécle*. Saint-Laurent, Quebec: Fides, 1990.

Brock, Robert Alonzo, ed. *The Official Records of Robert Dinwiddie, Lieutenant-Governor of the Colony of Virginia, 1751–1758*. 2 vols. Richmond: Virginia Historical Society, 1883–84.

Brodine, Charles. "Civil-Military Relations in Pennsylvania, 1758–1760: An Examination of John Shy's Thesis." *Pennsylvania History* 62 (1995): 213–33.

Broglie, [Jacques-Victor-] Albert, duc de. *L'Alliance autrichienne*. Paris: Calmann Lévy, 1895.

———. *Frédéric II et Louis XV, d'après des documents nouveaux, 1742–1744*. 2 vols. Paris: Calmann Lévy, 1885.

———. *Frédéric II et Marie-Thérèse, d'après des documents nouveaux, 1740–1742*. 2 vols. Paris: Calmann Lévy, 1883.

———. *The King's Secret: Being the Secret Correspondence of Louis XV with His Diplomatic Agents, from 1752 to 1774*. Translator not listed. 2 vols. Paris, London, New York: Cassell, Petter and Galpin, 1879.

———. *Marie-Thérèse impératrice, 1744–1746*. 2 vols. Paris: Calmann Lévy, 1888.

———. *Maurice de Saxe et le marquis d'Argenson*. 2 vols. Paris: Calmann Lévy, 1891.

———. *La Paix d'Aix-la-Chapelle*. Paris: Calmann Lévy, 1892.

Broglie, [Jacques-Victor-Albert], duc de, and Vernier, Jules, eds. *Correspondance inédite de Victor-François, duc de Broglie avec le prince Xavier de Saxe, comte de Lusace pour servir à l'histoire de la Guerre de Sept Ans (campagnes de 1759 à 1761)*. 4 vols. Paris: Albin Michel, 1903–05.

Brooke, John, ed. *Horace Walpole: Memoirs of King George II*. 3 vols. New Haven: Yale University Press, 1985.

———. *King George III*. New York, St. Louis, San Francisco, Mexico, Panama, Düsseldorf: McGraw-Hill, 1972.

Brown, Peter Douglas. *William Pitt, Earl of Chatham, the Great Commoner*. London: George Allen and Unwin, 1978.

Brown, Peter D., and Karl W. Schweizer, eds. *The Devonshire Diary: William Cavendish, Fourth Duke of Devonshire: Memoranda on State of Affairs, 1759–1762*. London: Royal Historical Society, 1982.

Browne, William Hand, ed. *Correspondence of Governor Horatio Sharpe*, vol. 1, *1753–57*; vol. 2, *1757–61*. Baltimore: Maryland Historical Society, 1888–90.

Browning, Reed. "The British Orientation of Austrian Foreign Policy, 1749–1754." *Central European History* 1 (1968): 299–323.

———. *The Duke of Newcastle*. New Haven: Yale University Press, 1975.

———. "The Duke of Newcastle and the Financing of the Seven Years' War." *Journal of Economic History* 31 (1971): 344–77.

———. "The Duke of Newcastle and the Imperial Election Plan, 1749–1754." *Journal of British Studies* 7 (1967): 28–47.

———. *The War of the Austrian Succession*. New York: St. Martin's Press, 1993.

Brumwell, Stephen. *Redcoats: The British Soldier and War in the Americas*. New York: Cambridge University Press, 2002.

———. "'A Service Truly Critical': The British Army and Warfare with the North American Indians, 1755–1764." *War in History* 5 (1998): 146–75.

Brun, Vincent-Félix. *Guerres maritimes de la France: Port de Toulon, ses armaments, son administration, depuis son origine jusqu'à nos jours*. 2 vols. Paris: Henri Plon, 1861.

Buchet, Christian. *La Lutte pour l'espace caraïbe et la facade atlantique de l'Amérique centrale et du sud (1672–1763)*. 2 vols. Paris: Librairie de l'Inde, 1991.

————. *Marine, économie et société: Un Exemple d'interaction: L'Avitaillement de la Royal Navy durant la guerre de sept ans.* Paris: Honoré Champion, 1999.

Buddress, Eckhard. *Die französische Deutschlandpolitik, 1756–1789.* Mainz: Philipp von Zabern, 1995.

Buffington, Arthur H. "The Canada Expedition of 1746: Its Relation to British Politics." *American Historical Review* 45 (1939–40): 552–80.

Bussemaker, Th. [Carel Hendrik Theodoor], ed. *Archives, ou correspondance inédite de la maison d'Orange-Nassau: Quatrième série.* 4 vols. Leiden: A. W. Sijthoff, 1908–14.

Butel, Paul. "Bordeaux et la Hollande au XVIIIᵉ siècle: L'Exemple du négotiant Pellet (1694–1772)." *Revue d'histoire économique et sociale* 45 (1967): 58–86.

————. *L'Economie française au XVIIIᵉ siècle.* Paris: SEDES, 1993.

————. "France, the Antilles, and Europe in the Eighteenth Century: Renewals of Foreign Trade." In James D. Tracy, ed., *The Rise of Merchant Empires: Long Distance Trade in the Early Modern World, 1350–1750,* 153–73. New York: Cambridge University Press, 1990.

Butler, Rohan. *Choiseul,* vol. 1, *Father and Son, 1719–1754.* Oxford: Clarendon Press, 1980.

Butterfield, Sir Herbert. *The Reconstruction of an Historical Episode: The History of the Enquiry into the Origins of the Seven Years' War.* Glasgow: Jackson, Son, 1951.

————. "Review Article: British Foreign Policy, 1762–5." *Historical Journal* 6 (1963): 131–40.

Cahen, Léon. "Les Mémoires du Cardinal de Bernis et les débuts de la guerre de Sept ans." *Revue d'histoire moderne et contemporaine* 12 (1909): 73–99.

Caix de Saint-Aymour, Amédé, vicomte de. *Une Famille d'artistes et des financiers au XVIIᵉ et XVIIIᵉ siècle: Les Boullongne.* Paris: Henri Laurens, 1919.

Campbell, Peter R. *Power and Politics in Old Regime France, 1720–1745.* London and New York: Routledge, 1996.

Canada, Public Archives. *The Northcliffe Collection: Papers Presented to the Government of Canada by Sir Leicester Harmsworth, Bt.* Ottawa: F. A. Acland, 1926.

————. *Report Concerning Canadian Archives for the Year 1905 in Three Volumes,* vol. 1. Ottawa: S. E. Dawson, 1906.

Captier, Jacques. *Etude historique et économique sur l'inscription maritime.* Paris: Bussière, Giard et Brière, 1907.

Caron, François. *La Guerre incomprise, ou, les raisons d'un échec (capitulation de Louisbourg, 1758).* Vincennes, France: Service historique de la marine, 1983.

Carter, Alice Clare. *The Dutch Republic in Europe in the Seven Years' War.* London: Macmillan, 1971.

Casgrain, Abbé Henri-Raymond, ed. *Collection des manuscrits du maréchal de Lévis.* 12 vols. Montreal: C.-O. Beauchemin & fils; Quebec: L.-J. Demers & frère, 1889–1895.

————. *Guerre du Canada, 1756–1760: Montcalm et Lévis.* 2 vols. Quebec: L.-J. Demers & frère, 1891.

————. *The Makers of Canada: Wolfe and Montcalm.* Toronto: Moreng, 1912.

————, ed. *Extraits des archives des ministères de la marine et de la guerre à Paris. Canada, correspondance général: MM. Duquesne et Vaudreuil, gouverneurs-généraux, 1755–1760.* Quebec: L.-J. Demers & frère, 1890.

Castex, Raoul-Victor-Patrice. *Les Idées militaires de la marine du XVIIIe siècle: De Ruyter à Suffren.* Paris: L. Fournier, 1911.

Cave, Alfred A. *The French and Indian War.* Westport CT: Greenwood Press, 2004.

Cayton, Andrew R. L., and Fredrika Teute, eds. *Contact Points: American Frontiers from the Mohawk Valley to the Mississippi, 1750–1830.* Chapel Hill: University of North Carolina Press, 1998.

Chabannes-La Paulice, E. de. "Au Seuil de la guerre de succession d'Autriche, 1741–1744." *Revue Maritime,* new ser., no. 151–53 (July–September 1932): 29–47, 187–204, 342–63.

Chabaud-Arnault, Ch. "Etudes historiques sur la marine militaire de France. XII: La Marine française sous la Régence et sous le ministère de Maurepas; XIII: La Marine française pendant la guerre de la succession d'Autriche; XIV: La marine française avant et pendant la guerre de Sept ans." *Revue maritime* 110 (1891): 49–85; 111 (1891): 86–131; 114 (1892): 56–84, 482–501; 115 (1892): 403–25, 609–22; 117 (1893): 591–628.

Chance, James Frederick, ed. *British Diplomatic Instuctions, 1689–1789,* vol. 3, *Denmark.* London: Royal Historical Society, 1926.

———, ed. *British Diplomatic Instructions, 1689–1789,* vol. 5, *Sweden, 1727–1789.* London: Royal Historical Society, 1928.

Chapais, Thomas. *Le Marquis de Montcalm (1712–1759).* Quebec: J.-P. Garneau, 1911.

Charteris, Evan. *William Augustus, Duke of Cumberland and the Seven Years' War.* London: Hutchinson, 1925.

Chassaigne, Philippe. "L'Economie des îles sucrières dans les conflits maritimes de la second moitié du XVIIIe siècle: L'Exemple de Saint-Domingue." *Histoire, economie et société* 7 (1988): 93–105.

Chelin, Antoine. *Une Ile et son passé: Ile Maurice (1507–1947).* Port Louis, Mauritius: Mauritius Print, 1973.

Chenevix Trench, Charles P. *George II.* London: Allen Lane, 1973.

Childs, John. *Armies and Warfare in Europe, 1648–1789.* Manchester: Manchester University Press, 1982.

Choiseul-Stainville, Etienne-François, duc de. *Mémoire historique sur la négotiation de la France et de l'Angleterre, depuis le 26 mars 1761 jusqu'au 20 septembre de la même année, avec les pièces justificatives.* Paris: Imprimerie royale, 1761.

Christelow, Allan. "Economic Background of the Anglo-Spanish War of 1762." *Journal of Modern History* 18 (1946): 22–36.

———. "French Interest in the Spanish Empire during the Ministry of the Duc de Choiseul, 1759–1771." *Hispanic American Historical Review* 21 (1941): 515–37.

Cisternes, Raoul de. *La Campagne de Minorque d'après le journal du commandeur de Glandevez et de nombreuses lettres inédites.* Paris: Calmann Lévy, 1899.

Clark, J. C. D. *The Dynamics of Change: The Crisis of the 1750s and English Party Systems.* New York: Cambridge University Press, 1982.

———, ed. *The Memoirs and Speeches of James, 2nd Earl Waldegrave, 1742–1763.* New York: Cambridge University Press, 1988.

Clayton, T. R. "The Duke of Newcastle, the Earl of Halifax, and the American Origins of the Seven Years' War." *Historical Journal* 24 (1981): 571–603.

Clowes, William Laird. *The Royal Navy: A History from the Earliest Times to the Present.* 7 vols. Boston: Little, Brown; London: Sampson Low, Marston, 1897–1903.

Cobbett, William, and Thomas C. Hansard, eds. *The Parliamentary History of England from the Earliest Period to the Year 1803.* 36 vols. London: T. C. Hansard, 1806–20.

Cole, Hubert. *First Gentleman of the Bedchamber: The Life of Louis-François-Armand, maréchal duc de Richelieu.* New York: Viking Press, 1965.

Colin, Jean. *Louis XV et les Jacobites: Le Projet de débarquement en Angleterre, 1743–44.* Paris: R. Chapelot, 1901.

Combeau, Yves. *Le Comte d'Argenson (1696–1764): Ministre de Louis XV.* Paris: Ecole de Chartes, 1999.

Conn, Stetson. *Gibraltar in British Diplomacy in the Eighteenth Century.* New Haven: Yale University Press; London: Humphrey Milford, Oxford University Press, 1942.

Cook, Chris, and John Stevenson, comps. *British Historical Facts, 1688–1760.* London: Macmillan, 1988.

———. *British Historical Facts, 1760–1833.* London: Macmillan, 1980.

Coquelle, P. *L'Alliance franco-hollandaise contre l'Angleterre, 1735–1788, d'après les documents inédits du ministère des affaires étrangères.* Paris: Plon-Nourrit et cie., 1902.

———. "L'Espionnage en Angleterre pendant la Guerre de Sept Ans d'après des documents inédits." *Revue d'histoire diplomatique* 14 (1900): 508–33.

———. "Les Projets de descente en Angleterre d'après les archives des affaires étrangères." *Revue d'histoire diplomatique* 15 (1901): 433–52, 591–624; 16 (1902): 134–57.

Corbett, Sir Julian S. *England in the Seven Years' War: A Study in Combined Strategy.* 2nd ed., 2 vols. London: Longmans, Green, 1918.

———. *Some Principles of Maritime Strategy.* London: Longmans, Green, 1911.

Corkran, David H. *The Cherokee Frontier: Conflict and Survival, 1740–62.* Norman: University of Oklahoma Press, 1962.

———. *The Creek Frontier, 1540–1783.* Norman: University of Oklahoma Press, 1967.

Corvisier, André. *L'Armée française de la fin du XVIIᵉ siècle au ministère de Choiseul: Le Soldat.* 2 vols. Paris: Presses universitaires de France, 1964.

Coste, Charles, ed. *Aventures militaires au XVIIIᵉ siècle d'après les mémoires de Jean-Baptiste d'Aleyrac.* Paris: Berger-Levrault, 1935.

Côté, André. *Joseph-Michel Cadet, 1719–1781: Négociant et munitionnaire du roi en Nouvelle-France.* Sillery, Canada: Septentrion; Paris: Christian, 1998.

Crankshaw, Edward. *Maria Theresa.* New York: Viking Press, 1969.

Creswell, John. *British Admirals of the Eighteenth Century: Tactics in Battle.* London: George Allen and Unwin, 1972.

Crouzet, François. "Angleterre et France au XVIIIᵉ siècle: Essai d'analyse comparée de deux croissances." *Annales: Economies-sociétés-civilisations* 21 (1966): 254–91.

———. "The Second Hundred Years' War: Some Reflections." *French History* 10 (1996): 432–50.

Crowhurst, R. P. "The Admiralty and the Convoy System in the Seven Years' War." *Mariner's Mirror* 57 (1971): 163–73.

──────. *The Defence of British Trade, 1689–1815.* Folkestone, Eng.: William Dawson and Sons, 1977.

Cruickshanks, Eveline. "101 Secret Agent." *History Today* 19 (1969): 273–76.

──────. *Political Untouchables: The Tories and the '45.* London: Gerald Duckworth, 1979.

Cushner, Nicholas P., ed. *Documents Illustrating the British Conquest of Manila, 1762–1763.* London: Royal Historical Society, 1971.

D'Agay, Frédéric. "Un Episode naval de la guerre de Sept Ans." *Marins et Océans* 2 (1991): 143–71.

Daney, Sidney. *Histoire de la Martinique depuis la colonisation jusqu'en 1815,* vol. 2. Fort Royal, Martinique: E. Ruelle, 1846.

Dann, Uriel. *Hanover and Great Britain, 1740–1760: Diplomacy and Survival.* Leicester: Leicester University Press, 1991.

Danvila y Collado, Manuel. *Reinado de Carlos III,* vol. 2. Madrid: El Progreso editorial, 1894.

Dardel, Pierre. *Navires et marchandises dans les ports de Rouen et du Havre au XVIIIe siècle.* Paris: S. E. V. P. E. N., 1963.

Debrett, John. *The History, Debates and Proceedings of Both Houses of Parliament of Great Britain from the Year 1743 to the Year 1774.* 7 vols. London: J. Debrett, 1792.

Delbrück, Hans. *History of the Art of War within the Framework of Political History,* vol. 4, *The Modern Era.* Translated by Walter J. Renfroe Jr. Westport CT: Greenwood Press, 1985.

Delmas, Jean et al. *Conflits de sociétés au Canada français pendant la guerre de Sept Ans et leur influence sur les operations: Colloque international d'histoire militaire, Ottawa, 19–27 août 1978.* Vincennes, France: Service historique de l'armée de terre, 1978.

──────. *Histoire militaire de la France,* vol. 2, *De 1715 à 1871.* Paris: Presses universitaires de France, 1992.

Demerliac, Alain. *La Marine de Louis XV: Nomenclature des navires français de 1715 à 1774.* Nice: Editions Omega, 1995.

Desbarats, Catherine M. "France in North America: The Net Burden of Empire during the First Half of the Eighteenth Century." *French History* 11 (1997): 1–28.

Dickson, P. G. M. *Finance and Government under Maria Theresa, 1740–1780.* 2 vols. Oxford: Clarendon Press, 1987.

Dobson, John. *Chronological Annals of the War: From Its Beginning to the Present Time.* Oxford: Clarendon Press, 1763.

Doerflinger, Thomas M. "The Antilles Trade of the Old Regime: A Statistical Overview." *Journal of Interdisciplinary History* 6 (1975–76): 397–415.

Doran, Patrick Francis. *Andrew Mitchell and Anglo-Prussian Diplomatic Relations during the Seven Years' War.* New York: Garland, 1986.

Dorn, Walter L. *Competition for Empire, 1740–1763.* New York: Harper Brothers, 1940.

Doughty, Arthur G., ed. *An Historical Journal of the Campaigns in North America for the Years 1757, 1758, 1759 and 1760 by Captain John Knox.* 3 vols. Toronto: Champlain Society, 1914–16.

———, ed. "Montcalm's Correspondence." In *Report of the Public Archives of Canada for the Year 1929*, 31–108. Ottawa: F. A. Acland, 1930.

Doughty, A., and G. W. Parmelee. *The Siege of Quebec and the Battle of the Plains of Abraham.* 6 vols. Quebec: Dussault & Proulx, 1901.

Dowd, Gregory Evans. *War under Heaven: Pontiac, the Indian Nations and the British Empire.* Baltimore: Johns Hopkins University Press, 2002.

Downey, Fairfax. *Louisbourg: Key to a Continent.* Englewood Cliffs NJ: Prentice-Hall, 1965.

Droysen, Johann Gustav et al., eds. *Politische Correspondenz Friedrich's des Grossen.* 47 vols. and supp. to date. Berlin: Alexander Duncker (and other publishers), 1879–.

Ducéré, Edouard. *Histoire maritime de Bayonne: Les Corsairs sous l'ancien régime.* Bayonne, France: E. Hourquet, 1895.

Duffy, Christopher, *The Army of Maria Theresa: The Armed Forces of Imperial Austria, 1740–1780.* North Pomfret VT: David and Charles, 1977.

———. *The Austrian Army in the Seven Years War*, vol. 1, *Instrument of War.* Rosemont IL: Emperor's Press, 2000.

———. *The '45.* London: Cassell, 2003.

———. *Frederick the Great: A Military Life.* London: Routledge and Kegan Paul, 1985.

———. *The Military Experience in the Age of Reason.* London: Routledge and Kegan Paul, 1987.

———. *Prussia's Glory: Rossbach and Leuthen 1757.* Chicago: Emperor's Press, 2003.

———. *Russia's Military Way to the West: Origins and Nature of Russian Military Power, 1700–1800.* London: Routledge and Kegan Paul, 1981.

Duffy, Michael, ed. *Parameters of British Naval Power, 1650–1850.* Exeter: University of Exeter Press, 1992.

Dunnigan, Brian Leigh, ed. *Memoirs on the Late War in North America between France and England by Pierre Pouchot.* Translated by Michael Cardy. Youngstown NY: Old Fort Niagara Association, 1994.

———. *Siege 1759: The Campaign against Niagara.* Youngstown NY: Old Fort Niagara Association, 1986.

Dupont, Maurice. *D'Entrecosteaux: Rien que la mer, un peu de gloire.* Paris: Editions maritimes et d'outre-mer, 1983.

Durand, Yves-René. *Les Fermiers Généraux au XVIIIᵉ siècle.* Paris: Presses universitaires de France, 1971.

———, ed. "Mémoires de Jean-Joseph de Laborde, fermier général et banquier de la cour." *Annuaire-Bulletin de la Société de l'histoire de France*, no. 478 (1968–69): 73–162.

Dussauge, André. *Etudes sur la guerre de sept ans: Le Ministère de Belle-Isle*, vol. 1, *Krefeld et Lütterberg (1758).* Paris: L. Fournier, 1914.

Dussieux, Louis-Etienne, ed. *La Canada sous la domination française d'après les archives de la marine et de la guerre.* 3rd ed. Paris: Victor Lecoffre, 1883.

Dussieux, L.-E., and E. Soulié, eds. *Mémoires du duc de Luynes sur la cour de Louis XV (1735–1758)*. 17 vols. Paris: Firmin Didot frères, fils & cie., 1860–1865.

Dziembowski, Edmond. *Un nouveau Patriotisme français, 1750–1770: La France face à la puissance anglaise à l'époque de la guerre de Sept Ans*. Oxford: Voltaire Foundation, 1998.

Eccles, William J. *The Canadian Frontier, 1534–1760*. Rev. ed. Albuquerque: University of New Mexico Press, 1983.

———. *Essays on New France*. Toronto: Oxford University Press, 1987.

———. *France in America*. New York, Evanston, San Francisco, London: Harper and Row, 1972.

Edwardes, Michael. *The Battle of Plassey and the Conquest of Bengal*. London: Batsford, 1963.

Egnal, Marc. *New World Economies: The Growth of the Thirteen Colonies and Early Canada*. New York: Oxford University Press, 1998.

Egret, Jean. *Louis XV et l'opposition parliamentaire, 1715–1774*. Paris: Armand Colin, 1970.

Eldon, Carl William. *England's Subsidy Policy towards the Continent during the Seven Years' War*. Philadelphia: Graduate School of the University of Pennsylvania, 1938.

Entick, John et al. *The General History of the Late War: Containing its Rise, Progress and Event, in Europe, Asia, Africa, and America*. 5 vols. London: Edward Dilly and John Millan, 1763–1764.

Erskine, David, ed. *Augustus Hervey's Journal: Being the Intimate Account of the Life of a Captain in the Royal Navy Ashore and Afloat, 1746–1759*. London: William Kimber, 1953.

Fauteux, Aegidus. "Journal du siège de Québec du 10 mai au 18 septembre 1759." *Rapport de l'archiviste de la province de Québec* 1 (1920–21): 137–241.

Félix, Joël. *Finances et politique au siècle des Lumières: Le ministère L'Averdy, 1763–1768*. Paris: Comité pour l'histoire économique et financière de la France, 1999.

Ferling, John E. "School for Command: Young George Washinton and the Virginia Regiment." In Warren R. Hofstra, ed., *George Washington and the Virginia Backcountry*, 195–222. Madison wi: Madison House, 1998.

Fernández Duro, Cesáreo. *Armada española desde la unión de los Reinos de Castilla y de Aragón*. 9 vols. Madrid: Tipográfico "Succesores de Rivadeneyra," 1895–1903.

Findlay, James Thomas. *Wolfe in Scotland in the '45 and from 1749 to 1753*. London: Longman, Green, 1928.

Flammermont, Jules. *Rapport à M. le ministre de l'instruction publique sur les correspondances des agents diplomatiques étrangères en France avant la Révolution conservées dans les archives de Berlin, Dresde, Genève, Turin, Gênes, Florence, Naples, Simancas, Lisbonne, Londres, La Haye et Vienne*. Paris: Imprimerie nationale, 1896.

Flassan, [Jean-Baptiste-]Gaétan de Raxis de. *Histoire générale et raisonnée de la diplomatie française, ou de la politique de la France, depuis la fondation de la monarchie jusqu'à la fin du règne de Louis XVI*. 2nd ed. 7 vols. Paris and Strasburg: Treuttel et Würtz, 1811.

Flexner, James Thomas. *Lord of the Mohawks: A Biography of Sir William Johnson*. Boston: Little, Brown, 1979.

Fortescue, Sir John W., ed. *The Correspondence of King George the Third from 1760 to December 1783*, vol. 1, *1760–1767*. London: Macmillan, 1927.

———. "Guadeloupe, 1759." *Blackwood's Magazine* 234 (1933): 552–66.

———. *A History of the British Army*, vol. 2, *First Part—To the Close of the Seven Years' War, vol. II*. 2nd ed. London: Macmillan, 1910.

France. Commission des Archives Diplomatiques. *Recueil des instructions données aux ambassadeurs et ministres de France depuis les traités de Westphalie jusqu'à la révolution française*. 30 vols. to date. Paris: Félix Alcan (and other publishers), 1884–.

France. Service historique de la marine. *Guerres et paix, 1660–1815: Journées franco-anglaises d'histoire de la marine organisées par la Service historique de la marine à la Corderie royale de Rochefort les 20, 21 et 22 mars 1986*. Vincennes, France: Service historique de la marine, 1987.

Francis, A. D. "The Campaign in Portugal, 1762." *Journal of the Society for Army Historical Research* 59 (1981): 25–43.

Fraser, David. *Frederick the Great: King of Prussia*. London: Allen Lane, 2000.

Freeman, Douglas S. *George Washington: A Biography*, vols. 1–2, *Young Washington*. New York: Charles Scribner's Sons, 1948.

Frégault, Guy. *Canada: The War of the Conquest*. Translated by Margaret M. Cameron. Toronto: Oxford University Press, 1969.

———. *François Bigot: administrateur français*. 2 vols. Montreal: Institut d'histoire de l'Amérique française, 1948.

———. *Le Grand Marquis, Pierre de Rigaud de Vaudreuil, et la Louisiane*. Montreal: Fides, 1952.

———. *Le XVIIIᵉ siècle canadien: Etudes*. Montreal: Editions HMH, 1968.

Friis, Aage, ed. *Bernstorffske Papirer*. 3 vols. Copenhagen: Gyldendalske boghandel, Nordiske forlag, 1904–13.

Fry, Bruce W. *"An Appearance of Strength": The Fortifications of Louisbourg*. 2 vols. Ottawa: Historical Parks and Sites Branch, Parks Canada, Environment Canada, 1984.

Fyers, Evan W. H. "The Loss and Recapture of St. John's, Newfoundland, in 1762." *Journal of the Society for Army Historical Research* 11 (1932): 179–215.

Gabriel, Charles-Nicolas. *Le Maréchal de camp Desandrouins, 1729–1792: Guerre du Canada, 1756–1760; guerre de l'indépendance américaine, 1780–1782*. Verdun: Renvé-Lallemant, 1887.

Gagliardo, John G. *Reich and Nation: The Holy Roman Empire as Idea and Reality, 1763–1806*. Bloomington: Indiana University Press, 1980.

Garnault, Emile. *Le Commerce rochelais au XVIIIᵉ siècle d'après les documents composant les anciennes archives de la chambre de commerce de la Rochelle*, vol. 4, *Marine et colonies de 1749 au traité de paix de 1763*. Paris: Augustin Challamel; La Rochelle: E. Martin, 1898.

Gibson, John S. *Ships of the '45: The Rescue of the Young Pretender*. London: Hutchinson, 1967.

Gipson, Lawrence Henry. *The British Empire before the American Revolution*. 15 vols. Caldwell ID: Caxton Printers (vols. 1–3); New York: Alfred A. Knopf (vols. 4–15), 1936–70.

———. "A French Project for Victory Short of a Declaration of War, 1755." *Canadian Historical Review* 26 (1945): 361–71.

Giraud, Charles, ed. "Mémoire de M. de Choiseul remis au roi en 1765." *Journal des savants* 66 (1881): 171–84, 250–57.

Glete, Jan. *Navies and Nations: Warships, Navies and State Building in Europe and America, 1500–1860*. 2 vols. Stockholm: Almqvist and Wiksell International, 1993.

Godfrey, William G. *Pursuit of Profit and Preferment in Colonial North America: John Bradstreet's Quest*. Waterloo, Ont.: Wilfrid Laurier University Press, 1982.

Gold, Robert L. *Borderland Empires in Transition: The Triple-Nation Transfer of Florida*. Carbondale: Southern Illinois University Press; London and Amsterdam: Feffer and Simons, 1969.

Goodwin, Albert, ed. *The New Cambridge Modern History*, vol. 8, *The American and French Revolutions, 1763–93*. Cambridge: Cambridge University Press, 1965.

Goubert, Jean-Pierre. *Malades et médecins en Bretagne, 1770–1790*. Paris: C. Klincksieck, 1974.

Gould, Eliga H. *Persistence of Empire: British Political Culture in the Age of the American Revolution*. Chapel Hill: University of North Carolina Press, 2000.

Gradish, Stephen F. *The Manning of the British Navy during the Seven Years' War*. London: Royal Historical Society, 1980.

Graham, Dominick. "The Planning of the Beauséjour Operation and the Approaches to War in 1755." *New England Quarterly* 41 (1968): 551–66.

Granier, Hubert. "Le Vice-Amiral Emmanuel-Auguste de Cahideuc, comte du Bois de la Motte (1683–1764)." *Marins et Océans* 3 (1992): 72–84.

Grant, William. "Canada versus Guadeloupe, An Episode of the Seven Years' War." *American Historical Review* 17 (1911–12): 735–743.

———. "The Capture of Oswego by Montcalm in 1756: A Study in Naval Power." *Transactions of the Royal Society of Canada*, 3rd ser., 8 (1914): 193–214.

———. "La Mission de M. de Bussy à Londres en 1761." *Revue d'histoire diplomatique* 20 (1906): 351–66.

Great Britain. Historical Manuscripts Commission. *Tenth Report of the Royal Commission on Historical Manuscripts*. London: Eyre and Spottiswoode, 1885.

Greene, Donald J., ed. *Samuel Johnson: Political Writings*. New Haven: Yale University Press, 1977.

Greene, Jack P. "'A Posture of Hostility': A Reconsideration of Some Aspects of the Origins of the American Revolution." *Proceedings of the American Antiquarian Society*, new ser., 87 (1977): 27–68.

———. "The Seven Years' War and the American Revolution: The Causal Relationship Reconsidered." *Journal of Imperial and Commonwealth History* 8 (1979–80): 85–105.

———. *Understanding the American Revolution: Issues and Actors*. Charlottesville: University Press of Virginia, 1995.

Gregory, Desmond. *Minorca, the Illusory Prize: A History of the British Occupations of Minorca between 1708 and 1802*. Rutherford NJ: Farleigh Dickinson University Press; London and Toronto: Associated University Presses, 1990.

Greiert, Steven G. "The Board of Trade and Defense of the Ohio Valley." *Western Pennsylvania Historical Magazine* 64 (1981): 1–32.

Grenier, Fernand, ed. *Papiers Contrecoeur et autres documents concernant le conflit anglo-français sur l'Ohio de 1745 à 1756*. Quebec: Presses Universitaires Laval, 1952.

Griffiths, Naomi E. S. *The Contexts of Acadian History, 1686–1784*. Montreal: McGill-Queen's University Press, 1992.

[Grimoard, Philippe-Henri, comte de, ed.] *Correspondance particulière et historique du maréchal duc de Richelieu en 1756, 1757 et 1758, avec M. Paris du Verney, conseiller d'état*. 2 vols. London and Paris: Buisson, 1789.

Groehler, Olaf. *Die Kriege Friedrichs II*. Berlin: Deutscher Militärverlag, 1966.

Grouchy, Emmanuel-Henri, vicomte de, and Paul Cottin, eds. *Journal inédit du duc de Croij, 1718–1784*. 4 vols. Paris: Ernest Flammarion, 1906–07.

Guicciardi, Jean-Pierre, and Philippe Bonnet, eds. *Mémoires du duc de Choiseul*. Paris: Mercure de France, 1982.

Guillon, Edouard-Louis-Maxime. *Port-Mahon: La France à Minorque sous Louis XV (1756–1763) d'après les documents inédits des archives de France et des Baléares*. Paris: Ernest Leroux, 1894.

Gwyn, Julian. *An Admiral for America: Sir Peter Warren, Vice Admiral of the Red, 1703–1752*. Gainesville: University Press of Florida, 2004.

———. "French and British Naval Power at the Two Sieges of Louisbourg: 1745 and 1758." *Nova Scotia Historical Review* 10, no. 2 (1990): 63–93.

———. *Frigates and Foremasts: The North American Squadron in Nova Scotia Waters, 1745–1815*. Vancouver: UBC Press, 2003.

———, ed. *The Royal Navy and North America: The Warren Papers, 1736–1752*. London: Navy Records Society, 1973.

Hackmann, William Kent. "The British Raid on Rochefort, 1757." *Mariner's Mirror* 64 (1978): 263–75.

———. "English Military Expeditions to the Coast of France, 1757–1761." Ph.D. dissertation, University of Michigan, Ann Arbor, 1969.

———. "George Grenville and English Politics in 1763." *Yale University Library Gazette* 64 (1990): 158–66.

Hagerty, Gilbert. *Massacre at Fort Bull: The Léry Expedition against Oneida Carry*. Providence: Mowbray Publications, 1971.

Haines, Michael R. and Richard H. Steckel, eds. *A Population History of North America*. New York: Cambridge University Press, 2000.

Halgouet, Hervé, vicomte du. *Nantes: Ses Relations commerciales avec les îles d'Amérique au XVIIIe siècle; ses armateurs*. Rennes: Oberthur, 1939.

Halpenny, Francess G., ed. *Dictionary of Canadian Biography*, vol. 3, *1741 to 1770*, and vol. 4, *1771 to 1800*. Toronto: University of Toronto Press; Les Presses de l'Université Laval, 1974–79.

Hamer, P. M. "Anglo-French Rivalry in the Cherokee Country, 1754–1757." *North Carolina Historical Review* 2 (1925): 303–22.

Hamilton, Charles, ed. *Braddock's Defeat: The Journal of Captain Robert Cholmley's Batman, the Journal of a British Officer, [and] Halkett's Orderly Book*. Norman: University of Oklahoma Press, 1959.

Hamilton, Edward P., ed. *Adventure in the Wilderness: The American Journals of Louis Antoine de Bougainville, 1756–1760*. Norman: University of Oklahoma Press, 1964.

Hamilton, Milton W. *Sir William Johnson, Colonial American, 1715–1763*. Port Washington NY: Kennikat Press, 1976.

Hamont, Tibulle. *La Fin d'un empire français aux Indes sous Louis XV: Lally-Tollendal d'après des documents inédits*. Paris: E. Plon, Nourrit et cie., 1887.

Harding, Richard. *Amphibious Warfare in the Eighteenth Century: The British Expedition to the West Indies, 1740–1742*. Woodbridge, Eng. and Rochester: Boydell Press for the Royal Historical Society, 1991.

———."Sailors and Gentlemen of Parade: Some Professional and Technical Problems Concerning the Conduct of Combined Operations in the Eighteenth Century." *Historical Journal* 32 (1989): 35–55.

———. *Seapower and Naval Warfare, 1650–1830*. London: UCL Press, 1999.

Harris, R. Cole, ed. *Historical Atlas of Canada*, vol. 1, *From the Beginnings to 1800*. Toronto: University of Toronto Press, 1987.

Hart, Francis Russell. *The Siege of Havana, 1762*. Boston and New York: Houghton Mifflin; London: G. Allen and Unwin, 1931.

Hatley, Tom. *The Dividing Paths: Cherokees and South Carolinians Through the Era of Revolution*. New York: Oxford University Press, 1993.

Hattendorf, John B., ed. *Maritime History*, vol. 2, *The Eighteenth Century and the Classic Age of Sail*. Malabar FL: Krieger, 1997.

Hattendorf, John B., R. J. B. Knight, A. W. H. Pearsall, N. A. M. Rodger, and Geoffrey Till, eds. *British Naval Documents, 1204–1960*. Aldershot, Eng.: Scolar Press for the Navy Records Society, 1993.

Hatton, Ragnhild, and M. S. Anderson, eds. *Studies in Diplomatic History: Essays in Memory of David Bayne Horn*. London: Longman, 1970.

Haudrère, Philippe. *La Compagnie française des Indes au XVIIIe siècle (1719–1795)*. 4 vols. Paris: Librairie de l'Inde, 1989.

Hebbert, F. J. "The Belle-Ile Expedition of 1761." *Journal of the Society for Army Historical Research* 64 (1986): 81–93.

Hébert, Jean-Claude, ed. *The Siege of Québec in 1759: Three Eye-Witness Accounts*. Quebec: Ministère des affaires culturelles, 1974.

Héliot, Pierre. "La Campagne du régiment de la Sarre au Canada (1756–1760)." *Revue d'histoire de l'Amérique française* 3 (1949–50): 518–36.

Henretta, James A. *"Salutary Neglect": Colonial Administration under the Duke of Newcastle*. Princeton: Princeton University Press, 1972.

{Herpin, Clara Adèle Luce]. *Un Petit-nevue de Mazarin: Louis Mancini-Mazarini, duc de Nivernais*. 7th ed. Paris: Calmann Lévy, 1899.

Hervey, Frederic et al. *The Naval History of Great Britain: From the Earliest Times to the Rising of the Parliament in 1779*, vol. 5. London: J. Bew, 1779.

Higginbotham, Don. *George Washington and the American Military Tradition*. Athens: University of Georgia Press, 1985.

Higonnet, Patrice Louis-René. "The Origins of the Seven Years' War." *Journal of Modern History* 40 (1968): 57–90.

Hill, S. C., ed. *Indian Record Series: Bengal in 1756–1757: A Selection of Public and Private Papers Dealing with the Affairs of the British in Bengal during the Reign of Siraj-Uddaula*. 3 vols. London: John Murray, 1905.

Hitsman, J. Mackay. "Order before Landing at Louisbourg, 1758." *Military Affairs* 22 (1958): 146–48.

Hitsman, J. Mackay, and C. C. J. Bond. "The Assault Landing at Louisbourg, 1758." *Canadian Historical Review* 35 (1954): 314–30.

Hoffman, Philip T., and Kathryn Norberg, eds. *Fiscal Crises, Liberty and Representative Government, 1450–1789*. Stanford: Stanford University Press, 1994.

Horn, David Bayne. "The Cabinet Controversy on Subsidy Treaties in Time of Peace, 1749–50." *English Historical Review* 45 (1930): 463–66.

———. "The Duke of Newcastle and the Origins of the Diplomatic Revolution." In J. H. Elliot and H. G. Koenigsberger, eds., *The Diversity of History: Essays in Honor of Sir Herbert Butterfield*, 245–68. Ithaca: Cornell University Press, 1970.

———. *Great Britain and Europe in the Eighteenth Century*. Oxford: Clarendon Press, 1967.

———. "The Origins of the Proposed Election of a King of the Romans, 1748–1750." *English Historical Review* 42 (1927): 361–70.

———. *Sir Charles Hanbury Williams and European Diplomacy (1747–58)*. London, Bombay, Sydney: G. G. Harrap, 1930.

Hotblack, Kate. *Chatham's Colonial Policy: A Study in the Fiscal and Economic Implications of the Colonial Policy of the Elder Pitt*. London: G. Routledge and Sons; New York: E. P. Dutton, 1917.

———. "The Peace of Paris, 1763." *Transactions of the Royal Historical Society*, 3rd. ser., 2 (1908): 235–67.

Hudson, Ruth Strong. *The Minister from France: Conrad-Alexandre Gérard, 1729–1790*. Euclid OH: Lutz Printing and Publishing, 1994.

Hull, Anthony. *Charles III and the Revival of Spain*. Washington: University Press of America, 1981.

Hunt, W. "Pitt's Retirement from Office, 5 Oct. 1761." *English Historical Review* 21 (1906): 119–32.

Hunter, William A. *Forts on the Pennsylvania Frontier, 1753–1758*. Harrisburg: Pennsylvania Historical and Museum Commission, 1960.

Hyam, Ronald. "Imperial Interests and the Peace of Paris, 1763." In Ronald Hyam and Ged Martin, *Reappraisals in British Imperial History*, 21–43. London: Macmillan, 1975.

Ilchester, Giles Stephen Holland Fox-Strangways, Earl of. *Henry Fox, First Lord Holland, His Family and Relations*. 2 vols. London: J. Murray, 1920.

————, ed. *Letters to Henry Fox, Lord Holland, with a Few Addressed to His Brother Stephen, Earl of Ilchester*. London: privately printed for the Roxburghe Club, 1915.

Ireland, Bernard. *Naval Warfare in the Age of Sail: War at Sea, 1756–1815*. New York: W. W. Norton, 2000.

James, Alfred Procter, ed. *Writings of General John Forbes Relating to His Service in North America*. Menasha, Wis: Collegiate Press, 1938.

James, Alfred Procter, and Charles Morse Stotz. *Drums in the Forest: Decision at the Forks / Defense in the Wilderness*. Pittsburgh: Historical Society of Western Pennsylvania, 1958.

Jarrett, Derek, ed. *Horace Walpole: Memoirs of the Reign of King George III*. 4 vols. New Haven: Yale University Press, 2000.

Jennings, Francis. *Empire of Fortune: Crown, Colonies and Tribes in the Seven Years War in America*. New York: W. W. Norton, 1988.

John, A. H. "War and the English Economy, 1700–1763." *Economic History Review*, 2nd ser., 7 (1954–55): 329–44.

Jones, Colin. *The Great Nation: France from Louis XIV to Napoleon, 1715–99*. New York: Columbia University Press, 2002.

Jucker, Ninetta S., ed. *The Jenkinson Papers, 1760–1766*. London: Macmillan, 1949.

Kaplan, Herbert H. *Russia and the Outbreak of the Seven Years' War*. Berkeley: University of California Press, 1968.

Kaunitz-Ritberg, Wenzel-Anton, Fürst. "Mémoire sur la cour de France, 1752." *Revue de Paris* 11, part 4 (July–August 1904): 441–54, 821–47.

Kellogg, Louise P., ed. "La Chapelle's Remarkable Retreat through the Mississippi Valley, 1760–61." *Mississippi Valley Historical Review* 22 (1935–36): 63–81.

Kennett, Lee. *The French Armies in the Seven Years' War: A Study in Military Organization and Administration*. Durham NC: Duke University Press, 1967.

Kent, H. S. K. *War and Trade in Northern Seas: Anglo-Scandinavian Economic Relations in the Mid-Eighteenth Century*. Cambridge: Cambridge University Press, 1973.

Keppel, Sonia. *Three Brothers at Havana, 1762*. Wilton, Eng.: Michael Russell, 1981.

Keppel, Thomas. *The Life of Augustus, Viscount Keppel, Admiral of the White and First Lord of the Admiralty in 1782–3*. 2 vols. London: Henry Colburn, 1842.

Kerrebrouck, Patrick van. *Nouvelle Histoire généalogique de l'auguste maison de France*, vol. 4, *La Maison de Bourbon, 1256–1987*. Villeneuve d'Ascq, France: privately printed, 1987.

Kimball, Gertrude Selwyn, ed. *Correspondence of William Pitt When Secretary of State with Colonial Governors and Military and Naval Commissioners in America*. 2 vols. New York: Macmillan, 1906.

Koch, Chr. [Christophe-Guillaume de], ed. *Table des traités entre la France et les puissances étrangères depuis la paix de Westphalie jusqu'à nos jours*. 2 vols. Basel: J. Decker; Paris: Ch. Pougens, 1802.

Koehn, Nancy F. *The Power of Commerce: Economy and Governance in the First British Empire*. Ithaca: Cornell University Press, 1994.

Konopczynski, W. "La Deuxième Mission du comte du Broglie: Un Supplément aux

'Instructions de Pologne' (1755–1756)." *Revue d'histoire diplomatique* 21 (1907): 495–508.

Koontz, Louis K. *The Virginia Frontier, 1754–1763*. Baltimore: Johns Hopkins Press, 1925.

Kopperman, Paul E. *Braddock at the Monongahela*. Pittsburgh: University of Pittsburgh Press, 1977.

Kroener, Bernard R., ed. *Europa im Zeitalter Friedrichs des Grossen: Wirtschaft, Gesellschaft, Kriege*. Munich: R. Oldenbourg, 1989.

Kuethe, Allan J. *Cuba, 1753–1815: Crown, Military and Society*. Knoxville: University of Tennessee Press, 1986.

Kunisch, Johannes. *Das Mirakel des Hauses Brandenburg: Studien zum Verhältnis von Kabinettspolitik und Kriegführung im Zeitalter des Siebenjährigen Krieges*. Munich and Vienna: R. Oldenbourg, 1978.

Kwass, Michael. *Privilege and the Politics of Taxation in Eighteenth-Century France: Liberté, Egalité, Fiscalité*. Cambridge, New York, Oakleigh, Australia: Cambridge University Press, 2000.

Kyte, E. C., ed. *An Impartial Account of Lieut. Col. Bradstreet's Expedition to Fort Frontenac*. Toronto: Ross and Mann, 1940.

Labaree, Leonard W. "Benjamin Franklin and the Defense of Pennsylvania, 1754–1757." *Pennsylvania History* 29 (1962): 7–23.

Labaree, Leonard W., et al., eds. *The Papers of Benjamin Franklin*, 37 vols to date. New Haven: Yale University Press, 1959–.

Labrousse, Ernest, Pierre Léon, Pierre Goubert, Jean Bouvier, Charles Carrière, and Paul Harsin. *Histoire économique et sociale de la France*, vol. 2, *Des derniers temps de l'âge seigneurial aux préludes de l'âge industriel (1660–1789)*. Paris: Presses universitaires de France, 1970.

La Condamine, Pierre de. *Un Jour d'été à Saint-Cast: L'Epopée de la Bretagne*. Cohélais-Saint-Molf, France: La Bateau qui vire, 1977.

Lacour-Gayet, Georges. *La Marine militaire de la France sous le règne de Louis XV*. Rev. ed. Paris: Honoré Champion, 1910.

Lamontagne, Roland. *Aperçu structural du Canada au XVIIIᵉ siècle*. Montreal: Lémeac, 1967.

———. *La Galissionière et le Canada*. Montreal: Presses de l' Université de Montréal; Paris: Presses universitaires de France, 1962.

———. "La Galissionière et ses conceptions coloniales d'après le Mémoire sur les colonies de la France dans l'Amérique septentrionale (decembre 1750)." *Revue d'histoire de l'Amérique française* 15 (1961–62): 163–170.

La Morandière, Charles de. *Histoire de la pêche française de la morue dans l'Amérique septentrionale (des origines à 1789)*. 2 vols. Paris: G. P. Maisonneuve et Larose, 1962.

Lanctôt, Gustave. *A History of Canada*, vol. 3, *From the Treaty of Utrecht to the Treaty of Paris, 1713–1763*. Translated by M. M. Cameron. Cambridge: Harvard University Press, 1965.

Langford, Paul. *The Eighteenth Century, 1688–1815*. London: J. Adam and Charles Black, 1976.

————. "William Pitt and Public Opinion, 1757." *English Historical Review* 88 (1973): 54–80.

La Pause, Jean-Guillaume-Charles de Plantavit de Margon, chevalier de. "Mémoire et observations sur mon voyage en Canada." *Rapport de l'archiviste de la province de Québec* 12 (1931–32): 3–125.

Laughton, Sir John Knox. *Studies in Naval History*. London: Longmans, Green, 1887.

Lavery, Brian. *The Ship of the Line*, vol. 1, *The Development of the Battlefleet, 1650–1850*. Annapolis: Naval Institute Press; London: Conway Maritime Press, 1983.

Lawson, Philip. *George Grenville: A Political Life*. Oxford: Clarendon Press, 1984.

Leach, Douglas Edward. *Arms for Empire: A Military History of the British Colonies in North America, 1607–1763*. New York: Macmillan; London: Collier-Macmillan, 1973.

————. *Roots of Conflict: British Armed Forces and Colonial Americans, 1677–1763*. Chapel Hill: University of North Carolina Press, 1986.

Lee, David. "The Contest for Isle aux Noix, 1759–1760: A Case Study in the Fall of New France." *Vermont History* 37 (1969): 96–107.

Le Fevre, Peter, and Richard Harding, eds. *Precursors of Nelson: British Admirals of the Eighteenth Century*. London: Chatham, 2000.

Legg, L. G. Wickham, ed. *British Diplomatic Instructions, 1689–1789*, vol. 7, *France, part IV, 1745–1789*. London: Royal Historical Society, 1934.

Le Goff, T. J. A. "Offre et productivité de la main-d'oeuvre dans les armaments français au XVIIIᵉ siècle." *Histoire, économie et société* 2 (1983): 457–73.

————. "Problèmes de recrutement de la marine française pendant la Guerre de Sept Ans." *Revue historique* 283 (January–June 1990): 205–33.

Legohérel, Henri. *Les Trésoriers généraux de la marine, 1517–1788*. Paris: Cujas, 1965.

Lemisch, Jesse. "Jack Tar in the Streets: Merchant Seamen in the Politics of Revolutionary America." *William and Mary Quarterly*, 3rd ser., 25 (1968): 371–407.

Le Moing, Guy. *La Bataille navale des "Cardinaux."* Paris: Economica, 2003.

Lenman, Bruce P. *Britain's Colonial Wars, 1688–1783*. Harlow, Eng. and elsewhere: Longman, 2001.

Leonard, Carol S. *Reform and Regicide: The Reign of Peter III of Russia*. Bloomington: Indiana University Press, 1993.

Le Roy Ladurie, Emmanuel. *The Ancien Régime: A History of France, 1610–1774*. Translated by Mark Greengrass. Oxford, Eng. and Cambridge MA: Blackwell, 1996.

Lever, Evelyne. *Madame de Pompadour: A Life*. Translated by Catherine Temerson. New York: Farrar, Straus and Giroux, 2002.

Levot, Prosper-Jean. *Histoire de la ville et du port de Brest*, vol. 2, *Le Port depuis 1681*. Paris: Bachelin-Deflorenne, 1865.

Lewis, W. S. et al., eds. *The Yale Edition of Horace Walpole's Correspondence*. 48 vols. New Haven: Yale University Press; Oxford: Oxford University Press, 1937–83.

Lincoln, Charles Henry, ed. *Correspondence of William Shirley, Governor of Massachusetts and Military Commander in America, 1731–1760*. 2 vols. New York: Macmillan, 1912.

Lincoln, Margarette. *Representing the Royal Navy: British Sea Power, 1750–1815*. Burlington VT: Ashgate, 2002.

Lind, Gunner. "The Making of the Neutrality Convention of 1756: France and Her Scandinavian Allies." *Scandinavian Journal of History* 8 (1983): 171–92.

Lindner, Thomas. *Die Peripetie des Siebenjährigen Krieges: Der Herstfeldzug 1760 in Sachsen und der Winterfeldzug 1760/61 in Hessen.* Berlin: Duncker & Humblot, 1993.

Lindsay, J. O., ed. *The New Cambridge Modern History,* vol. 7, *The Old Regime, 1713–1763.* Cambridge: Cambridge University Press, 1963.

Linijer de La Barbée, Maurice. *Le Chevalier de Ternay: Vie de Charles Henry Louis d'Arsac de Ternay, chef d'escadre des armées navales, 1723–1780.* 2 vols. Grenoble: Editions des 4 seigneurs, 1972.

List and Index Society. *Ships' Muster Series I and II: Adm. 36 and Adm. 37.* 2 vols. Kew, Eng.: List and Index Society, Public Record Office, 1992.

Little, C. H., ed. *The Battle of Restigouche: The Last Naval Engagement between France and Britain for the Possession of Canada.* Halifax: Maritime Museum of Canada, 1962.

———, ed. *Despatches of Rear-Admiral Philip Durell, 1758–1759 and Rear-Admiral Lord Colville, 1759–1761.* Halifax: Maritime Museum of Canada, 1958.

———, ed. *Despatches of Rear-Admiral Sir Charles Hardy, 1757–1758 and Vice-Admiral Francis Holburne, 1757.* Halifax: Maritime Museum of Canada, 1958.

———, ed. *Despatches of Vice-Admiral Charles Saunders, 1759–1760: The Naval Side of the Capture of Quebec.* Halifax: Maritime Museum of Canada, 1958.

———, ed. *The Recapture of Saint John's, Newfoundland: Despatches of Rear-Admiral Lord Colville, 1761–1762.* Halifax: Maritime Museum of Canada, 1959.

Lloyd, Christopher. *The British Seaman, 1200–1860: A Social Survey.* London: Collins, 1968.

———, ed. *The Naval Miscellany,* vol. 4. London: Navy Records Society, 1952.

Lloyd, E. M. "The Raising of the Highland Regiments in 1757." *English Historical Review* 17 (1902): 466–69.

Lodge, Sir Richard. *Great Britain and Prussia in the Eighteenth Century.* Oxford: Clarendon Press, 1923.

———. "Sir Benjamin Keene, K. B.: A Study in Anglo-Spanish Relations." *Transactions of the Royal Historical Society,* 4th ser., 15 (1932): 1–43.

———. *Studies in Eighteenth-Century Diplomacy, 1740–1748.* London: John Murray, 1930.

———, ed. *The Private Correspondence of Sir Benjamin Keene, K. B.* Cambridge: Cambridge University Press, 1933.

Love, Robert William et al., eds. *Changing Interpretations and New Sources in Naval History: Papers from the Third United States Naval Academy History Symposium.* New York: Garland, 1980.

Loyer, P. "La Défense des côtes de Bretagne pendant la guerre de Sept Ans: La Bataille de Saint-Cast." *Revue Maritime,* new ser., no. 156 (December 1932): 721–739 and no. 157 (January 1933): 75–98.

Lunn, Jean Elizabeth. "Agriculture and War in Canada, 1740–1760." *Canadian Historical Review* 16 (1935): 123–36.

Lydon, James G. *Struggle for Empire: A Bibliography of the French and Indian War.* New York: Garland, 1986.

Lyon, David, comp. *The Sailing Navy List: All the Ships of the Royal Navy Built, Purchased and Captured, 1688–1860.* London: Conway Maritime Press, 1993.

Lyon, E. Wilson. *Louisiana in French Diplomacy, 1759–1804.* Norman: University of Oklahoma Press, 1934.

Maas, John R. "'All This Poor Province Could Do': North Carolina and the Seven Years' War, 1757–1762." *North Carolina Historical Review* 79 (2002): 50–89.

Macdonald, James. *A Free Nation Deep in Debt: The Financial Roots of Democracy.* New York: Farrar, Straus and Giroux, 2003.

Mackay, Ruddock F. *Admiral Hawke.* Oxford: Clarendon Press, 1965.

———, ed. *The Hawke Papers: A Selection 1743–1771.* Aldershot, Eng.: Scolar Press for the Navy Records Society, 1990.

Mackesy, Piers. *The Coward of Minden: The Affair of Lord George Sackville.* London: Allen Lane, 1979.

MacLeod, D. Peter. *The Canadian Iroquois and the Seven Years' War.* Toronto and Oxford: Dundurn Press, 1996.

———. "The Canadians against the French: The Struggle for Control of the Expedition to Oswego in 1756." *Ontario History* 80 (1988): 143–57.

———. "The French Siege of Oswego in 1756: Inland Naval Warfare in North America." *American Neptune* 49 (1989): 262–71.

———. "Microbes and Muskets: Smallpox and the Participation of the Amerindian Allies of New France in the Seven Years' War." *Ethnohistory* 39 (1992): 42–64.

Madariaga, Isabel de. *Russia in the Age of Catherine the Great.* New Haven: Yale University Press, 1981.

Mahon, R. H. *Life of General the Hon. James Murray, a Builder of Canada.* London: John Murray, 1921.

Malartic, Gabriel de Maurès, comte de, ed. *Journal des campagnes au Canada de 1755 à 1760 par le comte de Maurès de Malartic.* Paris: E. Plon, Nourrit et cie., 1890.

Malcomsom, Robert. *Warships of the Great Lakes, 1754–1834.* London: Chatham, 2001.

Malo, Henri. *Les Dernières Corsaires: Dunkerque (1715–1815).* Paris: Emile-Paul frères, 1922.

Malvezin, Théophile. *Histoire du commerce de Bordeaux, depuis les origines, jusqu'à nos jours,* vol. 3, *XVIIIᵉ siècle.* Bordeaux: A. Bellier, 1892.

Mante, Thomas. *The History of the Late War in North-America, and the Islands of the West-Indies, including the Campaigns of MDCCLXIIII and MDCCLXIV against His Majesty's Indian Enemies.* London: W. Strahan and T. Cadell, 1772.

Mapp, Paul. "French Reaction to the British Search for a Northwest Passage from Hudson Bay and the Origins of the Seven Years' War." *Terrae Incognitae* 33 (2001): 13–32.

Marcus, Geoffrey. "Hawke's Blockade of Brest." *Journal of the Royal United Service Institution* 104 (1959): 475–88.

———. *Quiberon Bay.* Barre MA: Barre, 1963.

Marion, Marcel. *Histoire financière de la France depuis 1715*. 6 vols. Paris: A. Rousseau, 1914–31.

Marley, David F. "Havana Surprised: Prelude to the British Invasion, 1762." *Mariner's Mirror* 78 (1992): 293–305.

Marsangy, Louis Bonneville de. *Le Chevalier de Vergennes: Son Ambassade à Constantinople*. 2 vols. Paris: E. Plon, Nourrit et cie., 1894.

Marsh, A. J. "The Taking of Goree, 1758." *Mariner's Mirror* 51 (1965): 117–30.

Marshall, P. J., ed. *The Oxford History of the British Empire*, vol. 2, *The Eighteenth Century*. Oxford: Oxford University Press, 1998.

Martin, Gaston. *Nantes au XVIIIe siècle*, vol. 2, *L'Ere des négriers (1714–1774) d'après des documents inédits*. Paris: Félix Alcan, 1931.

Martin, Ronald D. " Confrontation at the Monongahela: The Climax of the French Drive into the Upper Ohio Region. *Pennsylvania History* 37 (1970): 133–50.

Masson, Frédéric. *Le Cardinal de Bernis depuis son ministère, 1758–1774*. Paris: Plon, Nourrit et cie., 1884.

————, ed. *Mémoires et lettres de François-Joachim de Pierre, Cardinal de Bernis (1715–1758)*. 2 vols. Paris: E. Plon et cie., 1878.

Mathias, Peter, and Patrick O'Brien. "Taxation in Britain and France, 1715–1810: A Comparison of the Social and Economic Incidence of Taxes Collected for the Central Governments." *Journal of European Economic History* 5 (1976): 601–650.

Mathieu, Jacques. "La Balance commerciale: Nouvelle-France-Antilles au XVIIIe siècle." *Revue d'histoire de l'Amérique française* 25 (1971–72): 465–97.

————. *Le Commerce entre la Nouvelle-France et les Antilles au XVIIIe siècle*. Montreal: Fides, 1981.

[Mauduit, Israel]. *Considerations on the Present German War*. London: J. Wilkie, 1760.

Maupassant, Jean de. "Les Armateurs bordelais au XVIIIe siècle: Les Deux Expéditions de Pierre Desclaux au Canada (1759 et 1760)." *Revue historique de Bordeaux* 8 (1915): 225–40, 313–30.

————. *Un Grand Armateur de Bordeaux, Abraham Gradis (1699?-1780)*. Bordeaux: Ferret et fils, 1917.

Mayo, Lawrence Shaw. *Jeffrey Amherst: A Biography*. London: Longmans, Green, 1916.

McConnell, Michael N. *A Country Between: The Upper Ohio Valley and Its People, 1724–1774*. Lincoln: University of Nebraska Press, 1992.

McCulloch, Ian M. " 'Like roaring lions breaking from their chains': The Battle of Ticonderoga, 8 July 1758." In Donald E. Graves, ed., *Fighting for Canada: Seven Battles, 1758–1945*, 23–80. Toronto: Robin Bass Studio, 2000.

McCusker, John J. *Money and Exchange in Europe and America, 1660–1775: A Handbook*. Chapel Hill: University of North Carolina Press, 1978.

————. *Rum and the American Revolution: The Rum Trade and the Balance of Payments of the Thirteen Continental Colonies*. New York and London: Garland, 1989.

McGill, William J. "The Roots of Policy: Kaunitz in Vienna and Versailles, 1749–1753." *Journal of Modern History* 43 (1971): 228–44.

McLachlan, Jean O. "The Uneasy Neutrality: A Study of Anglo-Spanish Disputes over Spanish Ships Prized, 1756–1759." *Cambridge Historical Journal* 6 (1938–40): 55–77.

McLennan, J. S. *Louisbourg from Its Foundation to Its Fall, 1713–1758.* London: Macmillan, 1918.

McLynn, Frank Edward. *Charles Edward Stuart: A Tragedy in Many Acts.* London and New York: Routledge, 1988.

———. *France and the Jacobite Rising of 1745.* Edinburgh: Edinburgh University Press, 1981.

———. *1759: The Year Britain Became Master of the World.* London: Jonathan Cape, 2004.

McManners, John. *Church and Society in Eighteenth-Century France.* 2 vols. Oxford: Clarendon Press, 1998.

McNeill, John Robert. *Atlantic Empires of France and Spain: Louisbourg and Havana, 1700–1763.* Chapel Hill: University of North Carolina Press, 1985.

Meng, John J., ed. *Despatches and Instructions of Conrad-Alexander Gérard, 1778–1780.* Baltimore: Johns Hopkins Press, 1939.

Merino Navarro, José P. *La armada española en el sigo XVIII.* Madrid: Fundación Universitaria Española, 1981.

Merrell, James H. *Into the American Woods: Negociators on the Pennsylvania Frontier.* New York and London: W. W. Norton, 1999.

Merrick, Jeffrey W. *The Desacrilization of the French Monarchy in the Eighteenth Century.* Baton Rouge: Louisiana State University Press, 1990.

Merritt, Jane T. *At the Crossroads: Indians and Empires on a Mid-Atlantic Frontier, 1700–1763.* Chapel Hill: University of North Carolina Press, 2003.

Meyer, Jean. *L'Armement nantais dans la deuxième moitié du XVIIIe siècle.* Paris: SEVPEN, 1969.

Meyer, Jean, and John Bromley. "The Second Hundred Years' War (1689–1815)." In Douglas Johnson, François Crouzet, and François Bédarida, eds., *Britain and France: Ten Centuries,* 139–72. Folkestone, Eng.: William Dawson and Sons, 1980.

Michel, Jacques. *La Vie aventureuse et mouvementée de Charles-Henri, comte d'Estaing.* [Paris]: privately printed, 1976.

Middleton, Richard. *The Bells of Victory: The Pitt-Newcastle Ministry and the Conduct of the Seven Years' War, 1757–1762.* New York: Cambridge University Press, 1985.

———. "The British Coastal Expeditions to France, 1757–1758." *Journal of the Society for Army Historical Research* 71 (1993): 74–92.

———. "British Naval Strategy, 1755–1762: The Western Squadron." *Mariner's Mirror* 75 (1989): 349–67.

———. "Pitt, Anson and the Admiralty, 1756–1761." *History,* new ser., 55 (1970): 189–98.

———. "A Reinforcement for North America, Summer 1757." *Bulletin of the Institute of Historical Research* 41 (1968): 58–72.

Miquelon, Dale. *Duggard of Rouen: French Trade to Canada and the West Indies, 1729–1770.* Montreal: McGill-Queen's University Press, 1978.

Mitchell, B. R., and Phyllis Deane, comps. *Abstract of British Historical Statistics.* Cambridge: Cambridge University Press, 1962.

Moore, Christopher. "The Other Louisbourg: Trade and Merchant Enterprise in Ile Royale, 1713–58." *Histoire sociale-Social History* 12 (1979): 76–96.

Morineau, Michel. "Budgets de l'état et gestion des finances royales en France au dix-huitième siècle." *Revue historique* 264 (July–December 1980): 289–336.

[Mouffle d'Angerville, Barthélemy-François-Joseph.] *Vie privée de Louis XV, ou principaux évenémens, particularités et anecdotes de son règne.* 4 vols. London: John Peter Lyton, 1781.

Muhlmann, Rolf. *Die Reorganisation der Spanischen Kriegsmarine im 18. Jahrhundert.* Cologne and Vienna: Bohlau, 1975.

Muret, Pierre. *La Prépondérance anglaise (1713–1763).* 3rd ed. Paris: Presses universitaires de France, 1949.

Murphy, Orville T. *Charles Gravier, Comte de Vergennes: French Diplomacy in the Age of Revolution, 1719–1787.* Albany: State University of New York Press, 1982.

Murrin, John M. "The French and Indian War, The American Revolution, and the Counterfactual Hypothesis: Reflections on Lawrence Henry Gipson and John Shy." *Reviews in American History* 1 (1973): 307–18.

Myers, James P., Jr. "Pennsylvania's Awakening: The Kittanning Raid of 1756." *Pennsylvania History* 66 (1999): 399–420.

Namier, Sir Lewis. *England in the Age of the American Revolution.* 2nd ed. New York: St. Martin's Press, 1961.

Nash, Gary B. *The Urban Crucible: Social Change, Political Consciousness, and the Origins of the American Revolution.* Cambridge: Harvard University Press, 1979.

Neal, Larry. "Interpreting Power and Profit in Economic History: A Case Study of the Seven Years War." *Journal of Economic History* 37 (1977): 20–35.

Nester, William R. *The First Global War: Britain, France, and the Fate of North America, 1756–1765.* Westport CT and London: Praeger, 2000.

Neuville, Didier, ed. *Etat sommaire des archives de la marine antérieures à la Révolution.* Paris: L. Baudoin, 1898.

Newbold, Robert C. *The Albany Congress and Plan of Union of 1754.* New York: Vantage, 1955.

Newman, Aubry. *The World Turned Inside Out: New Views on George II: An Inaugural Lecture Delivered in the University of Leicester 10 October 1987.* Leicester, Eng.: History Department, University of Leicester, 1988.

Nicolai, Martin L. "A Different Kind of Courage: The French Military and the Canadian Irregular Soldier during the Seven Years' War." *Canadian Historical Review* 70 (1989): 53–75.

Niedhart, Gottfried. *Handel und Krieg in der britischen Weltpolitik, 1738–1763.* Munich: Wilhelm Fink, 1979.

Nolan, J. Bennett. *General Benjamin Franklin: The Military Career of a Philosopher.* Philadelphia: University of Pennsylvania Press; London: Humphrey Milford, Oxford University Press, 1936.

Nordmann, Claude. "Choiseul and the Last Jacobite Attempt of 1759." In Eveline Cruick-shanks, ed., *Ideology and Conspiracy: Aspects of Jacobitism, 1689–1759*, 201–17. Edinburgh: John Donald, 1982.

Norkus, Nellie. "Virginia's Role in the Capture of Fort Duquesne, 1758." *Western Pennsylvania Historical Magazine* 45 (1962): 291–308.

Nosworthy, Brent. *The Anatomy of Victory: Battle Tactics, 1689–1763*. New York: Hippocrene Books, 1990.

O'Callaghan, E. B. et al., eds. *Documents Relative to the Colonial History of the State of New-York*. 15 vols. Albany: Weed, Parson, 1853–1887.

O'Gorman, Frank. *The Rise of Party in England: The Rockingham Whigs, 1760–82*. London: G. Allen and Unwin, 1975.

Oliphant, John. *Peace and War on the Anglo-Cherokee Frontier, 1756–63*. Baton Rouge: Louisiana State University Press, 2001.

Oliva, L. Jay. *Misalliance: A Study of French Policy in Russia during the Seven Years' War*. New York: New York University Press, 1964.

Olson, Alison Gilbert. "The British Government and Colonial Union, 1754." *William and Mary Quarterly*, 3rd ser., 17 (1960): 22–34.

Olson, Donald W., William D. Liddle, Russell L. Doescher, Leah H. Behrends, Tammy D. Silakowski, and François-Jacques Saucier. "Perfect Tide, Ideal Moon: An Unappreciated Aspect of Wolfe's Generalship at Québec, 1759." *William and Mary Quarterly*, 3rd ser., 59 (2002): 957–74.

Oresko, Robert, G. C. Gibbs, and H. M. Scott, eds. *Royal and Republican Sovereignty in Earl Modern Europe: Essays in Memory of Ragnhild Hatton*. Cambridge: Cambridge University Press, 1997.

Ormesson, François D., and Jean-Pierre Thomas. *Jean-Joseph de Laborde: Banquier de Louis XV, mécène des Lumières*. Paris: Perrin, 2002.

Owen, John B. "George II Reconsidered." In Anne Whiteman, J. S. Bromley, and P. G. M. Dickson, eds., *Statesmen, Scholars, and Merchants: Essays in Eighteenth-Century History Presented to Dame Lucy Sutherland*, 113–34. Oxford: Clarendon Press, 1973.

Ozanam, Didier. "La Disgrace d'un premier commis: Tercier et l'affair De L'Esprit (1758–1759)." *Bibliothèque de l'Ecole de chartes* 113 (1955): 140–70.

———. "Les Origines du troisième pacte de famille (1761)." *Revue d'histoire diplomatique* 75 (1961): 307–40.

Ozanam, Didier, and Michel Antoine, eds. *Correspondance secrète du comte de Broglie avec Louis XV (1756–1774)*. 2 vols. Paris: C. Klincksieck, 1956–61.

Paine, Gary. "Ord's Arks: Angles, Artillery, and Ambush on Lakes George and Champlain." *American Neptune* 58 (1998): 105–22.

Pajol, Charles-Pierre-Victor, comte. *Les Guerres sous Louis XV*. 7 vols. Paris: Firmin-Didot, 1881–1891.

Palacio Atard, Vicente. *El Tercer Pacto de familia*. Madrid: Escuela de Estudios Hispano-Americanos de la Universidad de Sevilla, 1945.

Pares, Richard. *Colonial Blockade and Neutral Rights, 1739–1763*. Oxford: Clarendon Press, 1938.

————. *The Historian's Business, and Other Essays*. Oxford: Clarendon Press, 1961.

————. *War and Trade in the West Indies, 1739–1763*. Oxford: Clarendon Press, 1936.

————. *Yankees and Creoles: The Trade between North America and the West Indies before the American Revolution*. Cambridge: Harvard University Press, 1956.

Pargellis, Stanley McCrory. "Braddock's Defeat." *American Historical Review* 41 (1935–36): 253–69.

————. *Lord Loudoun in North America*. New Haven: Yale University Press; London: Humphrey Milford, Oxford University Press, 1933.

————, ed. *Military Affairs in North America, 1748–1765: Selected Documents from the Cumberland Papers in Windsor Castle*. New York: D. Appleton-Century, 1936.

Parry, Clive, comp. *The Consolidated Treaty Series*. 243 vols. Dobbs Ferry NY: Oceana, 1969–86.

Parscau du Plessis, Louis-Guillaume. "Journal d'une campagne au Canada à bord de *la Sauvage* (mars–juillet 1756)." *Rapport de l'archiviste de la province de Québec* 9 (1928–29): 211–26.

Pease, Theodore Calvin, ed. *Anglo-French Boundary Disputes in the West, 1749–1763*. Springfield: Illinois State Historical Library, 1936.

————. "The Mississippi Boundary of 1763: A Reappraisal of Responsibility." *American Historical Review* 40 (1934–35): 278–86.

Peters, Marie. *The Elder Pitt*. London: Longman, 1998.

————. "The Myth of William Pitt, Earl of Chatham, Great Imperialist. Part I: Pitt and Imperial Expansion, 1738–1763." *Journal of Imperial and Commonwealth History* 21 (1993): 31–74.

————. *Pitt and Popularity: The Patriot Minister and London Opinion during the Seven Years' War*. Oxford: Clarendon Press, 1980.

Petrie, Sir Charles. *King Charles III of Spain: An Enlightened Despot*. London: Constable, 1971.

Peyser, Joseph L., ed. *Jacques Legardeur de Saint-Pierre: Officer, Gentleman, Entrepreneur*. East Lansing MI: Michigan State University Press; Mackinac Island MI: Mackinac State Historical Park, 1996.

————, ed. *On the Eve of the Conquest: The Chevalier de Raymond's Critique of New France in 1754*. East Lansing: Michigan State University Press; Mackinac Island MI: Mackinac State Historic Park, 1997.

Pfister-Langanay, Christian. *Ports, navires et négotiants à Dunkerque (1662–1792)*. Dunkirk: Société dunkerquoise, 1985.

Piccioni, Camille. *Les Prémiers commis des affaires étrangères au XVIIᵉ et au XVIIIᵉ siècles*. Paris: E. de Bocard, 1928.

Pick, Robert. *Empress Maria Theresa: The Earlier Years, 1717–1757*. New York: Harper and Row, 1966.

Plank, Geoffrey. *An Unsettled Conquest: The British Campaign Against the Peoples of Acadia*. Philadelphia: University of Pennsylvania Press, 2001.

Pocock, Tom. *Battle for Empire: The Very First World War, 1756–63*. London: Michael O'Mara Books, 1998.

Pope, Dudley. *At Twelve Mr. Byng Was Shot.* Philadelphia: J. B. Lippincott, 1962.

Preston, Richard, and Leopold Lamontagne, eds. *Royal Fort Frontenac.* Toronto: Champlain Society, 1958.

Price, Jacob M. *France and the Chesapeake: A History of the French Tobacco Monopoly, 1674–1791, and of Its Relationship to the British and American Tobacco Trades.* 2 vols. Ann Arbor: University of Michigan Press, 1973.

—————. "Who Cared about the Colonies? The Impact of the Thirteen Colonies on British Society and Politics, circa 1714–1775." In Bernard Bailyn and Philip D. Morgan, eds., *Strangers within the Realm: Cultural Margins of the First British Empire,* 395–436. Chapel Hill: University of North Carolina Press, 1991.

Pritchard, James. *Anatomy of a Naval Disaster: The 1746 French Naval Expedition to North America.* Montreal: McGill-Queen's University Press, 1995.

—————. "Fir Trees, Financiers, and the French Navy during the 1750's." *Canadian Journal of History* 23 (1988): 337–54.

—————. "The French Naval Officers Corps during the Seven Years' War." In *New Aspects of Naval History: Selected Papers from the 5th Naval History Symposium,* 59–67. Baltimore: Nautical and Aviation Publishing Company of America, 1985.

—————. "From Shipwright to Naval Constuctor: The Professionalization of Eighteenth-Century French Naval Shipbuilders." *Technology and Culture* 28 (1987): 1–25.

—————. *Louis XV's Navy, 1748–1762: A Study of Organization and Administration.* Montreal: McGill-Queen's University Press, 1987.

—————. "The Pattern of French Colonial Shipping to Canada before 1760." *Revue française d'histoire d'outre-mer* 63 (1976): 189–210.

Proulx, Gilles. "Le dernier Effort de la France au Canada: Secours ou fraude?" *Revue d'histoire de l'Amérique française* 36 (1982–83): 413–26.

—————. *Fighting at Restigouche: The Men and Vessels of 1760 in Chaleur Bay.* Ottawa: National Historic Sites, Parks Canada, 1999.

Ram Gopal. *How the British Occupied Bengal: A Corrected Account of the 1756–1765 Events.* New York: Asia Publishing House, 1963.

Rashed, Zenab Esmat. *The Peace of Paris, 1763.* Liverpool: Liverpool University Press, 1951.

Rathery, E. J. B., ed. *Journal et mémoires du marquis d'Argenson.* 9 vols. Paris: Mme Veuve Jules Renouard, 1859–1867.

Rawlyk, George A. *Nova Scotia's Massachusetts: A Study of Massachusetts–Nova Scotia Relations, 1630 to 1784.* Montreal: McGill-Queen's University Press, 1973

—————. *Yankees at Louisbourg.* Orono ME: University of Maine Press, 1967.

Reese, Armin. *Europäische Hegemonie und France d'Outre mer: Koloniale Fragen in der französischen Aussenpolitik 1700–1763.* Stuttgart: Steiner, 1988.

Reid, Marjorie G. "Pitt's Decision to Keep Canada in 1761." In *The Canadian Historical Association: Report of the Annual Meeting Held in the City of Ottawa, May 17–18, 1926,* 21–32. Ottawa: Department of Public Archives, n.d.

Reilly, Robin. *The Rest to Fortune: The Life of Major-General James Wolfe.* London: Cassell, 1960.

Renaut d'Oultre-Seille, Francis P. *Le Pacte de famille et l' Amérique: La Politique coloniale franco-espagnole de 1760 à 1792*. Paris: Editions Leroux, 1922.

Richmond, Sir Herbert W. *The Navy in the War of 1739–48*. 3 vols. Cambridge: Cambridge University Press, 1920.

———, ed. *Papers Relating to the Loss of Minorca in 1756*. London: Navy Records Society, 1913.

———. *Statesmen and Sea Power*. Oxford: Clarendon Press, 1946.

Riker, Thad W. "The Politics Behind Braddock's Expedition." *American Historical Review* 13 (1907–08): 742–752.

Riley, James C. "French Finances, 1727–1768." *Journal of Modern History* 59 (1987): 209–43.

———. *The Seven Years War and the Old Regime in France: The Economic and Financial Toll*. Princeton: Princeton University Press, 1986.

Ritter, Gerhard. *Frederick the Great: A Historical Profile*. Translated by Peter Paret. Berkeley: University of California Press, 1968.

Robbie, Enid. *The Forgotten Commissioner: Sir William Mildmay and the Anglo-French Commission of 1750–1755*. East Lansing: Michigan State University Press, 2003.

Roberts, Michael. *The Age of Liberty: Sweden, 1719–1772*. New York: Cambridge University Press, 1986.

———. *British Diplomacy and Swedish Politics, 1758–1773*. Minneapolis: University of Minnesota Press, 1980.

———. *Splendid Isolation, 1763–1780*. Reading: University of Reading, 1970.

Robinson, Dwight E. "Secret of British Power in the Age of Sail: Admiralty Records of the Coasting Fleet." *American Neptune* 52 (1992): 5–21.

Robitaille, abbé Georges. *Montcalm et ses historiens: Etude critique*. Montreal: Granger frères, 1936.

Rochambeau, [Jean-Baptiste-Donatien de Vimeur], comte de. *Mémoires militaires, historiques et politiques de Rochambeau, ancien maréchal et grand officier de la Legion de Honneur*. 2 vols. Paris: Fain, 1809.

Rodger, N. A. M. "The Continental Commitment in the Eighteenth Century." In Lawrence Freedman, Paul Hayes, and Robert O'Neill, eds., *War, Strategy, and International Politics: Essays in Honor of Sir Michael Howard*, 39–55. Oxford: Clarendon Press, 1992.

———. "Image and Reality in Eighteenth-Century Naval Tactics." *Mariner's Mirror* 89 (2003): 280–96.

———. *The Insatiable Earl: A Life of John Montagu, 4th Earl of Sandwich, 1718–1792*. New York and London: W. W. Norton, 1994.

———. "Recent Books on the Royal Navy of the Eighteenth Century." *Military Affairs* 63 (1999): 683–703.

———. "Stragglers and Deserters from the Royal Navy during the Seven Years' War." *Bulletin of the Institute of Historical Research* 57 (1984): 56–79.

———. "The Victualing of the British Navy during the Seven Years' War." *Bulletin du Centre d'histoire des espaces Atlantiques*, n.s., 2 (1985): 37–53.

———. *The Wooden World: An Anatomy of the Georgian Navy*. London: Collins, 1986.

———, ed. *The Naval Miscellany*, vol. 5. London: George Allen and Unwin for the Navy Records Society, 1984.

Rogers, Alan. *Empire and Liberty: American Resistance to British Authority, 1755–1763*. Berkeley: University of California Press, 1974.

Rogers, H. C. B. *The British Army of the Eighteenth Century*. London: George Allen and Unwin, 1977.

Rogister, John. *Louis XV and the Parlement of Paris, 1737–1755*. New York: Cambridge University Press, 1995.

Romano, Ruggiero. "Documenti e prime considerazioni intorno alla 'balance du commerce' della Francia dal 1716 al 1780." In *Studi in onore di Armando Sapori*, 2 vols., 2:1266–1300. Milan: Instituto Editoriale Cisalpino, 1957.

Rossel, Louis-Auguste, chevalier de. "Journal de ma campagne à l' Ile Royale (1757)." *Rapport de l'archiviste de la province de Québec* 12 (1931–32), 369–87.

Rousseau, François. *Règne de Charles III d'Espagne (1759–1788)*. 2 vols. Paris: Plon-Nourrit et cie., 1907.

Rousset, Camille, ed. *Correspondance de Louis XV et du maréchal de Noailles*. 2 vols. Paris: Didier et Cie., 1869.

Rowland, Dunbar, A. G. Sanders, and Patricia Kay Galloway, eds. *Mississippi Provincial Archives*, vol. 5, *French Dominion, 1749–1763*. Baton Rouge: Louisiana State University Press, 1984.

Roy, Antoine, ed. "Les Lettres de Doreil." *Rapport de l'archiviste de la province de Québec* 25 (1944–45): 1–171.

Roy, Pierre-Georges. *Bigot et sa bande et l'Affaire du Canada*. Lévis QC: privately printed, 1950.

———, ed. "Les Chambres de commerce de France et la cession du Canada." *Rapport de l'archiviste de la province de Québec* 5 (1924–25): 199–228.

———, ed. "La Mission de M. de Bougainville en France en 1758–1759." *Rapport de l'archiviste de la province de Québec* 4 (1923–24): 1–70.

Russell, Lord John, ed. *Correspondence of John, Fourth Duke of Bedford, Selected from the Originals at Woburn Abbey*. 3 vols. London: Longman, Brown, Green, and Longmans, 1842–1846.

Russell, Nelson Vance. "The Reaction in England and America to the Capture of Havana, 1762." *Hispanic American Historical Review* 9 (1929): 303–16.

Russell, Peter E. "Redcoats in the Wilderness: British Officers and Irregular Warfare in Europe and America, 1740 to 1760." *William and Mary Quarterly*, 3rd ser., 35 (1978): 629–652.

Ruville, Albert von. *William Pitt, Earl of Chatham*. Translated by H. J. Chaytor and Mary Morison. 3 vols. London: W. Heinemann; New York: G. P. Putnam's Sons, 1907.

Saint Hubert, C. de. "Ships of the Line of the Spanish Navy (1714–1825)." *Warship* 10 (1986): 65–69, 129–34, 208–11, 283–85.

Salagnac, Georges Cerbelaud. "La Reprise de Terre-Neuve par les Français en 1762." *Revue française d'histoire d'outre-mer* 63 (1976): 211–22.

Salmon, Edward. *Life of Admiral Sir Charles Saunders, K. B.* London: Isaac Pitman and Sons, 1914.

Samoyault, Jean-Pierre. *Les Bureaux du secrétariat d'état des affaires étrangères sous Louis XV: Administration, personnel.* Paris: A. Pedone, 1971.

Samuel, Sigmund, ed. *The Seven Years' War in Canada, 1756–1763.* Toronto: Ryerson Press, 1934.

Sareil, Jean. *Les Tencin: Histoire d'une famille au dix-huitième siècle d'après de nombreux documents inédits.* Geneva: Droz, 1969.

Sautai, Maurice. *Montcalm at the Battle of Carillon (Ticonderoga) (July 8, 1758).* Translated by John S. Watts. Ticonderoga NY: Fort Ticonderoga Museum, 1941.

Sauvageau, Robert. *Acadie: La Guerre de cent ans des Français d' Amérique aux Maritimes et en Louisiane, 1670–1769.* Paris: Berger-Levrault, 1987.

Savelle, Max. "The American Balance of Power and European Diplomacy, 1713–78." In Richard B. Morris, ed., *The Era of the American Revolution: Studies Inscribed to Evarts Boutell Greene,* 140–69. New York: Columbia University Press, 1939.

———. *The Diplomatic History of the Canadian Boundary, 1749–1763.* New Haven: Yale University Press; Toronto: Ryerson Press; London: Oxford University Press, 1940.

———. "Diplomatic Preliminaries of the Seven Years' War in America." *Canadian Historical Review* 20 (1939): 17–36.

———. *The Origins of American Diplomacy: The International History of Angloamerica, 1492–1763.* New York: Macmillan; London: Collier-Macmillan, 1967.

Savory, Sir Reginald. *His Britannic Majesty's Army in Germany during the Seven Years' War.* Oxford: Clarendon Press, 1966.

Schaefer, Arnold. "Urkundliche Beiträge zur Geschichte des siebenjährigen Kriegs." *Forschungen zur Deutschen Geschichte* 17 (1877): 1–106.

Schieder, Theodor. *Frederick the Great.* Translated by Sabina Berkeley and H. M. Scott. London and New York: Longman, 2000.

Schilling, Lothar. *Kaunitz und das Renversement des alliances: Studien zur aussenpolitischen Konzeption Wenzel Anton von Kaunitz.* Berlin: Duncker & Humblot, 1994.

Schlenke, Manfred. *England und des friderizianische Preussen, 1740–1763: Ein Beitrag zum Verhältnis von Politik und öffentlicher Meinung im England des 18. Jahrhunderts.* Freiburg and Munich: Karl Alber, 1963.

Schomberg, Isaac. *The Naval Chronology; or, An Historical Summary of Naval and Maritime Events from the Time of the Romans to the Treaty of Peace of Amiens.* 5 vols. London: T. Egerton, 1815.

Schöne, Lucien. "La Politique de la France au XVIIIᵉ siècle à l'égard des colonies." *Revue coloniale,* new ser., 6 (1906): 84–113, 173–92, 246–56, 297–328, 359–408.

Schutz, John A. "Cold War Diplomacy and the Seven Years' War." *World Affairs Quarterly* 26 (1955–56): 323–37.

———. "The Disaster of Fort Ticonderoga: The Shortage of Muskets during the Mobilization of 1758." *Huntington Library Quarterly* 14 (1950–51): 307–15.

———. "Imperialism in Massachusetts during the Governorship of William Shirley, 1741–1756." *Huntington Library Quarterly* 23 (1959–60): 217–36.

————. *Thomas Pownall, British Defender of American Liberty: A Study of Anglo-American Relations in the Eighteenth Century.* Glendale CA: Arthur H. Clark, 1951.

————. *William Shirley: King's Governor of Massachusetts.* Chapel Hill: University of North Carolina Press, 1961.

Schweizer, Karl W. "Britain, Prussia and the Prussian Territories on the Rhine, 1762–1763." *Studies in History and Politics* 4 (1985): 103–14.

————. *Frederick the Great, William Pitt, and Lord Bute: The Anglo-Prussian Alliance, 1756–1763.* New York and London: Garland, 1991.

————. "Israel Mauduit: Pamphleteering and Foreign Policy in the Age of the Elder Pitt." In Stephen Taylor, Richard Connors, and Clyve Jones, eds., *Hanoverian Britain and Empire: Essays in Memory of Philip Lawson*, 198–209. Woodbridge, Eng.: Boydell Press, 1998.

————. "Lord Bute and William Pitt's Resignation in 1761." *Canadian Journal of History* 8 (1973): 111–22.

————. "The Seven Years' War: A System Perspective." In Jeremy Black, ed., *The Origins of War in Early Modern Europe*, 242–60. Edinburgh: John Donald, 1987.

————. *William Pitt, Earl of Chatham, 1708–1788: A Bibliography.* Westport CT: Greenwood Press, 1993.

————, ed. *Lord Bute: Essays in Re-Interpretation.* Leicester: Leicester University Press, 1988.

Schweizer, Karl W., and J. Bullion. "The Vote of Credit Controversy, 1762." *British Journal for Eighteenth-Century Studies* 15 (1992): 175–88.

Schweizer, Karl W., and Carol S. Leonard. "Britain, Prussia, Russia, and the Galitzin Letter: A Reassessment." *Historical Journal* 26 (1983): 531–56.

Scott, H. M. *British Foreign Policy in the Age of the American Revolution.* Oxford: Clarendon Press, 1990.

————. *The Emergence of the Eastern Powers, 1756–1775.* New York: Cambridge University Press, 2001.

————. "France and the Polish Throne, 1763–1764." *Slavonic and East European Review* 53 (1975): 370–88.

————. "Religion and Realpolitik: The Duc de Choiseul, the Bourbon Family Compact, and the Attack on the Society of Jesus, 1758–1775." *International History Review* 25 (2003): 37–62.

Sedgwick, Romney, ed. *Letters from George III to Lord Bute, 1756–1766.* London: Macmillan, 1939.

Ségur, Pierre-Marie-Maurice, Henri, marquis de. *Le Maréchal de Ségur (1724–1801) ministre de la guerre sous Louis XVI.* Paris: Plon, Nourrit et cie., 1895.

Selesky, Harold E. *War and Society in Colonial Connecticut.* New Haven: Yale University Press, 1990.

Severance, Frank H. *An Old Frontier of France: The Niagara Region and Adjacent Lakes under French Control.* 2 vols. New York: Dodd, Mead, 1917.

Shafroth, John F. "The Capture of Louisbourg in 1758: A Joint Military and Naval Operation." *United States Naval Institute Proceedings* 64 (1938): 78–96.

————. "The Capture of Quebec in 1759: A Joint Military and Naval Operation." *United States Naval Institute Proceedings* 64 (1938): 187–201.

Shannon, Timothy J. *Indians and Colonists at the Crossroads of Empire: The Albany Conference of 1754.* Ithaca NY: Cornell University Press, 2000.

Shennan, J. H. "Louis XV: Public and Private Worlds." In A. G. Dickens, ed., *The Courts of Europe: Politics, Patronage, and Royalty, 1400–1800,* 304–24. London: Thames and Hudson, 1977.

Shepherd, William R. "The Cession of Louisiana to Spain." *Political Science Quarterly* 19 (1904): 439–58.

Sherrard, O. A. *Lord Chatham: Pitt and the Seven Years' War.* London: Bodley Head, 1955.

Showalter, Dennis E. *The Wars of Frederick the Great.* London and New York: Longman, 1996.

Shy, John. "Armed Force in Colonial North America: New Spain, New France, and Anglo-America." In Kenneth J. Hagen and William R. Roberts, eds., *Against All Enemies: Interpretations of American Military History from Colonial Times to the Present,* 3–20. New York, Westport CT, and London: Greenwood Press, 1986.

————. *Toward Lexington: The Role of the British Army in the Coming of the American Revolution.* Princeton: Princeton University Press, 1965.

Siebert, Wilbur H. "How the Spaniards Evacuated Pensacola in 1763." *Florida Historical Quarterly* 11 (1932): 48–57.

————. "Spanish and French Privateering in Southern Waters, July, 1762, to March, 1763." *Georgia Historical Quarterly* 16 (1932): 163–78.

Simmons, R. C., and P. D. G. Thomas, eds. *Proceedings and Debates of the British Parliaments Respecting North America, 1754–1783.* 6 vols. to date. Millwood NY: Kraus International Publications, 1982–.

Sinéty, André-Louis-Waldemar-Alphée, marquis de. *Vie du maréchal de Lowendal.* 2 vols. Paris: Bachelin-Deflorenne, 1867–1868.

Skaggs, David Curtis, and Larry E. Nelson, eds. *The Sixty Years' War for the Great Lakes, 1754–1814.* East Lansing: Michigan State University Press, 2001.

Smelser, Marshall. *The Campaign for the Sugar Islands, 1759: A Study of Amphibious Warfare.* Chapel Hill: University of North Carolina Press, 1955.

Smith, Mrs. Gillispie, ed. *Memoirs and Correspondence (Official and Familiar) of Sir Robert Murray Keith, K. B.* 2 vols. London: Henry Colburn, 1849.

Smith, William James, ed. *The Grenville Papers: Being the Correspondence of Richard Grenville, Earl Temple, K. G. and the Right Hon. George Grenville, Their Friends and Correspondents.* 4 vols. London: John Murray, 1852–1853.

Soltau, Roger H. *The Duke de Choiseul: The Lothian Essay, 1908.* Oxford: B. H. Blackwell; London: Simpkin, Marshall, 1909.

Sorel, Albert. *Essais d'histoire et de critique.* 4th ed. Paris: Plon-Nourrit et cie., 1913.

————. *Europe and the French Revolution: The Political Traditions of the Old Regime.* Translated by Alfred Cobban and J. W. Hunt. Garden City NY: Doubleday, Anchor Books, 1971.

Sosin, Jack M. "Louisbourg and the Peace of Aix-la-Chapelle, 1748." *William and Mary Quarterly*, 3rd ser., 14 (1957): 516–35.

————. *Whitehall and the Wilderness: The Middle West in British Colonial Policy, 1760–1775*. Lincoln: University of Nebraska Press, 1961.

Soulange-Bodin, André. *La Diplomatie de Louis XV et le pacte de famille*. Paris: Perrin et cie., 1894.

Speck, W. A. "The International and Imperial Context." In Jack P. Greene and J. R. Pole, eds., *Colonial British America: Essays in the New History of the Early Modern Era*, 384–407. Baltimore: Johns Hopkins University Press, 1984.

Spencer, Frank. "The Anglo-Prussian Breach of 1762: An Historical Revision." *History*, new ser., 41 (1956): 100–112.

Spinney, David. *Rodney*. London: George Allen and Unwin, 1969.

St. John Williams, Noel T. *Redcoats along the Hudson: The Struggle for North America, 1754–1763*. London and Washington: Brassey's, 1997.

Stacey, C. P. "The Anse au Foulon, 1759: Montcalm and Vaudreuil." *Canadian Historical Review* 40 (1959): 27–37.

————. *Quebec, 1759: The Siege and the Battle*. Toronto: Macmillan, 1959.

————. "Quebec, 1759: Some New Documents." *Canadian Historical Review* 47 (1966): 344–55.

Stanley, George F. G. *New France: The Last Phase, 1744–1760*. Toronto: McClelland and Stewart, 1968.

Starkey, David J. *British Privateering Enterprise in the Eighteenth Century*. Exeter: University of Exeter Press, 1990.

————. "War and the Market for Seafarers in in Britain, 1736–1792." In Lewis R. Fisher and Helge W. Nordvik, eds., *Shipping and Trade, 1750–1950: Essays in International Maritime Economic History*, 25–42. Pontefract, Eng.: Lofthouse, 1990.

Steele, Ian K. *Betrayals: Fort William Henry and the "Massacre."* New York: Oxford University Press, 1990.

————. "Exploding Colonial American History: Amerindian, Atlantic and Global Perspectives." *Reviews in American History* 26 (1998): 70–95.

————. *Guerillas and Grenadiers: The Struggle for Canada, 1689–1760*. Toronto: Ryerson Press, 1969.

————. *Warpaths: Invasions of North America*. New York: Oxford University Press, 1994.

Stein, Robert. "The French Sugar Business in the Eighteenth Century: A Quantitative Study." *Business History* 22 (1980): 3–17.

Stenberg, Richard R. "The Louisiana Cession and the Family Compact." *Louisiana Historical Quarterly* 19 (1936): 204–9.

Stephenson, R. S. "Pennsylvania Provincial Soldiers in the Seven Years' War." *Pennsylvania History* 62 (1995): 196–212.

Stevens, Sylvester K., Donald H. Kent, and Autumn L. Leonard, eds. *The Papers of Henry Bouquet*, vol. 2, *The Forbes Expedition*. Harrisburg PA: Pennsylvania Historical and Museum Commission, 1951.

Stone, Lawrence, ed. *An Imperial State at War: Britain from 1689 to 1815.* London and New York: Routledge, 1994.

Stotz, Charles Morse. *Outposts of the War for Empire: The French and English in Western Pennsylvania: Their Armies, Their Forts, Their People, 1749–1764.* Pittsburgh: University of Pittsburgh Press for the Historical Society of Western Pennsylvania, 1985.

Stout, Neil R. *The Royal Navy in America, 1760–1775: A Study of the Enforcement of British Colonial Policy in the Era of the American Revolution.* Annapolis: Naval Institute Press, 1973.

Sturgill, Claude C. "The French Army's Budget in the Eighteenth Century: A Retreat from Loyalty." In David G. Troyansky, Alfred Cismaru, and Norwood Andrews Jr., eds., *The French Revolution in Culture and Society,* 123–34. Westport CT: Greenwood Press, 1991.

Sullivan, James et al., eds. *The Papers of Sir William Johnson.* 14 vols. Albany: University of the State of New York, 1921–65.

Sutherland, Lucy. "The East India Company and the Peace of Paris." In Aubrey Newman, ed., *Politics and Finance in the Eighteenth Century: Lucy Sutherland,* 165–76. London: Hambledon Press, 1984.

Sutton, John L. *The King's Honor and the King's Cardinal: The War of the Polish Succession.* Lexington: University Press of Kentucky, 1980.

Swann, Julian. "Parlements and Political Crisis in France under Louis XV: The Besançon Affair, 1757–1761." *Historical Journal* 37 (1994): 803–28.

———. *Politics and the Parlement of Paris under Louis XV, 1754–1774.* New York: Cambridge University Press, 1995.

Syrett, David. "American Provincials and the Havana Campaign of 1762." *New York History* 49 (1968): 374–90.

———. "The British Landing at Havana: An Example of an Eighteenth-Century Combined Operation." *Mariner's Mirror* 55 (1969): 325–331.

———. "The Methodology of British Amphibious Operations during the Seven Years and American Wars." *Mariner's Mirror* 58 (1972): 269–80.

———, ed. *The Siege and Capture of Havana, 1762.* London: Navy Records Society, 1970.

Szabo, Franz A. J. *Kaunitz and Enlightened Absolutism, 1753–1780.* Cambridge: Cambridge University Press, 1994.

Tamussino, Ursula. *Isabella von Parma, Gemahlin Joseph II.* Vienna: Osterreichischer Bundesverlag Gesellschaft, 1989.

Tashereau, Jules-A., ed. "Conseils des ministres sous Louis XV." In *Revue retrospective, ou bibliothèque historique, contenant des mémoires et documents authentiques, inédits et originaux, pour servir à l'histoire proprement dite, à la biographie, à l'histoire de la littérature et des arts,* 20 vols., 20 (3rd ser., 3): 343–72. Paris: H. Fournier aîné, 1833–38.

Taylor, Robert J. "Israel Mauduit." *New England Quarterly* 24 (1951): 208–30.

Taylor, William Stanhope, and John Henry Pringle, eds. *Correspondence of William Pitt, Earl of Chatham.* 4 vols. London: John Murray, 1838–1840.

Temperley, H. W. V. "The Peace of Paris." In J. Holland Rose, A. P. Newton and E. A.

Benians, eds., *The Cambridge History of the British Empire*, vol. 1, *The Old Empire from Its Beginnings to 1783*, 485–506. Cambridge: Cambridge University Press, 1929.

———. "Pitt's Retirement from Office, 1761." *English Historical Review* 21 (1906): 327–30.

Thackeray, Francis. *A History of the Right Honourable William Pitt, Earl of Chatham*. 2 vols. London: C. and J. Rivington, 1827.

Thomas, Peter D. G. *George III: King and Politician, 1760–1770*. Manchester: Manchester University Press, 2002.

Thomas-Lacroix, P. "La Guerre de course dans les ports des Amirautés de Vannes et de Lorient, 1744–1783." *Mémoires de la Société d'histoire et d'archéologie de Bretagne* 26 (1946): 159–215.

Thorpe, Frederick J. *Remparts lointains: La Politique française des travaux publiques à Terre-Neuve et à l'île Royale, 1695–1758*. Ottawa: Editions de l'Université de Ottawa, 1980.

Thrapp, Dan L., ed. *Encyclopedia of Frontier Biography*. 4 vols. Glendale CA: Arthur H. Clark, 1988–94.

Titus, James. *The Old Dominion at War: Society, Politics and Warfare in Late Colonial Virginia*. Columbia: University of South Carolina Press, 1990.

Townshend, C. V. *The Military Life of Field Marshal George, First Marquess Townshend, 1724–1807*. London: J. Murray, 1901.

Toynbee, Arnold, Fred L. Israel, and Emanuel Chill, eds. *Major Peace Treaties of Modern History, 1648–1967*. 4 vols. New York: Toronto, London, Sydney: McGraw-Hill, 1967.

Tracy, Nicholas. "The Capture of Manila, 1762." *Mariner's Mirror* 55 (1969): 311–23.

———. *Manila Ransomed: The British Assault on Manila in the Seven Years War*. Exeter: University of Exeter Press, 1995.

———. *Navies, Deterrence, and American Independence: Britain and Seapower in the 1760s and 1770s*. Vancouver: University of British Columbia Press, 1988.

Troude, O. *Batailles navales de la France*, vol. 1. Paris: Challamel aîné, 1867.

Trudel, Marcel. "The Jumonville Affair." Translated by Donald H. Kent. *Pennsylvania History* 21 (1954): 351–81.

Tunstall, William Cuthbert Brian. *Naval Warfare in the Age of Sail: The Evolution of Fighting Tactics, 1650–1815*. Edited by Nicholas Tracy. Annapolis: Naval Institute Press, 1990.

———. *William Pitt, Earl of Chatham*. London: Hodder and Stoughton, 1938.

Ultee, Maarten, ed. *Adapting to Conditions: War and Society in the Eighteenth Century*. University: University of Alabama Press, 1986.

Valori, Henri Zosime, marquis de, ed. *Mémoires des négociations du marquis de Valori, ambassadeur de France à la cour de Berlin*. 2 vols. Paris: Firmin Didot, père et fils, 1820.

Vandal, Albert. *Louis XV et Elisabeth de Russie: Etude sur les relations de la France et de la Russie au dix-huitième siècle d'après les archives du Ministère des affaires étrangères*. 3rd ed. Paris: E. Plon, Nourrit et cie., 1896.

Van Kley, Dale E. *The Damiens Affair and the Unraveling of the Ancien Régime, 1750–1770*. Princeton: Princeton University Press, 1984.

————. *The Jansenists and the Expulsion of the Jesuits from France, 1757–1765.* New Haven: Yale University Press, 1975.

Van Royen, Paul, Jaap Bruijn, and Jan Lucassen, eds., *"Those Emblems of Hell"? European Sailors and the Maritime Labour Market, 1570–1870.* St. John's, Newfoundland: International Maritime Economic History Association, 1997.

[Vedel, Peter August Frederik Stoud, ed.] *Correspondance entre le comte Johan Hartvig Ernst Bernstorff et le duc de Choiseul, 1758–1766.* Copenhagen: Gyldendal, 1871.

Velde, François, and David R. Weir. "The Financial Market and Government Debt Policy in France, 1746–1793." *Journal of Economic History* 52 (1992): 1–39.

Vergé-Franceschi, Michel. *Les Officiers généraux de la marine royal (1715–1774): Origines-conditions-services.* 7 vols. Paris: Librairie de l'Inde, 1990.

Vignes, Pierre. *L'Armament en course à Bayonne de 1744 à 1783.* Bordeaux: Imprimerie Bière, 1942.

Villiers, Patrick. "Commerce coloniale, traite de noirs et cabotage dans les ports du Ponant pendant la guerre de Sept Ans." *Centre de recherches sur l'histoire du monde Atlantique-enquêtes et documents* 17 (1990): 21–46.

————. *Marine royale, corsaires et trafic dans l'Atlantique de Louis XIV à Louis XVI.* 2 vols. Dunkirk: Société Dunkerquoise d'Histoire et d'Archéologie, 1991.

Villiers du Terrage, Baron Marc. *Les Dernières Années de la Louisiane française: Le Chevalier de Kerlérec, d'Abbadie, Aubry, Laussat.* Paris: Librairie orientale & américaine, 1904.

Volz, Gustav Berthold, and George Küntzel, eds. *Preussische und Osterreichische Acten zur Vorgeschichte das Siebenjährigen Krieges.* Leipzig: S. Hirzel, 1899.

Waddell, Louis M. "Defending the Long Perimeter: Forts on the Pennsylvania, Maryland, and Virginia Frontier, 1755–1765." *Pennsylvania History* 62 (1995): 171–95.

Waddington, Richard. *La Guerre de Sept Ans: Histoire diplomatique et militaire.* 5 vols. Paris: Firmin-Didot et cie., 1899–1914.

————. *Louis XV et le renversement des alliances: Préliminaires de la guerre de Sept Ans, 1754–1756.* Paris: Firmin-Didot, 1896.

Wall, Robert Emmet, Jr. "Louisbourg, 1745." *New England Quarterly* 37 (1964): 64–83.

Wallace, Anthony F. C. *King of the Delawares: Teedyuscung, 1700–1763.* Philadelphia: University of Pennsylvania Press, 1949.

Ward, Harry M. *Major General Adam Stephen and the Cause of American Liberty.* Charlottesville: University Press of Virginia, 1989.

Ward, Matthew C. "An Army of Servants: The Pennsylvania Regiment during the Seven Years' War." *Pennsylvania Magazine of History and Biography* 119 (1995): 75–93.

————. *Breaking the Backcountry: The Seven Years' War in Virginia and Pennsylvania, 1754–1765.* Pittsburgh: University of Pittsburgh Press, 2003.

————. "'The European Method of Warring Is Not Practiced Here': The Failure of British Military Policy in the Ohio Valley, 1755–1759." *War in History* 4 (1997): 247–63.

————. "Fighting the 'Old Women': Indian Strategy on the Virginia and Pennsylvania Frontier, 1754–1758." *Virginia Magazine of History and Biography* 103 (1995): 297–320.

Webb, James L. A., Jr. "The Mid-Eighteenth-Century Gum Arabic Trade and the British

Capture of Saint-Louis du Sénégal, 1758." *Journal of Imperial and Commonwealth History* 25 (1997): 37–58.

Weber, David J. *The Spanish Frontier in North America.* New Haven: Yale University Press, 1992.

Webster, John Clarence. *The Forts of Chignecto: A Study of the Eighteenth-Century Conflict between France and Great Britain in Acadia.* Shediac, New Brunswick: privately printed, 1930.

———, ed. *The Journal of Jeffrey Amherst: Recording the Military Career of General Amherst in America from 1758 to 1763.* Toronto: Ryerson Press; Chicago: University of Chicago Press, 1931.

Weslager, C. A. *The Delaware Indians: A History.* New Brunswick: Rutgers University Press, 1972.

Western, John R. *The English Militia in the Eighteenth Century: The Story of a Political Issue, 1660–1802.* London: Routledge and Kegan Paul; Toronto: University of Toronto Press, 1965.

White, Eugene Nelson. "Was There a Solution to the Ancien Régime's Financial Dilemma?" *Journal of Economic History* 49 (1989): 545–68.

White, Richard. *The Middle Ground: Indians, Empires, and Republics in the Great Lakes Region, 1650–1815.* New York: Cambridge University Press, 1991.

Whitworth, Rex. *Field Marshal Lord Ligonier: A Study of the British Army, 1702–1770.* Oxford: Clarendon Press, 1958.

———. *William Augustus, Duke of Cumberland: A Life.* London: Leo Cooper, 1992.

Wiggin, Lewis Merriam. *The Faction of Cousins: A Political Account of the Grenvilles, 1733–1763.* New Haven: Yale University Press, 1958.

Williams, Judith Blow. "The Development of British Trade with West Africa, 1750 to 1850." *Political Science Quarterly* 50 (1935): 194–213.

Wilson, Arthur McCandless. *French Foreign Policy during the Administration of Cardinal Fleury, 1726–1743: A Study in Diplomacy and Commercial Development.* Cambridge: Harvard University Press; London: Humphrey Milford, Oxford University Press, 1936.

Winfield, Rif. *The 50-Gun Ship.* London: Caxton Editions, 2001.

Wood, George A. "Céleron de Blainville and French Expansion in the Ohio Valley." *Mississippi Valley Historical Review* 9 (1922–23): 302–19.

———. *William Shirley, Governor of Massachusetts, 1741–1756.* New York: Columbia University Press; London: P. S. King and Son, 1920.

Woodbridge, John D. *Revolt in Prerevolutionary France: The Prince de Conti's Conspiracy against Louis XV, 1755–1757.* Baltimore: Johns Hopkins University Press, 1995.

Woodfine, Philip. *Britannia's Glories: The Walpole Ministry and the 1739 War with Spain.* Woodbridge, Eng. and Rochester: Boydell Press for the Royal Historical Society, 1998.

Wright, J. Leitch, Jr. *Anglo-Spanish Rivalry in North America.* Athens: University of Georgia Press, 1971.

Wright, Wyliss E. *Colonel Ephraim Williams: A Documentary Life.* Pittsfield M A: Berkshire County Historical Society, 1970.

Wyczynski, Michel. "The Expedition of the Second Battalion of the Cambis Regiment to Louisbourg, 1758." *Nova Scotia Historical Review* 10, no. 2 (1990): 95–110.

Wylly, H. C. *"Primus in Indis": A Life of Lieutenant-General Sir Eyre Coote, K. B.* Oxford: Clarendon Press, 1922.

Yaple, Robert L. "Braddock's Defeat: The Theories and a Reconsideration." *Journal of the Society for Army Historical Research* 46 (1968): 194–201.

Yorke, Philip C. *The Life and Correspondence of Philip Yorke, Earl of Hardwicke, Lord High Chancellor of Great Britain.* 3 vols. Cambridge: Cambridge University Press, 1913.

Index

University of Nebraska Press